AF789917

Proceedings

Workshop on Principles of Advanced and Distributed Simulation

PADS 2005

Proceedings

Workshop on Principles of Advanced and Distributed Simulation *(PADS 2005)*

Monterey, California

June 1–3, 2005

Sponsored by

ACM, IEEE Computer Society, and SCS

David M. Nicol, General Chair

Christopher D. Carothers and Stephen J. Turner, Program Co-Chairs

IEEE COMPUTER SOCIETY

http://computer.org

Los Alamitos, California

Washington • Brussels • Tokyo

Copyright © 2005 by The Institute of Electrical and Electronics Engineers, Inc.
All rights reserved.

Copyright and Reprint Permissions: Abstracting is permitted with credit to the source. Libraries may photocopy beyond the limits of US copyright law, for private use of patrons, those articles in this volume that carry a code at the bottom of the first page, provided that the per-copy fee indicated in the code is paid through the Copyright Clearance Center, 222 Rosewood Drive, Danvers, MA 01923.

Other copying, reprint, or republication requests should be addressed to: IEEE Copyrights Manager, IEEE Service Center, 445 Hoes Lane, P.O. Box 133, Piscataway, NJ 08855-1331.

The papers in this book comprise the proceedings of the meeting mentioned on the cover and title page. They reflect the authors' opinions and, in the interests of timely dissemination, are published as presented and without change. Their inclusion in this publication does not necessarily constitute endorsement by the editors, the IEEE Computer Society, or the Institute of Electrical and Electronics Engineers, Inc.

IEEE Computer Society Order Number P2383
ACM Order Number 577050
ISBN 0-7695-2383-8
ISSN 1087-4097

Additional copies may be ordered from:

IEEE Computer Society
Customer Service Center
10662 Los Vaqueros Circle
P.O. Box 3014
Los Alamitos, CA 90720-1314
Tel: + 1 800 272 6657
Fax: + 1 714 821 4641
http://computer.org/cspress
csbooks@computer.org

IEEE Service Center
445 Hoes Lane
P.O. Box 1331
Piscataway, NJ 08855-1331
Tel: + 1 732 981 0060
Fax: + 1 732 981 9667
http://shop.ieee.org/store/
customer-service@ieee.org

IEEE Computer Society
Asia/Pacific Office
Watanabe Bldg., 1-4-2
Minami-Aoyama
Minato-ku, Tokyo 107-0062
JAPAN
Tel: + 81 3 3408 3118
Fax: + 81 3 3408 3553
tokyo.ofc@computer.org

Individual paper REPRINTS may be ordered at: reprints@computer.org

Editorial production by Randall Bilof
Cover art production by Joe Daigle/Studio Productions
Printed in the United States of America by The Printing House

IEEE COMPUTER SOCIETY

IEEE

IEEE Computer Society
Conference Publishing Services
http://www.computer.org/proceedings/

Contents

Proceedings of the Workshop on Principles of Advanced and Distributed Simulation

PADS 2005

Performance Prediction and Real-Time

Network Simulation

Optimistic Simulation

(MMSM) Analysis of Worms

Advanced Simulation Techniques

(MMSM) Malware Defense

HLA and Virtual Environments

Message from the General Chair

PADS 2005

Welcome to the 2005 Workshop on Principles of Advanced and Distributed Simulation (PADS 2005), held this year in Monterey, California. It is a beautiful location that offers many attractions, in addition to the exciting and very full set of technical offerings at the conference. This is the first year PADS sallies forth with a different interpretation of the acronym; for 18 years PADS stood for "Parallel and Distributed Simulation," but a year ago the community decided to formalize its interest in expanding the conference scope with a new title, "Principles of Advanced and Distributed Simulation." With an eye toward jump-starting the desired diversity, we created within PADS a topically focused track that was advertised separately, the Symposium on Measurement, Modeling, and Simulation of Malware (MMSM). The response to this overture was excellent, and we are happy to have an MMSM session each day. To those new to PADS, welcome!

A production like PADS succeeds due to the efforts of many helpers. I am particularly grateful for the efforts of Chris Carothers and Steve Turner, the Program Co-Chairs, for leading the development of the technical program, to Michael Liljenstam who spear-headed the MMSM program development, and Jason Liu who put together the website describing the technical meeting itself. Special thanks are due to the Program Committee and outside reviewers, who (as we have come to expect) provided yet again thorough and discerning reviews of the many submissions. Finally, I'm thankful for the meeting experts at IEEE who are practiced at leading neophyte General Chairs such as myself through the paces of budgeting, planning, and reporting.

Enjoy the conference and the locale!

David M. Nicol
University of Illinois, Urbana-Champaign

Message from the Program Co-Chairs

PADS 2005

We welcome you to the first Workshop on Principles of Advanced and Distributed Simulation (PADS 2005). Like its predecessor, PADS continues to be the most highly regarded venue for the publication of ground-breaking research in parallel and distributed simulation. Additionally, with its expanded scope PADS now reflects a more holistic view of advances in modeling and simulation. That view has come full circle this year with our Symposium on Measurement, Modeling and Simulation of Malware (MMSM).

The PADS/MMSM programs are high quality, and we believe will be extremely interesting to a wide range of researchers and practitioners of modeling and simulation. In response to both PADS and MMSM Calls for Papers, we received forty-six submissions. As done in the past, a double-blind review process was employed by leveraging the WIMPE paper management system. Each paper received four reviews of which three were done by a member of the Program Committee in a majority of the cases. The Program Committee meeting was held Saturday, December 4, in conjunction with the Winter Simulation Conference that was held in Washington, D.C. From that meeting it was decided that fourteen papers would be accepted and eight papers were conditionally accepted. These eight papers were assigned "shepherds" by the Program Chairs who provided constructive guidance as part of the revision process. Through great efforts on the part of the authors and their "shepherds," all eight of these papers were cleared for acceptance. In a pipeline fashion, MMSM papers were collected and separately reviewed by the General Chair, the Program Chairs, and other outside reviewers. For the final program, we have a total of thirty papers, one keynote address, and a work-in-progress session.

On behalf of the PADS 2004 Program Co-Chairs, Ernie Page and Thom McLean, we are delighted to confirm that the winner of the PADS 2004 Best Paper is:

> "Detailed OFDM Modeling in Network Simulation of Mobile Ad Hoc Networks," by Gavin Yeung, Mineo Takai, Rajive Bagrodia, Alireza Mehrnia, and Babak Daneshrad

As is customary a Best Paper for this year will be announced at the workshop and will be cited in next year's PADS proceedings. The five most highly ranked papers were considered for the 2005 Best Paper award. These five were characterized as having all reviewers recommend acceptance, with at least two program committee members giving "strong" (as opposed to "weak") accept recommendations. A panel of three program committee members (other than these authors) selected the Best Paper for 2005, the winner will be announced at the conference. The five papers considered are:

> "Transparent State Management for Optimistic Synchronization in the High Level Architecture" by Andrea Santoro and Francesco Quaglia

> "Simulation of Network Traffic at Coarse Timescales" by David M. Nicol and Guanhua Yan

"RINSE: The Real-Time Immersive Network Simulation Environment for Network Security Exercises" by Michael Liljenstam, Jason Liu, David M. Nicol, Yougu Yuan, Guanhua Yan, and Chris Grier

"Optimistic Parallel Discrete Event Simulations of Physical Systems Using Reverse Computation," by Yarong Tang, Kalyan S. Perumalla, Richard M. Fujimoto, Homa Karimabadi, Jonathan Driscoll, and Yuri Omelchenko

"Routing Worm: A Fast, Selective Attack Worm Based on IP Address Information" by Cliff C. Zou, Don Towsley, Weibo Gong, and Songlin Cai

These authors will be invited to expand their scope and be considered for a Special Issue in the journal SCS Simulation. Announcement of the winning paper will be made at the conference.

In the creation of this workshop there are numerous folks to thank. We would like to express our gratitude to David Nicol, the General Chair, for taking on the daunting task of bring the workshop's expanded scope to fruition, and finding our amazing venue site as well as more mundane tasks such as that of WIMPE creator and administrator. Special thanks to Fred Wieland and AEgis Technology Group for allowing us the use of their facilities to hold the Program Committee meeting. Additionally, we express our thanks to the PADS Steering Committee for their guidance and to the Program Committee for their time and effort in the final review process as well as the referees for creating well constructed reviews—all within a compressed schedule. And finally, we wish to thank all those who submitted articles to both PADS and MMSM. For without your current and continued participation we would not have PADS!

Enjoy the program!!

Christopher D. Carothers
Rensselaer Polytechnic Institute, Troy New York

Stephen J. Turner
Nanyang Technological University, Singapore

Workshop Committees

PADS 2005

General Chair

David M. Nicol

Program Co-Chairs

Christopher D. Carothers
Stephen J. Turner

Steering Committee

Stephen J. Turner (Chair)
Simon J. E. Taylor
Adel S. Elmaghraby
Peter S. Magnusson
Brian W. Unger
George Riley
Richard M. Fujimoto (Honorary)

Program Committee

Azzedine Boukerche
Doug Degroot
Lorenzo Donatiello
Adel S. Elmaghraby
Richard M. Fujimoto
Axel Lehmann
Michael Liljenstam
Jason Liu
Jhonnes Luethi
Ernest H. Page
Kalyan Perumalla
Francesco Quaglia
George Riley
Rob Simmonds
Emin G. Sirer
Boleslaw K. Szymanski
Greg Tackett
Mineo Takai
Simon J. E. Taylor
Carl Tropper
Adelinde Uhrmacher
Brian W. Unger
Fred Wieland
Phil Wilsey

Reviewers

PADS 2005

Cameron Kiddle
Shiyan Hu
Maloan Chetlur
Andrea Santoro
Gilbert Chen
Boon Ping Gan
Yan Gu
Nasser Kalantery
Wentong Cai
David Xu
Gabriele D'Angelo
Luciano Bononi
Young-Jun Lee
Monirul Sharif
Dan Chen
Dheeraj Reddy
Xiaoguang Wang
Suiping Zhou
Malcolm Low
Regina Santana

Introduction and Keynote Address

Modeling and Simulating the Brain as a System
Extended Abstract

Doug DeGroot
LIACS, Leiden University, The Netherlands
and Techsus, USA

Advances in the neurosciences and related fields are occurring at such rapid rates that they are engendering a compartmentalization across the research activities within these fields. Neuroscience, computational neuroscience, cognitive psychology, and computer science largely continue to proceed separately; cognitive and neural models remain largely disjoint or even orthogonal; and the relations between brain structures, brain processes, and mind—especially as they relate to emergent, dynamic phenomena—remain largely unexplored. Thus while monumental successes have been achieved in many arenas within the neurosciences, little progress has been made toward developing a unified theory of the brain. Many potential sources of this failure can be identified, including: the sheer complexity of the brain, the credit assignment problem, the scarcity of cross-field researchers, and even the reductionist approach to science, among many others.

Certainly one major source is the huge gap between the speeds and capacities of modern computers and the human brain. Current software, modeling tools, visualization packages, and the like are quite slow, weak, and isolationist by any reasonable measure. Hopes of computationalizing a theory or model and performing actual experiments often forces researchers to: tackle toy problems; to scale their neural structures and problems to very small sizes and levels of complexity; to abstract away critical system-level details; to perform sub-critical numbers of experiments; and to make frail extrapolations from components to structures. Further, the isolationist nature of the tools does little to encourage and support hierarchical integration and the essential and complementary process of synthesis (or reconstruction). These problems and their resultant research practice limitations, coupled with the inherent complexity of the brain, contribute to the ongoing lack of a comprehensive theory of the brain.

The situation may be about to change, however. By some estimates, the human brain's raw processing power is equivalent (sic) to approximately 100 teraflops (100 trillion floating-point operations per second), at least in terms of neuron firings. This is a daunting number, yet parallel supercomputers are nearing and will soon exceed these numbers. For example, Japan's NEC Earth Simulator delivers performance at 35.8 Tflops—about one-third that of the human brain. The joint DOE/IBM Blue Gene/L computer targeted a full petaflop of performance, or 10 times the estimated raw performance of the human brain. Amazingly, one of the major milestones predicted by Moore's law is that by 2020 single computer chips will be capable of this brain-scale performance (actually, by 2020, one human; by 2050, the entire human race). The costs for such brain-scale power will also decline exponentially. Within the near future, therefore, brain-scale machines will become highly affordable and broadly available, making possible for the first time large-scale, integrated simulations of entire mammalian brains.

This is a massively significant, near-term, technological discontinuity that promises unprecedented opportunities for the brain sciences. It's attraction is not simply being able to access more computing power in order to model increasing levels of detail or biological fidelity of small neural structures (such as the impressive efforts in modeling single Purkinje cells on a Cray supercomputer); it is more about exploiting brain-scale computing to target the high-fidelity simulation of the human brain and nervous systems, using formally developed holistic frameworks and computing platforms for integrating advances in brain, mind, computing, sensing, and behaving into a comprehensive, systematic whole. Success in this "brain as system" approach will easily require truly integrative, interdisciplinary research at "grand challenge" levels, rethinking the problems, paradigms, approaches, and goals in many cases, and institutionalized innovation across the involved research communities.

New methods of experimental and theoretical neuroscience research, coupled with new computational methods, will need to be developed—ones involving reusable, plug-and-play functional-model libraries, massive computational experimentation approaches, large-scale evolutionary computing and cognitive models, direct methods of developing and evaluating emergent properties, "in silico" neurophysiological experimentation, and even integration of silicon sensory and motor systems to create complete, end-to-end, artificial nervous systems. Many of these methods involve computer science and engineering technologies that are already widely applied to other fields but that have not yet targeted brain-scale computing and integrated theories of the brain. However, several such efforts are already emerging that hope to address these problems and opportunities.

This presentation provides an overview of several of these activities and discusses some of the key research roles that may be played by simulation and modeling, performance engineering, distributed computing, architectures, visualization and other key technologies of interest to the PADS community. In particular, the discussion will present a concept for the development of isomorphic, hierarchical architectures and principles of operation of the brain at multiple levels, using interactive visualization and distributed simulation techniques.

New Applications

Towards Time-Parallel Road Traffic Simulation

Tobias Kiesling
Fakultät für Informatik
Universität der Bundeswehr München
85577 Neubiberg, GERMANY
kiesling@informatik.unibw-muenchen.de

Johannes Lüthi
Studiengang Wirtschaftsinformatik
FHS Kufstein Tirol
6330 Kufstein, AUSTRIA
Johannes.Luethi@fh-kufstein.ac.at

Abstract

As an alternative to spatial parallelization of simulation models, time-parallel simulation offers the potential for massive parallelism with a high level of independence between the parallel processes. Unfortunately, due to inherent problems, the applicability of time-parallel simulation is restricted. Therefore, it has been proposed recently, to use approximation with time-parallel simulation in order to facilitate its application and to extend the class of models suitable for time-parallel simulation. As a proof-of-concept, this work shows how approximate temporal parallelization can be applied to the simulation of road traffic. Traffic simulation is used extensively in transportation research for various purposes, e.g. analysis of traffic phenomena, traffic forecast, and optimization of traffic flow. Depending on the level of fidelity, a traffic model exhibits a state space of moderate to high complexity. This paper is intended to discuss the basic properties of time-parallel traffic simulation and to examine its feasibility. Experiments with a sequential microscopic traffic simulator, that emulates important aspects of a corresponding time-parallel simulator, suggest this feasibility.

1. Introduction

Transportation research is concerned with the analysis of phenomena occurring in real world traffic. As the amount of traveling, as well as transport of goods, is increasing continuously, existing transportation resources get more and more overloaded, resulting in congestion or breakdown of resources. The situation is especially bad with road traffic, where a limited amount of road capacity must accommodate an increasing amount of traffic. Transportation research can help to understand the characteristics of traffic and propose solutions for existing problems. To achieve these goals, computer simulation of traffic is an important tool. A lot of work has been invested in the past to develop simulation models appropriately representing the reality of road traffic.

There are two fundamentally different types of models in traffic simulation. Macroscopic models try to characterize traffic flow with fluid-dynamical approaches [5, 11], giving an aggregated view of the problem. Microscopic simulation, in contrast, represents all entities (e.g. vehicles, traffic lights, intersections) of the simulated system as individual objects. Besides more accurate simulation results, this has the advantage that individual choices of travelers can be considered. A straightforward approach is to describe the movement of vehicles by equations, directly or indirectly derived from physical laws, e.g. [18]. In order to reduce computation time, more recent approaches model traffic as cellular automata [19], where the dynamical behavior of vehicles is discrete in time and space. An example of this is the Nagel/Schreckenberg model [15], which is recognized as simple and computationally efficient, yet exhibiting realistic behavior.

The original cellular-automaton-based model of Nagel and Schreckenberg was developed for single lane traffic. Afterwards it has been extended to support multi lane [16] and urban traffic [3]. Among other applications, it has been used for traffic forecasts [2] and as the central part of the large-scale TRANSIMS project [17].

Due to the high fidelity of the Nagel/Schreckenberg model, computational demands of large-scale traffic simulators can be high, leading to the need for efficient parallelization. Existing parallelizations [13, 14] use a domain decomposition approach where a graph representing the street network to be simulated is decomposed into subgraphs that are simulated concurrently on different processing nodes. To exchange information about vehicles traveling from one subgraph to another, the parallel processes operate synchronously in the simulated time, i.e. at every time, all processors execute the same simulation time step. For small numbers of processors this poses no problem and impres-

1087-4097/05 $20.00 © 2005 IEEE

sive performance increases can be achieved. However, due to the significant synchronization overhead, these solutions do not scale well to higher numbers of processors [1], if a fixed problem size is supposed.

For a potential improvement of the scalability of parallel traffic simulations, the method of time-parallel simulation [4] can be applied to reduce synchronization between processes. This is done by temporal decomposition of the simulation model, a partitioning of the simulated time into time slices, which are simulated concurrently by parallel processes. However, without further mechanisms this approach is doomed to fail, as the correct states of the simulation at the boundaries of time slices are unknown prior to the simulation. Several solutions to this problem have been proposed for various types of models [6, 7, 12], but none of them with a simulation state as complex as in traffic simulation. To be able to use temporal parallelization with traffic simulation, the approach of approximate state matching [10] can be used, which has also been successfully applied to the simulation of least-recently-used caching [9].

This paper is intended as a first step in the direction of time-parallel road traffic simulation. Some preliminaries are introduced in Sections 2 and 3. Section 4 shows how time-parallel traffic simulation can be applied to the Nagel/Schreckenberg model. The feasibility of time-parallel road traffic simulation is examined experimentally in Section 5. Finally, Section 6 concludes the work.

2. The Nagel/Schreckenberg model

Cellular Automata [19] are of an increasing significance in the field of experimental physics to describe natural phenomena with discrete and computationally efficient models. In a cellular automaton, a one-, two, or multidimensional space is divided into cells of a fixed size with a discrete state attributed to each cell. The state of an individual cell changes discrete in time and depends only on the *neighborhood* of the cell which is most often defined as a set of cells located nearest in the geometrical sense.

The basic Nagel/Schreckenberg model [15] is a one-dimensional stochastic cellular automaton, where a road segment is divided into cells of a fixed size (typically 7.5m, which is enough to accommodate a single passenger car with sufficient space before and after the car). A cell can either be empty or occupied with a car traveling at a discrete velocity $v \in \{0, \ldots, v_{max}\}$. The behavior of a vehicle located at a i is specified by four simple rules [15], which are applied in the given order to all vehicles during a time step. The rules are applied in parallel to the vehicles, operating on the old state of the simulation (i.e. the state of the simulation before any calculations of the current time step have been performed).

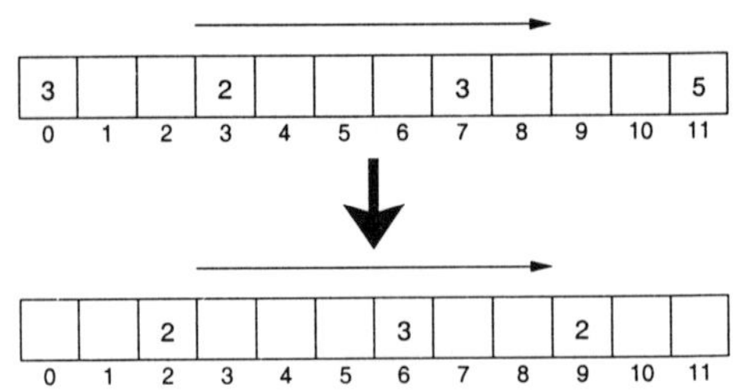

Figure 1. Example of vehicle movement

1) **Acceleration:** if the velocity v of the vehicle is lower than v_{max}, then it is increased by one $[v \rightarrow v+1]$
2) **Slowing down:** if there is a vehicle at site $i+j$ (with $j \leq v$), the velocity is reduced to $j-1$ $[v \rightarrow j-1]$
3) **Randomization:** if $v > 0$, then with probability p, the velocity v of the vehicle is decremented $[v \rightarrow v-1]$
4) **Vehicle motion:** the vehicle is advanced v cells

Figure 1 shows an example of vehicle motion in a short road segment with 12 cells. The vehicles moving from left to right are depicted by numbers inside the cells which also indicate their velocity. The state of the segment is shown before (first line) and after (second line) performing the state update of a particular time step. Note that the vehicle located in cell 9 after performing state changes chose to decrease the maximally possible velocity of 3 due to the probabilistic rule number 3).

Although extremely simple, the Nagel/Schreckenberg model exhibits realistic behavior. While at low traffic densities laminar flow of traffic can be observed, congestion clusters are formed at higher densities. Further, the formation of start-stop waves found in real freeway traffic is adequately represented by the model. This is illustrated in Figure 3, where the occupation of a road section (x-axis from left to right) is plotted against the simulation time (y-axis from top to bottom). A cell occupied by a vehicle is plotted as a black dot, while unoccupied cells are left blank. If the movement of a vehicle from left to right is not constricted by a congestion, its path over the road segment can be identified as a decreasing diagonal line. Further, congestion clusters (black areas) can be seen, where multiple vehicles are located close together.

3. Time-Parallel Simulation with Approximate State Matching

In most traditional parallel and distributed simulation approaches, work is mapped to a number of nodes by distributing *spatial* regions of the state variables to these nodes. Every node is subsequently responsible for computing changes of its subset of the state variables over time.

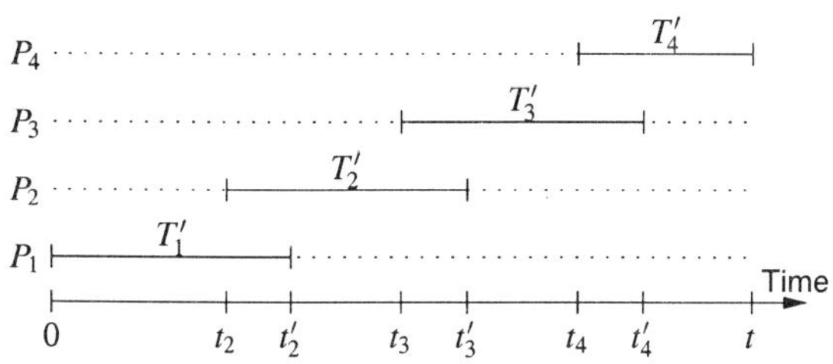

Figure 2. Overlapping time intervals

In contrast to that, time parallel simulation maps *time intervals* $T_i = [t_i, t_{i+1}]$ with $i \in \{1, \ldots, m\}$, where $t_1 = 0$ and $t_2, \ldots, t_m \in (0, t_{final})$ and $t_{m+1} = t_{final}$, to the computing nodes. Every node i is responsible for computing the evolution of all state variables over its time interval T_i.

There are two main advantages of this approach: Firstly, partitioning the state variables in a way that keeps dependencies (and thus communication) between nodes low is usually a nontrivial task, whereas partitioning of the time axes is often straightforward. To be more specific, time parallel simulation can even be applied where no reasonable partitioning of state variables is available. Secondly, during the simulation of each time interval, there is no need for communication between simulation nodes. I.e., every node can simulate its time interval independently from the other nodes.

However, in general the initial state at the beginning of every time interval is unknown with the exception of time interval T_1. Thus, all nodes simulating time intervals T_i, $i > 1$, do so by using a guessed initial state. When all nodes have simulated their time interval, usually the final state Z_{i-1} of interval T_{i-1} and the initial state z_i of the next interval T_i will not be identical. Thus, a so-called *fix-up operation* is applied. This means that node i continues simulation until some simulation time t for which its state matches that computed by node $i+1$ for simulation time t. This problem in time-parallel simulation is known as the *state-match problem* [4]. The fix-up computations may have to be applied repeatedly until the states match at all interval boundaries.

Another disadvantage of time-parallel simulation is the necessity of storing simulation states for state match performance. This might be a significant burden with a long overall simulation time, resulting in serious scalability issues.

In the sequel, we apply an alternative view of these iterative fix-up computations that is illustrated in Figure 2: every processor computes a time interval that overlaps with the time interval of the successor. The overlap has to extend to a simulation time for which the originally computed state equals that computed by the processor producing the simulation time overlap. To be more specific, the *fix-up period* of process P_i is the time interval $[t_{i+1}, t'_{i+1}]$. Now every process P_i is responsible for calculating the simulation results of the time interval $[t'_i, t'_{i+1}]$, hence the fix-up period of P_i can also be interpreted as a *warm-up period* of process P_{i+1}. In order to produce simulation results identical to that of a sequential simulation, the times t'_{i+1} have to be chosen such that the simulation states of each pair (P_i, P_{i+1}) of adjacent processes match at t'_{i+1}. In the worst case this may lead to a situation where node 1 has to compute the evolution of state variables for the whole simulation time. In this case, time parallel simulation degrades to sequential simulation. Note that this is only a different view on time-parallel simulation with exactly the same behavior as the more traditional views.

In order to have a reasonable chance that one of the states produced during the fix-up computation matches an originally computed state, the *behavior* of the simulation entities must be strictly repeatable. Hence, special care has to be taken for stochastic aspects of the model. Repeatability can be achieved by pre computation of random number sequences used in the model. As a cost efficient alternative, it is sufficient if the seeds for random number streams are preselected/precomputed for every time interval. This allows to use the same random number sequences for original simulations and fix-up computations.

The state-match problem renders time-parallel simulation for many models useless, especially for classes of models with complex states. However, in cases where the deviation of final and initial states of adjacent time intervals is only marginal, it may be feasible to accept the corresponding simulation run, although incorrect simulation results are produced. This concept of *approximate state matching* was successfully applied to time parallel simulation of simple queueing systems [10] and to cache simulation [9]. It can be interpreted as a toleration of incorrect state changes at inter val boundaries. The obvious advantage is the considerable gain in speedup due to lower computation and synchronization overhead. However, the increase in performance comes at the cost of an error that is introduced in the simulation results. If no further measures are taken, the error may seriously invalidate results.

In order to decide whether or not to accept states at interval boundaries, a distance measure between states has to be defined. Using such a measure, the deviation between the final state Z_{i-1} of interval T_{i-1} and the initial state z_i of the next interval T_i can be computed. Let δ_i be the deviation of states at interval boundary t_i. Furthermore, a tolerance Δ is defined. A simulation execution of an interval T_k is accepted if $\delta_k \leq \Delta$. If $\delta_k > \Delta$, fix-up computations have to be performed as in the original time-parallel simulation approach. However, these fix-up computations need not proceed until the corresponding states match exactly. It is sufficient that the difference of states is less than Δ.

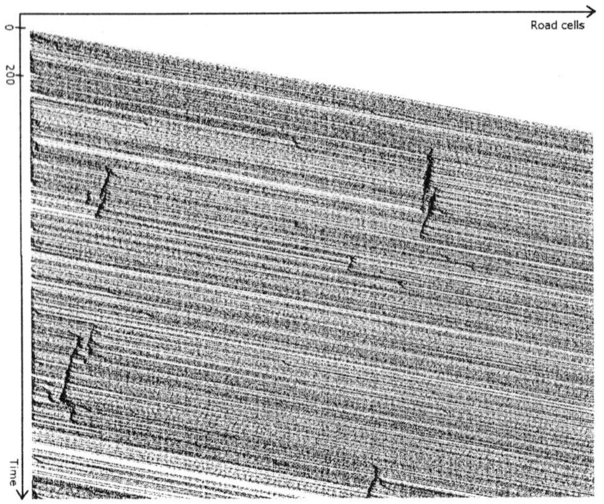

Figure 3. Trace of simulation starting at time 0

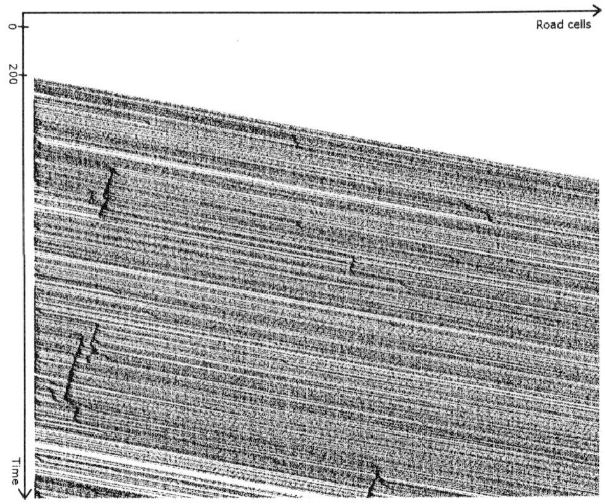

Figure 4. Trace of simulation starting at time 200

Tolerating incorrect state changes in approximate time parallel simulation induces an error in the simulation results. In general it is nontrivial to determine the error introduced to the simulation results depending on the tolerated deviation of states. In special cases, bounds for the error in simulation results can be computed based on the local deviations of states at all time interval bounds [9].

4. Time-Parallel Traffic Simulation

Parallelization approaches of traffic simulations based on the Nagel/Schreckenberg model using spatial decomposition, reported limited scalability with increasing number of processors [13, 14]. In these approaches, space parallel simulation requires communication after every single simulation time step. Thus, communication overhead becomes high for not tightly coupled processing nodes. For a similar model, Cetin et al. derive an upper bound on the number of processors that can be utilized efficiently, given the latency of the underlying communications network [1]. To be more specific, Cetin et al. report experiments using Ethernet for communication between processes, where speedup levels out at about 32 processes. This bound can be improved using faster means of communication, e.g. to about 64 processors with a Myrinet network.

4.1. Time Decomposition of the Traffic Model

Time-parallel simulation may be applied to overcome these parallelization limitations. As discussed in Section 3, for time parallel simulation the simulation time is partitioned into intervals $T_i = [t_i, t_{i+1}]$, where each interval contains a given number of time steps of the cellular automaton. Obviously, the processing done in each time step t depends on the state of the simulation after the preceding step $t-1$. Thus, the only time where the simulation state is known prior to execution is the initial state at simulation time zero. In analogy to time-parallel cache simulation [7], this problem can be approached by pretending that the road network is completely empty at the beginning of each time slice. This will produce incorrect simulation results which have to be corrected by the use of fix-up computations.

It appears to be manifest that this case occurs frequently in microscopic traffic simulation, rendering temporal parallelization useless here. Fortunately, microscopic traffic simulation is more robust to incorrect state changes than might be supposed. This is confirmed qualitatively in Figures 3 and 4, which show the trace of vehicle movements starting at two different simulation times with an empty road section as initial state. When comparing the state development of the simulation starting at a later time (Figure 4) with the simulation starting at time 0 (Figure 3), a fast state convergence can be noted. A quantitative analysis of the state convergence behavior of microscopic traffic simulation is presented in Section 5.

4.2. State Match Detection

An important aspect during fix-up computations of time-parallel simulation is to detect when two simulation states are identical (state matching). The original time parallel simulation approach requires an exact match of the associated states. In the cellular automaton traffic model, the comparison of two states is of the same order of complexity as the simulation of a time step. This means that exact state matching would cut down the amount of potential parallelism significantly. Furthermore, for exact state matching it is required to store all states of a simulation execution, which extends the memory requirement extraordinarily. Finally, in order to apply approximate state matching, a deviation measure has to be defined that allows to identify *similar* states. The definition of similarity of states can only be done in the context of the objectives of the simulation study. This means that two simulation states should only be viewed as similar if the simulation results produced as a consequence of these states are sufficiently close.

In order to define and study similarity of states, we introduce two different deviation measures: (a) a microscopic measure based on the comparison of single cells and (b) a macroscopic measure based on traffic densities in road sections. A variety of additional deviation measures have been considered that cannot all be discussed here.

4.3. State Deviation Measures

The *microscopic* deviation measure compares the cells of two states s_1 and s_2 in the driving direction of the model until the state of a cell in state s_1 differs from that in s_2. Let p be the index of the first cell from the beginning of the road whose cell state is equal in s_1 and s_2, i.e. all cells before p have a different cell state in s_1 and s_2. If there is no difference at all, $p = N$, the number of cells in the model. The microscopic measure (ranging from 0 to 1) is defined to be

$$\delta_{micro}(s_1, s_2) = 1 - \frac{p}{N}.$$

This means that the microscopic measure corresponds to 1 minus the percentage of the road (starting from cell zero) where the cell states are identical. An important property of this measure is that $\delta_{micro}(s_1, s_2) = 0 \leftrightarrow s_1 = s_2$. Thus, this measure can be used for exact as well as approximate state matching. However, the overhead for this measure is prohibitive (computational and memory complexities are identical to that of exact state matching). Hence, we only use it as a comparison basis for other aggregated deviation measures.

The *macroscopic* deviation measure that is used in Section 5.2 is called the *local density deviation*. It is computed as follows: the total number of cells N is partitioned into n sections (bins) of size $b = \frac{N}{n}$. In each bin, a local vehicle density is computed. This yields the following deviation measure:

$$\delta_{locdens}(s_1, s_2) = \frac{1}{N} \sum_{i=1}^{n} |\gamma(s_1, i) - \gamma(s_2, i)|$$

where $\gamma(s, i)$ is the number of vehicles in section i of state s. Note that if the number of bins is 1, two states are considered being equal if the number of vehicles in the two states is equal. On the other hand, if the number of bins equals the number of cells, two states are equal only if the occupation status of every single cell is equal in the two states.

It is important to realize that an aggregated (macroscopic) deviation measure may identify two states as being equal (i.e., yield a deviation of 0) even if they may not be exactly identical. Thus, using aggregated deviation measures, approximate state matching is performed implicitly, even if no explicit tolerance is applied. However, aggregated deviation measures are constructed in a way that gives rise to the speculation that similarity w.r.t. an aggregate measure corresponds to similarity w.r.t. the microscopic measure. This speculation is confirmed by experiments presented in Section 5.2 that show a significant correlation between the two proposed measures. The feasibility study in the following section also discusses the applicability of the proposed deviation measures to approximate state matching along the lines of [10].

5. Feasibility Study

Time-parallel traffic simulation, as introduced in Section 4, is feasible if only a small part of time intervals has to be re simulated during fix-up computations. The amount of fix-up computations is determined by the time until state matching occurs, which can be controlled with a tolerance in the case of approximate state matching. Here, the speed of state convergence in time-parallel traffic simulation is examined by emulating the fix-up computations as they would be performed by a time-parallel road traffic simulator. For a given time interval and trace of arriving vehicles, two different simulation executions are performed: One execution starts with an empty road segment, representing the determination of incorrect results before fix-up computations would be performed in the time-parallel simulator. The other execution starts with the *correct* state, where occupation of cells in the road segment has been determined by a warm-up phase. Now the states of both simulation executions can be compared at every time step and the convergence of states can be examined.

The results of experiments presented in this section were obtained with a prototypical implementation of the Nagel/Schreckenberg model for a unidirectional one-laned road segment without intersections consisting of 2000 cells. Vehicles arrive at one end of the road according to the given trace of vehicle arrivals and are put into an input queue. If at least one cell from the beginning of the road is empty, the first vehicle in the queue enters the road section. This allows for multiple vehicle arrivals in the same time step and ensures correctness in the case of a congestion spreading back to the beginning of the segment. All of the simulations were executed for 2000 time steps.

ρ	matching	mean	stdev	min	max
0.05	500	452.99	26.55	411	700
0.06	499	502.35	117.66	422	1340
0.07	360	752.61	385.75	435	1989
0.08	123	764.85	429.66	435	1993

Table 1. State match times of parallel simulations

5.1. Microscopic State Matching

As explained in Section 4.2, there is a prohibitively large overhead in exact state match detection. However, to gain insight into the state match behavior of time-parallel traffic simulation, a look at state match times (i.e. the times when exact state matching occurs) is worthwhile. Table 1 shows the results of experiments with average traffic densities ρ ranging from 0.05 (i.e. 5% of available cells are occupied in average) to 0.08 and 500 repetitions for every density level. Note that in this model, saturation of the road occurs with a traffic density of 0.08 [15]. With lower traffic densities, the states of almost all of the repetitions match before the end of the observed time interval $[0, 2000]$ (column *matching*) and the average time of matching (column *mean*) is close to the average vehicle travel time. With increasing traffic density, the fraction of successful state matching before the end of simulation decreases and the average time of matching increases. Judging from Table 1 alone, time-parallel traffic simulation with exact state matching seems to be reasonable for traffic densities up to some value between 0.06 and 0.07.

Especially for an application of approximate state matching, the speed of convergence of simulation states is of importance. The convergence of states for 500 replications of experiments is shown in Figures 5 to 7, using the microscopic state deviation measure introduced in Section 4.3. In Figure 5, the averages of all repetitions are presented

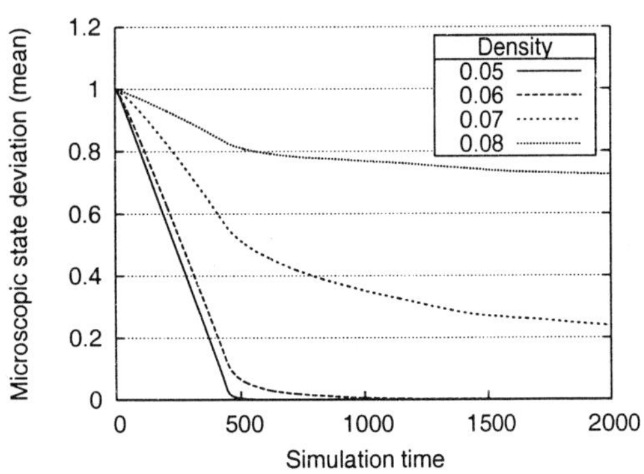

Figure 5. Microscopic state deviation over time

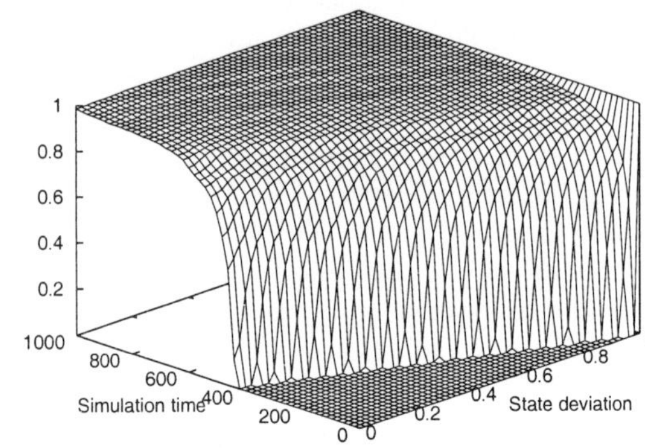

Figure 6. Deviation distribution over time (ρ = 0.06)

for various densities. With the smaller densities of 0.05 and 0.06, the deviation of states falls rapidly to zero, while with higher densities, only a gradual decrease can be observed.

Figures 6 and 7 show the evolution of the distribution of state deviations (y and z axes) against simulation time (x-axis) of two selected densities. While convergence of states is fast for all of the repetitions with $\rho = 0.06$ (Figure 6), the situation is different with $\rho = 0.07$ (Figure 7). With this density a large part of the repetitions exhibit rapidly converging states. However, there is a significant number of repetitions with no convergence at all (a state deviation of 1 – noticeable by the almost vertical lines near the right back plane of the diagram).

Hence, using the microscopic state deviation measure, time-parallel traffic simulation seems to be feasible only for traffic densities below 0.07. However, better results might be obtained for specific simulation objectives by utilizing alternative deviation measures (cf. Section 5.3).

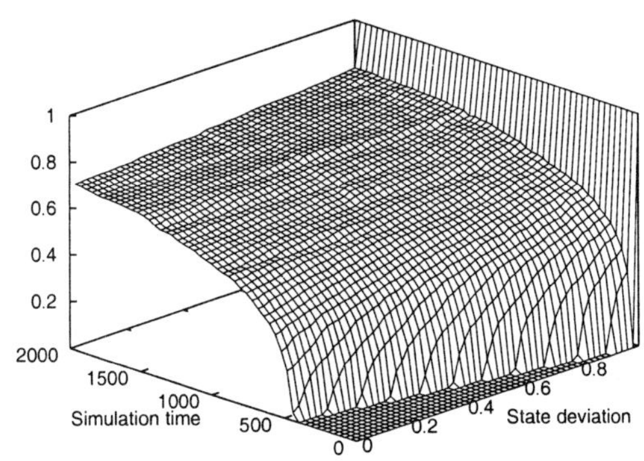

Figure 7. Deviation distribution over time (ρ = 0.07)

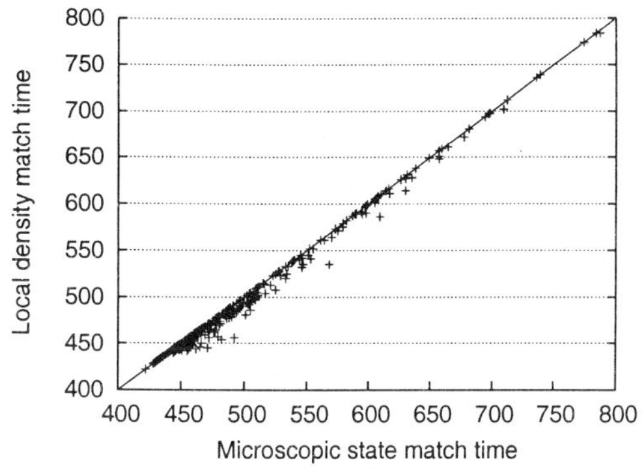

Figure 8. Microscopic state vs. local density ($\rho = 0.06$)

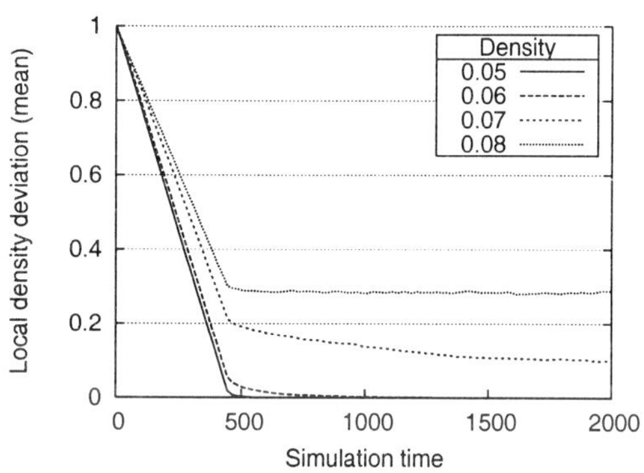

Figure 9. Local density deviation over time

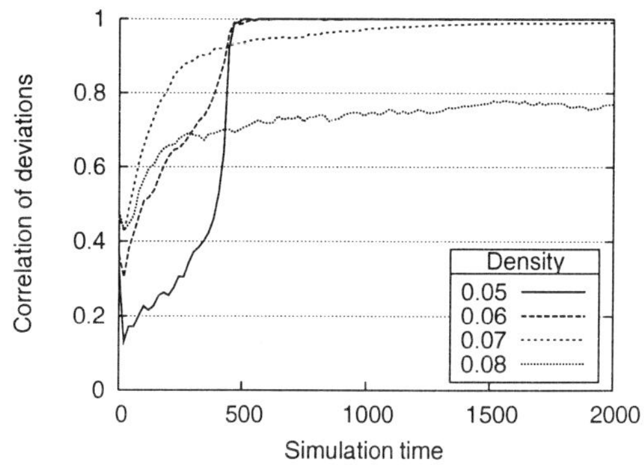

Figure 10. Correlation of microscopic state and local density

5.2. Aggregated Deviation Measures

Section 4.3 discussed the need for aggregated deviation measures to allow for an efficient detection of state matching and suggested one such measure. Here, the local density deviation measure is examined experimentally in order to validate its use in comparison to the microscopic state deviation measure. A moderate bin size of 50 cells has been used.

Figure 8 shows the match times of 500 repetitions with a density of $\rho = 0.06$ using the microscopic state deviation (x-axis) against the local density deviation (y-axis). It can be noted that all data points are located on or closely below the diagonal $y = x$. The situation is very similar for other densities not illustrated here. Hence, if only the times of exact matching are of interest, local density deviation seems to be an appropriate measure for state match detection, although a small bias towards the beginning of the simulation is introduced.

However, if the convergence behavior of states is of interest (e.g. if approximate state matching is to be applied), further investigation is necessary. Figure 9 shows the evolution of the local density deviation over simulation time (results are averages of 500 repetitions). To be able to compare experiments with different traffic densities, the graphs have been normalized by dividing the absolute deviation at every simulation time by the maximum of all deviations (which is in fact always the deviation at the beginning of the simulation). It can be noted that the curves of the lower global densities of $\rho = 0.05$ and $\rho = 0.06$ are very similar to that of the microscopic state deviation (Figure 5). With a global density of $\rho = 0.07$, the local density deviation drops faster than the corresponding state deviation, but still exhibits a similar shape of the curve. Only with $\rho = 0.08$, the relationship between local density and microscopic state deviations seems to be weak.

These observations are confirmed by Figure 10, which shows the correlation between microscopic state and local density deviations of 500 repetitions over simulation time (Spearman's r [8] has been used as correlation coefficient, because of its resistance to outliers occurring frequently at later times during the simulations). Correlation is generally low before the first vehicle has completely passed the road, but is significant afterwards. Therefore, the local density deviation is an appropriate measure after this event. An exception is the traffic density of $\rho = 0.08$, where no significant correlation can be observed.

5.3. Travel Time Deviations

In Section 5.1, time-parallel road traffic simulation was found not to be feasible with a traffic density of 0.07 and above, which was determined using the microscopic state deviation measure. However, in the case of approximate state matching, it is not necessarily the case that the microscopic state deviation properly reflects the error in the simu-

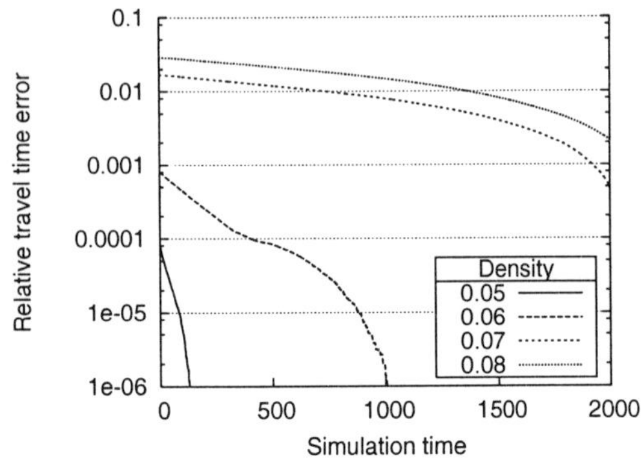

Figure 11. Average error due to approximate state matching

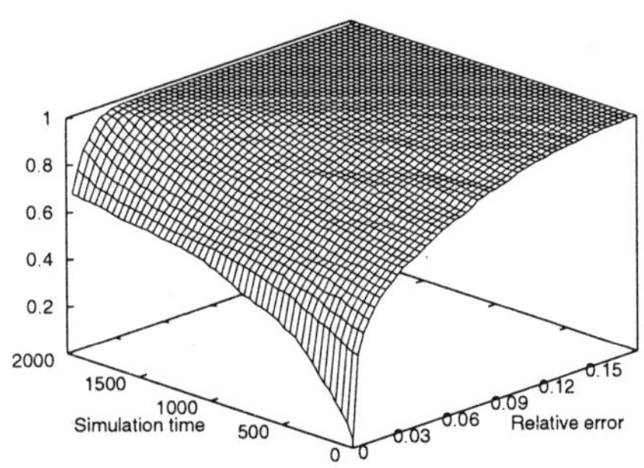

Figure 12. Evolution of error distributions

lation results introduced by the approximation. In that case, alternative deviation measures should be utilized, which may extend the applicability of time-parallel traffic simulation.

As an example of alternative measures, this section evaluates the case, where the simulation objective is to determine average travel times of vehicles over a road segment. A direct comparison between deviations of vehicle travel times and microscopic state deviation is hard to perform, as the travel time of a vehicle does not depend on a single state of the simulation alone, but rather on the set of all states of times where the vehicle is located somewhere on the road segment. On the other hand, there is only a weak dependency on the exact state of a single time step, viz. only on that part of the road where the vehicle is located during the time step. Hence, using microscopic state deviation is not reasonable in this case.

Figure 11 shows the relative errors in mean vehicle travel time (averaged over 500 repetitions) that would be introduced by an approximate state matching at a specific simulation time. The introduced error is generally low, not exceeding 1.5% of the correct vehicle travel time even with higher densities and it decreases monotonically with time, due to the accuracy of the simulation increasing with a growing amount of fix-up computations. For the smaller densities of $\rho = 0.05$ and $\rho = 0.06$, errors drop rapidly to zero, whereas there is a significant amount of error introduced with higher densities. However, when studying the distribution of errors over the 500 repetitions with $\rho = 0.08$, presented in Figure 12, it can easily be recognized that a large part of the average error is caused by a few outliers, especially at later simulation times.

6. Conclusions

Road traffic simulation is an important part of transportation research. Applications range from the investigation of small domains to large-scale simulation models. With increasing size of models, parallel and distributed simulation techniques can be applied to achieve a required level of performance. For the Nagel/Schreckenberg microscopic traffic simulation model examined in this work, domain decomposition has been used successfully as a parallelization approach. Unfortunately, the scalability of this approach is limited, depending strongly on the latency of the underlying communications network. This paper discusses the alternative possibility to apply temporal parallelization to road traffic simulation with the Nagel/Schreckenberg model and evaluates its feasibility.

To date, time-parallel simulation has mainly been applied to simulation models with rather simple complexities of simulation states. In contrast, microscopic traffic simulation exhibits high-dimensional and complex states, which cannot easily be predicted. However, with the fix-up-computation-based approach, it is possible to apply temporal parallelization: At the beginning of time intervals to be simulated concurrently, the road is supposed to be empty, creating preliminary results after an initial simulation phase and correcting these afterwards by the use of fix-up computations. The difficulty here is the efficient detection of state matching, which is necessary to stop fix-up computations. This can be solved by using aggregated state match measures, which should appropriately represent the matching of microscopic states and be efficient to calculate. Furthermore, if state deviation measures can be found, it is possible to use approximate state matching, which allows to increase the performance of the simulation by cost of an introduced error.

The feasibility of time-parallel road traffic simulation has been examined with varying traffic densities for a simple road topology. With lower densities, the states of concurrent simulations converge rapidly, indicating a low overhead due to fix-up computations in a time-parallel simulator. With higher densities, the feasibility of time-parallel traffic simulation seems to be restricted, although for specific simulation objectives, approximate state matching can be used to achieve reasonable simulation results. The measure of local density deviation has been examined and found to appropriately represent microscopic state deviations.

It remains to be seen if time-parallel traffic simulation is feasible for more complex road topologies, e.g. multi-lane traffic or road crossings. Based on the results of experiments with single-lane traffic, it might be speculated that with low traffic densities, convergence of states might be fast, even with more complex topologies. However, this depends on the exact topology and on the overall problem size.

References

[1] N. Cetin, A. Burri, and K. Nagel. A large-scale agent-based traffic microsimulation based on queue model. In *Proceedings of the 3rd Swiss Transport Research Conference*, 2003.

[2] R. Chrobok, J. Wahle, and M. Schreckenberg. Traffic forecast using simulations of large scale networks. In *Proceedings of the 4th International IEEE Conference an Intelligent Transportation Systems*, pages 434–439, 2001.

[3] J. Esser and M. Schreckenberg. Microscopic simulation of urban traffic based on cellular automata. *International Journal of Modern Physics C*, 8(5):1025–1036, 1997.

[4] R. M. Fujimoto. *Parallel and Distributed Simulation Systems*. John Wiley & Sons, New York, 2000.

[5] N. H. Gatner and N. H. M. Wilson, editors. *Transportation and Traffic Theory*. Elsevier, New York, 1987.

[6] A. G. Greenberg, B. D. Lubachevsky, and I. Mitrani. Algorithms for unboundedly parallel simulations. *ACM Transactions on Computer Systems*, 9(3):201–221, 1991.

[7] P. Heidelberger and H. S. Stone. Parallel trace driven cache simulation by time partitioning. In *Proceedings of the 1990 Winter Simulation Conference*, pages 734–737, 1990.

[8] G. W. Heiman. *Basic Statistics for the Behavioral Sciences*. Houghton Mifflin Academic, 4th edition, 2002.

[9] T. Kiesling. Approximate time-parallel cache simulation. In *Proceedings of the 2004 Winter Simulation Conference*, 2004.

[10] T. Kiesling and S. Pohl. Time-parallel simulation with approximative state matching. In *Proceedings of the 18th Workshop on Parallel and Distributed Simulation*, pages 195–202, 2004.

[11] W. Leutzbach. *Introduction to the Theory of Traffic Flow*. Springer, Berlin, 1988.

[12] Y. Lin and E. Lazowska. A time-division algorithm for parallel simulation. *ACM Transactions on Modeling and Computer Simulation*, 1(1):73–83, 1991.

[13] K. Nagel and M. Rickert. Parallel implementation of the TRANSIMS micro-simulation. *Parallel Computing*, 27:1611–1639, 2001.

[14] K. Nagel and A. Schleicher. Microscopic traffic modeling on parallel high performance computers. *Parallel Computing*, 20:125–146, 1994.

[15] K. Nagel and M. Schreckenberg. A cellular automaton model for freeway traffic. *Journal de Physique I*, 2:2221–2229, 1992.

[16] K. Nagel, D. E. Wolf, P. Wagner, and P. Simon. Two-lane traffic rules for cellular automata: A systematic approach. *Physical Review E*, 58(2):1425–1437, 1998.

[17] TRANSIMS – transportation analysis and simulation system. http://transims.tsasa.lanl.gov/.

[18] R. Wiedemann. Simulation des Straßenverkehrsflusses. In *Schriftenreihe des Instituts für Verkehrswesen*, 8. Universität Karlsruhe, Germany, 1974.

[19] S. Wolfram. *Theory and Applications of Cellular Automata*. World Scientific, Singapore, 1986.

Parallel Event-Driven Neural Network Simulations Using the Hodgkin-Huxley Neuron Model

Collin J. Lobb[1], Zenas Chao[2], Richard M. Fujimoto[1], Steve M. Potter[2]

[1] *College of Computing*
Georgia Institute of Technology
{collin,fujimoto)@cc.gatech.edu

[2] *Laboratory for Neuroengineering*
Georgia Institute of Technology
zenas@neuro.gatech.edu
stpotter@ece.gatech.edu

Abstract

Neural systems are composed of a large number of highly-connected neurons and are widely simulated within the neurological community. In this paper, we examine the application of parallel discrete event simulation techniques to networks of a complex model called the Hodgkin-Huxley neuron[1]. We describe the conversion of this model into an event-driven simulation, a technique that offers the potential of much greater performance in parallel and distributed simulations compared to time-stepped techniques. We report results of an initial set of experiments conducted to determine the feasibility of this parallel event-driven Hodgkin-Huxley model and analyze its viability for large-scale neural simulations.

1. Introduction

Much work in parallel and distributed simulation focuses on synchronizing time in hundreds or thousands of entities. Researchers have been able to create scalable algorithms that efficiently coordinate the temporal activities of these entities. However, there are many domains in which one must synchronize a massive number of entities. Many of these domains have not been investigated. In this paper, we will examine a relatively new domain in parallel and distributed simulation whose scale could eventually reach billions of entities making trillions of connections: the nervous system.

In parallel and distributed simulation, there are two main techniques for incrementing time: a time-stepped approach and an event-driven approach. Event-driven simulations have been shown to offer better performance. Thus, many efforts are devoted to creating suitable event-driven models. This allows one to abstract out the partitioning and synchronizing algorithms. In this paper, we will discuss the transformation of the Hodgkin-Huxley model [1] of a neuron, hence referred to as the "HH model", into an event-driven process and discuss some of our preliminary findings in simulating a large scalable number of these neurons.

We are investigating how network scale and interconnectivity affect the emergence of a large synchronous burst of neural activity called a "superburst" [2]. In order to investigate these network-level questions, we need the ability to run large network simulations. The computational requirements for such networks are much greater than those currently available on typical desktop computers. The effective use of parallel and distributed computation can help address these ever-increasing computational demands.

This paper is organized into eight sections. In section 2, we provide a brief introduction to neural systems. In section 3, we discuss previous work in simulating these neuron models. In section 4, we describe how we converted the continuous HH model into a discrete event-driven simulation model. In section 5, we discuss the implementation of the HH model using a parallel discrete event simulation engine called μsik [3] and the methods by which we create networks of these HH neurons. In section 6, we describe efforts to verify this model. In section 7, we discuss some initial scalability experiments on this event-driven HH model. Finally in section 8, we provide some concluding thoughts on these results and how one might go about improving them.

2. Neural Systems

Like most biological systems, neural systems are typically comprised of cells and the fluid that they inhabit (extracellular medium). These cells are able to communicate with one another. For many cells, these communication mechanisms involve the movement of ions, which are atoms with an electric charge. Most cells, including neurons, have a charged membrane but only a few types of cells (e.g. neurons and cardiac cells) are

1087-4097/05 $20.00 © 2005 IEEE

considered to be "electrically excitable" and are able to produce "electrical" responses that can be transmitted from cell to cell. It is important to remember that these "electrical" responses are in the form of ion flows, not flows of electrons.

A neuron (depicted below in Figure 1) is an electrically-excitable cell found in the nervous system. A neuron lives in a medium similar to seawater, which contains various ions. The *soma* is the cell body and has a charge due to the presence of these *ions*. The soma is surrounded by a selectively permeable *cell membrane*. The soma of a "pre-synaptic" neuron can produce an electrical response called an "action potential" that is transmitted down its *axon* to its *synaptic terminals* with some transmission delay. This "output" charge is then received from the *synaptic cleft* by the "post-synaptic" neuron via its *dendrites*.

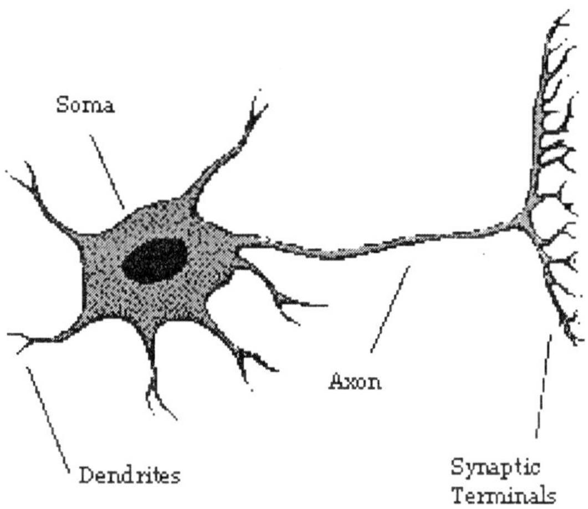

Figure 1: A schematized neuron

In the absence of any outside forces (i.e., at equilibrium), there will be differences in the amount of each ion on either side of the neuron's membrane. When we account for all of the forces due to (a) differences in concentration of each type of ion (i.e., "diffusion") and (b) the differences in the amount of positive and negative ions on each side (i.e., "electrostatic pressure"), we find that typically a neuron at equilibrium has a negative "membrane potential" (the charge difference on the neuron's membrane) in the range of -65 mV to -90 mV.

In the presence of outside forces, e.g., due to an injected current or the reception of a transmitted electrical response from another neuron, ions will flow into or out of the neuron through pores in the membrane called "ion channels". One can think of these ion channels as small gates that are each operated by a gatekeeper according to the laws of chemistry and physics. A gatekeeper will only allow the flow of certain types of ions at certain times at certain rates and in certain conditions. The membrane potential of the neuron is governed by a combination of how open each of these gates is and thus what ion flow is permitted across the membrane (i.e. its permeability). This "combination" is modeled by a set of differential equations that many experimenters such as Hodgkin and Huxley have quantified.

One of the most important processes that a neuron undergoes is the action potential, shown in Figure 2 (henceforth called an "AP"). It is characterized electrically as a very large increase in the membrane potential (on the order of 100mV) followed by a sharp decrease in potential that sends the membrane potential below its equilibrium value, followed by a slow return to equilibrium. This also defines the shape of the AP. Consider this in terms of gates and gatekeepers. The gatekeepers manipulate these gates, much like an operator controlling floodgates at a reservoir, trying to maintain equilibrium. For the neuron, there are two main types of gatekeepers: sodium gatekeepers that permit sodium flow into the neuron, and potassium gatekeepers that permit potassium flow out of the cell. Since both sodium and potassium ions are positive, all of these gatekeepers must work together in order to maintain equilibrium.

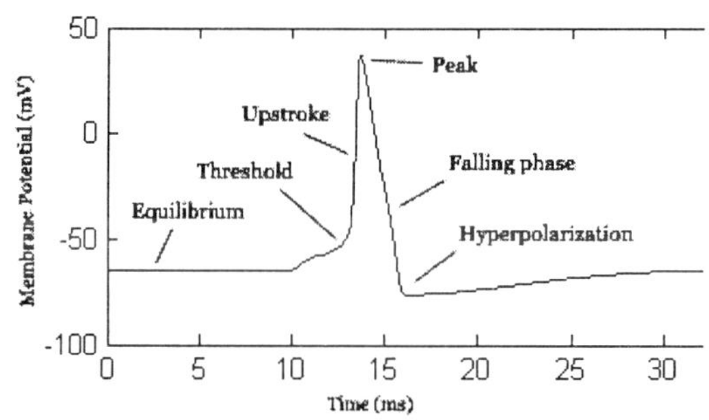

Figure 2: An action potential generated from a HH neuron in our simulation

In response to a sufficiently large positive input (e.g., injecting current into the cell) the sodium ion gatekeepers begin to open their gates to let sodium ions into the cell. This starts to increase the membrane potential, which in turn tells the sodium gatekeepers to let more sodium ions in. Meanwhile, there is a large number of potassium gatekeepers that prior to this sodium influx have been inactive and kept their gates closed. One of their jobs is to monitor the membrane potential and open up their gates when the membrane potential becomes too high. As the sodium level (and thus the membrane potential) begins to rise these potassium gatekeepers begin to take notice and open their gates to let potassium out of the cell. This would lower the membrane potential and return the cell to equilibrium. However, these potassium gatekeepers (letting potassium out) operate more slowly than the sodium gatekeepers (letting sodium in) so the membrane potential keeps rising. When the sodium ion gatekeepers let in enough sodium ions to raise the membrane potential above some threshold, a flood of additional sodium ions rush into the cell and quickly raise the membrane potential (the "upstroke"). The sodium gatekeepers try to quickly close the gates to control the flood of incoming sodium ions and are only able to effectively do so after letting in a large number of sodium ions. The potassium gatekeepers try to compensate by opening their gates further. Through the combination of the sodium gates closing and the potassium gates opening the large influx of positive ions is controlled and the membrane potential stops rising (the "peak" of the AP). However, at this point much potassium efflux is being allowed through the open potassium gates and the membrane potential begins to drop dramatically (the "falling phase"). The potassium gatekeepers slowly begin to notice that the membrane potential is dropping rapidly (this is their other responsibility) and that they need to close their gates. By the time they close their gates, the membrane potential has shot well below its equilibrium value ("hyperpolarization"). The sodium gatekeepers, however, quickly recover and begin to open their gates up just enough to increase the membrane potential to its equilibrium value. It is this process that experimenters such as Hodgkin and Huxley have mathematically modeled with a set of differential equations.

Neuroscientists have created a wide range of neuronal models but are split concerning how to deal with the action potential. One class of models called integrate-and-fire (henceforth called "IF") or "spiking" neuron models [4, 5], does not model the AP itself. These models effectively model the relationship between the neuron and its responses to various input currents but when this "threshold" is crossed they assume that a "spike" is generated and the neuron is instantaneously reset to some reset voltage. Think of this spike as taking the action potential from Figure 2 and compressing it from both ends until it approaches a vertical line. They are unable to capture the shape of the AP or accurately capture how the neuron responds to input during the action potential and during recovery. Despite being biologically unrealistic, the differential equations that govern their behavior are much simpler, easier to analyze, and are solvable. Models such as the HH model that are more biologically realistic are typically governed by a more complex set of differential equations that cannot be solved explicitly and therefore must be approximated using numerical analysis. To put it more quantitatively, 1 ms. of simulation time of the IF model requires around 5 FLOPS while the HH requires 1200 FLOPS [6]. For reasons such as these, large network simulations have been primarily limited to IF models. How might we be able to efficiently run large simulations of these more complex models? This is the driving question behind this work.

3. Related Work

Since IF models are primarily used in large scale network models, many iteratively-stepped parallel simulators have been created to efficiently simulate them: NEOSIM[13], the "Neocortex" simulator[11], SPIKELAB[14], SPIKENET [15] and Brettle and Niebur [16] to mention a few.

Using an iterative approach, one would iterate the governing differential equations for each dt and determine if its threshold has been crossed. If so, it would fire a spike. However, since the governing equations of the IF model can be solved, one can determine when the next time the IF neuron will fire. One could just keep an estimate of this "firing time" and update it if any more input is received. This is an event-driven approach and can be used to dramatically speed up the simulation[10, 17-19].

There are several existing parallel simulators capable of running networks of HH neurons: PNEURON, a parallel version of NEURON [7], PGENESIS [8], PARALLEL NEUROSYS[9], and the "Neocortex" simulator [10, 11]. Thomas [12] completed some work on running HH networks, which parallelizes time-stepped subsystems through waveform relaxation. As far as the authors are aware, only the "Neocortex" simulator has looked into partitioning algorithms. All of these simulators use an iterative approach. This paper explores the use of an event-driven framework on such HH networks.

4. Model Design

Muresan [10] states that ideally a large-scale neural simulator would support a high degree of interoperability in both the types of neurons that can be used and the techniques that each neuron employs. It would allow for both "implicit" and "explicit" synaptic representations. An explicit representation is one that says that neuron A connects to neuron B; in contrast, an implicit representation is one where neuron A connects to some other neuron as defined by some "rule of connectivity" [10]. This is in addition to the stereotypical desires of high accuracy, computational efficiency (speed), and minimal memory requirements.

Two major, interrelated aspects that one must consider when designing a parallel, event-driven HH simulation are (a) how to define the distinct entities making up the network and (b) the time intervals inherent in the model that can be used to extract lookahead. It is well known that good lookahead properties are desirable for optimistic synchronization mechanisms and essential for conservative techniques. The means by which network entities are defined will determine the types of events that are exchanged between entities, greatly affecting the partitioning strategy, and the types of optimizations that might be later applied.

One can define the neural system as being composed of at least four components: the soma, the axon, the synapse (i.e., the synaptic terminals, the dendrites and the synaptic cleft) and the extracellular medium (environment). One important question is how one would represent each of these neural components in such a way that performance is maximized for the types of experiments that will be performed. There are two things that we should keep in mind as we go about defining these components. First, for scalability purposes, a fairly compact representation for these components is desirable as memory requirements will be large. It is also important that we keep in mind that there are many simplifying assumptions that one makes in order to investigate network behavior. These can be made for a general class of neural systems or can be made purely on the nature of the experiment at hand.

Foremost, we describe several general simplifications that one might make when looking at network-level questions. The first simplification is that we are not modeling changes in the environment. We assume isopotentiality in the neuron, i.e., space is uniform and does not have to be explicitly considered in our equations. We are not modeling the interactions of the AP as it travels down the axon (e.g. by cable equations). We characterize the axon purely in terms of the delay in which an AP is transmitted. This delay is typically much larger than the timesteps that are used in these types of simulations. This transmission is also one-way. These two facts suggest that the axon would provide a good means of separating the neuron components from the synapse components.

Other important considerations arise when we consider a model for our synapses. The interactions between the post-synaptic neuron and the synapse itself are assumed to be instantaneous; i.e., the dendrites are not explicitly modeled. After an AP has been transmitted down the axon with some delay, it is considered to be instantly transmitted to the receiving neuron. Learning mechanisms inherent in a typical synaptic model (e.g., [20, 21]) describe instantaneous messages to be passed between the post-synaptic neuron and the synapse model. Unfortunately, this means that separating the neuron model from the synapse model would result in a zero-lookahead simulation. To avoid this and to improve the efficiency of interaction between these components, the representations of the neuron model and the synaptic model are combined into a single "synapse-neuron" simulation entity (i.e., are mapped to a single logical process), allowing instantaneous messages to be implemented as manipulations of shared state. However, combining these representations can be potentially disastrous if one has to replicate and coordinate multiple synaptic models. Because of our desire to obtain good lookahead, we wish to partition the network by splitting a neural connection by its axon and base our lookahead on the axonal transmission time. Fortunately, the standard synaptic models employed here are unidirectional, meaning that the synapse only affects the post-synaptic neuron and does not need to pass messages back to the pre-synaptic neuron. Therefore, we incorporate the synaptic model into the post-synaptic neuron's representation. The pre-synaptic neuron only needs to know to which synapses it should fire and what delays are involved in these firings. On the other hand, the post-synaptic neuron doesn't need to know this delay since it will receive this action potential as an event. The only replication of the synapse that is needed is the unique synaptic identifier.

An important consideration that arises from this combined representation is a hierarchical notion of variable scope. A neuron "owns" many synaptic representations. Thus, variables that are common to all of its synapses may be abstracted from the synaptic representation and put in the neuron representation. As this is a one-to-many relationship this can result in large memory savings. Computationally, a common means of speeding up various synaptic calculations (e.g. how much current is being received by a neuron at this moment) is to allow these calculations to be performed in batch for all of the synapses thus making the calculation more computational efficient (see [22] for an excellent example of this technique). One can extend this variable abstraction technique two more levels and say that state common to all neurons in a simulation process can be abstracted to that simulation process itself and that variables common to all simulation processes can become "constants" in the simulation. Such abstraction is a powerful means for limiting memory consumption.

One of the most challenging issues concerns how to define the "action potential event" and how to determine not only what it looks like but exactly when it occurred. Typically, they can be defined in terms of timing, kinetic models, and sometimes their "waveforms" (i.e., shape). Here we have chosen to use the synaptic model described in [22], which uses kinetic models to exhibit STDP[21] and short-term depression[20], but are not currently using any of the optimizations that they describe. STDP is a Hebbian learning mechanism based purely on timings of received and fired action potentials. Short-term depression describes a synapse as having limited resources and its output is affected by recent synaptic activity.

We can effectively model the AP here as a singular event where we only need to know the time it is received. The advantage of this is that we are effectively modeling the relationship between the voltage on the soma and any input current at all times. The disadvantage of this is that any small variation in AP shape is not transmitted to a receiving neuron. We could effectively transmit a waveform to a receiving neuron by knowing where it "starts" and "stops". This event-driven approach can theoretically handle all three types of synaptic models and thus promotes interoperability.

Since we are measuring the AP purely in terms of timing, we need to determine when the AP needs to be received. If we know the axonal delay then we need to determine when the AP was fired. This is essentially the same issue as the problem of finding the exact moment threshold crossing for an IF neuron (e.g. see the work in [17, 19, 24, 25]). For most IF models this is determined by explicitly solving the governing equations (see Brette [19] for an unsolvable IF model).

The HH model does not explicitly have any notion of a "threshold". However, this notion is quite useful here. For an event-driven HH model, one could set the "threshold" to be a voltage on the action potential with the idea that if this "threshold" was reached then a neuron must be firing an action potential (by definition, we must because the threshold is *on* the action potential). By experimentally varying the amount of a constant input current we can determine that the HH neuron will fire if the voltage is increased above -50mV. Thus we can say that -50mV is our threshold. This leaves us with the problem of determining the exact moment in which the threshold was crossed. One possible solution lies in the fact that the APs generated from a neuron generally have a narrow range of possible shapes. Given this, it seems plausible that we could better interpolate the exact crossing from the range of slopes that will occur at threshold crossing.

As the reader may have noticed it is not absolutely necessary to determine when this HH threshold was crossed. In the above paragraphs, this notion of "threshold" was used because it is a convenient place to define the moment when the action potential event occurred. However, one must keep in mind that the focus of events in discrete event simulation is not when an event actually is "sent" but when it is received. Instead of calculating the threshold and using that to determine when the action potential event should be received, one could determine this received time from the current stepped value of time directly. This would conflate the issue of what lookahead would be used but it is indeed possible especially for optimistic protocols. This type of approach may be very useful for more complex neurons where the shape of the AP is not as well defined.

The above description of an event-driven HH model affords several advantages. One such advantage is that it allows one to make various modeling optimizations concerning when the state of the neural components need not be updated. As an illustrative example, consider the 'synapse-neuron' representation at equilibrium. In the absence of noise, none of the values are changing so there is no point in updating it during these times. This is essentially the same type of rationale that led to the creation of event-driven IF models. The next time that it must be updated is when it comes out of equilibrium. Or do we? If the input is small and enough time would pass that the system would quickly respond back to equilibrium, one might be able to ignore it completely. This type of optimizations would be more acceptable for many network-level questions where the concern is typically about the generation of action potentials and not minute changes in a neuron's membrane potential.

A vital point to be made here is that in these neural systems there is a significant amount of noise. This noise is accounted for in many of the models as a "noise current". How might we be able to efficiently have random noise in the system? Does this make it a highly irregular problem and inherently more difficult to solve using this type of an approach? Does this dismiss the possible optimizations that are discussed above? These types of questions deserve further exploration (see [18] for an account of how to deal random noise in IF neurons).

5. Model Implementation

We chose to implement the neural system using the simulation engine μsik [3] (pronounced "Musik"), which is written in C++. μsik was developed to be able to efficiently simulate large-scale discrete-event simulations while allowing for maximum flexibility in its synchronization algorithm. It uses a micro-kernel design analogous to the one employed in operating systems. These inherent advantages are reminiscent of the design goals that were discussed in the previous section. As such, μsik is well-suited as a simulation engine for modeling this neural system. It also will provide a seamless way for testing different synchronization methodologies and comparing the performance advantages and disadvantages of each.

In μsik, a physical process is referred to as a 'Simulator' and is composed of many logical processes. Each logical process has its own synchronization algorithm. Logical processes communicate via discrete events. For conservative approaches, time is synchronized by determining the next event for each logical process via a global lower bound timestamp (LBTS) computation. Lookahead is important in these approaches for efficient synchronization as it allows the simulation engine to know when the federate will not schedule any new events.

The neural simulation is implemented using the 'synapse-neuron' representation as the logical process. Presently, a conservative protocol is used for synchronization. LPs send "action potential" events when their threshold is crossed. In order to meet the constraints of the conservative approach, each neuron updates its state at regular intervals. The reasoning behind this is outlined below.

In μsik, the physical process, called *NeuralSimulator,* is defined as a subclass of 'Simulator'. Inside this federate, there are pointers to output files for recording data. The logical processes are implemented as the class *Neuron*, a subclass of 'NormalSimProcess'. Inside *Neuron,* several state variables are defined including the current timestep, the threshold of excitation, the membrane potential, the time the neuron was last updated, and two ids. One id serves as the unique LP identifier for a *NeuralSimulator* instance. The other id is defined to be unique over the entire simulation and is used for determining noise current. In the previous section, the state of the synapse was described as being an explicit component in the representation for the post-synaptic neuron and only an identifier and a delay for the pre-synaptic neuron. We have implemented this as two C++ maps to which *Neuron* holds a pointer: one that holds a list of pointers to this *Synapse* class and the other that holds a list of neurons, their federate ids and the appropriate axonal transmission delay (in a *ConnectionInfo* class) to whom this neuron fires. Both maps are keyed on the unique synapse id.

The *Neuron* class sends and receives two types of messages. The first is an event called an "AP_ARRIVAL", that signals the neuron that an action potential has arrived at the neuron. When this event is received, the neuron will update its time from the last time it was updated and then update the appropriate state variables. An adaptive Runge-Kutta timestep method with error control, as described in [23], is used to perform the necessary numerical approximations. This algorithm allows one to set a tolerance on the calculated error and lets the timestep grow or shrink as needed in order to minimally meet this tolerance. This timestep is bound to a certain range and will grow/shrink at a constant rate. Each neuron LP has its own timestep value which is retained between events. This adaptive timestep method is also consistent with the event-driven philosophy.

One challenge is determining when this action potential event will actually be received. If the exact "firing time" were known then the AP event would need to be received at the firing time plus the axonal transmission time. For this implementation we simply see if the threshold was crossed during some timestep dt. If it was crossed then a neuron will fire an AP_ARRIVAL event at the end of this dt. We perform no interpolation to get a more exact crossing moment (within dt).

Unlike the IF event models, it is not known deterministically when this threshold will be crossed and one cannot employ a simpler LBTS-maintained system-wide "spike estimate" priority queue with conservative synchronization. To meet the constraints of the conservative protocol that we are currently using, we update the neuron periodically with a "WAKEUP" event. If the threshold has not been crossed then we could theoretically fire at any time (e.g. a supra-threshold input current arrives). In order to ensure that the received event occurs in the LPs future and meets the constraints of the conservative protocol we require that the WAKEUP event occurs at one-half the minimum axonal transmission delay. As a result of this, we must define our lookahead as also being one-half the minimum axonal transmission delay.

However, if a threshold has been crossed and we are currently generating the AP we know that we cannot fire again until the AP finishes and a period of time that the neuron cannot fire again (called the "absolute refractory period") has passed. We have experimentally calculated a very conservative estimate of the sum of these two periods as 10ms. Thus, one-half the minimal transmission time plus 10ms is the next time that our neuron would have to be updated.

The use of this WAKEUP event has an interesting consequence in that the more the neuron fires the less often we need to update its state via a WAKEUP event. This suggests that the simulation may get better performance if there is a moderate amount of activity. We investigate this quantitatively in section seven.

To model noise in the system, we added a noise current to the HH model. The value used is obtained by a Gaussian distribution with a mean of 700nA and standard deviation of 7500 and is sampled upon every time increment. This was defined with the intuition that most of the noise will generate sub-threshold responses but occasionally a neuron will receive supra-threshold noise, generating an action potential. Experimentally, if these large noise currents did not exist then the dynamics of our ion channels would simply converge to a steady-state range of a few millivolts above equilibrium.

The creation of these networks and its partitioning is done by a separate C++ program. This program will generate a network configuration based on [26]. The network generated is consistent with biological data in that synaptic connections between two neurons are much more likely if those neurons are near each other. It is important to note that the number of synapses generated will grow as the amount of neurons in the simulation grows! This relationship is shown in Figure 3. The current version of this program is extremely memory intensive and limits us to creating a network below 10,000 neurons.

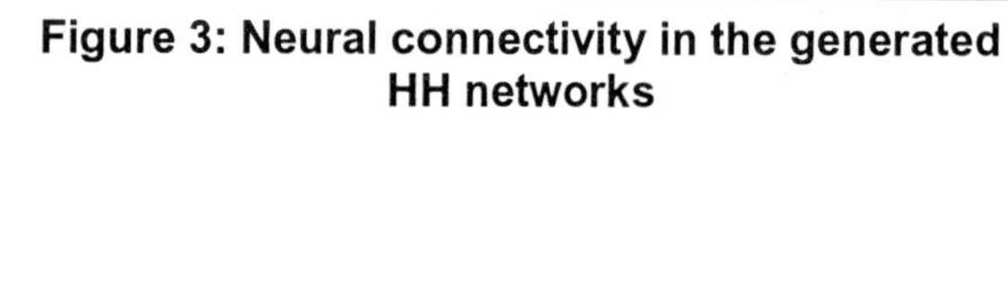

Figure 3: Neural connectivity in the generated HH networks

The partitioning of these networks is currently done through a simple scoring system where each synapse is given a weighted score based on the transmission delay and the number of synapses that are firing to the same neuron. Qualitatively, this weighted score is a measure of how often events will be received by the post-synaptic neuron. We iterate through the synapses from highest score to lowest score assigning neurons to processors. If both neurons for a synapse are unassigned then both are assigned in a round robin order to the next processor. If only one of the neurons is unassigned then it is either assigned to the same processor as the already assigned neuron or to the next processor. The greater the score of the synapse the more likely it is that it will be assigned to the same processor. The partitioned network for each processor is written to a unique input file that a *NeuralSimulator* reads in when it is initialized.

6. Model Verification

It is very difficult to verify that the network that we have created will generate reasonable neuronal activity in the absence of experimental data. Such verification requires a fair amount of parameter tuning. In the present paper, we are more concerned with if the basic mechanisms are correct and how different parameters (e.g. those that increase the chance that a neuron will fire an AP) will affect simulator performance. In order to investigate this, we have conducted several efforts to verify the neuron and synaptic models used in our implementation.

In order to verify our model of the HH neuron, we compared the event-driven model to a standard time-stepped HH model. The event-driven model appears to generate a normal action potential shape (see Figure 2) and respond similarly to sub-threshold input currents. It is worth noting here that since we are using numerical approximation the results of the comparison will not be exact.

We have completed some preliminary verification on our synaptic model. Initial testing on the mechanisms of STDP in our synaptic model and each of these variables indicates it appears to be responding correctly. We have done no testing with our short-term depression implementation so we have not included it in the experiments below. Verification of the biological accuracy of the networks that we generated remains an area of future work.

7. Initial Results

An initial set of simulation runs were conducted in order to test the feasibility of this event-driven Hodgkin-Huxley model and to access its scalability and performance. The simulations were run on a single cluster node consisting of 8 550 MHz PIII Xeon SMP processors with an available 4GB RAM. All simulations were conducted on a single node and thus there is no overhead due to intern-node communications.

Networks of size 25, 50, 100, 200, and 400 neurons were created according to the description in section five and simulated for 15 seconds of simulation time using 1, 2, 4, and 8 processors. Each neuron initially received between zero and four action potentials at random times in the first twenty milliseconds of the simulation. These inputs were designed to augment the spontaneous activity of these networks. All synapses in these networks were excitatory, meaning that input currents increase the membrane potential of the neuron. The speedups for these networks are shown in Figure 4.

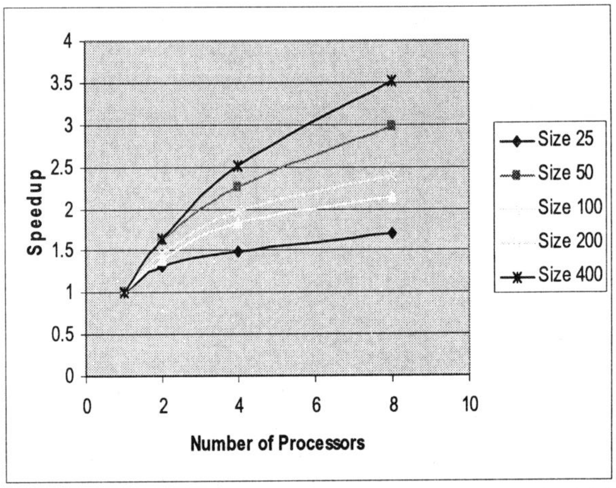

Figure 4: Speedup for networks of 25, 50, 100, 200, and 400 neurons on 1, 2, 4 and 8 processors.

As can be seen from the results in Figure 4, we are able to achieve good speedup in our neural networks. The network of 50 neurons offers particularly good speedup here because there are fewer remote events due to the way the network is partitioned. One might be able to achieve better speedup with other networks with better partitioning. These results suggest that one may be able to effectively run larger networks of these event-driven Hodgkin-Huxley neurons.

Next, we conducted an experiment to determine how simulation performance changes as network activity increases. In order to test this, we varied the maximal synaptic conductance (g_{max}) in a set of 15 second simulations on a network of size 100 on a single processor. The results are shown in Table 1. This experiment demonstrates that we are able to achieve better performance when there is a moderate amount of activity.

Table 1: Effects of Network Activity on Execution Time of a 100 HH Neuron Network

g_{max}	APs Fired	Total Elapsed Time (s)
0.010	402	11761.8
0.015	425	11745.2
0.030	398	11747.2
0.050	399	11699.6
0.065	412	11708.8
0.075	461	11445.6
0.090	417	11403.5
0.100	427	11518.3
0.130	481	10772.0

Important factors that determine the execution time are the number of events that must be processed and the amount of computation required to process each event. In our model there are two types of events: a WAKEUP event and an AP_ARRIVAL event. In Table 2 below, we list the percentage of each event that we process in our simulations. As one can see the number of WAKEUP events is far greater than the number of AP_ARRIVAL events. Efforts to reduce the number of WAKEUP events needed or the regularity in which they occur would greatly reduce the number of events that need to be processed and could yield much better performance.

Table 2: Percentage of Each Event in Simulations

	% AP_ARRIVAL Events	% WAKEUP Events
25	0.0677	99.9323
50	0.0787	99.9213
100	0.0604	99.9396
200	0.1046	99.8954
400	0.1567	99.8433

It is important to be able to characterize the computation time of each of these events. In order to determine this, the time taken to process each type of event was recorded in a separate set of simulations that were setup as described above but ran for only 1s of simulation time.

In Figure 5, we can see the amount of time to process each event increases as the size of our network increases. The WAKEUP event updates the state of the neuron to the timestamp in that event. The time to process this event grows roughly linearly with network size because the number of synapses for which we must calculate the synaptic input grows linearly (see Figure 3). Optimizations that try to pull out computations from individual synapses may greatly help speed up the computation here (e.g., see [22]).

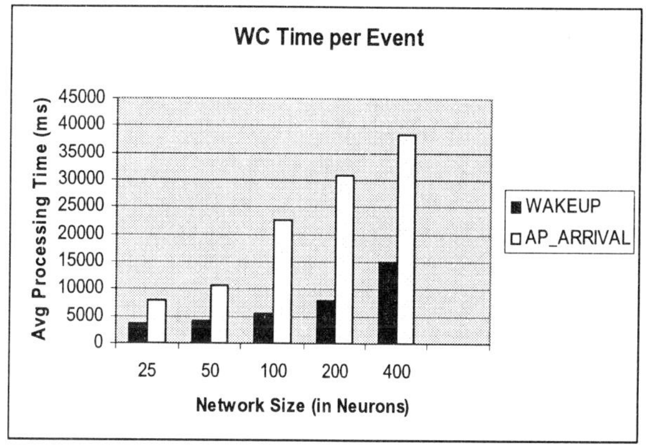

Figure 5: Wall clock processing time for WAKEUP and AP_ARRIVAL events for networks of size 25, 50, 100, 200, and 400 neurons

The AP_ARRIVAL event updates the state of our neuron to the timestamp of that event and then updates the state of the synapses for the arrival of an action potential. The time to process an AP_ARRIVAL event will grow similar to the WAKEUP event because of linear synaptic growth. In addition, we must find and update the appropriate synapse in our synaptic representation (a C++ map). This computation is logarithmic and accounts for the difference between the two types of events.

8. Conclusion

In this paper, we have described an event-driven Hodgkin-Huxley neuron that offers promise for effective parallel simulation of larger networks. This technique offers good performance as the networks size increases, better performance when there is moderate activity in the network, and meets several of the design criteria described in [10] for large scale neural simulators.

From the simulation side, there are many future directions that could be pursued. These include: improving the partitioning algorithm; investigating the use of other synchronization algorithms, experimentation on larger networks with a larger number of processors; achieving a lookahead based on action potential events only; characterizing and limiting the memory consumption of the simulation; and performing a comparison with a time-stepped approach to determine what, if any, savings result from using this event-driven approach.

From the modeling side, there are equally as many directions that deserve further investigation. These include: further verification of the neuron and synapse models and networks for biological realism and parameter sensitivity; a better characterization of the noise current and the questions that it begs; and investigating other techniques and optimizations that may be employed to improve the computational speed in which events are processed.

Appendix: Model Details

The Hodgkin-Huxley model is a set of four differential equations (1-4). The synaptic model is also a set of four differential equations (5-8).

(1) $-C * dV/dt = I_{noise} - (I_{Na} + I_K + I_{leak})$

a. $I_{Na} = g_{na} * m(t)^3 * h(t) * (V - E_{Na})$

b. $I_K = g_K * n(t)^4 * (V - E_K)$

c. $I_{leak} = g_{leak} * (V - E_{leak})$

(2) $dm/dt = (m_{inf} - m) / \tau$

(3) $dn/dt = (n_{inf} - n) / \tau$

(4) $dh/dt = (h_{inf} - h) / \tau$

(5) $dg_{ex}/dt = -g_{ex} / \tau_{ex}$ (Excitatory Synapses)

(6) $dg_{in}/dt = -g_{in} / \tau_{in}$ (Inhibitory Synapses)

(7) $dM/dt = -M/\tau_-$

(8) $dP_a/dt = -P_a/\tau_+$

Equation 1 was solved using adaptive Runge-Kutta using a tolerance of 10^{-11}. Equations 2-8 were formulated in terms of an update rule (of the form $x(t + dt) = \dots$) and evaluated for the appropriate value of V. These parameters resulted in average timesteps in the range of 0.001 ms. to 0.00004 ms. for the first set of experiments described in section seven.

Parameter values for these equations were given in their respective papers. Similar to [21], we set the initial value of g_a to g_{max} in order to maximize network activity (g_{max} = 150 pS).

Acknowledgements

This research was supported in part by NSF grant ATM-0326431.

References

[1] A. L. Hodgkin and A. F. Huxley, "A quantitative description of membrane current and its application to conduction and excitation in nerve." *Journal of physiology*, vol. 117, pp. 500-544, 1952.

[2] Nadasdy Z. , W. D. A., Potter S.M. (2003). "Attractor dynamics of superbursts in living neural networks." SFN 2003, New Orleans, LA.

[3] K.Perumalla, "Musik – A Micro-kernel for Parallel/Distributed Simulation Systems", PADS 2005.

[4] L. Lapicque, "Recherches quantitatives sur l'excitation electrique des nerfs traitée comme une polarisation," vol. 9, pp. 620-635, 1907.

[5] W. Gerstner and W. M. Kistler, *Spiking neuron models: single neurons, populations, plasticity*. New York: Cambridge University Press, 2002.

[6] E. M. Izhikevich, "Which model to use for cortical spiking neurons?" *IEEE transactions on neural networks*, vol. 15, pp. 1063-1070, 2004.

[7] M. Hines and N. T. Carnevale, "The NEURON Simulation Environment," *Neural Computation*, vol. 9, pp. 1179-1209, 1997.

[8] J. M. Bower and D. Beeman, *The book of GENESIS: exploring realistic neural models with the GEneral NEural SImulation System*. Santa Clara, Calif.: Telos, 1995.

[9] P. Pacheco, M. Camperi, and T. Uchino, "PARALLEL NEUROSYS: a system for the simulation of very large networks of biologically accurate neurons on parallel computers," *Neurocomputing, July 1999*, vol. 32-33, pp. 1095-1102, 2000.

[10]I. I. Muresan R.C., "Principles of Design for Large Scale Neural Simulators," presented at International Conference on Automation, Quality and Testing, Robotics, Cluj-Napoca, 2004.

[11]I. I. Muresan R.C., "The "Neocortex" Neural Simulator. A Modern Design," presented at International Conference on Intelligent Engineering Systems, Cluj-Napoca, 2004.

[12]E. A. Thomas, "A parallel algorithm for simulation of large neural networks," *Journal of Neuroscience Methods*, vol. 98, pp. 123-34, 2000.

[13]N. Goddard, G. Hood, F. Howell, M. Hines, and E. De Schutter, "NEOSIM: portable large-scale plug and play modelling," *Neurocomputing*, vol. 38-40, pp. 1657-61, 2001.

[14]C. Grassman and J. K. Anlauf, "Fast digital simulation of spiking neural networks and neuromorphic integration with SPIKELAB," *International Journal of Neural Systems*, vol. 9, pp. 473-8, 1999.

[15]A. Delorme, J. Gautrais, R. van Rullen, and S. Thorpe, "SpikeNET: a simulator for modeling large networks of integrate and fire neurons," *Neurocomputing*, vol. 26-27, pp. 989-996, 1999.

[16]D. Brettle and E. Niebur, "Detailed parallel simulation of a biological neuronal network," *IEEE Computational Science & Engineering*, vol. 1, pp. 31-43, 1994.

[17]M. Mattia and P. Del Giudice, "Efficient event-driven simulation of large networks of spiking neurons and dynamical synapses," *Neural Computation*, vol. 12, pp. 2305-29, 2000.

[18]J. Reutimann, M. Giugliano, and S. Fusi, "Event-driven simulation of spiking neurons with stochastic dynamics," *Neural Computation*, vol. 15, pp. 811-30, 2003.

[19]R. Brette, "Event-driven simulation of integrate-and-fire neurons with exponential synaptic conductances," *Submitted*, 2005.

[20]H. Markram, Y. Wang, and M. Tsodyks, "Differential signaling via the same axon of neocortical pyramidal neurons," *Proceedings of the National Academy of Sciences of the United States of America*, vol. 95, pp. 5323, 1998.

[21]S. Song, Miller, K.D. and Abbott, L.F., "Competitive Hebbian Learning Through Spike-Timing Dependent Synaptic Plasticity," *Nature Neurosci*, vol. 3, pp. 919-926, 2000.

[22]M. Giugliano, M. Bove, and M. Grattarola, "Fast calculation of short-term depressing synaptic conductances," *Neural Computation*, vol. 11, pp. 1413-26, 1999.

[23]W. H. Press, *Numerical recipes in C: the art of scientific computing*, 2nd ed. Cambridge; New York: Cambridge University Press, 1992.

[24]M. J. Shelley and L. Tao, "Efficient and accurate time-stepping schemes for integrate-and-fire neuronal networks," *Journal of Computational Neuroscience*, vol. 11, pp. 111-19.
[25]T. Makino, "A discrete-event neural network simulator for general neuron models," *Neural Computing & Applications*, vol. 11, pp. 210-23, 2003.
[26]R. Segev and E. Ben-Jacob, "Generic modeling of chemotactic based self-wiring of neural networks," *Neural Networks*, vol. 13, pp. 185-99, 2000.

Optimistic Parallel Discrete Event Simulations of Physical Systems using Reverse Computation

Yarong Tang, Kalyan S. Perumalla, Richard M. Fujimoto
College of Computing, Georgia Institute of Technology
Atlanta, Georgia 30332-0280
{yarongt, kalyan, fujimoto}@cc.gatech.edu
and
Homa Karimabadi, Jonathan Driscoll, Yuri Omelchenko
SciberNet Inc.
Solana Beach, CA 92075
{homak, driscoll, yurio}@scibernet.com

Abstract

Efficient computer simulation of complex physical phenomena has long been challenging due to their multi-physics and multi-scale nature. In contrast to traditional time-stepped execution methods, we describe an approach using optimistic parallel discrete event simulation (PDES) and reverse computation techniques. We show that reverse computation-based optimistic parallel execution can significantly reduce the execution time of a plasma simulation without requiring a significant amount of additional memory compared to conservative execution techniques. We describe an application-level reverse computation technique that is efficient and suitable for complex scientific simulations involving floating point operations.

1. Introduction

Parallel Discrete Event Simulation (PDES) has been an active research area in the high performance computing community for many years. Synchronization techniques for PDES systems are usually classified into two pricipal categories: conservative approaches that avoid violating the local causality constraint, and optimistic approaches that allow violations to occur, but provide a mechanism to recover. The operation of recovering a previous state in an optimistic parallel simulation is known as a *rollback,* and involves undoing incorrect computations.

A widely used technique for implementing rollback is *state-saving* that saves the values of state variables prior to an event computation and restores them by referring to these saved values upon rollback. *Copy state saving* creates an entire copy of a process's state; *incremental state saving* keeps a log of changes to individual state variables; *infrequent state saving* periodically saves the entire copy of the state. A relatively new technique for rollbacks, *reverse computation* [1], realizes rollbacks by performing the inverses of the individual operations executed in the event computation. These techniques have been exploited in small- and large-scale parallel simulations.

However, advances in PDES research to date have yet to be explored in space physical science, where multi-physics and multi-scale physical systems are modeled by partial differential equations and particles. Traditionally, simplified models of such physical systems have been simulated using time-driven or time-stepped approaches [2]. The inherent limitations of the time-stepped approach prevent the simulation of more complex physical systems that are important in plasma physics and other areas of science. Even the latest techniques developed in time-stepped research such as adaptive mesh refinement (AMR) [3] are constrained by excessive computational requirements and the necessity to update all cells within a given mesh patch based on the Courant-Friedrichs-Levy (CFL) condition in that patch. Discrete event simulation was recently used to model spatially discretized physical systems [4] where it was shown that this approach not only alleviates the constraint of the CFL condition but also provides a significant performance advantage over the time-stepped approach.

In our work, we extend this work and apply optimistic

1087-4097/05 $20.00 © 2005 IEEE

parallel discrete event simulation techniques to this problem. Because memory constraints are often a severe limitation in the size of the computations that can be performed, reverse computation offers greater promise than traditional state saving techniques. We explore the use of reverse execution for plasma simulations to gain new insights for such challenging, complex physical systems. The combination of DES methodology and reverse computing techniques offers the potential to dramatically reduce the amount of time required to perform plasma simulations without incurring a large penalty in additional memory requirements.

The main contributions in this work can be summarized as follows. To our knowledge, this is the first work to apply reverse computation techniques to parallel physical system simulations and to show performance advantages using this approach. In addition, we provide a simple model and guidelines for creating reverse simulation codes at the application level that may help physicists or astrophysicists to develop simulation prototypes without comprehensive knowledge of PDES mechanisms.

The remainder of this paper is organized as follows. The next section discusses related research. Section 3 provides an overview of the physical system we simulate and the reverse computation approach. Section 4 gives an in-depth discussion of the reverse computation implementation and discusses its challenges. Section 5 presents experimental results from a preliminary performance evaluation study. We conclude by reporting current and future work in this area and provide guidelines for reversing parallel physical simulation codes.

2. Related Work

A limited amount of research has examined physical system simulation using parallel discrete event simulation techniques. Perhaps the earliest was the "colliding pucks" application developed for the Time Warp Operating System (TWOS) [5]. This work, modeling a set of pucks traveling over a frictionless plane, was used to benchmark an early implementation of the Time Warp protocol. Lubachevsky discusses the use of conservative simulation protocols to create cellular automata models of Ising spin [6]. Other work describes challenges in using discrete event simulation techniques for a few other physical system problems [7]. A formal approach to both discrete event and continuous simulation modeling based on DEVS (Discrete EVent System Specification), was proposed by Zeigler et al. [8] and some numerical solutions have been examined based on the DEVS formalism [9].

Seminal work in optimistic parallel discrete event simulation was completed by Jefferson [10]. State saving has historically been the dominant approach to enabling the rollback of computations. Much work has been done to reduce the cost of state saving both using hardware [11] and software support. The less costly software approaches reported in the literature include copy state saving, incremental state saving [12, 13] and infrequent state saving [14, 15, 16, 17]. A different approach avoiding the cost of state saving was first described in [1], where reverse execution is used to roll back computations. Their reverse procedures were automatically generated by a compiler. More recent work using reverse execution for parallel network simulations, using manually generated code, was reported in [18]. Our work is different in that it applies reverse execution techniques to the simulation of physical systems that involve complex floating point operations and generates reverse code based on application semantics.

Traditionally, complex physical systems described by partial differential equations and particles are modeled by time-stepped simulations. The authors in [4] recently demonstrated both the feasibility and efficiency of applying discrete event simulation (DES) methodology to model such complex systems. Their study shows that a performance improvement of up to two orders of magnitudes is achievable by switching from a time-stepped approach to an event-driven approach. Our study is based on their work and focuses on *parallel* execution techniques for their DES models. In particular, we examine the feasibility of optimizing the parallel synchronization mechanism by applying reverse computation techniques.

3. Overview

In this section we describe the computational plasma simulation model that is used as a case study. A more detailed discussion on the DES modeling methodology and the physics behind the models can be found in [4]. Since our focus is on the use of reverse execution techniques in optimistic simulation, a high level description of the model suffices for our purpose.

3.1. Computational Model: PIC Simulation

One of the great challenges in space physics is to understand how the solar wind interacts with the earth's magnetosphere. The work presented in [4] was the first to use a DES approach to simulating such complex physical systems. A feasibility study based on the well-known particle-in-cell (PIC) model [19] was described to provide the foundation for development of such multi-physics and multi-scale simulations. We choose this same model for our feasibility study.

The PIC modeling approach serves as a good starting point in theoretical research in plasma dynamics. This model is conceptually simple, yet captures the characteristics of physical phenomena involved and can be extended to more complex models. However, the PIC simulation is nontrivial in that it simulates movements of millions of particles and their interactions with the fields. There has been considerable interest in improving its performance in the high performance computing community. Although we apply reverse computation method only to this particular model in our study, the programming model and methodology used here are representative of grid-based physical systems. Therefore, the approach presented here may be applicable to a wider range of physical systems.

We limit our simulations to a one-dimensional electrostatic model using spherical coordinates. Figure 1 illustrates a plasma PIC simulation of charging a spacecraft immersed in neutral plasma by injecting a charged beam from its surface [19]. The spacecraft is initially charge-neutral and immersed in the charge-neutral plasma of the solar wind. A charged beam is periodically injected from the spacecraft surface. The effect of beam injection is two-fold: the surface charge of the spacecraft incurs a change equal in magnitude but with an opposite sign to the injected beam particles; the field in the plasma space incurs a change equal to the beam both in magnitude and sign. The change in plasma field would affect the plasma particles' movement which in turn affects the plasma field.

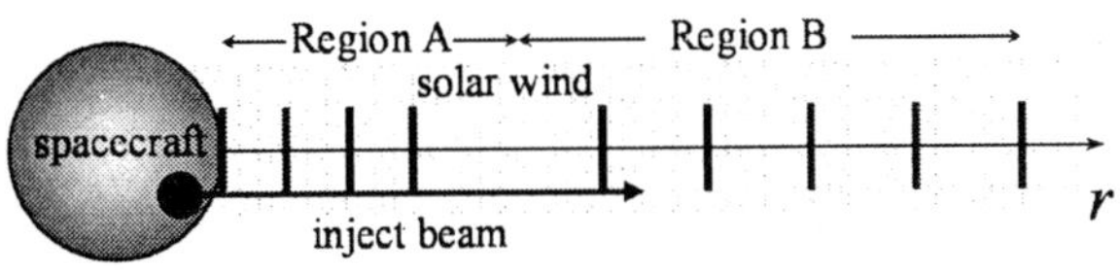

Figure 1. Schematic of the PIC model

3.2. Parallelization

In PDES of a PIC model, the simulation domain is divided into "cells" with each cell mapped onto one logical process (LP). In our spacecraft model, each cell is called a "shell", and is modeled as a Shell class (we will use the terms cell and shell interchangeably). Two distinct regions are shown in figure 1, based on different grid spacing. The state of each LP includes the cell field variables and the states of all particles within the cell boundaries. The dynamic behavior of the system is driven by particle movements that are modeled by events. Whenever a particle moves across a cell boundary, the electric field in the affected cells is updated by keeping track of the charge that crosses the boundary [4]. Note that field updates are limited to active cells in which events are allowed to be scheduled.

There are three types of events associated with particle movements: *ParticleArrivalEvent, ParticleDepartureEvent* and *ParticleInjectEvent*. The corresponding event handlers are outlined in figure 2. When the simulation starts, all active cells are initialized, including electric fields and particle states (velocities, positions, etc.). In particular, each particle's movement is determined by its *MoveTime* or cell exit time (a time in the future when the particle will exit the hosting cell). Whenever a particle is created or inserted in a cell, its exit time must be calculated and a pair of departure and arrival events scheduled at the exit time. In addition, a particle's exit time needs to be recalculated whenever the hosting cell "wakes up". A wakeup happens when a cell's field changes beyond a threshold value, resulting in the need for recalculation of exit times of all its particles. The physical activities associated with each component shown in figure 2 will be explained in detail in section 4.

```
Shell::arrival( ParticleArrivalEvent *e ) {
    if ( this cell is active ) {
      update cell state;
      insert particle in cell;
    } else if ( e is a beam particle ) {
      activate cell;
    }
}
Shell::departure( ParticleDepartureEvent *e ) {
    if ( particle bounced from right neighbor ) {
      bounce particle back; // no cell state change
    } else {
      update cell state;
    }
}
Shell::inject( ParticleInjectEvent *e ) {
    update cell state;
    insert beam particles;
}
```

Figure 2. A simplified PIC model

3.3. Reverse Computation Approach

The characteristics of this plasma simulation present three major challenges concerning the synchronization of parallel computations. The rationale for the parallelization approach used here is based on the following considerations.

- **Lookahead.** The simulation is highly dynamic. The amount of parallelism can vary dramatically as the simulation progresses. Dependencies among events are governed by each particle's exit time, but this time can be arbitrarily close into the near future. This low level of "predictability" results in a low, dynamically changing value of lookahead that makes efficient execution using conservative synchronization techniques difficult. This suggests that optimistic synchronization [10] may be a more natural choice for this simulation.

- **Memory**. Realistic plasma simulations involve a large number of events, on the order of billions. Complex data structures are often needed. This makes traditional approaches to optimistic execution using state saving problematic: the amount of memory required can be prohibitively large. Further, the amount of model-level computation performed for each event tends to be relatively small, on the order of a few microseconds on a contemporary CPU. This suggests that the time overhead for state saving may be significant, and hence could significantly degrade performance, even utilizing techniques such as incremental state saving. While various techniques to reduce the cost of state-saving-based rollbacks have been developed [20, 21], our experiences indicate much memory is still needed to achieve efficient parallel execution [22]. For this reason, reverse computation was selected for the parallelization of this plasma simulation code. However, comparison of the reverse execution approach with other advanced check-pointing approaches remains an area of future investigation.

- **Floating point.** The reverse computation approach proposed in [1] uses an automated approach to creating the reverse execution code for each line of forward execution code. For example, a decrement statement is generated to undo an increment statement in the forward execution code. This approach becomes problematic when floating point arithmetic is used because the computation may not be easily reversed due to effects such as round-off error. Here, we explore a different approach where the program is viewed at a higher level of abstraction, and suitable reverse computation code is developed manually.

These factors motivate the approach that was adopted for optimistic synchronization using manually derived reverse computation code. We believe this can be used to build a foundation for future work in developing scalable parallel simulators for complex physical systems.

4. Parallel Simulation Code

Here we use a one-dimensional model of the spacecraft electrostatic particle code as an illustrative example to discuss some of the challenges in generating the reverse code for this physical system simulation. There are two types of distinct physical entities in this simulation: particles and cells[1]. Particles move across cells and each cell keeps track of the particles residing within its own domain. The communication between adjacent cells occurs via particle movement events that contain information of particle physical states. The complex data structures housing the particles and physical processes being captured require a careful modeling of the system. The object-oriented design used here allows one to encapsulate physical properties via classes..

The code in Figure 2 includes three event handlers, one for each type of event. Much of the complexity of the event computation is encapsulated within the **insert** and **update** operations. An **insert** operation includes an "insert" queue operation (data structures representing particles in the cell are organized in a priority queue) and computation of the exit time of that particle from the cell based on an equation of motion. An **update** operation recomputes the cell's field value based on the arrival particle's charge. The change in the field value may trigger an expensive wakeup computation that again scans the particle list and updates each particle's exit time.

It may be noted that the reverse computation techniques introduced in [1] would generate the reverse code for each instruction without taking into account the semantics of the higher level operations that are being performed. This will clearly lead to inefficiencies for the queue management operations used in this code, and as mentioned earlier, leads to difficulties concerning the reversibility of floating point operations. The model-specific approach taken here involves generating the reverse code for the application by exploiting knowledge of the higher level semantics of the operations being performed. We call this approach *application-level* reverse computation. Here, each cell must manage a large number of particles within its domain. The choice of container class directly affects the efficiency of the simulation. We use the **list** class because of its efficient insertion and deletion operations. However, both insertion and deletion are destructive due to pointer assignments and thus irreversible. However, it is clear from a higher level examination of the operations being performed that insertion and deletion are perfect inverse operations of each other. Indeed, reverse computation in such queue operations are more memory-efficient than state-saving.

Careful readers may notice that the particle departure event handler depicted in figure 2 does not specify any deletion operation that matches the insertion operations in the particle arrival event handler. In fact, deletions are performed aggregately on an as-needed basis. This is done based on performance considerations. Instead of deleting each particle at its exiting time, a near-periodic deletion operation is used to amortize the cost of deletions in

[1] The spacecraft situated at one end of the spatial coordinate can be treated as a special cell that does not keep the physical states of particles. We use "cells" thereafter to refer to the regular cells unless otherwise specified.

queues. It is observed that wakeup events happen almost periodically with a frequency determined by physical conditions within the simulation; furthermore, each wakeup requires a scan of the cell's particle queue. We find that restricting deletion operations only at cell wakeup times reduces the total overhead of particle deletions without introducing excessive memory usage. Since the aggregate deletions are used to clean up the obsolete states for particles that have already exited, no rollbacks are needed to recover these obsolete states in the event of undoing a wakeup.

Figure 3 shows the reverse code of the simulation. Notice that after decomposing the forward code into components based on simulating physical processes, the reverse code is relatively easy to construct based on the operations shown in figure 3. The next step for generating the complete reverse code is just a matter of reversing each physical process. Examples of reversing some of the more difficult processes are shown in figure 3.

```
Shell::undo_arrival( ParticleArrivalEvent *e ) {
    if ( cell was activated ) {
      undo_activate cell;
    } else if ( cell already active ) {
      delete particle in cell;
      undo_update cell state;
    }
}
Shell::undo_departure( ParticleDepartureEvent *e ) {
    if ( particle was bounced from right neighbor ) {
      undo_bounce particle;
    } else {
      undo_update cell state;
    }
}
Shell::undo_inject( ParticleInjectEvent *e ) {
    delete beam particles;
    undo_update cell state;
}
```

Figure 3. A simplified reverse code of the PIC model

The **insert** operation appears in both particle arrival and injection event handlers. Its effect includes assigning memory for the new particle states in the queue and scheduling arrival/departure event pairs at each particle's future exiting time. Conversely, the **delete** operation in the reverse code should perform corresponding inverses of these processes. Particles in each cell are organized in a FILO (first-in last-out) queue, so the **delete** operation always removes the particle at the head of the queue that is exactly the same particle that was inserted in the forward computation. As for "undoing" event scheduling, it is assumed the underlying simulation engine provides the application with a primitive for explicitly retracting scheduled events; this is very useful to implement the **delete** operation.

The effect of the **activate** process is to load an inactive cell where previously no particle movements are allowed with particles of uniform distribution. Its basic operation is in fact multiple particle insertions. Its reverse code can utilize the **insert-delete** pair operations described above.

The cell state **update** process is in fact the most complex process and its reverse code is not trivial. Each **update** performs two major computations: computes the cell's new field values and then updates the cell's particle queue. Each cell computes its field locally and keeps track of field values at its left and right boundaries by summing the charges passing through that boundary. During a cell's field update, an addition of charge at its boundary can be simply reversed as a subtraction of the charge at the boundary upon rollback. The update on a particle queue, however, is not as easy. It requires a check of the wakeup condition (i.e., the field change exceeding a threshold) and triggers a wakeup event if necessary. Otherwise it makes no changes. As previously described, a cell wakeup is the single most costly operation in the plasma simulation. In the event of a wakeup, all particles' states are recomputed based on the new cell field values and obsolete particle states are erased. The destructive nature of the re-computation is one of the principal challenges in generating the reverse code for this simulation.

One example of an irreversible operation is the calculation of a particle's exit time *MoveTime*. It is calculated by finding the roots *dt* of the quadratic equations [4]:

$$\frac{1}{2} \square Acc \square dt^2 + Vel \square dt + Pos \square CellWidth = 0 \quad (1)$$

$$\frac{1}{2} \square Acc \square dt^2 + Vel \square dt + Pos = 0 \quad (2)$$

where Acc, Vel, Pos are particle acceleration, velocity and position in the cell, respectively. Equations (1) and (2) represent the right and left exit conditions, respectively. dt is the time difference between the current simulation time and the particle's last movement time. The smallest real value of dt is used for MoveTime. An initial inspection of the quadratic equations seems to suggest the impossibility of applying reverse computation to this process. However, if we apply the reverse computation approach at the application level, we find that the movement of the particle is highly reversible. Based on the physical laws of particle motion, the recovery of dt does not require the direct inverse of the quadratic equations. Indeed, as illustrated in figure 4, the particle's acceleration, velocity and position states can be simply rolled back by reverse computation and then the critical state dt can be reconstructed by carrying the forward computation using the recovered particle states. Note that the parameters cell_field and dt in the reverse code refer to the rolled-back cell_field value and the time difference between now and the time when the particle moved right before the wakeup. Finally, we note that random number generation is essential to this parallel simulation. Therefore, an efficient random number generator (RNG) that is reversible and has a long period is required. For this purpose, we use the reversible RNG that is described in [1].

```
Particle::update_position( double dt ) {
    Pos += Vel * dt + 0.5 * Acc * dt * dt;
}
Particle::update_velocity( double dt ) {
    Vel += Acc * dt;
}
Particle::update_acceleration( double cell_field ) {
    Acc = cell_field * particle_charge / particle_mass;
}
Particle::reverse_position( double dt ) {
    Pos = Pos - Vel * dt - 0.5 * Acc * dt * dt;
}
Particle::update_state( double cell_field, double dt ) {
    update_position(dt);
    update_velocity(dt);
    update_acceleration(cell_field);
    dt = update_dt(); // solve eq. (1) and (2)
    MoveTime = now + dt;
}
Particle::reverse_state( double cell_field, double dt ) {
    update_acceleration(cell_field);
    update_velocity( -dt );
    reverse_position(dt);
    dt = update_dt();
    MoveTime = now + dt;
}
```

Figure 4. The reverse code example of the particle states

5. Performance Evaluation

The application-level reverse computation approach is best implemented in a system that decouples implementation details of the simulation engine from the application in order to allow one to focus one's efforts on application semantics. As a result, a simulation engine that can support reverse computation at an application level and provide efficient management of large numbers of events with minimal storage requirement is needed. In addition, the simulation engine should have the flexibility and extensibility to support future refinement of the parallel simulation.

The parallel simulation code using reverse execution described in the previous section was implemented using μsik, a general-purpose parallel/distributed simulation engine based on a micro-kernel architecture [23]. μsik provides primitives supporting multiple synchronization approaches, including optimistic and conservative synchronization, as well as means to relax event ordering rules and mixing different approaches to synchronization within a single parallel execution. It therefore provides the capabilities needed for the parallel physical system simulations described here.

In a μsik simulation, logical (simulation) processes (LP) are fully autonomous entities that communicate via events. In our simulation model, each cell is implemented as an LP and can choose to run conservatively or optimistically. A conservative implementation of the simulation described here performed very poorly, due to poor lookahead, and is not discussed further. We focus on optimistic execution using our reverse handlers to support rollback.

5.1. Experiment Configuration

To demonstrate the feasibility and efficiency of reverse computation in the electrostatic plasma simulation, we carried out all experiments on a Symmetric Multi-Processor (SMP) machine running Red Hat Linux 7.3 with a customized 2.4.18-10smp kernel. The SMP machine is equipped with eight Pentium III 550MHz Xeon processors that share 4GB of memory.

We use normalized units throughout our simulation, where length, time and velocity are normalized to electron Debye length, electron plasma frequency and electron thermal velocity, respectively. The spacecraft is assumed to have a 500 unit radius and each cell has a width of 0.24 units. The solar wind plasma is initially loaded with uniformly distributed electrons and protons. We choose the initial values of 30 electrons and 30 protons per cell. The injected positron beam has energy of 10 kev with an injection period of 0.004. Upon initialization, there are up to 7000 cells of which the first 70 close to the spacecraft are "active"; as the simulation progresses up to time 60, the beam travels further away from spacecraft surface and thus more cells are activated.

5.2. Parallel Performance

Figure 5 shows a snapshot visualization of phase space structures for the solar wind electrons, protons and beam particles from a time-stepped simulation and the optimistic PDES simulation. Both simulations are run up to 60 time units, and with the same simulation parameters except using different random number generators (RNG). The PDES used a specialized reversible RNG in contrast to the generic single-stream RNG used in the time-stepped simulation. Despite this difference, the two phase space structures at the end of the simulations are rather close in form. The result from the PDES execution with reverse computation is verified to accurately capture the main features of movement for all three species of particles at the end of the simulation. In particular, it can be seen that the beam front in both simulations has propagated to the same distance and beam particles display a similar shape in phase space. It is also evident that the electron phase space has a finer resolution in the PDES case for up to 4000 cells. This is the result of its fine time-scale based on individual particles. A minor difference to note is that, in the PDES case, the phase space does not extend all the way to the right wall, whereas in the time-stepped model, it does. This is because we model an expanding box in PDES but not the time-stepped model. Overall, the results helped serve as validation of our optimistic simulation model against the original sequential simulation model.

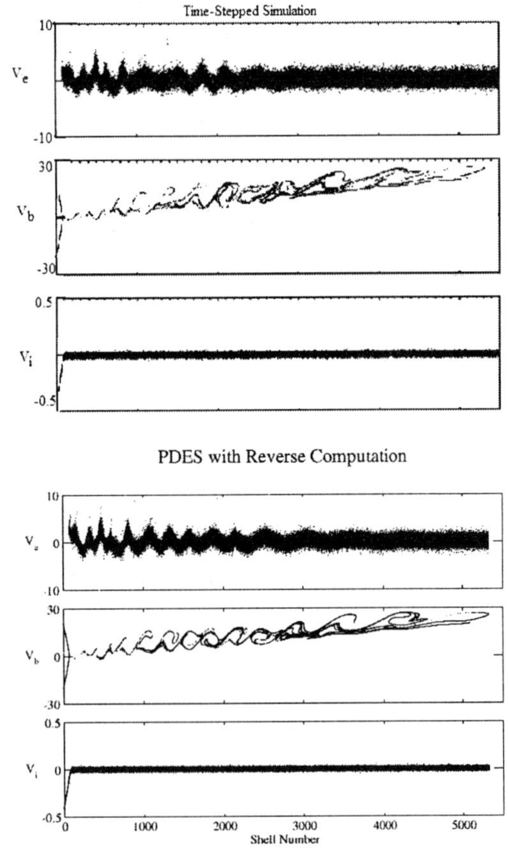

Figure 5. Validation by phase space comparison of time-stepped simulation and PDES with reverse computation.

The speedup of DES over TDS has been discussed in great detail in [4]. In our work, we focus on further improving the DES performance by realizing parallelization in the simulation and utilizing optimistic synchronization. All the parallel experiments discussed in the following section were run with the same physical parameters and resulted in the same number of committed events as the sequential runs. Figure 6 shows the parallel speedup in terms of execution time for up to 8 processors. The sequential data is measured by running the parallel code on a single processor. It should be noted that the single processor execution incurs neither rollbacks nor state saving overhead. Because μsik was designed for both efficient sequential and parallel execution, we believe these measurements reflect the performance one could expect to see using a reasonably efficient sequential simulation engine.

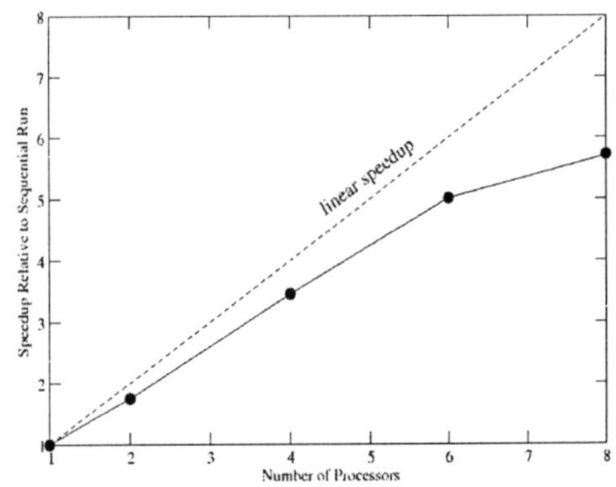

Figure 6. PDES vs. sequential DES

We observe that the optimistic parallel execution achieves a nearly linear speedup up to 4 processors, but the performance improvement is somewhat less in going from 4 to 8 processors. This phenomenon is largely due to the fact that there is relatively little computation per particle event. As the computation is distributed over more and more processors, the amount of computation between event communications decreases, resulting in reduced speedup. We expect that this problem will not persist if a larger, more complex physical model such as a three dimensional plasma code were used. An initial test with an increased simulation time of 2 units did show better speedup performance due to the fact that the longer the simulation runs, the more cells are activated, resulting in more balanced computation for each processor.

A second factor that results in less than optimal performance concerns the distribution of the workload. Figure 7 shows the amount of computation assigned to each processor in each of the runs. Here, the load is distributed by first dividing the physical area encompassed by the simulation into two regions (as illustrated in figure 1) with the initially active cells closer to the spacecraft in the "heavy activity" region, and other cells forming the "less active" region. Cells in the active regions are evenly grouped and distributed among the available processors, while other cells are grouped into sub-regions or "blocks" and distributed among processors in a round-robin fashion. All simulations shown in figure 7 have a fixed "block" size. We observe that during the lifetime of each simulation, the processor load shows significant variation as more and more cells become active. Upon simulation termination, the simulation with the largest number of processors tends to be the least balanced. The imbalance is inherent of such simulations due to their highly dynamic nature and the static load-balancing scheme. Further investigation of characteristics of electrostatic plasma simulations is needed to aid in the development of a more efficient load-balancing algorithm for this application that can lead to better parallel performance for large numbers of processors.

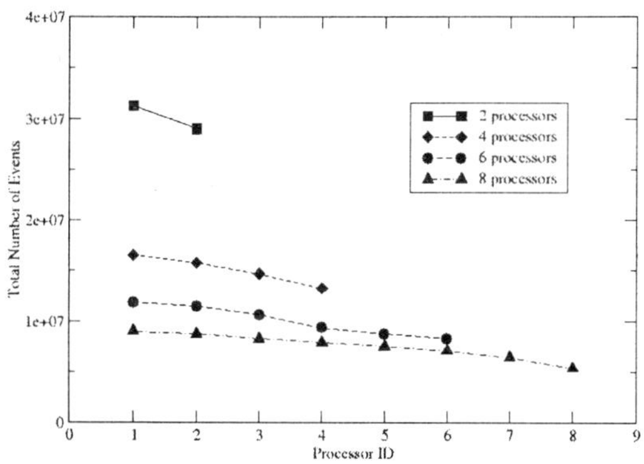

Figure 7. Event rate distribution

5.3. Efficiency

Intuitively, grid-based physical systems such as the electrostatic plasma simulation studied here have the desirable features of locally solved field values and queuing/dequeuing operations that are time-reversible, but the evolution of the system itself (beam injections, cell wakeups in our case) is not time-reversible. However, with the application-level reverse computation illustrated here, we have shown that numerical operations in the electrostatic plasma simulation chosen for this study are truly reversible, despite round-off errors and irreversible evolution processes. The most important discovery from our study is that application-level reverse computation may be quite efficient for these scientific simulations.

The efficiency mainly comes from two contributing factors: the smaller amount of additional memory required for optimistic execution, particularly, queue operations where no additional state is required to perform rollbacks; note the fact that the simulation is not constrained by arbitrarily small look-ahead values. However, there are still important practical issues related to reverse computation.

Ideally, one would like to apply reverse computation to all reversible operations. But reverse computation also comes at a cost: if the number of destructive operations is sufficiently large and no efficient application-level reverse computation can be found, employing reverse computation can result in worse performance than state-saving. One such case as pointed out in [1] is when a rollback spans several processed events. Merely switching pointers to restore a state based on the earliest rolled back event incurs a small cost in copy state-saving; while reverse computation must roll back one event at a time and thus excessive rollbacks can cause performance to degrade considerably. The effect of this is particularly severe in our simulation when a rollback spans multiple wakeup events.

Our solution to reducing the rollbacks of costly wakeup events is to limit the "optimism" of the parallel execution. The idea of controlling optimism is not new. One such approach is first described in the Moving Time Window (MTW) protocol [24], where LPs are not allowed to advance beyond a time window above the GVT. Although other approaches such as probabilistic rollbacks [25], local rollbacks [26], Breathing Time Buckets [27] and Wolf Call mechanism [28], have been proposed to counter the effect of over-optimism, we simply choose to a time window-based approach because of its simplicity and low overhead. μsik supplies simulation applications with a convenient facility for our purpose. A "*run-ahead*" parameter, which is in fact the moving window size, can be set by the model upon simulation initialization. This limits how far in simulation time each LP can run ahead of other LPs during optimistic execution. By tuning the run-ahead parameter based on cell wakeup frequency, we are able to reduce or eliminate consecutive rollbacks of wakeup events. The significant performance gain in our experiment indicates the extra operation associated with the window maintenance is a small cost to pay. Further improvement in parallel performance is possible by fine-tuning the run-ahead value. This is left for future investigation.

In addition to the basic reverse computation techniques discussed here, advanced reverse techniques can be applied to the plasma simulation. For example, compiler-supported reverse computation can be used to further optimize the parallel performance at run-time. This approach is beyond the scope of our discussion and will be studied in the future.

6. Conclusions

In this work, we have applied reverse execution to perform parallel discrete event simulations of a physical system. We demonstrated that application-level reverse computation can be used to manually generate efficient reverse code. These results suggest that reverse computation merits further investigation as an approach for parallel/distributed simulation of physical systems modeled using a discrete event simulation paradigm.

As previously mentioned, the PIC simulation considered in this paper is only a simplified example of reverse execution in simulating physical systems. The examples given in section 4 are representative and certainly do not encompass the diversity and complexity of all physical system simulations. However, the underlying reverse techniques can be used in other grid-based models without extensive modifications. Here we provide some guidelines for the development of parallel physical discrete event simulations using reverse computation. Since our exploration of reverse computation is an on-going research effort, the guidelines provided here should be used as references rather than strict rules for applying reverse computation in scientific simulations.

- Reverse computation is well-suited for fine-grained applications such as 1D electrostatic grid-based plasma models. It is especially useful where efficient queue management is needed. But other optimization techniques should also be considered in order to fully optimize parallel performance.
- Good knowledge of the application semantics, especially the underlying physics, can be beneficial in producing reverse code for physical systems. Model-specific optimization can be quite efficient but requires knowledge of application-level operations. The simple example of reversing the quadratic equation would not have been efficient, if at all possible, without knowledge of the physics involved (particle's motion in this case).
- The modeling process largely determines how successfully reverse computation will improve parallel performance. Initial analysis in [1] shows that complex use of jump instructions such as goto, break and continue are difficult to optimize in terms of memory usage.
- In modeling physical systems, one should attempt to avoid monolithic code for event handlers and use functions calls that are associated with each physical process. If an event handler only consists of a long sequence of simple instructions, it is difficult to extract application semantics and therefore reverse computation will degenerate to instruction-by-instruction reverse execution. Using many small function calls that reflect physical processes helps to develop reverse codes based on physical properties of the system. Another advantage is easier debugging and testing for the reverse code.

The work presented here is only an initial step based on a simplified physical system. Yet, the results show promise. Our goal is to build a scalable parallel simulator for complex physical systems by exploitation of more advanced reverse computation techniques.

Acknowledgements

This work was supported in part by the National Science Foundation grants ATM-0326431 and 0325046. Additionally the authors would like to thank the anonymous reviewers for their helpful comments on improving the paper.

References

[1] Carothers, C. D., K. Perumalla and R. M. Fujimoto. Efficient Optimistic Parallel Simulation Using Reverse Computation. *ACM Transactions on Modeling and Computer Simulation,* **9**(3): 224-253, 1999.

[2] Birdsall, C. K. and A. B. Langdon. Plasma Physics via Computer Simulation. *McGraw-Hill Book Company*, 1985.

[3] Dawson, C. and R. Kirby. High Resolution Schemes for Conservation Laws with Locally Varying Time Steps. *SIAM Journal of Scientific Computing*, **22**(6): p. 2256, 2001.

[4] Karimabadi, H., J. Driscoll, Y. A. Omelchenko, and N. Omidi. A New Asynchronous Methodology for Modeling of Physical Systems: Breaking the Curse of Courant Condition. *J. Computational Physics,* **205**(2): 755 - 775, 2005.

[5] Hontalas, P., B. Beckman, M. DiLorento, L. Blume, P. Reiher, K. Sturdevant, L. V. Warren, J. Wedel, F. Wieland and D. Jefferson. Performance of the Colliding Pucks Simulation on the Time Warp Operating System. *Distributed Simulation, Society for Computer Simulation International*, 1989.

[6] Lubachevsky, B. D. Efficient Distributed Event-Driven Simulations of Multiple-Loop Networks. *Communications of the ACM,* **32**(1): 111-123, 1989.

[7] Lubachevsky, B. D. Several Unsolved Problems in Large-Scale Discrete Event Simulations, in *Proceedings of the 7th Workshop on Parallel and Distributed Simulation*, 1993. p. 60-67.

[8] Zeigler, B. P., H. Praehofer and T. G. Kim. Theory of Modeling and Simulation: Second Edition. *Academic Press,* 2000.

[9] Nutaro, J. J. Parallel Discrete Event Simulation with Application to Continuous Systems. *Ph. D. Dissertation*. 2003. Electrical and Computer Engineering Dept, Univerisity of Arizona.

[10] Jefferson, D. Virtual Time. *ACM Transactions on Programming Languages and Systems,* **7**(3): 404-425, 1985.

[11] Fujimoto R. M., J. J. Tsai and G. Gopalakrishnan. The Roll Back Chip: Hardware Support For Distributed Simulation Using Time Warp, in *Proceedings of SCS Distributed Simulation Conference*, **19**(3): 81-86, 1988.

[12] Bauer H. and C. Sporrer. Reducing Rollback Overhead in Time Warp Based Distributed Simulation with Optimized Incremental State Saving, in *Proceedings of the 26th Annual Simulation Symposium*, 1993.

[13] Steinman J. Incremental State Saving in SPEEDES Using C++, in *Proceedings of the 1993 Winter Simulation*

Conference, 1993.

[14] Lin. Y. B. and E.D.Lazowska. The Optimal Checkpoint Interval in Time Warp Parallel Simulation, *Technical Report 89-09-04,* Dept. of Computer Science and Engineering, University of Washington, 1989.

[15] Bellenot S. State Skipping Performance with the Time Warp Operating System, in *Proceedings of the 6th Workshop on Parallel and Distributed Simulation,* 1992. p. 53-61.

[16] Franks S., F. Gomes, B. Unger, and J. Cleary. State Saving for Interactive Optimistic Simulation, in *Proceedings of the 11th Workshop on Parallel and Distributed Simulation*, 1997. p. 72-79.

[17] Fleischmann J. and P. Wilsey. Comparative Analysis of Periodic State Saving Techniques in Time Warp Simulators, in *Proceedings of the 9th Workshop on Parallel and Distributed Simulation*, 1995. p. 50-58.

[18] Yuan, G., C. D. Carothers and S. Kalyanaraman. Large-Scale TCP Models Using Optimistic Parallel Simulation, in *Proceedings of the 17th Workshop on Parallel and Distributed Simulation*, 2003. p. 153.

[19] Pritchett, P. L. and R. M. Winglee. The Plasma Environment during particle beam injection into space plasmas: 1. Electron-beams, *J. of Geophysical Res. – Space Physics*, 1987. **92** (A7): 7673-7688.

[20] Jefferson, D.R., Virtual Time II: Storage Management in distributed Simulation, in *Proceedings of the Ninth Annual ACM Symposium on Principles of Distributed Computing*, 1990. p. 75-89.

[21] Preiss, B.R. and W.M. Loucks. Memory Management Techniques for Time Warp on a Distributed Memory Machine, in *Proceedings of the 9th Workshop on Parallel and Distributed Simulation*, 1995. p. 30-39.

[22] Das, S.R. and R.M. Fujimoto. An Empirical Evaluation of Performance-Memory Tradeoffs in Time Warp. *IEEE Transactions on Parallel and Distributed Systems*, 1997. **8**(2): p. 210-224.

[23] Perumalla, K. µsik -- A Micro-kernel for Parallel/Distributed Simulation Systems, in *Proceedings of the 19th Workshop on Principles of Advanced and Distributed Simulation*, 2005.

[24] Sokol, L. M. and B. K. Stucky. MTW: Experimental results for a constrained optimistic scheduling paradigm, in *Proceedings of the SCS Multiconference on Distributed Simulations*, 1990. **22**: 169-173.

[25] Madisetti V., D. Hardaker and R. Fujimoto. The MIMDIX Operating System for Parallel Simulation. *Journal on Parallel and Distributed Computing*, 1993. **18**(4) : 473-483.

[26] Dickens, P.M. and P.F. Reynolds. SRADS with Local Rollback, in *Proceedings of the SCS Multiconference on Distributed Simulation*, 1990. **22**: 161-164.

[27] Steinman, J. S. Breathing Time Warp, in *Proceedings of the 7th Workshop on Parallel and Distributed Simulation*, 1993. p. 109–118.

[28] Madisetti V., J. Walrand and D. Messerschmitt, WOLF: a rollback algorithm for optimistic distributed simulation systems, in *Proceedings of the 20th Conference on Winter Simulation*, 1988. p. 296-305.

Optimistic and Hybrid Simulation

Seven-O'Clock: A New Distributed GVT Algorithm Using Network Atomic Operations

David Bauer, Garrett Yaun, Christopher D. Carothers
Murat Yuksel and Shivkumar Kalyanaraman
Department of Computer Science
Rensselaer Polytechnic Institute
Troy, NY 12180, U.S.A.
{bauerd,yaung,chrisc}@cs.rpi.edu, {yuksem,shivkuma}@ecse.rpi.edu

Abstract

In this paper we introduce a new concept, *network atomic operations (NAOs)* to create a zero-cost consistent cut. Using NAOs, we define a wall-clock-time driven GVT algorithm called *Seven O'Clock* that is an extension of Fujimoto's shared memory GVT algorithm. Using this new GVT algorithm, we report good optimistic parallel performance on a cluster of state-of-the-art Itanium-II quad processor systems for both benchmark applications such as PHOLD and real-world applications such as a large-scale TCP/Internet model. In some cases, super-linear speedup is observed.

1 Introduction

At the heart of an optimistic parallel simulation system is the ability to reclaim memory and re-use it to schedule future events as well as support state-saving operations as part of speculative event processing. Global virtual time (GVT) defines a lower bound on any unprocessed event in the system and defines the point beyond which events *should not* be reclaimed. Thus, it is imperative that the GVT computation operate as efficiently as possible.

Global virtual time (GVT) algorithms must solve two key problems. The first is *the transient message problem*. Here, a message is delayed in the network and neither the sender nor the receiver consider that message in their respective GVT calculation. Thus, a GVT algorithm must account somehow for all messages scheduled. The second problem is called *simultaneous reporting*. This problem arises "because not all processors will report their local minimum at precisely the same instant in wall-clock time" [8]. Here, the underlying assumption is that event processing is allowed to continue asynchronously during the GVT computation which enables better overall parallel performance.

Asynchronous GVT algorithms rely on the ability to create a "cut" across the distributed simulation that divides events into two categories: past and future [8, 18]. GVT is then defined by the lower bound on unprocessed events in the "past" of the cut, which is in effect an estimate of the true GVT since events are being processed during its computations. Creating a cut can be done in several ways depending on the architecture of the machine(s) being used. For distributed computing platforms, the primary method of creating a "cut" is via message-passing as was defined by Mattern [18]. Here, messages are sent such that at most two cuts are made. The first cut signals the "start" of the GVT computation. The second cut, if needed based on message counts computed in the first cut, consider any transient messages discovered from the first cut. Please note, that these cuts need not be *consistent*. A *consistent cut* is defined as a cut where there is no message that was scheduled in the future of the sending processor but received in the past of the destination processor. These messages can be ignored because by definition they must be scheduled at a time that is greater than GVT computed using a consistent cut. The "cuts", while not consistent, effectively divide past from future in a causally consistent manner to solve the simultaneous reporting problem. Additionally, because of the use of message counts, it is able to determine if a second "cut" round is needed and traps any transient messages.

In contrast, a shared memory multiprocessor greatly simplifies the GVT algorithm. Fujimoto's GVT algorithm [7] generates a cut by setting a global flag positive. In a shared memory system this operation is observed on all processors in a causally correct order because the underlying hardware memory management mechanism ensures that no two processors will observe different orderings of memory references to a shared variable. Shared memory multiprocessor systems that adhere to this memory ordering model are called *sequentially consistent* [14]. The impact this memory model has on a GVT algorithm are that: (i) *no* messages are lost which prevents the transient message problem, and (b) the simultaneous reporting problem is solved because all processor effectively "observe" the start of the GVT calculation at the same instant of wall-clock time.

The motivation behind our research here is the question: *Is there a method to achieve some of the benefits of sequentially consistent shared memory but in a loosely coordinated, cluster computing environment?* The answer turns out to be *yes*. In this paper, we propose the idea of a *network atomic operation (NAO)*, which enables a zero-cost cut mechanism which greatly simplifies GVT computations in a cluster com-

Algorithm 1 Fujimoto's Shared Memory GVT Algorithm: Variable Definitions.

Global Variables

```
int gvt_flag;
lock_t gvt_lck; /* mutual exclusion variable */
int gvt_interval; /* number of time thru batch loop */
virtual_time_t lvt[npe]; /* LVT of each processor */
virtual_time_t gvt;
```

Processor Private Variables

```
virtual_time_t send_min_ts;
```

Algorithm 2 Fujimoto's Shared Memory GVT Algorithm: Initiate GVT.

Steps to Initiate GVT within the Scheduler Loop

```
if(this processor is the MASTER)
{
  gvt_cnt++;
  if( gvt_cnt >= gvt_interval AND
  processor status is GVT_NORMAL)
  {
    gvt_cnt = 0;
    if(gvt_flag == -npe)
    {
      lock(&gvt_lck);
      gvt_flag = npe;
      unlock(&gvt_lck);
    }
    set processor status to GVT_COMPUTE;
  }

}
else if (gvt_flag > 0 AND
         processor status is GVT_NORMAL)
  set processor status to GVT_COMPUTE;
```

Algorithm 3 Fujimoto's Shared Memory GVT Algorithm: Receive Events.

Steps to Receive Events and Anti-messages within Scheduler Loop

```
move positive messages from shared memory
message queue to processors priority queue.
process any rollbacks.
remove anti-messages from shared memory
''cancel'' queue.
process any message cancellations and
rollbacks.
```

puting environment. We demonstrate its reduced complexity by extending Fujimoto's shared memory algorithm to operate across a cluster of shared-memory multiprocessors (SMP). We present a performance study using the PHOLD benchmark and TCP network model.

Algorithm 4 Fujimoto's Shared Memory GVT Algorithm: Compute GVT.

Steps to Compute GVT Once Initiated within Scheduler Loop

```
if( processor status is GVT_COMPUTE )
{
  set processor status to GVT_WAIT
  lvt[my_pe] = min(send_min_ts,
                   smallest event in
                   priority queue);
  lock(&gvt_lck);
  gvt_flag--;
  if( gvt_flag == 0)
  {
    gvt = min( lvt[0] ... lvt[npe-1] );
    gvt_flag = -1;
    set processor status to GVT_NORMAL;
    reset send_min_ts to max time value;
    unlock(&gvt_lck);
    collect processed events and state < GVT;
    if( gvt > end time of simulation )
         goto DONE;
  } else
  {
    unlock(&gvt_lck);
    set processor status to GVT_WAIT;
  }
}
else if(processor status is GVT_WAIT AND
                               gvt_flag < 0 )
{
  lock(&gvt_lck);
  gvt_flag--;
  unlock(&gvt_lck);
  if( gvt > end time of simulation )
    goto DONE;
  collect processed events and state < GVT;
  set processor status to GVT_NORMAL;
  reset send_min_ts to max time value;
}
```

2 Fujimoto's GVT Algorithm and NAOs

We begin with an overview of Fujimoto's GVT algorithm, as shown in Algorithms 1 – 5. Please note, there are minor modifications from the original algorithm presented in [7], but the correctness and efficient execution is preserved. These 5 parts are described as follows:

1. **Variables (Algorithm 1):** The key shared variable is the `gvt_flag`, which contains a mutual exclusion variable, `gvt_lck`.

2. **Initiate GVT (Algorithm 2):** The algorithm is initiated when the "master" processor iterates through the event scheduler loop `gvt_interval` times before setting the `gvt_flag` equal to the number of processors

Algorithm 5 Fujimoto's Shared Memory GVT Algorithm: Process and Schedule Events.

Steps to Process and Schedule Events within Scheduler Loop

```
  Process smallest event in priority queue;
  if( sending a new event during
                       event processing )
  {
    enqueue message on destination
                receive queue;
    if( gvt_flag > 0 AND
         processor status is NOT GVT_WAIT )
        send_min_ts = min( send_min_ts,
                  time-stamp of new event);
  }

DONE:
compute parallel simulation stats and exit.
```

(i.e., npe). Here is where the algorithm exploits the sequentially consistent memory properties. Every processor will "observe" the start of the GVT at the same instant in wall-clock time. More precisely, once the flag has been set, any other messages sent, are the responsibility of the sender, as shown in Algorithm 5. This provides a true separation between events in the logical past and logical future. When another processor observes the start of a GVT computation, it changes its status to "needs to compute an local virtual time (LVT)" This is denoted by send_min_ts.

3. **Receive Events (Algorithm 3):** Here, new events and anti-messages are processed from arrival queues shared between processors. Each processor has its own externally exported queue that all other processors use to send events. A mutual exclusion lock is used around the queue to correctly serialize the arrival of either new events or anti-messages. Because of sequentially consistent memory, no message can be lost "in the network" and so the transient message problem is intrinsically solved. Observe that this "receive" and process rollbacks and anti-messages is a necessary step prior to computing any part of the GVT. It is also a normal step in every iteration through the scheduler loop.

4. **Compute GVT (Algorithm 4):** Once the new events and anti-messages are processed, each processor computes its local virtual time (LVT) value, which is the smallest unprocessed event that it is "aware" of, which includes any events it sent after the gvt_flag was set. This is denoted by send_min_ts. The last processor to compute its LVT also computes the minimum among all LVTs, which becomes the new GVT value. To inform other processors that the new GVT value is available, the gvt_flag is set to negative one. The last processor never "waits" for the GVT value and skips that state, while all other processors move to the "asynchronously waiting for GVT" state.

Algorithm 6 gvt_interval is a predefined number of iterations, and gvt_count is the current number of iterations.

```
CPU 0:
   a. If(gvt_interval == gvt_count)
   b.       set gvt_flag positive

CPU 1:
   c. if(gvt_flag)
   d.      start processing LVT
```

5. **Process Events (Algorithm 5):** In this last step, forward event processing commences. Here, the smallest event is removed from the pending event set and processed. If a new event is scheduled and the gvt_flag has been set greater than zero and the LVT value has not been reported (i.e., the processor should not be in the "wait" state), then it means *this* processor must consider this event in its LVT computation.

2.1 Network Atomic Operations

To directly extend Fujimoto's GVT algorithm to a network of machines, would require a sequentially consistent distributed memory model, similar to what is provided in a shared memory system. As we described above, each processor observes the "start" of the GVT computation at the same wall clock time because of sequentially consistent memory. In reality, a processor attempting to read the flag may be stalled while the underlying system updates the local cache with the correct value of the flag. Consider the following abstracted view of the algorithm run in parallel on an SMP machine as shown in Algorithm 6.

Running this code on a single processor defines the sequential consistency. The statements could be ordered on a single CPU as $O = \{a, b, c, d\}$. In this case both CPU 0 and 1 would begin computing GVT. However, if we change the interleaving of instructions to $O = \{a, c, b, d\}$ then the GVT computation would only begin on CPU 0. CPU 1 would begin processing more events, but when an event is sent, the gvt_flag would be checked per the algorithm to ensure the sender correctly accounts for events during the GVT computation. The instruction, call it e, would then be accounted for by CPU 1 because e occurred after instruction b, and the consistent cut is properly formed.

NAOs provide a similar functionality in a distributed system, however they are clock-based and not memory or state-based. **The general concept is that an operation may occur atomically within a network of machines if all machines "observe" the event at the same instant of wall clock time.** This functionality can be implemented on modern processors because most architectures now provide a time-stamp counter, or clock-cycle counter for performance measuring, such as the rdtsc instruction on all x86 series processors [11]. So we can compute wall-clock time based off of each processor's time-stamp counter and synchronize these counters to a common view of wall clock time. Calls to read-

Algorithm 7 Here, `gvt_interval` redefined as a measure of time usually in clock cycles, and not defined as the number of batch round through the scheduler.

```
CPU 0:
   a. if(local clock time >= gvt_interval)
   b.         start computing GVT

CPU 1:
   c. if(local clock time >= gvt_interval)
   d.       start computing GVT
```

ing the CPU clock adhere to the principles of a sequentially consistent memory model because wall clock time is consistent across all processors. Consider the following clock-based approach shown in Algorithm 7.

If we again attempt to create a sequential ordering of instructions, it becomes obvious that any permutation is guaranteed to be consistent. Consistency is guaranteed because instructions a and c in Algorithm 7 will evaluate to true if and only if the same instance of wall clock time has passed for each CPU. Because we can only read the current wall-clock time (as measured in clock cycles), any permutation of the possible orderings is valid because wall clock time is *assumed* to be the same for all processors. There are limitations which we will discuss later in the paper.

So NAOs may be characterized as a subset of the possible operations provided by a complete sequentially consistent memory model. For example, NAOs can only occur at predefined intervals, not dispersed throughout the time-scale of the running application. Not only must NAOs occur at agreed upon intervals, but they must also take on a specific meaning or value. In the case of the GVT algorithm, we use NAOs to generate a consistent cut. The system is either in a GVT computation, or it is not. Further, GVT computations occur at a predefined frequency through the runtime of the application. An NAO cannot be used to give some global variable any value, because the only global variable in an NAO is wall clock time. However, any sequence of operations can be performed once the clock has been read.

2.2 Clock Synchronization

The heart of a network atomic operation is the assumption that all processors share a highly accurate, common view of wall-clock time. For this to occur, each processor's time-stamp or cycle-counter must be synchronized in some fashion. This is a well researched problem in distributed computing. The most recent, relevant result for our operating environment is by Ostrovsky and Patt-Shamir [20]. Here, they present provably optimal clock synchronization scheme where the clocks have drift and the message latency may be unbounded. Previous to this result, all other optimal results were based on non-drifting clocks. Moreover, they suggest that operational clock synchronization algorithms *need not be general* and "that they should work for the particular system in which they are deployed". We take this view here. In particular, because of the time-scale of the clock is 1,000 times greater than message sends (i.e., nanoseconds vs. microseconds), clock drift rates can largely be ignored here.

Additionally, since our contribution is not about clock synchronization algorithms, we used a simplified approach. To synchronize the clocks across all processors, we use a *network barrier*. Here, a master time keeper sends a synchronization message to each node, which responds back with its local time-stamp-counter. The master time keeper then sends a message to each processor with an appropriate time-stamp counter value that would be when in real-time measure in cycles the first GVT is to occur. Upon receipt of that message, each processor is released from the barrier and begins processing events. We recognize that for a large 1000 processor cluster, this approach has some scalability limitations. For such an operating environment, we would implement Ostrovsky and Patt-Samir algorithm [20].

3 Seven O'Clock GVT Algorithm

We can now give a definition of a network atomic operation:

Definition: *An NAO is an agreed upon frequency in wall-clock time at which some event is logically observed to have happened across a distributed system.*

Each processor in the system uses the NAO to determine the current state of the system depending upon the logical meaning of the NAO. For example, we use an NAO to determine if a GVT computation has been started. There is no actual global variable, such as the `gvt_flag` in Algorithm 2, which signals the start of the GVT. Instead, we simply compute GVT every n units of wall-clock time.

We have affectionately call this algorithm the *"Seven O'clock Algorithm"*. Seven O'clock comes from the idea that if we could have synchronized wall clocks on each network node, then we could simply compute GVT at well-defined intervals, i.e., every minute starting from Seven O'Clock, where Seven O'Clock is simply the start time of the scheduler. During the discussion of this algorithm we assume that each processor's timestamp counter is perfectly synchronized with all of the other counters. We introduce the complexity of clock drift and jitter at the end.

As we previously indicated, if one were to open up the underlying hardware implementation of a sequentially consistent shared memory system, a number of messages would be observed being passed over the memory bus between memory and cache modules. Also, any memory reads to a shared location could be blocked while waiting for the memory address to be made consistent. In particular, these consistency messages would either be well synchronized in time over a memory bus or acknowledged over a network depending on the architecture [9, 15]. Because we assume a distributed message passing system without acknowledgments, we need some additional information about the communications environment to avoid the transient message problem (i.e., events lost in the network). This problem can be overcome by adding a small amount of time to the NAO expiration, *max_send_delta_t*.

Definition: *max_send_delta_t is a worst case bound on the time to send an event through the network.*

This delta allows for the sending processor to account for remotely sent events which may cross the cut boundary. Note that this is not the same as delta causality which allows for excessively old events to be discarded. While it may seem unreasonable to assume such a value can be determined in practice, current cluster computing networks rely on high-speed switching fabrics. These fabrics typically have extremely low loss probabilities ($1e-12$ or less) and can typically support the full bandwidth of all ports. Consequently, the worst case is experimentally computable and does not vary greatly from the average case.

The states of the Seven O'Clock algorithm are shown in Figure 1 and are discussed below.

- **State A:** Events are processed normally and not accounted for in GVT computation. This is no different from Fujimoto's GVT Algorithm.

- **GVT "start":** The NAO signals the consistent start of the GVT to all processors, just as setting the `gvt_flag` in Fujimoto's algorithm.

- **State B:** Events sent during the `max_send_delta_t` interval are accounted for on the sending side. This is similar to how Fujimoto's Algorithm uses `gvt_flag` to capture events the receiving processor might not consider in the sender's LVT computation. Here, our algorithm reads the processor's local cycle counter, determines if it is within the `max_send_delta_t time` of a GVT computation. If it is, then it captures this event's timestamp against the minimum of any previously scheduled events during the `max_send_delta_t` time.

- **State C:** Processors compute LVT by taking min(unprocessed events, events sent during B). This is identical to Fujimoto's GVT Algorithm.

- **State D:** Node 1 is first to complete local GVT algorithm and propagates this value to other nodes.

- **State E:** Node 0 completes it's local GVT algorithm and receives Node 1's. It takes the minimum of the two and retransmits this value back to Node 1. The other processors check for the new GVT value at some point in the future and read the value from the shared memory. The processors return to state A.

The only other differences between Fujimoto's GVT algorithm and Seven-O'Clock are: (a) physically receiving messages and (b) physically sending messages. In the receiving step (Algorithm 3), all remotely sent new event messages and anti-messages are read from a communications channel, such as a socket. This is in addition to the shared memory queuing structures. From the standpoint of the GVT algorithm, it captures messages sent over either communications medium. Likewise, when a message is sent, the algorithm does not differentiate between which events are shared memory or off-system messages.

3.1 Proof of Correctness

As previously noted, in order for a GVT algorithm to operate correctly, it must solve the transient message and simultaneous reporting problems.

First, we assume all processors clocks are perfectly synchronized and there are no clock drift or jitter problems. We will relax this constraint later.

Proof: To prove that a transient message cannot occur, assume that a transient message occurs in the scheduler. Then the time to send the event must be greater than the $max\_send\_delta\_t$. But by definition $max\_send\_delta\_t$ is a worst-case bound on the time to send an event. This leads to a contradiction because the transient event took longer to send than the worst-case bound.

Next, the simultaneous reporting problem occurs when all processors do not begin computing their local minimum at the same instant. In fact, this is exactly what happens in the Seven O'Clock algorithm. Because the consistent cut is generated using an NAO, each processor in the distributed system begins accounting for messages at precisely the same instant in wall clock time. Therefore this problem does not occur in this GVT algorithm.

Theorem: *The simultaneous reporting problem cannot occur in a system where a consistent cut is defined across all processors at precisely the same instant in wall clock time.*

Proof: *Assume to the contrary that the simultaneous reporting problem can occur.*

CASE 1: Assume each processor's clock is perfectly synchronized with all other processor clocks. For the simultaneous reporting problem to occur, at least two processors must have different views of wall clock time. This is a contradiction because there only exists one notion of wall clock time.

CASE 2: Each processor's clock is synchronized with some degree of error, which is bounded by $epsilon$. In order for the problem to occur now, at least two processors must have different views of wall clock time, which differs by at most $epsilon$. This means that in $epsilon$ time between two processors, a message was sent which was not accounted for. This is a contradiction because it is not possible to send a message in $epsilon$ time and not account for the event being sent. Consider the steps for remote sending of events:

1. *Send the event.*
2. *Read local time-stamp clock.*
3. *If* $time\_now + max\_send\_delta\_t >= gvt\_interval$, *then account for the event.*

Since $epsilon$ is a value far less than $max\_send\_delta\_t$, we must always account for the sent event. In the event that $epsilon >= max\_send\_delta\_t$, we simply change our $max\_send\_delta\_t$ to have a larger value to overcome $epsilon$.

3.2 Problems with Clock-Based Algorithms

While the discussion of clock synchronization and its associated problems are outside of the scope of this paper, the Seven

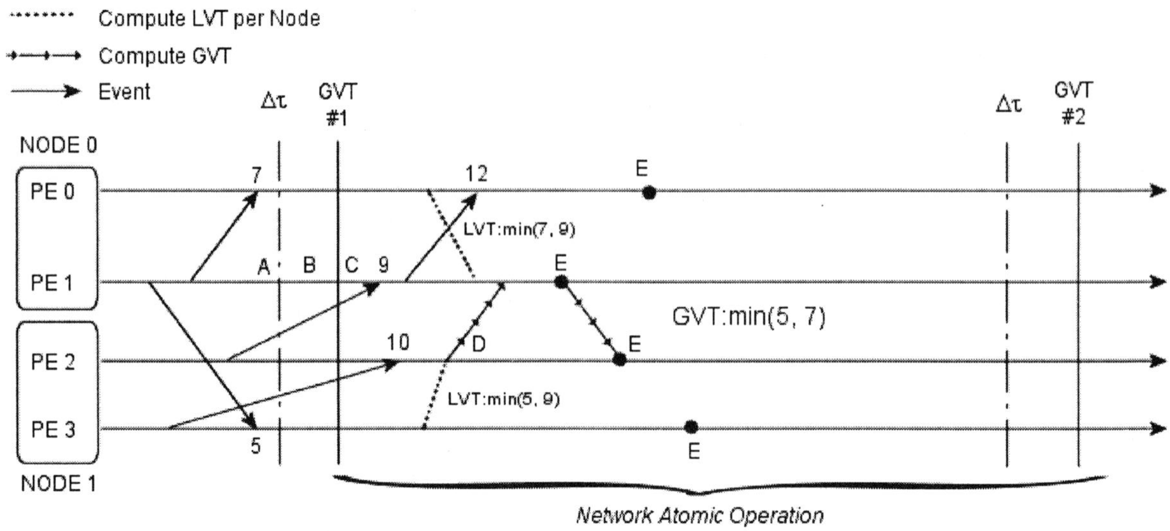

Figure 1: States of the Seven O'Clock Algorithm.

O'Clock algorithm does provide a mechanism to solve each of these problems. Three problems arise in any clock-based algorithm: drift, jitter and synchronization error. During the course of a simulation, clocks may drift together, or apart. In the later case, this can lead to a gradual disparate view of time. Clock jitter occurs when a time is discretized and the width of the time units is not uniform. This can be a cause of clock drift over time depending on the frequency and size of the jitter. Finally, it is difficult to synchronize clocks to a high degree of granularity. This can lead to two processors being synchronized, but off by an indeterminate amount. Each of these problems can be dealt with in the Seven O'Clock algorithm by adjusting the definition of $max\_send\_delta\_t$. Recall that this value is a worst-case bound on the time to send an event between two processors.

We now redefine max_send_delta_t as the maximum of:

1. worst-case bound on events sends
2. two times the synchronization error
3. two times the maximum clock drift during execution

We observe that the $max\_send\_delta\_t$ parameter is simply an adjustment to the NAO to compensate for in-transit events that the sender must account for if they will not be received prior to the NAO expiring at the receiver. The "two times" factor comes from the observation that one processor could have a max synchronization error or clock drift in the negative direction relative to the absolute real time (i.e., master node) and the other processor could have the max synchronization error or clock drift in the positive direction. Thus, these two processors are "out of synch" by at most a factor of two times maximum error or drift. However, in practice these error and drift values are several orders of magnitude smaller than the maximum time to send an event through the network, and can be safely ignored in most operating circumstances.

3.3 Limitations

Two issues arise from the introduction of the Seven O'Clock algorithm that do not exist in other GVT algorithms. Both stem from the general problem which is that the Seven O'Clock GVT algorithm cannot be "forced". First, GVT must advance for a simulation to determine that the simulation must end. In the *Rensselaer's Optimistic Simulation System(ROSS)* parallel scheduler this happens quickly because events to be scheduled past the end time are not processed and the GVT interval counter climbs quickly so that GVT may be computed when the system is effectively out of events. The Seven O'Clock algorithm cannot be forced because each node must wait for the NAO to expire. At the end of a simulation, the *ROSS* system has no events scheduled for processing, and is simply waiting for the CPU to compute the next GVT interval. This situation cannot be aborted early because each network node is unaware of other nodes still actively processing events. The time wasted is bounded in the worst case by the size of the GVT interval. It is reasonable to expect this value to be small in relation to the overall time spent in execution, and so we do not consider this to be a major loss because it can be effectively amortized away.

The fact we cannot force a GVT computation leads to the second limitation to the system. When all of the free events were consumed in the *ROSS* parallel scheduler, we were previously able to "jump" the GVT interval counter and force a GVT computation to occur. Refreshing the GVT value meant that we could reclaim at least one additional event in the system and continue forward processing. When free events are exhausted in the *ROSS* distributed scheduler we can no longer force GVT, and so must simply wait for the next GVT interval to pass. This problem occurs when we do not have sufficient optimistic memory to continue forward execution. The solution to this problem is to simply add more optimistic memory, *or more network nodes*, further distributing the model so that this does not occur. An indirect cause of this problem is spec-

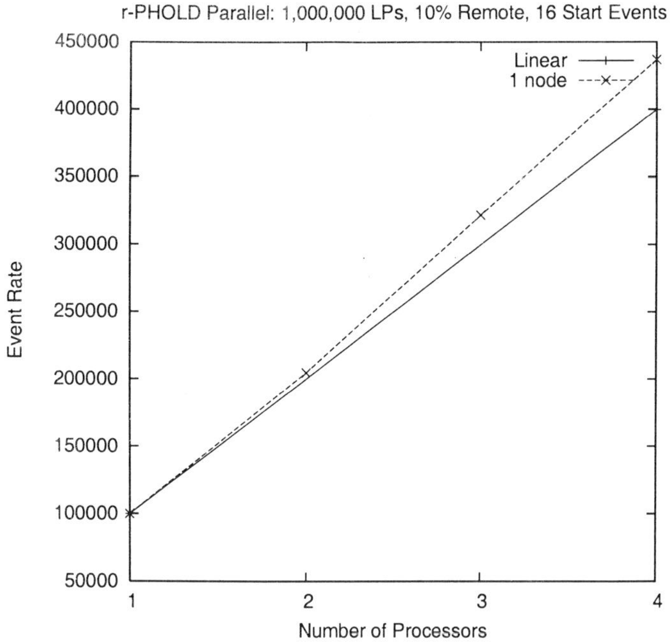

Figure 2: PHOLD results in parallel case.

ulative execution. In this case, stalled waiting for GVT to pass can act as a throttle on the faster nodes in the network such that they cannot overly speculatively execute, thereby creating the potential for long rollbacks. This problem is best solved by tuning the GVT interval to more closely match the amount of available memory.

4 Performance Study

There are two benchmark models used in this performance study. The first is a synthetic workload model called PHOLD. This commonly used benchmark has been modified to support reverse computation and is configured to have minimal LP state, message sizes and event processing. The forward computation of events involves computing three random numbers: one for computing if a remote event should be created, one used to compute the time-stamp and one used for the destination LP. The reverse computation involves "undoing" an LP's random number generator (RNG) in order to restore it's state. Because the RNG is perfectly reversible, the reverse computation restores seed state by computing the perfect inverse function as described in [3]. The destination LP is determined by calling a uniformly distributed random number generator in the range of 0 to 100. If the generated value is less than the specified percent of remote messages allowed, we choose the destination LP over an exponential distribution of LPs, otherwise, the event will be sent to the source LP. The third call determines the offset timestamp for events and is exponentially distributed with a mean of 1.0, with the model completing at timestamp 100. For all experiment runs, we mapped LPs to PEs in a round robin fashion. Each simulation run contained 1 million LPs, and the number of KPs was

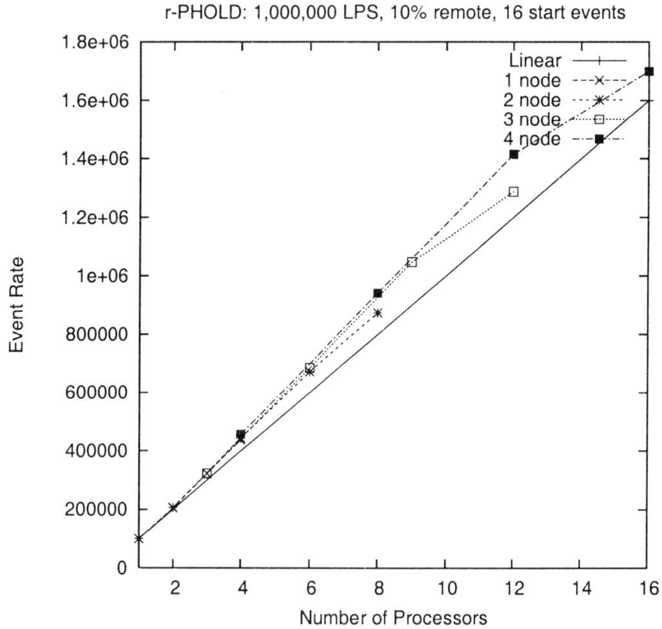

Figure 3: PHOLD results in the distributed cases with 1,2 or 3 processors utilized per node. The 4 processor cases are clearly affected by context-switching in the operating system for I/O operations.

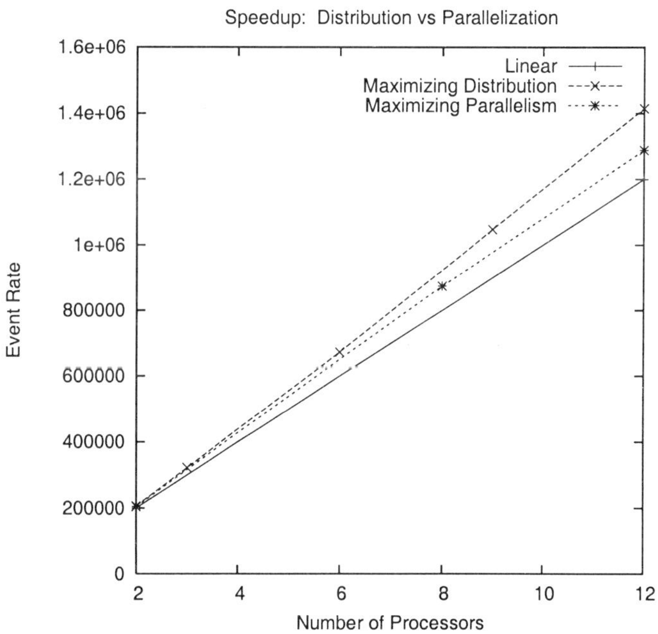

Figure 4: Maximizing nodes used generates better speedup than maximizing processors per node.

determined as $NPEs^2 * 4$. The message population per LP is 16. This model is a pathological benchmark which has minimal event granularity while producing a configurable number of remote events which can result in "thrashing" rollbacks.

The second application is a model of TCP and this implementation follows the Tahoe specification [5]. There are three main data structures in this model: the data packet which is sent between hosts in the data plane, the network router LPs which maintain queuing information and forward packets through the network and the host LPs which keep statistical information on the transferring of data. For detailed model design and implementation, we refer the interested reader to [25].

For all TCP experiments, each TCP connection maintained a consistent configuration. The transfer sizes are infinite and so each TCP sender/receiver pair operates for the duration of the simulation. Each host pair is generated randomly during the initialization of the model. The random nature of connections means that there is a high percentage of "long haul" links which results in a large number of remote events being scheduled between PEs. The synthetic topology is hierarchical, and contains 4 levels, the top-most being fully connected. A router in a given level has N lower level routers or hosts connected to it, so the total number of nodes in the system is equal to: $N^4 + N^3 + N^2 + N$. The nodes were enumerated in such a way that the next hop can be calculated based on the destination at each hop. The bandwidth, delay and buffer size for the synthetic topology is as follows:

- 2.48 Gb/s, a delay of 30 ms, 3MB buffer
- 620 Mb/s, a delay between 10 and 30 ms, 750 KB buffer
- 155 Mb/s, a delay of 5, 1o and 30 ms, and 200 KB buffer
- 45 Mb/s, a delay of 5 ms, and 60 KB buffer
- 1.5 Mb/s, a delay of 5 ms, and 20 KB buffer
- 500 Kb/s, a delay of 5 ms, and a 15 KB buffer

4.1 Computing Testbed and Experiment Setup

The Itanium2 processor [10] is a 64 bit architecture based on *Explicitly Parallel Computing (EPIC)* which intelligently bundles instructions together that are free of data, branch or control hazards. This approach enables up to 48 instructions to be in flight at any point in time. Current implementations employ a 6-wide, 8-stage deep pipeline. A single system can physically address up to 2^{50} bytes and has a full 64-bit virtual address capability. The L-3 cache comes in a 3 MBs configuration and can be accessed at 48 GBs/second which is the core bus speed. For all experiments here, up to 4, quad Itanium processor servers were use. TCP over Gigabit Ethernet was used as the interconnection network between quad processor systems.

When applicable, the parallel scheduler computed 64 events per batch loop, and computed GVT after 64 batch loops. Thus, up to 4096 events will be processed between GVT epochs. These settings have been determined in the past to yield high performance. For the Seven O'Clock Algorithm, the NAO is configured to fire every 250 milliseconds to compute GVT. Optimistic event memory was computed in each case from the following formula: $OptimisticMemory = C * NumPEs * Batch * GVT_{Interval}$ [3]. Here, $NumPEs$ is the number of processors used within the network, and C is a small constant factor. Each processor can consume $Batch * GVT_{Interval}$ events per GVT epoch and C determines an amount of reserve buffers for optimistic execution during the asynchronous GVT computations. During distributed execution, each processor can consume approximately the NAO time interval (in cycles) divided by the average time (in cycles) to compute one event per GVT epoch.

4.2 PHOLD Performance Data

For the Itanium cluster results, we configured PHOLD with 10% remote messages with 16 seed event per LP and used the Myrinet network. Shown for completeness, Figure 2 shows that *ROSS* parallel scheduler continues to provide linear speedup. In fact, it proved difficult to derive a sequential case which did not show a slight super-linear speedup. Comparing the results in the parallel and distributed case in Figure 3 is complicated because we have results based both on the number of processors used and on the number of nodes used. We start by considering two nodes maximizing the processors before increasing the number of nodes. Then we consider three nodes, and finally four nodes.

When a fourth processor is allocated per node, performance degrades. We attribute this phenomenon to our simulation processes competing with other operating system service processes resident on each node, such as Network File System (NFS) daemons, for processing time. For two and three processors cases, the Linux scheduler would bind those service jobs to other available processors. When all four processors are used, the Linux scheduler now must multiplex our simulators' threads and these service processes among all processors leading to an increase in context switch overheads. To confirm this hypothesis, we measured the amount of context switches which occurred in each case. For the two and three processor cases we observed 12 and 14 involuntary context switches respectively. However, for the four processor case, we found 1123 involuntary context switches. This is a 100 fold increase.

After close analysis of the parallel and distributed system we conclude that there are two possible speedups in a parallel and distributed system: speedup due to parallelism and speedup due to distribution. In Figure 4 we see that the system is in fact generating a better speedup as we go more distributed. Besides context switching, other problems may arise such as memory bus overloading or serialized memory references [2, 15, 19], which limit the possible speedup due to parallelism. By maximizing the number of nodes used in a simulation it is possible to avoid or reduce these problems by de-coupling the hardware systems which are limiting performance.

4.3 TCP Performance Data

Computing the LP to PE mapping for the TCP-TAHOE model becomes difficult when the number of processors available is not some multiple of 32. Therefore we present here the results for the 2- and 4-node simulation runs. Figure 5 shows that we again generate a very linear speedup. However, the speedup is sub-linear because of the available num-

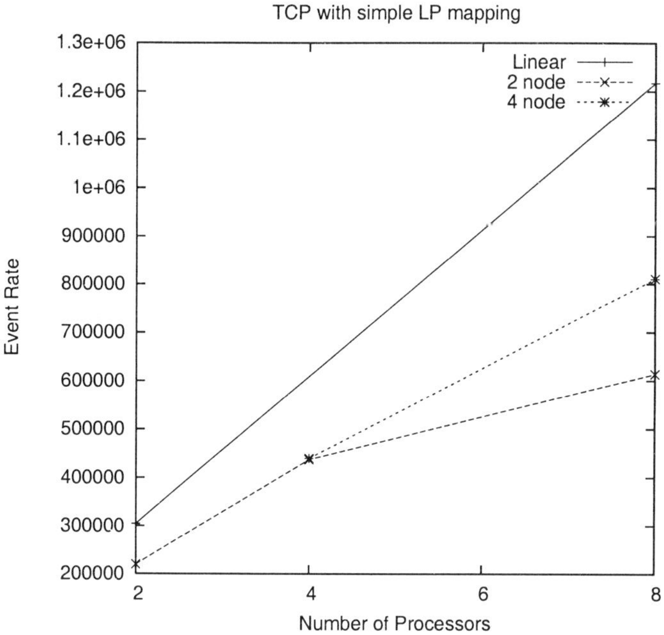

Figure 5: Results for TCP-TAHOE running on 2 and 4-nodes.

ber of kernel processes (KPs). In [3], KPs where introduced as an aggregation structure for reducing LP fossil collection and rollback overheads. In our implementation of this optimization, we hypothesize that we are seeing the same performance problem here, but on a much larger scale. With 1 million LPs, each modeling some end (either source or destination) of a TCP connection, the model requires far greater than 32 KPs in order to achieve good performance. So it is constrained by the way the topology of the TCP network was mapped to LPs/KPs/PEs. However, we believe with a better mapping, the performance would improve.

5 Related Work

Samadi's algorithm [24] solves the simultaneous reporting problem through the use of message acknowledgments. Here, processors will tag any "ack" message that it sends in the period from when the processor reports its LVT until it receives the new GVT value. This process prevents any messages from "slipping through the cracks" [8].

In addition to Fujimoto's and Mattern's GVT algorithms, there have been a number of predecessors. Preiss [22] introduced a scheme which places the PEs into a ring. The first round completes when a token has been passed around the ring and returns to the initiating PE. When the initial token is received, a PE begins accounting for remotely sent messages which may or may not complete prior to the GVT computation. On receiving the second token, a local GVT value is computed as the minimum between the value stored in the token and the PEs local minimum. Improvements to this algorithm have been proposed by Bellenot [1] which reduce the complexity of message passing by organizing PEs into trees rather than a ring. Lin and Lazowska [16] propose a new data structure that reduces the frequency of acknowledgment messages. The work done by Tomlinson and Garg [23] uses counters to detect transient messages. However, this scheme does not employ the use of a "cut" as Mattern's algorithm does. Pancerella [21] propose a hardware based scheme whereby host systems using custom network interface cards are interconnected to form an efficient reduction network to rapidly compute GVT.

In follow-up research, Lin [17] uses control messages to efficiently find/flush out transient messages. At about the same time, D'Souza et. al [4], proposes a statistical approach to estimating GVT.

Prior to Fujimoto's GVT algorithm, Xiao et al. [26], proposes an asynchronous GVT algorithm that exploits shared-memory multiprocessor architectures. Here the concept of "cages" is used, where each processor own some set of "cages" that it places or lays down in order to track the LVT of that processor. It is interesting to note, that here a global *Cage Flag* much like the `gvt_flag` in Fujimoto's Algorithm, is used to "kick off" the GVT computation.

Related to both "consistent cuts" and sequentially consistent memory is the issue of causality. Most recently, Zhou et al [27], propose a "relaxed" causal receive ordering algorithm called *critical causality* for distributed virtual environments.

6 Conclusions

We present a new idea of Network Atomic Operations, and apply it to solving the global virtual time problem. We use an NAO to generate a zero-cost cut in a distributed system which is both scalable and efficient. Our experimental results indicate a super-linear speedup over sequential. We also propose that there are two forms of speedup, one due to parallelization and one due to distribution. The parallel scheduler results were already super-linear, however there is more speedup inherent to distribution because we eliminate bottlenecks such as the memory bus and context switching. Finally, NAOs lead us to viewing the behavior of Time Warp in the frequency domain because they define the relationship between virtual time and wall-clock time. In the future, such a view may potentially prove beneficial in better understanding Time Warp behavior.

Acknowledgments

This research is supported by NSF CAREER Award CCR-0133488, NSF CNS Award CNS-0435259, DARPA Network Modeling and Simulation (NMS) program, contract #F30602-00-2-0537 and a AT&T University Relations Program Grant.

References

[1] S. Bellenot, "Global Virtual Time Algorithms", In *Proceedings of the SCS Multiconference on Distributed Simulation*, Vol. 22, pp. 122–127, 1990.

[2] C. D. Carothers, K. S. Perumalla, and R. M. Fujimoto, "The effect of state-saving in optimistic simulation on a cache-coherent non-uniform memory access architecture," in *Proceedings of the 1999 Winter Simulation Conference*, 1999.

[3] C. D. Carothers, D. Bauer, and S. Pearce, "Ross: A high-performance, low memory, modular time warp system," *Journal of Parallel and Distributed Computing*, 2002.

[4] L. M. D'Souza, X. Fan, and P. A. Wilsey, "pGVT: An Algorithm for Accurate GVT Estimation", In *Proceedings of the 8th Workshop on Parallel and Distributed Simulation (PADS '94)*, pp. 102–109, 1994.

[5] K. Fall and S. Floyd, "Simulation-based comparison of tahoe, reno, and sack tcp," *Computer Communication Review*, vol. 26, pp. 5–21, 1996.

[6] R. M. Fujimoto, "Time warp on a shared memory multiprocessor," in *Proceedings of the 1989 International Conference on Parallel Processing*, vol. 3, pp. 242–249, August 1989.

[7] R. M. Fujimoto and M. Hybinette, "Computing global virtual time in shared-memory multiprocessors," *ACM Trans. Model. Comput. Simul.*, vol. 7, no. 4, pp. 425–446, 1997.

[8] R. M. Fujimoto, *Parallel and Distributed Simulation Systems*. "John Wiley and Sons, Inc.", 2000.

[9] K. Garachorloo et al. "Memory Consistency and Event Ordering in Scalable Shared-Memory Multiprocessors", *Proceedings of the 17th Annual Symposium on Computer Architecture*, pp. 15–26, 1988.

[10] Intel, "Intel Itanium-II Reference Manuals", Available via the web at: `http://www.intel.com/design/itanium/documentation.htm?iid=ipp_srvr_proc_itanium2+techdocs&`

[11] Intel, "Intel Pentium 4 and Xeon Processor Optimization Reference Manual," Available via the web at: `http://developer.intel.com/design/pentium4/manuals/248966.htm`

[12] D. Jefferson, "Virtual Time", *ACM Trans. Prog. Lang. and Systems*, vol. 7, no. 3, July, pp. 404–425, 1985.

[13] D. Jefferson, "Virtual Time II: Storage Management in Distributed Simulation", In *Proceedings of the 9th Annual ACM Symposium on Principles of Distributed Computing*, August, pp. 75–89, 1990.

[14] L. Lamport, "How to Make a Multiprocessor Compute that Correctly Executes Multiprocess Programs", *IEEE Transactions on Computers*, vol. 28, no. 9, September, pp. 690–691, 1979.

[15] J. Laudon and D. Lenoski, "The sgi origin: a ccnuma highly scalable server," pp. 241–251, 1997.

[16] Y-B. Lin and E. D. Lazowska, "Determining the Global Virtual Time in a Distributed Simulation", In *Proceedings of the 1990 International Conference on Parallel Processing*, vol. 3, August, pp. 201–209, 1990.

[17] Y-B. Lin, "Determining the Global Progress of Parallel Simulation with FIFO Communication Property", *Information Processing Letters*, 50, pp. 13–17, 1994.

[18] F. Mattern. "Efficient Distributed Snapshots and Global virtual Time Algorithms for Non-FIFO Systems", *Journal of Parallel and Distributed Computing (JPDC)*, vol. 18, no. 4, August, pages 423–434, 1993.

[19] D. Nagle, R. Uhlig, T. Stanley, S. Sechrest, T. N. Mudge, and R. B. Brown, "Design tradeoffs for software-managed TLBs," in *ISCA*, pp. 27–38, 1993.

[20] R. Ostrovsky and B. Patt-Shamir, "Optimal and efficient clock synchronization under drifting clocks" In *Proceedings of the 18th Annual ACM Symposium on Principles of Distributed Computing*, pp. 3 - 12, 1999.

[21] C. M. Pancerella, and P. F. Reynolds, "Disseminating Critical Target-Specific Synchronization Information in Parallel Discrete-Event Simulation", In *Proceedings of the 7th Workshop on Parallel and Distributed Simulation (PADS '93)*, pp. 52–59, 1993.

[22] B. R. Preiss, "The Yaddes Distributed Discrete Event Simulation Specification Language and Execution Environments", In *Proceedings of the SCS Multiconference on Distributed Simulation*, vol. 21, March, pp. 139–144, 1989.

[23] A. Tomlinson and V. K. Gang, "An Algorithm for Minimally Latent Global Virtual Time", In *Proceedings of the 7th Workshop on Parallel and Distributed Simulation (PADS '93)*, pp. 35–42, 1993.

[24] B. Samadi. "Distributed Simulation, Algorithms and Performance Analysis", Ph. D. Thesis, University of California, Los Angeles (UCLA), 1985.

[25] G. Yaun, C. D. Carothers, and S. Kalyanaraman, "Large-scale TCP models using optimistic parallel simulation," In *Proceedings of Workshop on Parallel and Distributed Simulation (PADS 2003)*, June 2003.

[26] Z. Xiao, J. Cleary, F. Gomes, and B. Unger. "A Fast Asynchronous Continuous GVT Algorithm for Shared Memory Multiprocessors Architectures", In *9th Workshop on Parallel and Distributed Simulation (PADS '95)*, June, 1995.

[27] S. Zhou, W. Cai, S. J. Turner and F. Lee, "Critical Causality in Distributed Virtual Environments", In *Proceedings of the 16th Workshop on Parallel and Distributed Simulation (PADS '02)*, pp. 53–59, 2002.

Optimistic Protocol Analysis in a Performance Analyser and Prediction Tool

Peihan Teo[1], Stephen John Turner[1], Zoltan Juhasz[2,3]
[1]*School of Computer Engineering, Nanyang Technological University, Singapore*
[2]*Department of Information Systems, University of Veszprem, Hungary*
[3]*Department of Computer Science, University of Exeter, United Kingdom*
S8133753E@ntu.edu.sg, ASSJTurner@ntu.edu.sg, juhasz@irt.vein.hu

Abstract

Parallelising sequential discrete event simulation programs is often a tedious process, with no guarantee for speedup. This paper describes a performance analyser tool developed to predict the execution performance of parallel discrete event simulation programs, using either optimistic or conservative protocols. The tool aims to provide the user with the flexibility of choosing the simulation protocol desired, and to make useful comparisons between the results obtained. The novel feature of the analyser is that it predicts the parallel execution performance based on a sequential simulation run, without the parallel implementation developed. This paper describes the structure and operation of the analyser program focusing on the analysis of the optimistic simulation protocol. As the prediction of the optimistic protocol is very different from the conservative one, its uniqueness will be illustrated in this paper. The performance analyzer and prediction tool can be used to explore different protocols and parameters in order to provide faster decision making about the final implementation strategy.

1. Introduction

Simulation is a central tool in science and industry, enabling scientists and engineers to investigate many phenomena that would be impossible to study and understand with other methods. Since simulation programs are used extensively to study the behaviour of complex systems in detail, they are computationally intensive and require long execution times.

Although parallel computing technology can potentially speed up the execution of large and complex discrete event simulations, it is not yet widely accepted within the discrete event simulation community, despite years of parallel simulation research. The two main factors that have been hindering the acceptance of the technology are: developing parallel simulation programs is a tedious and difficult process requiring special expertise, and also there is no guarantee that the end product will deliver improved performance.

The first issue can be addressed by developing and accepting high-level, visual parallel simulation programming environments. The second issue calls for easy-to-use performance analysis and prediction tools. Unfortunately, the prediction of parallel performance is a complex and difficult task, as the achievable performance gain for any parallel simulation problem depends on the particular simulation problem (application) as well as on many software and hardware related parameters. As there is no best parallel simulation protocol suitable for all situations, selecting the best parallel implementation is still frequently done by trial and error.

The structure of the paper is as follows. Section 2 gives a brief overview of previous work in the parallel simulation performance analysis and prediction area. Section 3 introduces the conservative protocol analyser that is the basis of our current work. Section 4 describes the structure and operation of the optimistic protocol performance analyser. Then, Section 5 illustrates some potential use cases for our tool as well as results obtained with simple test cases. The paper ends with conclusions and a short discussion of future directions.

2. Related Work

As previously mentioned, analysing the behaviour of parallel simulation protocols is very difficult. One

1087-4097/05 $20.00 © 2005 IEEE

approach is to build analytical models of parallel simulation algorithms. An early example of this type of work is given in [1], where it is shown that for a worst-case simulation model, an optimistic Time Warp algorithm [2] can arbitrarily outperform a conservative Chandy-Misra protocol [3], but the converse is not true (the conservative algorithm can only outperform the optimistic one by a constant factor). A good summary of early work on analytical performance analysis can be found in [4]. Most of the analytical models described in the literature are based on very simple assumptions, such as zero communication time, and are often limited to two or a small number of logical processes. Our approach differs from this work in that it emphasises the *engineering* aspects of performance analysis: using the prediction tool to explore different protocols and parameters in order to provide faster decision making about the final implementation strategy.

There are two fundamentally different ways for creating such a parallel simulation performance analyser. The first is to base the analysis on the execution of a *parallel simulation* run. The other is to use a *sequential simulation* as the basis of predicting parallel behaviour [5]. While the first method is potentially more accurate, its main disadvantage is that it requires the existence of the parallel simulation program, hence it cannot really predict performance, it can only be used for performance evaluation of a given parallel implementation.

Analysers based on a sequential execution run rely on trace information generated during the sequential simulation. Depending on whether the analysis is performed during or after the sequential run, one can distinguish between integrated or post-mortem analysis. Two integrated systems are described in [6, 7]. The former is used for the Chandry-Misra conservative protocol, while the latter is for the synchronous conservative protocol. The advantage of the integrated approach is its memory efficiency; only limited trace information needs to be stored for analysis.

Post-mortem analysis offers more flexibility and predictive power at the price of using larger trace files. A general purpose performance analyser and prediction tool for conservative protocols has previously been developed [8, 9] that enables users to determine whether or not a parallel implementation is worthwhile, and if so, which approach is the best for the given simulation problem. The tool allows developers to experiment with various simulation protocols, process-to-processor mappings, and the effects of communication and other parameters. The work discussed in this paper extends this tool with the capability to analyse optimistic protocols.

3. The Conservative Protocol Analyser

The conservative performance analyser is a post-mortem parallelism analyser that predicts parallel execution time for different conservative simulation protocols [10] based on run-time trace information gathered during the execution of a sequential simulation program. This tool allows one to explore the behaviour of different simulation protocols as well as the effects of different process-to-processor mappings and hardware parameters, prior to implementing the parallel simulation program. Using this new tool, the developer can gain important insight into the execution of the simulation in question, and determine which approach is the best for the given simulation problem. The parallel version then needs to be developed only if proven to be successful.

The overall architecture of the analyser is shown in Figure 1. The detailed discussion of the design and operation can be found in [8, 9].

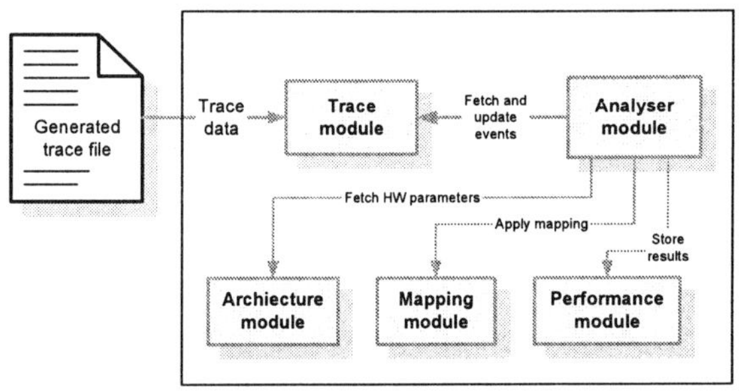

Figure 1. The overall architecture of the performance analyser.

4. The Optimistic Protocol Analyser

The conservative simulation protocol works on the basis of avoiding causality errors and allowing only safe events to be processed. In many cases, this results in an overly pessimistic execution sequence, not fully exploiting the potential parallelism inherent in the simulation.

Optimistic approaches use a detection and recovery approach: causality errors are detected, and a rollback mechanism is invoked to recover from errors. The main advantage of this method is that it has the ability to allow a simulation to exploit parallelism in situations where parallel event processing is possible and causality errors do not occur.

The Time Warp [2, 11] mechanism based on the Virtual Time paradigm is the most well-known optimistic simulation protocol. In Time Warp, a causality error is detected whenever an event message is received with a timestamp smaller than the current simulation time of the receiving process. Recovery is accomplished by undoing the effects of all events processed prematurely by the process receiving the event causing rollback.

4.1. Design of the Optimistic Analyser

Since the optimistic protocol works differently from the conservative one, the performance analyser has to be modified significantly to handle the different protocol analysis operations.

The sequential execution trace contains events in correct timestamp order. These can be processed and analysed directly by the conservative protocol analyser. As opposed to this, the optimistic algorithm executes events as they arrive, without checking if they are safe to process in the first place. This algorithm resolves causality errors by rolling back events that are not executed in the correct timestamp order. The different behaviour requires changes in the protocol analysis as well as the data structures used.

As a result, the execution flow within the analyser is divided into three main phases: (*i*) *Input*, (*ii*) *Analysis* and (*iii*) *Output*. In the following description, the term processor is used to refer to a Time Warp simulation process (i.e. we assume there is one simulation process per processor). The performance analyser tool has a mapping module [9] that can be used to investigate the effect of different mappings when there are more processes than processors.

Input phase:

This phase is responsible for performing the necessary trace data pre-processing for the subsequent analysis phase since the optimistic protocol requires events to be executed in arrival (not necessarily timestamp) order. We use the term *real time* to mean the wall clock time of the optimistic simulation algorithm we are analysing.

A pending list is created for each processor and is populated by events as the trace file is being input. Since the trace file contains information about to which processor events are sent, events can be inserted into their respective pending list. At the end of the input phase all events in the list are initially marked as *unarrived*.

Analysis phase:

The execution flowchart of the analysis phase is shown in figure 2.

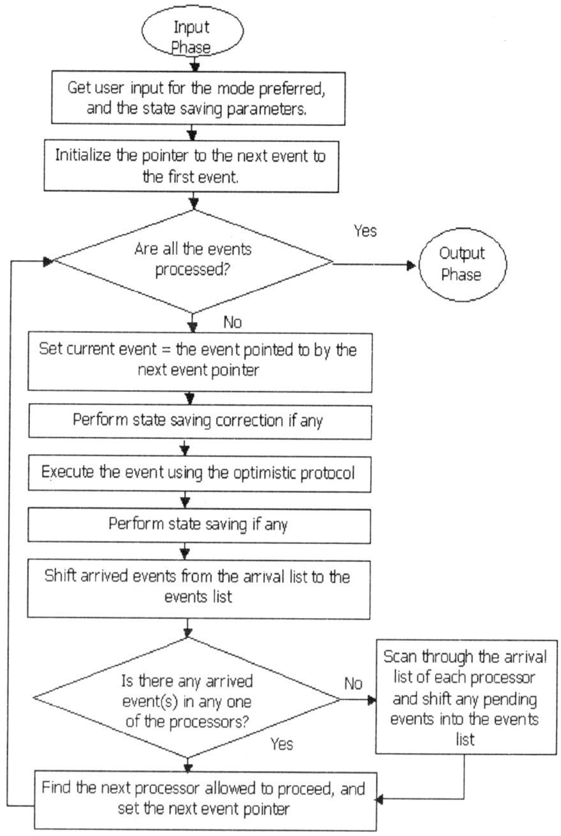

Figure 2. Execution flowchart of the protocol analysis phase.

The performance analysis of the optimistic protocol is carried out in the analysis phase using the following operations.

- A *shift-events* operation is used to move events from the pending list to the event list according to the real time they actually arrive. Each processor has an event list that contains events in timestamp order. Each event list has a next event pointer pointing to the next event to be executed for that particular processor. The events preceding the next event pointer have already been executed. The events following the next event pointer are waiting to be executed.
- A *find-next-processor* operation is used to find the next processor that is allowed to execute in the simulation analysis. This is required as the arrival times of the events depend on the execution of the events that generated them and other factors such as communication latency. Hence, it is essential to scan through the processors to determine which processor should execute. Also, in the case when

there are no unprocessed events in the event list, the pending list of each processor has to be scanned to check if there are any arrived events.

- A *rollback* operation is required to handle rollbacks. This involves restoring the original state (before the rolled back events) and re-executing the events in the correct order. Anti-messages are sent to the relevant processors, which may cause cascaded rollbacks. Another operation is used to handle anti-messages, where consideration is needed to check if annihilation has occurred. Also, various state saving strategies need to be handled.

Output phase:

This phase is responsible for displaying and visualising the results of the protocol performance analysis. Additional features need to be added to the original conservative visualisation system to distinguish rolled back events from ordinary ones.

4.2. Data Structures Required

There are various data structures in addition to those for the conservative analyser that are required to implement the optimistic protocol analysis. The following data structures are created with one element for each processor and are indexed by the processor number:

1. The *ptrNextEvent* array stores the pointer to the next event to be executed on that processor.
2. The *eventList* array stores the events that have arrived at that processor (i.e. have an arrival time less than or equal to the processor's real time). Events that have already been executed are also kept in this list in case of rollback.
3. The *pendingList* stores all the events that have not yet arrived at that processor (i.e. *unarrived* events where the arrival time has not yet been calculated or events with an arrival time greater than the processor's real time).
4. The *antiMsgList* array stores all the anti-messages that have arrived at that processor before the corresponding event message and have yet not been annihilated. This is required as it is necessary to keep track of the anti-messages, so that it is possible to annihilate the corresponding events.
5. The *stateSavingList* array stores the list of virtual times when the processor's state was saved, so that the appropriate state in the case of a causality error can be identified and restored.
6. The *stateSavingTrigger* array stores the data needed to trigger state saving. This is the count of events executed if we are performing state saving after every *n* events, or the real time if we are performing state saving after every T_{state} time units. State saving strategies are discussed later in Section 4.3.2.

4.3. The Optimistic Analysis Algorithm

After the input phase, all events are assigned to their respective pending lists and are marked *unarrived.*

Prior to starting the analysis, user parameters governing the analysis (e.g. state saving mode, other state saving parameters) are input. A variable *nextProcessor* is initialized to the processor that executes the first event. The first event is shifted to the eventList of that processor and the next event pointer is initialized to point to that event.

After executing each event, the next processor must be determined. If there are still events to be executed, *nextProcessor* will be set to the processor on which the next event will be executed. If there are no more events to be executed, *nextProcessor* will be set to null and the simulation terminates.

An outline of the optimistic analysis algorithm is as follows:

```
while ( nextProcessor != null ) do
i.   currentEvent := eventList[nextProcessor]->
         GetEvent(ptrNextEvent[nextProcessor]);
ii.  call OptimisticProtocol(currentEvent)
iii. call StateSaving(processorNo, SSOverhead, mode,
         eventsInterval, timeInterval);
iv.  call ShiftEvents(currentEvent->processor);
v.   nextProcessor := FindNextProcessor();
end do
```

The main steps of the algorithm are discussed in detail in the remaining subsections of this section.

4.3.1. The OptimisticProtocol Function. After the current simulation event has been identified in Step i., this function searches for any events that could annihilate the current event. If such a corresponding event exists, the current event is annihilated; otherwise the current event is processed. The current event could be either a normal event or an anti-message.

If the current event is a normal event, we first scan through the antiMsgList to see whether there is a corresponding anti-message that has arrived before this event. If the anti-message exists, the current event will be shifted back to its pending list, marked *unarrived.* This is because the same event will be rescheduled at a later time. The anti-message is deleted accordingly. If there is no corresponding anti-message, the current event is executed and the processor's real time is incremented. The current event may generate other events to be sent out to the other processors. Communication overheads are also taken into consideration for calculating the arrival times of these generated events. The corresponding events are marked *arrived* in the pending lists of the appropriate processors. The arrived events in the pending list are ordered according to the real time that the events arrive.

If the current event is an anti-message and the corresponding event message has not been processed, the anti-message is executed like a normal event but it will not affect the real time of the processor as the execution time of the anti-message is set to 0. This 'execution' step is required for keeping track of anti-messages for future cancellations. If, however, an event that needs to be cancelled has been executed before its anti-message arrives, the rollback algorithm is called upon immediately to undo that particular event, as well as the events that were executed afterwards. This is handled in the ShiftEvents function.

4.3.2. The StateSaving Function. This function is responsible for determining the cost of state saving in the optimistic simulation protocol. To be able to perform a rollback the state of each process is saved periodically. There are two modes of how the analyser can save states: saving state periodically after every n events or after every T_{state} time units.

The *mode* variable specifies which of these two modes the user has selected. The *eventsInterval* variable stores the number of events between state saving. The *timeInterval* variable stores the length of the real time between consecutive state saving points. The *SSOverhead* stores the state saving overheads that might be incurred during state saving.

4.3.3. The ShiftEvents Function. This function takes as input the processor number of the currently executed event and shifts the events that have arrived at that processor from the pendingList to the eventList. It is only necessary to look at the processor that has just executed the event because only this processor has incremented its real time as a result of the event execution. The real time of other processors is unchanged.

Each event in the pendingList is checked to see whether it has actually arrived at that processor in real time. Only events with an arrival time less than or equal to the processor's real time are shifted to the eventList. The events in the eventList are arranged in timestamp order according to the Time Warp algorithm, and hence, the arrived events are shifted into the eventList in timestamp order.

If the arrived event has a timestamp that is less than that of the event that was executed last, a causality error has occurred and the rollback operation is called to undo all events that have been processed prematurely.

If the arrived event has a timestamp greater than that of the event that was executed last, the event will be simply inserted into the eventList according to its timestamp. The next event pointer is also updated accordingly to point to the next event to be executed. This is the event after the one that has just been executed if there is such an event, otherwise the next event pointer is set to null.

If the pendingList is empty, it means that no events will arrive at the processor in the future (except possibly for anti-messages). Also, if all arrived events in the pendingList have an arrival time greater than the real time of the processor, it means none of them has actually arrived in real time. In both cases, no events are shifted to the eventList. If there are no unprocessed events already in the eventList, the next event pointer is set to null.

4.3.4. The FindNextProcessor Function. This function is used for selecting the next processor that is allowed to execute for the optimistic protocol analysis. The next processor is determined by calculating the minimum real time at which the next event would be executed in the optimistic simulation algorithm. This represents the most significant difference between the conservative and optimistic analysers.

There are two arrays required by this function, they are both indexed by the processor number. An array of integers, *arrivalEventIndex,* is required to store the index of the event in the pendingList with the minimum arrival time for each processor, its values are initialized to –1. An array of double, *time*, stores the real time at which each processor would execute its next event, and its values are initialized to 0.0. Note that this information has to be recalculated after executing each event as event execution can generate new events for other processors that may affect the calculation.

For each processor, the eventList and pendingList are inspected. If there are unprocessed events in the eventList (i.e. the ptrNextEvent is pointing to a valid event in the eventList), time[currentProcessor] is set to the real time of the processor.

Then, if the pending list is not empty, it will be checked for events that are marked arrived. time[currentProcessor] is set to the minimum of the time[currentProcessor] and the minimum arrival time of the arrived events. If this time is that of an event in the pendingList, arrivalEventIndex[currentProcessor] is also set to the index of this event. Hence if time[currentProcessor] is zero after scanning through the pending list, this indicates that there are no arrived events in the pendingList and no unprocessed events in the eventList.

Then, the values stored in the *time* array are compared to the real time of the processors. The values in the *time* array will be set to the real time of the processor if the real time of the processor is larger than that of the value stored in *time*. Then, the processor with the smallest *time* value is selected as the winner. To summarize, the processor with the minimum value of maximum(real time of processor, minimum arrival time of next event) is selected. The real time of the winner must also be set to its *time* value as it is possible that the processor has been idle waiting for the next event to arrive.

If the next event is already in the eventList (as indicated by arrivalEventIndex[winner] < 0), the winner is simply returned as the next processor to execute. Otherwise the timestamp of the event indicated by arrivalEventIndex[winner] is checked. If its timestamp is less than that of the event pointed to by ptrNextEvent[winner] or ptrNextEvent[winner] is not pointing to any event, the event will be inserted into the eventList according to its timestamp. This can lead to a causality error if it is inserted into the eventList before a previously executed event. In this case, the rollback algorithm is required to undo the error before returning the winner as the next processor to execute.

4.3.5. The Rollback Function. This function implements the rollback mechanism. For each event to roll back, the event is added into the rollback list, so that we can properly record the previous execution information of the event for visualisation. If the event has sent out any other message, there is a need to send out the corresponding anti-messages to the respective processors for cascading rollbacks. The stateSavingList is used to determine the virtual time of the restored state and the ptrNextEvent is updated to point to the next event in the eventList greater than or equal to this virtual time.

5. Performance Evaluation and Prediction Methodology

The analyser tool developed in our project helps developers answer the following types of questions: (i) What is the shortest possible simulation execution time (or largest speedup) that a parallel implementation could provide? (ii) Which simulation protocol will give the best results for my particular application? (iii) How will the speedup scale if we increase the number of processors or the size of the problem? (iv) Which parallel architecture is the most suitable for our implementation?

In the rest of this section we illustrate a few potential ways of using the analyser. For space limitations and easier understanding we have selected a set of very simple test cases and discuss only a few representative examples. The results of the analyses are shown in tabular format as well as by screenshots of the actual analyser screens.

5.1 Test Cases

There were six different test cases we used for demonstrating the optimistic performance analyser:

1. Events executing on 4 processors. This is the test case used to illustrate state saving in section 5.2 (see Figure 7).
2. Events executing on 4 processors with delay. This trace file is almost the same as the earlier one, except the event 6@1's execution time is lengthened so that the event 2@3 will arrive after event 1@3 has finished executing[1].
3. Events executing on 5 processors without rollback. This test case has no rollbacks in the optimistic protocol.
4. Events executing on 5 processors with deliberate rollback. This trace file is almost the same as Test Case 3, except that events 4@1 and 6@1's execution times are lengthened so that event 2@4 will have to be rolled back (see Figure 4).
5. Events executing on 4 processors with cascaded rollback. This trace file is a variation of Test Case 1, except the event 6@1's execution time is lengthened, and the timestamps of events 4@1, 1@3 are changed so that there will be cascaded rollbacks.
6. Events executing on 4 processors with cascaded rollbacks and late anti-messages. This trace file is a variation of Test Case 5, in that event 2@1's execution time is lengthened so that in addition to the cascaded rollback, the anti-messages sent by processor 3 will be late, causing more rollbacks in processor 4 (see Figure 6).

[1]An event identifier is written *n@p* where *n* is the event count and *p* is the source processor.

5.2 Conservative vs. Optimistic Protocol

In this section, we illustrate how the analyser can be used to predict the parallel execution performance of a simulation for different simulation protocols. This can help a developer to choose the most beneficial protocol (variation) for implementation.

First, Test Case 4 is assumed to execute under the conservative protocol. The execution schedule is displayed in the screenshot of Figure 3. As expected with conservative simulation, events always execute in correct timestamp order. The predicted parallel execution time T_{par} is 2.5 time units. The sequential execution time T_{seq} is 2.8 time units (marked by a red dashed vertical line on the analyser screen), hence the achievable speedup S_p with this protocol is $S_p = T_{seq} / T_{par} = 2.8 / 2.5 = 1.12$.

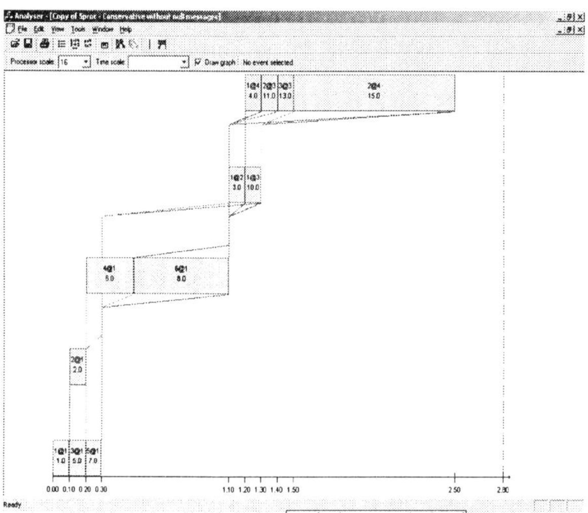

Figure 3. The results obtained from test case 4, using the conservative protocol.

Figure 4 shows the predicted execution of the simulation using the optimistic protocol. It can be seen that event execution starts earlier on processors 4 and 5 than in the conservative case. It can also be seen that event 2@4 with timestamp 13 is executed prematurely and has to be rolled back (rolled back events are shown as yellow by the analyser as opposed to correctly executed blue ones). The predicted parallel execution time T_{par} is 2.7 time units. The sequential execution time is 2.8 time units, hence the achievable speedup S_p with this protocol is $S_p = 2.8 / 2.7 = 1.037$. In this case, the conservative protocol gives a better performance.

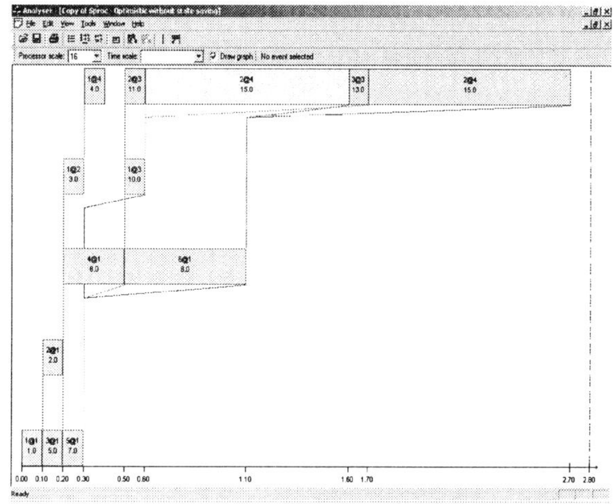

Figure 4. The results obtained from test case 4, using the optimistic protocol.

The next case (Test Case 6) illustrates a situation when the optimistic protocol provides better performance. The execution of the test case under the conservative protocol is shown in Figure 5.

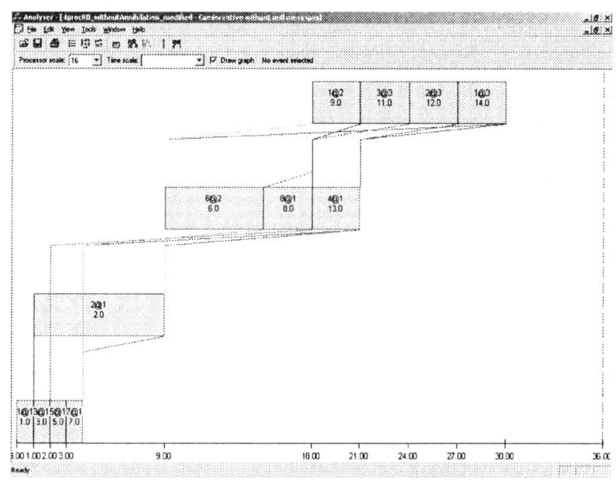

Figure 5. The results obtained from test case 6, using the conservative protocol.

The conservative simulation took 30 time units. The speedup $S_p = 36 / 30 = 1.2$. The optimistic simulation is shown in figure 6 and took 29 time units. During this execution there are six events that are rolled back, events 1@3, 3@3, 2@3, 4@1, 8@1 and 4@1. The speedup for the optimistic execution is $S_p = 36 / 29 = 1.241$. In this case, the optimistic protocol gives a better performance even with the presence of multiple rollbacks.

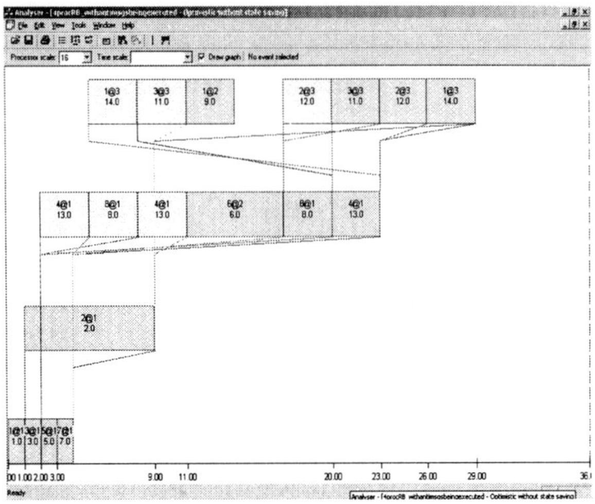

Figure 6. The results obtained from test case 6, using the optimistic protocol.

The predicted speedup values for all test cases for the conservative and optimistic protocols are listed in Table 1.

Table 1. Predicted speedup values for the optimistic and conservative protocol.

Test case	Trace file	Optimistic Speedup	Cons. Speedup
1	4 processors	**1.473**	1.400
2	4 processors with delay	**1.550**	1.348
3	5 processors	**1.710**	1.330
4	5 processors with rollback	1.037	**1.120**
5	4 processors with early anti-messages	**1.348**	1.192
6	4 processors with late anti- messages	**1.241**	1.200

5.2 The Effect of State Saving

The use of the optimistic protocol requires periodic state saving whose cost can greatly influence the simulation performance. In this section we demonstrate how the analyser supports the investigation of state saving effects. There are two different approaches to saving the state periodically. The first is to save state after every *n* events on each processor, where *n* is specified by the user. The other one is to save state after every T_{state} time units, where T_{state} *is* specified by the user.

Saving state less frequently obviously reduces the state saving overheads. On the other hand, it might result in even higher rollback overheads. This might mean that events are being rolled back further in simulation time than is required, reducing performance by unnecessarily re-executing past events. Figure 7 illustrates state saving when $n = 2$. It can be observed that there is a state saving overhead after every second event for each process.

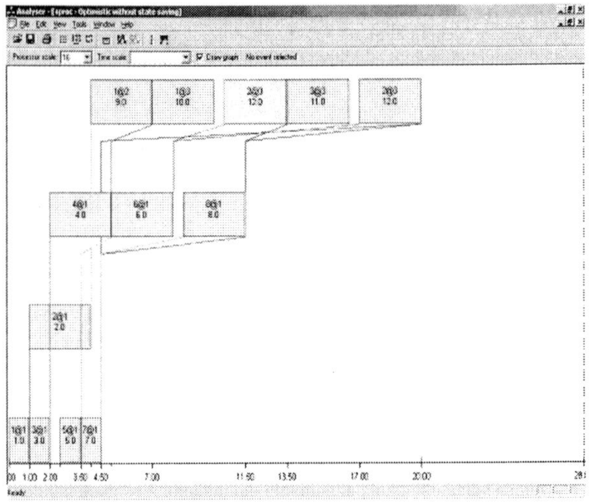

Figure 7. Results obtained with state saving after every 2 events for test case 1.

When *n* is large, the state saving overheads will be greatly reduced, as the frequency of state saving is decreased. However, when a rollback occurs in this case, a significant rollback overhead can be created as we have to roll back more than the necessary number of events. The predicted effect of state saving as a function of *n* is shown in Table 2. The value for n = 0 is the hypothetical case when there is no state saving cost. The table indicates that for this particular problem, the optimum state saving frequency is n = 2.

Table 2. Speedup values predicted for performing state saving after event(s).

Event Interval *n*	Speedup
0	1.473
1	1.333
2	1.400
3	1.077
4	1.098
5	1.098

For state saving at time intervals, the state is saved after every T_{state} time units for each processor. This state saving scheme does not take into consideration the number of events that are executed in that time period. Whenever a rollback occurs, the most recent state that is saved before the rolled back events is restored, and execution is resumed. This scenario is shown in Figure 8. Event 3@3 arrives at processor 4 while 2@3 is executing and so causes a causality error. But the most recent saved state is the one before 1@3 so event 1@3 also has to rolled back and re-executed.

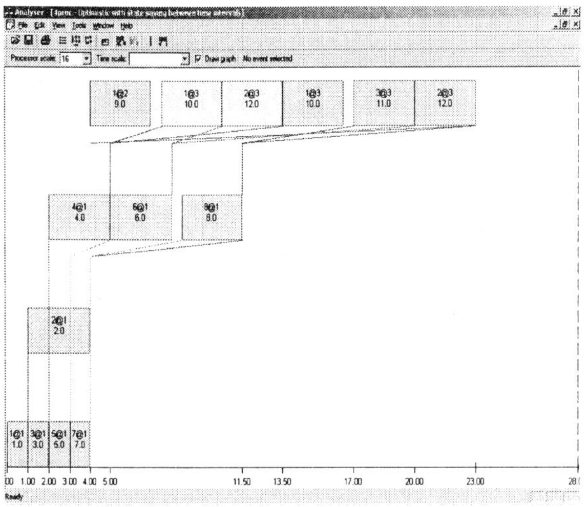

Figure 8. Results obtained with state saving every 0.007 sec for test case 1.

The state saving at time intervals scheme makes it easier to predict the rollback overheads as the states are saved at regular time intervals. Similar to the previous scheme, as T_{state} increases, state saving overhead decreases, but the rollback overhead increases. The inverse happens when T_{state} decreases.

From Table 1 and Table 2, we can draw the following conclusions. If the events that are rolled back have approximately the same execution time as the normal events, the results show that the optimistic protocol performs better than the conservative one. However, if the events that are rolled back have a longer execution time as compared to the events that need not be rolled back, the conservative protocol is observed to have better performance than the optimistic one.

The reason for this is that if the execution times for the events that are rolled back are significant, having to execute these events more than once will definitely result in inefficiency and high overheads. Hence, in the conservative scheme, where the events are only executed once, the time taken for the simulation will be less.

6. Conclusions

This paper describes a post-mortem performance analyser and prediction tool that provides an easy and quick way for developers to analyse and predict the behaviour of parallel discrete-event simulation programs based upon sequential run-time trace information. Our approach emphasises the *engineering* aspects of performance analysis: using the prediction tool to experiment with various simulation protocols, and the effects of communication and other parameters. We believe that such a tool can help programmers in choosing the best approach for an efficient parallel implementation of a given simulation program. Moreover, the analysis can be carried out without the actual development of the parallel simulation program. The work reported in this paper extended the existing analyser with ability to investigate the performance of the optimistic parallel discrete event simulation protocol.

Since the optimistic protocol works differently from the conservative one, new analysis mechanisms had to be developed to deal with the order of event execution, event cancellation, rollbacks and state saving. Our results show that with the analyser it is relatively simple to compare the execution characteristics of the simulation under the conservative and optimistic protocols, and study the effect of state saving. As discussed in [9], the analyser also supports evaluating the effects of communication and process-to-processor mapping. These can also influence performance since if the communication cost of the rolled back events is much longer than the remaining events, then it will have a similar effect as when the execution times of the rolled back events are much larger. This happens if the event that has to be rolled back consists of large amount of data, hence the communication time required is significant.

During our tests, the conservative analyser used a default small lookahead value. The performance of the conservative scheme, however, improves as the lookahead increases [12]. Hence, an optimistic scheme might not be able to outperform a conservative one, as its lookahead increases. By extending the tool to allow the specification of lookahead values, further experiments may be performed to investigate the effects of lookahead on performance.

Although the analyser is a promising tool already, further work is required to incorporate support for more subtle protocol variations dealing with more complex state saving mechanisms (e.g. incremental state saving) and event cancellation policies (e.g. lazy cancellation), as well as hybrid protocols. Also, stress testing with large simulation trace files is also necessary to investigate the speed of analysis as well as the robustness of the analyser.

References

[1] R.J. Lipton, and D.W. Mizell, "Time Warp vs. Chandy-Misra: A Worst-Case Comparison", In *Proceedings of the SCS Multiconference on Distributed Simulation*, San Diego, 1990, pp.137-143.

[2] D.R. Jefferson, "*Virtual Time*", *ACM Transactions on Programming Languages and Systems*, Vol. 7, No. 3, July 1985, pp. 404-425.

[3] K.M. Chandy, and J. Misra, "Distributed simulation: A case study in design and verification of distributed programs", IEEE on Transactions on Software Engineering, SE-5, No. 5, 1979, pp. 440--452.

[4] D.M. Nicol, and R.M. Fujimoto, "Parallel Simulation Today", *Annals of Operations Research*, vol. 53, 1994, pp. 249-286.

[5] Y.-B. Lin, "Parallelism Analysers for Parallel Discrete Event Simulation". *ACM Transactions on Modeling and Computer Simulation*, Vol. 2, No. 3, 1992, pp. 239–264.

[6] Y.-C. Wong, S.-Y. Hwang, and J.Y.-B. Lin, "A Parallelism Analyser for Conservative Parallel Simulation", *IEEE Transactions on Parallel and Distributed Systems*, Vol. 6, No. 6, June 1995, pp. 628–638.

[7] C.-C. Lim, Y.H. Low, B.-P. Gan, S. Jain, W. Cai, W.J. Hsu, and S.Y. Huang, "Performance Prediction Tools for Parallel Discrete-Event Simulation", In *Proceedings of 13th Workshop on Parallel and Distributed Simulation*, Atlanta, 1999, pp. 148–155.

[8] Z. Juhasz, S.J. Turner, M. Gerzson, and K. Kuntner, "A Performance Analyser and Prediction Tool for Parallel Discrete Event Simulation", In *Proceedings of 5th UK Simulation Society Conference*, Cambridge, UK, 2001, pp. 8–13.

[9] Z. Juhasz, S.J. Turner, M. Gerzson and K. Kuntner, "A Traced-based Performance Prediction Tool for Parallel Discrete Event Simulation", *International Journal of Simulation Systems, Science & Technology*, Vol. 4, No. 1–2, 2003, pp. 7–22.

[10] R.M. Fujimoto, "Parallel Discrete Event Simulation", *Communications of the ACM*, Vol. 33, No. 10, October 1990, pp. 30–53.

[11] D.M. Nicol and X. Liu, "The Dark Side of Risk (What your Mother never told you about Time Warp)", *In Proceedings of 11th Workshop on Parallel and Distributed Simulation*, Lockenhaus, 1997, pp. 188–195.

[12] R.M. Fujimoto, "Lookahead in Parallel Discrete Event Simulation". In *Proceedings of the International Conference on Parallel Processing*, 1988, pp.34–41.

μsik – A Micro-Kernel for Parallel/Distributed Simulation Systems

Kalyan S. Perumalla
www.cc.gatech.edu/fac/kalyan
College of Computing, Georgia Institute of Technology
Atlanta, Georgia, USA

Abstract

*A novel micro-kernel approach to building parallel/distributed simulation systems is presented. Using this approach, a unified system architecture is developed for incorporating multiple types of simulation processes. The processes hold potential to employ a variety of synchronization mechanisms, and could even alter their choice of mechanism dynamically. Supported mechanisms include traditional lookahead-based conservative and state saving-based optimistic execution approaches. Also supported are newer mechanisms such as reverse computation-based optimistic execution and aggregation-based event processing, all within a single parsimonious application programming interface. The internal implementation and a preliminary performance evaluation of this interface are presented in **μsik**, which is an efficient parallel/distributed realization of the micro-kernel architecture in C^{++}.*

1. Introduction

High-performance parallel and distributed discrete event simulation (PDES) systems have traditionally been built from the ground up, one for each major variant of various PDES techniques. However, it is desirable to have the freedom to add new techniques without having to develop entirely new systems from scratch for each variant. To this end, we are interested in isolating the core invariant portion of PDES techniques, and in providing a generalized framework for building traditional as well as newer techniques on top of the core. The core constitutes the micro-kernel, and the traditional implementations (conservative or optimistic) form the system services on top of the micro-kernel. This permits the incorporation of newer techniques on top of the core, as well as optimization of existing system services, without the need for system-wide changes.

The PDES micro-kernel approach is based on analogy with operating systems[1]. In operating systems that are based on micro-kernel architecture, a very basic set of services is provided by the operating system core (e.g., process identifiers and address spaces). Using such primitive services, the rest of the system services are in fact built outside the core (e.g., file systems and networking). We borrow this approach in our system. A micro-kernel operating system provides an easy and safe way of adding new system/kernel services, such as new network protocols and file systems. Similarly, a PDES micro-kernel provides an easy way to add new types of simulation processes without the need for an overhaul of the entire PDES system implementation.

Our micro-kernel approach is experimental in nature to test the feasibility of developing such a system that can accommodate multiple synchronization techniques and endure additions over time, while at the same time maintaining high-performance execution without undue performance penalty.

The rest of the document is organized as follows. Section 2 presents the motivation and background for the design and development of the micro-kernel approach. The micro-kernel concepts for PDES are introduced in Section 3. Implementation details of the micro-kernel interface are described in Section 4. A preliminary performance study of our microkernel implementation on a distributed platform is presented in Section 5. Finally, current status and future work are presented in Section 6.

2. Motivation and Background

In some of our current projects in collaboration with modeling experts in physical sciences, we are pursuing development of physics simulation models (e.g., of Earth's magnetosphere). These physics simulations are complex, and employ fine-grained events. It is unknown as to which synchronization method works best for these models, hence a specific synchronization scheme cannot be chosen *a priori*. More ideally, the models can benefit from a single engine that not only semi-transparently supports multiple synchronization approaches, but also entails execution with sufficiently low overheads. A generalization of the goals is for the simulation system to allow simulation processes the freedom to adopt any event processing scheme, or freely switch between schemes at runtime. Additionally, since our focus is on very large-scale simulations, especially of physics models in our current projects, we need scalable parallel/distributed execution capabilities.

2.1. Traditional vs. New Systems Approach

The method of prevalence in building PDES systems is to build the system specifically for one synchronization method (e.g., one conservative algorithm, or one optimistic variant). This tradition has two fallouts. First, additions to the underlying framework involve major overhauls. Secondly, modelers need to either determine

1087-4097/05 $20.00 © 2005 IEEE

and stick to one mechanism, or re-code their models to switch to a new mechanism. Such a limitation is deplorable: the PDES research community has developed a host of techniques for high-performance execution; yet, an elegant *systems* framework is lacking for incorporating the multitude of techniques in an incremental, modular fashion.

Our thesis is that a large number of PDES techniques can be *transparently* supported in a single unified framework, with a small set of fundamental primitives. Based on this premise, we develop a unified application program interface (API) that encompasses most, if not all, synchronization approaches. Using this interface, simulation models can be written in a manner that is resilient to changes and optimizations.

2.2. Related Work

The High Level Architecture (HLA)[2] defined by the US Department of Defense provides services for integrating a wide variety of simulator implementations, including space and/or time parallel (conservative, optimistic) discrete event simulations, and time-stepped continuous simulations. However, the architecture has been designed for interoperation of coarse integration entities, such as distributed programs communicating over the network. As such, it is not well-suited for integration of fine-grained entities, as in the hosting of multiple event-oriented logical processes and/or threads within a single UNIX process. In particular, primitives to facilitate efficient process scheduling are not addressed in the standard; such primitives turn out to be the key to efficient execution of fine-grained autonomous entities.

A more closely related work is by Jha and Bagrodia[3] in which a unified framework is presented to permit optimistic and conservative protocols to interoperate and alternate dynamically. (A variation of Jha and Bagrodia's protocols is later discussed in [4], but in the context of VLSI applications). High-level algorithms are presented in [3] that elegantly state the problem along with their solution approach. However, they do not address system implementation details or performance data. Their treatment provides proof of correctness, but lacks an implementation approach and a study of runtime performance implications. Our work differs in that we are interested in defining the interface in a way that guarantees efficient implementation, and we describe details of a high-performance implementation of such a unified interface. Some of our terms share their definitions with analogous terms in their work, but our interface uses fewer primitives and diverges in semantics for others. For example, our interface does not require the equivalent of their Earliest Output Time (EOT). Also, in contrast to their need for lookahead, we do not require that the application always specify a non-zero lookahead. Their related PARSEC system supported an API for processes to dynamically switch between optimistic and conservative modes, but we differ in our systems approach in implementing similar functionality. Another related work is by Rajaei, Ayani and Thorelli [5] on a hierarchical system to combine Time Warp with conservative execution; this work overlaps in goals with our work, but differs in approach.

SPEEDES[6] is a commercial optimistic simulation framework that is capable of distributed execution; however, we were unable to find evidence on its large-scale parallel performance capabilities for fine-grained applications. GTW[7] and ROSS[8] are representative of high-performance implementations of optimistic simulators, but they are restricted to parallel execution on symmetric shared memory multiprocessor (SMP) platforms. The SMP-only constraint sometimes limits the user's choice of hardware as well as scalability. An exception is the WARPED simulator[9], a shared-memory time warp system extended to execute on distributed memory platforms, but it has only been evaluated on relatively small hardware configurations. We are interested in scalable execution on large-scale computing platforms, such as large clusters (hundreds) of quad-processor SMP machines typically available in supercomputing installations for academic research. The cluster-of-SMPs platform is appealing since it is relatively less expensive as compared to a comparable SMP system for large number of processors.

We note that, while the possibility of switching between types of protocol is not entirely new, our parsimonious API and our high-performance implementation approach are novel.

3. PDES Micro-Kernel Concepts

In this section, we introduce some terminology and concepts, and provide high-level descriptions of important micro-kernel operations. It is assumed that PDES models are written in terms of simulation processes that exchange events. Multiple simulation processes (also called logical processes) hosted on each processor. Operationally, one operating system process (e.g., a UNIX process) hosts several simulation processes.

In the PDES micro-kernel system view, simulation processes are fully autonomous entities. They are free to determine for themselves when and in what internal order they would process their received events. The micro-kernel does not process events in and by itself – it only acts as a router of events. In particular, it does not generate, consume or buffer any events. It does not examine event contents, except for the event's header (source, destination and timestamp). The micro-kernel does not distinguish between regular events, retraction events, anti-events or multicast events. It also does not perform event buffer management (memory reuse, fossil collection, etc.), in contrast to traditional parallel/distributed simulation engines. The distinctions among event types and their associated optimizations are deferred to protocol-specific functionality of services outside the kernel proper. The responsibility of a micro-kernel is restricted to only providing services to the simulation processes such that the processes can efficiently communicate events with each other, and collectively accomplish "asymptotic" time-ordered processing of events.

3.1. Core Services

The micro-kernel core consists of *naming*, *routing* and *scheduling* services, as follows:

- **Naming**: The micro-kernel provides a uniform way for simulation processes to locate and refer to each other, within and across processors in a parallel/distributed execution setting. A list of valid identifiers is maintained to map identifiers to processes and vice versa.
- **Routing**: The routing services ensure that events are transparently forwarded to the receiver process, regardless of whether the sender and receiver are co-located or distributed across processors. This is coupled with a guarantee that no event timestamp is overlooked in global timestamp-ordered processing.
- **Scheduling**: The micro-kernel takes care of allocating CPU cycles among multiple simulation processes in a manner that best promotes simulation progress, and ensures absence of livelock or deadlock.

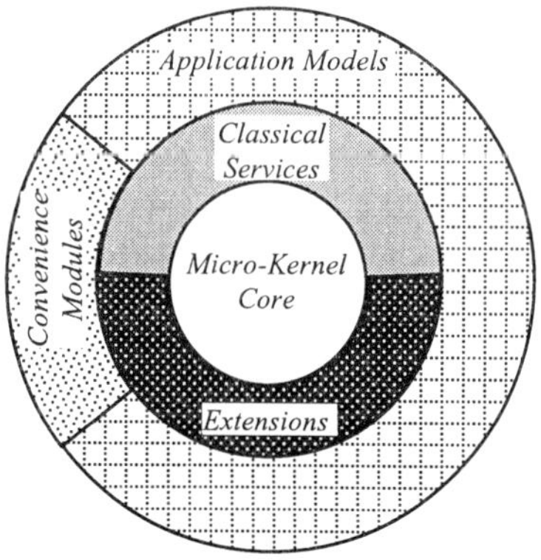

Figure 1: Elements of the micro-kernel architecture, and their inter-relationships.

A wide variety of PDES mechanisms can be built around this parsimonious set of core services, as outlined in Figure 1. Classical services include support for conservative and optimistic processing – event processing/commitment, rollback support and lookahead specification services. They also include kernel process support for remote communication, retractions and multicast (group) communication. Extensions are placeholders for newer techniques in the future, such as "aggregate event processing", "constrained out-of-order execution" and the like (to appear in later publications). Convenience services include routines such as initialization, timers, and reversible random number generation.

3.2. Event Lifecycle and Categories

Events can be considered to go through different stages in their life cycle. First an event is allocated and scheduled by a sender simulation process. Next, the receiver simulation process performs initial processing of the event. This stage includes executing application (model) code associated with that event type. Eventually, in a following stage, final actions associated with the event are committed. Finally, the memory used by the event is released and recycled.

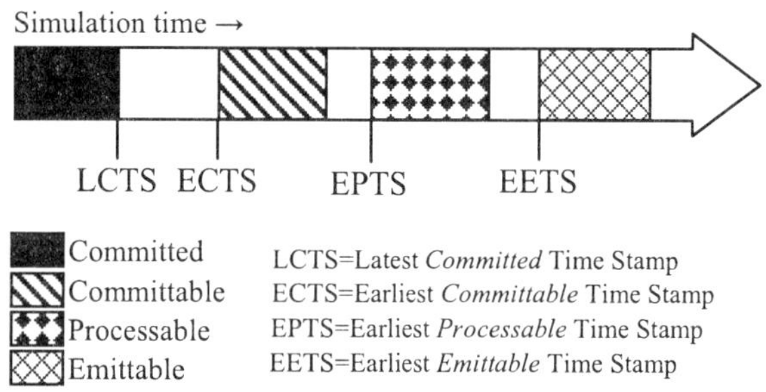

Figure 2: Illustration of the simulation timeline and important event categories in each simulation process. The relation LCTS≤ECTS≤EETS always holds.

Based on the disposition of event lifecycle stages, at any given snapshot moment during simulation, all events belonging to a simulation process can be categorized into four distinct classes – committed, committable, processable and emittable. The first set of events (committed set) is those that have been processed, committed and whose memory has been released for reuse. The second set (committable set) consists of those that have been processed but are waiting to be committed. The third set (processable set) consists of events received by this simulation process that are waiting to be processed. The final set (emittable set) is a logical set that comprises those events that are potentially schedulable by this simulation process to other simulation processes (excluding itself) during the processing of its current set of committable and processable events. Event categories and their mutual ordering are illustrated in Figure 2.

In purely conservative processes, all application code executes during "commit" stages of events. In optimistic processes, revocable portions (slices) of code execute during the "process" stage, while irrevocable portions are done in the "commit" stage.

A Lower Bound on Time Stamp (LBTS) value is defined as a distributed snapshot[10, 11] of the least EETS value among all processes in the simulation. It is essentially a guarantee on the value of the smallest timestamp receivable by any process in future.

When LBTS advances to/beyond the timestamp of a committable event, examples of actions performed when committing the event include, but are not limited to, the following:

- **State vector release**: Release of state vectors, if any, used for state saving during optimistic processing of the event.
- **Input/Output**: Operations such as conservatively printing output to the terminal, or reading from a file.
- **Memory allocation/release**: Finalizing the effect of dynamic memory operations initiated by the application while processing the event.

3.3. Determining Event-Category Times

For classical services, assume that the events in a process are *logically* stored in two data structures: FEL and PEL. The Future Event List (FEL) consists of events in the process' processable event set. Processed Event List (PEL) consists of events in the process' committable event set. For a simulation process i, let FEL_i^{top} be the minimum timestamp in FEL_i (infinity if FEL_i is empty) and PEL_i^{top} be the minimum timestamp in PEL_i (infinity if PEL_i is empty). Note that PEL_i^{top} is always infinity for conservative simulation processes.

The earliest time stamp for each event category is determined as follows:

1.	$ECTS_i$	=	$Min(FEL_i^{top}, PEL_i^{top})$
2.	$EPTS_i$	=	*infinity* if conservative FEL_i^{top} if optimistic
3.	$EETS_i$	=	$Min(FEL_i^{top} + Lookahead_i, PEL_i^{top})$

In the preceding equations, $EETS_i$ is defined rather simplistically, but could accommodate additional complexity if so desired. For example, if lookahead is highly variable across events, $EETS_i$ could be defined on a per-event basis: $EETS_i=min(E_j+LA_j)$ for each event E_j in FEL_i, and LA_j is the lookahead for event E_j. Similar refinements can be made based on limiting it by the set of destination processes of process i. Additional refinements can be made for optimistic processes as well. The main idea is that the event categories provide simple yet powerful abstractions that enable several types of synchronization.

3.4. Process Scheduling

On each processor, the scheduling algorithm proceeds by executing the code in Figure 3 within a loop:

```
1. if( ECTS_min < LBTS )
2.     P_ECTS-min.advance( LBTS )
3. else
4.     P_EPTS-min.advance_opt( EPTS_min2 )
```

Figure 3: Micro-kernel's (simplified) scheduler loop.

$ECTS_{min}$ is the minimum ECTS among all processes on that processor. $Process_{ECTS\text{-}min}$ is the process with the minimum ECTS value. $Process_{EPTS\text{-}min}$ is the process with the minimum EPTS value. $EPTS_{min2}$ is the second least EPTS value among all processes on that processor. The method P.advance(T) conservatively processes all events of process P with timestamps less than or equal to time T. The method P.advance_opt(T) optimistically processes all events of process P with timestamps less than or equal to time T. Either method is a no-op if P is null. The operation of this loop will become clearer in the following two subsections.

The LBTS itself is computed as the minimum EETS among all processes across all processors. Any transient event (in transit across processors) is accounted for by the sender process' queues until the event reaches its receiver process. The LBTS computation can either be performed concurrently with the scheduler, or, periodically inside the scheduler loop just prior to each optimistic processing step (line 4).

3.5. Conservative Processing

During normal processing, the micro-kernel only schedules conservatively executable actions in increasing order of their committable timestamps. Only those processes whose ECTS values are less than or equal to the LBTS value are considered for conservative scheduling. The process with the least ECTS value is scheduled, and it is permitted to advance up to and including the current LBTS value. When that process is finished with its processing, the micro-kernel schedules the process with the next minimum ECTS value, and so on. Note that new events, if any, generated by the scheduled process will necessarily have timestamps greater than or equal to the current LBTS value.

If no process exists whose ECTS value is less than or equal to the current LBTS, then the micro-kernel initiates a new LBTS computation (if one is not already in progress). A new LBTS value typically takes time to be computed, due to communication latency across processors. It is this delay that induces blocking of conservative computation. This blocking period can be utilized as an opportunity to perform optimistic event processing. Hence, while a new LBTS value is being computed, the micro-kernel schedules those processes that are capable and willing to perform optimistic event processing, as described next.

3.6. *Optimistic Processing*

In optimistic mode, the micro-kernel schedules the process that has the least EPTS value. Recall that the EPTS value for conservative processes is infinity, and for optimistic processes it is equal to the minimum timestamp among unprocessed events (or, infinity if FEL is empty). Thus, if there are any optimistic processes, their EPTS values can make them schedulable for optimistic processing.

When at least one optimistic process exists for scheduling, optimistic execution is scheduled as follows: two processes with the minimum and the next minimum EPTS values (say, $EPTS_{m1}$ and $EPTS_{m2}$) are selected. If only one optimistic process exists, $EPTS_{m2}$ is set to infinity (in this case, this limit needs to be customized, if necessary, to throttle unbounded optimism). Then, the process with $EPTS_{m1}$ is allowed to optimistically process its events with timestamps less than or equal to $EPTS_{m2}$.

Initiating optimistic execution only when all conservative processing is blocked ensures that time spent in correct execution is maximized, and the potential for incorrect execution (in optimistic mode) is minimized.

4. Micro-Kernel Implementation

We now describe our implementation of the micro-kernel approach in a new software system named μsik (**micro si**mulation **k**ernel, pronounced "mew-seek"). μsik is written in C^{++}, linkable to an application as a library, and provides class hierarchies rooted at base classes corresponding to micro-kernel concepts.

A naïve implementation of the micro-kernel approach could entail significant overheads, as compared to the traditional monolithic simulator implementations. In a monolithic simulator, it is possible to optimize the implementation by employing centralized data structures such as event buffers, event lists and state vectors. On the other hand, in a micro-kernel, the key data structures are, by design, encapsulated inside simulation processes. The challenge is to find efficient ways of implementing the micro-kernel framework so as to minimize or eliminate overheads.

A key issue is the problem of always accurately tracking the ordering among processes with respect to their ECTS, EPTS and EETS values. For example, when a new event is sent from one simulation process to another, the receiver's ECTS, EPTS and EETS values can change. Similarly, a simulation process will have its values changed at the end of processing an event. Event retractions need to be dealt with appropriately, as they too alter timestamp ordering.

It is clear that the right choice of data structures determines the efficiency of micro-kernel operation. As its main components, the micro-kernel maintains a list of local user processes, a hash table for mapping process identifiers to processes, and a list of "kernel processes". For scheduler operations, three important priority queues are maintained. Each of these components is described next.

4.1. *Naming Services*

To provide naming services, the micro-kernel maintains a mapping of process identifiers to process instances. Process identifiers are specified as a pair of integers: (processor number, local process number). Simulation processes can be "kernel processes" or user processes. Kernel processes are used for internal implementation of services on top of the micro-kernel (see Section 4.3). User processes are part of application model.

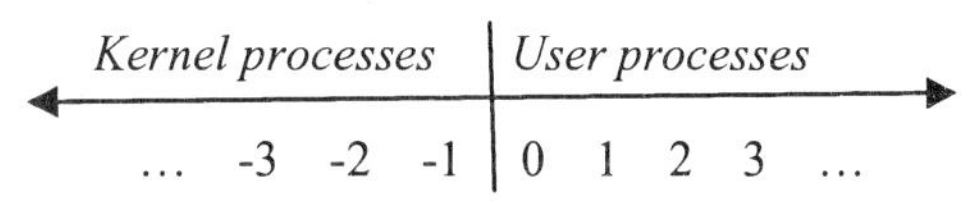

Figure 4: Every simulation process is assigned a locally unique identifier as soon as it is added to the simulation. User processes are assigned positive identifiers starting with 0, while kernel processes are assigned negative identifiers.

User processes are assigned local identifiers as positive integers, starting at 0, while kernel processes are assigned negative integers, as shown in Figure 4. The rationale behind this scheme is that it allows applications to rely on their processes being identified from 0 to n-1 (this is a common way in which models are written). Using negative identifiers for kernel processes makes them transparent to the application, and will not interfere with the traditional modeling methods. Special identifiers are also defined for specifying an invalid identifier, and to specify multicast destinations.

4.2. *Scheduling Services*

The scheduler is implemented as a loop inside a micro-kernel method.

Process Ordering

Three in-place *min-heaps* are used, one each for tracking the ECTS, EPTS and EETS values of simulation processes. Each heap maintains the minimum time-stamped process at the top. For example, the process with the least ECTS value is always available as the top of ECTS heap. The heaps are designed to rapidly update and readjust the elements when the key of an element is increased or decreased. This rapid update is essential to quickly keep the heaps consistent before and after every scheduling action by the scheduler (see also Section 4.4).

Readjusting Timestamp Orders within Scheduler

When events are sent or received by simulation processes, the processes' relative ordering can change with respect to their ECTS, EPTS, and EETS values. The heaps of the micro-kernel scheduler need to be readjusted to restore correct timestamp order. This readjustment is accomplished via a pair of before_dirtied() and after_dirtied() methods within the base simulation process. These methods keep track of whether any changes occurred to the key timestamps. If (and only if) any of the ECTS, EPTS or EETS values of an affected process changes, the corresponding scheduler heap is readjusted. The affected process that needs to be updated could be the active (sending) process that is currently scheduled, or, it could also be the set of processes to which the currently scheduled process generates new events.

Distributed Time Synchronization

To compute LBTS values, we employ the distributed snapshot algorithm described in [12]. We use the publicly available implementation [13] of this algorithm. Its current implementation includes two different modules: one is based on efficient global hierarchical reductions[12, 14], while the other is based on an optimized variant[15] of the Chandy-Misra-Bryant null message algorithm[16]. These are reported to have been tested by their authors on large-scale platforms, and demonstrated to scale very well, even up to supercomputing configurations of more than 1500 processors[14, 15, 17].

4.3. *Routing Services*

Local event exchange is trivially handled by enqueueing the event in the local destination process. Remote communication is implemented via a special delegation mechanism using kernel processes (see next). The micro-kernel itself never stores or buffers any events at any time. Every event routed through the micro-kernel is immediately delegated either to the destination process (if it is a local user process), or delegated to a local kernel process (if the destination is a remote process or a multicast group). We omit discussion of multicast communication due to space limitations.

Kernel Processes

Kernel processes are used to implement remote federate communication and multicast event exchanges. The reason they are implemented this way is that the functionality can be quite seamlessly implemented using the scheduling services provided by the micro-kernel core. This is fairly analogous to operating system micro-kernels. Services such as networking, file I/O, etc. are implemented as processes outside the micro-kernel core, which themselves utilize many of the services that normal user processes utilize.

A notion of kernel processes for PDES is introduced (for improving rollback efficiency) in ROSS[8]. Our concept of kernel processes and its usage is quite different and unrelated, serving a different notion and purpose.

Remote Event Communication

On each processor, one kernel process is instantiated for every other (remote) processor. These kernel processes for remote communication act as local representative proxies for the corresponding remote processors. This scheme operates as follows.

Let us denote by KP^i_m the m'th kernel process on processor i. When a user process on processor i attempts to send an event to a user process on a remote processor m, the micro-kernel on processor i delegates that event to its local kernel process KP^i_m. KP^i_m is then responsible for forwarding the event to KP^m_i, which is its peer kernel process on processor m. When KP^m_i receives that event, it forwards to the destination user process (guaranteed to be local) via the micro-kernel.

This scheme, despite its simplicity, affords elegant implementation of a wide range of features and optimizations studied in PDES literature. Sophisticated variants can be incorporated with few changes to the rest of the system. Here we briefly discuss a few possibilities:

Optimistic Sends: In this most common method, an event scheduled to a remote process is immediately sent over the wire to its corresponding remote processor. A downside with this scheme is that the network communication cost becomes a wasted overhead if the event is later retracted. The event retraction could be initiated either by the user (in conservative or optimistic processing) to take back a previously scheduled event, or by the kernel for event cancellation (anti-messages for secondary rollbacks in optimistic processing).

Lazy Sends: Instead of forwarding the event immediately over the wire to the remote processor, the event could be withheld within the kernel process for dt simulation time units, where $0<dt\leq(T_{event}-T_{now})$. Delaying the event longer will postpone the network communication cost, which is beneficial in case the event is retracted later. On the flip side, it might increase the event communication latency, and stall the receiving processor waiting to receive the event for its own progress. Adaptive schemes could be devised and implemented in the kernel process to exploit this "lazy send" optimization.

Non-aggressive Sends: The kernel process can also be used to easily implement non-aggressive sends – i.e., to send remote messages if and only if they cannot be retracted in the future. This is a well-known PDES variant in optimistic simulation to separate risk and aggressiveness [18], in which events are processed optimistically *locally*, but only "correct" events are propagated *across* processors. The kernel process adds the event in its FEL, and "processes" the events in a conservative fashion. The event is actually sent over the wire to the remote processor only when it is committed. Since events are committed only when they are guaranteed to be not retracted, non-aggressiveness is assured.

Message Bundling: To amortize the cost of network communication, it is possible to bundle multiple events into one message. The cost savings can be good especially when events are small in size, as compared to network message headers (e.g., TCP header size). Again, such bundling techniques can be incorporated into the kernel process responsible for remote communication.

All KP^i_m are responsible for maintaining a mapping from event identifiers to event buffers. Such a mapping is necessary in order to implement event retractions (during conservative and/or optimistic execution) and anti-events (to realize secondary rollback/cancellation in optimistic execution). The kernel process is also responsible for periodically flushing the hash table when events are committed and can no longer be retracted or canceled.

The beauty of this kernel process scheme lies in the fact that the kernel processes themselves are time-synchronized automatically (since they are simulation processes themselves). This fact can be exploited to easily and modularly implement the aforementioned variants.

4.4. *Optimized Queues and Lists*

The micro-kernel uses priority queue and list data structures in its implementation. The efficiency of these data structures is critical for keeping runtime overheads low. We define our own heap and list data types, to avoid overheads of dynamic memory allocation of conventional libraries. Our definitions are different from other standard library templates in that our definitions permit the same object to be linked into multiple instances of the same container type, without the need to allocate container headers to hold the elements. Standard template libraries are difficult to use or inefficient when the same element needs to belong to multiple instances of the same type of container *simultaneously*.

For example, in our micro-kernel, we need to link each simulation process into three different priority queues, all at the same time. This is to order the processes along their three basic timestamps: ECTS, EPTS and EETS. The key used for ordering in each queue is different, yet, the container data type is exactly the same (a min-heap priority queue).

5. Performance Study

We now turn to a study of runtime performance.

Platform: Our implementation currently runs on a network of shared-memory multiprocessors, and is portable across homogeneous configurations of Windows, Mac and Unix/Linux platforms. All performance data reported here are collected on a cluster of 8-way Intel SMP systems, each system with 8 Intel Xeon 550MHz processors and 4GB memory.

Applications: μsik is currently being used in multiple projects, exercising its conservative and optimistic execution modes, as well as experimenting with a few newer mechanisms. It has successfully been used as the engine for a conservative parallel execution (on up to 128 processors) of discrete event models of 1-dimensional particle-in-cell physics[19]. Another application of μsik is in parallel simulation of the nervous system, presented in [20]. Yet another application of μsik is in optimistic parallel execution of a plasma simulation model of spacecraft charging in outer space. Reverse computation is used for rollback in this application, and a performance study is reported in [21]. Here, we focus on performance study using a synthetic benchmark, namely, the classical PDES benchmark known as Phold[22].

In our Phold implementation, *NLP* simulation processes are evenly mapped to all available processors. A fixed population of events, *NLP*R*, is generated at initialization, with random destinations. *R*, an integer, is the ratio of number of events to number of processes. When a process receives an event, it schedules a new event into the future to another random destination (possibly to itself) with a minimum time increment called lookahead. With probability *L*, the destination is on the same processor as the source. We use a uniform random number generator (URNG) to randomly determine event destinations, and another URNG stream to determine time increment. Since Phold is fine-grained, with very little computation performed per event, it represents a worst-case scenario that can expose runtime overheads of the simulation engine.

In the following, we evaluate μsik for its sequential execution performance, its parallel time-synchronization costs, its optimistic execution performance and mixed conservative-optimistic performance.

5.1. *Sequential Performance*

Figure 5 shows the average time taken to process an event in Phold, for increasing number of simulation processes and events. The time per event includes send/receive costs, process scheduling costs, as well as random number generation costs.

Context Switching Cost: The process scheduling costs are accentuated when the event population is low. For example, when R=1, each simulation process has a single event to process on average, and holds a high probability that its next send is not to self. This forces a "context switch" from one process to another for each and every event. In a context switch, the micro-kernel is required to update the time queues for the scheduled process as well as the destination process for the newly scheduled event. When R=10, each process has ten events to process on average, which implies processing an average of ten events between two context switches.

It is seen that our micro-kernel implementation scales excellently with the number of simulation processes, without drastic overheads for the maintenance of ECTS, EPTS and EETS values. In the largest sequential configuration on one processor, we are able to simulate an event population of 10 million events and 100,000 simulation processes, with less than 10 microseconds per event.

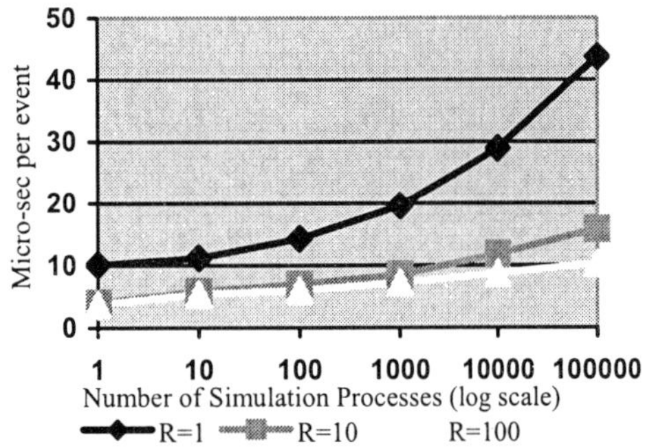

Figure 5: Performance of µsik on Phold, demonstrating scalability up to 10 million events and hundred thousand simulation processes on one processor.

5.2. Parallel Time-Synchronization Cost

Figure 6 shows the average processing time per event while the number of processors is varied. This experiment is intended to measure the cost of synchronizing simulation time across processors in isolation from remote event exchange costs. This is achieved (L=100%) by choosing random destinations only from among local processes (i.e., no event goes across processors). The entire distributed execution, however, is still time synchronized – LBTS computations are performed, and time advances of simulation processes are permitted only upon LBTS advances. For comparison, performance with a slight amount of inter-processor event communication is also plotted (L=99%).

While Figure 6 shows performance for relatively large simulation configurations (million LPs and events), Figure 7 is intended to show that significantly lower runtime costs can be observed when the number of context switches is low. This is done by using one million event population as in Figure 6, but using only 1000 LPs, resulting in a event/process ratio of R=1000, which in turn results in 1000-fold reduction in the average number of context switches.

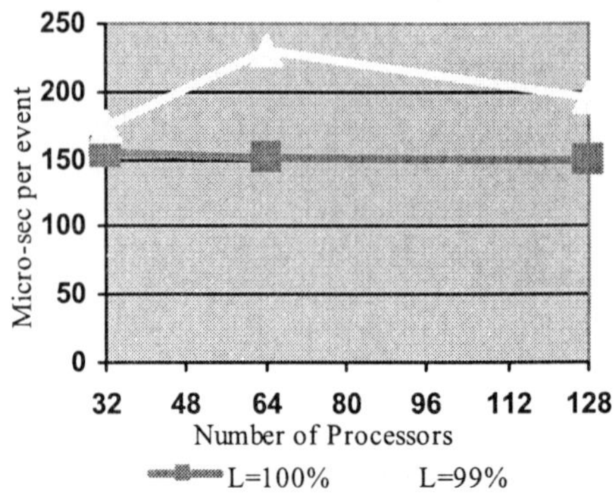

Figure 6: Conservative parallel performance of µsik on Phold with 1 million LPs and 1 million event population.

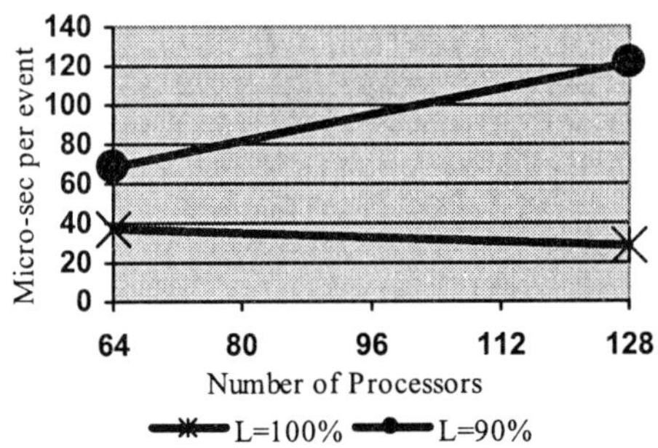

Figure 7: Conservative parallel performance of µsik on Phold with 1000 LPs and 1 million event population.

5.3. Optimistic Simulation Performance

In the optimistic configuration, each of the Phold processes executes its events optimistically ahead in time. Rest of the application is unmodified. In fact, the only source-code change between the conservative and optimistic executions is setting an optimistic execution flag in the simulation process.

Figure 8 shows the performance of optimistic parallel execution on a 1-million LPs & 1-million event configuration of Phold. This execution is intended to demonstrate the capability as a working proof-of-concept of our prototype. Further work is needed to reduce overheads in larger parallel executions, especially by incorporating flow-control mechanisms that can adaptively throttle over-optimistic execution. In particular, we are incorporating non-blocking TCP communication to send events across processors, to overcome potential deadlocks due to blocking sends.

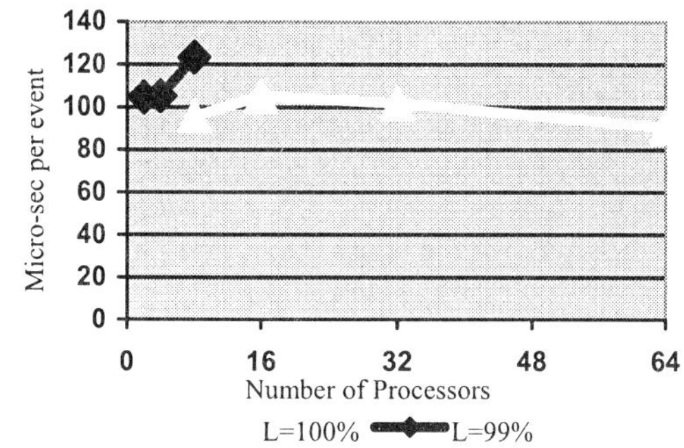

Figure 8: Optimistic parallel performance of μsik on Phold with 1 million LPs and 1 million event population.

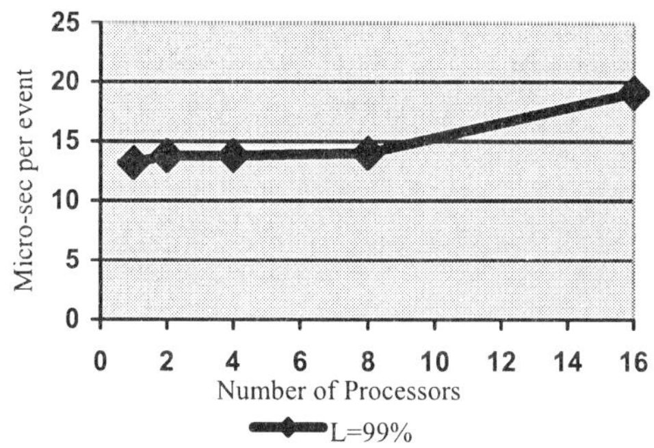

Figure 9: Optimistic parallel performance of μsik on Phold with 1000 LPs and 100,000 event population.

On smaller number of processors, the application is relatively well balanced, and optimistic mode delivers excellent performance. Figure 9 shows costs under 15 microseconds per event when operating entirely with shared memory communication (up to 8 processors), and under 20 microseconds per event even involving TCP communication across the 8-CPU SMPs nodes. It is worth noting that these experiments were executed on 550MHz CPUs, and can be expected to be significantly better on more recent platforms (e.g., 3GHz CPUs).

5.4. *Mixed Simulation Performance*

A simple change of the configuration yields an example in which every alternate process in Phold is conservative, and every other process is optimistic. This configuration is once again intended to serve as proof-of-concept demonstration of the micro-kernel approach that can accommodate both types of processes. Figure 10 shows the performance of such a mixed configuration executing in parallel on up to 128 processors.

5.5. *Memory Usage*

Figure 11 demonstrates that memory is recycled efficiently on large configurations. With active time-synchronized committing of events, events are committed (and hence freed) as early & aggressively as possible, in a scalable fashion.

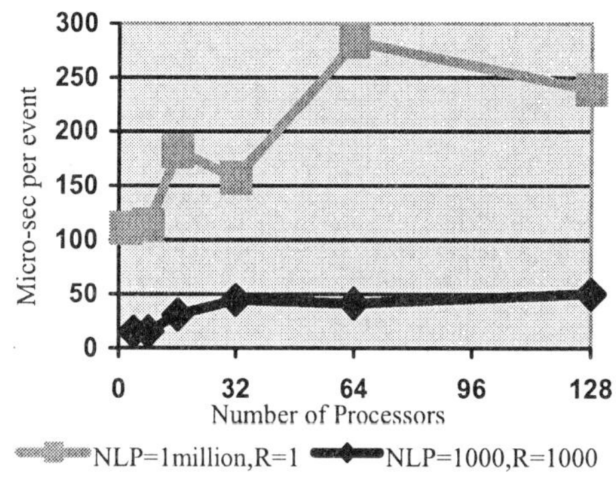

Figure 10: Parallel performance of μsik on Phold, with mixture of optimistic and conservative processes, one million event population, and localized communication.

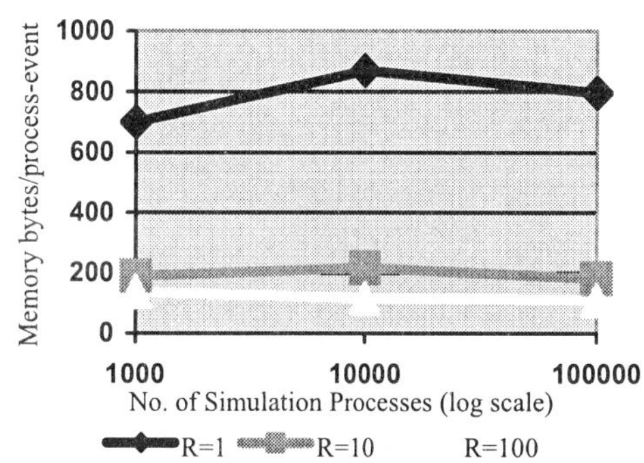

Figure 11: Memory usage of μsik in sequential execution of Phold.

Memory usage in bytes on the *y*-axis is computed as: $(M_{RP}-M_1)/(R*P+P)$. Here, M_{RP} is the memory usage for a Phold execution of P simulation processes and $R*P$ event population. M_1 is the memory usage of 1 process and 1 event (fixed cost of the simulator). When R=1, processes and events are equally weighted in the average. When R=100, event memory usage dominates, showing that each event on the average consumes 110 bytes. This includes optimistic processing overheads, such as causal list pointers. The data shows that μsik's usage of memory per event is bounded in proportion to the actual number of events, and scales with the both number of events as well as the number of simulation processes.

6. Status and Future Work

μsik is a general-purpose parallel/distributed

simulation kernel built upon a micro-kernel architecture consisting of autonomous simulation processes. Simulation processes hold and manage their own events, and can be optimistic or conservative in their event processing, or adopt other techniques such as aggregate event processing. The micro-kernel overhead is kept very low by design. µsik also uses the concept of kernel processes, which serve to push kernel-functionality to outside the micro-kernel.

The current implementation is portable across UNIX/Linux and Windows platforms. The micro-kernel source-code is compact (~4000 lines of C^{++} code). The µsik release includes the micro-kernel source code, example applications, and a user's manual. The most recent version can be obtained from www.cc.gatech.edu/fac/kalyan/musik.htm.

µsik currently supports: lookahead-based conservative execution; rollback-based optimistic execution with both state-saving and reverse computation; resilient computation (zero rollbacks) and any combination of them; per-process limits to optimism; user-level retractions; dynamic process addition/deletion; automated network-throttled flow control; shared-memory/distributed execution; and (conservative) process-oriented views based on POSIX threads). It is being successfully used in non-trivial applications with both conservative as well as optimistic modes.

Analogous to micro-kernel based operating systems, observed performance depends on process context switches. We are profiling the run-time performance to identify the most time-critical paths in execution, and envision further reduction in runtime overheads for process scheduling, and distributed synchronization on larger number of processors. We are also porting our system to supercomputing platforms for scalability to hundreds of processors. Further exercising generality and extensibility, we are exploring accommodation of Critical Channel Traversal[23] algorithms, Lookback[24], and Approximate Time[25] notions over the micro-kernel.

Acknowledgements

This work was supported in part by the National Science Foundation grant ATM-0326431.

References

[1] J. Liedtke, "On Micro-Kernel Construction," ACM Symposium on Operating Systems Principles, 1995.
[2] "IEEE Std. 1516: High Level Architecture," in *Institute of Electrical and Electronic Engineers*, 2000.
[3] V. Jha and R. Bagrodia, "A unified framework for conservative and optimistic distributed simulation," PADS, 1994.
[4] D. Lungeanu and C.-J. R. Shi, "Distributed simulation of VLSI systems via lookahead-free self-adaptive optimistic and conservative synchronization," IEEE/ACM International Conference on Computer-Aided Design, 1999.
[5] H. Rajaei, R. Ayani, et al., "The Local Time Warp Approach to Parallel Simulation," PADS, 1993.
[6] Metron, "SPEEDES: Synchronous Parallel Environment for Emulation and Discrete-Event Simulation," 2004, www.speedes.com.
[7] S. R. Das, R. M. Fujimoto, et al., "GTW: A Time-Warp System for Shared Memory Multiprocessors," WSC, 1994.
[8] C. Carothers, D. Bauer, et al., "ROSS: A High-Performance, Low Memory, Modular Time Warp System," *Journal of Parallel and Distributed Computing*, vol. 62, 2002.
[9] G. D. Sharma, R. Radhakrishnan, et al., "Time Warp Simulation on CLUMPS," PADS, 1999.
[10] K. M. Chandy and L. Lamport, "Distributed Snapshots: Determining Global States of Distributed Systems," *ACM Transaction on Computer Systems*, vol. 3, 1985.
[11] F. Mattern, "Efficient Algorithms for Distributed Snapshots and Global Virtual Time Approximation," *Journal of Parallel and Distributed Computing*, vol. 18, 1993.
[12] K. S. Perumalla and R. M. Fujimoto, "Virtual Time Synchronization over Unreliable Network Transport," PADS, 2001.
[13] K. S. Perumalla, "libSynk Homepage," 2004, www.cc.gatech.edu/computing/pads/kalyan/libsynk.htm.
[14] K. S. Perumalla, A. Park, et al., "Scalable RTI-based Parallel Simulation of Networks," PADS, 2003.
[15] A. Park, R. M. Fujimoto, et al., "Conservative Synchronization of Large-scale Network Simulations," PADS, 2004.
[16] K. M. Chandy and J. Misra, "Asynchronous Distributed Simulation via a Sequence of Parallel Computations," *Communications of the ACM*, vol. 24, 1981.
[17] R. M. Fujimoto, K. S. Perumalla, et al., "Large-Scale Network Simulation -- How Big? How Fast?" MASCOTS, 2003.
[18] P. F. Reynolds, Jr., "A Spectrum of Options for Parallel Simulation," WSC, 1988.
[19] H. Karimabadi, Y. Omelchenko, et al., "A New Approach to Modeling Physical Systems: Discrete Event Simulations of Grid-based Models," Workshop on State-Of-The-Art in Scientific Computing (PARA), 2004.
[20] C. J. Lobb, Z. Chao, et al., "Parallel Event-Driven Neural Network Simulations Using the Hodgkin-Huxley Neuron Model," PADS, 2005.
[21] Y. Tang, K. S. Perumalla, et al., "Optimistic Parallel Discrete Event Simulations of Physical Systems using Reverse Computation," PADS, 2005.
[22] R. M. Fujimoto, "Performance of Time Warp Under Synthetic Workloads," SCS Multiconference on Distributed Simulation, 1990.
[23] Z. Xiao, B. Unger, et al., "Scheduling Critical Channels in Conservative Parallel Discrete Event Simulation," PADS, 1999.
[24] G. Chen and B. Szymanski, K., "Four Types of Lookback," PADS, 2003.
[25] R. M. Fujimoto, "Exploiting Temporal Uncertainty in Parallel and Distributed Simulations," PADS, 1999.

(MMSM) Worm Simulation Techniques

Distributed Worm Simulation with a Realistic Internet Model

Songjie Wei, Jelena Mirkovic, Martin Swany

Computer & Information Sciences
University of Delaware
Newark, DE 19716
(weis, sunshine, swany@cis.udel.edu)

Abstract

Internet worm spread is a phenomenon involving millions of hosts, who interact in complex and diverse environment. Scanning speed of each infected host depends on its resources and the defenses at work in its network. Aggressive worms further interact with the underlying Internet topology – the dynamics of the spread is constrained by the limited bandwidth of network links, and high-volume scan traffic leads to BGP router failure thus affecting global routing. Worm traffic also interacts with legitimate background traffic competing for (and often winning) the limited bandwidth resources. To faithfully simulate worm spread and other Internet-wide events such as DDoS, flash crowds and spam we need a detailed Internet model, a packet-level simulation of relevant event features, and a realistic model of background traffic on the whole Internet. The memory and CPU requirements of such simulation exceed a single machine's resources, creating a need for distributed simulation. We propose a design and present implementation of a distributed worm simulator, called PAWS. PAWS runs on Emulab testbed, which facilitates its use by other researchers. We validate PAWS in a variety of scenarios, and evaluate costs and benefits of distributed worm simulation.

1. Introduction

First step in designing early detection and response techniques for Internet worms must be the understanding of this threat. We need high-fidelity simulators that faithfully replicate each worm copy's behavior and reproduce all the elements interacting with the spreading worm. A simulator's fidelity has to be three-fold:

(1) *Internet-level fidelity.* Worm spread dynamics depend on the underlying Internet fabric such as Autonomous System (AS) and router topology, link bandwidth and routing table information. Worms also affect global Internet by causing router failure under heavy scan traffic and thus introducing routing changes.

(2) *Packet-level fidelity.* Worm spread is affected by the host diversity (infected hosts will spread the worm with different speed based on their hardware and OS specifics), network diversity (networks will have different ratios of live and vulnerable hosts), scanning techniques and presence of worm defenses. To capture all these effects we must simulate worm spread at the packet level.

(3) *Background-traffic fidelity.* Both the worm traffic and the worm defenses interfere with legitimate background traffic. We need to simulate *realistic* background traffic to gauge the damage of the worm spread, and evaluate the benefit and collateral damage of any proposed defense. Recent work on measuring the available bandwidth of inter-AS links [8] offers starting data for estimating legitimate traffic load on those links, and simulating legitimate traffic at an aggregate level. It is currently unclear if packet-level simulation of background traffic is necessary for accurate worm spread simulation, but it may be needed for detailed evaluation of worm defenses. Some substantial work will be needed to develop background traffic's connection-level models which are representative of Internet traffic patterns, and incorporate them in packet-level worm simulators.

Mathematical models of worm propagation [14, 15, 17] are built upon epidemiological equations that describe spread of real-world diseases. These models offer valuable insight into the infection dynamics and can be simulated efficiently, but they cannot capture effects of different scanning and infection techniques, and the interactions of the worm with the Internet topology, protocols, and security mechanisms. Mathematical models that are easily applicable to random scanning techniques require considerable work and multiple approximations to be extended to sophisticated scanning techniques, such as subnet scanning [18].

Single-node worm spread simulators [10, 11, 12, 13] require a set of simplifications and approximations, to be able to run at a reasonable speed on a single machine. They ignore or simplify the specifics of the Internet topology, congestion created by the worm spread, and the diversity of network fabric. These simplifications are necessary to reduce simulation's memory requirements and accommodate them at a single-machine. Further, packet-level simulation of worm scans requires a large number of CPU cycles, making simulation length prohibitive. Current single-machine worm simulators avoid packet-level simulation of worm scans, instead simulating most or all worm scans at a fluid-level using mathematical models of the worm spread.

Some notable success was achieved with distributed worm simulation [9]. Using PDNS (a distributed version of NS-2 simulator) and GTNetS, Perumalla et al. simulated worm propagation among 1.28 million vulnerable nodes at a dedicated 128-CPU cluster. In another paper on distributed simulation of Internet events [26] the authors note that PDNS and GTNetS can simulate about 95K packet transmissions per wall-clock second (PTS) at a single machine and 5.5M packet transmissions on a

1087-4097/05 $20.00 © 2005 IEEE

dedicated 136-CPU cluster. This is an excellent result, given that both PDNS and GTNetS simulate connection-level behavior such as TCP 3-way handshake and congestion control mechanism, and thus must keep and update connection state for each packet transmission.

We note two main problems with the approach used in [9] for worm spread simulation:

(1) To achieve reasonable simulation speed (5.5M PTS) one needs a powerful 100+ node cluster. Not every researcher has access to such a cluster, yet many researchers work in the worm detection and response field and need a high-fidelity worm simulator that can run in reasonable time on multiple common PCs to validate their ideas.
(2) Packet-level simulation in [9] generates a network message for each packet sent to a different simulation node which incurs huge overhead when simulating worm scans. Instead, these transmissions can be aggregated and sent in a single network message at the end of a simulated time unit.

We further note that work in [9] does not replicate a realistic Internet topology or background traffic and thus cannot faithfully evaluate congestion effects caused by the spreading worm.

In this paper we present a design and implementation of a distributed worm simulator called PAWS. Our simulator runs on multiple common PCs that synchronize over a TCP/IP network. We replicate a realistic Internet topology at the Autonomous System level, and the background traffic at the aggregate, inter-AS link level. Link bandwidth and background traffic values are inferred using Pathneck [8] measurements of Internet bottlenecks as a starting point for estimation. PAWS is implemented in the Emulab testbed [1] which facilitates its use by other researchers, and is extensible to support different scanning techniques and host and network diversity.

PAWS is a dedicated worm spread simulator - it simplifies certain worm spread behavior to achieve higher simulation speed. Worm scans are simulated as single packet transmissions, without connection-level semantics. While this is a correct model for UDP worms, TCP worms need several packet transmissions for successful infection and will perform TCP SYN retransmissions in case of dropped scans. We believe that TCP connection establishment and payload transmission only influence the speed of worm scan generation in case of successful and unsuccessful infection. These features can be modeled by setting two per-host parameters and avoiding TCP stack simulation for each scan. TCP SYN retransmissions will increase a number of scans in the Internet but should not increase congestion effects due to very small size of TCP SYN packets (20 Bytes). PAWS currently does not replicate TCP SYN retransmission behavior but will be extended to do so as a part of our future work. PAWS further deploys time-discrete packet-level simulation – worm scans that need to be transmitted from one simulation node to another over the network, during one time unit, are grouped together and sent in a single network message. This minimizes network traffic and overhead of network communication, while having a very small effect on fidelity. PAWS replicates AS level Internet topology using Routeviews data [3] and simulates background traffic at an aggregate, inter-AS link level. Routing path of each worm scan through ASes is replicated and bandwidth consumption on inter-AS links is simulated to capture congestion effects.

PAWS can currently simulate propagation of a random scanning worm in a 10M vulnerable population using 8 Emulab machines and achieving 4.7M packet transmissions per wall-clock second. Note that PAWS simulates 8 times more vulnerable nodes than work presented in [9], with comparable performance, using 8 common PCs. PAWS simulation of Code Red v2-like worm propagating with a 10M vulnerable population is shown in Figure 1.

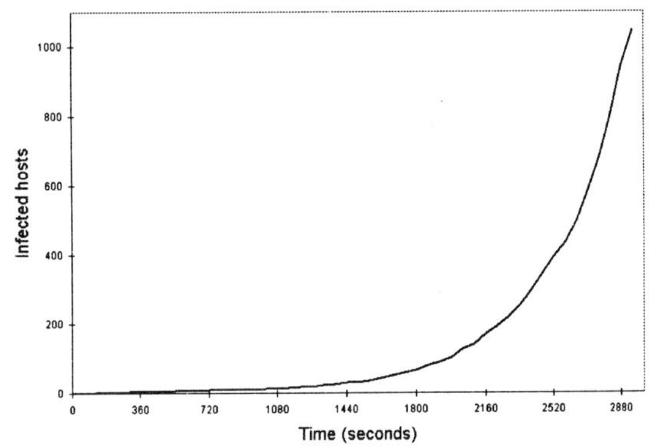

Figure 1: Code Red v2 worm propagating in 10M vulnerable population

2. Related Work

The closest work to PAWS is described in [9], and the differences between PAWS and [9] are given in the introduction. We here briefly survey other work on worm simulation and modeling.

Worm models: Staniford et al. [14] use SIR epidemiological model of worm spread to evaluate effectiveness of various worm scanning techniques. Zou et al. [15] present a "two-factor" model that extends SIR epidemiological model to capture the effects of human countermeasures and the congestion due to the worm spread. Shen et al. [16] provide a discrete-time worm model that considers patching and cleaning effect and can model worms with local scanning techniques. All these approaches abstract specifics of the Internet topology, change in the size of vulnerable population as the worm spreads, and the effect of the individual host and network defenses (except for patching, in case of [16]) on the spread.

Single-machine simulation with AS-level topology: Savage et al. [13] model Internet topology at the AS level, along with epidemiological worm spread model, to measure the effectiveness of different containment strategies and deployment patterns. Wagner et al. [12] model delay and bandwidth differences between vulnerable hosts by dividing all Internet hosts into four groups, then modeling interactions between and within groups. This approach achieves better Internet-level fidelity than prior simulators but the division of hosts into four same-bandwidth same-latency groups heavily approximates the underlying Internet topology. The simulation cannot model individual host or network actions, congestion at routers and the scan traffic received by a given host or a network. Liljenstam et al. [10, 11] describe an add-on worm propagation model for SSFNet simulator. This model adds simulation of countermeasures at router level to the simple epidemiological model, and simulates those actions assuming a single router per AS. A realistic AS topology from Route Views project [3] is used in a scaled-down form, due to single-machine memory constraints. Worm scans are simulated using hybrid packet/fluid level simulation. Riley et al. [25] developed a packet-level worm simulator GTNetS that captures connection-level semantics of TCP worm propagation, and can simulate worms with different payload size, infection delay, scanning rate, number of parallel scanning threads, etc. GTNetS captures congestion effects due to worm spread but uses a simple Internet topology replicating only the bandwidth of first-hop links that connect to "the core". [25] experiments do not model background traffic, and cannot simulate more than several thousands of vulnerable hosts.

3. PAWS Design

We next explain various models deployed in PAWS.

3.1. Internet Topology and Routing Model

Worm spread features depend heavily on the underlying Internet characteristics such as connectivity, topology, bandwidth, link utilization, etc. It is necessary to faithfully model the Internet to achieve high-fidelity worm spread simulation. On the other hand, because of the Internet's heterogeneity and rapid change [2], there will be a limit on the number and level of Internet details we can replicate in a simulation.

PAWS currently models the Internet on the Autonomous System (AS) level. We obtain global connectivity data from Route Views[3] project, which provides BGP table snapshots of a small number of participating ASes. AS_PATH information from these snapshots can be used to infer peering relationships between ASes and the ownership of IP addresses and build an AS-connectivity map. We note here that this map is the subset of the real AS topology as some peering relationships will not be reflected in Route Views data if neither of the peers participates in Route Views.

To faithfully model Internet routing, one could attempt to discover and then simulate all the routers in the Internet, loading the corresponding routing tables obtained from the real routers into the simulation. This approach is not reasonable, because (i) it is impossible to discover router-level topology of the whole Internet[1], (ii) very few routing tables are publicly accessible and (iii) routing table information changes dynamically. PAWS currently applies the Dijkstra's algorithm on the AS map to compute the shortest routing paths between ASes, assuming the constant cost per AS hop. In the future work we plan to improve this model by (i) using the available BGP data from Route Views to partially populate BGP tables, and (ii) inferring the remaining routing information by using AS customer-provider-peer relationships and rules for sharing BGP information as described in [22, 23].

To take the most advantage of parallel simulation, nodes have to evenly divide the processing and communication load. For simple worm spread scenarios that include uniform distribution of vulnerable hosts and defenses, a node's processing load depends on the size of IP address space assigned to it. We develop a heuristic to split IP address space evenly among simulation nodes, which results in uneven distribution of ASes among nodes due to high variance of AS IP size.

PAWS models hop-by-hop Internet routing to account for inter-AS bandwidth consumption. A scan sent from an infectious to a susceptible host traverses all the intermediate ASes. To minimize a node's network communication load our heuristic assigns neighboring ASes to the same simulation node, up to a node's IP size limit. This means that most of the ASes assigned to a simulation node form a connected graph, which minimizes the number of network messages generated by scans. Grouping all worm scans sent from one simulation node to another within a time unit in a single network message further reduces communication cost.

We distribute routing information across simulation nodes; each node only stores routing tables of the ASes it simulates. When a worm scan is generated, the simulation node determines the destination AS for the given IP address using shared data which maps IP ranges to ASes. The node then uses its view of routing tables to calculate the path to the destination AS and the bandwidth consumption on this path. Scans to invulnerable hosts will increase bandwidth consumption but will be dropped at source simulation node. Successful scans will be either be delivered to another simulation node via a network message (if the AS path traverses more than one simulation node) or will generate a function call on the same simulation node.

Worm spread events produce huge volume of probes, which frequently lead to serious network congestion. To simulate this phenomenon, we need to model the limited bandwidth of each inter-AS link in our map. We also should take into account the portion of this bandwidth consumed by legitimate user traffic and the interaction of

[1] There are some published router-level topologies of large ASes [21] and there are several Internet mapping efforts [5, 20]. Authors of [24] build a detailed router-level map of US backbone ISPs along with inferred bandwidth and delay information. However, a large portion of the Internet is still not mapped.

this traffic with the worm traffic. There is currently no available data on AS-to-AS link bandwidth and there is scarce data on bandwidth utilization provided by Pathneck [8] project for a small number of inter-AS links.

Following a philosophy that large ASes will have bigger links than small ASes, and that AS size is proportional to its connection degree, we classify ASes into three categories by their connection degree, and then attempt to infer link bandwidth values for each category using bottleneck information obtained by Pathneck project as a starting point. Some ASes, like AS 1 and AS 701, have thousands of peers and contain huge portions of the IP address space. These ASes are part of the Internet backbone and they likely have high-bandwidth links to other large ASes, to route high-volume transit traffic. On the other end of the AS connectivity chart, ASes like 14364 and 14369 have a single connection to a better-connected AS. These ASes are stub networks whose links only carry their customers' traffic and thus have small bandwidth.

According to the discussion in [4, 6], there is a power-law distribution pattern on AS vertex degree. We first classify the ASes into three categories based on the connection degree: *small* ASes with less than 3 peers, *medium* ASes with 4–300 peers, and *large* ASes with more than 300 peers. We next determine likely bandwidth values for links between any two AS categories. Since we have three different categories of ASes, there are six link categories and thus six bandwidth values used in PAWS Internet model.

We use the data from Pathneck [8] project to aid our choice of bandwidth values. Pathneck project provides measurements of an upper bound on the available bandwidth on bottleneck links between ASes. This bound is measured by sending a train of packets on a path, and measuring packet interarrival times at routers along the path. The measurements provide only an instantaneous sample of the upper bound of the available bandwidth. The real available bandwidth fluctuates as traffic patterns change, and so does the upper bound. Pathneck tool can further provide an accurate available bandwidth measurement only for links *preceding* a bottleneck, as only those links can be filled with measurement traffic. After the packet train passes through a bottleneck, it is slowed down and only partially fills the remaining links. Pathneck provides a lower bound on the available bandwidth for links following the bottleneck link. Note that some links will have no records in Pathneck data as they have not been traversed by a measurement train, while other links may have multiple records since they have been traversed by multiple measurement trains.

We divide Pathneck-supplied data into 6 bins, based on the category of the ASes on a link's endpoints. We further select the maximum value x from a bin, and choose a bandwidth limit y, where y is the smallest value from the list of possible link bandwidths (OC1, OC3, etc), that satisfies $y \geq x$ requirement. Table 1 shows the chosen bandwidth values for different link categories:

Category	BW1 (Mbps)	Type1	BW2 (Mbps)	Type2	BW3 (Mbps)	Type3
1-1	155.52	OC3	32.064	J3	100.00	Fast Ethernet
1-2, 2-1	622.08	OC12	34.368	E3	155.52	OC3
1-3, 3-1	622.08	OC12	34.368	E3	466.56	OC9
2-2	1866.24	OC36	89.472	DS3-C	466.56	OC9
2-3, 3-2	1866.24	OC36	89.472	DS3-C	622.08	OC12
3-3	9953.28	OC192	9953.28	OC192	9953.28	OC192

Table 1: Selected bandwidth values for inter-AS links

In this paper we have examined two approaches to modeling the background traffic on inter-AS links, starting from the information provided by Pathneck data. The first approach averages the available bandwidth samples for a given AS-to-AS link, calculating value x_i. We then assume that the legitimate user traffic occupies the remaining bandwidth on this link: $z_i = y - x_i$, where y is our bandwidth limit estimate for this link's category. The second approach models the legitimate traffic amount on a link as an exponentially distributed random variable, whose parameters are obtained from the bins for a given link's category. We chose an exponential model since bin samples appear to be heavy tailed, following an exponential-like distribution.

3.2. Congestion Model

With the above Internet model, we simulate the bandwidth saturation and traffic congestion, which occur at aggressive worm propagation. If y_j is bandwidth of a link j, z_j is the legitimate traffic on this link, and w_j is the worm scan traffic on this link, then for each individual worm packet: (i) if $y_j \geq z_j+w_j$ the worm packet can pass through the link, and if $y_j < z_j+w_j$ the worm packet passes through the link with probability of $y_j/(z_j+w_j)$. A worm packet reaches the destination if and only if it is not dropped on any link along the routing path between two ASes.

3.3. Vulnerable Host Model

Each AS "owns" a set of IP ranges and each IP from these ranges may correspond to a physical host. PAWS uses per-AS ratio of "live" hosts, and generates a data structure to store both the basic information and the run-time status of each live host. This information specifies host features that may affect worm propagation, such as the type of OS and applications running on this host, how much resources it has (CPU speed, memory, bandwidth), whether this host has vulnerabilities that may be attacked by the worm, etc. The run-time status of a host includes its status (vulnerable, infected, patched, etc.) how many times it has been scanned and if infected, how many scans it has sent out and how many new hosts it has infected.

3.4. Worm Model

PAWS builds a worm description file for each specific worm, containing the following customizable parameters: (1) vulnerable ratio, (2) scanning rate, (3) infection delay which defines time between receipt of a worm probe by a vulnerable host, and the first scan sent from this host, (4) worm scan size and (5) scanning strategy. PAWS currently implements random and subnet scanning, but due to its modular design it can be easily extended with new scanning strategies.

3.5. Worm Scan Model

The simulation of worm spread on PAWS is a time-discrete procedure. Every time unit, each infected host produces a list of target IP addresses to scan. The target addresses are generated based on both the scanning strategy of that specific worm and the features (hardware, network connection, bandwidth) of the infected hosts. Each worm scan is time-stamped and buffered as an event. At the end of a time unit, those events are carried out together. To enhance simulation performance, scans to invulnerable IP addresses are sent to other simulation nodes individually, but their effects (the used bandwidth and the possible congestion caused) are simulated and the congestion information is exchanged between simulation nodes.

4. PAWS Implementation

Emulab testbed [1] at the University of Utah provides publicly available resources for real-machine testing, simulation and emulation. Emulab real-machine testbed features 212 PCs that can be interconnected and configured using a user-friendly, web-based interface and ns-compatible scripts or Java GUI. We chose to implement PAWS on Emulab testbed [1] to make it easily accessible to other researchers. While simulation code will run on any machine with a C compiler, our scripts are specifically tailored to Emulab environment.

Emulab PCs come in different CPU speeds. To maximize the simulation speed we use only PCs with 850MHz CPU (*pc850*). The hardware and software information of *pc850* machine is shown in Table 2. One machine is a master node that synchronizes the simulation and the remaining machines are slaves that carry out the simulation. All the nodes are connected on a 100M LAN. Both the latency and the loss rate of this LAN are set to zero.

Type:	pc850
Processor:	PIII
Speed:	850 MHZ
RAM:	256 MB
Disk Size:	39.00 GB
OS:	RHL-STD

Table 2: Emulab node hardware specification

4.1. Inter-Node Communication

In Emulab PAWS implementation, simulation nodes communicate and exchange data in two ways. First communication method is via a shared project directory which is NFS-mounted. This provides easy means of sharing data needed by all the slave nodes. This data is stored in the following files:

- *Per-AS information file* containing per-AS IP range list
- *Inter-AS routing file* containing inter-AS routing paths.
- *Worm description file* containing the information described in worm model section.
- *Vulnerable host list file* containing IPs of all the vulnerable hosts simulated on a specific simulation node.
- *PAWS configuration file* containing all the other simulation-related information, such as a number of simulation nodes, their names, distribution of the AS map and simulation tasks among the nodes, etc..

Another method for inter-node communication in PAWS is through stream sockets. During the initialization stage, each node sets up a stream socket and connects to all other simulation nodes. During the simulation, TCP packets are used for worm scan propagation and status reports exchange among the nodes.

4.2. Dynamic Update Interval (Time Unit Scaling)

A significant portion of the simulation time is used for inter-node communication, mostly for worm scan propagation and for the broadcasting IPs of newly infected hosts. An obvious design approach is that at the end of each time unit, all the simulator nodes communicate and synchronize with each other, so that they reach a consistent view of the simulated network. However, some time units will contain very few events of interest (for instance in the early stage of the worm spread, or when the worm reaches saturation) and do not warrant heavy message exchange. PAWS optimizes network communication by exchanging inter-node messages at specific intervals whose size is a multiple of simulation time units and is dynamically adjusted using *time-unit scaling*, according to the formula

$$i = \left\lceil \frac{N}{c \cdot m} \right\rceil$$

where i is the new value of update interval, N is size of the vulnerable population, m is the number of newly infected hosts in the previous time unit, and c is a constant. For example, if c equals to 1000, and during the last time unit, 0.01% of the vulnerable population became infected, next update interval will occur after 10 time units.

5. Experiments

To validate correctness of PAWS, we simulate two well-known worm spread events: Code Red v2 (July 19th, 2001) [27] and SQL Slammer (January 25th, 2003) [7].

5.1. Simulation of CodeRed v2

During the outbreak of CodeRed v2 worm, more that 359,000 infected hosts were observed by CAIDA [8]. In our simulation, we set the Code Red vulnerable population

N=360,000. Each infected host tries to infect a different list of randomly generated IP addresses at an observed peak rate of roughly 6 probes per second. Initially there are 2 infected hosts at time 0. We reproduce AS-level map from July 19th, 2001, 10am UTC in this simulation.

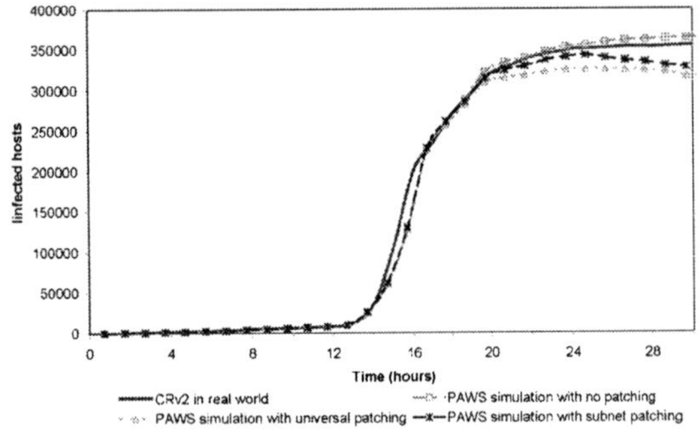

Figure 2: Simulation of CRv2

Figure 2 shows simulated number of infected hosts (lines with marks) compared with the measured number during worm propagation (line without marks) published in [8]. We simulate three worm spread events:

- *CRv2 propagation without patching:* worm propagates without any defenses applied. Once a vulnerable host is infected, it starts to probe others with a constant speed.
- *CRv2 propagation with universal patching:* Patching is a good defense to fight slow-propagating worms. In this experiment we set the initial patching rate of a host at 32/100,000 per second. AS the worm spread progresses, the user awareness increases and the patching rate increases linearly. Patching starts 16 hours after the worm breakout. The initial patching rate, speed of the linear increase and start time for patching are estimated from the graph depicting measured host deactivation after Code Red v2 spread [27]
- *CRv2 propagation with subnet patching:* This experiment simulates an organized patching of all the machines in a subnet administered by a single organization. We use a constant patching rate of 1/100,000 per second per subnet and define the subnet as an IP range belonging to an AS, no greater than 2^{16} hosts. All the machines inside a selected subnet are patched within the same time unit. For subnets larger than 2^{16} addresses, PAWS patches a randomly selected portion of 2^{16} hosts. Patching starts 16 hours after the worm breakout.

From Figure 2, we see that "no-patching" case generates the best match with the real worm. Further, two patching scenarios, especially subnet patching, generate the decline in the number of infected hosts after the worm reaches its peak which resembles the effect measured at one Internet subnetwork during CRv2 re-emergence and shown in [7].

5.2. Simulation of SQL Slammer

SQL Slammer [7] propagated on January 25, 2003, starting from 05:30am UTC and infected more than 90% of vulnerable hosts within 10 minutes. Total of 75,000 infected hosts are observed. In the simulation, we use 75,000 as the vulnerable population size, and the average scan rate of is 4,000 probes per second. We replicate routing at the worm spread start using Route Views data.

Figure 3 shows Slammer simulation results. In addition to congestion-constrained worm spread (line with cross marks), we also simulate the occurrence of router failures due to large volume of scan traffic (line with square marks), assuming a single router per AS peer. When the traffic on an inter-AS link is two times bigger than its bandwidth value, PAWS simulates router failure by removing this inter-AS link. In both simulation runs congestion builds up as the worm spreads, causing dropped scans and slowing down propagation. For comparison, we show the worm propagation with unlimited bandwidth (line without marks). We note here that the propagation can be "slowed down" more by choosing smaller bandwidth values and thus increasing congestion effects. The simulation with three different bandwidth value assignments in Table 1 is shown in Figure 4. We note that the worm propagation is slowed by about 5 minutes by using significantly lower bandwidth values than in Figure 3.

Figure 3 also shows the number of scans in the Internet for worm propagation with and without the router failure. We note that we drop around 18 million scans due to router failures when the network is fully congested. The curve with network failure reaches 80 million of scans around 300 seconds which matches the measured Slammer scan activity in [7].

Among the three bandwidth assignments shown in Table 1, we believe the values in column 6 are most reasonable and nearest to the real applications of current Internet. Many small ASes are owned by universities or institutes, who normally use 100Mbps Fast Ethernet network, while major ISPs with medium size ASes tend to provide OC-9/OC-12 services. OC-192 techniques are used for backbone network with 10Gbps data rate.

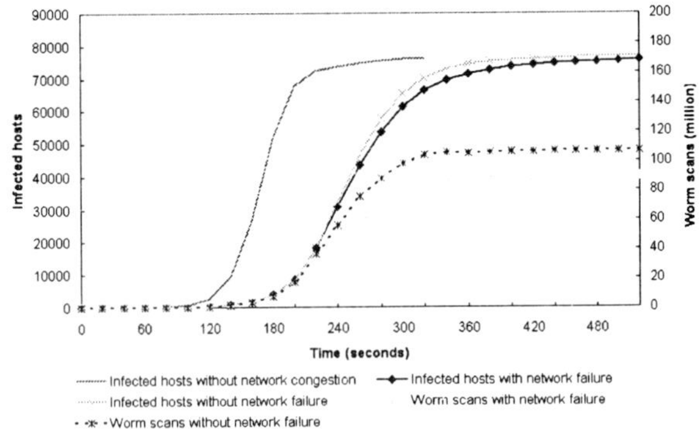

Figure 3: Simulation of Slammer

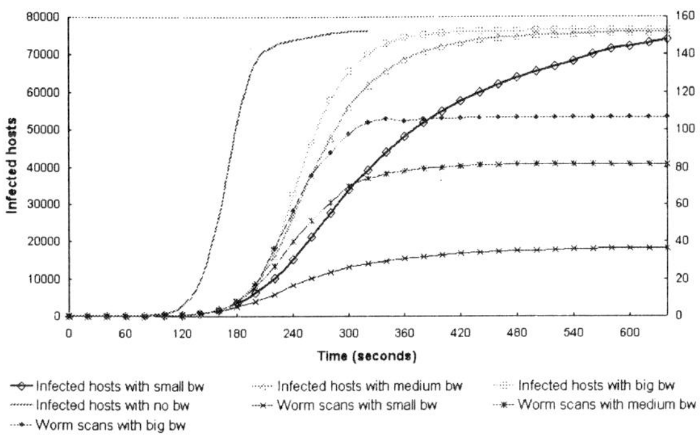

Figure 4: Simulation with different bandwidth values assignments in Table 1

Zou et al [28] analyzed the effect of dynamic quarantine as a worm defense. To demonstrate PAWS ability to provide accurate evaluation of defense system performance, we have also implemented dynamic quarantine approach. We further replicate the experiment from [28] where the quarantine rate of infectious hosts is $\lambda_1 = 0.2$ per second and the quarantine rate of susceptible hosts is $\lambda_2 = 0.2$ per second. The quarantine time T is 10 seconds. In figure 5, we show the simulation result with and without network congestion. We note that our simulation result without considering bandwidth and congestion match the result in [28]. With bandwidth consideration, the dynamic quarantine significantly slows down the worm. The bandwidth values in Table 1 column 6 are used for this experiment.

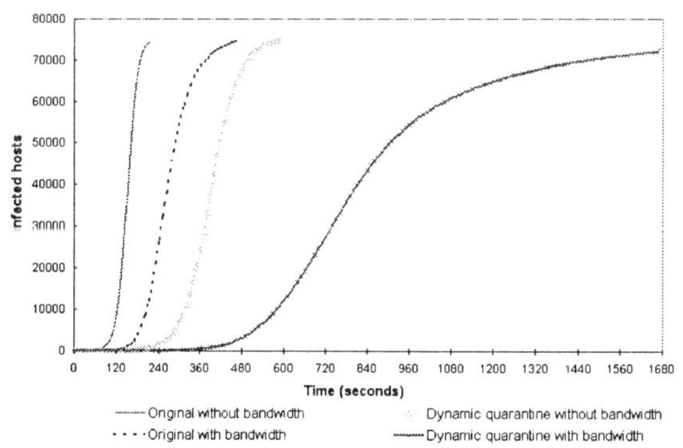

Figure 5 Simulation of Slammer with dynamic quarantine defense

5.3. Effect of Time-Unit Scaling

We measure the loss of simulation fidelity due to time-unit scaling, and show the results in Figure 6 depicting the number of infected hosts by Slammer with and without time-unit scaling. In these simulations we used bandwidth values from Table 1, column 4. Time-unit scaling slows slightly worm propagation in the early stage, but the propagation "catches up" with the no-scaling curve (solid lines) during the exponential stage of the spread. The difference between curves is very small, while the gain in simulation time is almost 30%. Figure 7 shows the value of the scaled interval (dashed line) as simulation progresses.

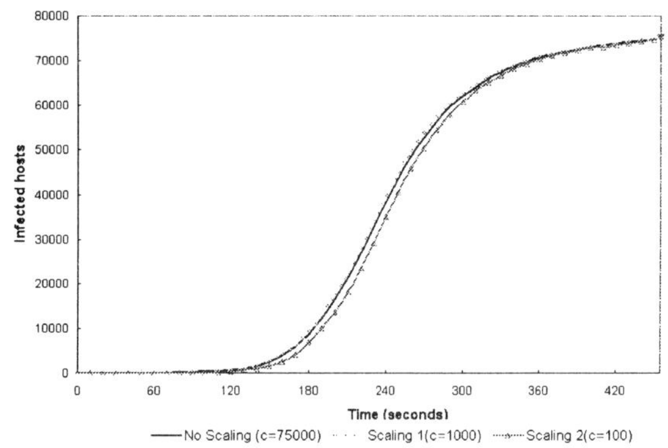

Figure 6: Time-unit scaling effect on simulation fidelity

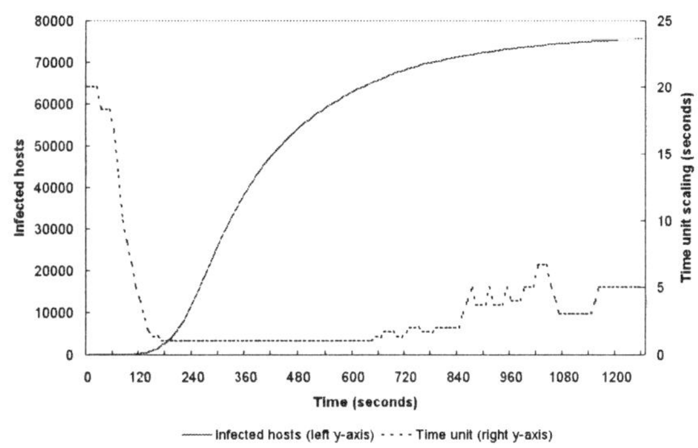

Figure 7: Value of the scaled interval

Slammer in case of constant and random traffic assignment. Simulations use the link bandwidth values from Table 1, column 4. Two curves are identical, which indicates that the worm spread is not very sensitive to the amount of the background traffic present in the Internet. We attribute that to the fact that Slammer was very aggressive UDP worm which easily prevailed over the small amount of well-behaved background traffic. Aggressive TCP worms may exhibit greater sensitivity to background traffic values.

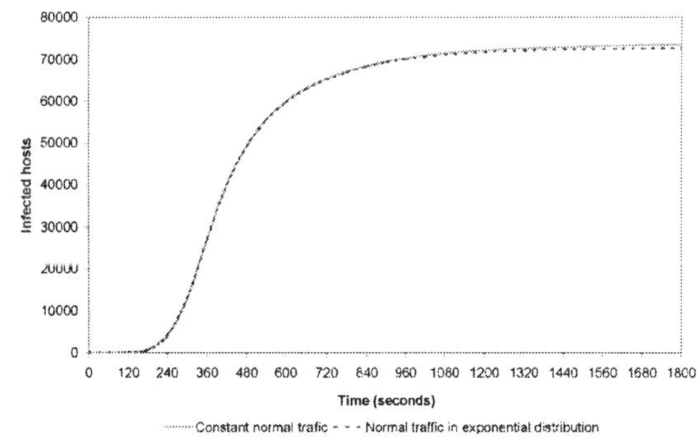

Figure 8: Slammer propagation with constant and random assignment of background traffic values

6. PAWS Performance

Two major PAWS' activities during worm propagation are processing and transmitting of worm scans. Worm scan processing encompasses the operation of sending a worm scan from each infected host and receiving and processing this scan on the target host. This is the major task of a worm simulator and consumes most of the CPU time. As there are more infected machines in the simulation, PAWS scan processing overhead grows. Higher distribution degree reduces the processing overhead on individual simulation nodes and thus decreases scan processing time for the simulation.

Transmission activity encompasses the transfer of a worm scan from the source (an infected host) to the destination (the targeted host). Most of the time, source and destination hosts are not collocated on the same simulation node, and transferring worm scans leads to network communication that produces additional simulation delay. As there are more scans in the simulation, transmission overhead grows as the scan message must be split into several network packets. Higher distribution degree also increases communication among simulation nodes and the overall scan transmission time.

These two opposite factors influence the overall simulation time. In Figure 9 we show the simulation time and the CPU utilization for a varying number of simulation nodes, simulating the first twenty hours of CodeRed v2 propagation. Figure 10 shows the exact time used for communication and processing on single node with different number of simulation nodes. The volume of inter-node traffic increases with the number of simulation nodes, which is shown in Figure 11.

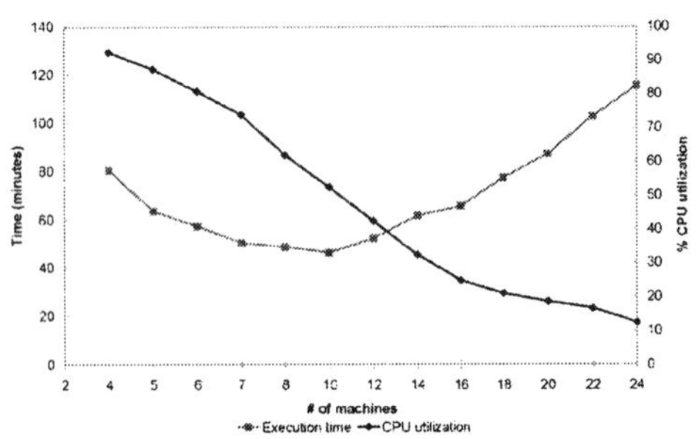

Figure 9: Simulation time and CPU load

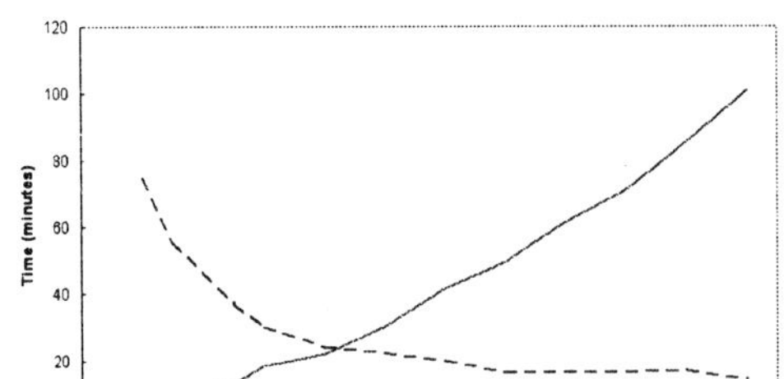

Figure 10: Communication and processing time

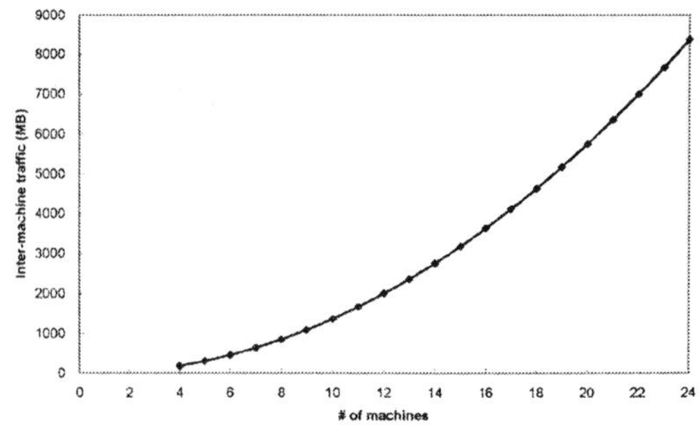

Figure 11: Inter-node traffic

Execution time is smallest with 10 nodes for this simulation (first twenty hours of CodeRed v2 propagation), and benefits of using multiple simulation machines balance the cost of inter-node communication. As we use more than 10 nodes, the inter-node communication increases yielding higher execution time. When using less than 10 nodes, per-node processing load is the key overhead factor. Please note that the scanning strategy used by CodeRed v2 is a simplest one (random scan), and no monitoring or defense is simulated. For more complex experiments or sophisticated worm simulations, the scan processing time should increase, shifting the minimum shown in Figure 9 to the right and to higher values. The CPU utilization decreases as the number of simulation nodes grows, because a large portion of the CPU time is spent initiating and waiting for inter-node communication. In the future work, we will investigate approaches to reduce and simplify the inter-node communication and thus get better usage of CPU resources.

7. Conclusion

We present a design and implementation of a distributed worm simulator, PAWS, that runs on common PCs and achieves largest packet-level simulation of worm spread to date. PAWS simulates a realistic Internet model and background traffic load, enabling investigation of congestion effects of the worm spread and its interactions with the background traffic. PAWS further supports a variety of user-customizable parameters that enable testing of various host and network diversity models, worm scanning strategies and Internet topologies. PAWS' modular design, variety of features, high-fidelity and Emulab-based implementation make it a useful tool for worm researchers.

References

[1] B. White, J. Lepreau, L. Stoller, R. Ricci, S. Guruprasad, M. Newbold, M. Hibler, C. Barb, and A. Joglekar, "An Integrated Experimental Environment for Distributed Systems and Networks," OSDI 2002.

[2] S. Floyd and V. Paxson, "Difficulties in Simulating the Internet," IEEE/ACM Transactions on Networking, Vol.9, No.4, pp. 392-403, August, 2001.

[3] University of Oregon Route Views Project, http://www.Route Views.org

[4] H. Chang, S. Jamin, W. Willinger, "On Inferring AS-level connectivity from BGP Routing Tables," Proceedings of SPIE ITCom 2001.

[5] B. Cheswick and H. Burch, "The Internet Mapping Project," http://research.lumeta.com/ches/map/

[6] H. Tangmunarunkit, R. Govindan, S. Jamin, S. Shenker, W. Willinger, "Network Topology Generator: Degree-Based vs. Structural, Proceedings of SIGCOMM 2002.

[7] D. Moore, V. Paxson, S. Savage, C. Shannon, S. Staniford, N. Weaver, "Inside the Slammer Worm," *Security and Privacy*, 1(4):33-39, July 2003.

[8] Ningning Hu, Li Erran Li, Zhuoqing Morley Mao, Peter Steenkiste, Jia Wang, "Locating Internet Bottlenecks: Algorithms, Measurements, and Implications," Proceedings of SIGCOMM 2004.

[9] K.S. Perumalla, S. Sundaragopalan, "High-Fidelity Modeling of Computer Network Worms," Annual Computer Security Applications Conference (ACSAC), December 2004.

[10] M. Liljenstam, Y. Yuan, B. J. Premore, "A Mixed Abstraction Level Simulation Model of Large-scale Internet Worm Infestations," International Symposium on Modeling, Analysis and Simulation of Computer and Telecommunication Systems (MASCOTS 2002).

[11] M. Liljenstam, D. Nicol, V. Berk, and R. Gray, "Simulating Realistic Network Worm Traffic for Worm Warning System Design and Testing," Proceedings of the 2003 ACM Workshop on Rapid Malcode (WORM 2003).

[12] A. Wagner, T. Dübendorfer, B. Plattner and R. Hiestand, "Experiences with Worm Propagation Simulations," In Proceedings of the 2003 ACM Workshop on Rapid Malcode, 2003.

[13] D. Moore, C. Shannon, G. M. Voelker and S. Savage, "Internet Quarantine: Requirements for Containing Self-Propagating Code," INFOCOM, 2003.

[14] S. Staniford, V. Paxson and N. Weaver, "How to 0wn the Internet in Your Spare Time," Proceedings of the 11th USENIX Security Symposium, 2002.

[15] C. C. Zou, W. Gong and D. Towsley, "Code Red Worm Propagation Modeling and Analysis," In Proceedings of the 9th ACM conference on Computer and communications security, 2002.

[16] Z. Shen, L. Gao and K. Kwiat, "Modeling the Spread of Active Worms," In Proceedings of INFOCOM 2003.

[17] J.O. Kephart and S.R. White, "Measuring and Modeling Computer Virus Prevalence," Proceedings of the 1993 IEEE Symposium on Research in Security and Privacy, Oakland, CA, May 1993.

[18] C. C. Zou, W. Gong, D. Towsley and L. Gao, "Monitoring and Early Detection for Internet Worms," In Proceedings of 10th ACM Conference on Computer and Communication Security, 2003.

[19] S. Floyd and E. Kohler, "Internet Research Needs Better Models," Proceedings of Hotnets-I. October 2002.

[20] M. Dodge, "An Atlas of Cyberspaces," http://www.cybergeography.org/atlas/more_isp_maps.html.

[21] R. Haynal, "Major Internet Backbone MAPs," http://navigators.com/isp.html.

[22] F. Wang and L. Gao, "Inferring and Characterizing Internet Routing Policies," ACM SIGCOMM Internet Measurement Conference 2003

[23] L. Gao, "On Inferring Autonomous System Relationships in the Internet ," IEEE Global Internet, Nov 2000.

[24] M. Liljenstam, J. Liu, and D. Nicol, "Development of an Internet Backbone Topology for Large-Scale Network Simulations," Proceedings of 2003 Winter Simulation Conference.

[25] G. F. Riley, M. I. Sharif and W. Lee, "Simulating Internet Worms," Proceedings of the 12th Annual Meeting of the IEEE/ACM International Symposium on Modeling, Analysis, and Simulation of Computer and Telecommunication Systems (MASCOTS), 2004.

[26] R. Fujimoto, K. Perumalla, A. Park, H. Wu, M. Ammar and G. Riley, "Large-Scale Network Simulation – How Big? How Fast?," IEEE/ACM International Symposium on Modeling, Analysis and Simulation of Computer Telecommunication Systems (MASCOTS), October 2003.

[27] D. Moore, C. Shannon, J. Brown, "Code-Red: a Case Stud On the Spread and Victims of an Internet Worm," Proceedings of the Internet Measurement Workshop, 2002.

[28] C.C. Zou, W. Gong, D. Towsley, "Worm Propagation Modeling and Analysis under Dynamic quarantine defense," Proceeding of ACM CSS Workshop on Rapid Malcode (WORM'03), October 2003.

Mobile Contagion: Simulation of Infection & Defense

Everett Anderson — Computer Science
Kevin Eustice — Computer Science
Shane Markstrum — Computer Science
Mark Hansen — Statistics
Peter Reiher — Computer Science

University of California, Los Angeles

Abstract

For worms with known signatures, properly configured firewalls can prevent infection of a network from the outside. However, as several recent worms have shown, portable computers provide worms with an entry point into such networks, since these computers are connected behind the firewall. Once inside, the firewall provides no protection against the worm's further spread. Wireless networks are particularly dangerous in this regard, as the act of connection is often invisible, and improperly configured wireless networks will allow anyone within radio range to connect. In this paper, we use real data on a large-scale wireless deployment to analyze the speed with which a worm could spread if it used only this propagation vector. We discuss several possible solutions and provide analysis on how much protection those solutions would provide.

1. Introduction

The worms that achieved the largest infected populations have been designed to spread across arbitrary networks. In most cases, they travel from one wired node through the Internet to another wired node. Along the way, they are likely to either pass through or be rejected by a firewall that separates the target node from the rest of the Internet. Since worms typically make use of known vulnerabilities, rather than zero-day exploits, one method of controlling their spread is to install filtering rules in firewalls that look for either particular worm payloads or attempts to exploit known vulnerabilities. Substantial research is ongoing in developing methods to automatically detect and analyze worm behavior, with a goal of spreading signature information to firewalls, which can then stop further infections by filtering on the signature.

The Blaster and Sasser worm events, however, demonstrated that this approach is not sufficient. Sites whose firewalls were fully cognizant of the infection vector and well prepared to reject any such messages still found their internal networks infected by these worms.

Why? In general, not because of imperfections in the firewalls, but rather because mobile computing allows nodes to move from network to network without traversing any firewall. A mobile computer is plugged into an already infected or unprotected network, is infected with the worm, and is then disconnected. Later it is brought into a protected office environment, where it connects to the network behind the firewall. Its packets are never examined for the worm, since they don't go through the firewall, and it is thus free to infect the entire network. Many sites had serious problems with these worms for precisely this reason.

Further, many of the proposed solutions to detecting and handling worms are based on the presumption that the worm is both aggressive and noisy. By acting in characteristically different ways than the infected node would ordinarily behave, in its attempt to infect as many nodes as possible, as quickly as possible, the worm offers defenders an opportunity to detect its presence and take responsive measures. Some have postulated that if effective defenses of this type are built, they could be stymied by a worm that was slower, more careful, and less aggressive [1]. Propagating only on human movement is one simple way to achieve that effect.

These problems are unlikely to go away. In fact, they will get worse. With wired networks, there is an explicit step that a user takes to connect up to the protected network: he plugs in a cable. Perhaps users can be educated to regard this as an event with security significance, requiring them to perform extra actions, such as a virus scan.

With wireless networks, there is no such user-initiated event. Typically, wireless nodes automatically detect and join local wireless networks. The user does not necessarily even know it has happened. Wireless networks are becoming increasingly common, and wireless advocates are working diligently towards a world with nearly ubiquitous coverage and transparent mobility from network to network. In addition to the popularity of wireless PDAs and laptop computers, cell phones powerful enough to download and run Java code are widespread [2], increasing their utility and offering users, as well as malware authors, many new possibilities.

1087-4097/05 $20.00 © 2005 IEEE

Existing research has modeled the spread of worms that rely on the standard method of using some IP transport protocol to move across arbitrary networks, but it has not yet provided any insight on how fast and how far a worm could spread by making use of mobile computers and wireless networks. This paper addresses that question. We use existing data of real users working in a campus-wide wireless environment over the course of several months to provide realistic data on mobility and connectivity patterns. We perform simulations based on this data to observe how a worm might propagate using only local wireless connections and human user mobility. Further, since various groups are already building defenses against this form of infection based on examining and quarantining dangerous machines as they enter networks behind the firewall, we analyze several strategies of this kind of defense.

2. Worm Models

As detailed in [1] and [3], an Internet worm such as Code Red can be modeled by applying the Susceptible-Infected (SI) epidemic formula, deriving an equation for the number of infected users over time based on an average contact rate. Moore et al went on to define this rate for Internet worms as the product of scanning frequency and the probability of finding a vulnerable host in the search space (2^{32} when scanning the entire IP address range), but a worm written specifically with behavior for wireless environments would take a different approach to infecting other hosts.

The intensive scanning performed by normal Internet worms would quickly give away their presence on a bandwidth-constrained device. In order to avoid detection, a worm on a mobile host would try to limit scanning of the wide area network and focus on peers with the assumption that eventually those peers would travel behind security boundaries and allow it to reach more hosts. If the worm has multiple attack vectors, it might switch to a more aggressive one suitable for a wired environment once it found an unprotected or particularly well-connected point.

For our theoretical worm, the average contact rate becomes a function of variables such as the number of access points users visit, their session lengths, the number of users per access point or subnet, and whether the worm can monitor the channel to discover new targets. Many of these factors lead back to mobility, and users currently seem to use the network in highly variable ways – large differences may exist between users or even in the same user's behavior over time. As wireless networks become more widely used and reliable models of mobility are discovered, a formula for the contact rate of our hypothetical worm should emerge. Work has already begun on extracting mobility models from traces gathered by Dartmouth College. [4]

In our work, we use a simple model of worm activity. The worm only propagates across wireless networks. Whenever a worm successfully associates with a new subnet, it attempts to infect any other nodes already associated with that subnet. The access points themselves cannot be infected. In our analysis, we assume that all other devices in the simulation are susceptible to the exploit the worm uses to attack new machines, and that once a machine is infected, it continues to try to spread the infection until the machine is disinfected and patched.

In our simulations, we always assume that only a single user in the system starts off with the infection, received either by contact with a hypothetical host outside the scope of the simulation or through some other attack vector. This assumption may not be realistic, as it would be likely that a successful worm might enter a population of mobile wireless users through several hosts. We plan to examine the effects of multiple infection points in future experiments.

Similarly, there are many other variants of worm behavior that could be studied this way, including a worm that sometimes propagates stealthily across wireless networks and sometimes propagates rapidly when well connected. A comprehensive analysis of these variants is beyond the scope of this paper, but several will be addressed in future work.

3. Dartmouth Trace Description and Interpretation

Performing our simulations required a source of data describing how users move between different access points. Rather than use a synthetic model of user mobility, we relied on extensive traces of real behavior.

Kotz and Essien presented a detailed study of traces for Dartmouth College's 802.11b campus network for the Fall 2001 semester in [5], and have continued to collect and make available large amounts of data online. The trace archive now contains full system logs from early in 2001 through the present with few interruptions, making it the largest public source available for studying real user behavior. These logs contain records of many events of interest in the wireless networks they studied, some of which are precisely the data we needed for our simulations.

The Dartmouth campus environment is especially useful for user mobility research since it spans 200 acres and over 160 buildings, and is saturated with 802.11b connectivity throughout. All students are required to have computers, and 70% of students purchasing computers from the campus store in 2001 bought laptops, all of which had 802.11b adapters.

3.1. Dartmouth System Logs

The system logs available from the Dartmouth archive were altered by Kotz et al to add timestamps, sanitize client MAC addresses, and change the names of access points to a format that identifies the class of building (academic, residential, etc).

We interpreted the entries closely following the methods in [5], including adjusting deauthentications due to user inactivity and removing users when access points rebooted.

3.2. Filtering

The system logs of the trace, covering September 23, 2003 through December 10, 2003 (Fall 2003 semester), were filtered as follows. We discarded entries with corrupted data, those with MAC addresses not in the trace format, and messages that do not represent one of the above user events.

Since the logs do not provide information about the organization of the network, we chose to form subnets out of the set of access points in each building. Network cards can freely switch access points if they find a stronger signal, but reassociating with an AP out of the subnet would interrupt the user's experience. Grouping our access points this way makes an association with a new subnet more closely correspond to a change in location. Using building scope is also practical since the outer walls would affect signal strength.

While [5] performed a more sophisticated session analysis, we assume that as long as the user stays within one subnet, the session continues until a disassociate or deauthenticate message appears from the AP with which the user was last connected. Thus, the user's machine remains addressable at the same network location and any connections with other computers continue even if the network card reassociates with a stronger AP signal within the building.

Our resulting data set had 6630 unique MACs which we assume correspond to unique users, 165 subnets (buildings), 3,746,005 entries, 2,590,365 unique timestamps at the granularity of seconds, 1,164,458 Associates, 1,753,640 Reassociates, 380,159 Deauthenticates, 446,501 Disassociates, and 175 Reboots.

3.3. General Analysis

Since user mobility and sharing of access points are the main drivers behind the spread of our envisioned worm, it is helpful to look at related features in the trace.

Our median user visited just over 9 buildings, had a session length of 16.21 minutes, initiated 82 sessions during the simulation, and shared a subnet with 892 other unique users. Time spent online varied widely, with the median user active 582 hours, and including 14% who used the network less than 10 hours.

The subnets in the trace had a median of 17 maximum simultaneous users, received a median of 7,073 visits, and saw a median of 228 unique users. These numbers provide hints as to how likely an infected user would be able to come in contact with others, and thus contribute to forming the average contact rate. Interestingly, even when only simulating at the access point level so that each AP was its own subnet and movements to other APs broke connections, the infection results were equally severe.

Obviously, this trace and our use of it represent only one model of mobility and access point sharing. However, the trace is real, fairly recent, and representative of a reasonably large class of users whose mobile computing experience is largely limited to one large area. These experiments could obviously be run with other mobility models based on different assumptions or traces, likely yielding different results. Such investigations must be deferred to future work, however.

4. Worm Simulation

After filtering the trace, we ran a custom simulator written in Java to determine how worms would behave in this environment. For each of the 6630 users in the trace, we performed a simulation of what would happen if that user began the semester infected with a idealized worm that required 30 seconds to scan and infect the other machines on the subnet, and was capable of infecting any uninfected target, but not the APs. Even if the worm couldn't switch its host's network adapter to promiscuous mode to monitor new connections, since the maximum number of simultaneous users at any subnet in the simulation was 334 (at a library), the subnets would probably be small enough to scan quickly for susceptible hosts.

Figure 1 shows the resulting maximum, median, and lower quartile curves of the number of infected hosts over time. Please note that the x-axis has been normalized such that 0 is the first appearance of the initial infecting user. This allows us to compare infection rates across initial infectors.

The normalized curves show that the idealized worm exhibits similar infection behavior to the SI model, with a rapid jump in victims followed by a smoothing out as the worm finds fewer and fewer new targets. [1] discussed the reaction time of a containment system necessary to limit an infection to a given proportion of users. For the median curve of Figure 1, such a system would need to react within 1 hour and 50 minutes to contain the infection to 10% of the population and within 34 hours to contain it within 50%.

This is considerably better news for network administrators than the "Warhol worm" described in [3] that could infect all vulnerable hosts on the Internet in just minutes, and reflects the contagion approach of our hypothetical wireless worm.

Since mobility patterns and different patterns of use of the network clearly affect how likely this form of worm is to spread widely, we also present data on how many users would ultimately be infected given different users who were the original point of the infection. We found that 86 of the 6630 users in the semester were poor infectors, incapable of infecting any other systems due to low and/or short contact with peers. For the following results, we removed the simulations where one of these users was chosen as the initial infector.

As Figure 2 shows, even with just a single initial infector, most users are capable of causing near total contamination of the network. 83% of the users were able to infect over 90% of their peers. Except for the 86 users who had almost no contact with anyone on the network, almost all of the users were able to infect two thirds of the overall population. Clearly, while this method of spreading a worm is not incredibly fast, it can be extremely effective.

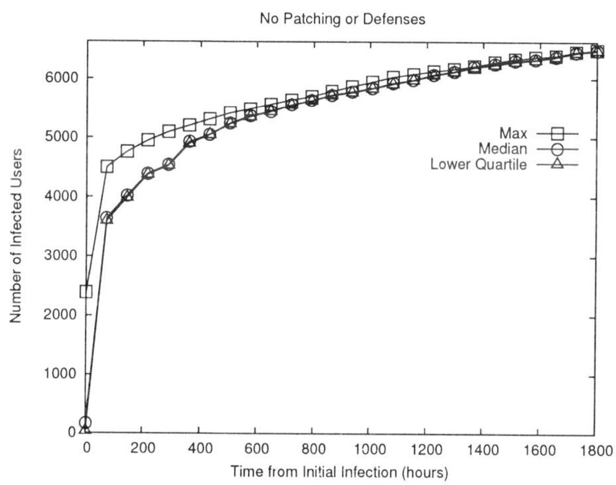

Figure 1. Plot of max, median, and lower quartile summaries of infection over time when there are no defense mechanisms.

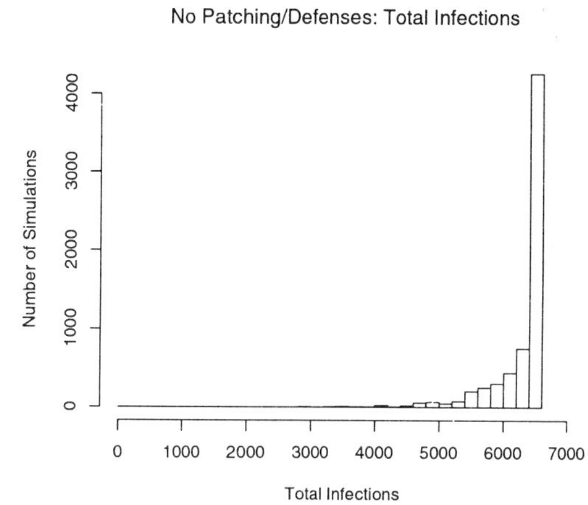

Figure 2. Histogram of total number of users infected across simulations of the 6544 initial infectors.

5. Defense Systems

How can a worm that uses this type of propagation be stopped? We modeled a variety of types of defense systems to see how well they contain the threat, performing tens of thousands of simulations per type. For all simulations, we assume that users run virus-scanning software and disinfect before installing patches.

One important note is that due to the fact that we are replaying recorded trace log data in hopes of having an accurate user mobility model, we are ignoring the possibility that the users would change their network usage when infected or when interacting with one of the defense systems. For instance, if a defense that denied access to infected users were only partially deployed, infected users might decide to walk to a location that didn't have it after being denied access at locations that do.

We simulated random 25% deployments of the defense models across the subnets, as well as the combination of users patching their own systems with the infrastructure solutions. We evaluate the results based on four metrics: percent of simulations where the worm never infected more than 1% of the users, the number of total infections that occurred, the number of infected users who remain infected by the end of the semester, and the general shape of the infection over time plots.

The following are descriptions of the models and their individual results, with comparison and analysis in section 6. Figures 3, 4, and 5 compare data for the several models.

5.1. Unpatched User Shunning (US)

These systems are capable of detecting that a user is vulnerable and send him a warning message that if he doesn't install the patch within a certain period of time, he will be shunned from using the network, presumably until he fixes his system and reports to an administrator to request removal from the shun list. This model allows infections on its subnet and communication between its users. We used the following parameters: The users were given 5 days to patch, 95% would patch some time within that period, and all the users who became shunned would patch within 3 days. We also assumed that the shun list is global – all the installations of this system are coordinated by a campus-wide administrator.

For 25% deployment, in about 2.5% of the simulations, the US defense model contained the infection to less than 1% of the users. In the median case, it still allowed a total 89% of the users to become infected. Figure 4 shows that it flattens the infected population, keeping up the rate of disinfection with the worm, until eventually all the users who are going to travel to one of the US systems do so and the infectable population is exhausted.

5.2. Infected/Unpatched User Shunning (IUS)

This model is the same is the Unpatched User Shunning case except it also prevents infections attempted at defense locations, warns infected users, and then adds them to the global shun list. An IUS system might actively analyze traffic looking for signatures or anomalies and be able to cut off an infected system before it contaminates others. We assumed that all users warned that they are infected will disinfect and patch within 24 hours.

IUS performed much better in containing the threat to less than 1% of the users, doing so in almost 20% of the simulations. It allowed 65% of users to become infected in the median case, and flattened the infected population to about 25%.

5.3. Active Disinfect/Patch (Active)

In an active defense model similar to [6], users who connect to the network are quarantined until they prove that they are up to date with the latest patches and are uninfected. Infected users are disinfected and unpatched users are provided the patch. In our simulations, we assumed 10 seconds are required to disinfect and patch an infected user. Infected users who leave the network before the time is up are not disinfected. Thus, in most cases an infected machine will be disinfected if it ever visits a location where the defense is deployed.

Active reduced the infected population by the end of the simulation to about the same level as IUS; however it was able to contain the threat to less than 1% of the population in almost 27% of the cases and reduced the number of users ever infected to 51% in the median case. This suggests that it did its work faster and was more likely to prevent the outbreak in the first place. Nonetheless, even a strong and aggressive defense of this kind can frequently permit a high degree of infection if its deployment is limited to merely 25% of all systems. Clearly, higher degrees of deployment will be required to achieve greater protection, rather than merely more sophisticated defenses at a limited number of locations.

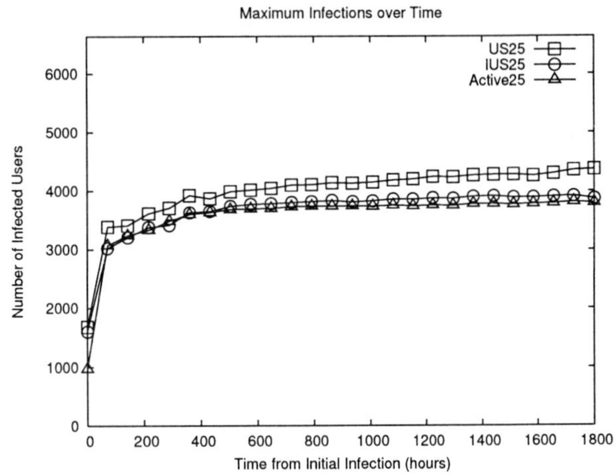

Figure 3. Maximum infection over time curves for US, IUS, and Active at 25% deployment.

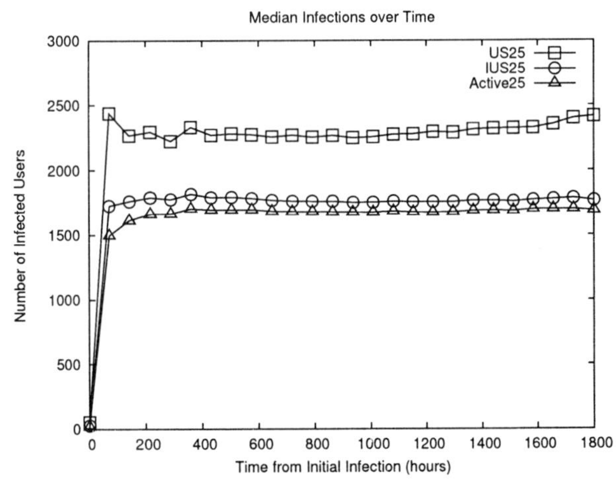

Figure 4. Median infection over time curves for US, IUS, and Active at 25% deployment.

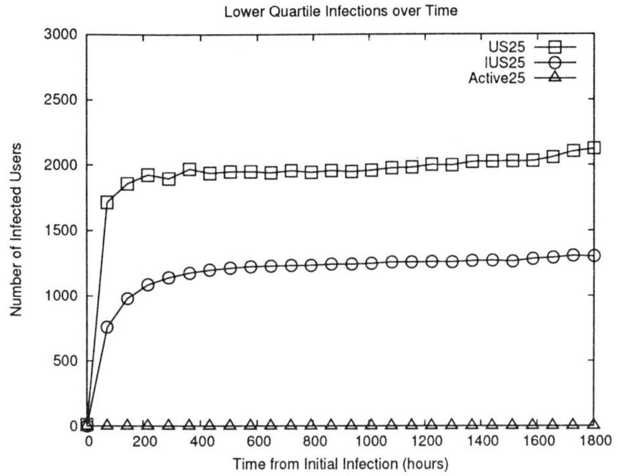

Figure 5. Lower quartile infection over time curves for US, IUS, and Active at 25% deployment.

5.4. Proactive Patching

Since most popular consumer operating systems now support automatic warnings of new vulnerabilities and make it easy to install patches, we expect more users will keep their systems up to date. To examine the impact of this effect, we used the following schedule for patch installation starting at the beginning of the trace data: 50% of users patch some time within the first 7 days, 25% in the next 7 days, 10% in the third 7, and finally 15% will never patch on their own. Users were allowed to patch even if they were not on the wireless network, since we generally assume that they have other sources for network connectivity.

If users patch their own systems according to the schedule we devised, they can have a significant effect. However, the worm is still fast enough to infect a large percentage of the population. In less than 1% of the simulations, the worm was contained to 1% or less of the users, and in the median case, 63% of the users were infected, though only 15% were still infected by the end of the simulation due to our schedule. One of the curves on Figure 6 shows the effect of relying only on patching (with this pattern) to combat a worm.

5.5. Combining Proactive Patching and Infrastructure Defense

While the combination of proactive patching with the defense systems had significantly better results than any single system alone, the relative performance of US, IUS, and Active remained about the same. Due to space constraints, we will only show the infections over time graph of the median cases, and present a complete summary in section 6. Note that even the best combined defense still left around 250 users infected in the median case.

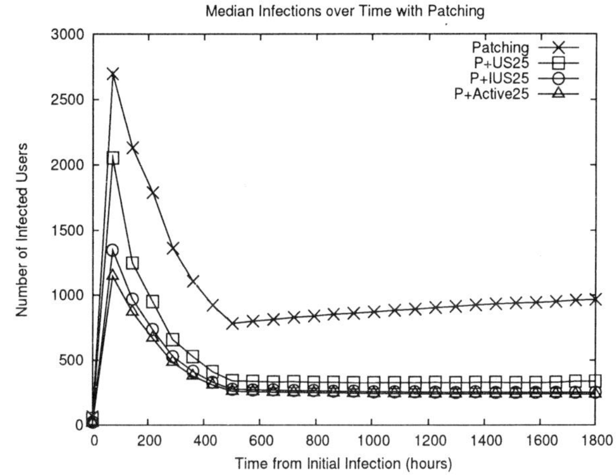

Figure 6. Median infection over time plots for the combination of Proactive Patching and the three defense systems at 25% deployment.

6. Comparison and Analysis

Tables 1, 2, and 3 summarize results for three of our metrics. The two most important results are for the percentage of simulations for which the defense contained the infection to less than 1% of the population and the total number of users infected. With a random 25% deployment, the best solution across all our metrics is the combination of proactive patching plus an active network defense system.

Table 1

Percentage of simulations in which the defense strategy contained the threat to 1%, 25%, and 50% of the total users.

Containment	1%	25%	50%
No Protection	0.02%	0.05%	0.17%
US25	2.56%	4.99%	21.07%
IUS25	19.67%	24.35%	39.07%
Active25	26.68%	31.92%	49.35%
Patching	0.93%	9.36%	20.19%
P + US25	3.54%	16.18%	26.80%
P + IUS25	20.56%	32.21%	56.45%
P + Active25	28.28%	41.47%	96.10%

Table 2

Summaries of the total number of users infected during each type of simulation.

	Max	3rd Qu.	Median	1st Qu.	Min
No Protect.	6541	6538	6506	6282	2
US25	6487	6335	5912	3644	1
IUS25	6295	5380	4292	1736	1
Active25	6034	4430	3353	1	1
Patching	4390	4241	4188	3722	1
P + US25	4263	4106	4016	3094	1
P + IUS25	4099	3528	3202	574	1
P + Active25	3841	2852	2230	1	1

Table 3

Summaries of the number of infected users who remained infected at the end of the simulation.

	Max	3rd Qu.	Median	1st Qu.	Min
US25	4384	2622	2303	1980	0
IUS25	3881	2032	1643	1113	0
Active25	4008	1992	1567	0	0
Patching	1098	989	968	946	0
P + US25	708	385	337	288	0
P + IUS25	589	306	246	165	0
P + Active25	599	298	233	0	0

7. Future Work

It remains to be seen whether results from the Dartmouth traces are applicable to other large wireless networks, such as those at other universities or those from commercial providers such as T-Mobile. More traces must be gathered and analyzed to develop credible mobility models. Alternately, mobility models developed from traces that are not directly available could be used to drive the simulation, instead of actual traces. In addition, as the number of wireless access points increases and devices that use network resources become more ubiquitous, early models of user behavior may become irrelevant. Therefore, work on determining how changing models of user mobility and behavior affect worm propagation should continue.

The results shown here obviously suggest that a higher degree of defense employment than the 25% tested here is needed to really stop spread of this kind of worm. We must perform further experiments to determine the degree of deployment required to stop worms reliably for various forms of defense.

One approach to getting more value from the defense systems is to strategically place them on subnets based on heuristics such as the maximum number of simultaneous users, number of unique users seen, and number of visits. Initial results suggest that a good heuristic can improve defense by over 50% for the same percentage of deployment.

For a given wireless network trace, more work can be done to identify what aspects of user mobility are the greatest contributors to the contact rate parameter of the SI epidemic model, thus yielding a contact rate formula for the network. Another approach might be to look at the "infection potential" of users based on aspects of their mobility or their system configurations, and explore the ways that an attacker could most efficiently achieve a large infection base in the shortest amount of time through releasing the worm at targeted locations or hosts. A larger experiment could be conducted to take random users at random times as the initiators of the infection, allowing multiple infectors. This might provide a stronger guarantee of the effectiveness of the defense systems.

As mentioned earlier, studies of worms that combine different modes of infection depending on circumstances are needed. A simple example is a worm that spreads at high speed to random addresses when it has infected a site with a high speed wired link, but spreads more slowly when connected only to a wireless network. Another example is making use of two entirely different types of wireless connection, such as Bluetooth and 802.11, to spread. Other varying patterns are also possible and worthy of study.

Finally, the simulations run here generated a vast amount of data, only some of which was presented in this paper. Closer examination of this data might well reveal other interesting phenomena, such as the relationship of worm infection rates to real world events.

8. Related Work

After the seminal paper on worm models [3], others have looked at worm modeling. [7] describes their general-purpose simulator for worm propagation. It is unclear whether their model would capably support a wireless environment simulation. [8] uses measurements to show that active worms seem to propagate slightly slower than standard models indicates, but have a very similar, if more limited, overall behavior. [9] discusses the spread of the Slammer worm. They do not provide a model, but show that more damaging worms can similarly propagate quickly throughout the Internet. [10] uses a somewhat different quarantine model to study protection against standard worms in a wired environment.

In addition to Kotz et al, others have analyzed different networks for user mobility and performance, and have made their own trace data available from the Dartmouth trace archive. Tang and Baker have examined several levels of networks, from a single wireless LAN [11] to a seven-week trace of a large metropolitan Ricochet-based network called Metricom with nearly 25,000 users. [12]. Balazinska and Castro analyzed SNMP records from a corporate LAN in [13], and Balachandran, Voelker, Bahl, and Rangan looked at traces recorded at the ACM

SIGCOMM'01 conference [14]. These studies could be used to examine the worm discussed here in other environments.

Inspired by recent worm incidents, a number of parties have examined systems that quarantine and sometimes try to disinfect mobile computers brought into a network behind the normal firewall. The best known is Cisco's Network Admission Control [15]. InfoExpress, ZoneLabs, Sygate, Symantec, Network Associates, and other companies and research groups offer products with functionality of this kind, as well, differing in ways not relevant to this paper [16].

9. Conclusion

The increasing penetration of wireless networks and mobile computing are likely to make these technologies attractive to those who write worms. As shown by previous worms, mobility offers a back door for entry into otherwise protected networks, and wireless networks exacerbate the problem. To understand how to combat this propagation vector, we must first understand the characteristics of worms that use it. This paper is a first step towards such an understanding.

Our results, based on simulations using real trace data gathered at Dartmouth College from wireless networks supporting mobile computers, suggest that a worm using this attack vector would have a characteristic infection curve similar in shape to that of other worms, but would spread much more slowly However, given sufficient time, even a single infected user is highly likely to infect virtually the entire susceptible population.

The combination of users proactively patching their machines plus an active network defense system that prevents infection, disinfects the infected, and patches the unpatched can significantly reduce the reach of the worm we modeled. But with defense deployment limited to 25% of susceptible systems, worms can still frequently achieve high infection rates.

All of these results are based, of course, on a single set of mobility data. More study is required to generalize these results to the wider community, but the initial results are promising. Dartmouth's situation matches many other institutions that are installing widespread wireless networking, and their users are likely to behave in similar ways. Generally, more study is needed on the likely infection rates and patterns of worms using different infection strategies, and on the effects of deploying varying kinds of defenses to stop them.

10. References

[1] D. Moore, C. Shannon, G. M. Voelker, and S. Savage, "Internet Quarantine: Requirements for Containing Self-Propagating Code", *INFOCOM 2003.*

[2] Sun Microsystems, "Sun Strengthens Lead in Worldwide Mobile Data Services with Java," http://www.sun.com/smi/Press /sunflash/2003-10/sunflash.20031014.4.html, October 14, 2003.

[3] S. Staniford, V. Paxson, and N. Weaver, "How to 0wn the Internet in Your Spare Time," *Proceedings of the 11th USENIX Security Symposium,* August 2002.

[4] R. Jain, A. Shivaprasad, X. He, and D. Lelescu, "Towards an Empirical Model of User Mobility and Registration Patterns," poster, *Proceedings of MobiHoc 2004.*

[5] D. Kotz and K. Essien, "Analysis of a Campus-Wide Wireless Network, *Proceedings of MobiCom 2002.*

[6] K. Eustice, L. Kleinrock, S. Markstrum, G. Popek, V. Ramakrishna, P. Reiher, "Securing Wi-Fi Nomads: The Case for Quarantine, Examination, and Decontamination," *Proceedings of the New Security Paradigms Workshop (NSPW) 2003.*

[7] A. Wagner, T. Dubendorfer, B. Plattner, and R. Hiestand, "Experiences with Worm Propagation Simulations," *10th ACM CCS Workshop on Rapid Malcode (WORM '03)*, 2003.

[8] Z. Chen, L. Gao, and K. Kwiat, "Modeling the Spread of Active Worms," *INFOCOM 2003.*

[9] D. Moore, V. Paxson, S. Savage, C. Shannon, S. Staniford, and N. Weaver, "Inside the Slammer Worm," *IEEE Magazine of Security and Privacy,* August 2003.

[10] C. C. Zou, W. Gong, and D. Towsley, "Worm Propagation Modeling and Analysis under Dynamic Quarantine Defense," *10th ACM CCS Workshop on Rapid Malcode (WORM '03),* 2003.

[11] D. Tang and M. Baker, "Analysis of a Local-Area Wireless Network," *Proceedings of MobiCom 2000.*

[12] D. Tang and M. Baker, "Analysis of a Metropolitan-Area Wireless Network," *Proceedings of MobiCom 1999.*

[13] M. Balazinska, P. Castro, "Characterizing Mobility and Network Usage in a Corporate Wireless Local-Area Network," *Proceedings of MobiSys 2003.*

[14] A. Balachandran, G. M. Voelker, P. Bahl, and P. V. Rangan, "Characterizing User Behavior and Network Performance in a Public Wireless LAN," *SIGMETRICS 2002.*

[15] Cisco, "Cisco NAC: The Development of the Self-Defending Network," http://www.cisco.com/warp/public /cc/so/neso/sqso/csdnl_wp.htm.

[16] J. Vijayan, "Extended Enforcement," *Computer World,* May 10, 2004.

Comparative Study between Analytical Models and Packet–Level Worm Simulations *

Monirul I. Sharif[1]
George F. Riley[2]
Wenke Lee[1]

[1]College of Computing
Georgia Institute of Technology
Atlanta, GA 30332-0280
{msharif,wenke}@cc.gatech.edu

[2]School of Electrical and Computer Engineering
Georgia Institute of Technology
Atlanta, GA 30332-0250
riley@ece.gatech.edu

Abstract

The threat of Internet worms has been, and continues to be, one of the most important issues faced by networking researchers and network users. The need for accurate and efficient modeling and analysis methods cannot be understated. Models that accurately reflect the behavior of existing and yet-to-be deployed worms is critical to understanding how to deal with this ongoing threat. Recently developed analytical models, have been used to generate propagation trends that match with historic worm outbreaks. However in this effort, the values used for some of the parameters are different from empirically measured information, such as probe rate per unit of IP address space. Although not found in simpler models, new analytical models are under development that can take into account various network and worm characteristics. But in order to build and test them accurately real world data has been used. In our work, we have focused on packet–level detail in the simulation models, which can take into account realistic network characteristics that include, queuing delay, packet-loss, link delays and also realistic worm characteristics at the expense of additional computational complexity. Using our simulator we show how it can be a useful tool in analyzing and evaluating analytical worm models. We study the worm propagation pattern predicted by one particular analytical model and compare it to our packet–level simulations.

1. Introduction

Internet worms have now become the one of the greatest threats to the Internet community. The outbreak of the *Code Red* worm in 2001[11], was the first global-scale worm attack on the Internet, after the worm approach was first conceived and developed by *Moris* more than a decade ago. The worm, which infected more than 359,000 computers in less than 14 hours, showed how ill–prepared the current Internet infrastructure is to deal with such attacks. Since then there have been an increasing number of incidents of various worm outbreaks that show improving skills and troubling innovations on the part of the worm authors. The *Slammer* worm outbreak in January 2002[10] reached 90% of its susceptible 75,000 hosts in less than 10 minutes. Although there are no exact statistics available, it is estimated that the *Blaster* worm of 2003 reached more than 500,000 hosts in just a few hours. And also in 2004, the *Witty* worm[17] was the first worm ever to introduce a damaging payload that, in addition to continuing to spread to others, also formats portions of the hard drive of infected hosts. Almost all of these autonomous worm outbreaks have caused wide-spread network outages as the tremendous amount of network traffic generated by the worm during propagation hampers legitimate network traffic flow.

Worms are generally defined as malicious programs that are able to spread from an infected host computer to other systems by means of exchanging network packets in an autonomous fashion. The autonomous spreading is achieved by exploiting security vulnerabilities in target systems that enables the worm to execute unauthorized instructions contained in specially formed packets. Unlike *computer viruses*, which can be dealt with by systematic detection and removal techniques, worms only leave a small time window after its initial outbreak to perform defensive measures to effectively stop the spread. Therefore modeling the spreading behavior of these autonomous worms has become essential in order to understand and predict the nature of wide-scale worm outbreak and also develop and validate defensive measures that can be used to mitigate and stop such incidents.

* This work is supported in part by NSF under contract number ANI-0240477, and in part by DARPA under contract number N66002-00-1-8934.

Relying on the global scanning nature of worms and using the gathered propagation data of recent large scale worm outbreaks, several researchers have attempted to identify this trend and to develop analytic models that can explain the nature of worm propagation. The work of Staniford *et al.* [18] described the propagation of Code Red using the classical simple epidemic model of disease spread. By assuming that worms select targets by randomly selecting a host from the pool of susceptible hosts, he suggested that worm propagation in the Internet can be adequately expressed using this model.

Moore *et al* [11], presented a good analysis based on observed data collected during the Code Red outbreak. Their analysis showed that the worm propagation rate slowed down considerably a few hours after the initial outbreak, as a result of human countermeasures (e.g. patching the vulnerability or rebooting the infected systems), as well as a built in shut–off mechanism in the worm itself. Zou *et al* introduced an analytical model called the *Two-Factor worm model* [21, 20], that tries to better match the propagation of Code Red by taking human counter-measures into account. Gao *et al* recently introduced a discrete time analytic model called the *Active Analytical Worm Propagation* or *AAWP* model [2], that also supports patching and rebooting of infected machines. Gao argues that the classical epidemic model and its derivatives use continuous time differential equations which is less realistic. Instead, Gao uses a discrete time model to better represent the actual steps used by the worms to infect others. The Gao model also supports the notion of local preference scanning. Gu *et al.*in the work [8] used a modified version of the AAWP which assumes infected hosts are uniformly distributed in the used *IP* address space.

The primary benefit of the analytical models is computational efficiency, in that the numerical solutions to these models are largely independent of population size (topology size), and can easily predict worm behavior on networks of millions of elements. Furthermore, recent models [12] can incorporate the effects of packet loss and protocol behavior on coarse timescales.

The benefit of packet–level models are ease of implementation, accuracy, and ability to interact with any proposed detection or defensive mechanism, at the cost of potentially lengthy simulation executions. Once the observable behavior of a worm is understood, addition of models for that worm in any existing packet level simulation tool should be a straightforward activity. But because of its inefficiency, doing large–scale simulations in this much detail has been difficult. We have built worm models into *GTNetS* [13] which is a highly scalable packet–level network simulator that supports millions of nodes [7]. By making some careful design changes in the underlying simulation tool to tackle with the malicious, non–standard behavior of worms and the immense number of packets generated during simulation, we have been able to improve simulation performance substantially [16]. Nonetheless, simulation of packet–level detail for the complete Internet is still well beyond the capability of any packet-level simulation tool. Here, we focus on simulations of no more than 256K hosts, and focus the study on comparison of packet–level simulation results with an analytical model on similar sized network. We chose the AAWP worm model for analysis and evaluation here.

The remainder of the paper is organized as follows. In Section 2 we provide some related work and a brief description of the AAWP model. Section 3 describes our worm model of *GTNetS* and its various parameters. In Section 4 we give a basis for evaluation and discuss the evaluation technique between *GTNetS* worm models and analytic models. We provide several experimental results in Section 5 to evaluate and compare analytic worm models and our worm models, and also several interesting experiments that highlight the capabilities of our worm models. Section 6 gives a concluding discussion on this work.

2. Background

In this section we first discuss about previous worm simulation work. Then we give a brief description of the AAWP model which we select as the representative of current analytical worm models for our study.

2.1. Related Work

One of the first significant works on packet–level worm simulations was done by Liljenstam *et al.* [9]. In this work, the *SSFNet* [4, 5] simulator was extended with models of behavior of Internet worms, and used to measure the worm's effect on network dynamics. Their approach was to incorporate a computationally efficient analytic model for the whole network, and use packet–level details for a small section. In this hybrid approach, the packet–level network dynamics do not affect the analytic worm model parameters, and therefore the global spread trend only depends on the analytic part. But this approach has its benefits of being able to simulate very large scale scenarios with packet-level details for a small portion of the network.

In [19], Wagner discusses an efficient simulator for worm propagation implemented in the *Perl* scripting language. In his work, he used models of large groups of nodes for the Internet rather than single hosts to reduce complexity. Simplified models of *UDP* and *TCP* behavior were also incorporated. This enabled very large topologies to be simulated but without packet–level detail. But the lack of realistic network topology and protocol models makes it prone to assumptions of parametric values and adjustments for it to match real worm propagation trends.

The *ns2* [1] simulator has recently been extended to include some models for worm behavior. Their approach is similar to the hybrid approach used by *SSFNet*. Further, *ns2* has no built in mechanism for assigning *IP* addresses to nodes and thus making complex and realistic address scanning models hard to model. The simulation tools also lack scalability for worm simulations as moderate topologies involving a few thousand nodes require a long time to simulate.

Our simulation technique has a different view of modeling worm propagation. Rather than relying on analytical models to estimate the infected hosts in the susceptible population we simulate the worm infection by creating a model of worm activities that follow the activities of real worms, and incorporated these models into our *GTNetS* [13] packet level network simulator, which accurately models the activities and actions of the worms in packet–level detail. This leads to a worm spreading model that takes into account almost all aspects of the network behavior, including queuing delay, link congestion, TCP slow-start and congestion management, and packet losses.

2.2. The AAWP model

The AAWP model [2] is a discrete time continuous state deterministic approximation model to describe the propagation of active worms. In this model, a worm in an infectious machine will simultaneously scan many machines and will not re-infect a machine that is already infected. It assumes a simplified model of infection in which the time taken to scan a host includes the communication time and the time to infect a susceptible target.

Two human countermeasures are taken into account in this model – patching and rebooting. Patching a system removes it from the population of vulnerable machines and as well as the population of infectious machines. Sometimes a user might notice an infected machine is not working properly, and simply reboot it. This temporarily removes the infection but leaves it vulnerable for future infections. To make the rate of patching and rebooting dynamic over time, these effects are computed as a fraction of the total infectious hosts at a given time in this model. Therefore, as the infectious population grows, people become more aware, and as it reduces, the rate of these events happening also reduce.

If N denotes the initial vulnerable population size, m_i the total number of vulnerable systems, (including hosts currently infectious), and n_i the number of infectious machines at time tick i, every time tick n_i is reduced by $(p+d)n_i$, where p is the patching rate and d is the rebooting rate. The vulnerable population m_i is also reduced by pm_i. Assuming the worm scans 2^{32} addresses with a scan rate of s, the number of infectious systems and vulnerable systems at time tick $i+1$ are:

$$n_{i+1} = n_i + (m_i - n_i)[1 - (1 - \frac{1}{2^{32}})^{sn_i}] - (d+p)n_i \quad (1)$$

$$m_i = (1-p)^i N \quad (2)$$

Because of the discrete time nature of this model, care must be taken in selecting the time-step. As we shall see in our experiments, because of the small network size, all vulnerable hosts are infected in a very small time frame. Having a time-step in seconds will give a very coarse plot of the propagation trend. If however we reduce the time-step to fraction of a second, a much cleaner plot can be produced, but the scanrate s has to be appropriately scaled. The time-step should not be smaller than $1/s$, because in that case fractional infected host infected in a fraction of time will contribute to the infection of new hosts, skewing the results of the discrete-time model.

3. Our Worm Simulation Models

In this section, we discuss in details the design of our worm models for *GTNetS*. We modeled the life–cycle of a self–propagating worm by closely following the steps that a worm takes when infecting others. Although there is at present no such universally agreed upon formulation, [6] provides a good in depth description of a typical worm's life–cycle. We have made our initial design as generic as possible, allowing easy extension and customization to account for worm behaviors not yet known.

As mentioned earlier, self–propagating worms exploit a software vulnerability, usually a buffer overflow [3], that is known to exist in software running on a large number of computers connected to the Internet. The vulnerability generally resides in a module that relies on network communication. A worm program executing in an infected host typically selects new hosts, called victims, by randomly generating *IP* addresses or by using other more sophisticated scanning techniques [18]. It then sends specially formed packets addressed to the vulnerable software module in the victims. if the vulnerability does exist, it enables the execution of unauthorized code contained in the packets on the system and the system becomes infected. The worm starts propagating from the newly infected host by finding additional targets and sending out network packets in the same way.

The transport layer protocols of the Internet are basically *TCP* and *UDP*. Due to distinct differences in the protocols, worms based on them have different characteristics and need to be modeled separately. As *UDP* does not require any connection establishment and acknowledgments for sent data, worms based on this protocol can send out packets at the highest possible rate allowed by the first–hop link. *TCP* on the other hand is connection oriented. Therefore *TCP* worms require to separate connections to target hosts to send malicious packets. They mostly use the use the multi-threading capability of host operating system to simultaneously connect to multiple targets.

3.1. Worm Model

In *GTNetS*, every host computer or router is modeled by a class called *Node*. This class provides a model of the abstract behavior of networked systems, and supports multiple *Interfaces* that represent NIC's. These interfaces connect to communications links and support separate *IP* addresses. *GTNetS* provides an *Application* class that models the behavior of a typical application. This class can be attached to a given host node in the network, and can respond to *events* such as packet arrivals, timer events etc. The application model can use any number of transport level protocols for communication. Models of both *UDP* and *TCP* protocols are available in *GTNetS*. Our base worm model is a derivative of this Application class with the generic behavior of worms built into it. Two separate derivatives of this class have been created to model the behavior of *UDP* and *TCP* based worms. Any new worm functionality can be added into the generic worms, by creating derivatives with additional events and properties.

Parameter	Description
Vulnerability	The probability that a host is vulnerable to the worm attack
Length	Length of worm data sent over the Internet
Port	Port of vulnerability
BaseIP	Base *IP* address for target scanning
Scanrange	The range of *IP* addresses to scan.
TargetVector	Target scanning module, (supports Random, LocalPref, Sequential, user defined)
Protocol	The transport layer protocol (actually the specific descendant of worm class is used)
Inf. Packet Rate	Number of infectious data packets sent out per second by each worm (for *UDP*)
Threads	Number of parallel connections (for *TCP*)

Table 1. List of parameters that can be set for the worm model.

In the real world, executable code (or scripts) need to be sent inside network packets destined to some transport layer port to be executed upon receipt by vulnerable machine to make a system infected. As we are interested in propagation dynamics we can simplify this behavior inside a network simulator. Rather than dynamically attaching worm application models to newly infected hosts, we initially attach *inactive* worm application instances to all vulnerable machines in the network. Therefore properties common to the worms are defined as static members in the class, and accessible by all instances. Every instance of class keeps state and activity information about itself and the node it is attached to. At any point in time, each worm is in one of three states: *vulnerable*, *infected* or *removed*. These worm applications listen to specific network ports which we call the *infection port* for packets containing the signature of the worm. The signature may be any sort of text string that separates it from normal traffic packets. Once such a packet is received, if the worm application instance is in a vulnerable state, it activates its worm activities after changing its state to infected. Otherwise the packet is ignored. This approach has the benefit of letting us simulate non–worm applications in the same host as well as multiple worm outbreaks in the same scenario.

The parameters defining worm behavior (including *TCP* and *UDP* variants) are given in table 1. There are several other parameters, mostly related to the network environment, that affect worm propagation as well. These network related parameters are discussed in section 3.2. The *BaseIP*, *Scanrange* and *TargetVector* parameters define how a worm selects its target victims and are discussed in section 3.3. The length parameter is used to define the size of infectious data sent over the network. The protocol is selected by using the appropriate class or deriving from it. The *Infected Packet Rate* is defined for the *UDP* worm. It is the rate in which a single *UDP* worm instance sends out infectious packets. This is not to be confused with the scan rate defined in the analytical models, which refers to the rate in which a worm's infectious packets *reach* target hosts. On the other hand, for *TCP* based worms, a rate similar to the *UDP* worm is meaningless. To infect a host or attempt an infection on a target, a connection handshake needs to be performed, acknowledgment packets need to be received for sent data and connections must be terminated. All of this depends on the latency or RTT of the connection between the hosts. Furthermore, for target *IP*'s that are unused, a *TCP* timeout is required before the source knows that target does not exist. In *GTNetS* the default connection timeout is 6 seconds, but can be any value specified by the user. Further, the presence or absence of *ICMP unreachable* messages, and the operating system type initiating the connection, can have an affect on the actual connection failure rate. We have defined the parameter *threads* which defines the maximum number of parallel connection attempts made by the *TCP* worm. Once a connection is closed or fails, that same thread can be used to make another connection attempt.

3.2. Network Environment

Since we are using our worm models on a detailed packet level simulator, the network topology itself affects the worm propagation. *GTNetS* allows the freedom to setup topologies of arbitrary complexity by creating any number of nodes, and connecting them with links of specified bandwidth and delays. In our topology models, nodes that are at the end of stub networks are considered host computers running application programs (and also vulnerable to worm attack). The other intermediate nodes are considered as routers. A simplified and efficient assumption of routing is used [14, 15] for scalability. As mentioned earlier, several issues relating to efficiently and realistically simulating worms using packet–level simulators were addressed in [16]. Those improvements have allowed us to simulate worm traffic with full packet–level detail of very large networks. Figure 1 shows a 256K host network [1] worm simulation done in packet level detail. The population was infected up to 85% in 1.5 hours and 99% in 3 hours on a single processor workstation.

Parameter	Description
Topology	How nodes are connected in the network. Several stub networks, can be defined connected by a backbone
Bandwidth	The bandwidth of host connecting links, intermediate links and backbone links (can be set separately)
Delay	The link delays, (selectable as with bandwidth)
Address	*IP* address ranges.
Unused *IP*	Percentage of *IP* addresses being used

Table 2. Parameters that are settable to define the network environment for the worm propagation.

We list the parameters that can be changed in the network environment in table 2. In our work, we used a simplified topology generation scheme consisting of a simplified backbone connecting several stub networks generated as *RandomTrees* [16]. A Randomtree stub network topology tries to capture the notion of hierarchical sub–netting of the *IP* address space.

Furthermore, we simulate the effect of unused *IP* address ranges. In the Internet almost 50% of *IPv4* address space is unused. In our network environment, while generating the random trees, portions of subnets are randomly pruned depending on a specified probability. Therefore it is possible to generate, for example, a stub network with /20 address space consisting of only 2K hosts, resulting in a 50% utilization of *IP* addresses. At present work on a more realistic topology to represent the Internet is underway.

3.3. Scanning Strategies

In our simulation environment every host has an assigned *IP* address. Therefore we can introduce any sort of scanning strategy that can be defined in a real worm. There is a user definable *Target Vector* module for each worm that is called to select the next target address. To provide flexibility, we have defined an abstract *WormTargetVector* class that can be derived to define any required scanning strategy. For experimental purposes we have defined the usual uniform random scanning, local preference scanning and sequential scanning. Every worm instance gets an individual scanning module, and therefore can generate random sequences that are independent. Complicated strategies like permutation scanning, hit–list scanning can created easily. It is also possible to add the facility of excluding specific ranges of addresses, such as the well–known non-routable addresses.

The *BaseIP* and *Scanrange* worm parameters select the range in which the target vector will return an *IP* address. Although Internet worms can potentially scan a 2^{32} address range, we can define it to have a smaller range, thereby leading to a realistic hit probability factor in scaled down networks.

The local preference scanning supports any number of local preferences. For a worm having address a, a scan–range s and k choices of local preference, we can define tuples (p_i, s_i), for i=1, 2, ..., k, where p_i is the probability of selecting s_i as the scanrange. Therefore a target is generated from the complete scanrange with probability $(1 - \sum p_i)$ or in the range s_i with probability p_i.

3.4. Human Counter-measures

As in the case of the analytical worm models, we assume a single patching factor p and reboot factor d. We assumed the rate in which the patching and rebooting is proportional to the number of infectious hosts at any given time. Therefore if the number of infectious hosts and vulnerable hosts at time t is $I(t)$ and $V(t)$ respectively, by the time $t+1$, $pI(t)$ vulnerable hosts will be patched and $dI(t)$ infectious hosts will be rebooted. This means that some non-infectious vulnerable machines will also get patched. Unlike the *AAWP* model, our patching rate is directly proportional to the infectious population.

To simulate this effect, we calculate at regular intervals the probability that a single infectious host is being patched ($P_p(t)$) or rebooted ($P_r(t)$). Then we traverse the list of hosts and use two independent uniform random variables to decide if a host should be patched or rebooted.

$$P_p(t) = \frac{pI(t)}{V(t)} \tag{3}$$

$$P_r(t) = \frac{dI(t)}{I(t)} = d \tag{4}$$

Once a vulnerable machine is patched, it is no longer activated by incoming worm packets. A patched infected machine becomes inactive right away and becomes invulnera-

1 This is the number of end–hosts only, the actual number of nodes including intermediate nodes in the network is somewhat higher

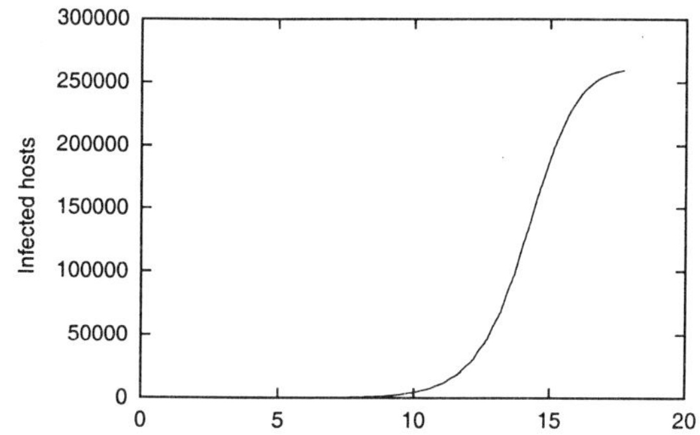

(a) 256K GTNetS UDP worm simulation

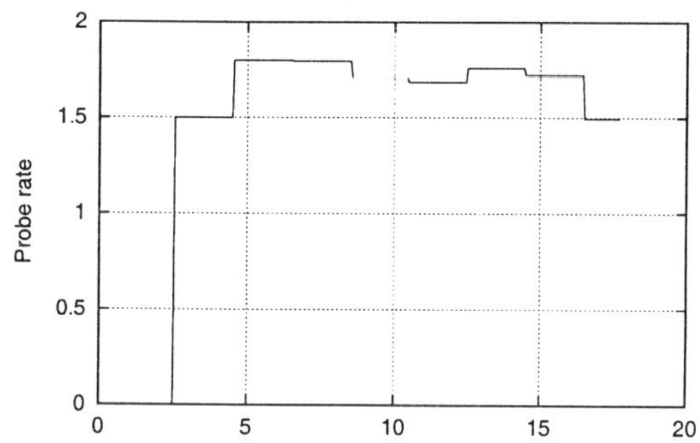

(b) Globally observed avg. probe rate for the 256K host sim

Figure 1. Initial UDP worm experiment in GTNetS.

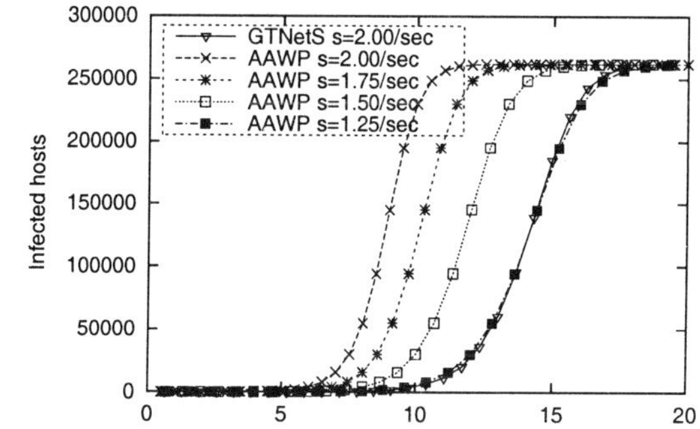

(a) GTNetS and AAWP models using different scan rates

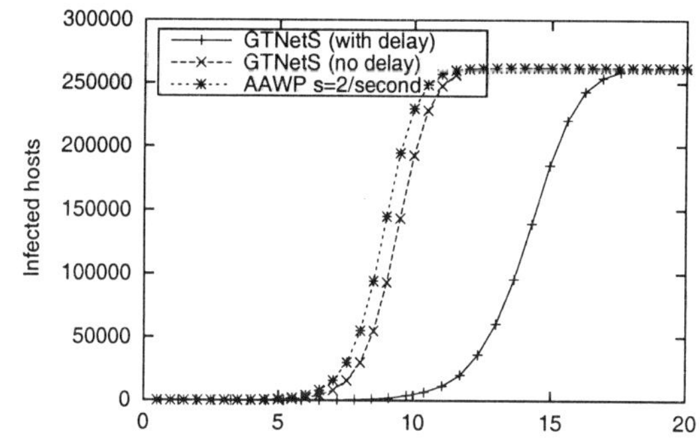

(b) GTNetS 256K host simulation removing link delays

Figure 2. Comparison between GTNetS worm model and AAWP.

ble. A rebooted infected machine, assumes vulnerable state and can be infected again.

4. Comparing Our Simulation Models with Analytical Models

To provide a comparative study of the AAWP model and our packet–level simulation models, we need to provide both models with similar parameters. The biggest problem in this case is that the AAWP model has simplified parameters that abstracts or acts as a combination of several other parameters. For example, the *scan rate* parameter in the AAWP model which specifies the number of infection attempts done by the worm per unit time, has no counterpart in our simulation. Since we assume that network propagation delays and loss for the packets exist, this parameter is hard to specify in terms of the behavior of each infected host, but it can be observed as the simulation progresses. The transport protocol used by the worm, the size of the worm payload, the bandwidth and propagation delay on the links being used and the network topology all contribute to the observed scan rate used in the AAWP model.

In order to compare the these models, we define an observed metric in our simulation environment called the *probe rate*. This is the observed average infection attempts done by the worm per unit time. We give this name so that it is not confused with our *UDP* worm model's scan rate parameter discussed previously. Now we can calculate the observed probe rate from a particular worm scenario from our simulation and use it to plot a corresponding AAWP model propagation trend. In an ideal case, if no other parameters affect the AAWP model and the *scan rate* is a representative of all worm and network parameters, the plots should be identical. In order to do this effectively the method in which the *probe rate* is observed has to be reliable. For the Internet, large corporations use big address spaces to observe incoming data to the network and predict several, worm characteristics based on them. For example the Code Red data gathered by CAIDA, was done by one /16 and two /8 network address spaces [11]. Although there is a question of the effectiveness of the size of address space to gather data, in [2] the authors suggest that a /8 network is sufficient to characterize the spread of an active worms. As our simulation environment provides access to all nodes and all data in the simulation environment, we can have the advantage of calculating this parameter globally, which should give a more accurate value for comparison. To calculate globally observed average *probe rate*, we can measure the number of scan attempts to targets done by every unique infectious host in a specific interval and perform the average. In the beginning phase of the simulation, the number of infectious hosts can be small, but as time proceeds the growing number of infectious hosts should cause the average to be a better representation of the global average scan rate for the worm outbreak. The *UDP* worms' scan attempts are counted every time an infectious packet reaches a destination host. The packet's source *IP*address is looked up to increase the necessary count value. For *TCP* worms, a scan count is increased when all the data are successfully sent to the target host (for unused *IP* addresses, it is increased when a SYN packet arrives).

As stated in [11], the observed scan rate/probe rate for the Code Red worm was almost 11/second at some instance. The AAWP model was matched with the worm infection trend by using a scan rate of 2/second [2]. This discrepancy raises the question why such mismatch exists and to what extent. We have tried to answer this question by performing comparative experiments given in section 5.

5. Experiments

In the first experiments we use our simulation and the AAWP model with similar parameters and compare results. Then we show using our model how link delays affect worm propagation and the observed *scan rate* parameter. We comment on how much effective an observation can be due to network parameters. We then show how bandwidth dynamically changes worm propagation and discuss why AAWP cannot express the effect. We have attempted to provide a more realistic evaluation of local scanning strategy with the help of our realistic network environment. Finally we provide experimental results to show how our worm model can deal with various worm parameters and transport protocol effects.

We first attempt to compare our worm simulation model with the AAWP model. For this purpose we use the method described in section 4. We initially simulate a worm propagation in *GTNetS* and observe the global average probe rate for use in the AAWP model. We choose a 256K host network for this purpose where all *IP* addresses are used and all systems are vulnerable. Utilizing all *IP* addresses eases the scan counting which otherwise would require router elements to count packets destined for unused addresses that would get dropped somewhere in the middle of the network.

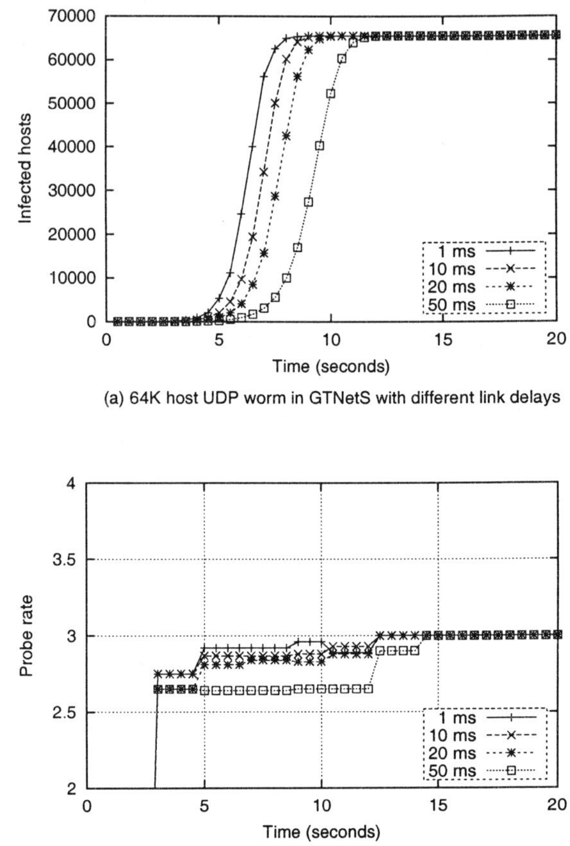

(a) 64K host UDP worm in GTNetS with different link delays

(b) Globally observed average probe rate

Figure 3. The effect of link delays on observable scan rate.

We use a normal link latency of 50ms for non backbone links and 20ms for backbone ones. The network bandwidth is set to an extremely large value so that we do not have to deal with the affects of link saturation. We also keep the patching and reboot rate 0, so as not to interfere with the results. The observed scan rate measurement was initiated at 0.5 seconds, with a sampling interval of 2 seconds. We released a *UDP* worm with a infectious packet rate of 2/second into the network and observed the results. The worm was kept a small size of less than 400 bytes and the scanning range was the entire /14 address space of the network or 2^{18} addresses.

Figure 1(a) shows the results of the experiment. The single worm propagation curve shows the number of infected (same as infectious in this case) hosts over time. Our simulation shows that the entire host population is infected in almost 18 seconds. From this experiment we also gather the measured probe rate over the whole simulation time. The re-

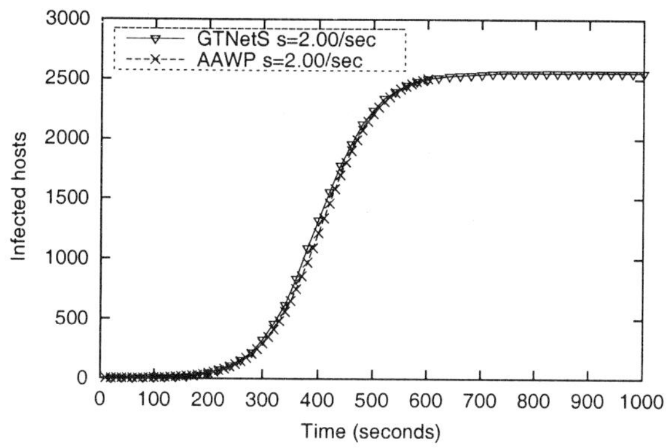

GTNetS and AAWP models using 1% vulnerable hosts

Figure 4. An experiment for link delays with 1% vulnerable hosts.

sults are shown in figure 1(b). It is interesting to see that the measured probe rate varies over time starting and ending around 1.5/second with a peak of 1.75/second. First of all the measured scan rate is less than the 2/second infectious packet rate of the worm. This makes sense since the infectious packets coming out at a constant rate need to propagate the network to reach their specific targets. The targets might be scattered at different locations in the network. There will be a delay of some amount before hosts get infected and they start sending out packets.

To compare the results with the AAWP model, we first change the formula to incorporate a scanning space of 2^{18} rather than 2^{32}. We then do three separate runs with three values of the *scan rate*, *s* with 1.5/second, 1.75/second and 2/second. The results are given in figure 2(a) along with our result. The results show that in the AAWP model, the worm propagates much faster. Even with the scan rate of 1.5/second all hosts are infected in less than 15 seconds where our model requires 18 seconds. To match the results of AAWP with our simulation results we needed to put a scan rate of 1.25/second. This means that in our simulation even though observed scan rate was between 1.5/second to 1.75/second, the AAWP model required a smaller value of 1.25/second to match the propagation trend. This discrepancy can be compared with the 2/second scan rate used in the AAWP model of the CodeRed worm to match the actually measured 11/second scan rate.

5.1. Comparison Experiment

To find the reason behind this difference between the observed scan rate and used scan rate, we first looked into the reason behind the varying and low observed probe rate. As we conjectured, the the propagation delays in the network might be the reason, we set the link delays in all links inside the 256K host network to 1ms. We then reran the simulation and obtained results are shown in figure 2(d). By al-

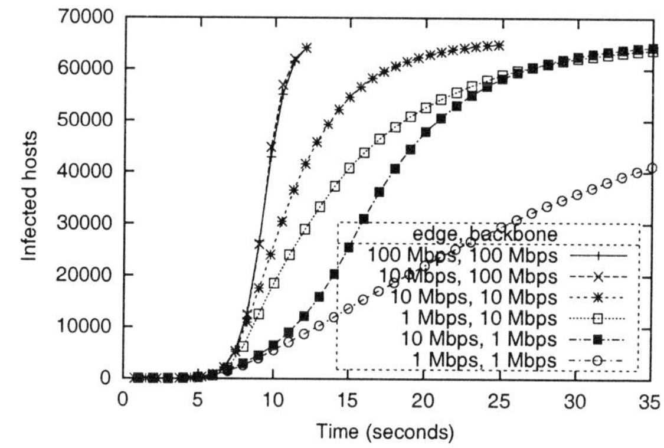

(a) Network bandwidth effect on UDP worm propagation

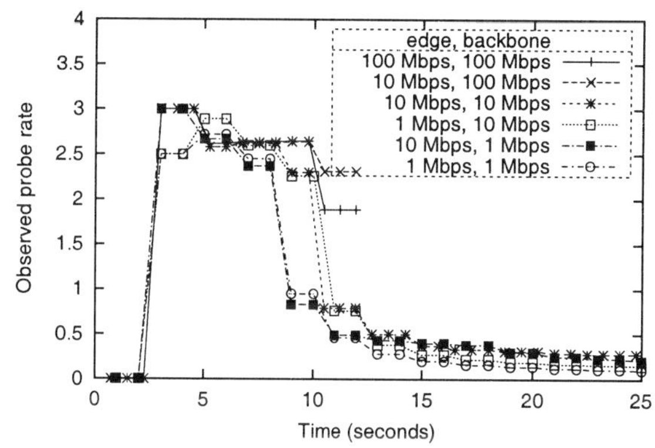

(b) Observed probe rate for the bandwidth experiment

Figure 5. The effect of link bandwidth on *UDP* worm propagation in a 64K host network

most removing the link delays the worm propagated faster and this time it requires 12 seconds to infect almost all the hosts. This is result almost matches with the 2/second scan rate AAWP model result. This slight mismatch can be attributed to the effect of transmission delay, which we cannot remove from our simulation environment.

For showing the effect of link delays on worm propagation more clearly, we conducted an experiment on a 64K host network with various link delays in *GTNetS*. We used a *UDP* worm with a infectious packet rate of 3/second. We used delay values of 1ms, 10ms, 20ms and 50ms. The delay parameters were set for all links in the network.

Figure 3(a) shows the propagation trends the different link delays in the network. It can be seen that, the lower the link delays the faster the worm propagated through the network. The worm with 50ms link delay spread 50% slower than the one with almost no delays. Figure 3(b) shows the observed probe rate for all the runs with different link de-

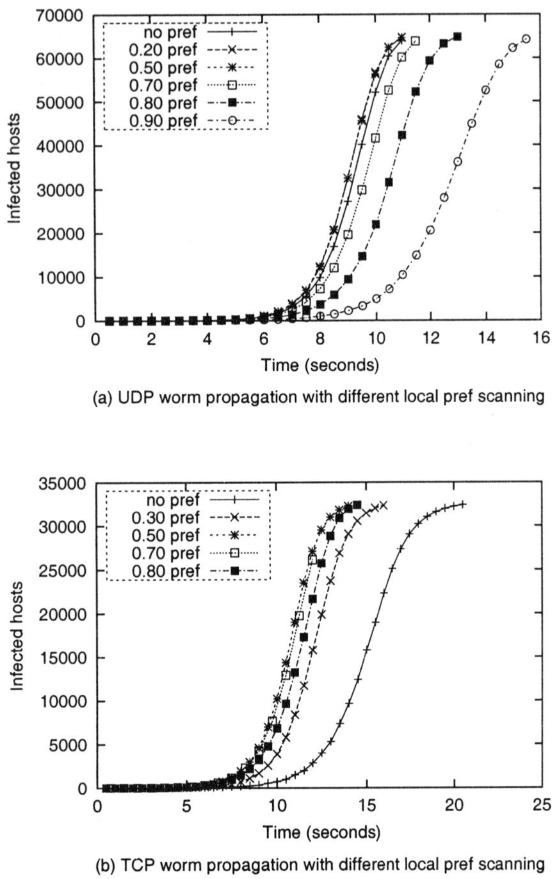

(a) UDP worm propagation with different local pref scanning

(b) TCP worm propagation with different local pref scanning

Figure 6. The effect of local preference scanning on *UDP* and *TCP* based worms

lay values. It must be noted that the maximum theoretical scan rate should be 3/second, as that is the rate in which the infectious packets are being sent out.

The lower link delay experiments showed an observed probe rate that increased faster and reached the theoretical highest of 3/second earlier. less the delay the more closer its final value was to the rate of 3/second. This also shows that worm propagation would get faster as delays are decreased, and the values would go closer to the theoretical maximum. It must be noted that we performed the experiment long enough to show that the probe rate does reach 3/second at some point. This is because the link delay causes a skew every time a new host is infected. But the longer the infected host keeps infecting other nodes, the closer the rate of infection reaches the rate in which packets are sent out. But during the initial phase of worm outbreak and as long as there are uninfected vulnerable hosts left, the delays should have some effect. It must also be noted, that keeping all hosts vulnerable causes the skew of time due to link delays happens for every infection attempt.

The prior experiments used vulnerability probability of 1.0, meaning every host is susceptible to worm attacks. Historical worms have in fact been able to infect only a much smaller fraction of Internet hosts, although there is no guarantee that future worms will have similar limitations. To make a more realistic scenario, we conducted an experiment with 256K scan address space, but with only 1% hosts being vulnerable which is more in line with prior worm outbreaks. We use a scan rate of 2/second in the simulation, and also generate results using the AAWP model with s=2.0, and scan rate and $m = 2560$. In figure 4, we show the results of both the simulation and the analytical model. Interestingly both give almost exact results. The AAWP model does not seem to be affected by the link delays as before. Clearly, the AAWP analytical model (and presumably other similar models) can give very accurate results in this case.

Therefore we can say that the AAWP model provides an upper bound on the speed of propagation of a worm with a specific scan rate s. This upper bound can be reached when all network latencies are ignored. We have seen, that in cases where the scanned target address space is much larger than the vulnerable population, as is with almost all worm outbreaks to date, the analytical model does provide reasonable accurate results for *UDP* worm models. Due to the inherent lack of the AAWP model to account for network delays, care must be taken in using it for cases with higher vulnerability ratio and faster propagation rates.

5.2. Effects of Network Bandwidth

In order to find the effect of network bandwidth on worm propagation we ran a *UDP* worm in a 64K host network with various network bandwidth settings. The backbone links had a delay of 20ms and 50ms for all other links. As we fixed the scan range of the worm to the entire host address space. The length of the worm was fixed at 1000 bytes. Figure 5(a) shows the worm propagation trends for these experiments and figure 5(b) shows the measured scan rate. Initially we performed a run with 100 Mbps bandwidth on all links. For such a small network this bandwidth is hard to saturate. The worm propagation showed a natural trend. After reducing the bandwidth of all links except for the backbone to 10 Mbps the results did not vary much. When we set all link bandwidths to 10Mbps the worm propagation was different. After the initial exponential rise, the super–linear growth had a reducing rate which created a long tail. It took almost double time to infect 90% of the population. The probe rate also showed a drop after 6 seconds. We can attribute this effect to saturation of the bandwidth of the backbone links in the network. The loss of worm packets reduced the rate in which hosts were getting infected. Further reduction of bandwidth to 1 Mbps showed a more slower propagation. When all links were set to 1 Mbps the bandwidth was so low that the worm showed an almost lin-

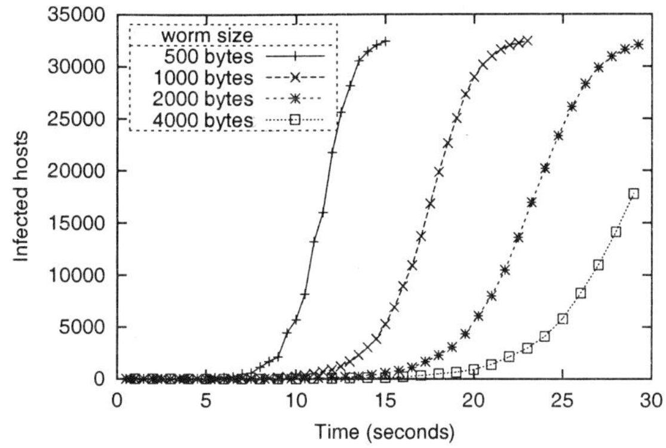

(a) The effect of payload size on TCP worm propagation

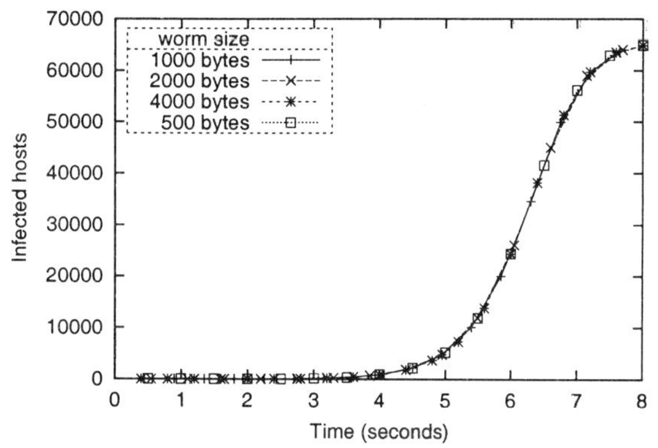

(b) The effect of payload size on UDP worm propagation

Figure 7. Larger payload shows negative impact on *TCP* worms, but *UDP* worms are unaffected

ear growth in infected population. The observed scan rates in figure 5(b) show how they drastically reduce when network bandwidth start to saturate. The AAWP model does not support the variation of the scanrate parameter. Therefore the long tails due to bandwidth saturation cannot be expressed by the model.

5.3. Evaluation of Local Preference Scanning

To test the effects of local preference scanning we take both *UDP* and *TCP* based worms into account. The LAAWP model suggests that local preference scanning does not improve worm propagation, and in some cases might worsen it. We set up a 64K host network and a 32K host network with almost infinite bandwidth for the *UDP* and *TCP* worms respectively. The results in figure 6(a) show the effect of local preference scanning on *UDP* based worms. The experiment was conducted in a 64K host network with all nodes susceptible. We set the worm to select targets within the same /28 network with probability p. From the results it can be seen that for *UDP* worms, local preference above 0.5 does actually reduce worm spread, the worst being for $p = 0.9$. This is the case because the worm spends more time, trying to infect local addresses, which after sometime might already be infected. Preference of $p = 0.2$ improves performance slightly. On the other hand for *TCP* based worm experiment, local preference scanning let the worm propagate faster for any value of p as shown in figure 6(b). The reason for such improvement can be related to the delay of communication between hosts on closer networks being less than that of farther ones. As *TCPś* connection oriented nature makes it RTT dependent, trying to infect hosts that require less delay improves worm propagation.

This definitely agrees with the intuition used by worm writers to use local scanning in their worms in order to try to propagate faster. It is interesting to see the result that such effort with a *UDP* worm will not prove fruitful, whereas for a *TCP* worm it seems that it will propagate faster and infect more hosts in less time.

5.4. Worm Characteristics

Another worm parameter might be its size. The AAWP has no parameter to directly account for varying size in worm payload, although payload size is a contributing factor to the scan rate parameter. But the modeling of *TCP* based worms raises a question on how much time it would take to infect another host if *TCP* is used. Large worms might require several RTT's to complete the transfer of the worm payload. Even congestion control of *TCP* might have an effect too. We therefore do an experiment using *TCP* based worms with different sizes in a 32K host network. Figure 7(a) shows that larger size of payload slows down worm propagation considerably. But as *UDP* worms are not dependent on RTT's of the network, the payload size should not have any significant effect on propagation. Figure 7(b) shows supporting results for this claim. The worm propagation is similar for all payload sizes. It must be noted that the bandwidth in this experiment was kept high so that packets would not get dropped. In the real world scenario larger *UDP* worms might cause more traffic and more packet loss. Higher packet loss might slow down the propagation of the worm due to *UDP*'s unreliable nature.

6. Conclusion

Our simulation models for Internet worms show that packet-level details provide us with many insights into a worm's propagation nature. We have shown how a realistic network model and a worm model can let us validate analytic models and to predict how they would perform for various cases. However, we also conclude that the AAWP model, and presumably other similar analytical models, shows a high degree of agreement with our simulation model in some cases, which gives us increased confidence in both models. In particular, for scenarios with relatively small infection probability and those that use UDP as the worm transport protocol, the analytic models give accurate results with substantial computation advantage over packet–level models.

It is clear that both analytical models and packet–level models can be used to study worm behavior, effects of varying network conditions, and potential defensive mechanisms. Packet–level models, built on top of a well designed and efficient network simulation tool can easily model worm infections of up to 256k hosts. Any alarm or defense that can be implemented on actual network hardware can easily be modeled in simulations that correctly model network router and host actions at packet–level detail. Analytical models are much more computationally efficient, and when used in conjunction with more abstract models of network behavior can also be used to measure and predict worm behavior, assuming that derived metrics (such as worm scan rate) can be accurately determined.

References

[1] Network Simulator 2. http://www.isi.edu/nsnam/ns.

[2] Z. Chen, L. Gao, and K. Kwiat. Modeling the spread of active worms. In *Proceedings of INFOCOM '2003*. IEEE Computer Society, 2003.

[3] C. Cowan, F. Wagle, C. Pu, S. Beattie, and J. Walpole. Buffer overflows: attacks and defenses for the vulnerability of the decade. In *DARPA Information Survivability Conference and Exposition 2000*, Jan 2000.

[4] J. Cowie, H. Liu, D. Nicol, and A. Ogielski. Towards Realistic Million-node Internet Simulations. In *Proceedings of International Conference on Parallel and Distributed Processing Techniques and Applications*, Jun 1999.

[5] J. H. Cowie, D. M. Nicol, and A. T. Ogielski. Modeling the Global Internet. In *Computing in Science and Engineering*, Jan 1999.

[6] D. Ellis. Worm anatomy and model. In *Proceedings of the 2003 ACM workshop on rapid malcode*, Oct 2003.

[7] R. Fujimoto, G. Riley, K. Perumalla, A. Park, H. Wu, and M. Ammar. Large–scale network simulation: How big? how fast? In *Proceedings of Eleventh International Symposium on Modeling, Analysis and Simulation of Computer and Telecommunication Systems*, Oct 2003.

[8] G. Gu, M. Sharif, X. Qin, D. Dagon, W. Lee, and G. Riley. Worm detection, early response and response based on local victim information. In *20th Annual Computer Security Applications Conference*, Dec 2004.

[9] M. Liljenstam, D. Nicol, V. Berk, and R. Gray. Simulating realistic network worm traffic for worm warning system design and testing. In *Proceedings of the 2003 ACM workshop on rapid malcode*, Oct 2003.

[10] D. Moore, V. Paxon, S. Savage, C. Shannon, S. Staniford, and N. Weaver. Inside the slammer worm. *IEEE Security and Privacy Magazine*, 1(4), July 2003.

[11] D. Moore, C. Shannon, and K. Claffy. Code–Red: a case study on the spread and victims of an Internet worm. In *Proceedings of the second ACM workshop on Internet Measurement*, Nov 2002.

[12] D. M. Nicol and G. Yan. Simulation of Network Traffic at Coarse Time-scale. In *Proceedings of 19th Workshop on Principles of Advanced and Distributed Simulation*, Jun 2005.

[13] G. F. Riley. The Georgia Tech Network Simulator. In *Proceedings of the ACM SIGCOMM workshop on Models, methods and tools for reproducible network research*, 2003.

[14] G. F. Riley, M. H. Ammar, and R. M. Fujimoto. Stateless Routing in Network Simulations. In *Proceedings of the Eighth International Symposium on Modeling, Analysis, and Simulation of Computer and Telecommunication Systems*, Aug 2000.

[15] G. F. Riley, M. H. Ammar, and E. W. Zegura. Efficient Routing Using NIx-Vectors. In *2001 IEEE Workshop on Hgh Performance Switching and Routing*, May 2001.

[16] G. F. Riley, M. Sharif, and W. Lee. Simulating internet worms. In *Proceedings of 12th Annual Meeting of IEEE/ACM International Symposium on Modeling, Analysis and Simulation of Computer and Telecommunication Systems*, Oct 2004.

[17] C. Shannon and D. Moore. The spread of the witty worm. *IEEE Security and Privacy Magazine*, July 2004.

[18] S. Staniford, V. Paxon, and N. Weaver. How to own the Internet in your spare time. In *Proceedings of the 11th Usenix Security Symposium*, August 2002.

[19] A. Wagner, T. Dubendorfer, B. Plattner, and R. Hiestand. Experiences with worm propagation simulations. In *Proceedings of the 2003 ACM workshop on rapid malcode*, Oct 2003.

[20] C. Zou, L. Gao, W. Gong, and D. Towsley. Information warfare: Monitoring and early warning for Internet worms. In *Proceedings of the 10th ACM conference on Computer and communication security*, Oct 2003.

[21] C. Zou, W. Gong, and D. Towsley. Code red worm propagation modeling and analysis. In *Proceedings of the 9th ACM Conference on Computer and Communications Security*, Nov 2002.

Performance Prediction and Real-Time

Performance benchmark of a parallel and distributed network simulator

Samson Lee, John Leaney, Tim O'Neill, Mark Hunter
Institute for Information and Communication Technologies, University of Technology, Sydney
PO Box 123, Broadway NSW 2007, Australia
{samlee,jrleaney,toneill}@eng.uts.edu.au, mark.hunter@alcatel.com.au

Abstract

Simulation of large-scale networks requires enormous amounts of memory and processing time. One way of speeding up these simulations is to distribute the model over a number of connected workstations. However, this introduces inefficiencies caused by the need for synchronization and message passing between machines. In distributed network simulation, one of the factors affecting message passing overhead is the amount of cross-traffic between machines. We perform an independent benchmark of the Parallel/Distributed Network Simulator (PDNS) based on experimental results processed at the Australian Centre for Advanced Computing and Communications (AC3) supercomputing cluster. We measure the effect of cross-traffic on wall-clock time needed to complete a simulation for a set of basic network topologies by comparing the result with the wall-clock time needed on a single processor. Our results show that although efficiency is reduced with large amounts of cross-traffic, speedup can still be achieved with PDNS. With these results, we developed a performance model that can be used as a guideline for designing future simulations.

1. Introduction

Simulation of telecommunications networks allows researchers to investigate and reason about the qualities of a new or proposed system without the high cost and risk of disruption associated with experimenting on the real system. By carefully analyzing the hypothetical system, problems can be avoided when the real system is built. In the UTS-Alcatel Management of Enriched Experience Networks (MEEN) project, simulation is seen as a critical component in the verification, validation and demonstration of the proposed network management system. However, the scale of the new-generation Enriched Experience Network (EEN) [1] makes detailed packet-level simulation difficult because of the enormous amounts of memory and processing time needed.

Given the need to speed up network simulations so that larger and more complex networks can be represented, Liu, et al. [2] described three categories of methodologies for speeding up network simulation: *simulation technology*; *simulation model abstraction*; and *computational power*.

In the simulation technology category, more efficient algorithms for implementing the event-list manipulation such as the calendar queue [3] (used in ns-2) instead of the basic linked-list can speed up simulation. In the simulation model abstraction category, simplifying the model attempts to improves efficiency such as by representing traffic as fluid-flows [2, 4] instead of individual packets. The third approach to speeding up simulations is to use more resources such as faster machines or by distributing the model over a number of connected machines [5].

The focus of this paper is in the third category. In parallel distributed network simulation, multiple processors are used simultaneously for executing a single simulation. However, the absence of a global clock introduces the need for synchronization algorithms to ensure that cause-and-effect relationships are correctly produced by the simulator. Two methods to ensure correct temporal order of the asynchronous event execution are: *conservative* and *optimistic* methods. The conservative approach [6] strictly imposes the correct temporal order of events. The optimistic approach [7] uses a detection and recovery mechanism: whenever the incorrect temporal order of events is detected, a rollback mechanism or Time Warp is invoked to recover.

In the conservative approach one instance of the simulator can only process an event when it has a guarantee no other event containing a smaller time-stamp may arrive at some later time. An inefficiency of this approach called *message passing overhead* is due to the delay incurred by serializing event data (sometimes

1087-4097/05 $20.00 © 2005 IEEE

called marshalling), transferring the serialized event to the remote processor, and rebuilding the event from the serialized data (sometimes called un-marshalling) [8]. In general, simulations where much of the traffic crosses the boundary of a simulator instance is more susceptible to message passing overhead. In view of that, our objective is to measure the effect of *cross-traffic* on wall-clock execution time to complete a simulation.

Our main contribution is an independent benchmark of the conservative Parallel/Distributed Network Simulator (PDNS) developed at Georgia Institute of Technology based on experimental results processed at the Australian Centre for Advanced Computing and Communications (AC3) cluster. We measure the effect of cross-traffic and interaction on wall-clock time needed to complete a two processor simulation for a set of basic network topologies by comparing the result with the wall-clock time needed on a single processor.

This work is part of a UTS-Alcatel research group that seeks to understand and manage large-scale complex networks, where large scale means millions of entities and users. Firstly, we are investigating the efficacy of Policy-Based Network Management (PBNM) to reduce the complexity of the management task, augmented by advanced simulation to predict effects. Secondly, we are exploring the needs, wants and expectations of users to better understand and accommodate them, under the banner of Quality of Experience (QoE). Thirdly, we are modeling, developing and visualizing the evolving system using the approach of Architecture-based Engineering to ensure the realization of a system design which will achieve its functional and non-functional qualities.

The remainder of this paper is organized in five sections. In Section 2, we provide an overview of the parallel and distributed simulator. In Section 3, we describe the design of the experiments conducted for this paper. In Section 4, we give details of the individual experiments. In Section 5, the results of the experiments are analyzed and discussed. Finally in Section 6, are our conclusions and future work. Additional related work is described in Section 7.

2. Parallel/Distributed Network Simulator

The PADS research group at Georgia Tech [9] has developed extensions and enhancements to the popular ns-2 [10] simulator to allow a network simulation to be run in a parallel and distributed fashion, on a network of workstations. We chose PDNS instead of alternatives, such as GTNetS [11] and DaSSF [12] among others because of the familiarity, availability and wide-spread use of ns-2 models. For the purposes of this work, we will not be examining the other parallel discrete event network simulators.

PDNS uses a federated simulation approach where separate instantiations of ns-2 modeling different subnetworks execute on different processors. PDNS uses a conservative approach to synchronization. No federate in the parallel simulation will ever process an event that would later have to be undone due to receiving messages in the simulated past.

PDNS uses a new scheduler called RTI instead of the default calendar scheduler in ns-2. The RTI scheduler uses the time management functions of the libSynk/RTIKIT libraries [13, 14] for synchronization.

3. Experimental design

The experiments presented in this paper have been conducted as part of an experimental design life-cycle. Previously, pre-structural experiments have been performed, which has contributed to our evolution in understanding the problem. For a detailed discussion of the experimental design life-cycle, see our previous paper [1].

For all experiments, we have simplified the choice of network topology, traffic characteristics, and transport protocols. They represent abstractions of the access and core of any telecommunications network, and are not meant to be complete or accurate representations of a real EEN. These baseline experiments could serve as a reference when designing more realistic simulations. Although not as realistic, our topologies provide more control over the ratio of cross-traffic compared to the commonly used benchmark specification developed by the research group at Dartmouth College [15].

All simulation experiments were processed on resources at the Australian Centre for Advanced Computing and Communications (AC3) [16]. We used Barossa, which is a Linux Beowulf cluster with 155 dual 3GHz Pentium 4 nodes (152 compute nodes), each with 2GB RAM. It is located within the Australian Technology Park in Redfern, Sydney.

There were a number of environmental factors that needed to be considered to control error in our experiments. Since the processor, disk and memory resources can be shared between users simultaneously, care was taken to minimize the effect due to this.

Barossa uses the Portable Batch System (PBS), which is a batch scheduling system that allocates requested resources to jobs submitted in a queue. It is possible that PBS allocates one processor in a compute node where the other processor is in use by another user. To ensure that exclusive use of that node could be obtained, it was necessary to request both processors of a compute node even though only one processor was used (i.e. the two processor experiments were conducted using one processor on each of two computers).

The home directory of Barossa is shared among all nodes, meaning that there is a higher potential for disk access delays when the fileserver is busy. Although our experiments did not require extensive reading or writing, initial experiments had occasional standard output messages used for debugging and monitoring time/memory during a simulation. Even for such trivial operations, there were intermittent delays of up to 15 seconds. To ensure this did not affect our final results, these messages were turned off, and all files were written to the scratch space on the compute node's local hard drive during a simulation and subsequently copied to the home directory.

The focus of this work is the effect of cross-traffic on simulation wall-clock execution time, and not on simulation memory usage. However, we also monitored memory usage for all the experiments to ensure that there was sufficient physical memory available so that simulation wall-clock execution time would not be affected by virtual memory "disk thrashing".

4. Details of experiments

The experiments were conducting using PDNS version 2.27-v1a with libSynk dated 15 July 2004. For consistency, the same RTI scheduler was used for both one and two processor simulations, with message compression enabled. Scheduler look ahead was 10ms for two processor simulations, and 999999 for one processor simulations. Additionally, we disabled all unnecessary packet headers and used nix-vector routing to optimize memory usage and execution speed.

We studied the effect of cross-traffic on wall-clock execution time for a set of basic network models. First is the dumbbell topology, and the second is an extension of the dumbbell topology. TCP traffic generators were used in both models and a number of parameters including wall-clock time to complete a simulation were observed and sampled. These are described in the following subsections.

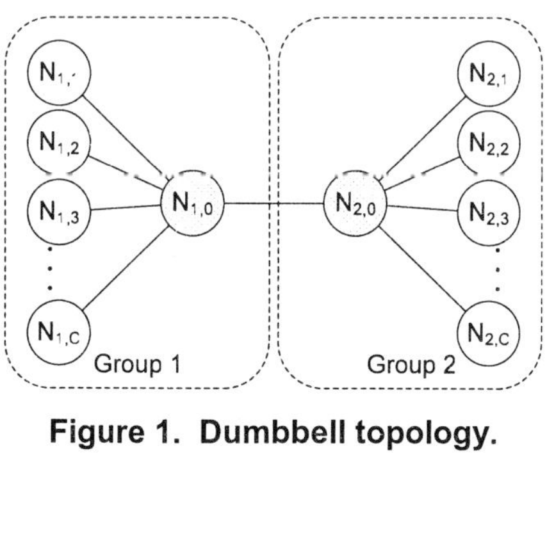

Figure 1. Dumbbell topology.

4.1. Dumbbell topology

The network model that we examined first is the familiar dumbbell topology that is frequently used in network research studies. Our dumbbell topology has C leaf nodes that are connected to routers $N_{1,0}$ and $N_{2,0}$ on both ends of a shared link. Each of the leaf nodes are connected to the corresponding router with 512 Kbps full-duplex links with an arbitrary 5 ms delay. The shared link has an over-provisioned full-duplex bandwidth of $C \times 512$ Kbps to minimise the effect of congestion on wall-clock execution time, and has an arbitrary delay of 10 ms. There is a total of $2C + 2$ nodes in this network model. For the purposes of these experiments, one end of the dumbbell is labelled Group 1, and the other end is labelled Group 2, as depicted in Figure 1. Each group can be distributed onto two separate processors, or they can be combined and simulated on one processor.

Each leaf node is a source of traffic, and there are C sources in each group. Since the objective of this work is to study the effect of cross-traffic on wall-clock execution time, we define two types of traffic connections. Remote connections are source-destination pairs where the source $N_{1,r}$ or $N_{2,r}$ is in one group and the corresponding destination $N_{2,r}$ or $N_{1,r}$ is in the other group. There are R remote connections in each group. Local connections are source-destination pairs where the source $N_{1,l}$ or $N_{2,l}$ and destination $N_{1,l+1}$ or $N_{2,l+1}$ are neighbours in the same group. The last local source $N_{1,C}$ or $N_{2,C}$ in each group connects to the first local source $N_{1,R+1}$ or $N_{2,R+1}$ also in the same group. There are L local connections in each group. The number of traffic sources in each group is C=R+L. The total number of traffic sources in this network model is $2C$.

To illustrate the above, let C=500, R=100, L=400.

Remote connections: $N_{1,r}$ sends traffic to $N_{2,r}$ and $N_{2,r}$ also sends traffic to $N_{1,r}$ where r=[1, 2, ..., 100].

Local connections: $N_{G,l}$ sends traffic to $N_{G,(l+1)}$ where l=[101, 102, ..., 499] and G=[1, 2]. $N_{G,500}$ sends traffic to $N_{G,101}$ where G=[1, 2].

With this model, we could vary the amount of cross-traffic in a two processor simulation by keeping C constant and using different values of R. For constant C in two processor simulation, there is minimum cross-traffic when R/C=0, and there is maximum cross-traffic when R/C=1. Accordingly, for a two processor simulation there will be more message passing overhead due to cross-traffic when R/C=1 than when R/C=0.

Part of the wall-clock execution time depends on the number of events that need to be processed by the simulator. Events include packet-level operations such as entering and exiting a queue at each packet hop. In the dumbbell topology above, each remote connection requires packets to be sent to a destination that is three hops away. In comparison, each local connection requires packets to be sent to a destination that is only two hops away.

4.2. Extended dumbbell topology

The dumbbell topology previously described does not provide symmetry in terms of number of packet hops as R/C is varied. The network model that we examined next is an extension of the dumbbell topology that attempts to provide symmetry and therefore a more constant wall-clock execution time. This topology also contains C leaf nodes connected to routers $N_{1,0}$ and $N_{2,0}$ on both sides of a shared link, with one side labelled Group 1 and the other side labelled Group 2. In addition, a second router $L_{1,0}$ and $L_{2,0}$ is connected to the original router in both groups, and there are C leaf nodes connected to these second routers. The link characteristics are the same as before. There is now a total of $4C + 4$ nodes in this network model. Each group can be distributed onto two separate processors, or they can be combined and simulated on one processor. The model is depicted in Figure 2.

Each leaf node connected to $N_{1,0}$ and $N_{2,0}$ is a source of traffic, and there are C sources in each group. Remote connections are source-destination pairs where the source $N_{1,r}$ or $N_{2,r}$ is in one group and the corresponding destination $N_{2,r}$ or $N_{1,r}$ is in the other group. There are R remote connections in each group. Local connections are source-destination pairs where the source $N_{1,l}$ or $N_{2,l}$ and corresponding destination $L_{1,l}$ or $L_{2,l}$ is in the same group. There are L local connections in each group. The number of traffic sources in each group is still C=R+L. The total number of traffic sources in this network model is still 2C.

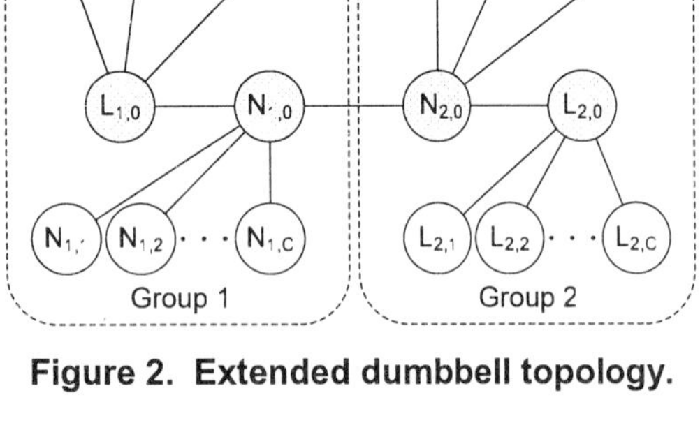

Figure 2. Extended dumbbell topology.

To illustrate the above, let C=500, R=276, L=224.

Remote connections: $N_{1,r}$ sends traffic to $N_{2,r}$ and $N_{2,r}$ also sends traffic to $N_{1,r}$ where r=[1, 2, …, 276].

Local connections: $N_{G,l}$ sends traffic to $L_{G,l}$ where l=[277, 278, …, 500] and G=[1, 2].

As with the dumbbell model, we could vary the amount of cross-traffic in a two processor simulation by keeping C constant and using different values of R. Wall-clock execution time can be measured in one and two processor simulations with different amounts of cross-traffic.

The key difference with this extended dumbbell model is that both remote and local connections require packets to be sent to a destination that is three hops away.

It must be noted that a different number of L nodes participate in a connection when R/C is varied. Hence the number of nodes for which state is accessed during the course of a simulation is different. Although not evident in the results presented in Section 5, there is a possibility for cache performance to be affected due to the different amount of state that is accessed during the course of the simulation.

4.3. Traffic

The traffic was kept homogeneous for simplicity and to make the results more predictable. We used Tahoe TCP transport agents with default parameters and simulated FTP applications for bulk data transfer. Each of the FTP applications were configured to start sending at a random time uniformly distributed throughout the duration of the simulated time, t. They were configured to continue sending for a random duration exponentially distributed with a mean of $t/4$, after which the application stops sending. This is representative of a number of data bursts within the simulated time, and distributes the TCP slow-start behaviour throughout the simulated time.

It was expected that this type of traffic is sensitive to cross-traffic in a two processor simulation because of the interaction that is necessary between sender and receiver. For this type of traffic, the sender is only able to process the current window of packets before having to wait for an acknowledgement sent from the receiver.

4.4. Sampling of data

Since the dumbbell and extended dumbbell models are divided into groups, each group can be simulated as a federate on two processors. Alternatively, the groups can be combined into a one processor simulation. The wall-clock execution times for one processor and two processor simulations can be measured and compared. The expectation is that in general, two processor simulations with minimal cross-traffic will outperform the one processor equivalent. Also, the expectation is that two processor simulations with maximum cross-traffic will not outperform the one processor equivalent due to message passing overhead. If these expectations are correct then the objective of the experiment is to find the value of R/C where one processor simulation wall-clock execution time is less than two processor simulation wall-clock execution time.

We performed simulations of the network model described above with C=500 for [20, 30, 40, 50, 60] minutes of simulated time, t. We took samples of each value of R from 0 to C in single increments. For each simulation, we recorded wall-clock time, described next.

The total wall-clock execution time to complete a simulation is $T_{total} = T_{init} + T_{run}$. Initialisation T_{init} begins when the script is first loaded and includes creating the simulated node and link objects in memory. The main factor determining T_{init} is the number of nodes and links in the simulated topology. T_{init} finishes and T_{run} begins when the event scheduler begins processing packet-level events, and finishes when the scheduler is halted. The main factor determining T_{run} is the simulated time, t and the number of packet hops as a result of traffic being sent through the network from source to destination. Additionally, for two processor simulations, T_{run} is also dependent on the amount of cross-traffic between simulator instances.

We did not record packet-level events to a trace file, so disk access was not a major factor affecting T_{total}. Available physical memory should also affect T_{total}, but was not considered in our experiments because our values of C were chosen such that there was sufficient available physical memory to avoid "disk thrashing". These values were determined through exploratory experiments.

5. Results analysis and comments

To illustrate our analysis of results for dumbbell and extended dumbbell topologies, the charts in Figure 3 and Figure 4 show the total wall-clock execution time required for simulating 60 minutes (t = 3600) as R/C is varied from 0 to 1. Note the points where one processor (1p) and two processor (2p) wall-clock execution times intersect. For brevity, charts for the other values of simulated time t are not included, but are summarized in the performance models shown in Table 1 and Table 2.

The results of T_{init} were approximately constant for all values of t and R/C, so we used the averages of those results in our performance models. The results of T_{run} for each value of t were dependent on R/C, especially for two processor simulations due to message passing overhead. The trendlines of T_{run} were approximately linear for each value of t, so we fitted it to the simple equation $T_{run} = m \times (R/C) + b$. The gradient, m and y-intercept, b are functions of t, and we observed that they are actually proportional to t. Therefore, m/t and b/t were calculated for each value of t and the averages used in our performance models. These performance models of T_{total} for one and two processor simulations with C=500 are shown beneath the corresponding sections of Table 1 and Table 2. They were verified by plotting theoretical values with actual data.

For small values of t, most of the computations only involve initialization and calculating the routes for connections since the number of packet-level events is also small. Because of this, there were cases where two processor simulations always completed faster than the one processor simulation, regardless of R/C. There were also cases where one processor simulation is more efficient than the two processor simulation, depending on the value of R/C.

We used our performance model to solve for t when R/C=1 (i.e. when the two processor simulation is least efficient) to find the value of t such that two processor simulation would be more efficient than one processor simulation regardless of R/C. For the dumbbell topology, this value of t was 48 seconds. For the extended dumbbell topology, this value of t was 81 seconds. If the simulated times are less than these values, then there is a clear performance gain in using PDNS with two processors instead of one processor.

For simulated times that are greater than the above

Table 1. Dumbbell topology results

1 processor simulation, C=500

t	T_{sim_init}	$T_{run}(m)$	$T_{run}(m/t)$	$T_{run}(b)$	$T_{run}(b/t)$
1200	15.80	139.52	*0.12*	540.75	*0.45*
1800	15.76	208.74	*0.12*	807.81	*0.45*
2400	15.71	278.36	*0.12*	1075.87	*0.45*
3000	15.79	350.00	*0.12*	1345.27	*0.45*
3600	15.91	426.22	*0.12*	1616.78	*0.45*
Avg:	**15.80**		***0.12***		***0.45***

1p T_{total} $= 15.8 + t \times [0.12 \times (R/C) + 0.45]$

2 processor simulation, C=500

t	T_{sim_init}	$T_{run}(m)$	$T_{run}(m/t)$	$T_{run}(b)$	$T_{run}(b/t)$
1200	8.42	539.61	*0.45*	291.97	*0.24*
1800	8.28	828.77	*0.46*	437.13	*0.24*
2400	8.36	1099.16	*0.46*	585.37	*0.24*
3000	8.43	1338.58	*0.45*	728.46	*0.24*
3600	8.48	1779.38	*0.49*	823.38	*0.32*
Avg:	**8.39**		***0.46***		***0.26***

2p T_{total} $= 8.39 + t \times [0.46 \times (R/C) + 0.26]$

Table 2. Extended dumbbell topology results

1 procesor simulation, C=500

t	T_{init}	$T_{run}(m)$	$T_{run}(m/t)$	$T_{run}(b)$	$T_{run}(b/t)$
1200	22.39	-45.93	*-0.04*	699.39	*0.58*
1800	24.40	-74.15	*-0.04*	1105.19	*0.61*
2400	24.45	-93.49	*-0.04*	1473.78	*0.61*
3000	22.33	-111.20	*-0.04*	1732.15	*0.58*
3600	24.50	-126.98	*-0.04*	2192.66	*0.61*
Avg:	**23.92**		***-0.04***		***0.60***

1p T_{total} $= 23.92 + t \times [-0.04 \times (R/C) + 0.6]$

2 processor simulation, C=500

t	T_{init}	$T_{run}(m)$	$T_{run}(m/t)$	$T_{run}(b)$	$T_{run}(b/t)$
1200	11.80	500.23	*0.42*	379.10	*0.32*
1800	11.80	701.89	*0.39*	584.56	*0.32*
2400	11.90	913.32	*0.38*	775.16	*0.32*
3000	11.81	1145.98	*0.38*	972.25	*0.32*
3600	11.90	1369.66	*0.38*	1179.47	*0.32*
Avg:	**11.84**		***0.39***		***0.32***

2p T_{total} $= 11.84 + t \times [0.39 \times (R/C) + 0.32]$

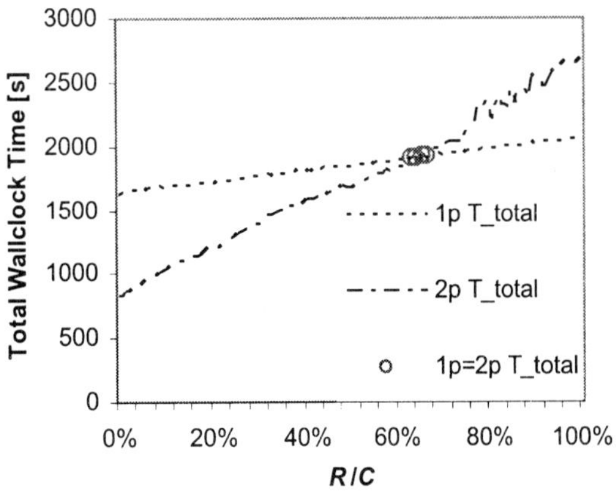

Figure 3. Results for dumbbell topology, C=500, t=3600

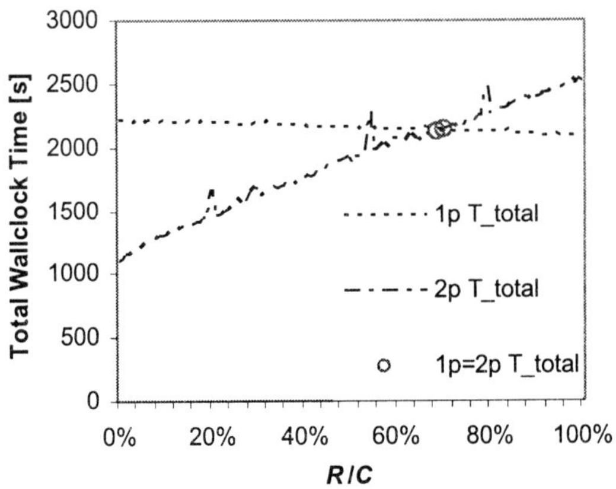

Figure 4. Results for extended dumbbell topology, C=500, t=3600

values, we can find the maximum value of R/C before one processor simulation becomes more efficient than two processor simulation due to message passing overhead. We used our performance model and found that:

$R/C = 21.46/t + 0.55$ for the dumbbell topology, and

$R/C = 28.21/t + 0.65$ for the extended dumbbell topology.

From the above equations, we can estimate the maximum value of R/C before the effect of cross-traffic outweighs the performance gains of two processors. For very large simulated times (as $t \rightarrow \infty$), R/C=0.55 for the dumbbell topology. The value is R/C=0.65 for the extended dumbbell topology. This means that for any R/C less than these values, two processor simulations will be more efficient than the one processor simulation. We can use this value as a general rule to keep remote connections versus total connections to be less than 0.55 for dumbbell topology and 0.65 for extended dumbbell topology.

5.1. Comments on dumbbell topology

As described in section 4.1, our dumbbell topology is not symmetrical, and there are three hops from source to destination for remote connections, and only two hops for local connections. Accordingly, for a one processor simulation, there will be slightly more packet-level events that need to be processed by the simulator when R/C=1. If there is sufficient bandwidth on the shared link, the expected wall-clock execution time should therefore increase slightly as R/C is varied from 0 to 1. For two processor simulation, it was expected that the effect of cross-traffic would result in a more significant increase in wall-clock execution time as R/C is varied from 0 to 1.

Our results showed that this was true. The gradient m was positive for both one and two processor simulations, with the latter being more significant.

5.2. Comments on extended dumbbell topology

As described in section 4.2, our extended dumbbell topology is more symmetrical and there are two hops from source to destination for both remote and local destinations. Accordingly, for a one processor simulation, there will be similar numbers of packet-level events that need to be processed by the simulator for all values of R/C. This model is more symmetrical in terms of packet hops as R/C varies. If there is sufficient bandwidth on the shared links, the expected wall-clock execution time should therefore remain more constant as R/C is varied. However, since remote connections only are bi-directional, the link bandwidth will be shared with returning TCP acknowledgements. Accordingly, it was expected that there will be a slight decrease in wall-clock execution time as R/C is varied from 0 to 1. For two processor simulation, it was expected that the effect of cross traffic would result in a more significant increase in wall-clock execution time as R/C is varied from 0 to 1.

Our results showed that this was true. The gradient m was negative for one processor simulations, and was positive for two processor simulations. The latter was more significant.

6. Summary and future work

We studied the effect of cross-traffic on wall-clock execution time in the Parallel/Distributed Network Simulator (PDNS) for a set of basic network topologies by benchmarking the results from simulations on one and two processors. We defined our first topology based on a dumbbell network to include variables for remote and local connections. By controlling these variables, we were able to control the amount of cross-traffic in our experiments. We defined our second topology as an extension of the first such that there is the same amount of packet hops to destinations for both remote and local connections. For both topologies, we defined the variables that were sampled, including components of total wall-clock time execution time.

The experimental results were processed on a Beowulf cluster at the Australian Centre for Advanced Computing and Communications (AC3). We reduced error due to the shared computing environment by ensuring exclusive use of a compute node's processors, as well as by writing to local scratch space instead of to the shared filesystem. Our experience gained from using these resources will be useful for future simulation studies.

Our results showed that for C=500, when simulated time is less than 48 seconds for our dumbbell topology, or less than 81 seconds for our extended dumbbell topology, two processor PDNS simulations outperforms one processor simulations regardless of our defined unit of cross-traffic, R/C. When simulated time is more than these values, two processor PDNS simulations will be more efficient than one processor simulation if $R/C < 21.46/t + 0.55$ for our dumbbell topology, and if $R/C < 28.21/t + 0.65$ for our extended dumbbell topology. Finally, these results can help us estimate the maximum value of R/C before the effect of cross-traffic outweighs the performance gains of using two processors in parallel.

The current results do not fully exploit the potential of the 155 node Beowulf cluster at AC3. Future work includes extending the experiments with more complex network models using more than two processors. We did not include results for shared memory communications, which is also future work.

The details of the results and analysis are only applicable to the testing environment and models used and not to other scenarios. As such, the results must be interpreted in light of this. The models and methodology of varying the ratio of remote and local connections versus total connections that have been described in this paper need to be extended to other models. Further generalization of the performance models will be useful to help understand the relative advantages of using PDNS for our network simulations.

Additionally, other methods for speeding up simulations, such as the other two categories described in the introduction of this paper can be examined in the future. We are particularly interested in the fluid-flow models.

7. Related work

The creators of PDNS and libSynk at the Georgia Institute of Technology have published several papers that include benchmarks of PDNS, including the following.

In [17], Perumalla et al show that RTI-based parallel simulations can scale extremely well and achieve very high speedup. Their experiments yielded more than 80-fold scaled speedup in simulating large TCP/IP networks, demonstrating performance of up to 6 million simulated packet transmissions per second on a Linux cluster. Networks containing up to two million network nodes were simulated. In [18], Fujimoto et al presents results from experiments utilizing as many as 1536 processors yielding performance as high as 106 Million packet transmissions per second. In [19], Riley et al present experimental results achieving nearly 2 million network nodes with linear efficiency up to 128 federates.

This paper differs from the abovementioned related works in that this is an independent benchmark that focuses on the overhead effects of simulated traffic crossing simulator boundaries. Although it is well known that increasing the ratio of remote traffic will degrade parallel distributed simulation performance, it is less well known the quantitative conditions where parallel distributed simulations become slower than an equivalent simulation performed on a single processor. As an independent research group, our experiences gained with PDNS have been very positive, and our results demonstrate certain conditions that need to be considered when designing future experiments.

8. Acknowledgement

Thanks to AC3 for their support in using the cluster.

Thanks to the PDNS group for the simulator software and support through the PDNS mailing list.

We acknowledge the funding by UTS, Alcatel and the ARC via grant LP 0219784, which includes an APA(I) for Samson Lee.

8. References

[1] S. Lee, N. Sheridan-Smith, T. O'Neill, J. Leaney, K. Sandrasegaran, and S. Markovits, "Managing the Enriched Experience Network -- Learning-Outcome Approach to the Experimental Design Life-Cycle," presented at Australian Telecommunication Networks and Applications Conference (ATNAC'03), Melbourne, Australia, 2003.

[2] B. Liu, D. R. Figueiredo, Y. Guo, J. Kurose, and D. Towsley, "A Study of Networks Simulation Efficiency: Fluid Simulation vs. Packet-level Simulation," presented at IEEE INFOCOM'2001, Anchorage, Alaska, 2001.

[3] R. Brown, "Calendar queues: A fast O(1) priority queue implementation for the simulation event set problem," *Communications of the ACM*, vol. 31, pp. 1220-1227, 1988.

[4] G. F. Riley, T. M. Jaafar, and R. M. Fujimoto, "Integrated Fluid and Packet Network Simulations," presented at MASCOTS'02, Fort Worth, Texas, 2002.

[5] R. M. Fujimoto, *Parallel and Distributed Simulation Systems*: Wiley Interscience, 2000.

[6] K. M. Chandy and J. Misra, "Distributed Simulation: A Case Study in Design and Verification of Distributed Programs," *IEEE Transactions on Software Engineering*, vol. 5, pp. 440-452, 1979.

[7] D. R. Jefferson, "Virtual time," *ACM Transactions on Programming Languages and Systems*, vol. 7, pp. 404-425, 1985.

[8] S. Bhatt, R. Fujimoto, A. Ogielski, and K. Perumalla, "Parallel Simulation Techniques for Large Scale Networks," *IEEE Communications Magazine*, vol. 36, pp. 42-47, 2002.

[9] "PDNS - Parallel/Distributed NS." http://www.cc.gatech.edu/computing/compass/pdns/, 2004.

[10] "The Network Simulator - ns-2." http://www.isi.edu/nsnam/ns/, 2004.

[11] "GTNetS - Georgia Tech Network Simulator." http://www.ece.gatech.edu/research/labs/MANIACS/GTNetS/, 2004.

[12] "Dartmouth Scalable Simulation Framework (DaSSF)." http://www.cs.dartmouth.edu/research/DaSSF/, 2004.

[13] Georgia Tech, "Federated Simulations Development Kit." http://www.cc.gatech.edu/computing/pads/fdk.html, 2001.

[14] K. Perumalla, "libSynk library." http://www.cc.gatech.edu/computing/pads/kalyan/libsynk.htm, 2004.

[15] J. H. Cowie, D. M. Nicol, and A. T. Ogielski, "Modeling the Global Internet," *Computing in Science and Engineering*, 1999.

[16] "Australian Centre for Advanced Computing and Communications." http://www.ac3.edu.au/edu/, 2004.

[17] K. S. Perumalla, A. Park, R. M. Fujimoto, and G. F. Riley, "Scalable RTI-Based Parallel Simulation of Networks," presented at Parallel and Distributed Simulation, San Diego, CA, USA, 2003.

[18] R. M. Fujimoto, K. Perumalla, A. Park, H. Wu, and M. H. Ammar, "Large-Scale Network Simulation: How Big? How Fast?," presented at Meeting of the IEEE International Symposium on Modeling, Analysis, and Simulation of Computer and Telecommunication Systems (MASCOTS), 2003.

[19] G. F. Riley, M. H. Ammar, R. M. Fujimoto, A. Park, K. Perumalla, and D. Xu, "A Federated Approach to Distributed Network Simulation," *ACM Transactions on Modeling and Computer Simulation*, vol. 14, pp. 116-148, 2004.

Performance Prediction using Simulation of Large-scale Interconnection Networks in POSE

Terry L. Wilmarth, Gengbin Zheng, Eric J. Bohm, Yogesh Mehta,
Nilesh Choudhury, Praveen Jagadishprasad and Laxmikant V. Kalé
Department of Computer Science
University of Illinois at Urbana-Champaign
{*wilmarth, gzheng, ebohm, ymehta, nchoudh2, jagadish, kale*}*@cs.uiuc.edu*

Abstract

Parallel discrete event simulation (PDES) of models with fine-grained computation remains a challenging problem. We explore the usage of POSE*, our Parallel Object-oriented Simulation Environment, for application performance prediction on large parallel machines such as BlueGene. This study involves the simulation of communication at the packet level through a detailed network model. This presents an extremely fine-grained simulation: events correspond to the transmission and receipt of packets. Computation is minimal, communication dominates, and strong dependencies between events result in a low degree of parallelism. There is limited look-ahead capability since the outcome of many events is determined by the application whose performance the simulation is predicting. Thus conservative synchronization approaches are challenging for this type of problem. We present recent experiences and performance results for our network simulator and illustrate the utility of our simulator through prediction and validation studies for a molecular dynamics application.*[1]

1. Introduction

PDES applications with fine-grained computation present a significant challenge. We present our simulation environment, POSE, in which we have studied the major obstacles to effective parallelization of discrete event models. We have focused our studies on models with fine computation granularity and a low degree of parallelism. POSE addresses these difficulties with a flexible object model based on the concept of virtualization, adaptive synchronization strategies, communication optimizations and load balancing. We discuss POSE in Section 2.

Simulating communication at the packet-level of a real application on a detailed contention-based network model for a large parallel computer is a good example of a discrete event simulation that is difficult to parallelize. This application presents us with all the challenges we would like POSE to overcome. It is also an area of immediate interest. New parallel computers with tremendous computational power are being constructed with surprising frequency. One example is the IBM BlueGene/L which will have 128K processors and achieve 360 TeraFLOPS peak performance. Developing and/or porting applications for/to such machines will present new challenges in getting applications to scale to such large machines. To make use of such machines efficiently, it would help to know how target applications might perform on them. If we can simulate how the application would behave on the large machine, we might be able to improve the design of the machine before it is built. We could also predict and optimize the performance of the application so that it is ready as soon as the machine is available. Another motivation for this approach is that even for existing machines, execution time for large applications is costly and often involves considerable waiting periods. A simulator could be used to prepare the application by enabling the programmer to perform debugging and optimization on the application before running on the target machine.

The BigSim[29, 30] project incorporates several levels of simulation to accurately predict performance of parallel applications on specific large parallel machines. This paper focuses on simulation of detailed contention-based network models for large parallel machines. It is impossible to use sequential simulation for large appli-

1 This work was supported in part by the National Science Foundation (NGS 0103645), the National Institutes of Health (PHS 5 P41 RR05969-04), the Defense Advanced Research Project Agency (NBCH30390004) and the Department of Energy (B341494).

1087-4097/05 $20.00 © 2005 IEEE

cations due to the size of the data involved. As we shall see, parallel simulation of networks with common network traffic patterns is difficult, while simulating the network with traffic generated by a real application is even more challenging. The dependencies that exist between events are strong and can result in an availability of work on only a portion of the network at a time, in turn resulting in a low degree of parallelism. Further, each individual message results in a long critical path of events. In addition, since application computation is performed in an earlier stage and recorded in log files, we are only modeling packet transmissions in postmortem simulation. Thus there is very little actual computation, resulting in an extremely small grainsize. Finally, execution of a log-based simulation makes it difficult to use look-ahead to determine the safety of an event. This limits us to the use of optimistic synchronization. We discuss BigSim further in Section 3.

We present our recent experiences with network simulation and show performance results of our detailed network simulator in Section 4. We illustrate the utility of our simulator through validation and prediction studies for a molecular dynamics application in Section 5. Finally we discuss our future plans for POSE and BigSim and present our conclusions in Section 6.

1.1. Related work

As an optimistically-synchronized PDES environment, POSE is based on the Time Warp[10, 7] mechanism. POSE uses a variety of adaptive[6] protocols. One of the throttling mechanisms used by POSE is the time barrier described in MTW[22]. Breathing Time Warp[24] followed a similar approach. POSE adapts the size of the time window (similar to [5]) according to simulation behavior. A new throttling mechanism used by POSE uses an adaptable tolerance which caps the quantity of *speculative* events that can be executed based on the concept of *useful work*[17]. This approach is particularly effective at dealing with bursts of events at the same timestamp. POSE uses a variant of *speculative execution*[16] which was originally developed to make conservative protocols more aggressive. POSE uses speculation to increase aggressiveness to compensate for the throttling mechanisms used and to complement the virtualization-based object model. The approach is lighter-weight but riskier than Breathing Time Buckets[23] and Breathing Time Warp because it allows speculative events to generate future events normally.

SMART [18] is a sequential simulator for simulating diverse traffic patterns for some common network architectures. The sequential simulator would limit the scalability of the network and traffic. Another serial simulation of IBM SP systems was [26]. A conservative parallel simulation of IBM SP2 network was shown in [3]. MINSimulate [25] focuses on multistage interconnection, limiting it to a subset of current network topologies. [2] and [13] focus their efforts on K-ary N-cube interconnection networks.

Program simulation is used to study the performance of complex applications when analytical performance prediction is impractical. It is well known that simulations of such large systems tend to be slow. The direct-execution [21, 1, 20] approach uses available hardware resources to directly execute application code to simulate architectural features of interest. Á la carte[4] is a Los Alamos computer architecture toolkit for extreme-scale architecture simulation which uses a conservative synchronization engine, the Dartmouth Scalable Simulation Framework (DaSSF)[14]. They have also targeted their simulations to thousands of processors. LAPSE[8] is another system which simulated message-passing programs. However, most existing simulators are designed for MPI applications. They do not readily apply to the broader class of parallel languages such as message-driven paradigms like CHARM++. In message-driven parallel applications, computation is invoked when a message arrives. Computation order depends on message arrival order. In direct execution, messages are not delivered in the simulating environment in the same order as they would be on the target machine. This behavior of parallel execution complicates simulation further.

2. POSE

POSE is a general-purpose optimistically-synchronized PDES environment designed for simulation models with fine computation granularity and a low degree of parallelism. POSE[27] is implemented in CHARM++[12], a C++-based parallel programming system that supports the *virtualization* programming model. Virtualization involves the decomposition of a problem into N entities that will execute on P processors[11]. N is independent of P, though ideally $N>>P$. The application programmer's view of the program is of these entities and their interactions; the underlying run-time system keeps track of the mapping of entities to processors and handles any remapping that might be necessary at run-time.

In CHARM++, these entities are known as *chares*. Chares are C++ objects with special *entry* methods that are invoked asynchronously from other chares. Since many chares are mapped to a single processor, CHARM++ uses *message-driven execution* to determine which chare gets control on a proces-

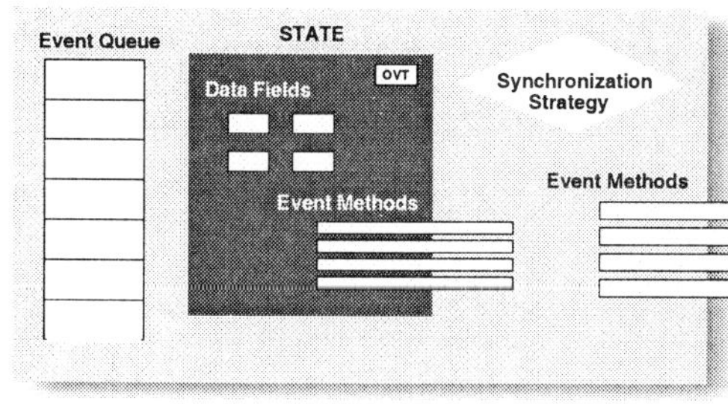

Figure 1: Components of a poser

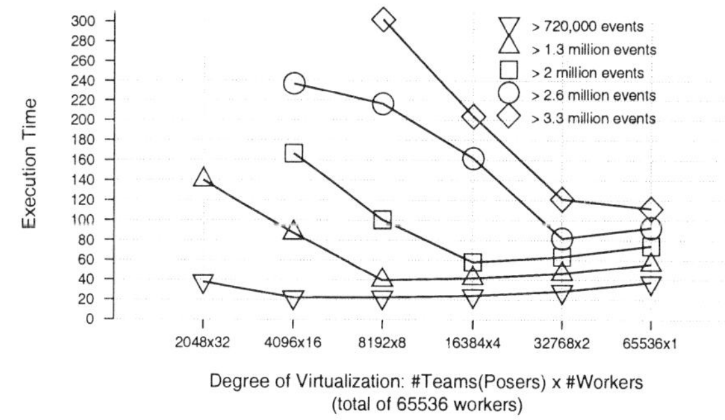

Figure 2: Effects of virtualization

sor. A dynamic scheduler runs on each processor and has a list of *messages* (entry method invocations) to select from. The messages are sorted according to a queuing strategy (FIFO by default). The user can attach priorities to messages. The scheduler takes the next message from its queue and invokes the corresponding entry method on the appropriate object. One advantage of this approach is that no chare can hold a processor idle while it is waiting for a message. Since $N>P$, there may be other chares on the same processor that can run in the interim. Thus, using virtualization allows us to maximize the degree of parallelism. The logical processors (LPs) from PDES (called *posers* in POSE) are implemented with CHARM++'s chares. We use timestamps on messages as priorities and the CHARM++ scheduler serves as a presorting event queue.

2.1. The POSE object model

Posers represent sequential entities in the simulation model. They are similar to LPs, but should encapsulate much smaller portions of state. POSE requires that parallelism in the model be represented by posers in the simulation handling events in parallel, but the responsibility for decomposing a simulation model into the smallest components possible (maximizing N, the number of posers) lies with the programmer. This approach differs from timelines[15] in DaSSF and similar approaches in that it encourages the maximum amount of decomposition without regard for how objects might relate. As we shall see, this choice does not result in significant drawbacks.

Figure 1 illustrates the structure of a poser. Each poser has an *object virtual time* (OVT). This is the virtual time that has passed since the start of the simulation relative to the object. Posers have *event methods* which are CHARM++ *entry methods* receiving *timestamped* messages. The poser encapsulates the state specified by the programmer and contains a local event queue. Incoming events are redirected from the CHARM++ scheduler into the appropriate poser's local event queue. Events are processed according to an instance of a synchronization strategy associated with the poser.

In addressing the problem of fine-granularity, this approach seems counterintuitive to approaches that cluster entities together. However, decomposing a model into posers has many benefits. The poser event queue limits the scope of simulation activity to the poser itself; since different entities may have dramatically different behaviors, this limits the effects of those behaviors to a smaller scope. When checkpointing is performed periodically according to the number of events received by a poser, this structure enables less frequent checkpointing on smaller states, reducing overhead and memory usage. Rollbacks are less likely to occur when the scope affected by incoming events is smaller. When they do occur, they cause shorter rollbacks. Decomposing state into smaller objects makes LP migration simpler. Finally, this structure paves the way for adaptive synchronization strategies that can fine-tune each LP's behavior.

The drawbacks of a high degree of virtualization are the management of information for a much larger quantity of simulation entities, coupled with the cost of switching from one such entity to another for each event.

Thus, we need to examine the tradeoffs. We ran a set of experiments varying the degree of virtualization of a fixed-size problem using a basic optimistic strategy with no throttling mechanisms. We wanted to see how virtualization could improve performance by reducing the overheads previously mentioned, but we also wanted to measure the increased overheads at the highest degree of virtualization. These experiments were executed on Cool[2] with a synthetic benchmark that allows parallel *workers* to be grouped together into `team` posers (*i.e.* each team corresponds to a logical process). Each worker has a single event type. When it receives an event, it performs some busy work and generates an event for another worker. The event communication pattern organizes the workers in rings such that 50% of the

2 Cool is a Linux cluster of 8 quad Xeon SMPs with fast Ethernet.

Table 1: Overhead cost breakdown

	Teams × Workers per Team				
	4096×16	8192×8	16384×4	32768×2	65536×1
FE	38.18	36.19	31.15	31.64	32.33
GVT	61.22	11.26	1.09	1.11	1.27
Sync	1.35	2.37	1.08	1.24	1.42
CP	3.96	3.45	0.98	0.78	0.55
FC	15.40	12.70	1.78	1.89	2.00
RB	0.00	0.00	0.00	0.00	0.00
Com	14.57	14.00	13.98	14.42	15.62
Other	16.28	7.90	6.10	10.90	19.20
Total	149.61	87.87	56.16	61.98	72.39

workers communicate locally and the rest remotely. We simulated a total of 65,536 workers in each experiment grouped together in different sized teams. We started with a low degree of virtualization, 2048 teams of 32 workers each, and ended with maximum virtualization, 65,536 teams of 1 worker each. We ran these experiments on 16 processors on 4 nodes of Cool with several different program sizes (in terms of number of events handled). The results are shown in Figure 2.

We found that the benefits of higher degrees of virtualization strongly outweighed the added costs. Further, as the problem size increased, higher degrees of virtualization consistently outperformed lower degrees of virtualization. It should be noted that we designed our benchmark to make rollbacks very unlikely, so what we see in Figure 2 is purely the cost of optimistic synchronization running optimally. Less optimal simulations with rollbacks would be more likely to incur higher costs for lower degrees of virtualization. Missing points for a curve indicate that those degrees of virtualization ran out of either memory or time allotted for the run.

We show a breakdown of the performance in Table 1. This table shows the costs in s (averaged per processor) for various overhead types for the >2 million event problem size, varying the degree of virtualization. FE is forward execution, CP is checkpointing, FC is fossil collection and RB is rollback and cancellation. The optimal performance for this set of runs occurs with 16,384 teams of 4 workers each. Activities which are highly dependent on the quantity of objects in the simulation (GVT, synchronization, fossil collection) are slightly elevated as the degree of virtualization increases from there. The most significant type of overhead affected by higher degrees of virtualization is the "Other" category which includes the cost of creating, distributing and managing the objects in the CHARM++ runtime system. Checkpointing costs decrease consistently as degree of virtualization increases. The most significant performance differences are attributable to higher memory usage for lower degrees of virtualization. As memory becomes scarce, the types of overhead that frequently deallocate and, to a lesser extent, allocate memory are most affected. These include GVT, fossil collection and forward execution. A small amount of rollback occurs at the lowest degree of virtualization. It is not enough to result in significant rollback overhead, but there is some event re-execution cost included in the forward execution times.

What Figure 2 does not show is that a higher degree of virtualization allows us to run a program on more processors than we could with lower degrees of virtualization, further increasing the chances of obtaining a better speedup. Thus, this "fine granularity of entities" does not incur significant additional cost and has further benefits that we are not yet taking advantage of. For example, having more fine-grained entities is a great benefit when we use load balancing in our simulations. As we shall see in the next section, high degrees of virtualization will enable fine-tuned adaptive synchronization.

2.2. Adaptive synchronization

In POSE, an object gets control of a processor when it either receives an event or cancellation message via the scheduler, or when a new GVT estimate has been calculated. In the first case, the object's synchronization strategy is invoked. In the second case, we perform fossil collection before invoking the strategy. Our basic optimistic strategy handles cancellation messages first and then checks for any stragglers that may have arrived and rolls back to the earliest. Finally, it is ready to perform forward execution steps.

This is where the opportunity to perform *speculative computation* arises. In traditional optimistic approaches, an event arrives, is sorted into the event list and the earliest event is executed. The event is the earliest on the processor, but may not be the earliest in the simulation, so its execution is speculative. In our approach, we have a *speculative window* that governs how far into the future beyond the GVT estimate an object may proceed. Speculative windows are similar to the time windows[22] used to throttle optimism in other systems. They differ in how events within the window are processed. In POSE, *all* events on a poser with timestamp within the speculative window are executed as a *multi-event*. The later events are probably not the earliest in the simulation and it is likely that they are not even the earliest on that processor. The strategy speculates that those events are the earliest that the *poser* will receive. This approach is more aggressive than traditional approaches because our version of speculative execution does not "hold back" events that are spawned, to be sent later when we are sure it is "safe". Rather they are executed in the standard way; spawned events are actually sent to other, possibly remote, posers. Multi-events are discussed in detail in [28].

Using multi-events, we reduce scheduling and context switching overhead and benefit from a warmed cache, eliminating some of the drawbacks associated with the high degree of virtualization. This form of speculation may increase rollback overhead. However, since the speculative window itself is the throttling mechanism, and since rollback costs are reduced by being highly localized due to the high degree of virtualization, we have many ways to keep rollback cost under control. We now combine the concepts of poser virtualization and speculation with adaptive synchronization.

In POSE, each entity is created with its own instance of an adaptive strategy which adapts the speculation on the object to the object's past behavior, current state and likely future behavior (given what future events and cancellations are queued on the object).

POSE allows for any strategy to be used for posers of a particular type, and many strategies have been written. Our ultimate goal however has been to develop a single default strategy flexible enough to adapt to a variety of situations. For this paper, we describe the behavior of this default strategy called *Adept*.

Adept applies three throttling mechanisms to the aggressive speculation behavior. First, the speculative window size can be adapted. This controls how far into the future a poser can progress. Initially, the window size is infinite. When a rollback occurs, the window is reduced to the interval between the GVT estimate and the time at which the straggler arrived. Assuming no other stragglers arrive, the window is rapidly expanded to infinity again after the poser has control only a few times.

The second throttling mechanism limits the *quantity* of events comprising a multi-event. A *speculative tolerance* is a percentage of total events executed that did not prove useful. If a poser is under the tolerance, it may execute however many events it can that would keep it under the tolerance, assuming none of the events turned out to be useful. A non-zero minimum guarantees progress.

The third throttling mechanism takes a snapshot of the memory footprint of an object, and if it exceeds a maximum, does not allow the object to process more events until fossil collection has been performed. Again, if the object has work that would restrict GVT advancement, it is executed to guarantee progress.

The last two throttling mechanisms are adapted to each poser. However, the criteria used to determine when to throttle is collected at processor level, so there is additional flexibility in how objects can behave. For example, if some objects are using very little memory, others which need more can be allowed to use it.

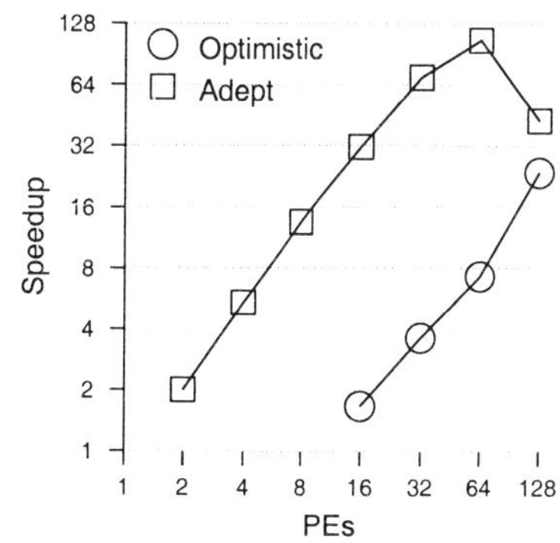

Figure 3: Adept vs. Optimistic

2.3. POSE performance

Early experiments with a simple synthetic benchmark indicated that Adept performed nearly identically to Optimistic under ideal (infrequent rollback, small problem size) conditions. Adept suffered a small performance hit for synchronization but ultimately performed with similar speedup to Optimistic on fewer processors, and slightly better on more processors. However, under less ideal conditions with more likelihood of rollback, high memory usage and high message density for example, Adept is far superior at adapting to the problem. We show a Turing[3] run of Adept vs. Optimistic in Figure 3 on a Multiple Rings benchmark. This program implements a set of overlapping rings of events, one started by each worker object. In this run, there are 10240 objects and an event density of 20 events per virtual time unit. The program terminates when all objects have each received 2000 events. Thus the total number of events handled is 20,480,000. The average grainsize of the events is 5 microseconds on Turing. Since the sequential run of this benchmark ran out of memory, we used the 2 processor time for Adept as our base sequential time to illustrate the speedup. Optimistic was unable to complete runs due to insufficient memory until the 16 processor experiment. Adept was able to complete a run on 2 processors and achieve excellent speedup up to 64 procs. The superlinearity of the curves is due to the decrease in the impact of insufficient memory as the number of processors increases. At 64 processors the program completed in 5 seconds and could not speedup beyond that.

As our default strategy for POSE, Adept exhibits excellent scalability. Figure 4 shows how POSE using Adept scales with problem size using the Multiple Rings benchmark. In one experiment, we double the number of events handled per object. Doubling processors then

3 *Turing* is a cluster of 640 dual 2GHz G5 processors 4 GB RAM Apple Xserves connected by Myrinet.

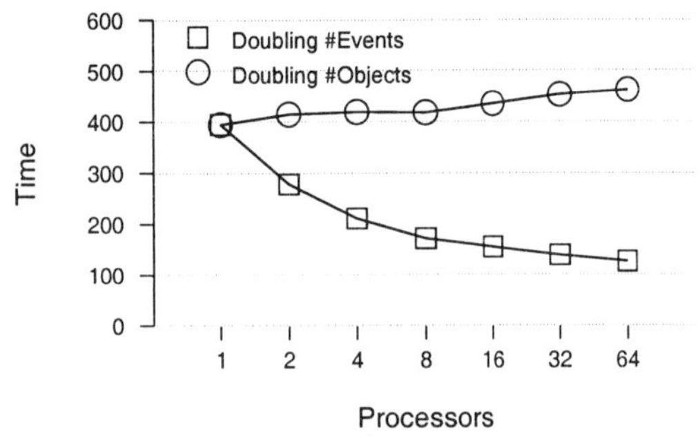

Figure 4: Scaling problem size

results in a decrease in the time taken to execute the double-size simulation. This is largely due to the increase in the size of the multi-events. More events can be handled in less time since there is less synchronization overhead and improved cache performance. Doubling problem size by doubling the number of objects has quite a different result and clearly illustrates the cost of increasing the degree of virtualization. The time gradually increases as processors and objects double. This is largely due to the startup time taken to construct the additional objects on the additional processors, but also includes extra overhead for object management. Since the number of events per objects remains constant, the size of multi-events cannot increase.

3. Network simulation

The BigSim project aims at developing techniques and methods to facilitate the development of efficient scalable applications on very large parallel machines. BigSim is based on simulation and performance prediction techniques including network simulation.

Our work in this project has focused on two distinct user groups. For the scientific community we have produced a simulation environment[31, 30] for performance prediction of scientific applications running on large machines. For designers of HPC systems we have created a detailed simulation environment for the performance prediction of future high speed large scale interconnects.

3.1. Application performance prediction

The core of the application performance prediction system is the BigSim emulator [29, 31]. Using the virtualization of CHARM++ [11], the BigSim emulator presents the execution environment of a petaflops class machine. CHARM++ or AMPI[9] applications are compiled to run on the emulator just as though it were any other architecture. They can then be run on an existing parallel computer and their performance captured in an

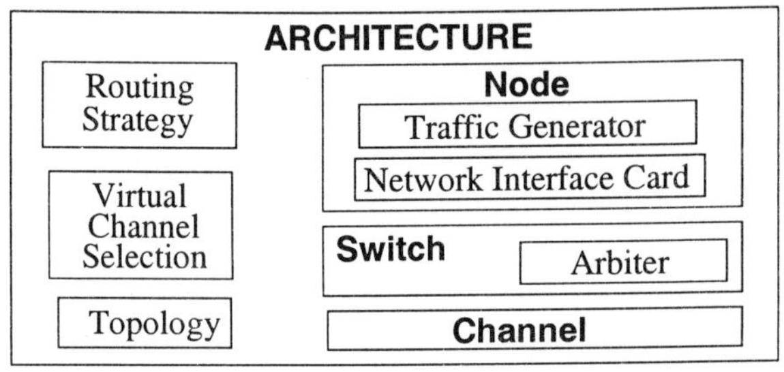

Figure 5: BigNetSim conceptual model

event trace log file. The trace log can then be used for performance analysis. The network simulation included within BigSim is a simple latency based network model.

When more precise network behaviors must be studied, the trace can be loaded into the POSE-based BigNetSim which corrects the recorded timestamps based on network contention, adaptive routing, hybrid networks, etc. as determined by the particular model chosen.

3.2. Network performance prediction

BigNetSim facilitates informed decision making for the design of high speed interconnects. As such it provides a configurable runtime environment where network parameters, such as buffer size, number of virtual channels, packet size, adaptive vs fixed routing, etc. can be set at run time. Furthermore, the design is modular to support easy extensions by the addition of new topologies, routing algorithms and architectures (see Figure 5). BigNetSim currently includes support for Torus, 3D-Mesh, Fat-Tree and Hypercube topologies.

In Figure 5, the traffic generator, NIC, Switch and Channel are modeled as posers. They rely exclusively on event messages to communicate with other simulation objects. Messages created on a node are passed to the NIC, which packetizes the message and sends the packets to a Channel. The Channel forwards a packet to a Switch. The Switch has an Arbiter, which uses the configured routing logic, to select the output Channel to route the packet. Switch models Virtual Channels and flow control based on feedback from downstream Switches and VC selection strategies. Channels in the path to the destination node receive the packets and pass them up through Switches. Finally the last channel in the path passes it to the NIC, which reassembles packets to form a message and sends it to the node. Several network parameters such as packet-size, channel-bandwidth, channel-delay, switch-buffer-size and a host of NIC delay parameters can be set in a network configuration file, which the simulation reads at runtime.

BigNetSim's modular nature and the detail of model entities should enable accurate modeling of current and future interconnection networks with minimal additional

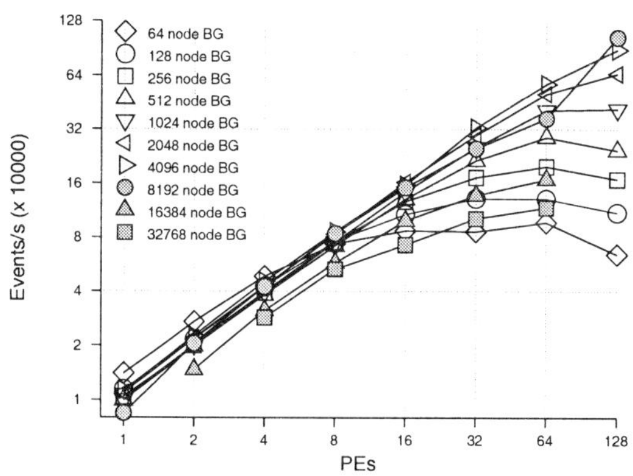

Figure 6: BigNetSim events/sec with TrafficGen

code. Higher resolution modeling of NIC behavior is planned. No modeling is done of message handling processes, such as message protocol stack manipulations.

When evaluating a network, it is essential to be able to study network performance based on expected traffic loads. The user may choose to load the network by executing an application trace or create standard network load patterns using the TrafficGen interface. TrafficGen sends messages from a source node to a destination node chosen according to a predefined pattern (k-shift, ring, bit transpose, bit reversal, bit complement and uniform distribution). These patterns are based on communication patterns in specific applications. Messages are generated by a deterministic or Poisson distribution.

As shown in Section 4, POSE's support for virtualization enables BigNetSim to perform and scale well despite the seemingly heavyweight object implementation.

4. Performance

We have evaluated the performance of our network simulator by simulating a uniform distribution of random traffic using our TrafficGen module on a simulated 3D Torus network ranging in size from 4x4x4 to 64x32x32. This pattern was chosen because it would more closely resemble the behavior of an arbitrary collection of applications running on a supercomputer than the other standard patterns. The randomly chosen destinations result in a repeatable but random asymmetric load on the network. The network parameters were selected to simulate the direct torus network of the Blue-Gene/L machine. All runs were made on Turing.

Figure 6 shows the number of POSE-committed events per second on average. From a network simulation perspective, a single packet-hop in a network translates to 6 or 7 events on an average. The system scales well up to 64 processors, with larger networks exhibiting the best scaling beyond 64 pro-

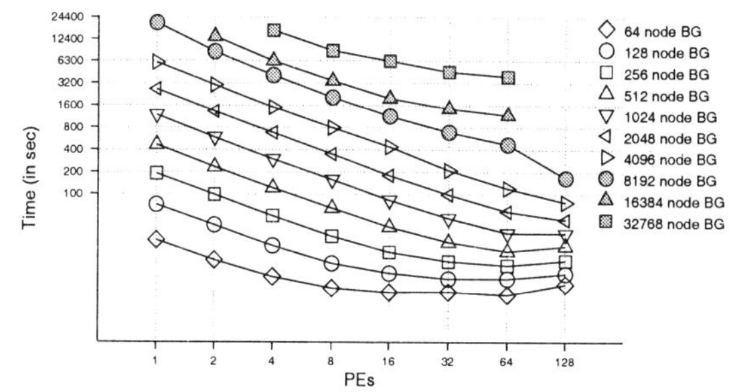

Figure 7: BigNetSim time with TrafficGen

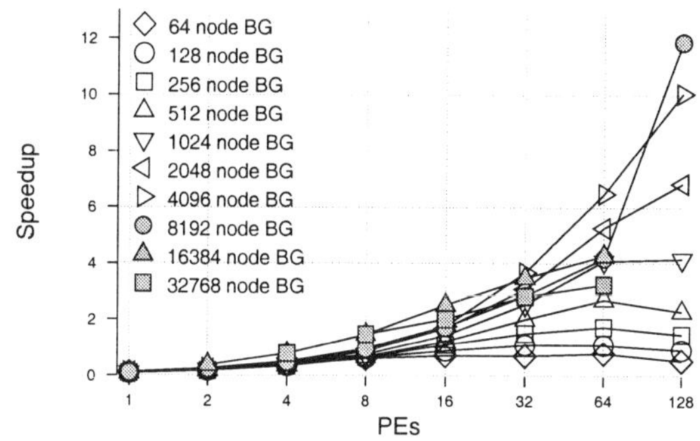

Figure 8: BigNetSim speedup with TrafficGen

cessors. At the peak we achieve 1 million committed events (150,000 packet-hops) per second on 128 processors for the 8192-node network. We observe that with increasing number of posers per processor, the number of events/s decreases. Another observation is that the number of events/s seems to scale well with increasing number of processors regardless of the problem size or the number of posers.

Figure 7 shows the execution time of BigNetSim for various network sizes. In this plot, the amount of work per poser is constant, but the number of posers/processor doubles with doubling network size. Hence, the time doubles too. BigNetSim shows good scalability upto a point beyond which it saturates. This can be explained by the tradeoff between virtualization and the costs associated with increasing the number of processors as expected from our discussion in Section 2. The point of saturation is around 16 processors for smaller problem sizes (simulation of a 4x4x4 network) and it increases with the problem size. Thus, BigNetSim scales better with increasing problem size. If we were to look at self-speedup (speedup relative to 1 processor parallel simulation), we observe linear speedup (evident from Figure 7).

Figure 8 shows a plot of speedup relative to sequential simulation time. The distinction between sequential and parallel simulation should be well understood. Sequential simulation orders events and executes them without communication or synchronization overhead.

Parallel simulation has to execute events based on optimized predictions, which could cause out of order execution and hence rollbacks. Therefore, parallel simulation on one processor is nearly 10 to 12 time slower than sequential simulation, but it has the promise that with good scaling on a large number of processors it can perform much better than sequential simulation. Furthermore, parallel simulation is essential for problems which are too large for a single machine. So, we look for a small break-even point and good scaling above that. Our simulation demonstrates both these features. The average breakeven point is 8 or 16 processors and it scales well beyond that. A promising way to decrease the discrepancy between sequential and parallel execution on one processor is by further decomposing the posers into a greater quantity of smaller objects, thus, increasing the degree of virtualization. This is expected to improve performance as shown in the virtualization benchmark of Section 2.3.

In the three figures, there are certain missing points. These are for large number of posers on a small number of processors which causes it to run out of memory. This strenghtens the need for a parallel simulation. For a network size above 8192 nodes, a single processor run (whether sequential or parallel) runs out of memory. In the speedup plot we have estimated values for these missing points based on available sequential data for smaller network sizes.

5. Performance prediction and validation

We have evaluated BigNetSim for real applications on very large numbers of processors. One such application is the simulation of biomolecules using Molecular Dynamics. It is one of the important applications for BlueGene/L and other large parallel machines. The application we chose is NAMD [19], which is the current state-of-art high performance molecular dynamics code designed for large biomolecular systems. It is one of the recipients of 2002 Gordon Bell Award for the achievement of scaling parallel simulation to 3000 processors.

5.1. NAMD validation

We have compared the actual execution time of NAMD with our simulation of it using BigSim on LeMieux[4]. Our validation approach is as follows. We first run NAMD on a number of real processors and record the actual run time. Then we run NAMD on BigSim emulator with a much smaller number of processors simulating the same number of processors used in the original run. This emulation generates log files that we then simulate with BigNetSim running the simple latency-based network model. We record the run time predicted by the simulator and compare with the original run time.

As a NAMD benchmark system we used Apo-Lipoprotein A1 with 92K atoms. The simulation runs for a total of 15 timesteps. A multiple time-stepping scheme with PME (Particle Mesh Ewald) involving a 3D FFT every four steps is performed. The result is shown in Table 2. The first row shows the actual execution time per timestep of NAMD on 128 to 2250 processors on LeMieux. The second row shows the predicted execution time per timestep using BigNetSim on a Linux cluster with network parameters based on Quadrics network specifications. It shows that the simulated execution time is reasonably close to the actual execution time. The predicted run time is not as accurate when number of real processors grows larger. One possible reason is that we might not have modeled the cache performance and the memory footprint effects in enough detail.

Table 2: Actual vs. predicted time (in *ms*) per timestep for NAMD

PEs	128	256	512	1024	2250
Actual time	71.5	40.3	23.9	17.6	12.8
Predicted time	75.8	43.6	25.1	20.8	16.13

5.2. Parallel performance

To evaluate the parallel performance of the simulator itself, we ran the BigSim emulator on 64 real processors with the NAMD program on 2048 simulated nodes configured in a 3D Torus topology with Bluegene/L characteristics. The emulation traces were then used with BigNetSim on a varying number of processors.

We show simulation execution time for BigNetSim with NAMD from 2 to 128 processors in Figure 9 and a corresponding speedup plot relative to one processor parallel time in Figure 10. It shows that BigNetSim scales linearly to 8 processors and sub-linearly to 26 on 32 processors. The simulator continues to scale to 63 on 128 processors.

The results in Figure 10 show that BigNetSim has decent parallel performance even when applied to performance prediction of a real world application. This is much more challenging than a synthetic benchmark due to complex dependencies among events resulting in relatively limited parallelism in the simulation. Performance

4 LeMieux is 750 Quad Alphaserver ES45 node machine at Pittsburgh Supercomputing Center (PSC)

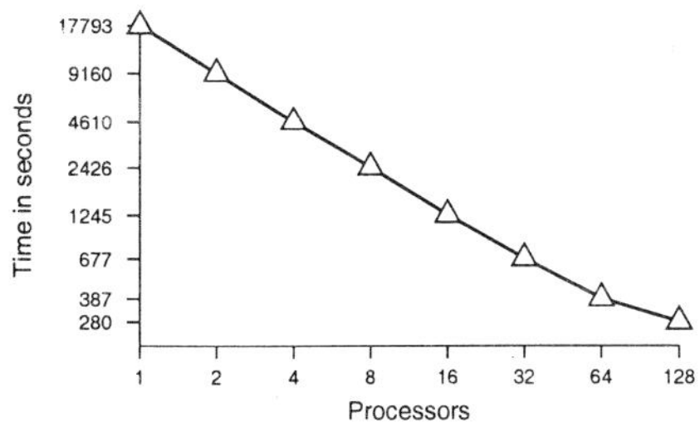

Figure 9: BigNetSim execution time with NAMD

is further complicated by the addition of several objects for each simulated node to handle trace input and perform message delivery confirmation.

This particular simulation achieved breakeven with the sequential simulator at 128 processors. BigNetSim was able to achieve a much earlier breakeven (16 processors, see Figure 8) for the 2048 node network when using TrafficGen. The reduced parallelism of the application trace revealed some implementation problems in BigNetSim which had been masked by the greater parallelism of artificial network loads. On closer inspection of the execution statistics provided by POSE, we found that BigNetSim execution time was dominated by rollback and GVT overhead. Closer analysis of the BigNetSim implementation indicates that the Switch object is too large and should be decomposed into smaller objects. Smaller objects take advantage of POSE performance characteristics as described in Section 2.

Simulation of detailed contention-based network models for predicting parallel performance is still quite challenging, but we have also achieved decent speedups relative to one-processor parallel time in [30]. An additional challenge is that the Apo-Lipoprotein A1 benchmark itself does not scale well beyond 3000 processors. This meant we could not get a credible result for the large network sizes (i.e. 8192) where BigNetSim achieves its best performance. The 2048 node run resulted in a small problem size of 3.5 million events, resolved by the sequential version of BigNetSim in a few minutes on a single processor.

6. Conclusions and future research

We have seen that simulation of interconnection networks for very large parallel computers presents a significant challenge, particularly when we wish to simulate their behavior for performance prediction of real applications. This problem presents two of the major drawbacks that make PDES challenging: fine granularity of computation and low degree of parallelism.

POSE has made it possible to study this and other problems by improving the chances of being able to scale such problems to greater numbers of processors. It

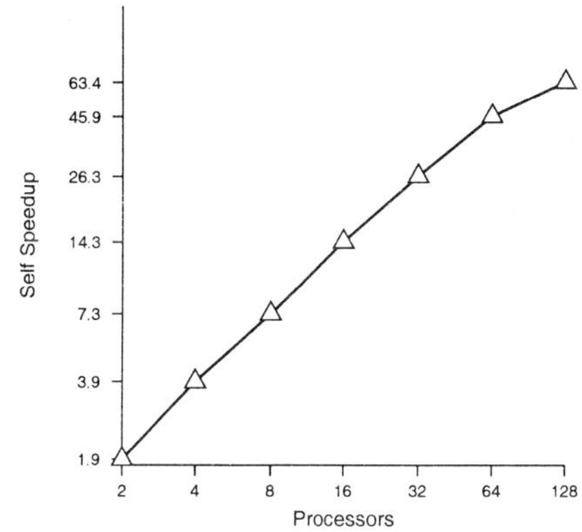

Figure 10: BigNetSim speedup with NAMD

incorporates a new object model based on virtualization and adaptive speculative strategies that can tune simulation behavior to a variety of applications. For our TrafficGen detailed network simulations, BigNetSim achieves excellent problem-size scaling, particularly for larger problem instances on greater numbers of processors. BigNetSim also exhibits excellent self-scaling (relative to single processor parallel runs). It is also capable of achieving break-even points relative to sequential time at 8 processors.

In the future, we plan to explore and expand the POSE load balancing framework as that seems key to improving the performance of this particularly challenging application. We also plan to enhance the adaptive capabilities of our synchronization strategies. BigNetSim's oversized Switch object will be broken up into smaller objects to lower the breakeven point and increase overall performance. Furthermore, higher fidelity modeling, specifically NIC performance constraints, will be studied. Performance prediction for other applications (such as Finite Element Simulations, larger NAMD benchmarks and Car Parinello Ab Initio Molecular Dynamics) will be undertaken. We anticipate that imminent access to actual Bluegene/L machines will allow us to improve the overall fidelity of the BigSim Project.

References

[1] V. S. Adve, R. Bagrodia, E. Deelman, and R. Sakellariou. Compiler-optimized simulation of large-scale applications on high performance architectures. *Journal of Parallel and Distributed Computing*, 62:393–426, 2002.

[2] A. Agarwal. Limits on Interconnection Network Performance. In *IEEE Transactions on Parallel and Distributed Systems*, October 1991.

[3] C. Benveniste and P. Heidelberger. Parallel simulation of the IBM SP2 interconnection network. In *Winter Simulation Conference*, 1995.

[4] K. Berkbigler, G. Booker, B. Bush, K. Davis, and N. Moss. Simulating the Quadrics Interconnection

Network. In *High Performance Computing Symposium 2003, Advance Simulation Technologies Conference 2003*, Orlando, Florida, April 2003.

[5] S. R. Das. Estimating the cost of throttled execution in time warp. In *Proceedings of the 10th Workshop on Parallel and Distributed Simulation*, pages 186–189, May 1996.

[6] S. R. Das. Adaptive protocols for parallel discrete event simulation. In *Winter Simulation Conference*, pages 186–193, 1996.

[7] S. R. Das, R. Fujimoto, K. S. Panesar, D. Allison, and M. Hybinette. GTW: a time warp system for shared memory multiprocessors. In *Winter Simulation Conference*, pages 1332–1339, 1994.

[8] P. M. Dickens, P. Heidelberger, and D. M. Nicol. A distributed memory lapse: parallel simulation of message-passing programs. *SIGSIM Simul. Dig.*, 24(1):32–38, 1994.

[9] C. Huang, O. Lawlor, and L. V. Kalé. Adaptive MPI. In *Proceedings of the 16th International Workshop on Languages and Compilers for Parallel Computing (LCPC 03)*, College Station, Texas, October 2003.

[10] D. Jefferson, B. Beckman, F. Wieland, L. Blume, and M. Diloreto. Time warp operating system. In *Proceedings of the eleventh ACM Symposium on Operating systems principles*, pages 77–93. ACM Press, 1987.

[11] L. V. Kalé. Performance and productivity in parallel programming via processor virtualization. In *Proc. of the First Intl. Workshop on Productivity and Performance in High-End Computing (at HPCA 10)*, Madrid, Spain, February 2004.

[12] L. Kalé and S. Krishnan. CHARM++: A Portable Concurrent Object Oriented System Based on C++. In *Proceedings of OOPSLA'93*, pages 91–108. ACM Press, September 1993.

[13] S. Kumarasamy, S. K. Gupta, and M. A. Breuer. Testing a K-Ary N-Cube Interconnection Network. In *IEEE International On-Line Testing Workshop*, June 1998.

[14] J. Liu and D. Nicol. *Dartmouth Scalable Simulation Framework User's Manual.* Dept. of Computer Science, Dartmouth College, Hanover, NH, February 2002.

[15] J. Liu, D. Nicol, B. J. Premore, and A. L. Poplawski. Performance prediction of a parallel simulator. In *PADS '99: Proceedings of the thirteenth workshop on Parallel and distributed simulation*, pages 156–164. IEEE Computer Society, 1999.

[16] H. Mehl. Speedup of conservative distributed discrete-event simulation methods by speculative computing. In *Proceedings of the Multiconference on Advances in Parallel and Distributed Simulation*, pages 163–166, January 1991.

[17] A. C. Palaniswamy and P. A. Wilsey. Adaptive bounded time windows in an optimistically synchronized simulator. In *Great Lakes VLSI Conference*, pages 114–118, March 1993.

[18] F. Petrini and M. Vanneschi. SMART: a Simulator of Massive ARchitectures and Topologies. In *International Conference on Parallel and Distributed Systems Euro-PDS'97*, Barcelona, Spain.

[19] J. C. Phillips, G. Zheng, S. Kumar, and L. V. Kalé. NAMD: Biomolecular simulation on thousands of processors. In *Proceedings of SC 2002*, Baltimore, MD.

[20] S. Prakash and R. L. Bagrodia. Mpi-sim: Using parallel simulation to evaluate mpi programs. In *Proceedings of IEEE Winter Simulation Conference*, 1998.

[21] S. K. Reinhardt, M. D. Hill, J. R. Larus, A. R. Lebeck, J. C. Lewis, and D. A. Wood. The wisconsin wind tunnel: Virtual prototyping of parallel computers. In *Measurement and Modeling of Computer Systems*, pages 48–60, 1993.

[22] L. M. Sokol, J. B. Weissman, and P. A. Mutchler. Mtw: an empirical performance study. In *Winter Simulation Conference*, pages 557–563. IEEE Computer Society, 1991.

[23] J. Steinman. SPEEDES: Synchronous Parallel Environment for Emulation and Discrete Event Simulation. In *Proceedings of the 1991 SCS Multiconference on Advances in Parallel and Distributed Simulation*, pages 95–103, January 1991.

[24] J. S. Steinman. Breathing time warp. In *Proceedings of the seventh workshop on Parallel and distributed simulation*, pages 109–118. ACM Press, 1993.

[25] D. Tutsch and M. Brenner. MINSimulate: A Multistage Interconnection Network Simulator. In *17th European Simulation Multiconference: Foundations for Successful Modeling and Simulation*, 2003.

[26] M. Uysal, A. Acharya, R. Bennett, and J. Saltz. A Customizable Simulator for Workstation Networks. In *11th International Parallel Processing Symposium (IPPS '97)*, Geneva, Switzerland.

[27] T. Wilmarth and L. V. Kalé. Pose: Getting over grainsize in parallel discrete event simulation. In *2004 International Conference on Parallel Processing*, pages 12–19, August 2004.

[28] T. L. Wilmarth. *POSE: Scalable General-purpose Parallel Discrete Event Simulation.* PhD thesis, Department of Computer Science, University of Illinois at Urbana-Champaign, 2005.

[29] G. Zheng, G. Kakulapati, and L. V. Kalé. Bigsim: A parallel simulator for performance prediction of extremely large parallel machines. In *18th International Parallel and Distributed Processing Symposium (IPDPS)*, Santa Fe, New Mexico, April 2004.

[30] G. Zheng, T. Wilmarth, P. Jagadishprasad, and L. V. Kalé. Simulation-based performance prediction for large parallel machines. In *International Journal of Parallel Programming*, number to appear, 2005.

[31] G. Zheng, T. Wilmarth, O. S. Lawlor, L. V. Kalé, S. Adve, D. Padua, and P. Guebelle. Performance modeling and programming environments for petaflops computers and the blue gene machine. In *NSF Next Generation Systems Program Workshop, 18th International Parallel and Distributed Processing Symposium(IPDPS)*, Santa Fe, New Mexico, April 2004. IEEE Press.

RINSE: the Real-time Immersive Network Simulation Environment for Network Security Exercises

Michael Liljenstam[1], Jason Liu[2], David Nicol[1], Yougu Yuan[1], Guanhua Yan[1], Chris Grier[1]

[1]University of Illinois at Urbana-Champaign
Coordinated Science Laborabory
1308 W. Main St., Urbana, IL 61801
{mili,nicol,yuanyg,ghyan,grier}@crhc.uiuc.edu

[2]Colorado School of Mines
Mathematical and Computer Sciences
Golden, CO 80401-1887
xliu@mines.edu

Abstract

The RINSE simulator is being developed to support large-scale network security preparedness and training exercises, involving hundreds of players and a modeled network composed of hundreds of LANs. The simulator must be able to present a realistic rendering of network behavior as attacks are launched and players diagnose events and try counter measures to keep network services operating. We describe the architecture and function of RINSE and outline how techniques like multiresolution traffic modeling and new routing simulation methods are used to address the scalability challenges of this application. We also describe in more detail new work on CPU/memory models necessary for the exercise scenarios and a latency absorption technique that will help when extending the range of client tools usable by the players.

1. Introduction

The climate on the Internet is growing increasingly hostile while organizations are increasingly relying on the Internet for at least some aspects of day-to-day operations. They are thus being forced to plan and prepare for network failures or outright attacks—how it might affect them and what actions to take. With current system complexity, tools to assist in preparedness evaluation and training are likely to become more and more important.

The October 2003 Livewire cyber war exercise [1] conducted by the Department of Homeland Security, is one particular instance of preparedness evaluation and training that involved companies across industrial sectors as well as government agencies. More exercises of this type are currently being planned, and based on experiences from the first event, there was a desire for improved tools to automatically determine the impact on the network from attacks and defensive actions and the extent to which the network is capable of delivering the services needed. Providing network simulation tool support for exercises such as Livewire is particularly challenging because of their scale. Future exercises are expected to involve as many as a couple of hundred participating organizations, and will thus involve many "players" and a network of significant size.

We are currently developing the Real-time Immersive Network Simulation Environment for network security exercises (RINSE) to meet this need and address the challenges inherent in this type of application. Hence, the goal for RINSE is to manage large-scale real-time human/machine-in-the-loop network simulation with a focus on security for exercises and training. It needs to be extensible so that it can evolve over time, and it needs to be designed with an eye towards security and resilience to hardware faults since these exercises involve many people and last for several days.

The spectrum of approaches to general large-scale network modeling being explored in the literature range from hardware emulation testbeds like Emulab [30], network emulators like ModelNet [29], to network simulators like IP-TNE [27], GTNetS [6], PDNS [6], and MAYA [31]. Hardware emulation excels in application code realism (running the real thing), while simulations tend to be more flexible and have an advantage in terms of scalability. However, the middle ground is increasingly being explored; for instance, through increasing emulation support in simulators. For security exercises we like the flexiblity and scalability of simulation, and the safety of unleashing attacks in a simulated environment rather than on a real network.

Several simulators offer similar capabilities, including parallel execution, real-time/emulation support, and discrete event/analytic models. However, we believe RINSE is unique in the way it brings together human/machine-in-the-loop real-time simulation support with multiresolution network traffic models, attack models that leverage the efficiency of the multiresolution traffic representations, novel

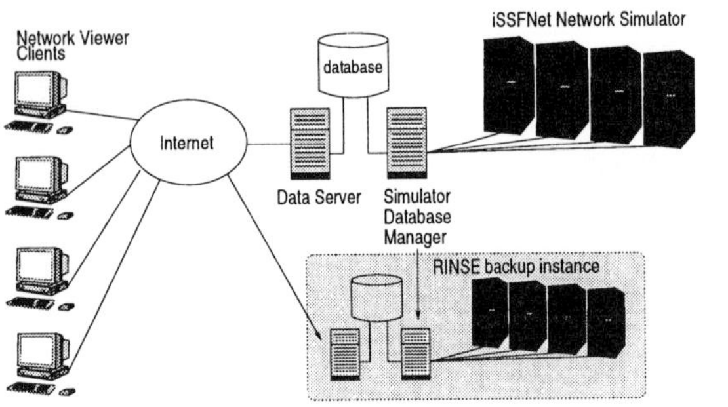

Figure 1: RINSE architecture

models of host/router resources such as CPU and memory, and novel routing simulation techniques. In this position paper we provide an overview of RINSE to show how these techniques are being brought to bear on the problem at hand. We also detail some specific new contributions: *i)* a technique for absorbing outside network latency into the simulation model and *ii)* models for including CPU and memory effects into network simulations.

The remainder of this paper is organized as follows. Section 2 describes the architecture of RINSE and outlines a simple example scenario that introduces the salient features of RINSE, described further in Sections 3 to 5. Finally, Section 6 summarizes and outlines future work.

2. RINSE Architecture

RINSE consists of five components: the iSSFNet network simulator, the Simulator Database Manager, a database, the Data Server, and client-side Network Viewers, as shown in Figure 1. The iSSFNet network simulator, formerly called DaSSFNet, is the latest incarnation of the C++ network simulator based on the Scalable Simulation Framework (SSF), an Application Programming Interface (API) for parallel simulations of large-scale networks [3]. iSSFNet runs on top of the iSSF simulation kernel, which handles synchronization and support functions. iSSF uses a composite synchronous/asynchronous conservative synchronization mechanism for parallel and distributed execution support [18], and has recently been augmented to include real-time interaction and network emulation support. iSSFNet runs on parallel machines to support real-time simulation of large-scale networks.

Each simulation node connects independently to the Simulator Database Manager, which delivers data from the simulator to the database and delivers control input from the database to the simulator. On the user/player side, the Data Server interfaces with client applications, such as the Java-based application "Network Viewer", which allows the user to monitor and control the simulated network. In the future, we plan to evolve the architecture towards using the emulation capabilities to support direct SNMP interaction with the simulated network devices, thus having regular networking utilities and network management tools as clients. In the current design, the Data Server performs authentication for each user, distributes definitions of the client's view of the network (using the Domain Modeling Language), and provides a simple way for the client applications to access new data in the database through XML-based remote procedure calls. The Network Viewer clients, a screen shot shown in Figure 2, provide the users with their local view of the network (usually only their organization's network) and periodically poll the Data Server for data. The Data Server responds with new data for each client, extracted from the database. The game managers, functioning as superusers of an entire exercise, also use Network Viewer clients, but can have a more global view of the network.

The Network Viewer clients have a simple command prompt where the user can issue commands to influence the model. User commands are sent in the opposite direction of the output data path and injected into the simulator. We currently divide the commands into five categories:

Attack– the game managers can launch attacks against networks or specific servers. RINSE focuses on Denial-of-Service effects on networks and devices, so attacks include DDoS and worms.

Defense– attacks can be blocked or mitigated, for instance by installing packet filters.

Diagnostic Networking Tools– functionality similar to some commonly used networking utilities, such as ping, are supported for the player to diagnose the network.

Device Control– individual devices, such as hosts and routers, can be shutdown or rebooted.

Simulator Data– commands can be issued to the simulator to control the output, turn on or off trace flow from a particular host, etc.

Depending on the type of a command, it may be addressing the whole simulator, a particular host or router, a particular interface, or a particular protocol or application on a host or router. A command handling infrastructure in the simulator passes the commands from the clients to the appropriate components of the simulation model.

2.1. Example Scenario

Consider a simple scenario where a player is responsible for a subnetwork, partially shown in Figure 2, containing among other things a server. Multiple clients are requesting information from the server through some form of transactions. By transaction we simply mean a request-response

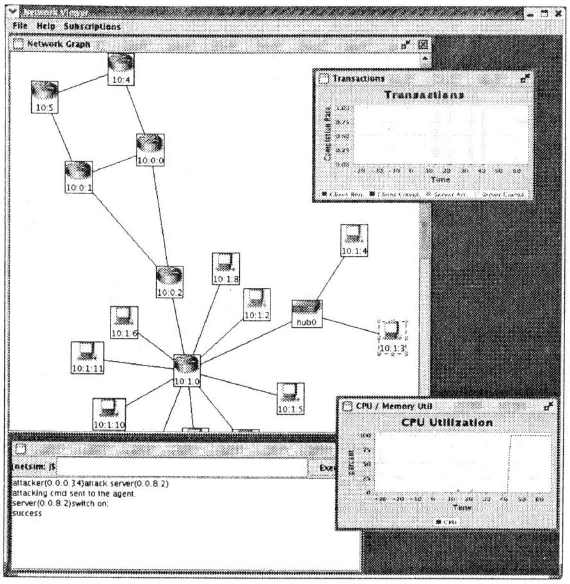

Figure 2: Network Viewer client screen shot

exchange between the client and the server. Section 4 outlines RINSE's models for efficient representation of traffic flows and route computation.

A game manager attempts to disrupt the operations of the server by launching a DDoS attack against open services on the server, and the player responsible for the network will need to diagnose what is going on and try to take remedial actions. The game manager launches the attack by issuing an attack command at the Network Viewer client:

```
ddos_attack attacker server 100 2000
```

Both `attacker` and `server` are symbolic names for the attacker's host and the targeted host, respectively. Upon receiving the command (via the command handling infrastructure), the attacker's host uses a simulated intermediate communication channel (e.g., Internet Relay Chat) to send attack signals to zombie hosts—hosts under the attacker's control. These zombie hosts then initiate the denial-of-service attack against the targeted victim. The attack is to last for 100 seconds and each zombie emits traffic at a rate of 2000 kbits/s. RINSE attack models leverage efficiencies in its high volume traffic representations (Section 4).

We will assume here that the DDoS traffic simply loads the open service daemons and thus induces a large CPU load on the server. This load disrupts the processing of legitimate transactions. As shown in the screen shot in Figure 2, the player managing the server can monitor the CPU utilization on the server and observe an abnormally high load. Models of host and router resources like CPU and memory are described in more detail in Section 5. After determining that the load likely stems from abnormal traffic, the player attempts to block traffic on a certain port that has been inadvertently left open by issuing the command:

```
filter server add 0 deny all all * all * 23
```

to install a filter on the server to deny packets coming in on `all` interfaces, using `all` protocols, from all source IP addresses ("*"), and `all` source ports, to all destination IP addresses ("*") and destination port 23. Successful filtering blocks packets from reaching the open service daemons and thus alleviates the load on the server at the expense of some processing cost for filtering.

We now proceed to describe aspects of the system mentioned here in more detail, starting with the real-time simulation support.

3. Real-time Simulation Support

In addition to supporting the RINSE Network Viewer client, we are currently developing support for the Simple Network Management Protocol (SNMP) to allow us to monitor and control the simulated network devices through industry-standard network management tools. For that reason, our real-time simulation support must be simple, flexible, and be able to accommodate real-time interactions at varying degrees of intensity, including both human-in-the-loop and machine-in-the-loop simulations. In this section, we describe the real-time support both in the iSSF parallel simulation kernel and in the network simulator supported by iSSF.

3.1. Kernel Support

Over the years, we have seen many network emulators, ranging from single-link traffic modulators to full-scale network emulation tools, e.g. [25, 29]. Most network emulators are time-driven. For example, ModelNet [29] stores packets in "pipes" sorted by the earliest deadline. A scheduler executes periodically (once every 100 μseconds) to emulate packet moving through the pipes. There are two main drawbacks associated with the time-driven approach: *i*) the accuracy of the emulation depends on the time granularity of the scheduler, which largely depends on the target machine or the target operating system, and *ii*) there has not been a good model used by network emulators to accurately characterize the background traffic and its impact on the foreground transactions (i.e., traffic connecting real-time applications). Simulation-based emulation (also referred to as *real-time network simulation*), on the other hand, provides a common framework for real application traffic to interact with simulated traffic, and therefore allows us to study both network and application behaviors with more realism. Examples of existing real-time network simulators include NSE [5], IP-TNE [27], MaSSF [16], and Maya [31]. IP-TNE is the first simulator we know that adopts parallel simulation techniques for emulating large-scale networks. The real-time support in iSSF inherits many features of these previous simulation-based emulators. Our approach, however, is unique in several ways, which we elaborate next.

Extending SSF API. The real-time support is designed as an extension to the SSF API, thus making an easy transition for other SSF models that require real-time support. In SSF, an `inChannel` (or `outChannel`) object is defined as a communication port in an entity to receive (send) messages from (to) other entities. We extended the concept of the in-channel using it as the conduit for the simulator to receive events from outside the simulator (e.g., accepting user commands arrived at a TCP socket). We extended the API so that a newly created in-channel object can be associated with a reader thread. The reader thread converts (external) physical events into (internal) virtual events and injects them into the simulator using the `putVirtualEvent` method. A virtual event is created to represent the corresponding physical event and is assigned with a simulation timestamp calculated as a function of *i*) the wall-clock time at which the event is inserted into the simulator's event-list, and *ii*) the current emulation throttling speed (which we will elaborate momentarily). The SSF entities receive events from the in-channel objects as before, regardless of whether they represent special devices that accept external events. From a modeling perspective, there is no distinction between processing a simulation event and a real-time event. Similarly, we also extended the concept of the out-channel using it as a device to export events (for example, reporting the network state to a client application over a TCP connection). In this case, a writer thread can be associated with the special `outChannel` object. The writer thread invokes the `getRealEvent` method to retrieve events designated for the external device and converts the virtual events into physical events. Each of these events is assigned with a real-time deadline indicating the wall-clock time at which the event is supposed to happen. The real-time deadline is calculated from the virtual time and again the emulation throttling speed. The writer thread is responsible for delivering the event upon the deadline.

Throttling Emulation Speed. The system can dynamically throttle the emulation speed (either by accelerating or decelerating the simulation execution with respect to real time). This feature is important for supporting fault tolerance. For example, if a simulator fails over a hardware problem, after fixing the problem, the simulator should be able to restart from a previously checkpointed state and quickly catch up with rest of the system. We can accelerate the emulation speed and use the same user input logged at the database server to restore the state. In order to regulate the time advancement, we modified the `startAll` method in the `Entity` class (which is used to start the simulation in SSF), adding an optional argument to allow the user to specify the emulation speed as the ratio between virtual time and wall-clock time—for example, a ratio of one means simulation in real-time, "infinity" means simulation as fast as possible, and zero means halting the simulation. An `Entity` class method `throttle` is also added to make it possible to dynamically change the ratio during the simulation.

Prioritizing Emulation Events: We use a priority-based scheduling algorithm in the parallel simulation kernel to better service events with real-time constraints. In SSF, the user can cluster entities together as timelines, i.e., logical processes, that maintain their own event-lists. Events on the timelines are scheduled according to a conservative synchronization protocol [18]. In a "pure" simulation scenario, where the simulation is set to run as fast as possible, a timeline can be scheduled to run as long as it has events ready to be processed safely without causing causality problems. For that reason, during the event processing session, the kernel executes all safe events of a timeline *uninterrupted* to reduce the context switching cost. When we enable emulation, however, the timelines that contain real-time events must be scheduled promptly.

To promptly process the events with real-time deadlines in the system, we adopted a greedy algorithm in iSSF assigning a high priority to emulation timelines. These timelines contain real-time objects—special in-channels and out-channels that are used for connecting to the physical world. Whenever a real-time event is posted and ready to be scheduled for execution on these emulation timelines, the system interrupts the normal event processing session of a non-emulation timeline and makes a quick context switch to load and process the real-time events in the emulation timeline. This priority-based scheduling policy allows the events that carry real-time deadlines to be processed ahead of regular simulation events. Note that, however, since normal simulation events may be on a critical path that affects a real-time event, this method is not an optimal solution. We are currently investigating other more efficient scheduling algorithms that can promptly process emulation events as well as events on the critical path, so that the real-time requirement can be satisfied in a resource-constrained situation.

3.2. Latency Absorption

We realize that the real-time demand not only puts a tight constraint on how we process events to reduce the chance of missed deadlines, but also on the connectivity between the simulator and the real applications. For example, consider a scenario in which a path is established between a client machine running the `ping` application and the machine running the network simulator, as shown in Figure 3. The client machine, which assumes the role of a host in the simulated network (with a virtual IP address 10.5.0.12),

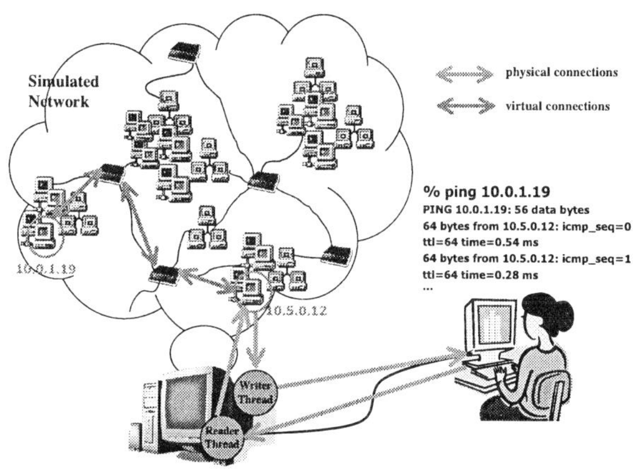

Figure 3: Emulation of a Ping Application

pings another host at 10.0.1.19. The ping application at the client machine generates a sequence of ICMP ECHO packets targeting 10.0.1.19. These packets are immediately captured by a kernel packet filtering facility [17] and then sent to the machine running the simulator. A reader thread receives these packets, and converts them to the corresponding simulation events. The simulator carries out the simulation by first putting the ICMP ECHO packets in the output queue of the simulated host 10.5.0.12. The packets are then forwarded over the simulated network to the designated host 10.0.1.19, which responds with ECHO REPLY packets. Once the packets return to the host 10.5.0.12, the simulator exports the events to a writer thread, which sends them to the client machine running the ping application. The client ping application finally receives the ECHO REPLY packets and prints out the result. Note that the segment of the path between the client application and the simulated host does not exist in the model. The problem is that the latencies of the physical connection can contribute a significant portion of the total round-trip delay. Simply on the forwarding path (from the client to the simulator), it may take hundreds of microseconds even on a high-speed local area network, before the emulation packet is eventually inserted into the simulator's event-list.[1] It can tremendously affect applications that are sensitive to such latencies.

Our solution to this problem is to hide the latencies due to the physical connection *inside* the simulated network. Since delays are imposed upon network packets transmitted from one router to another in simulation, we can modify the link layer model to absorb the latencies by sending the packet ahead of its due time. The simulator models the link-layer delay of a packet in two parts: the queuing time—the time to send all packets that are ahead of the packet in question, and the transmission time—the time for the packet to occupy the link before it can be successfully delivered, which we model as the sum of the link latency and the transmission delay—the latter is calculated by dividing the packet size by the link's transmission rate. Assuming that packets are sent in first-in-first-out (FIFO) order, the time required to transmit a packet is known as soon as the packet enters the queue at the link layer. Note that, if the FIFO ordering is not observed (e.g., packets are prioritized according to their types), one cannot predict the packet queuing time precisely. Furthermore, if we need to provide a more detailed model on lower protocol layers, the link state layer may play a significant role in determining the packet transmission time as well. In either case, we can still use a lower bound of the packet delays in our scheme. In the discussions to follow, we assume the delays are precise for better exposition.

We use a list to store the packets in the queue together with their precalculated transmission times. Let T_{now} be the current simulation time and P_0 be the last packet transmitted over the link. T_0 is the simulation time that P_0 starts transmission ($T_0 \leq T_{now}$). Let P_i be the ith packet in the queue, where $0 < i \leq N$ and N is the total number of packets currently in the queue. The time to transmit packet P_i is therefore $T_i = T_0 + \sum_{j=0}^{i-1}(\lambda + \beta_j)$, where λ is the link latency and β_j is the transmission delay of packet P_j. Suppose that an ICMP ECHO packet is created externally at wall-clock time t_R, and the corresponding simulation packet P_d is injected into the simulator at time t'_R. As a result, the packet carries a virtual time deficit of $\tau_d = (t'_R - t_R)/R$, where R is the proportionality constant that indicates the emulation speed (i.e., the ratio of virtual time to real time). Rather than appending the packet to the end of the queue, we insert the packet right before packet P_k, where $k = \max\{i | i \geq 0 \text{ and } \tau_d < \sum_{j=i}^{N}(\lambda + \beta_j)\}$.[2] After inserting the packet in the queue, we reduce deficit of the packet by the total transmission times of all packets behind the packet in the queue: $\sum_{j=k}^{N}(\lambda + \beta_j)$. Further improvement can be made to transmit the emulation packets even earlier. When a packet with a deficit becomes the head of the queue, we can simulate the packet transmission in zero simulation time. That is, we can further reduce the deficit by the packet's transmission time. Note that in iSSF the delay of the link that connects hosts belonging to two separate timelines is used to calculate the lookahead for the conservative parallel synchronization protocol. It is required that the link latency λ for cross-timeline links must be larger

1 The delay includes the time for the sender's operating system to capture and send the packet, the transmission time of the packet, the time for the reader thread to receive the packet, and the time for the simulator to finally accept the event and insert it into the appropriate event-list.

2 We do this by scanning the list from the packet at the tail of the list. k=0 means that the packet is inserted at the front of the list.

than zero. In this case, we can only reduce the deficit by as much as the expected packet transmission delay.

It is reasonable to insert an event with a time deficit ahead of others in the queue. After all, were the physical connection latencies not present, the event would have entered the queue much earlier. However, in cases where the deficit is larger than the sum of transmission time of all packets in the queue (the packet is therefore inserted at the head of the queue), we can only allow the packet to continue carrying the remainder of the deficit to the next hop, and therefore preempt events at the next hop. The process continues until the deficit is reduced to zero, or the packet reaches its destination. Since we do not "unsend" packets that have been sent before the emulation packet with the deficit arrives, this scheme is simply an approximation once the deficit is carried to the next hop.

Another issue concerns accommodating the physical connection latencies in the reverse path (from the simulator to the client application). A simple solution is to assume such latencies in the reverse path to be the same as in the forwarding path, and use a deficit of the same amount for all packets traveling in that direction. The problem with this approach is that the simulated network always tries to make up for the deficit within the first few hops, while in fact such a deficit is expected at the last segment of the path from the simulator to the application client. This means the interactions between the packets with deficits and other packets in simulation do not represent reality. We expect that, since in large-network simulations there are much fewer emulation packets than simulation packets, the effect of such a distortion may not be significant at all. We plan to quantify such effect in our future work.

4. Traffic, Attacks, and Routing

iSSFNet includes several novel techniques for modeling traffic, network attacks, and routing of traffic flows. A key technique employed in iSSFNet to make real-time simulation of large networks feasible is multi-resolution representations of traffic whereby the level of detail with which a traffic flow is simulated depends on how interested we are in the detailed dynamics of the flow. Traffic that is "in focus" (*foreground traffic*) is simulated with high fidelity at packet-level detail. Traffic that represents other things going on in the network (i.e., *background traffic*) is abstracted using fluid modeling, either using fine grained per-flow models, or coarse time-scale periodic fixed point solutions.

Fluid modeling [11, 15] is being explored also in other network simulators, such as MAYA [31], IP-TN [12], and HDCF-NS/pdns [24]. The models used in iSSFNet are based on our previous work to develop discrete-event fluid modeling of TCP and hybrid traffic interaction models such that the packet and fluid representations can coexist in the same simulation [21]. Recent work has addressed coarser models using fixed point solution techniques [22] of flow competition through a network, permitting several orders of magnitude speedups [19] and thus making it possible to represent larger networks and more flows in real time.

Attack models in RINSE focus on assets at a network resource level, i.e., things like network bandwidth, control over hosts, or computational or memory resources in hosts. Current attack models include DoS attacks, worms, and similar large-scale attacks typically involving large numbers of hosts and high intensity traffic flows. We are thus generally only interested in the coarse behavior of the attack traffic (a large volume of traffic) rather than the detailed traffic dynamics. Consequently, we leverage the coarser multi-resolution traffic models for efficient attack models, including zombie hosts emitting fluid DoS flows and fixed-point solutions of worm scan traffic intensities based on our previous work in multi-resolution worm modeling [14].

Memory and computational demands for routing of traffic have been identified as significant obstacles for large-scale network simulation and emulation. Some studies [23, 9, 2] start from the premise of shortest path routes and try to reduce computational and representational complexity through spanning tree approximations [9, 2] or lazy evaluation [23]. Others have achieved memory reductions in detailed protocol models, such as BGP (policy based routing) through implementation improvements [8, 4].

In iSSFNet we have developed a method for on-demand (lazy) computation of policy based routes, as computed by BGP [13]. For efficiency reasons and to ensure that traffic (attack traffic in particular) can address and reach a destination network even if the destination is missing, we need hierarchical addressing. Hence, our routing model is currently being extended to handle route aggregation. We are thus able to preload partial (precomputed) forwarding tables based on a priori known traffic patterns in the model, such as scripted background traffic, and compute routes for other flows as needed.

5. Modeling Device Resources

Earlier exercises of the type RINSE is targeting indicated the need to model not only limited network resources, like bandwidth, but also some aspects of constraints on computational resources in hosts and routers. Partly since they may be targeted for Denial-of-Service, but also to preclude unrealistic defensive strategies. For instance, zero cost packet filtering allows unrealistically large numbers of filters. Consequently, we need "light-weight" models of computational resources (CPU) and memory in RINSE, a problem that has not received much attention in network simulation to date since simple models have generally sufficed. For instance, a uniformly distributed compute delay has been used in studies of simulations of BGP routing [7], or a simple fixed cryptographic cost for S-BGP processing [20]. The sensor networking community, being very conscious of the constraints imposed by tiny sensors, are particularly interested in modeling the power consumption of different components, including the CPU [26].

5.1. CPU Model in RINSE

In RINSE a fair amount of detail is necessary and we identified the following requirements on our CPU model:

- *Interference* between different CPU intensive tasks.
- *Traffic delay* could result from high CPU load–in particular during abnormal (attack) conditions.
- Possibility of *packet loss* due to sustained high load.
- *Observable CPU load:* the user should be able to monitor CPU load to diagnose the system.
- *Light weight:* we must strive for the simplest possible models that can at least approximately represent the desired effects.

Thus, we require more behavior detail than many other applications do to be able to capture, at least coarsely, interactions between different tasks and traffic flows in terms of processing. This results in significant implementation hurdles, as will be described, and the situation is also complicated by the fact that the multi-resolution representation of traffic necessitates a multi-resolution representation of computational workload (i.e. hybrid discrete and fluid representations).

Interference: to observe interference between different tasks, we need to model how processing cycles are allocated. The generic UNIX process scheduling mechanism[3] [28] is based on priority scheduling, where process priorities are continuously recomputed to try to achieve good responsiveness and latency hiding for I/O bound tasks.

We do not want to get into the details of the scheduling mechanism, but be able to observe competition for resources. Within the CPU, a set of *tasks* are defined, where a task can be thought of as a process or thread. For instance, these could be application layer processes like web clients/servers, a database server, or lower layer functionality like a firewall process doing packet filtering on incoming packets. Figure 4 illustrates how each task services the work it has to do in FCFS order, but cycles are allocated among tasks using processor sharing. In this first model we simplify the problem by assuming that the tasks we consider have roughly the same priority (same range), so that

3 It varies somewhat between different flavors. Linux has a slightly different mechanism, but for the purposes of this discussion it's essentially the same.

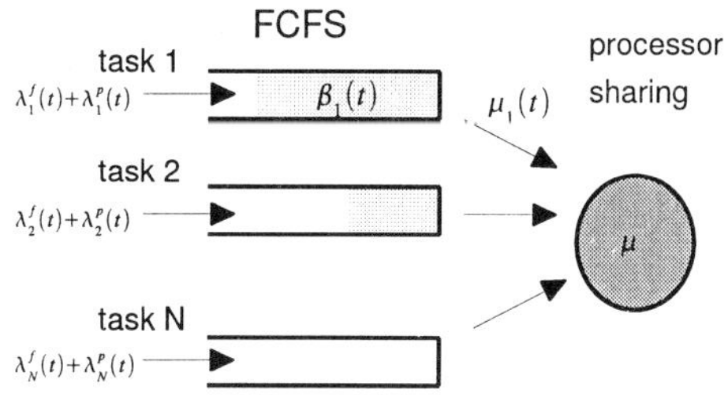

Figure 4: Processing work model where work is handled FCFS by tasks that are allocated "cycles" on the CPU

they are treated equally. The requests (incoming traffic) to each task may be a mixture of packets and fluid traffic flows. As in the hybrid packet/fluid traffic model in [21], we form a hybrid queue by fluidizing the packet load through estimating the packet rate. However, the service model interleaving the tasks actually make things even more complicated here than most hybrid traffic models since service is not FIFO. Assume there are N tasks. Let $\lambda_i^f(t)$ be the incoming fluid workload rate for task i (in cycles per second) at time t, and and μ is CPU service rate (i.e. its speed). A packet has an associated workload, w_t in cycles. By estimating the the packet arrival rate over a time window $[t', t]$, we get the estimated packet workload rate $\lambda_i^p(t)$. Let the total arriving workload for task i be $\lambda_i(t) = \lambda_i^f(t) + \lambda_i^p(t)$. We need to allocate a service rate to each task $\mu_i(t)$, determine backlog $\beta_i(t)$ and possibly lost work $\xi_i(t)$. A discrete workload arrival (packet workload) at t is always added to backlog on arrival $\beta_i(t) \leftarrow \beta_i(t) + w_t$. Note, however, that if no discrete arrivals preceded it in $[t', t]$, then $\lambda_i^p(t) = 0$.

We consider two cases:

Non-overload, the total incoming workload rate over all tasks is less than or equal to the workload service rate the CPU can handle, i.e. $\sum_i \lambda_i^f(t) + \lambda_i^p(t) \leq \mu$. In this case each task is first assigned the fluid service rate it requires $\mu_i(t) = \lambda_i^f(t) + \lambda_i^p$(t). Tasks that have any backlog ($\beta_i(t) > 0$), and this applies to any tasks processing packets, are marked as *greedy*. Let g be the number of greedy tasks. Any left-over cycles $\gamma(t) = \mu - \sum_i \mu_i(t)$ are allocated equally to greedy tasks $\mu_i(t) \leftarrow \mu_i(t) + \gamma(t)/g$. This ensures that the backlog gets drained as quickly as possible and thus packets are processed as quickly as possible. Consequently, fluid workload results in a processor utilization in proportion to the incoming rate, while discrete workload results in bursts of full utilization.

Overload, the sum of the incoming fluid workload rates and the averaged packet workload rates is greater than the service rate of the CPU. That is, there is a sustained overload condition. In this case the tasks are denied cycles in proportion to their fraction of the total workload, and what cannot be handled accumulates as backlog.

$$\mu_i(t) = \frac{\lambda_i(t) \cdot \mu}{\sum_i \lambda_i(t)} \tag{1}$$

An arriving discrete workload (packet) that does not yet have an average rate estimate poses a problem in this case. It is given $\mu_i(t) = 1$ (full utilization) without affecting other flows. This is unrealistic in that the total CPU service rate is now briefly more than μ, but is a reasonable approximation for occasional packets. If the packet is the first in a series with high average workload rate, then the service rates will be corrected the moment the first arrival rate estimate is calculated.

When a task is defined, a buffer space size b_i can be assigned to it to limit the backlog and introduce the possibility of loss of work if the task cannot keep up. Packets occupy buffer space according to their size until serviced. Fluid flows are assumed to have a simple linear relationship between the workload rate (cycles/second) and memory used for backlog rate (bytes/second). Modeling loss in hybrid queues is a delicate matter, as pointed out in [21]. If a discrete workload (packet) arrives to a back-logged task queue such that there is not enough space to fit it in the buffer we consider the state of the queue. If it is draining, the average arrival rate is less than the service rate, and we assume that it will fit (replacing fluid buffer space with the packet). If the queue is filling, we give the packet a probability of fitting into the queue equal to its proportion of the total task load $p = \lambda_i^p(t)/(\lambda_i^f(t) + \lambda_i^p(t))$.

In an overload condition tasks become coupled through competition for CPU and through the traffic flow, with fluid loads possibly leading to a cyclic dependency of traffic and CPU work; an unexpected complication. Figure 5 illustrates how we consider the cost of filtering and traffic forwarding in a firewall router, and if the CPU gets overloaded it needs to report back to the protocol layers so that they can reduce the traffic rate emitted. However, since the traffic flow passes first through filtering (A) and then forwarding (B) there is a feedback loop in terms of rate adjustments. When B changes its load to the CPU, it must update the serviced load for A. A must then update the traffic rate emitted to B, which must then perform another load update to the CPU. For n tandem tasks, where work is proportional to flow rate, the principle of proportional loss (equation 1) limits the feedback. Consider the i:th task. Let f_i be the inflow, $\lambda_i = k_i \cdot f_i$ be the (offered) workload, and c_i^n be the cycles allocated for task i. Initially, flow rate f_1 is sent through all tasks, so equation 1 implies we allocate cycles as $c_i^n = k_i / \sum_{j=1}^n k_j$. Tandem dependencies means

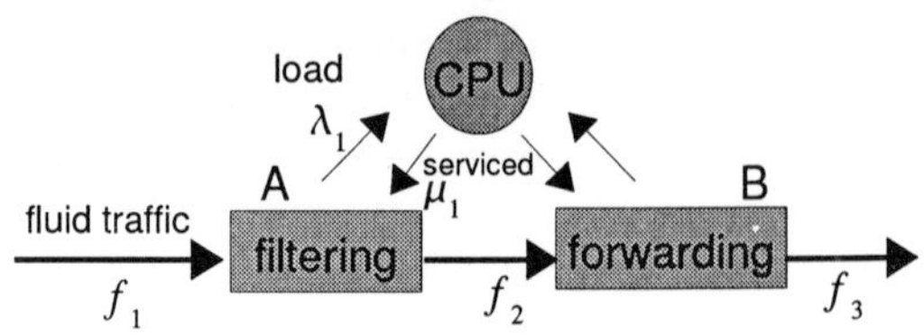

Figure 5: CPU control feedback on tasks and fluid flows

that $f_i = (c_{i-1}^n / \lambda_{i-1}) \cdot f_{i-1}$, and thus

$$\lambda_i = k_i \frac{c_{i-1}^n}{\lambda_{i-1}} f_{i-1} = \frac{k_i \cdot k_{i-1} f_{i-1} \cdot f_{i-1}}{\sum_{j=1}^n k_j f_{i-1} k_{i-1} f_{i-1}} = \frac{k_i}{\sum_{j=1}^n k_j}$$

That is, the required cycles λ_i to handle the adjusted inflow f_i equals the fraction of cycles assigned c_i^n, so the allocation stabilizes immediately. But completely avoiding this feedback loop does not appear possible, so we rate limit the feedback from the CPU to the protocol layers. Through this rate limiting, we mimic the control delay imposed by the scheduling mechanism and bound the computational costs in the model.

Traffic delay: one difficult issue was how to implement delays within the protocol stack without incurring significant overheads and code complexity. iSSFNet uses a protocol model inspired by the x-kernel design [10], where protocol sessions have a well defined common interface through which they can be plugged together. These are the push and pop methods. For maximum efficiency, the programming patterns used in the protocol stack are based on event-orientation through timer objects and continuations. Rather than switch to process-orientation to support arbitrary suspension points for packet processing delays, we opted to limit the possible suspension points to the push/pop entry interfaces (the socket API for the application layer). Thus, multiple delays on a packet within one protocol session will be merged into one delay that is not incurred until the point where the packet enters the next protocol session. The push/pop API's are good candidate suspension points because the state of processing of a packet (or a fluid flow) is passed in the packet itself along with a small number of additional parameters. Hence, we can safely assume that there are no additional state variables earlier in the execution stack that need saving. So, upon return we continue processing from the push or pop call without reconstructing the process stack. Other data structures in the protocol sessions, such as queues of packets that have been delayed pending some condition, evolve over time and thus do not require saving.

The accumulated delay for a packet within a protocol session is stored in the packet and thus detected as the packet reaches the next push/pop suspension point. Suspen-

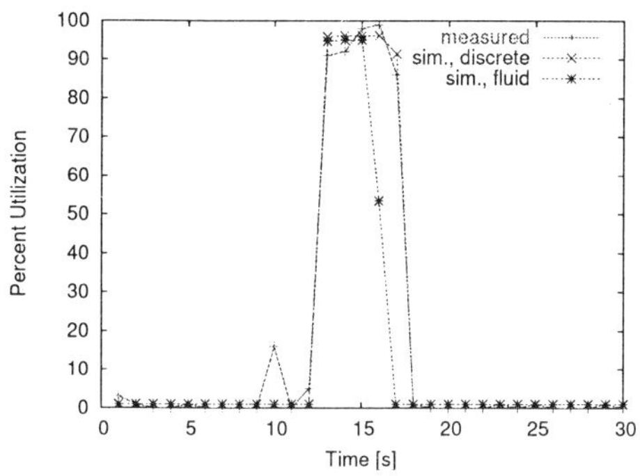

Figure 6: Example: `scp` transfer

sion points can be enabled or disabled through the DML configuration; the idea being to make it easy to aggregate delays, and thus aggregate events, by having fewer enabled suspension points. Displacing the suspension point from the point in the code where the delay should take place alters the causal ordering of state modifications in the model, i.e. the interleaving of updates in simulation time will be slightly altered. We believe this will not be a significant issue for the protocols under consideration here, but more experience with the model will be needed to bear this out.

5.2. Example

We illustrate the CPU model through a very simple example. In an experiment a 41.6 MB file was downloaded from a Linux laptop (acting as the server) using `scp` (secure copy). The CPU load on the data source (server) was monitored using `vmstat`. Figure 6 shows the CPU utilization during the transfer as "measured". This scenario was modeled in iSSFNet using its packet level TCP model. A client host is connected directly to a server host through a 100 Mb/s link. When modeling the CPU load, we have two choices: use a fluid representation of the load on the CPU, or use discrete chunks of work. The fluid representation is simple to use and has very low simulation cost. The drawback is that it is coarse and will not impose any delay on the the packets. Discrete work is more expensive to simulate, but is more fine-grained and delays packets.

Using fluid work, we simply call a `setFluid` method on the CPU, as the transfer starts, to set the instruction rate during the transfer (we simply match the observed utilization). When the transfer is completed the instruction rate is set back to zero. The result, shown as "fluid load", indicates a shorter transfer time than what was measured. Alternatively, we can use discrete workloads. Examining the OpenSSH scp implementation indicates that it transfers data through a 2 KB buffer, so we write data to the socket in 2 KB blocks and impose a compute delay on each block for data transfer and encryption. The computation cost is registered through a call to `cpu.use(...)` with the number of instructions used and a pointer to the socket being used. The socket `send()` code hides a call to `cpu.delay(...)` causing the socket processing to be suspended and delayed. We also use a timer to add a small idle delay between each block to model latencies. After tuning these delays, the result shown as "discrete load", can be made to match reality fairly well.

There is a significant difference in simulation cost between these two approaches. Using fluid CPU load, no extra events are added by the CPU model, but with the discrete workload model, each block requires a resource departure event and results in an event for drained backlog. Thus, the total event count increases by a factor of about 2.4 and the execution time by a factor of 4. It is up to the modeler to determine when the additional cost is justified.

Aside from approximations arising from implementation decisions, the current CPU resource model represents many simplifications. The principle of proportional loss is frequently used for fluid traffic and alleviates the allocation feedback issue mentioned previously. But we see the need for more emphasis on distinction of task priorities to better mimic prioritization of processes and threads. For instance, kernel level processes should be largely insulated from demands at the user level. We are looking into new allocation policies that can prioritize demands.

6. Summary and Future Work

RINSE incorporates recent work on *i)* real-time interaction/emulation support, *ii)* multi-resolution traffic modeling, *iii)* efficient attack models, *iv)* efficient routing simulation, and *v)* CPU/memory resource models, to target large-scale preparedness and training exercises. Described here were efficient CPU/memory models necessary for the scenario exercises, and a latency absorption technique that will help when extending the range of client tools usable by the players.

Aside from model refinements, our ongoing and future work includes more fundamental issues such as supporting fault tolerance and efficient real-time scheduling of compute intensive tasks like background traffic calculations and major routing changes. For example, we would like our simulation framework to permit certain background tasks, such as background traffic calculations, to be adaptively scheduled based on higher priority load.

Acknowledgements This research was supported in part by DARPA Contract N66001-96-C-8530, NSF Grant CCR-0209144, and DHS Office for Domestic Preparedness award 2000-DT-CX-K001. Thus, the U.S. Government retains a non-exclusive, royalty-free license to publish or reproduce this contribution. Points of view expressed are those of the authors and do not necessarily represent the official position of the U.S. Department of Homeland Security.

References

[1] T. Bridis. Gov't simulates terrorist cyberattack. Associated Press, `http://www.zone-h.org/en/news/-read/id=3728`, November 2003.

[2] J. Chen, D. Gupta, K. Vishwanath, A. Snoeren, and A. Vahdat. Routing in an Internet-scale network emulator. In *Symposium on Modeling, Analysis and Simulation of Computer and Telecommunication Systems (MASCOTS)*, October 2004.

[3] J. Cowie, D. Nicol, and A. Ogielski. Modeling the global Internet. *Computing in Science and Engineering*, 1(1):42–50, January 1999.

[4] X. Dimitropoulos and G. Riley. Large-scale simulation models of BGP. In *Symposium on Modeling, Analysis and Simulation of Computer and Telecommunication Systems (MASCOTS)*, October 2004.

[5] K. Fall. Network emulation in the Vint/NS simulator. In *4th IEEE Symposium on Computers and Communications (ISCC'99)*, pages 244–250, July 1999.

[6] R. Fujimoto, K. Perumalla, A. Park, H. Wu, M. Ammar, and G. Riley. Large-scale network simulation – how big? how fast? In *Symposium on Modeling, Analysis and Simulation of Computer Telecommunication Systems (MASCOTS)*, October 2003.

[7] T. Griffin and B. Premore. An experimental analysis of bgp convergence time. In *9th International Conference on Network Protocols (ICNP)*, November 2001.

[8] F. Hao and P. Koppol. An Internet scale simulation setup for BGP. *ACM SIGCOMM Computer Communication Review*, 33(3):43–57, July 2003.

[9] P. Huang and J. Heidemann. Minimizing routing state for light-weight network simulation. In *Symposium on Modeling, Analysis and Simulation on Computer and Telecommunication Systems (MASCOTS)*, August 2001.

[10] N. C. Hutchinson and L. L. Peterson. The x-kernel: An architecture for implementing network protocols. *IEEE Transactions on Software Engineering*, 17(1):64–76, January 1991.

[11] G. Kesidis, A. Singh, D. Cheung, and W. W. Kwok. Feasibility of fluid-driven simulation for atm network. In *Proceedings of IEEE Globecom*, November 1996.

[12] C. Kiddle, R. Simmonds, C. Williamson, and B. Unger. Hybrid packet/fluid flow network simulation. In *17th Workshop on Parallel and Distributed Simulation*, June 2003.

[13] M. Liljenstam and D. Nicol. On-demand computation of policy based routes for large-scale network simulation. In *2004 Winter Simulation Conference (WSC)*, December 2004.

[14] M. Liljenstam, D. Nicol, V. Berk, and R. Gray. Simulating realistic network worm traffic for worm warning system design and testing. In *2003 ACM Workshop on Rapid Malcode (WORM)*, October 2003.

[15] B. Liu, D. R. Figueiredo, Y. Guo, J. Kurose, and D. Towsley. A study of networks simulation efficiency: Fluid simulation vs. packet-level simulation. In *IEEE Infocom*, Anchorage, Alaska, April 2001.

[16] X. Liu, H. Xia, and A. Chien. Network emulation tools for modeling grid behavior. In *3rd IEEE/ACM International Symposium on Cluster Computing and the Grid (CC-Grid'03)*, May 2003.

[17] S. McCanne and Van Jacobson. The BSD packet filter: a new architecture for user-level packet capture. In *Winter USENIX Conference*, pages 259–269, January 1993.

[18] D. Nicol and J. Liu. Composite synchronization in parallel discrete-event simulation. *IEEE Transactions on Parallel and Distributed Systems*, 13(5):433–446, May 2002.

[19] D. Nicol, J. Liu, M. Liljenstam, and G. Yan. Simulation of Large-Scale Networks Using SSF. In *Winter Simulation Conference (WSC)*, December 2003.

[20] D. Nicol, S. Smith, and M. Zhao. Evaluation of efficient security for BGP route announcements using parallel simulation. *Simulation Pratice and Theory Journal, special issue on Modeling and Simulation of Distributed Systems and Networks*, June 2004.

[21] D. Nicol and G. Yan. Discrete event fluid modeling of background TCP traffic. *ACM Transactions on Modeling and Computer Simulation*, 14:1–39, July 2004.

[22] D. Nicol and G. Yan. Simulation of network traffic at coarse time-scales. In *Workshop on Principles of Advanced and Distributed Simulation (PADS)*, 2005.

[23] G. Riley, M. Ammar, and R. Fujimoto. Stateless routing in network simulations. In *Symposium on Modelling, Analysis, and Simulation of Computer and Telecommunication Systems (MASCOTS)*, May 2000.

[24] G. Riley, T. Jaafar, and R. Fujimoto. Integrated fluid and packet network simulations. In *Symposium on Modeling, Analysis, and Simulation of Computer and Telecommunication Systems (MASCOTS)*, October 2002.

[25] L. Rizzo. Dummynet: a simple approach to the evaulation of network protocols. *ACM SIGCOMM Computer Communication Review*, 27(1):31–41, January 1997.

[26] A. Savvides, S. Park, and M. B. Srivastava. On modeling networks of wireless micro sensors. In *SIGMETRICS*, June 2001.

[27] R. Simmonds and B. Unger. Towards scalable network emulation. *Computer Communications*, 26(3):264–277, February 2003.

[28] A. Tanenbaum. *Modern Operating Systems, 2nd ed.* Prentice Hall, Upper Saddle River, NJ, 2001.

[29] A. Vahdat, K. Yocum, K. Walsh, P. Mahadevan, D. Kostic, J. Chase, and D. Becker. Scalability and accuracy in a large scale network emulator. In *Proceedings of the 5th Symposium on Operating Systems Design and Implementation (OSDI'02)*, December 2002.

[30] B. White, J. Lepreau, L. Stoller, R. Ricci, S. Guruprasad, M. Newbold, M. Hibler, C. Barb, and A. Joglekar. An integrated experimental environment for distributed systems and networks. In *Fifth Symposium on Operating Systems Design and Implementation*, pages 255–270, December 2002.

[31] J. Zhou, Z. Ji, M. Takai, and R. Bagrodia. MAYA: integrating hybrid network modeling to the physical world. *ACM Transactions on Modeling and Computer Simulation (TOMACS)*, 14(2):149–169, April 2004.

Network Simulation

Efficient Simulation of Wireless Networks using Lazy MAC State Update *

Young J. Lee and George F. Riley

School of Electrical & Computer Engineering
Georgia Institute of Technology, Atlanta, GA 30332
Email: {young, riley}@ece.gatech.edu
Tel: (404) 894-9041; Fax: (404) 894-9959

Abstract

Scalable and efficient network simulation methods are the method of choice for evaluating and verifying wireless network protocols on a moderate to large scale. This need becomes obvious when simulating very large–scale wireless networks such as emerging ad hoc sensor networks in which the number of nodes can be the order of thousands or more, and with very high node density. Unfortunately, simulation of such large–scale wireless networks often requires excessively large amounts of computing resources and can be slow to complete. One approach to achieving higher performance in a large–scale network simulation is the use of parallel *or* distributed *simulation techniques. However, the efficient distributed simulation of wireless ad hoc networks is still a daunting task. Therefore, we turn our attention to more traditional sequential simulation methods, and seek to reduce the overhead incurred in the Medium Access Control (MAC) state update propagation between wireless nodes. We introduce a novel method called* LAMP *(LAzy MAC state uPdate), that substantially reduces this overhead, with no loss of accuracy. Using our wireless network simulation tool, we compare the efficiency of the* LAMP *approach to the more traditional approach, and show a performance improvement of up to a factor of eight, with no loss of accuracy.*

1 Introduction

The importance of effective evaluation and verification of wireless network protocols has been growing with the advancements and proliferation of wireless communications and computer technologies. A number of high–quality network simulation environments exist for analysis of the performance of wireless ad hoc networks, including *ns2* [1, 2], *GloMoSim* and its commercial counterpart *QualNet* [3], *OPNet* [4], and the Georgia Tech Network Simulator (*GTNetS*) [5]. All of these tools have detailed models of the IEEE 802.11 [15] wireless MAC protocol, as well as models for physical layer path loss. However, these tools also all suffer from degraded performance when simulating the wireless protocols, when compared to a similar sized *wired* network simulation. There are several contributing factors to the reduced performance for wireless simulation tools, including the complexity of accurate path loss and fading calculations in the physical layer, and the excessive number of simulation events needed to coordinate the MAC state updates between wireless nodes.

When the scalability property of a network protocol is especially of interest, scalable and efficient network simulation methods are required. This need becomes evident when one wishes simulation of very large–scale wireless networks such as emerging ad hoc sensor networks in which the number of nodes can be the order of thousands or more, and the node density can be very high. A traditional network simulation tool such as *ns2* is usually a poor choice in such an environment, due to excessive execution time and memory requirements.

One approach to address the performance issue is the use of *parallel* or *distributed* network simulation techniques, such as those used by *GloMoSim/QualNet* [3], *SSFNet* [7], *SWAN* [8], *pdns* [9], and *GTNetS* [5]. For the most part, these parallel simulation tools use a conservative synchronization approach, and rely on *lookahead* [10] to achieve reasonable performance. Usually, the lookahead value in parallel network simulations is obtained from the propagation delay of a signal going through a communication medium, as well as the packet transmission time on the link. However, in wireless networks, this propagation delay is usually very small (order of micro-seconds). Further, the MAC state information must be propagated to peers when the *first bit* of a packet is received by a receiver. Hence,

*This work is supported in part by NSF under contract numbers ANI-9977544, ANI-0136969, ANI-0240477, ECS-0225417, and DARPA under contract number N66002-00-1-8934.

the performance improvement of wireless network simulations through parallel simulation techniques has not been significant, and sometimes it is even worse than a *sequential* simulation [6].

In this paper, we introduce a different approach to improving the performance of wireless network simulations. Our approach, called *LAMP*, leads to substantial improvements in overall execution time and reduction in the size of the pending event list.

Our technique is motivated from the observation that informing all *potential* receivers of a given transmission is not necessary. In general, the MAC state of a node in a wireless network is only important *if the node wishes to transmit a packet.* More traditional approaches schedule a packet reception event at all potential receivers of a packet, including *undesignated* [1] receivers. The *designated* receivers of course must be able to sense and consequently receive the packet. However, undesignated receivers do not have to be aware of the transmission unless they are interested in accessing the communication medium in the near future. If one of the undesignated receiver nodes wishes to access the channel later, then it has only to update its MAC state related with the channel access according to the previous transmissions, i.e., according to the *history* of the medium access by other transmitter nodes.

The remainder of the paper is organized as follows. Section 2 gives an overview of the *LAMP* technique, with details given in Section 3. In Section 4, the performance evaluation results of *LAMP* are presented. We review some related work in Section 5, and then finalize the paper in Section 6 with conclusions and future work.

2 Overview of Lazy MAC State Update

As previously mentioned, with the *LAMP* method of delayed MAC state updates, the MAC state of each node is not updated needlessly. It is brought up-to-date only when a node wishes to join communications as a transmitter or a designated receiver. For example, let us suppose that there are three nodes, A, B, and C in a simple wireless network, and they share an IEEE 802.11 [15] wireless medium as shown in Fig. 1. Let us assume that each node is within the transmission range of the others, and node A wishes to send a unicast packet to node B with a preceding Request-To-Send (RTS) – Clear-To-Send (CTS) exchange. With a more traditional approach, every transmission from A and B will incur packet reception events and the relevant MAC state updates at C since C is within the transmission range of A and B. With *LAMP* however, no packet reception event will

[1] For unicast communications, there is only one receiver, and it is referred to as a designated receiver. The others that are not designated but hear the transmitted signal are called undesignated receivers.

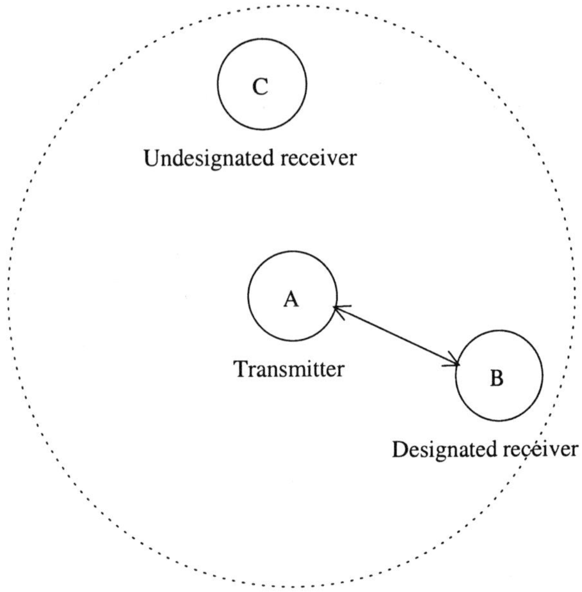

Figure 1. An example of a simple wireless network.

be scheduled at C and no MAC state update occur at C, because it is undesignated. If C wants to communicate with A while the communication between A and B is going on, C must become aware that it cannot access the medium at that time, and does so by updating its MAC state according to the medium access history. Thus, it behaves as if it heard the RTS-CTS exchange and performed the corresponding physical and virtual carrier sensing.

With *LAMP*, a *wireless link event list* is introduced and implemented as a medium access history buffer. This list contains full information necessary to bring the MAC state of undesignated receivers up-to-date. Its detailed structure will be discussed in the following sub-sections.

The wireless link event list is maintained per wireless link object that represents a wireless communication channel. [2] In addition, another list known as a *communicating entity list* is used. This list is used to guarantee that a node can safely change its MAC state without consulting the wireless link event list if it receives a packet. In a wireless network, a situation can occur where a node is both a communicating entity and an undesignated receiver, since a node can be involved in multiple communications at the same time. In such a case, the packet reception event from a communication in which the node is undesignated needs to be scheduled because the node is a communicating entity (as a transmitter or a designated receiver) for another com-

[2] The wireless link is a virtual channel object for scheduling of packet receipt events occurring through the channel. Note that it is not related with the channel state of a node.

munication and consequently needs to keep its MAC state updated.

The communicating entity list contains the nodes that are currently involved in communications. Therefore, any node that wishes to communicate through a medium will be added to this list, as well as all designated receivers. The added entities will be removed from the list as soon as the communication involving them completes.

When nodes want to communicate through a medium, they first must update their MAC states according to the wireless link event list. Then the nodes are added to the communicating entity list. When a node determines that it is allowed to access the medium, it transmits the packet, and records information about the transmission in the wireless link event list. The packet reception event due to this transmission is scheduled at the designated receivers normally, and is also scheduled for all nodes on the communicating entity list, excepting the transmitter itself. The fact that a node is on the communicating entity list means that the node must keep its MAC state updated. This is why the packet reception event should be scheduled at the nodes on the communicating entity list as well as the designated receivers. After the transmission completes, the transmitter and the corresponding designated receivers are removed from the communicating entity list.

In unicast communications, a data packet transmission completes when the sender finishes transmitting it and receives an ACK for the data packet from the view point of the sender. From the perspective of the receiver, the communication ends when the receiver of the data packet finishes transmitting an ACK to the sender. In the broadcast case, the communication ends as soon as the sender finishes transmitting the data packet and the receivers receive it. At the starting point of each communication, the sender and the designated receivers are entered into the communicating entity list, and they are removed from the list at the termination of the communication.

The overall effect of the *LAMP* method is a significant reduction in overall execution time due to the reduced number of MAC state update events, at the expense of the maintenance of the wireless link event list and the communicating entity list. We show later that benefits of the reduced event count are significant as compared to the relatively small overhead of the list maintenance.

3 The Detailed Structure and Algorithm

3.1 The List Structures

One of the key structures of *LAMP* is the wireless link event list. There is one such list for every wireless link object that represents a wireless medium, and it is accessible from each node in the network that shares the medium. Each item in the list consists of the following elements:

- Time that the transmission started
- Time that the transmission ended
- Location of the transmitter node
- Information of the transmitted frame

The first element is the timestamp for the start of a packet transmission event. The second element is used to compute the time of a packet reception event at each receiver. The propagation delay is added to this time to obtain the exact point of time for the packet reception. The third element is used to compute the distance between the transmitter and the receiver so that this distance can be used as one of the inputs to the propagation model, and the signal strength at the receiver can be calculated. The last element specifies the characteristics of the transmitted packet such as frame type and the type-specific information. For example, it will specify if the frame is RTS, CTS, Data, or Acknowledgment (ACK) as well as the corresponding information in the case of the IEEE 802.11 [15] as the MAC protocol.

The wireless link event list is implemented using a double-ended queue, with new items added at the end. Since the generation of the wireless link events are created strictly in timestamp order, this list is naturally sorted by ascending timestamps. When entries are added, old entries are removed when they become so old as to be no longer meaningful. Each node maintains a logical index pointer to the list that indicates the most recent item upon which its MAC state was updated.

The communicating entity list is simply a list of nodes (actually of wireless link interfaces) that are currently involved in communications as a transmitter and/or a designated receiver. Hence scheduling of a packet reception event must be done at each entity on this list if it is within transmission power range of a given packet transmission. In practice, it can be implemented in such a way that it holds a list of pointers to the corresponding objects. This list is also maintained per wireless link object, and each node that shares the medium can access this list.

3.2 Procedures for Lazy MAC State Update

There are a number of housekeeping details needed to properly maintain MAC state using *LAMP*. These can generally be classified into three main categories:

- Updating the MAC state (UPD_MAC)
- Joining the communicating entity list (JOIN_CE)
- Leaving from the communicating entity list (LEAVE_CE)

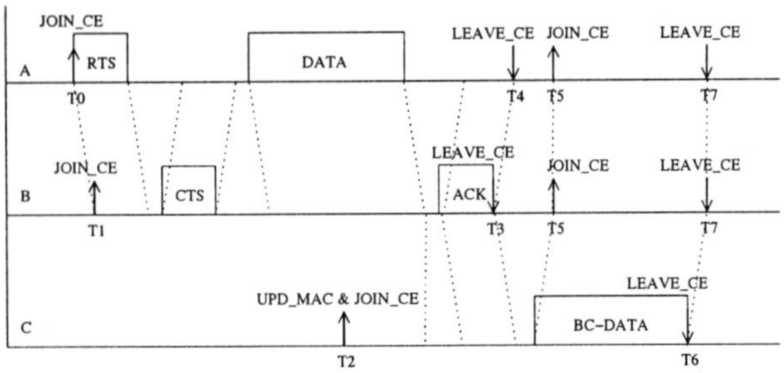

Figure 2. The timing diagram of lazy MAC state update.

The UPD_MAC procedure operates on the wireless link event list, and updates the MAC state of a node according to the packet transmission history. The other two procedures work with the communicating entity list, and they add or remove a node to or from the list.

Fig. 2 shows the timing diagram of the *LAMP* algorithm for the previous example of the simple wireless network described in Fig. 1. At time $T0$, A initiates a unicast communication by transmitting an RTS to B, and then the JOIN_CE procedure is called at A. B detects the first bit arrival of the RTS at time $T1$, joins the communicating entity list, and generates CTS for A. These RTS and CTS frames, however, are not scheduled for reception at C even if it is within the transmission range of A and B because it is not designated, and consequently no carrier sensing function is performed by the MAC layer of C. Let us suppose that there is a broadcast data request for C from the upper layer at time $T2$. C now updates its MAC state according to the wireless link event list that holds the past transmission records and behaves as if it heard the RTS-CTS exchange between A and B. After the update, C also joins the communicating entity list. After the unicast communication completes, and the corresponding LEAVE_CE procedure is performed at time $T3$ for B and at time $T4$ for A respectively, C is allowed to access the medium and transmits the requested broadcast data. This initiates another communication, and thus B and C perform the JOIN_CE procedure at time $T5$ when they hear the transmission, and the LEAVE_CE is requested at the end of the communication, i.e., at time $T6$ when A finishes transmitting the data packet and at time $T7$ when A and B successfully receive it. The detailed operation of each procedure is described as follows.

3.2.1 UPD_MAC Procedure

This procedure is called for just before a node joins the communicating entity list to bring the node's MAC state up-to-date. There are two right points in the method where this must be done. One is from a sender's perspective when a node has received a data send request from the upper layer, and the other is from a receiver's view point when a node has detected the first bit arrival from the sender.

In the UPD_MAC procedure, a node scans the wireless link event list and processes each item in the list. First, it examines if there are any items that need to be processed. If all the items are *old* (meaning they have already been processed), the procedure just returns without performing MAC state update. Otherwise, the corresponding items are processed according to the ascending order of time that each event occurred.

Generally, each update is done according to the following steps:

1. Compute the locations and the distance between communicating entities.
2. Calculate the signal strength after applying the propagation model.
3. Determine if the node can hear the transmission based on the signal strength and the transmission range.
4. Update the MAC state and perform carrier sensing functions as needed.

The MAC state variables involved in step 4 can be, for example, idle time, physical carrier sensing state, and network allocation vector (NAV) specified in IEEE 802.11. In step 4, scheduling of a packet reception event at its own node can happen if the first bit arrival time of the packet is past, and the last bit arrival is in the future. In that case, the node generates a corresponding packet according to the frame information in the wireless link event list, and schedules the reception at its own interface. Also, this procedure deals with overlapping of multiple signals if the *radio capture* capability of the MAC layer is enabled.

3.2.2 JOIN_CE Procedure

In the JOIN_CE procedure, a node is added to the communicating entity list after the corresponding update of its MAC state is done by the UPD_MAC procedure. For unicast communications, the designated receiver is added to the list as soon as the receiver detects the first bit arrival of a packet. For broadcasts, any node that can hear the transmission is added to the list. The transmitting node is also added to the list regardless of the communication type. This procedure first checks if there is already the same entity existing on it before adding a new entity.

Once a node is added to the communicating entity list, every packet that can be heard by the node is scheduled for reception at the node from that time on. The fact a node is on the list means that the MAC state of the node keeps being updated. This is to enable a communicating node to change its MAC state safely without preceding MAC state update when it has received a packet.

3.2.3 LEAVE_CE Procedure

The LEAVE_CE procedure deals with removal of a node from the communicating entity list. This procedure can be requested at multiple places once a node is added to the list by the JOIN_CE procedure.

Typically, this procedure is called at the end of each successful packet transmission. For the 802.11 protocol, this occurs from a sender's perspective when it has received an ACK frame for the packet, and from a receiver's perspective when the receiver has finished transmitting the ACK. For broadcast communications, it is the moment when the sender completes transmitting a packet and when the receivers successfully get the last bit of the packet.

The LEAVE_CE procedure must be handled carefully when a communication ends with an error. A communication error can occur due to collisions in a wireless network and result in unsuccessful transmission or erroneous packet reception. For that case, each node involved in the communication is withdrawn from the communicating entity list by the LEAVE_CE procedure.

4 Performance Evaluation

In this section, we present the performance evaluation results obtained from several different scenarios. The *LAMP* technique is compared to the traditional simulation method through extensive simulation experiments. The simulation environment is described in detail, and then the simulation results are presented and discussed.

4.1 The Simulation Environment

All of our simulation experiments were done using GTNetS [5]. GTNetS is a scalable simulation tool designed specifically to support large–scale simulations. The design of the simulator closely matches the design of real network protocol stacks and hardware.

The *LAMP* technique can apply to any type of MAC protocols, but we used the IEEE 802.11 [15] protocol for all experiments with two-ray ground reflection [16] as the propagation model.

We did two sets of experiments to measure the performance of the *LAMP* technique. First, we tested it for two extreme cases. One was for unicast only networks, and the other for broadcast only networks. As discussed, the key to *LAMP* is that we schedule packet reception events only at communicating entities so that unnecessary computation regarding MAC state maintenance can be saved. Therefore, the performance gain is expected to be great when there are a small number of communicating entities per transmission in the network. This is the case for the unicast only network. On the other hand, the performance may not be as good as in the former case if there are lots of entities involved in a transmission, which is the case for the broadcast only network since all the nodes within a transmission range are designated receivers in a broadcast. This is the reason that we want to test the new method for the two extreme cases. For this first set of experiments, we put all the nodes in such a way that every node can sense every other's transmission, i.e., every communication can happen in a single hop in order to remove effects of routing protocols. In this set of experiments, we executed simulations varying the number of traffic flows from 5 to 20, and the number of nodes in the simulated network was 100.

For the second set of experiments, we constructed more realistic networks with two mobility characteristics. One is with no mobility, and the other with the random waypoint mobility model [2]. For the latter case, the pause time was 200 seconds, and the node speed was uniformly distributed between 0 and 10 meters/second. In this experiment, the primary variables were node density and traffic volume. We varied the node density from 10 to 100, and the number of traffic flows from 5 to 20. We also performed experiments varying the network topology and traffic patterns. The ratio of the radio transmission range to the network radius was properly set to force multi-hop routing for this set of experiments. The number of nodes in the simulated network was 500.

For both experiments, all traffic was created with a constant-bit-rate (CBR) data source with a rate of 4 packets/second, with a fixed packet size of 512 bytes. We executed 10 simulation runs per scenario and averaged them to represent each data point in the simulation results. Each simulation executed for 500 simulated seconds.

A circular network topology was used for the simulated networks. In this context, the node density is defined as the number of nodes per unit area covered by a transmitter. Thus it can be computed by $D = \frac{N}{\pi R^2} \cdot \pi r^2$, where D is the node density, N the network size, R the network radius, and r the transmission range. For each experiment, the node density was pre-determined, and then the computed network radius was used to generate the network topology with radio transmission range of 250 meters.

We used as performance metrics the following:

- The memory usage
- The number of events processed
- The execution time

For the execution time, we convert it to *speedup* rather than directly specify the value. The speedup metric captures the performance improvement as compared to traditional methods.

4.2 Two Extreme Cases

Fig. 3 shows the simulation results from the unicast only experiment, and Fig. 4 the broadcast only experiment. As can be seen in Fig 3(a) and Fig. 4(a), the memory usage of *LAMP* is nearly identical to that of the traditional method. On the average, *LAMP* consumed only 57 KB more than the traditional method, which is less than 1 % with respect to the total memory footprint. This is because the only memory overhead incurred by *LAMP* is the use of the wireless link event list and the communicating entity list whose sizes are relatively small. This phenomenon can be observed throughout all of our experiments, and can be explained in the same way.

As expected, in Fig. 3(b), we can see that *LAMP* significantly reduces the number of events processed during the simulation. The event count was reduced by a factor of 15 for 5 traffic flows, a factor of 6 for 20 traffic flows, and a factor of 7 on the average. It can be also observed, for both methods, that the number of events increases with the number of traffic flows as expected. However, the total event count for *LAMP* shows a relatively gentle slope as compared to the traditional method.

As can be seen in Fig. 4(b), both simulation methods produced an identical number of events for the broadcast only experiment. This is as expected, since every node within a transmission range is a designated receiver in broadcast communications. With the *LAMP* method, therefore, a packet reception event was scheduled exactly in the same way as in the traditional method.

For the traditional method, it can be observed that the processed events in the unicast only experiment were much more than those in the broadcast only experiment. This is due to the increased number of packets for unicast communications using additional frames such as RTS, CTS, and ACK.

Fig. 3(c) shows speedup achieved by *LAMP* with respect to the traditional approach. The simulation with *LAMP* was up to about 5 times faster for 5 traffic flows, and about 2 times faster for 20 traffic flows. On the average, *LAMP* demonstrated speedup of about 3 in these experiments.

In Fig. 4(c), on the other hand, we can see that speedup by *LAMP* is less than one, which means that the simulation with *LAMP* was actually slightly slower than the one with the traditional method. Even though the difference is small (about 10 % slower on the average), one may wonder what made this difference while the both methods processed exactly the same number of events during the simulations. This question can be answered as follows. With *LAMP*, even though there is no action taken by the MAC_UPD procedure as every node is designated, there is still some computational overhead incurred by the JOIN_CE and LEAVE_CE procedures. These procedures are requested at the beginning and at the end of each communication respectively. For the unicast only experiment, this overhead was outweighed by the computation savings obtained from the lazy MAC state update. This was, however, not the case for the broadcast only experiment where there was no such computation benefit.

4.3 The 500-Node Experiments

Figure 5 and Figure 6 show the simulation results from the 500-node experiments with no mobility. The first was obtained using various node densities with a fixed number of traffic flows while the second varied the number of traffic flows with fixed node density.

Fig. 5(b) shows that *LAMP* substantially reduces the number of events processed during the simulation. It is worth noting that the number of events for *LAMP* remains almost constant with node density while the event count for the traditional method increases. For the traditional method, this phenomenon seems reasonable since a packet reception event needs to be scheduled at all nodes within a transmission range even for unicast communications. For *LAMP* however, the number of nodes that need scheduling of a packet reception event for unicast communications is no longer a function of node density. This implies that *LAMP* is scalable with respect to the node density of a network, and is responsible for the nearly flat graph with varying node densities.

In Fig. 6(b) we can see, for both methods, that the events increase with the number of traffic flows. But the slope of the line graph for the two method is quite different. The event count for the traditional method quickly increases with traffic flows, which is not the case for *LAMP*.

As can be seen in Fig. 5(c), a speedup of about up to 8 was achieved by *LAMP*. On the average, the simulation with *LAMP* was about 6.5 times faster than the traditional method. Speedup increases with node density because time for processing events with the traditional method increases with node density, while time for processing events with *LAMP* is largely unaffected by node density.

Fig. 6(c) shows speedup obtained from the 500-node experiment varying the number of traffic flows. We can see that speedup decreases as the number of traffic flows increases. The increased number of traffic flows translates to the increased number of nodes that need packet reception scheduling per unicast transmission. This is the main reason for the decreasing speedup with traffic flows. Another reason for this result is explained by the fact that the increased traffic volume incurs more collisions, packet losses, and occasional perceived link failures, resulting in more routing

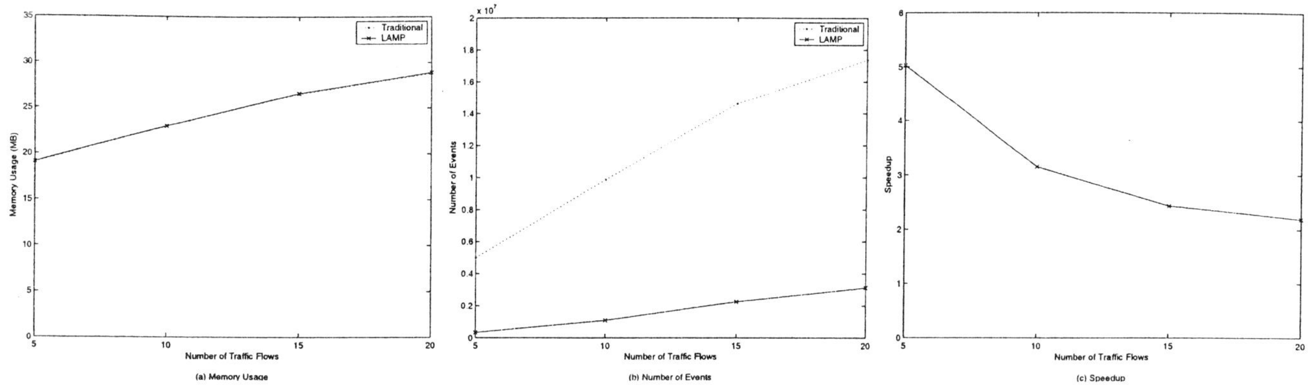

Figure 3. *Unicast only (100 nodes with varying traffic flows).*

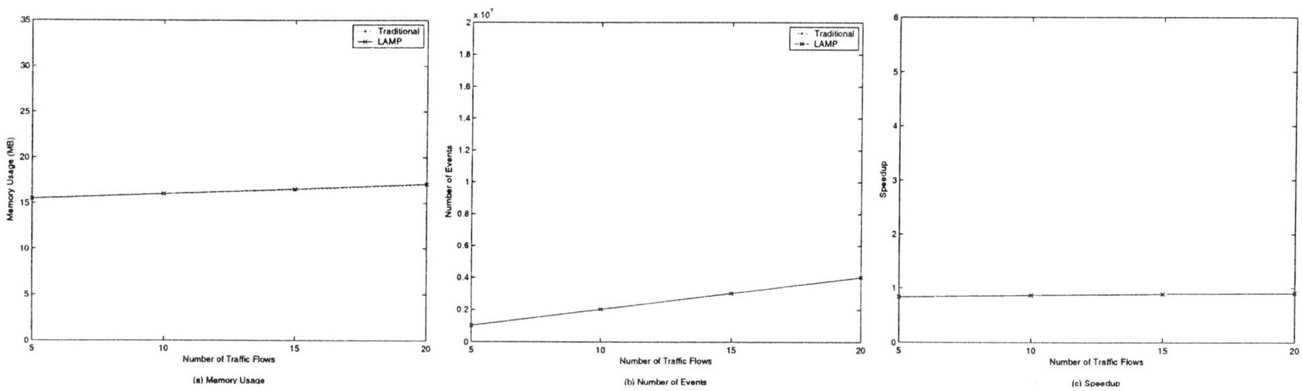

Figure 4. *Broadcast only (100 nodes with varying traffic flows).*

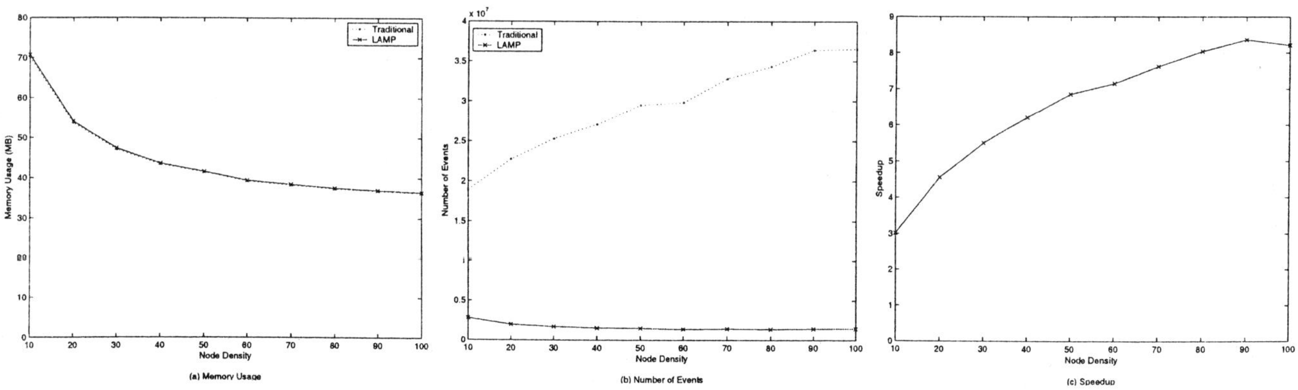

Figure 5. *500 nodes with no mobility (varying node densities with 10 traffic flows).*

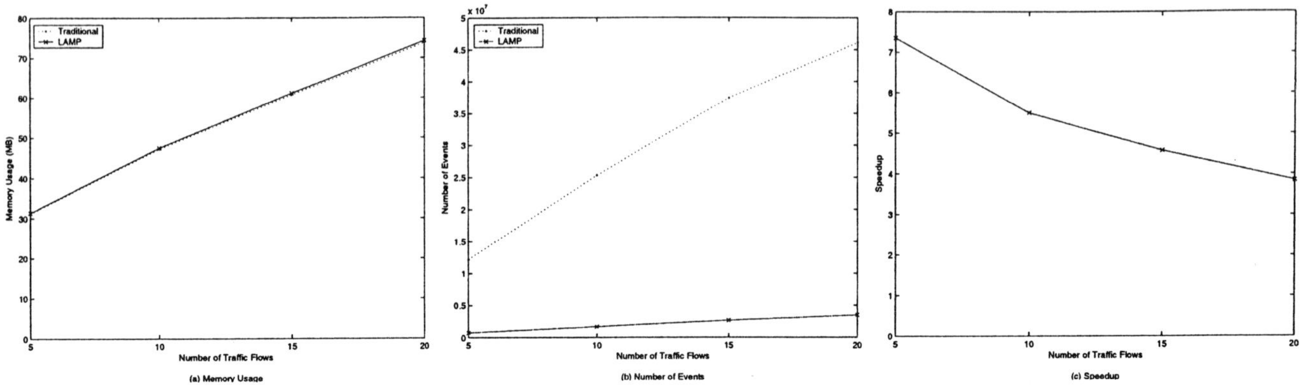

Figure 6. *500 nodes with no mobility (varying traffic flows with node density of 30).*

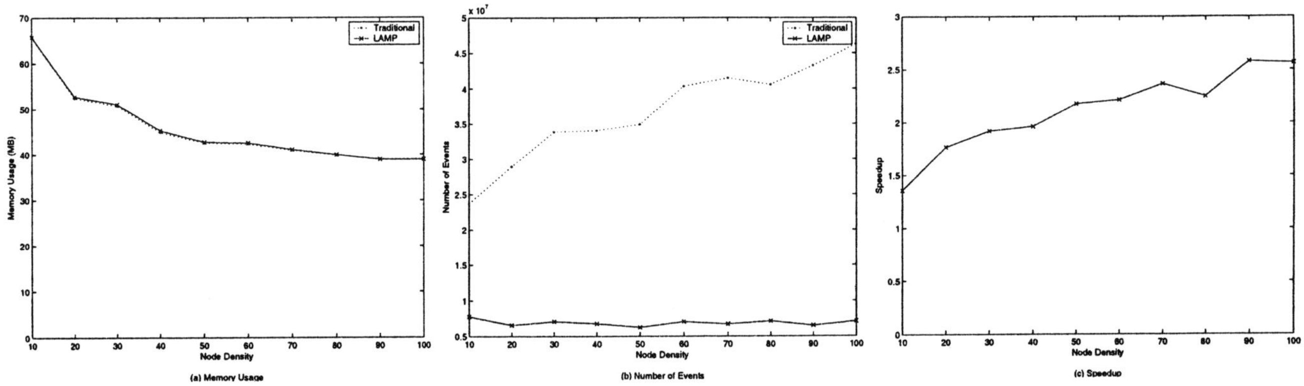

Figure 7. *500 nodes with mobility (varying node densities with 10 traffic flows).*

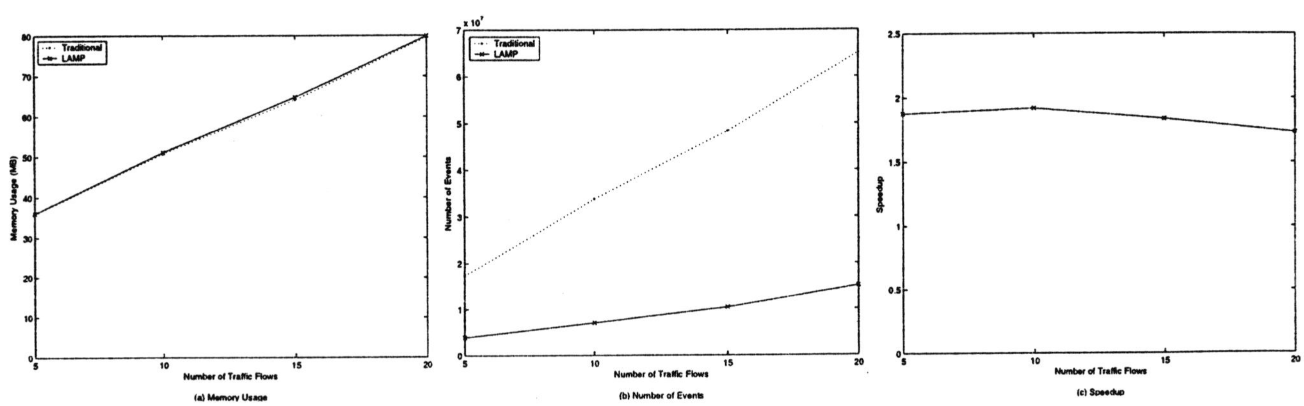

Figure 8. *500 nodes with mobility (varying traffic flows with node density of 30).*

message traffic. As discussed in the two extreme cases, the increased number of broadcast packets can adversely affect the performance of *LAMP* relative to the traditional method. For this experiment, speedup of up to 7 (for 5 traffic flows) was achieved. On the average, speedup of about 5 was achieved by *LAMP*.

Fig. 7 and Fig. 8 show the simulation results from the 500-node experiments with mobility. The first was obtained using various node densities with a fixed number of traffic flows while the second varied traffic flows with fixed node density. In general, as can be seen in these figures, the overall tendency is very similar to that for the previous experiment with no mobility.

The graphs in Fig. 7(b) look similar to those in the preceding case with no mobility. The number of events processed in the simulation with the traditional method grows with node density while the number for *LAMP* remains relatively stable. This again confirms that *LAMP* is scalable with respect to the network node density. For both methods, the absolute number of events increased as compared to the prior experiment with no mobility. This results from the increased number of routing related messages due to mobility induced link failures and subsequent additional routing messages.

The same tendency can be observed in Fig. 8(b). For both methods, the number of events processed during the simulation increases with the number of traffic flows, as discussed previously.

Fig. 7(c) shows the speedup values achieved by the *LAMP* method with mobility. Overall, speedup decreased as compared to the one with no mobility. The simulation with *LAMP* was nearly 2.6 times faster than the one with the traditional method, and about 2.1 times faster on the average. This reduced speedup as compared to the no mobility case is a result of the increased portion of broadcast packets due to route discovery.

Fig. 8(c) shows speedup obtained from the 500-node experiment with mobility varying the number of traffic flows. The maximum speedup was about 1.9, and the average speedup of 1.8 was achieved from this experiment. The reason for decreasing speedup with traffic flows was discussed above.

Even though it was omitted due to lack of space, the simulation with the *LAMP* method produced the identical simulation results as compared to the simulation with the traditional method, which means that *LAMP* can be used for simulation without loss of accuracy.

5 Related Work

There have been several other efforts to improve the performance of sequential wireless simulations and to enhance the existing simulation tools.

In [11], a simplified MAC model is developed and used. In this work, the claim is that a detailed model is both unwanted and unnecessary for protocol design purposes. Thus, this work is limited to the use of simulations for the purpose of higher layer protocol verification.

In [6, 12], a *network gridding* technique is proposed, where the physical network is divided into several partitions. With this approach, a radio signal is not allowed to propagate over the grids in which nodes are out of range from the transmitter. This technique is implemented at the layer that deals with channel propagation.

In [13], a *staged* approach is proposed, where a grid-based method is used to compute neighbors, and several optimizations are suggested to eliminate computational redundancies. Redundant computations are avoided by function caching. This approach differs from ours and the work in [6] in that our work focuses on optimizations in a single protocol stack layer, whereas theirs works across layers.

In [14], the *lazy event scheduling and corrective retrospection* technique is proposed, where a non-receivable signal is not scheduled for reception. Thus, it is determined based on the strength of a signal whether or not to schedule a packet receipt event. In ours, on the other hand, it is determined based on the state of a node, i.e., whether a node is a communicating entity that is involved in active communications.

All these works are complementary to our work. In addition, our work is unique in that it uses a *pull* technology for the MAC layer, in which necessary information is retrieved and computed on a demand basis. This is in contrast to existing wireless simulations where a *push* based approach has been adopted.

6 Conclusions and Future Work

We presented a novel simulation technique for mobile wireless networks, which is efficient in terms of the execution time and the event list size, and can be achieved with a sequential simulation. Our technique is motivated from the observation that scheduling of a packet reception event at undesignated receivers is not always necessary, since undesignated receivers do not have to be aware of the transmission unless they are interested in accessing the communication medium. The necessary information can be determined by the lazy MAC state update algorithm as needed. The new method is applicable to any kind of MAC protocols, but we implemented it for the IEEE 802.11 [15] MAC sub-layer for our simulation experiments.

Extensive simulation experiments were carried out to assess the performance of the proposed simulation technique, and the simulation results show that the new technique tremendously reduces the simulation events processed during the simulation and consequently shortens the execution time significantly.

Even though this work improves the efficiency and scalability of wireless network simulations, other issues such as a large amount of computing resources due to very large–scale network simulations still need to be addressed. Toward this end, we are planning to explore parallel and distributed simulation techniques as well.

References

[1] The network simulator – ns-2, available at `http://www.isi.edu/nsnam/ns/`.

[2] J. Broch, D. Maltz, D. Johnson, Y.-C. Hu, and J. Jetcheva, "A performance comparison of multi-hop wireless ad hoc network routing protocols," *ACM Int'l Conference on Mobile Computing and Networking (MobiCom'98),* October 1998.

[3] L. Bajaj, M. Takai, R. Ahuja, K. Tang, R. Bagrodia, and M. Gerla, "GloMoSim: A scalable network simulation environment," *Technical Report, UCLA Computer Science Department - 990027,* 1999.

[4] `http://www.opnet.com/`.

[5] G. Riley, "The Georgia Tech Network Simulator," *ACM SIGCOMM Workshop on Models, Methods and Tools for Reproducible Network Research (MoMeTools'03),* August 2003.

[6] M. Takai, R. Bagrodia, K. Tang, and M. Gerla, "Efficient wireless network simulations with detailed propagation models," *ACM/Kluwer Wireless Networks, Vol. 7, No. 3, pp. 297-305,* 2001.

[7] J. Cowie, D. Nicol, and A. Ogielski, "Modeling the global Internet," *Computing in Science & Engineering, Vol. 1, No. 1, pp. 42-50,* 1999.

[8] F. Perrone, D. Nicol, J. Liu, C. Elliot, and D. Pearson, "Simulation modeling of large-scale ad-hoc sensor networks," *Simulation Interoperability Workshop (SIW 2001),* 2001.

[9] G. Riley, R. Fujimoto, and M. Ammar, "A generic framework for parallelization of network simulations," *Int'l Symposium on Modeling, Analysis and Simulation of Computer and Telecommunication Systems (MASCOTS'99),* October 1999.

[10] R. Fujimoto, "Parallel discrete event simulation," *Communications of the ACM, Vol. 33, No. 10, pp. 30-53,* 1990.

[11] J. Liu, D. Nicol, L. Perrone, and M. Liljenstam, "Towards high performance modeling of the 802.11 wireless protocol," *Winter Simulation Conference (WSC 2001),* December, 2001.

[12] V. Naoumov and T. Gross, "Simulation of large ad hoc networks," *ACM Int'l Symposium on Modeling, Analysis and Simulation of Wireless and Mobile Systems (MSWiM'03),* September, 2003.

[13] K. Walsh and E. Sirer, "Staged simulation for improving the scale and performance of wireless network simulations," *Winter Simulation Conference (WSC 2003),* December 2003.

[14] Z. Ji, J. Zhou, M. Takai, and R. Bagrodia, "Scalable simulation of large-scale wireless networks with bounded inaccuracies," *ACM Int'l Symposium on Modeling, Analysis and Simulation of Wireless and Mobile Systems (MSWiM'04),* October, 2004.

[15] IEEE Computer Society, "802.11: Wireless LAN medium access control (MAC) and physical layer (PHY) specifications," June 1997.

[16] T. Rappaport, "Wireless communications: principles and practice," Prentice Hall, Upper Saddle River, 2nd edition, 2001.

Simulation of Network Traffic at Coarse Time-scales

David M. Nicol, Guanhua Yan
Coordinated Science Laboratory
University of Illinois, Urbana-Champaign

Abstract

Simulation of large-scale networks demands that we model some flows at coarser time-scales than others, simply to keep the execution cost manageable. This paper studies a method for periodically computing traffic at a time-scale larger than that typically used for detailed packet simulations. Applications of this technique include computation of background flows (against which detailed foreground flows are simulated), and simulation of worm propagation in the Internet. Our approach considers aggregated traffic between Internet Points of Presence, and computes the throughput of each POP-to-POP flow through each router on its path. This problem formulation leads to a non-linear system of equations. We develop means of reducing this system to a smaller set of equations, which are solved using fixed point iteration. We study the convergence behavior, as a function of traffic load, on topologies based on Internet backbone networks. We find that the problem reduction method is very effective, and that convergence is achieved rapidly. We also examine the comparative speedup of the method relative to using pure packet simulation for background flows, and observe speedups of exceeding 5000 using an ordinary PC. We also simulate foreground flows interacting with background flows, and compare the foreground behavior using our solution with that of pure packet flows. We find that these flows behave accurately enough in our approach to justify use of the technique in our motivating application.

1. Overview

Simulation of large-scale wireline networks has many applications. In some of these only a small fraction of traffic is of specific interest, e.g., the behavior of flows managed by a new transport protocol, or control traffic between BGP routers. However, the flows of interest are affected by, and may even (to a lesser degree) affect the other "background" flows. There is strong motivation to model background flows with less detail than foreground flows, with the objective of significantly lowering the computational requirements. Control traffic such as BGP announcements and DNS queries need to be modeled at the packet level, yet the network being simulated has hundreds of thousands of devices and (typically) tens of thousands of flows represented at any given time. The only hope we have of meeting real-time constraints is to significantly aggregate our treatment of background traffic. In other applications the traffic of interest can be modeled at a coarse time scale. For example, simulation of worm spread across the Internet can be usefully modeled at a time scale much larger than is usually used in network simulation, and the volume of traffic is so large that this becomes necessary.

Our problem is this : given a description of flow intensities at ingress points, efficiently determine link loads throughout the network interior, and determine flow intensities at egress points. Solution to this problem allows us to represent these flows to a more detailed traffic mode in terms of the demand they make on shared bandwidth (and potentially, buffer space). These demands are periodically recomputed, e.g., every 5 seconds. On large networks this method will compute bandwidth consumption significantly faster than will packet representation of the same flows.

These savings naturally come with a cost. Low resolution background flows may be less responsive to changes in network state, they may exhibit less burstiness, the degree to which a simulation using them differs from one with all flows at the same resolution will be unknown. Nevertheless there are contexts where the trade-offs in favor of computational speed are acceptable; indeed there are contexts where one really has no other option but to use highly abstracted representation of background traffic. Our research group is developing a network simulator that will be used in cyber-defense training exercises where the most important accuracy requirements are that the simulated behavior have a realistic "look and feel". The simulator computes the detailed effects on particular traffic flows (e.g. financial transactions) as cyber-attacks occur, and as defensive measures are taken. Two defining characteristics are that its application demands real-time performance (e.g., one second of simulation time takes no more than one second of wall-

1087-4097/05 $20.00 © 2005 IEEE

clock time to advance), and that its application involves networks with potentially hundreds of thousands of devices.

The simulation problem becomes non-trivial when we attempt to capture the effects of bandwidth sharing among flows across a common link. Our specific formulation targets time-scales larger than end-to-end latency, hence one assumes that flows pass instantaneously through the network. This leads to a system of non-linear equations whose solution gives the desired background flows. We propose a fixed point algorithm for its solution.

We empirically analyze this technique on models of real Internet backbone networks, with synthetic traffic generated using Pareto-Poisson Burst Processes (PPBP) [27]. We examine convergence behavior as a function of traffic load, the speedup it offers, and the accuracy of foreground traffic when it is used in place of packet simulation. Our experiments demonstrate the viability of the approach for our motivating application.

2. Related Work

Our problem is related to the area of network tomography, that likewise seeks to determine some network characteristics (e.g. the traffic matrix—volume of flows between any pair of ingress and egress points) from other traffic measurements (e.g. measured link loads on the network edge). There is a large and fascinating literature on the topic, e.g., see [25, 24, 7, 22, 20, 4, 1, 5]. A key difference between our problem and network tomography is that the latter is driven by difficulties in obtaining measurements of certain important quantities, and so works to use models to infer them from measurements that are available. In the virtual world of simulation we can measure anything we like; our problem is to compute those measurements given the offered load.

Our approach includes ideas found elsewhere. The notion of simulating traffic using simple rate functions was introduced almost ten years ago [8], a formulation that observes that FCFS service at a congested router port can be modeled by scaling the flows in portion to their input rates, which is a central facet of our model. Further development is found in [14]; application to TCP is developed in [16], which treats issues in simultaneous simulation of packet and fluid flows, as do [9], [26], and [15]. Specific application to the global Internet and practical problems therein are discussed in [2].

More detailed fluid models found in the literature include treatments of TCP [17], models containing stochastic elements [13], a time-stepped model [23], and a discussion of trade-offs [12, 11]. Use of fixed point iteration to solve for network measures of interest also appears in [3], a model that focuses much more on TCP and less on link loads. A very abstract rate-based model is discussed in [21], work that does not try to capture interflow dependencies in detail, as we do.

Against this backdrop our contribution is the development, optimized solution, and empirical study of a coarse-grained traffic model that focuses on the impact that bandwidth sharing on congested links has on flow rates throughout the entire network. Our fixed point approach is unique in that each approximated solution has internal consistency that can, in some contexts, allow it to be used even if the solution has not yet converged. The approach is a valuable and necessary component of our real-time cyber-defense training simulator.

3. Model

We are interested in how a network shapes coarse-grained traffic flows between many network points of presence (POPs). We assume that there are n of these, denoted by $P_1, P_2, \ldots, P_n$. Traffic is described by processes $\{T_{ij}(t)\}$, $(1 \leq i, j \leq n)$ that give the rate (bits per second) at which POP T_i injects traffic destined for POP P_j into the network at time t. We discretize time into units of length Δ seconds, and define time $t_k = k \cdot \Delta$, $k = 0, 1, 2, \ldots$. We make very few assumptions about how $\{T_{ij}(t)\}$ is defined, other than at time t_k the behavior of $P_{ij}(t)$ with $t \in [t_k, t_{k+1}]$ can be predicted. We may use this formalism to reflect an underlying random process, a recorded traffic trace, or even real-time measurements. We will work with "smoothed" values of $\{T_{ij}(t)\}$, as follows. Define $R_{ij}(t_k) = (1/\Delta) \int_{t_k}^{t_{k+1}} T_{ij}(t)\, dt$, and observe that the process that injects traffic at constant rate $R_{ij}(t_k)$ over $[t_k, t_{k+1}]$ injects exactly the same amount of traffic as does $T_{ij}(t)$ over that same period. We will use $\{R_{ij}(t)\}$ to describe injected traffic, in order to simplify the computation. Doing so we may dampen burstiness at scales smaller than Δ, but we will inject the same amount of traffic as the original process.

We model the network itself in terms of routers connected by uni-directional links, understanding that we can model a bi-directional link as a pair of uni-directional ones. The sending endpoint of a link is associated with a router's output port, and associated with each output port is a buffer size. Routing protocols establish forwarding tables that indicate for each router the output port to use for any particular POP destination. We assume that routing decisions are unaltered during a discretized epoch of length Δ. Link latencies are effectively assumed to be zero, which is an appropriate modeling assumption when Δ is large compared to the typical end-to-end latency of a flow.

At a given instant t_k we can examine the sum of the arrival rates to a router's port. Congestion and traffic loss may occur. We modified a congestion model commonly used in fluid traffic simulations (e.g. [8, 14]) for our time-stepped formulation, as follows. Suppose that at time t_k there are m flows mapped to a given port, with arrival rates $\psi_1^{(in)}(t_k), \psi_2^{(in)}(t_k), \ldots, \psi_m^{(in)}(t_k)$, and let $\Psi(t_k) = \sum_{i=1}^{m} \psi_i^{(in)}(t_k)$ be their aggregate arrival rate. Let μ denote the link bandwidth. The rate of the ith flow *out* of the port (denoted $\psi_i^{(out)}(t_k)$) is defined in terms of the relationships between $\Psi(t_k)$ and μ:

$$\begin{aligned} \psi_i^{(out)}(t_k) &= \begin{cases} \psi_i^{(in)}(t_k) \text{ for } \Psi(t_k) \leq \mu \\ \psi_i^{(in)}(t_k)\Big(\mu/\Psi(t_k)\Big) \text{ otherwise} \end{cases} \\ &= \psi_i^{(in)}(t_k) \times \min\{1, \mu/\Psi(t_k)\}. \end{aligned} \quad (1)$$

In the first case the port can completely serve all of the incoming flow; in the second case every flow's output bandwidth is scaled back by a constant factor, a device that models effect of FCFS service [8].

Equation (1) describes what the simulation needs to do in order to compute a link's utilization over the epoch $[t_k, t_{k+1}]$ as a function of the input flow rates to it at time t_k. However, we will see that this is a deceptively simple description; for, depending on the value of Δ, the flow rates into the port at time t_k may depend on the flow rates *out* of it at time t_k.

4. Algorithm

4.1. Time-step setup

The starting premise of our approach is that we can compute resource consumption of certain types of flows relatively infrequently, and treat that consumption as invariant between updates. These flows may be made sensitive to flows modeled with higher resolution, but only at the fixed update points. Upon reaching an update point we have the opportunity to re-assess the bandwidth allocated on each link. These decisions may be made as a function of observed past behavior. We also have the opportunity to adjust the offered load rate, e.g. , reduce it on flows for which loss has been observed in the last time, in order to model feedback (such as TCP provides). These issues are important, but are not the focal point of the present paper.

When we use this formulation to compute background traffic intensities it is important to capture the competition between foreground and background flows for link bandwidth. We use a simple mechanism for including the next epoch's anticipated foreground flow as we compute flow rates for background flows. At time t_k, for each port p_z, we compute an estimated foreground input rate $\lambda_f^{(in)}(p_z)$ based on recent observations (or even known predictions, if such were available). We model foreground flow passing through the port as though it is injected into the network at this point from a traffic source, crosses the link, and immediately disappears into a traffic sink. As we compute new flow rates, for that port we treat that flow exactly as any other flow. The "fair" contribution of foreground traffic is thus considered as we allocate bandwidth for the background traffic.

Since each flow is recomputed each time-step, we also have the opportunity to alter routing. This is particularly useful in applications where routing changes in response to changes in traffic loads, or where we simulate attacks on the routing infrastructure by disabling routers, eventually causing routing protocols to respond and create new routes. We assume that the routing for the next time step is known before we compute the flow updates.

4.2. Dependency Reduction

It is helpful to imagine the flow update computation in terms of the status of input flow variables. We describe the set of all flow variables at time t_k (including the ingress flow rates) by a vector $\Lambda(t_k)$. At any stage in flow update processing an element of this vector is either *settled* or *unsettled*. We say that a port is *resolved* once all of its input flows are settled, because then Equation (1) specifies its output rates. We say that the port is *transparent* if it is not resolved, but analysis shows that the sum of input rates cannot exceed the port's bandwidth; for such ports every flow's output rate is identical to its input rate. Our aim is to resolve as many flow variables as possible, in a sort of data flow analysis phase. Once finished we necessarily have circular dependencies among some flow variables, and another form of processing is needed. A key component to the flow resolution analysis is the computation and propagation of settled flow values—a settled flow value into a transparent port establishes a settled output value (and hence settled input to the next router in the path). Thus identification of transparent ports is important. Another key component is the observation that we sometimes may determine that a port is transparent if we know *upper bounds* on some of its inputs' as-yet-unsettled variables. A settled flow rate into a transparent but as-yet-unresolvable port produces a settled output rate (which in turn may be used to help make another port either transparent or resolvable.)

We describe the logic of this step in terms of production rules, such as one uses to build expert systems. A rule has a logical expression known as a precondition, and a set of actions to apply whenever the precondition is satisfied. Applied here, the precondition is a Boolean expression about settled/unsettled states of flow variables and the resolvable/transparent state of ports. The post conditions set flow variable values, and change the state of flow variables and ports.

A precise description of the rule set requires notation. We drop the notational dependence on t_k and use λ_i to be the

	Pre-condition	Action
1.	$\sim (\mathcal{S}[p] = \textit{resolved}) \wedge$ $\forall i \in I(p)\ \{\mathcal{S}[\lambda_i] = \textit{settled}\}$	$\mathcal{S}[p] \leftarrow \textit{resolved},$ $\forall i \in I(p)\ \{\mathcal{S}[\lambda_{n_p(i)}] \leftarrow \textit{settled},$ $\lambda_{n_p(i)} \leftarrow \lambda_i \times \min\{1, \mu_p / \sum_{j \in I(p)} \lambda_j\}\}\}$
2.	$\mathcal{S}[p] = \textit{unresolved} \wedge \sum_{i \in I(p)} \lambda_i \le \mu_p \wedge$ $\exists\ i \in I(p)\ s.t.\ \mathcal{S}[\lambda_i] = \textit{bounded}$	$\mathcal{S}[p] \leftarrow \textit{transparent},$ $\forall i \in I(p)\ s.t.\ \mathcal{S}[\lambda_i] = \textit{settled}\ \{\mathcal{S}(\lambda_{n_p(i)}) \leftarrow \textit{settled}\}$
3.	$\mathcal{S}[p] = \textit{transparent} \wedge \exists i \in I(p)\ s.t.$ $(\mathcal{S}[\lambda_i] = \textit{settled}) \wedge \sim (\mathcal{S}[\lambda_{n_p(i)}] = \textit{settled})$	$\mathcal{S}[\lambda_{n_p(i)}] \leftarrow \textit{settled},\ \lambda_{n_p(i)} \leftarrow \lambda_i$
4.	$\phi(p) \ge \mu_p \wedge \exists i \in I(p)\ s.t.$ $\lambda_{n_p(i)} > (\mu_p / \phi(p))\lambda_i$	$\lambda_{n_p(i)} \leftarrow (\mu_p / \phi(p))\lambda_i$
5.	$\exists i \in I(p)\ s.t.\ \lambda_i < \lambda_{n_p(i)}$	$\lambda_{n_p(i)} \leftarrow \lambda_i$

Table 1. Transition Rules for Dependency Reduction

i^{th} flow variable in vector Λ. The state of λ_i, denoted $\mathcal{S}[\lambda_i]$ is either *resolved*, or *bounded*. In the *settled* state λ_i has its final value, and in the *bounded* state we define λ_i to be the bound. As we will see, at initialization every flow variable is placed into one of these two states.

For every port p we denote the state of p by $\mathcal{S}[p]$, defined to be one of *resolved*, *transparent*, or *unresolved*. We also define $I(p)$ to be the set of indices such that if $i \in I(p)$, then λ_i is an input flow variable for p; we similarly define $O(p)$ as the indices of flow variables defined by flows leaving p. For every λ_i we let $f(i)$ denote the logical end-to-end flow associated with λ_i, and note that for every $i \in I(p)$ there exists a unique $j \in O(p)$ such that $f(i) = f(j)$; this j is denoted $n_p(i)$. μ_p denotes the port's bandwidth. We define $\phi(p)$ to be the sum of rates of all settled flows into p. This value necessarily changes as flows into p become settled in the course of the computation.

At initialization the flow variables describing network inputs are given state *settled* and their values set. Every other flow variable is put in the *bounded* state, and given the ingress value of its associated end-to-end flow. Every port is placed in the *unresolved* state. Table 1 gives five rules that are applied repeatedly, until no further pre-conditions are satified. Rule 1 says that if a port is not in the resolved state but all of its input flows are settled, then the port becomes resolved and all of its output flows become settled. Rule 2 says that if by summing the upper bounds on input flow values to an unresolved port we can determine that it will not be congested, then the port becomes transparent. Rule 3 says the if there is a settled input flow to a transparent port whose corresponding output flow is not settled, then that output flow becomes settled and takes the value of the input flow. Rule 4 observes that if the total volume of known settled flows into p exceeds the bandwidth, then the port will definitely be congested and the scale factor by which all input flows will be multiplied can be upper-bounded; thus application of that scale factor to either a settled flow or an upper bound on a flow produces an upper bound on the output flow value. Rule 4 reduces any output flow upper bound that can be so reduced. Finally, Rule 5 says that if the value (or bound) on an input flow to any port is less than the value or bound assigned to its corresponding output flow, then we can lower the value assigned to the output flow. Rules 4 and 5 are powerful in that they may let us push bounding information past an unresolved port. We note in passing that Rule 4 is the only rule in this set that depends fundamentally on the assumed FCFS service. Leaving out Rule 4, we can use this technique other disciplines, such as weighted fair queueing.

In the evaluation of a rule set such as this, at any time there may be a number of ports for which rule pre-conditions are satisfied. Prioritizing selection of which rules to fire is an important component of the solution. Rule 1 should always have highest priority, as the object is to resolve flow variables as quickly as possible. Next most important is Rule 2, for making a port transparent allows propagation of settled values through the port, potentially enabling a Rule 1 firing. Rule 3 has next priority, for the same reason. Rule 4 is next, for by decreasing upper bounds on output flows we may discover that a port is transparent. Rule 5 has lowest priority; Rule 4's lower bounds are sharper (hence it has priority when it applies), but Rule 5 nevertheless may help to identify the transparency of a port.

Efficient rule processing is possible. Our implementation visits each flow variable a small (constant) number of times. There is no ordering, sorting, or searching involved. The computational complexity is thus proportional to the number of flows times the average number of ports through which a flow passes—essentially linear in the size of the problem.

Figure 1 illustrates these concepts with an example topology, and description of the Rules processing that lead to each flow variable becoming settled.

4.3. Circular Dependencies

Unlike the example of Figure 1, it may happen that after dependency reduction is completed some input flow variables remain unsettled. When this occurs, there is a cycle of unresolved ports in the system graph. One small change in this example illustrates the point. If $\lambda_1 + \lambda_9 > \mu$ then p2 does not become transparent by Rule 2; the network is left with a cycle p2 $\rightarrow$ p4 $\rightarrow$ p6 $\rightarrow$ p2 of unresolved ports.

The next step focuses on solving flow variables on such cycles. The variables involved may be a subset of the variables still unsettled. In our running example we have to settle λ_2, λ_6, and λ_{10} on the loop before we can settle all the other unsettled variables. Fortunately it is easy to identify the cycles and restrict our attention to them. The network is a directed graph; the process of resolving ports and settling variables can be thought of as a kind of graph reduction where we remove nodes corresponding to ports, as they are resolved. After dependency reduction we can find cycles by identifying nodes that have out-degree 0 (egress ports), remove them and any edges directed to them. If the edge removal causes another node to have out-degree 0 it too is removed with all its in-edges, and so on. By this process we remove non-cyclical dependents of the cycles whose values we must compute. Once the variables on the cycles are determined we can compute the flow variables for the rest of the system.

We will say that a flow variable is *irreducible* if it is an output of a port whose node remains in the reduced graph. It may happen that the reduced graph has more than one connected component. In the reminder we describe what to do with a given connected component, understanding that different connected components can be solved for independently.

For the sake of notational simplicity, we suppose there are M irreducible flow variables, renamed as $\lambda_1, \lambda_2, \ldots, \lambda_M$; let Λ be the M-vector of these values. Every irreducible flow variable is the output from a port represented in the reduced dependency graph, and is thus expressed by Equation (1) as a function of the port's input flow rates—at least one of which must be irreducible. The port's non-irreducible input flows are known, having been computed either in a previous time-step, during the graph reduction, or as the result of computing flows from a port that will serve only backlogged traffic in the next epoch. From the point of view of Equation (1) applied at this point in the computation, non-irreducible flow variables are constants. Let $f_i(\Lambda)$ be the equation expressing λ_i, let $F_i(\Lambda) = \lambda_i - f_i(\Lambda)$, and let $F(\Lambda)$ express the system of M equations, the ith such being $F_i(\Lambda)$. Our problem is to find a solution to $F(\Lambda) = 0$.

This system of equations is non-linear, because the component equations $f_i(\Lambda)$ are not linear combinations of the variables. Our equations are more complex because the flows from a congested port have a decidedly non-linear response to changes in input flows.

The general problem of solving non-linear systems is known to be very hard. A non-linear system may have between 0 and many solutions, depending on the problem specifics. Solution approaches to non-linear systems are typically iterative, meaning that given an estimated solution Λ_k, one creates another estimate Λ_{k+1} that (hopefully) is closer to a true solution. Typically one iterates until some norm of the difference between successive iterations $||\Lambda_{k+1} - \Lambda_k||$ is less than a tolerance ϵ. Any given iterative algorithm may or may not converge to a solution, depending on the starting point Λ_0.

Some forms of iteration create Λ_{n+1} from Λ_n using derivative information. The widely known Newton-Raphson method [18] computes

$$\Lambda_{n+1} = \Lambda_n - J^{-1}(\Lambda_n)F(\Lambda_n)$$

where $J^{-1}(\Lambda_n)$ is the inverse of F's Jacobian evaluated at Λ_n, and $F(\Lambda_n)$ is the vector resulting from applying Λ_n to each equation F_i. Recall that the ij^{th} entry of F's Jacobi matrix is the value of the partial derivative of F_i with respect to λ_j. Newton's method converges fast on sufficiently well-behaved systems, using sufficiently close starting approximations Λ_0. It has the computational drawback of requiring, *at each iteration*, the inversion of a large dimension sparse matrix. That in itself is a significant computational challenge. It also leaves us with the issue of what traffic matrix to use if it should happen that the Jacobian cannot be inverted or the iterations diverge.

Equation (1) itself suggests an iterative method. We define the first approximation Λ_0 by computing the output of each port using as input a flow's ingress flow rate; the ap-

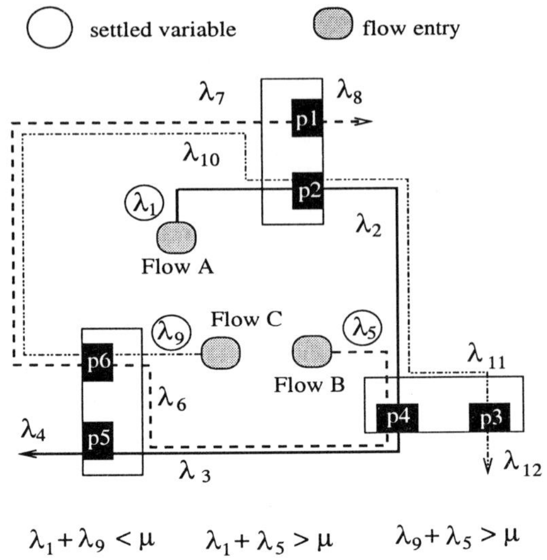

Topology

Step	Rule	Processing
1.	2	$S[p2] \leftarrow \mathit{transparent}, S[\lambda_2] \leftarrow \mathit{settled}$
2.	1	$S[p4] \leftarrow \mathit{resolved}, S[\lambda_6] \leftarrow \mathit{settled}$, $S[\lambda_3] \leftarrow \mathit{settled}$
3.	1	$S[p5] \leftarrow \mathit{resolved}, S[\lambda_4] \leftarrow \mathit{settled}$
4.	1	$S[p6] \leftarrow \mathit{resolved}, S[\lambda_7] \leftarrow \mathit{settled}$, $S[\lambda_{10}] \leftarrow \mathit{settled}$
5.	1	$S[p1] \leftarrow \mathit{resolved}, S[\lambda_8] \leftarrow \mathit{settled}$
6.	1	$S[p2] \leftarrow \mathit{resolved}, S[\lambda_{11}] \leftarrow \mathit{settled}$
7.	1	$S[p3] \leftarrow \mathit{resolved}, S[\lambda_{12}] \leftarrow \mathit{settled}$

Dependency reduction processing

Figure 1. Example Topology, and Sequence of Rules Applied

proximation is good if there is relatively little loss. Given approximate solution Λ_n, we compute

$$\Lambda_{n+1} = f(\Lambda_n) = (f_1(\Lambda_n), f_2(\Lambda_n), \ldots, f_m(\Lambda_n)).$$

This formulation is also known as a *fixed-point* computation. The intuition is that if we hold the flow rates into the network constant, over time the flows across each link should stabilize (although as yet we have no formal proof of this). If this were the case then the suggested iterative method is equivalent to pushing the network state along in time until it settles. The converged state is the "fixed-point", in the sense that reapplying the traffic shaping rules expressed by Equation (1) does not alter the flow rates. Naturally, a very significant question to ask is whether the fixed point computation will converge to some solution $\Lambda^* = f(\Lambda^*)$. The literature identifies a general condition under which convergence may be proven. Function $f : \mathbb{R}^n \rightarrow \mathbb{R}^M$ is said to be a *contraction mapping* if there exists $0 < q < 1$ such that for all $\Lambda_1, \Lambda_2 \in \mathbb{R}^M$ and norm $||x||$

$$||f(\Lambda_1) - f(\Lambda_2)|| < q||\Lambda_1 - \Lambda_2||.$$

The Banach fixed point theorem [6] states that there exists a unique fixed point Λ^*, e.g., $\Lambda^* = f(\Lambda^*)$, and that Λ^* may be found by choosing arbitrary Λ_0, and iterate as $\Lambda_n = f(\Lambda_{n-1})$. This sequence converges to the limit Λ^*.

Formally proving convergence, or circumstances under which convergence is achieved remains an important goal of our research. It is a challenging goal though, as it seems that to achieve it we will have to use specific properties of our problem domain. In particular, it seems that the contraction parameter q is dependent on the network being considered, which makes discovery of a general result for our application domain all the more challenging. Nevertheless, Banach's fixed point theorem gives the foundation for our approach. Our experimental section will directly study how convergence behaves on certain motivating networks.

We are in the uncomfortable position of lacking assurance of convergence by Newton's method or the fixed point method suggested by Equation (1). If it should happen that we observe *divergence* after some number of iterations, we have still to construct some representation of background traffic. In our training application context we can justify using a traffic matrix that doesn't satisfy Equation (1), but is in some weaker sense "plausible". Unfortunately intermediate steps of Newton's method may create an estimate Λ_n that is physically unrealizable, in the sense that it may assign outflow rates to a link such that their sum exceeds the link capacity, or in the sense that volume of a given flow that leaves the system exceeds the sum of what is entering plus what was buffered. These things can happen because the Newton method computes the next solution by following a linear projection out from the old solution. No constraints are placed on the solution that is so computed. Thus, if we should find that J is not invertible at some iteration, or that the iterations are diverging, we are left with the problem of using *something* reasonable for the traffic loads, and the intermediate solution Λ_n may not be reasonable.

The fixed point algorithm is a more attractive option with respect to this problem because respect for system constraints is built into Equation (1). We formalize this respect by the definition of a plausible approximation.

Definition 1 *Approximation* Λ_n *is* plausible *if*

1. *every flow rate expressed by Λ_n is non-negative,*
2. *across every link the sum of flow rates assigned by Λ_n to that link does not exceed the link bandwidth,*
3. *for every pair of POPs P_i and P_j, between times t_k and t_{k+1} the volume of P_i-to-P_j traffic leaving the subnetwork represented by the reduced graph is no larger than the sum of the volume of P_i-to-P_j traffic entering the subnetwork, plus the P_i-to-P_j traffic that is buffered along its path through the subnetwork.*

The fixed-point method suggested by Equation (1) ensures plausibility.

Theorem 1 *Let Λ_n be any approximation with non-negative flow values. Then $\Lambda_{n+1} = (f_1(\Lambda_n), f_2(\Lambda_n), \ldots, f_m(\Lambda_n))$ is a plausible approximation.*

Proof: Given non-negative values for flow variables, it is not possible for Equation (1) to create negative values, thus $f_i(\Lambda_n) \geq 0$ for all i and the first condition for plausibility is satisfied. By construction it is not possible for Equation (1) to assign flows across a link that exceed the link's allocated capacity for background traffic, so the second condition for plausibility is also satisfied. To establish the third condition, choose any flow P_i-to-P_j that passes through the subnetwork, and consider the sequence of ports $p_1, p_2, \ldots, p_z$ it follows through the subnetwork. Now in Equation (1) the value of the expression used in Case 1 is always larger than the value used in Case 2. Therefore an upper bound on the flow value associated with the flow leaving the subnetwork is obtained by assuming that the case 1 expression is used at each port along the path. That upper bound is simply the sum of the rate at which the P_i-to-P_j flow enters the subnetwork, plus $(1/\Delta)$ times the sum of P_i-to-P_j traffic buffered along the path. This establishes the third condition for plausibility. □

Our experience has yet to show a case where convergence did not occur; future work will look at firming up the theoretical basis for the convergence we observe.

5. Experimental Results

We now consider the results of experiments designed to examine the resource requirements of the algorithm, on four realistic topologies derived from the Internet, and flows across them. Their characteristics are given by the table below:

Topology	# routers	# links	# flows	Mbps
Top-1	27	88	702	100
Top-2	244	1080	12200	2488
Top-3	610	3012	61000	2488
Top-4	1126	6238	168900	2488

Top-1 is the a model of the ATT USA backbone, described in [10]. Each node is assumed to be a POP. We create a flow between every possible of the $27 * 26 = 702$ POPs. The link bandwidth (100Mbps) is artificially low to enable us to make a direct comparison of accuracy and performance with equivalent packet-based flows. Top-2, Top-3, and Top-4 are derived from topologies from the Rocketfuel [19] database. Top-2 is the Exodus backbone; every POP directs a flow to 50 others. Top-3 is Top-2 augmented through some peering points with the Above.Net backbone; and Top-4 is Top-3 augmented through some peering points with the Sprint backbone. Shortest-path routing is assumed. In Top-2, Top-3 and Top-4 each POP directs 50 flows to POPs in its own backbone, and 50 to each other backbone in the topology. Thus a Top-2 POP sends 50 flows, a Top-3 POP sends 100 flows, and a Top-4 POP sends 150 flows. Each flow is derived from a Poisson-Pareto-Burst-Process (PPBP) [27]. A Poisson process generates arrivals, each of which contributes a random traffic volume that is sampled from a Pareto distribution. The volumes are additive; one can describe a PPBP at time t in terms of the number of bursts that are active at time t. The PPBP is recognized as a good model of traffic arrival to a backbone. There are three parameters to a PPBP. In our experiments we choose them to create desired average link utilizations, and to a lesser degree, variance. The Hurst parameter for the Pareto distribution is 0.8.

5.1. Convergence Behavior

We first consider how the algorithm behaves in terms of the number of ports on cycles analyzed by the fixed point step, and the number of iterations required to achieve convergence. In all of these experiments we consider a solution to be converged when the maximum relative difference between successive approximations to any flow variable is 0.001, e.g., when $|\lambda_{n+1} - \lambda_n|/\lambda_n \leq 0.001$ for all flow variables λ.

Figure 2 gives histograms of the number of ports on cycles in a time-step, and the number of iterations used on a time-step, on single runs of 200 time-steps. A time-step spans 5 simulation seconds. Top-2, Top-3, and Top-4 topologies are represented. The Top-1 topology very rarely formed cycles, even at high utilitization. In the Top-2 and Top-4 experiments the traffic parameters are selected to create close to 50% link utilization. At these loads, and under these traffic patterns, to a first approximation the number of ports in dependency cycles is proportional to the square root of the number of ports, and the number of iterations is proportional to the square root of the number of ports on cycles. The same measurements at 10% link utilization confirm the intuition that cycles form very infrequently at low utilization.

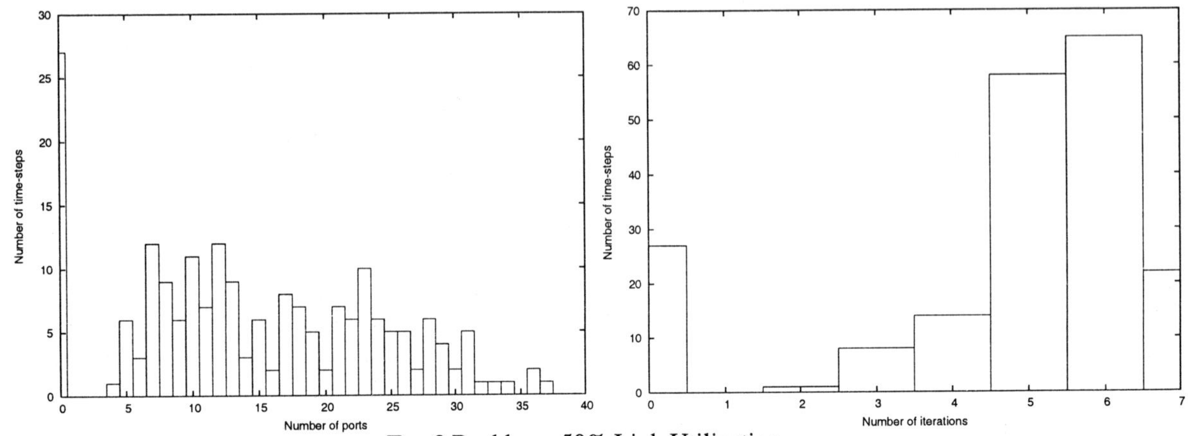

Top-2 Backbone 50% Link Utilization

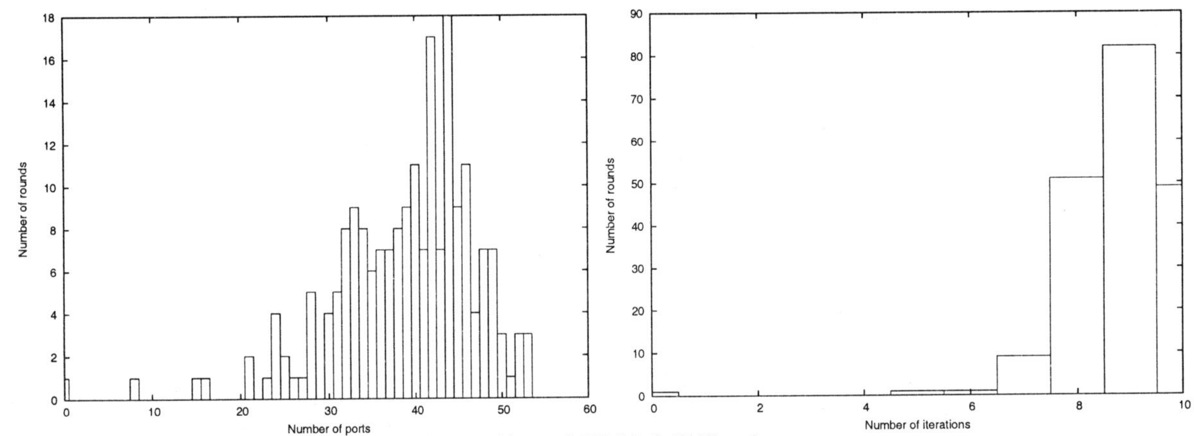

Top-3 Backbone 50% Link Utilization

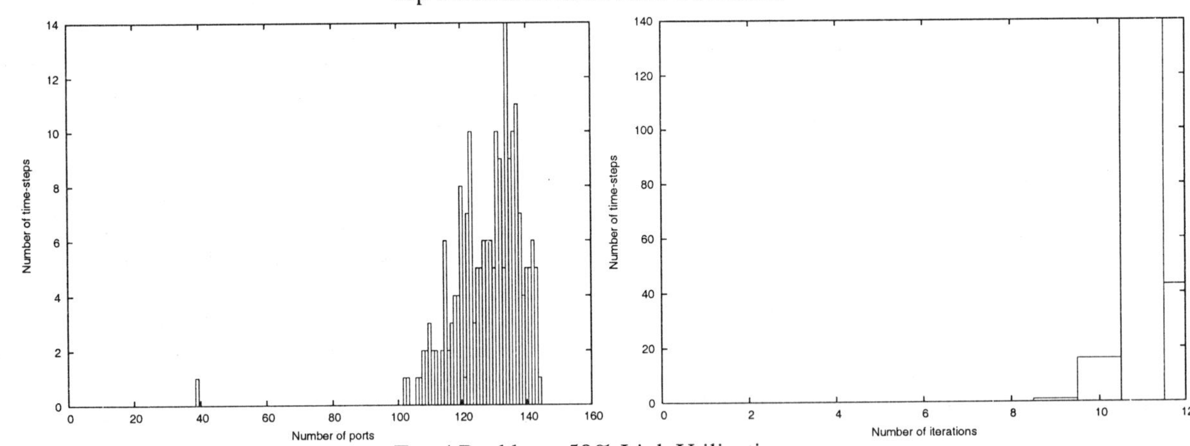

Top-4 Backbone 50% Link Utilization

Figure 2. Histogram of Ports on Cycles, and Iterations per Time-step, for Top-2, Top-3, and Top-4

5.2. Execution Time

Execution speed is a crucial aspect for us, because of our need to execute large network simulations in real-time. The table below gives the average time per time-step for these four topologies, at 20% and 50% link utilizations. The experiments were run using our high-performance simulation engine, on a 1.5GHz PC with 3Gb of memory, taking averages over 10 independent runs. For a given traffic load and topology, variation in run time was quite small.

Topology	secs/time-step (20% link util.)	secs/time-step (50% link util.)
Top-1	0.0026	0.0026
Top-2	0.051	0.051
Top-3	0.283	0.285
Top-4	0.852	0.907

Since a time-step takes 5 seconds, all of these experiments run much faster than real-time on a laptop scale machine. Observe that Top-4 at 50% utilization represents traffic movement equivalent to 970 million packet per second (assuming 1000 byte packets). To move this much traffic in real time on a packet-oriented parallel simulation engine that could scalably deliver 1 million simulated packets per second per CPU would require a supercomputer with 970 CPUs.

We did experiments on Top-1 computing the real speedup delivered by the coarse-grained algorithm against the equivalent packet-oriented flows, using our framework's simulation engine. The table below gives the results, as a function of link utilization. Each data point represents 10 independent experiments, variance was extremely small. Speedup initially increases with link utilization because the amount of work the packet simulator must do increases linearly, while the coarse grained solution's work remains comparatively stable. At higher link utilization we do see the effects though of more cycle resolution, which is more costly.

link util.	speedup	link util.	speedup
10	213	50	3436
20	1665	60	3725
30	2112	70	1023
40	2728	80	1135

5.3. Accuracy

The applications that motivate this work do not require close accuracy. Nevertheless, we ought to develop some sense, if we can, of the impact that using such a coarse-grained flow representation has on foreground traffic. In these experiments the foreground traffic consists of both TCP flows and UDP flows. We attach an end host to each router; the host has a TCP server, TCP client, UDP server, and UDP client. Each client's behavior is modeled by an on-off process. In the on phase the client chooses a server uniformly at random from among the other hosts in the network, and requests a 5Mb data transfer. The on phase ends when the transfer is completed, at which point the client is idle for 5 simulation seconds, and then repeats. On the server side, the inter-packet transmission time is 10 milliseconds. We ran the same foreground traffic against background traffic generated by packet processes, and against background traffic generated by our coarse flow approach. In the coarse grained approach the foreground traffic "sees" the effect of background traffic by a diminished available link capacity.

TCP behavior is very sensitive to random fluctuations in flows, because a single packet loss triggers a dramatic change in TCP sending behavior. We observed a great deal of variation in many TCP metrics across all our experiments. We have studied relative error in the number of bytes successfully delivered (e.g., the average goodput) for both UDP and TCP flows . While we hesitate to ascribe quantifiable statistical meaning to these results, the general trends are

- UDP traffic is relatively insensitive to the differences in background traffic generation
- TCP behavior is relatively insensitive when link utilization is low (because then its behavior is less driven by packet loss). With higher utilization more differences are observable. Indeed the largest differences appear when TCP behavior is most variant—in the middle range of low loss and high loss. Averaged over all the experiments we did, the relative error in goodput is 17%

Evidence from this study is that the accuracy of foreground flow behavior against coarse-grained background traffic will be quite adequate for the training application of interest.

6. Conclusions

This paper proposes an approach for simulating network traffic flows at a coarse scale. The approach is motivated by an application where we must deliver real-time performance, and "look-and-feel" accuracy. We develop an optimized means of performing the simulation, and study its behavior on a set of large topologies based on known Internet backbones. We find that it is fast—very very fast relative to packet-based flows—and accurate enough for our purposes.

Acknowledgements

This research was supported in part by DARPA Contract N66001-96-C-8530, and NSF Grant CCR-0209144. Accordingly, the U.S. Government retains a non-exclusive, royalty-free license to publish or reproduce the published form of this contribution, or allow others to do so, for U.S. Government purposes. In addition this project was supported under Award No. 2000-DT-CX-K001 from the Office for Domestic Preparedness, U.S. Department of Homeland Security. Points of view in this document are those of the author(s) and do not necessarily represent the official position of the U.S. Department of Homeland Security.

References

[1] A. Adams, T. Bu, R. Cáceres, N. Duffield, T. Friedman, J. Horowitz, F.L. Presti, S. Moon, V. Paxson, and D. Towsley. The use of end-to-end multicast measurement for characterizing internal network behavior. *IEEE Communications Magazine*, May 2000.

[2] C. Barakat, P. Thiran, G. Iannaccone, C. Diot, and P. Owezarski. A flow-based model for internet backbone traffic. In *Internet Measurement Workshop'02*, San Francisco, CA, November 2002.

[3] T. Bu and D. Towsley. Fixed point approximations for TCP behavior in an AQM network. In *Proceedings of ACM SIGMETRICS 2001*, Cambridge, Massachusetts, June 2001.

[4] J. Cao, D. Davis, S.V. Wiel, and B. Yu. Time-varying network tomography. *J. Americal Statistical Association*, 95:1063–1075, 2000.

[5] M. Coates, A. Hero, R. Nowak, and B. Yu. Internet tomography. *IEEE Signal Processing Magazine*, May 2002.

[6] L. Debnath and P. Mikusinksi. *Introduction to Hilbert Spaces with Applications*. Academic Press, San Diego, CA, 1990.

[7] Anja Feldmann, Albert G. Greenberg, Carsten Lund, Nick Reingold, Jennifer Rexford, and Fred True. Deriving traffic demands for operational IP networks: methodology and experience. In *SIGCOMM*, pages 257–270, 2000.

[8] G. Kesidis, A. Singh, D. Cheung, and W. W. Kwok. Feasibility of fluid-driven simulation for atm network. In *Proceedings of IEEE Globecom'96*, London, GB, November 1996.

[9] C. Kiddle, R. Simmonds, C. Williamson, and B. Unger. Hybrid packet/fluid flow network simulation. In *Proceedings of the Seventeenth Workshop on Parallel and Distributed Simulation (PADS'03)*, San Diego, California, June 2003.

[10] M. Liljenstam and A. Andy Ogielski. Tier-1 internet provider networks with multiple peering points. http://www.ssfnet.org/Exchange/gallery/usa/index.html.

[11] B. Liu, D. R. Figueiredo, Y. Guo, J. Kurose, and D. Towsley. A study of networks simulation efficiency: Fluid simulation vs. packet-level simulation. In *Proceedings of IEEE Infocom'01*, Anchorage, Alaska, April 2001.

[12] B. Liu, Y. Guo, J. Kurose, D. Towsley, and W. Gong. Fluid simulation of large scale networks: Issues and tradeoffs. In *Proceedings of the International Conference on Parallel and Distributed Processing Techniques and Applications*, Las Vegas, Nevada, June 1999.

[13] Y. Liu, F. L. Presti, V. Misra, D. Towsley, and Y. Gu. Scalable fluid models and simulations for large-scale ip networks. *ACM Transactions on Modeling and Computer Simulation*, 14(3):305–324, 2004.

[14] D. Nicol, M. Goldsby, and M. Johnson. Fluid-based simulation of communication networks using SSF. In *Proceedings of the 1999 European Simulation Symposium*, Erlangen, Germany, October 1999.

[15] D. Nicol, M. Liljenstam, and J. Liu. Large-scale network simulation using SSF. In *Proceedings of the 2003 Winter Simulation Conference*, New Orleans, LA, December 2003.

[16] D. Nicol and G. Yan. Discrete event fluid modeling of background TCP traffic. *ACM Transactions on Modeling and Computer Simulation*, 14:1–39, July 2004.

[17] J. Padhye, V. Firoiu, D. Towsley, and J. Kurose. Modeling TCP throughput: A simple model and its empirical validation. In *Proceedings of ACM SIGCOMM'98*, Vancouver, CA, September 1998.

[18] W. Press, S. Teukolsky, W. Vetterling, and B. Flannery. *Numerical Recipes in C++ : The Art of Scientific Computing (2nd Edition)*. Cambridge University Press, 2002.

[19] RocketFuel Project. `http://www.cs.washington.edu/research/networking/rocketfuel/`.

[20] C. Tebaldi and M. West. Bayesian inference on network traffic using link count data. *J. Americal Statistical Association*, 93:557–576, 1998.

[21] A. Vahdat, K. Yocum, K. Walsh, P. Mahadevan, D. Kostic, J. Chase, and D. Becker. Scalability and accuracy in a large-scale network emulator. In *Proceedings of 5th Symposium on Operating Systems Design and Implementation (OSDI)*, December 2002.

[22] Y. Vardi. Network tomography : Estimating source-destination traffic intensities from link data. *J. Americal Statistical Association*, 91:365–377, 1996.

[23] A. Yan and W. B. Gong. Time-driven fluid simulation for high-speed networks with flow-based routing. In *Proceedings of the Applied Telecommunications Symposium'98*, Boston, MA, April 1998.

[24] Y. Zhang, M. Roughan, N. Duffield, and A. Greenberg. Fast accurate computation of large-scale ip traffic matrices from link loads, 2003.

[25] Y. Zhang, M. Roughan, C. Lund, and D. Donoho. An information-theoretic approach to traffic matrix estimation, 2003.

[26] J. Zhou, Z. Ji, M. Takai, and R. Bagrodia. Maya:integrating hybrid network modeling to the physical world. *ACM Trans. on Modeling and Computer Simulation*, 14(2):149–169, April 2004.

[27] M. Zukerman, T. Neame, and R. Addie. Internet traffic modeling and future technology implications, 2003.

Simulating Realistic Packet Routing Without Routing Protocols *

George F. Riley
Dheeraj Reddy

Department of Electrical and Computer Engineering
Georgia Institute of Technology
Atlanta, GA 30332-0250
{riley,dheeraj}@ece.gatech.edu

Abstract

A fundamental requirement for any network simulation environment is the realistic forwarding of packets from a source to a destination in the simulated topology. The routing decisions at each hop along the path should accurately represent decisions made by actual routers with a similar topology. Further, the routing decisions must be affected by topology changes, such as link weight adjustments or node failures. The methods used by the simulation tools to achieve these requirements can be classified into three fundamental classes. First, the simulator can implement a model of any of the well known routing protocols, *such as* BGP, OSPF, *or* EIGRP. *Assuming the implemented models of these protocols are a reasonable representation of the deployed protocol, the routing decisions and routing updates in the presence of failures will highly accurate and will accurately model the real–world network. A second method is to use global topology knowledge within the simulator to pre–compute routing information using any of several graph theoretic algorithms that compute paths through a graph. Should any topology changes occur, the simulator can simply re–compute routes based on revised global knowledge. A third method is the use of on–demand routing computations using global topology knowledge, coupled with a source–based routing scheme, such as the well–know* NIx–Vector *method. Both of the first two methods suffer from excessive memory requirements for routing table storage, which can be* $O(N^2)$ *in the extreme case. The last two methods suffer from unrealistic routing decisions in the presence of topology changes, due to the use of instantaneous global topology knowledge. A link failure in some part of the topology is immediately known to all nodes, which results in instantaneous and unrealistic routing updates throughout the network. We present an approach to improve the realism of the on–demand methods, without incurring the* $O(N^2)$ *memory overhead of the routing protocol method.*

1 Introduction

Network simulation tools are a widely used and accepted method for studying the behavior of an arbitrary network under a variety of conditions. The class of network simulation tools known as *Packet–Level Detail* simulators include *ns2*[7], *SSFNet*[3, 2], *JavaSim*[12], and *GTNetS*[10] just to name a few. These *packet–level detail* simulators have detailed models for every packet on every communication link in the network, including models for packet transmission time, link propagation delay, queuing delay, and packet loss due to queue overflows or link errors. A fundamental requirement for this class of simulation tool is the correct and accurate forwarding of packets at each hop in a routing path from a source to a destination, and correct adjustments to the routing in the presence of link failures or link–weight adjustments.

The methods used by the various tools to achieve this goal of accurate packet routing can be categorized into three basic classes.

1. Use of routing protocols. In this method, the simulator includes a detailed model of the behavior of any of the well–known and widely used routing protocols, such as *BGP*[9], *OSPF*[8], or *EIGRP*[1, 6]. The models for these protocols exchange routing messages and updates in a fashion similar to the behavior of the actual deployed implementation of the protocol, and maintain detailed *routing tables* at each node which are consulted to make routing decisions. In the presence of failures or link–weight changes, the update messages propagate this information throughout the topology and packet routing decisions change appropriately

*This work is supported in part by NSF under contract numbers ANI-9977544, ANI-0136969, ANI-0240477, ECS-0225417, and DARPA under contract number N66002-00-1-8934.

1087-4097/05 $20.00 © 2005 IEEE

as the revised information becomes known. This results in highly accurate and realistic routing decisions, at the expense of excessive memory requirements for routing table storage. Indeed, in the extreme case the memory requirement is $O(N^2)$, where N is the number of nodes in the simulated topology.

2. Pre–computed static routes. This method leverages the fact that a network simulation environment has global topology knowledge, which can be represented as *graph* with vertices (nodes) and edges (links). Any shortest path graph algorithm, such as *breadth first search* for constant link weight graphs or *Dijkstra*[4] for variable link weight graphs, can be used to compute all–pairs routing paths and populate the routing tables appropriately. When topology changes occur, the shortest–path algorithm is executed again and the routing table information is updated to reflect the changes. This method suffers from both excessive memory usage (again $O(N^2)$) and lack of realism. In real networks, topology changes due to link failures are not immediately known to all routers and end–hosts in the network, but rather discover this information after potentially considerable delays while the routing protocol exchanges routing updates.

3. On–Demand route computation with source–based routing. This method reduces both the memory and CPU overhead incurred by the prior methods by calculating routing information only as needed, and by storing this information in the packet, rather than in routing tables at each node. A compact representation of source routes, such as the *NIx–Vector*[11] method, can lead to further memory savings. However, this method also suffers from unrealistic responses to topology changes, again due to the use of global topology knowledge for route computations. In the extreme case, any packet created at a source node immediately after a topology change event will take the best path to a destination even though the source cannot possibly be aware of the topology change event at that time.

We discuss the methodology used in our *Georgia Tech Network Simulator* (*GTNetS*) that overcomes the lack of realism suffered by both the static routing approach and the on–demand routing approach. Our method involves the introduction of a *route maintenance* time interval between the time that a topology change event occurs, and the time that the last node in the topology becomes aware of the change. During the *route maintenance* interval, the simulator incurs additional CPU overhead to validate and possibly recompute routing information as needed. When the *route maintenance* interval is over, overhead returns to normal. The fact that a topology change event has occurred is propagated through the topology using *Route Change Events*, that filter through the topology in a cascading fashion starting at the point where the change occurred. This results in routing updates that are somewhat less realistic than the routing protocol approach, but much more realistic than the existing approaches for static and on–demand routing; while at the same time maintaining the memory efficiency of the on–demand approaches.

The essential purpose of routing protocols in computer networks is to convey the topology changes in a network. Topology changes are not necessarily restricted to link failures, although this is the class of failures that we have chosen in this work. Change of costs of routes and expiry of quotas and other administrative trivia can also result in some links being rendered less desirable than others during the course of a data transmission. One of the ways in which this information is propagated across the network is by the exchange of routing messages (in case of BGP from one AS to another AS). In an actual network various routing protocols facilitate the propagation of these messages across the network so that appropriate routing decisions may be made.

In case of network simulations, it is not always convenient or necessary to implement a detailed model of a routing protocol to study, for example, a particular application behavior. Consequently, static routing, NIx-Vector routing and other methods are used which take into advantage the global knowledge of the topology that the simulator facilitates. Unlike real-world routing protocols which react to topology changes after finite delays, many routing protocols used in simulators react to these topology changes instantaneously by deriving their knowledge from the global state of the simulator.

On a broader scale, our proposed method facilitates propagation of any time-delayed information which has a causal effect on the phenomenon being studied, but where the details of such propagation do not effect the results of the simulation. In case of discrete event network simulations, topology change propagation without the use of detailed routing protocols present a very convincing example of the need for such a method.

The remainder of this paper is organized as follows. Section 2 introduces our cascading update approach when applied to static routing methods. Section 3 discusses the modifications needed in the on–demand routing approaches utilize our cascading route update approach. Section 4 discusses how our approach affects space–parallel distributed network simulations. Section 5 presents memory usage and CPU overhead statistics comparing our approach to more traditional routing methods. Finally, section 6 discusses conclusions from this work.

2 Static Routing Approaches

In this section, we discuss the often–used *static* routing approach, and show how our methods can add realism to this approach by delaying topology updates in a realistic way. In the next section, we show how the same approach can be used for on–demand routing methods, leading to both memory efficiency and realism.

Static routing approaches maintain a global topology database, which is essentially a global network connectivity graph. The most common use of this method simply pre–computes routing paths from every node to every other node, and stores the routing decision at each hop in a *routing table* that is consulted as routing decisions are needed. Should topology change events occur, such as a link or node failure, a revalidation or re-computation phase is needed, to recalculate routes that may be affected by the change. This method suffers from a lack of realism since all nodes react to the change instantaneously. In a real-life network, topology changes require some variable time delay to be propagated to all hosts. In fact, the farther a network element is from a the location of topology change, the longer it takes for the topology-change information to be known by the element.

One of the methods that can be used to calculate this time delay after which network elements know about a fault is Dijkstra's algorithm. Using this algorithm, one can calculate the shortest distance from the point of topological change to every other node in the simulation and inform them of the respective change after a time period proportional to the delay along the path. We define what is meant by *delay* in this context in the next paragraph. After the shortest–path algorithm completes, one could simply schedule events for every node in the topology at the appropriate time delay as computed by the algorithm (the *distance* from the change event). However, this approach requires one event per network node to be scheduled simultaneously in the event list, resulting in a potentially large sorted list and possible reduced performance.

The approach we have chosen to use is to progressively let the topology change information be propagated across the topology via the links. The network elements which are in the immediate vicinity of the change will notice the change immediately. These nodes will propagate the change to their neighbors, by scheduling an event after time a time period that represents the route update delay between the nodes. The route update delay between a pair of node is defined as:

$$d = P + S/B + U \qquad (1)$$

where P is the speed of light delay propagation delay between the nodes, B is the bandwidth of the link connecting the nodes, S is an arbitrary constant representing the average size of routing update message reflecting route changes, and U is another arbitrary constant representing the time delay required by a realistic routing protocol to determine a new route.

When neighbors later process the route update event, they will in turn inform their neighbors with similar delays, and so on. Care is taken by each node to suppress propagation of change on to the neighbor from which the update was received. Further, each topological change has a unique change-id, that is temporarily stored at each node to insure changes are not infinitely propagated due to possible loops in the topology. A network element acts upon a given change-id only once, and ignores any subsequent notification of the same change.

When network elements receive these change events, in addition to forwarding to neighbors, they also examine their routing tables and re-initialize them as needed. In our implementation, we delay this action until the next packet arrives, since there is some chance that another routing change event will supersede the current one prior to any packet forwarding actions. This delay leads to a small amount of state saving at each node but this is temporal and is deleted after a reasonable amount of time or if a change negating the earlier change arrives before the expiration. Hence, even if the number of topological changes is large, the amount of state required is still reasonably small.

One of the advantages of our method is that we need not store a catalog of changes and their respective impacts. The number of events in the simulator queue that are needed at any given point of time is limited, which results in minor increase in the memory requirements at each node. Section 5 gives measured results for this memory overhead.

3 On–Demand Routing Approaches

In this section, we discuss our approach to realistic routing decisions when on–demand route computations are used. The discussion is given specifically in the context of the well–known *NIx–Vector* [11] approach, but the techniques are applicable to other on–demand approaches as well. With the *NIx–Vector* routing approach, routing information for a given source and destination pair is only calculated when needed, in particular when a new packet is created at source S with a destination address D. Under the assumption that many more packets will be created with the same source and destinations, the calculated routing path is cached at source S and retrieved with an efficient *log k* lookup method (where k is the number of cached routes at source S). Further, to conserve memory, the routing informations is stored in the packet, rather than at each node along the path, and is stored in a memory efficient manner.

In the simplest approach, any routing topology

change could immediately delete any previously calculated and cached *NIx–Vectors*. At that point, any new packets created at any source node would require a new routing computation and would result in packets being routed properly in the revised topology. However, this is a poor approach for two reasons.

1. It is inefficient in terms of CPU use, in that the routing computations require at best $O(VE)$ steps, where V is the number of vertices (nodes) in the graph, and E is the number of edges (links). For large topologies this overhead can be significant.

2. It is unrealistic for the same reasons the static routing approach leads to unrealistic routing, namely that leaf nodes at the edge of a network will react instantaneously to routing changes at any point in the topology.

Our solution to proper routing in this case starts with the same routing update propagation events discussed in the previous section. Each node, starting with the failed node (or the node with a failed link) notifies its neighbors, which in turn notify their neighbors with appropriate delays. In addition, we introduce the notion of a *NIx–Vector validation time*, which indicates the last time at which each *NIx–Vector* was known to be valid. To describe the actions taken by each node when notified of routing topology changes, we look separately at *host* nodes (those with data generating applications) and *router* nodes (those with no applications).

- When a *host* node receives a notification of a topology change:

    1. If the topology change is a node or link failure, retrieve each previously calculated *NIx–Vector* and *validate* it. Validating a *NIx–Vector* simply means following the path specified by the *NIx–Vector* and insuring that each node and link in the path has not failed. If the *NIx–Vector* fails validation, simply discard it. If the validation succeeds, the calculated path is still the shortest path even in the revised topology, and the *NIx–Vector NIx–Vector* validation time is updated to the current time. The *NIx–Vector* validation is fairly efficient, requiring only $O(h)$ steps, where H is the hop count from the source to the destination in the *NIx–Vector* being validated.

    2. If the topology change is a node or link *repair* (a previously failed node or link has returned to normal operation), the we have no choice but to discard all existing cached *NIx–Vectors*. Since the addition of a new node or link in the topology may result in a new *shortest path* from a source, simply validating existing *NIx–Vectors* is not sufficient.

    Keep in mind however that both of the above actions are not instantaneous to the topology change, but rather become known to the *host* node after a realistic time delay by virtue of the route change propagation events previously discussed

- When a *router* node receives a notification of a topology change, the processing is slightly more complicated. It first notes the change event (i.e, which link or node has failed or restored), and the time that this change became known. Then:

    1. On receiving a packet with a *NIx–Vector*, check if the validation time of the *NIx–Vector* is more recent than any pending topology change event.
        (a) If so, this *NIx–Vector* can be used and the packet is forwarded normally.
        (b) If not, search for a previously cached *NIx–Vector* to the specified destination. If one exists, retrieve it and proceed to the next step. If one does not exist, calculate a new *NIx–Vector* from the router node to the specified destination, cache it for future reference, and proceed to the next step.

    2. If the next hop specified by the new (or existing) *NIx–Vector* is the same one from which the packet was received, this is a routing loop and the packet is dropped. Otherwise, replace the *NIx–Vector* on the received packet with the new one and route the packet normally.

    3. Since the above two steps result in the creation and caching of *NIx–Vectors* at routers, the same validation and discarding method discussed in item 1 under host actions must also be performed. If the topology change event indicates a node or link repair action, any cached *NIx–Vectors* must be discarded. If the change event indicates a link or node failure, then the validation method previously discussed is applicable.

In either case, once a given topology change indication has propagated to all nodes in the topology, all routing update states and temporarily cached *NIx–Vectors* in the routers are no longer needed and can be discarded.

The actions taken by each node in response to route change notification and packet reception events are best illustrated by an example. Consider the simple topology shown in figure 1. Suppose that source node 20 and destination node 21 have an existing connection and are exchanging packets. At some arbitrary time, say $t = 4.0$, the link connecting nodes 2 and 3 fails. In our scenario, both nodes 2 and 3 are immediately aware of the link failure due to error bits reported from the corresponding

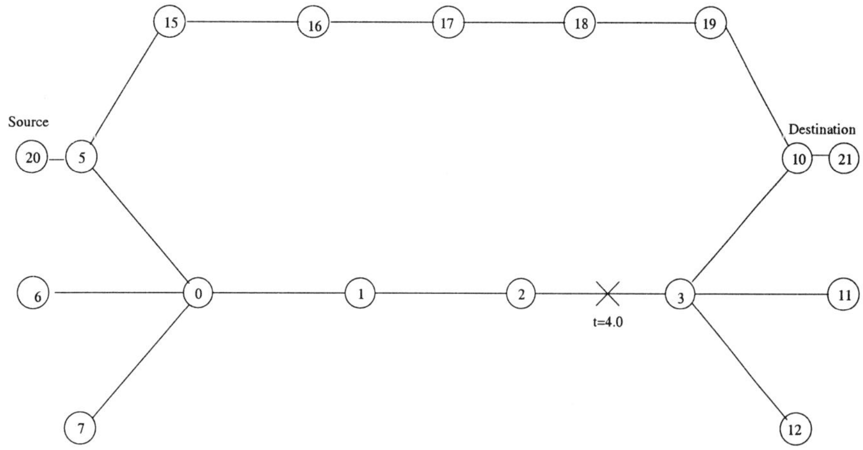

Figure 1. Simple Topology

interfaces. At that time, they schedule the route change update events for their neighbors (nodes 1 and 10, 11, 12 in our example) to be scheduled at the appropriate delay in the future. For this discussion, assume the delay is calculated to be 1 second for each node pair. In our scenario, source node 20 is still generating packets, and is not aware of the routing change and still sending them through nodes 5, 0, 1 and 2, towards node 20. Any packet arriving at node 1 before time $t = 5.0$ will still be forwarded to node 2. In addition, node 2 determines that the *NIx–Vector* in any arriving packet originated at node 20 is *out–of–date*, meaning that the validation time for that *NIx–Vector* is earlier than the most recent routing change event. This causes node 2 to re–calculate a *NIx–Vector* to reach destination 21, and discovers the shortest path is through node 1, indicating a routing loop. Node 2 drops this packet, and caches the calculated *NIx–Vector* to avoid costly re–computation. Any subsequent packet from node 20 to node 21 will also be dropped due to the same routing loop. At time $t = 5.0$, node 1 becomes aware of the change, and schedules a notification for node 0 at time $t = 6.0$. Additionally, node 1 also creates a new *NIx–Vector* for destination 21, and starts dropping all packets to node 21 due to same routing loop just discussed. The cascading of the route update events continues until time $t = 7.0$, when node 5 becomes aware of this change. At this time, the new *NIx–Vector* for destination 21 is through node 15, and all future packets to node 21 take this (correct) path.

It is easy to see that our approach results in somewhat realistic behavior, in that a significant number of packets (either those already in flight or newly created packets at a source) are incorrectly routed and dropped due to routing loops or routing to failed links. This mis–routing of packets will continue until a source becomes aware of the topology change and begins routing packets correctly. This is of course quite realistic since actually deployed networks would exhibit the same basic behavior.

One final note of clarification is needed here. Both in our simulation environment and in real networks, leaf nodes such nodes 20 and 21 in our topology have little interest or participation in routing decisions. Since these nodes have only one routing neighbor, any packet not addressed to the local host are simply forwarded to the single routing neighbor without regard to the ultimate destination. This is similar to the *default gateway* specification in most network configuration scripts, which specifies where to send packets not addressed locally. Similarly, our simulator excludes single–neighbor leaf nodes from all routing computations, and simply uses a default route in that case. Thus, in the discussion above when referring to the *source* of a packet, we are actually referring to the first point where a routing decision is made (node 5 in our sample topology).

4 Distributed Simulation

In a space-parallel distributed simulation, the topology being simulated is distributed between a number of independent processes that communicate using some *runtime infrastructure*, such as the *Federated Simulation Developers Kit*[5] from Georgia Tech. Each process is responsible for state maintenance for some subset of the overall topology. There is no easily accessible shared global state between the processes, and thus any information shared between the processes must be accomplished via exchange of event messages. Assuming the use of a conservative synchronization protocol, an important aspect of the distributed simulation is the *lookahead* between the processes. *Lookahead* is defined as the minimum simulated time delay between the creation of an event message at one process, and the time that the event messages affects state on the receiving process. For a typical distributed network simulation, the lookahead between any two simulating nodes will be equal to the sum of the minimum transmission time and the propagation delay between any two nodes that are involved in the parallel simulation. On a commodity 10/100 Mbps full duplex ethernet, it will be of the order of 8-10 microseconds.

Since our design for realistic routing state updates is patterned after the behavior of real networks, our approach has a natural counterpart in distributed simulations as well. Since we use event messages to exchange routing update information, there is no need for instantaneous global knowledge shared between processes. Instead, if a node in process A needs to inform a neighbor in process B of a routing update, it simply generates the routing update event normally (with the appropriate delay) and forwards it to process B using the same runtime infrastructure used to forward packet receipt events between processes A and B. Further, using our calculation of the *delay* time between updates given previously in equation 1, we have guaranteed that update messages propagate between processes no faster than normal packet events, and thus our approach has no effect on the lookahead between the processes.

The only issue is the lack of a universal *change–id* value, since each process independently assigns the topology change identifiers. This problem is easily solved by pre–pending a *process–id* to each *change–id*, resulting in globally unique topology change identifiers.

5 Experimental Results

To demonstrate the correct behavior of our approach, and to measure the overhead associated with this method, we designed two sets of experiments. The first is a simple topology similar to figure 1. Using our animation tool, we can visually observe the affect of the cascading routing change approach and determine that it behaves as expected. The second set of experiments uses a much larger topology, and is designed to measure the overhead of this approach, both in terms of memory and CPU consumptions.

We choose the simple topology for the first set of experiments so that we can easily observe packets in–flight, and can see the cascading effect of the routing updates as discussed previously. In this scenario, we have a simple UDP data source at node 20 sending packets at a constant rate to a single destination at node 21. The source generates data at a constant rate of 500 kbps. With no link failures, the shortest path is 20-5-0-1-2-3-10-20. At time $t = 4.0$, we modeled the failure of the link connecting nodes 2 and 3. For simplicity we assumed that all the link delays are equal, and set the delay value to 10 milliseconds each. The simulations were

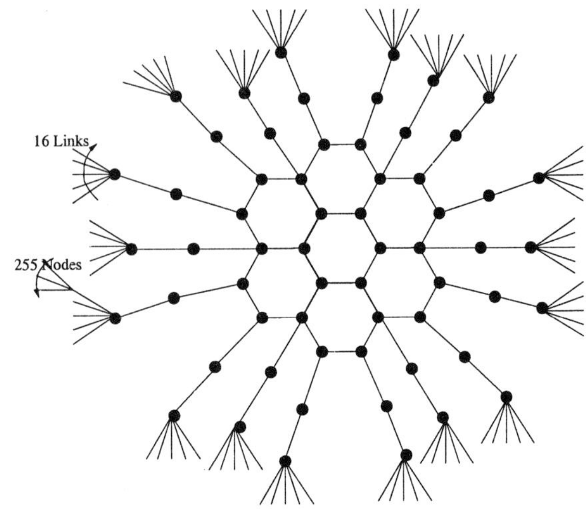

Figure 2. Large scale Topology

run for 10 seconds of simulation time, and the number of dropped packets along the path was measured.

We ran this simulation using both the unrealistic *instantaneous* route change knowledge, as well with our cascading update approach. In the unrealistic approach, source node 20 immediately is aware of the topology change, and begins using the new route 5-15-16-17-18-19-10-21. The only packets that would be mis–routed are those already in flight along the failed path. Our experiments confirmed that only 4 packets were lost in this case. Further, visual inspection of the simulation animation shows the instantaneous re–routing of packets after the link failure.

Using our cascading update approach, we measured 35 packets being lost at various points between the source and the destination. Further, visual inspection of the simulation animation confirms that packets continue to be improperly routed until the source node becomes aware of the topology change.

Clearly, a real–world implementation of a topology similar to figure 1 would result in a significant number mis–routed packets between nodes 20 and 21, until such time as node 20 became aware of the change and began routing packets along a valid path. We are not arguing that our approach is an exact model of what a real network would do in this situation, since the amount of time for the updates to propagate to a source node is hard to determine and certainly not a constant for each link. Rather, we claim that our approach is much more realistic than the instantaneous update approach commonly used in simulation tools. Further, our three terms used in the delay formula could be determined by empirical measurements, leading to more realistic route update propagations.

The second set of experiments was designed to show

Table 1. Overhead Measurement for a 73464 node topology

	Max Memory Usage	Execution Time	Max Event Queue Size
0 (Pristine)	240 MB	3.0 secs	50
1 Failure	243 MB	3.70 secs	14492
2 Failures	245 MB	9.5 secs	19956
3 Failures	247 MB	14.25 secs	19956
4 Failures	248 MB	16.52 secs	19987

the overhead incurred by our approach, both in terms of memory and CPU usage. The topology for these experiments consists of a 73464 node topology as shown in Figure 2. We defined five UDP flows with the same data generation parameters as in the previous experiments, but had different sets of source and destinations pairs resulting in five different routing paths through the central part of the topology. The flows scheduled were from one leaf to another leaf such that the route completely traverses the core hexagon.

This simulation was run twice, once with no topology change events (i.e, no link failures) and a second time with five different failures, each affecting one or more of the UDP flows. Results are shown in table 1. As we can see, the memory overhead for this particular experiment using our approach is about 1.2%. Further, the extra memory is only allocated during the topology change propagation, and is freed afterwards. Therefore, after the topology change has propagated completely, this memory overhead is near zero. The total time taken for the simulation increases by about 20%. This represents the time required to re–compute the source routes when routing change events are known. We point out that for any other approach that responds to routing changes there will also be significant CPU time for route re-computation. The comparison here is simply between a simulation with no topology changes as compared to one with several.

The maximum event list size observed shows a rather large increase. This is due to the regularity of our topology, with all link speeds and link delays the same. This results in time synchronized updates, and in fact a large number of leaf nodes end up with simultaneous update events being queued. Even with this excessive event list size, the overall execution time increase was modest. With more variation in link characteristics, the maximum event list size would be more reasonable.

To observe the scalability of our method, with respect to increasing number of fault events (these events cause topology changes in the network), we chose a 31044 node network topology similar to the slightly larger one shown in figure 2 and induced an increasing number of faults keeping all other conditions constant. The results of this study are tabulated in table 1. The total time taken by the simulation increases linearly with the number of fault events. This is along expected lines because each fault event generates a cascading sequence of events that convey the topology change information across the network. The is also a very small increase in the memory that is consumed. This is fairly negligible at around 0.5%.

Table 2. Scalability Measurements for varying failures / nodes

Nodes	Failures	Max Memory Usage	Execution Time (secs)	Max Event Queue Size
10644	1	61 MB	1.43	4892
10644	2	61 MB	2.42	6756
10644	3	62 MB	3.29	6785
10644	4	62 MB	3.78	6787
20844	1	104 MB	2.14	9692
20844	2	104 MB	3.96	13356
20844	3	105 MB	5.85	13385
20844	4	105 MB	6.82	13387
31044	1	147 MB	2.96	14492
31044	2	147 MB	5.72	19956
31044	3	147 MB	8.49	19985
31044	4	148 MB	9.7	19987
41244	1	189 MB	3.90	19292
41244	2	190 MB	7.51	26556
41244	3	190 MB	11.14	26585
41244	4	191 MB	12.88	26587
51444	1	231 MB	4.92	24092
51444	2	233 MB	9.36	33156
51444	3	233 MB	13.92	33185
51444	4	234 MB	16.13	33187

The results of the scalability study of our method with respect to increasing number of nodes as well as the number of failure events is shown in table 2. As the number of nodes increases in the simulation, the memory used increases in a linear fashion. As the number of link failures (topology changes) increase, the execution time of the simulation increases linearly with little or no change in memory usage. As the number of nodes increase the execution time of the simulation also increases due to the fact that the topology changes have to propagate across a larger network topology, and the longer time to calculate *NIx–Vector* routes. All the experiments were run on a Debian Linux box with 2.6.8

kernel and 1 G of RAM. Three runs of the experiment was carried for each data point and the mean recorded.

6 Conclusions

We have introduced an approach for network simulation tools to realistically model effects of route change events without requiring the excessive overhead of routing tables and routing protocol models. Our approach allows for routing changes to propagate through a topology in a realistic fashion, and captures the effect of mis–routing due to incomplete information at nodes not yet aware of changes. The overhead for our approach is minimal, both in terms of memory usage and CPU overhead. Our design is such that the rate of propagation of change events can be tuned to model time delays needed for routing protocols to converge on new routing information. Our simulation experiments demonstrated the effectiveness of our approach in terms of dropped packets due to incomplete information, and in terms of memory and CPU overhead. Each node simply processes a single event route update at an appropriate time, reacts to the routing change information, and forwards the change event to neighbors. Thus, routing change actions, such as link failures, become known to nodes in the topology in cascading waves, similar to the propagation of route updates in real networks.

References

[1] B. Albrightson, J. J. Garcia-Luna-Aceves, and J. Boyle. EIGRP – a fast routing protocol based on distance vectors. In *Proceedings of Networld/Interop*, May 1994.

[2] J. Cowie, H. Liu, J. Liu, D. Nicol, and A. Ogielski. Towards realistic million-node internet simulations. In *International Conference on Parallel and Distributed Processing Techniques and Applications*, June 1999.

[3] J. H. Cowie, D. M. Nicol, and A. T. Ogielski. Modeling the global internet. *Computing in Science and Engineering*, January 1999.

[4] E. W. Dijkstra. A note on two problems in connexion with graphs. *Numerische Mathematik*, (1):269–271, 1959.

[5] R. Fujimoto, S. Ferenci, M. Loper, T. McLean, K. Perumalla, G. Riley, and I. Tacic. Fdk users guide. Georgia Institute of Technology, March 2001.

[6] J. J. Garcia-Luna-Aceves. Loop–free routing using diffusing computations. *IEEE/ACM Transactions on Networking*, 1(1), Feb 1993.

[7] S. McCanne and S. Floyd. The LBNL network simulator. Software on-line: http://www.isi.edu/nsnam, 1997. Lawrence Berkeley Laboratory.

[8] J. Moy. Internet RFC2328: Ospf version 2. Network Working Group, April 1998.

[9] Y. Rekhter and T. Li. RFC 1771, border gateway protocol 4, March 1995.

[10] G. F. Riley. The Georgia Tech Network Simulator. In *Proceedings of the ACM SIGCOMM workshop on Models, methods and tools for reproducible network research*, pages 5–12. ACM Press, 2003.

[11] G. F. Riley, M. H. Ammar, and R. M. Fujimoto. Stateless routing in network simulations. In *Proceedings of the Eighth International Symposium on Modeling, Analysis and Simulation of Computer and Telecommunication Systems*, August 2000.

[12] J.-Y. Tyan and C.-J. Hou. Javasim: A component-based compositional network simulation environment. In *Proceedings of the Western Simulation Multiconference, Communication Networks And Distributed Systems Modeling And Simulation*, Jan 2001.

Optimistic Simulation

The WarpIV Simulation Kernel

Jeffrey S. Steinman, Ph.D.
RAM Laboratories, Inc.
10525 Vista Sorrento Parkway, Suite 220
San Diego, CA 92121
steinman@ramlabs.com

Abstract

This paper provides an overview of the WarpIV Simulation Kernel that was designed to be an initial implementation of the Standard Simulation Architecture (SSA). WarpIV is the next generation replacement for the Synchronous Parallel Environment for Emulation and Discrete Event Simulation (SPEEDES) framework that has supported a number of DoD simulation programs including MDWAR, EADTB, JSIMS, and others.

This paper first provides a look back at the historical evolution of SPEEDES, the evolution of the SSA, and the development of WarpIV. This historical background is followed by a description of the layered SSA and design of WarpIV. Capabilities and new algorithms or data structures provided by each layer of the architecture are mentioned, but are not described in full detail. Several benchmarks for the underlying communications infrastructure and internal event-processing engine are given. The summary and conclusions section highlights the main technical points of the paper and describes future research and development goals for WarpIV.

1 Introduction

WarpIV[1] traces its origins back to the late 80's at the Jet Propulsion Laboratory and Caltech where the Time Warp Operating System (TWOS) was initially researched and developed [1,2]. Following TWOS, the Synchronous Parallel Environment for Emulation and Discrete Event Simulation (SPEEDES) framework was constructed to provide better flow control techniques that facilitate stable execution of optimistic simulations [3]. SPEEDES started out as *Time Warp without antimessages*. Later, as SPEEDES began to extend its capabilities to support additional event-scheduling techniques (both conservative and optimistic), this initial optimistic scheduling strategy became known as *Breathing Time Buckets* (BTB) [4]. An analytic model describing the fundamental BTB concept, known as the *Event Horizon*, was derived to accurately predict how many events would be processed on the average per BTB processing cycle [5].

In 1993, a new scheduling approach was developed in SPEEDES to integrate the strengths of pure Time Warp with the risk-free flow control benefits of BTB. The result was the *Breathing Time Warp* (BTW) algorithm that reduced message-sending risk in optimistic simulations while not being overly pessimistic in terms of when to release messages to remote nodes [6].

Other significant advances were made to SPEEDES in the early 90's including automatic incremental state saving [7], lazy reevaluation [8], parallel proximity detection [9], new event management data structures [10], two-way interactions between optimistic simulations and real-world systems [11], high-speed communications through shared memory [12], and scalable GVT update algorithms [13]. The early 90's were best characterized as a time of innovative research and development of the SPEEDES underlying technologies.

The late 90's saw SPEEDES transition from JPL/Caltech to industry and into several large DoD simulation programs. Significant improvements were made to the modeling framework [14]. These improvements abstracted the message parameter packing/unpacking mechanisms and allowed applications to schedule and process events as remote method invocations with strong type checking on the event signatures. A process model capability was further developed to allow events to behave more like threads that can wait for specified periods of time, or can be interrupted when certain conditions occur. An object proxy system provided initial capabilities for distributed objects to publish and subscribe to registered attributes [15]. Object discovery, removal, and attribute update reflections were automated. Initial data distribution management capabilities were provided [16]

In 2000, the Joint Simulation System (JSIMS) program [17] made sweeping changes to its architecture to execute as a High Level Architecture (HLA) federation

[1] WarpIV derives its name by combining the word *Warp* with the Roman numeral *IV* that is used to symbolize *Time* as the fourth dimension. Thus, the *WarpIV Simulation Kernel* articulates an infrastructure based on concepts from *Time Warp*.

1087-4097/05 $20.00 © 2005 IEEE

[18], and to use SPEEDES as its Common Component Simulation Engine (CCSE) [19,20]. Because some of the JSIMS federates were required to operate in a classified environment, the JSIMS program required CCSE-SPEEDES to be maintained in a controlled Trusted Software Development Methodology (TSDM) environment. Configuration management of the software was brought into a secure government laboratory environment with tight controls over software integration. Only upgrades that were specific to JSIMS could be merged into the baseline. Unfortunately, this caused SPEEDES to splinter into multiple baselines as different DoD programs independently made upgrades to SPEEDES, fixed problems, and improved overall performance.

Several important improvements were made to CCSE-SPEEDES between 2000 and 2004 that not only simplified the development process of building models, but also significantly revolutionized the modeling paradigm. Borrowing ideas from HLA, CCSE-SPEEDES expanded interoperability concepts beyond just coarse-grained federates executing in a federation. CCSE-SPEEDES not only automated HLA interoperability [21], but it also provided an interoperability paradigm for (1) entities executing within a parallel federate, and (2) components hierarchically residing within entities.

Other SPEEDES-based programs such as the HLA High Performance Computing Run Time Infrastructure (HPC-RTI) effort showed how SPEEDES could itself become an RTI [22]. The significant difference between the HPC-RTI and other RTIs is that the foundation of the HPC-RTI is an optimistic discrete-event simulation engine. This means that all operations provided by the HPC-RTI are potentially time managed, including Declaration Management (DM), Data Distribution Management (DDM), and Ownership Management (OWM). Very interesting techniques were developed in 2001 to demonstrate how optimistic event processing, occurring within the HPC-RTI, could be coordinated with conservative processing in the application federate. It was also demonstrated how models executing in SPEEDES could directly interoperate with models executing in legacy HLA federates.

In early 2001, it became clear that a next generation replacement for SPEEDES was badly needed to bring the splintered technologies from different programs into a common baseline, while also applying lessons learned from the many years of SPEEDES development and support. Other issues such as NASA patents, licensing rights, and software distribution had to be resolved in order to provide a more flexible mechanism to market and distribute the high-performance computing capability to a broader user base.

For these reasons, RAM Laboratories, Inc. chose to develop the core of the WarpIV Simulation Kernel from scratch. However, some of the peripheral utilities and algorithms developed exclusively by RAM Laboratories engineers for SPEEDES were refactored and then integrated back into WarpIV. This ensured that RAM Laboratories could distribute and license WarpIV without infringing on any SPEEDES patents or software licensing issues. WarpIV does not require the use of any third-party software. It is completely self-contained. To expand the potential user base, RAM Laboratories obtained a WarpIV export license from the Department of Commerce.

2 Architecture and Design

While the origins of WarpIV derive from parallel and distributed simulation, the infrastructure was designed to be more than simply a high performance simulation framework. WarpIV combines (1) *communications*, (2) *software utilities*, and (3) *compute engines* into a synergistic infrastructure to facilitate the development of high performance sequential, parallel, and distributed applications.

The WarpIV architecture was constructed by combining the capabilities of various SPEEDES programs into a single system with the goal of standardizing each of the internal modules. Over time, this evolved into a proposed Standard Simulation Architecture (see **Figure 1**) [23]. It became clear that while SPEEDES provided most of the capabilities of the SSA, it would require significant code refactoring to cleanly separate the standardized modules. The WarpIV implementation strictly adhered to the layered SSA design, resulting in a significantly cleaner and easier to maintain system. WarpIV also made many performance improvements along the way.

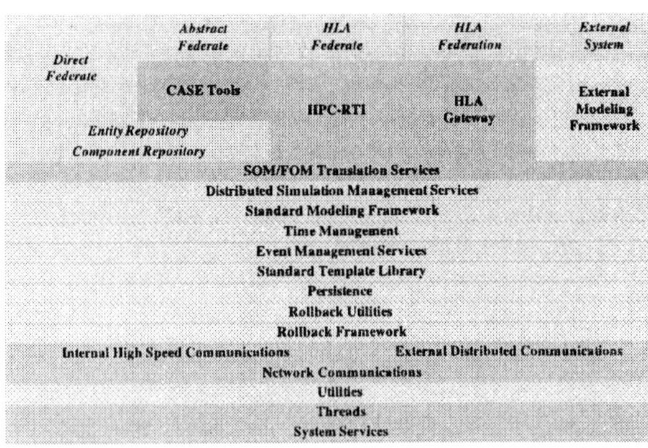

Figure 1: The Standard Simulation Architecture.

The layered architecture identifies the dependencies of each layer. Each layer depends at most on only the layers below and not above. This has several advantages. It forms a clean separation between the functionality of each layer, while offering a clear methodology to construct high-level capabilities by leveraging lower level capabilities.

3 Layered Capabilities

This section provides highlights of the WarpIV implementation of the SSA. The goal of this section is to give a broad overview of the capabilities and important internal algorithms that were implemented within WarpIV.

3.1 Utilities

WarpIV provides a large suite of software utilities that are heavily used internally and can be reused by applications to simplify model development. Most of the utilities described here have rollbackable counterparts that will be briefly discussed in the rollback capabilities section. Utilities include:

Container classes, various arrays, random number generation [24], object factories, various data parsers and run time classes, mathematical motion and coordinate system transformations [25], statistical algebra [26], strings, error handling, multi-resolution grids [27, 28], timers, spreadsheet data support,

3.2 High Speed Communications

WarpIV provides a standalone High Speed Communications (HSC) package that was developed to support both simulation and generic high-performance computing applications [29,30]. The WarpIV HSC has been highly optimized to support shared memory multiprocessors and small clusters of such machines. However, its interface was designed to be generic in order to allow construction of optimized implementations for different hardware or networked systems.

The HSC provides eight categories of services. These services are (1) startup and shutdown services, (2) miscellaneous services to obtain node information and set various performance tuning parameters, (3) global synchronization, (4) global reductions, (5) synchronized data distribution services, (6) asynchronous message passing, (7) coordinated message passing, and (8) ORB services that support distributed object remote method invocations.

3.3 Network Communications

WarpIV provides a self-contained robust network-based client/server ORB infrastructure [31] to support communication between heterogeneous platforms. Type-checked interfaces are generated by macros to create interface functions and mapping functions that register methods to interfaces. Three types of interfaces are supported. *Asynchronous* interfaces allow clients to invoke methods on the server, or for the server to invoke methods asynchronously back on the client. *Two-way* interfaces allow the client to synchronously invoke a method on the server, and for the server to return values back to the client through the argument list. *Function* interfaces are similar to two-way interfaces except that the remote method can actually return a non-void value like a normal function.

Building on the ORB, WarpIV provides a grid computing capability that allows *workers* to connect to a grid manager, while *taskers* issue commands that are performed by the workers [32]. The WarpIV grid solution is unique from other grid computing systems in that it allows applications to define their own strongly type-checked interfaces that can be embedded within their applications. The grid manager only assigns work to those workers that match the tasked interface. If a task does not complete because of an error condition, the grid manager automatically reassigns the task to another available worker.

3.4 Rollback Capabilities

WarpIV provides an optimized incremental state-saving rollback framework that hosts a wide variety of rollbackable data types and operations. The rollback framework can be used in a non-simulation context to automate undo and redo operations. However, in a WarpIV simulation, each event contains a rollback manager that automatically tracks rollbackable operations performed by the event. Events are individually rolled back as necessary when straggler messages or antimessages are received.

The rollback manager contains a doubly linked list of rollback items, which are automatically generated as rollbackable operations occur. The doubly linked list efficiently supports both rollback and rollforward operations. The base class rollback item provides four virtual functions: *Rollback*, *Rollforward*, *Commit*, and *Uncommit*. WarpIV invokes these methods as necessary to rollback, rollforward, commit, or uncommit events.

WarpIV provides a collection of rollbackable data types to represent integers, doubles, Booleans, pointers, and strings. These primitive data types are implemented as C++ classes that use operator overloading to capture changes. Default conversion operators allow these rollbackable primitive data types to be used as their native counterparts. Applications employing optimistic event processing must construct their state from these rollbackable data types.

Rollbackable container classes and arrays are provided to permit applications to store elements in lists, trees, hash tables, and arrays. These data structures use reverse operations to support rollback and rollforward operations. For example, an element that is inserted into a container is rolled back by subsequently removing the element from the container. The rollback item automatically performs the reverse operation.

Dynamic memory is managed through two mechanisms. The most straightforward approach is to identify a class to be rollbackable using a WarpIV-provided macro. The macro generates allocation and deallocation functions that automatically create rollback items to manage the memory when rollbacks occur. The second, and higher performing, dynamic memory approach is to identify a class with an object factory. Again, a macro is used to generate the allocation functions. Object factories provide a more efficient caching technique that helps reduce overheads by reusing allocated memory.

Many more rollback operations are provided by the rollback system. Some of these rollbackable operations include: sorted parallel output with optional data logging capabilities, memory copies and string duplication, functions that can be specified during commit phase, C-style malloc and free operations, assert statements, random number generation, and block memory state saves. The rollback framework was designed to be extensible, so new rollbackable operations are easily constructed if necessary.

3.5 Persistence

The WarpIV persistence framework fundamentally keeps track of memory allocations and pointer references within a high-speed internal database linked with applications [33]. With persistence, an object, and the collection of objects it recursively references through pointers, can be automatically packed into a buffer that is written to disk or sent as a message to another machine. Later, that buffer can be used to reconstruct the object and all of its recursively referenced objects. Upon reconstruction, the objects will be instantiated at different memory locations. The persistence framework automatically updates all affected pointer references to account for this fact.

3.6 Standard Template Library

WarpIV provides a rollbackable and persistent version of the Standard Template Library (STL) to accommodate mainstream C++ programmers [34]. The STL was developed from scratch and is based on the macro-generated container class algorithms. STL containers supported are: pair, string, list, map, multimap, set, multiset, vector, priority queue, stack, and queue. An extensive test suite was developed to test every API of these classes. The test suite can be compiled to operate with other STL implementations, which was used to validate the overall correctness of the tests.

3.7 Event Management

WarpIV provides an elaborate event management infrastructure that facilitates event processing, message sending and receiving, Global Virtual Time (GVT) updates, handling of rollbacks and antimessages, event cancellation, event queues, statistics gathering, and other miscellaneous operations such as startup and shutdown mechanisms.

One of the differences between SPEEDES and WarpIV is the clean separation between *logical processes* [35] and *simulation objects*. SPEEDES combines the functionality of these two types of WarpIV objects into a single simulation object class, while WarpIV separates event management functionality from modeling framework functionality. To facilitate the layered separation, simulation objects in WarpIV inherit from logical processes. The logical process class plays a significant role in the event management services layer, but does not provide any APIs for modelers. This separation is necessary to standardize the individual layers of the SSA.

Logical processes play a fundamental role in WarpIV. They are automatically distributed during startup to different nodes and are sources and syncs of events. Three kinds of logical processes exist: (1) a *master logical process manager* is provided on every node, (2) a *logical process manager* is automatically created on each node for each type of simulation object defined and plugged in by the application, and (3) *regular logical processes* that provide the base class for application-defined instances of simulation objects.

Logical processes manage pending events, and processed but uncommitted events when running optimistically. A more optimized event management mechanism is used when running sequentially or conservatively. A class diagram depicting the relationships between the three types of logical processes and events is shown in **Figure 2**.

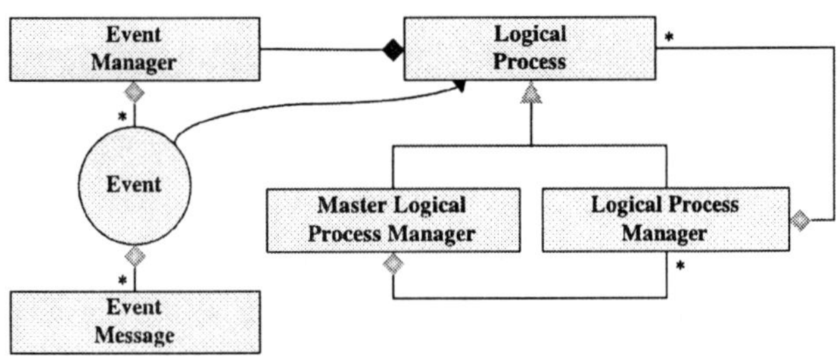

Figure 2: Event management classes.

The master logical process manager on each node stores its logical process managers in a local array, where the array index is the simulation object type. WarpIV automatically provides simulation object type Ids as applications *plug in* their simulation objects. Each logical process manager stores its local set of logical processes in a hash table that behaves like a high-speed array until new logical processes are created dynamically during the execution of the simulation. When dynamic simulation object creation is employed by the application, the array of logical processes automatically transforms into a high-speed hash table.

Logical process managers play a fundamental role in dynamic logical process creation and deletion. Because logical processes are dynamically created through time-tagged events, and because these events can be rolled back, the only legitimate way to implement this capability is to schedule creation and deletion events for logical process managers, whose role is to manage logical processes as part of its state. Thus logical process managers use rollbackable hash tables instead of regular hash tables to store logical processes.

Logical processes are identified through an abstract object handle composed of three integer values: *<NodeId, TypeId, LocalId>*. The object handle specifies the target logical process when scheduling events. When an event is scheduled, WarpIV automatically constructs an appropriate event message. Among other things, the message header includes object handle and event time information. If the event is scheduled for a remote node, the message is sent through the HSC to the receiving node. Once the message arrives, it is queued for processing. If necessary, those events incorrectly processed by the target logical process with time tags greater than the scheduled event time are rolled back. This may induce secondary rollbacks and the release of antimessages. Antimessages may induce further rollbacks when they cancel remote events that have already been processed. Locally scheduled events use a more optimized cancellation mechanism, and do not operate through the distributed antimessages formalism to cancel events that were scheduled by events that were rolled back.

WarpIV provides an abstract C++ representation of time that consists of a double-precision unit-less logical time value followed by four tie-breaking fields. The first two tie-breaking fields (Priority_1 and Priority_2) can be set by the application to specify the desired ordering of simultaneous events. WarpIV automatically sets the last two tie-breaking fields (Counter and UniqueId) when events are scheduled. Each logical process stores an integer event counter that is incremented as events are scheduled. Coupled with the logical process UniqueId, each event scheduled has a unique simulation time. One important correction must be made to the Counter. If an event that was scheduled by another logical process has a counter value of 100, while the logical process actually processing the event has a counter value of 50, then it is possible for the event to schedule new events with the same logical time value backward in time. To solve this problem, the logical process Counter is set to the Counter value in the event before the event is processed if its value is less than the event Counter. It is important to note that the Counter stored within the logical process must be rollbackable. Otherwise, non-repeatable simulation times would be generated as rollbacks occur.

Applications can schedule events for all three types of logical processes. The safest way to schedule an event for every object in the simulation at a given time is to first schedule an event for each master logical process manager on each node. As these events are simultaneously processed on each node, the events can schedule new events for each logical process manager, which in turn can access the information from its manager to schedule an event for each logical process for its type. This approach guarantees that all simulation objects active at a given time receive the event.

The event management layer collects statistics as events are processed. Each event is timed to measure its processing granularity. Statistics are gathered to count the number of events processed and rolled back by event type and by logical process type. A running critical path analysis computation is performed and displayed to users during GVT updates to indicate the maximum application speedup. Memory usage statistics can be displayed to indicate memory consumption for events and messages. Users may also display object factory information to further analyze their memory usage.

WarpIV also provides a trace file generation capability that stores critical information about each event that is processed and committed. The information is tailorable at run time and may include: the type of event, information about the object processing the event, all events scheduled by the event, rollback items created by the event, and application-specific streamed messages associated with the event. Unlike SPEEDES, WarpIV merges the trace-file output generated by each node into a single sorted file. This ensures that traces generated from sequential runs are identical to trace files generated when executing in parallel. It also simplifies debugging complex event sequences that span multiple nodes.

3.8 Time Management

WarpIV provides three time management algorithms to support sequential, conservative, and optimistic event processing [36]. **LightSpeed** executes on a single processor and eliminates all parallel processing overheads. **RamSpeed** provides a highly optimized lookahead-based conservative time management windowing algorithm with minimal overheads. Event management is dramatically simplified by organizing all events in a single event queue that is managed by the scheduler on each node. Events are attached to logical processes just before they are processed. RamSpeed removes virtually all rollback overheads during execution. **WarpSpeed** supports parallel optimistic event processing using several new flow control techniques to promote run-time stability. These are discussed below.

WarpSpeed offers several new time management techniques that reduce overheads while providing better flow control over event processing. While SPEEDES made great strides to promote stability through its BTW algorithm, WarpIV goes further and provides additional features to ensure stability.

The *first* flow control feature in WarpSpeed is to use event processing times instead of simply counting events to determine when to throttle messages, when to stop processing events optimistically, and when to update GVT. Event processing time is a better metric to use than event counters because it applies a more legitimate weighting scheme. An event that takes ten times longer to process than another event in SPEEDES has the same counting weight, while WarpIV takes the processing time differences into account. The end result is better process coordination between the nodes.

The *second* flow control feature in WarpSpeed uses a *Risk Lookahead* value specified at run time to determine which individual messages to release after an event is processed. In the BTB algorithm, SPEEDES either releases all generated messages from an event, or it holds back all of the messages for later sending. WarpSpeed only releases those messages with time tags less than the Risk Lookahead value. The benefit gained by the WarpSpeed approach is that events scheduled far into the future, and have no critical requirement to be processed right away, are held back until the event is committed, while events scheduled more tightly in time are released right away. Antimessages are not required for messages that have not yet been released, so this approach offers the opportunity for significant performance improvement over SPEEDES.

The *third* flow control feature that can be enabled or disabled in WarpSpeed eliminates cascading antimessages altogether. WarpIV includes both the time tag of the originating event and of the new event in each event-message. If cascading antimessages are disabled, WarpSpeed will not release messages from those events whose originating time is less than GVT. This guarantees that antimessages never trigger secondary antimessages. Antimessages are only triggered by straggler messages. The benefit of this approach is to provide rollback and antimessage stability. However, it is important to only enable this feature for applications that are large and exhibit instabilities due to rollbacks. For small simulations, this feature can actually reduce parallelism by not being aggressive enough in message sending.

The *fourth* flow control feature in WarpSpeed is still experimental. This technique dynamically modifies risk and optimistic processing parameter based on performance metrics. Traditional dynamic performance optimization algorithms try to balance the competing goals of maximizing committed event processing while minimizing rollback overheads. WarpSpeed takes a different approach by focusing on flow control and stability. WarpSpeed collects samples of antimessages and rollbacks during GVT updates. If the number of antimessages grows in a non-linear fashion, then this indicates that message-sending risk is too high so the parameters are adjusted to reduce the risk. The same consideration is made for rollbacks. If the number of rollbacks over time grows in a non-linear manner, then this means that the optimistic event processing parameters are too aggressive. If either numbers are stable, then the dynamic parameter settings are slightly loosened to be more aggressive. The goal is to provide the most aggressive parameter settings while keeping antimessage and rollback growth linear over time. Parameter settings must also account for non-steady state behavior, which leads to the use of non-trivial control-system feedback techniques. This work is currently ongoing and is an interesting topic for future research and development.

3.9 Modeling Framework

WarpIV offers a rich modeling framework that supports all of the SPEEDES capabilities and more. **Figure 3** depicts the various classes in the modeling framework.

The simulation object class, provided by the modeling framework, inherits from the logical process class that is defined in the event management services layer. Users inherit from the simulation object class to provide their specific models. A simulation object manager class for each user-defined simulation object type is automatically generated by a macro. An instance of each type of simulation object manager is created on each node. The master logical process manager manages each simulation object manager in an array that is indexed by object type.

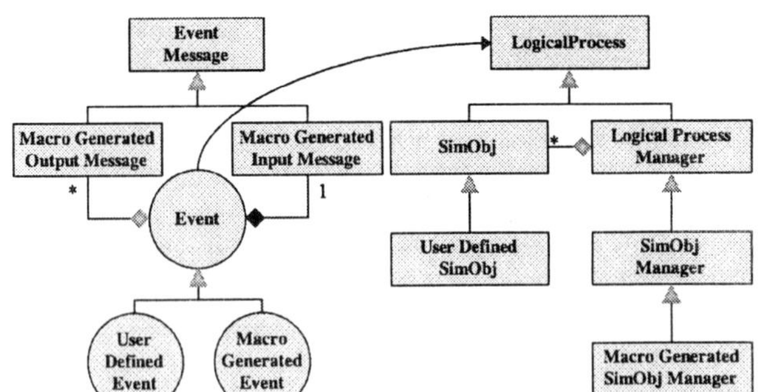

Figure 3: Modeling framework classes.

The simulation object manager provides the capability of creating and deleting simulation objects. It also provides lookup services to obtain object handles given the enumerated Id of a particular type of simulation object. During initialization, two decomposition strategies are provided. *Block* decomposition allocates consecutive blocks of simulation objects to nodes. For example, six objects identified by integer instance Ids are block decomposed to three nodes as (0,1), (2,3), and (4,5). *Scatter* decomposition "card deals" simulation objects to nodes. For example, six objects are scatter decomposed to three nodes as (0,3), (1,4), and (2,5). Lookup algorithms are provided to obtain object handles given an enumerated object Id.

After initialization, simulation objects can be dynamically created or deleted in logical time on local or remote nodes. This is implemented through a creation and deletion events that operate on the simulation object managers. An object handle is returned to the invoker of the create simulation object service.

Two types of interfaces are provided to dynamically create simulation objects. The first interface allows applications to define their own constructors with specified arguments. WarpIV automatically constructs simulation objects by invoking their constructor with arguments. The second interface allows applications to define simulation objects with their own initialization methods that are invoked after the default (no-argument) constructor is called. Type-checked arguments are passed into the specified initialization method.

Events always have one input message and zero or more outgoing messages that are generated as new events are scheduled. Event messages provide a header that is followed by the actual parameters of the event. Applications never manipulate event messages because all events are defined as method invocations. The low-level message-passing interface is never exposed to applications. Scheduling and processing events is similar to CORBA-style remote method invocation where interfaces are defined and then implemented as methods. Macros are used to define event interfaces and to map those methods that implement the interface to the event. For generality, actual method names are not required to match the event interface name. Four basic types of event services are supported.

Autonomous events are implemented as event objects that act on passive simulation objects. Applications define autonomous events by inheriting from the event base class. Applications provide a method on the derived autonomous event with the same signature as the event interface. WarpIV automatically creates autonomous event objects as messages are received and queues the events in logical time for processing. WarpIV provides each Autonomous event with a pointer to the target simulation object. This allows applications to operate on simulation objects from the outside by invoking their methods from the Autonomous event. This agent-like behavior can be used to preserve the integrity of a model, while supporting additional modeling capabilities without violating object-oriented encapsulation principles.

SimObj events are implemented as methods provided by user-defined simulation objects. Unlike Autonomous events, SimObj events directly invoke specified methods on the Simulation Object. Simulation objects are permitted to schedule events for other simulation objects using either the Autonomous event or SimObj event mechanisms. The event recipient is designated during scheduling by its object handle.

Local events allow simulation objects and their contained classes to conveniently schedule events using an object pointer to reference the event recipient. Local events are always scheduled for the same logical process. Simulation objects are never permitted to schedule local events for other simulation objects because this would violate encapsulation principles. A simulation object should never have access to the pointer of an object contained by another simulation object. Local events provide a natural mechanism for scheduling events between objects within a simulation object.

Polymorphic events allow simulation objects and their components to dynamically register and unregister handlers to specified events. This interoperability strategy decouples software components and provides the foundation for supporting mixed resolution models. Polymorphic events trigger zero or more handlers when they are processed.

Any event can become a *process* through the use of a few simple macros. A process is nothing more than an event that passes time (maybe several times) before exiting. Sometimes, processes are called persistent events because they persist over a range of simulation time. Processes support several ways of passing time.

Processes can wait a specified amount of time using the WAIT command. Processes can wait for various types of *semaphore* variables to be set or change state using the WAIT_FOR command. A timeout can be provided to wake the process up after a specified amount of time has elapsed, even if the semaphore has not been set. The following semaphore types are supported:

Logical semaphores can take on values of 0 or 1. Processes waiting on a logical semaphore wake up when the semaphore is set to 1. **Integer semaphores** allow processes to wake up when the integer value is non-zero. **Double semaphores** allow processes to wake up when the double-precision value is non-zero. **Counter semaphores** allow processes to wake up when the counter value is non-zero. This is useful when a model needs to wait for work to arrive before processing.

Processes can also wait for *interrupts* to occur. A timeout may be specified to allow the process to wake up even if no interrupts have been set. Interrupts are enumerated and are stored in a 32-bit integer bitfield. Interrupts can be masked to selectively determine which interrupts are of interest to the process.

The *resource* data type works with the process model to allow processes to wait until a specified amount of a quantity becomes available. Processes are prioritized according to the selected queuing discipline. Examples are First In First Out (FIFO), Last In First Out (LIFO), by amount requested (high or low can be selected), and general priority assignments. The following resource types are supported:

Integer resources are used to represent numbers of resources. An example might be workers serving customers. **Double resources** are used to represent an amount of a continuous resource. An example might be fuel in an aircraft.

The modeling framework provides a *sensitivity list* mechanism that automatically invokes registered methods when specified attributes are modified. This capability can be extended to processes to allow them to wake up from process-model WAIT statements when arbitrary complex expressions involving attributes are satisfied. Because the invoked functions themselves are allowed to modify other variables in sensitivity lists, a powerful capability is provided to support cognitive algorithms, neural networks, and rule-based logic in expert systems. These services are critical for developing reusable Human Behavior Representation (HBR) components.

Simulation objects may be internally decomposed into components that can be decomposed into further subcomponents, etc. This provides a rich hierarchically managed recursive infrastructure for decomposing model functionality. Polymorphic methods with component-based scope resolution provide a powerful mechanism to decouple interactions between components while promoting their interoperability and reuse.

Like callback systems, a component can invoke a polymorphic function that in turn activates polymorphic methods registered by other components. This is similar to general-purpose GUI callback systems that allow applications to register handlers when buttons are mouse-clicked, etc., except that the polymorphic method system is object-oriented.

The polymorphic method approach does not require inheritance and virtual functions to achieve polymorphism. Instead, a special macro defines the polymorphic interface. This macro generates a new polymorphic function with the specified interface that can be invoked to activate corresponding polymorphic methods that have been registered. Note that the invoker of the polymorphic function only references the interface and has no knowledge of how the interface is implemented, or which classes are used to implement the interface. Through another macro, any object (no inheritance is required and the object can be named anything) may register one or more of its methods (the method can also have any name) to implement the polymorphic interface. This double abstraction barrier facilitates the development of interoperable components that can be reused in different applications because there are no hard-coded object dependencies.

3.10 Distributed Simulation Management Services

The Distributed Simulation Management Services (DSMS) layer was implemented in CCSE and mirrors HLA functionality with automated easy-to-use interfaces [37]. The DSMS layer will be rehosted and further optimized in WarpIV by the end of summer, 2005.

The CCSE DSMS layer provides a standard set of interfaces for supporting Federation Objects (FOs), Interactions, Interest Management, and Ownership Management. The DSMS layer provides an efficient and scalable interest management for FOs and Interactions based on abstract multiresolution hierarchical grids.

Without efficient interest management, performance breaks down quickly when the numbers of entities gets large. All of the interest management filter overlap processing is distributed to avoid computational bottlenecks. Efficient destination-based multicast techniques distribute the filtered data through shared memory and networks to reduce message-passing overheads in large systems.

3.11 HLA Gateway

The HLA Gateway was implemented in CCSE to provide connectivity to existing HLA Federations using any HLA-compliant RTI. The gateway will be rehosted in WarpIV by the end of summer, 2005. It coordinates the flow of data (i.e., Federation Objects and Interactions) through the RTI while also coordinating the advancement of logical and/or real time.

The CCSE gateway was implemented as an entity that publishes and subscribes to Federation Objects and Interactions with both the RTI and the DSMS layer. For example, an Interaction received by the gateway from the RTI is passed to entities within the Federate by scheduling the Interaction in the DSMS layer. Similarly, the gateway forwards Interactions through the RTI as it receives them from the DSMS layer.

3.12 HPC-RTI

A logical-time HPC-RTI prototype [38] was developed for CCSE. This effort was based on the version 1.3 standard [39], and proved all of the critical algorithms for integrating conservative simulations with an RTI based on optimistic internal scheduling techniques. These time-managed techniques will be reimplemented in WarpIV by the end of summer, 2005.

WarpIV currently features a highly optimized real-time HPC-RTI prototype that was developed to showcase high-speed communications performance on clusters of shared memory multiprocessor machines.

4 Performance

WarpIV was designed to improve modularity, functionality, robustness, and performance over SPEEDES. This section highlights network performance, shared memory performance, and overall event-processing performance.

4.1 Network Communications

Network performance measurements were collected for several configurations involving machines at RAM Laboratories and at the University of California, San Diego. At RAM Laboratories, up to 75,000 *short* one-byte messages per second were exchanged between two personal computers connected through standard gigabit Ethernet. Sustained bandwidth for *large* one-megabyte messages was measured to be about 15 megabytes per second. Similar experiments using the UCSD Beowulf cluster demonstrated more than 50% improvement over the results obtained at RAM Laboratories.

4.2 High Speed Communications

High-speed communications performance benchmarks have been collected and are shown in **Figure 4**.

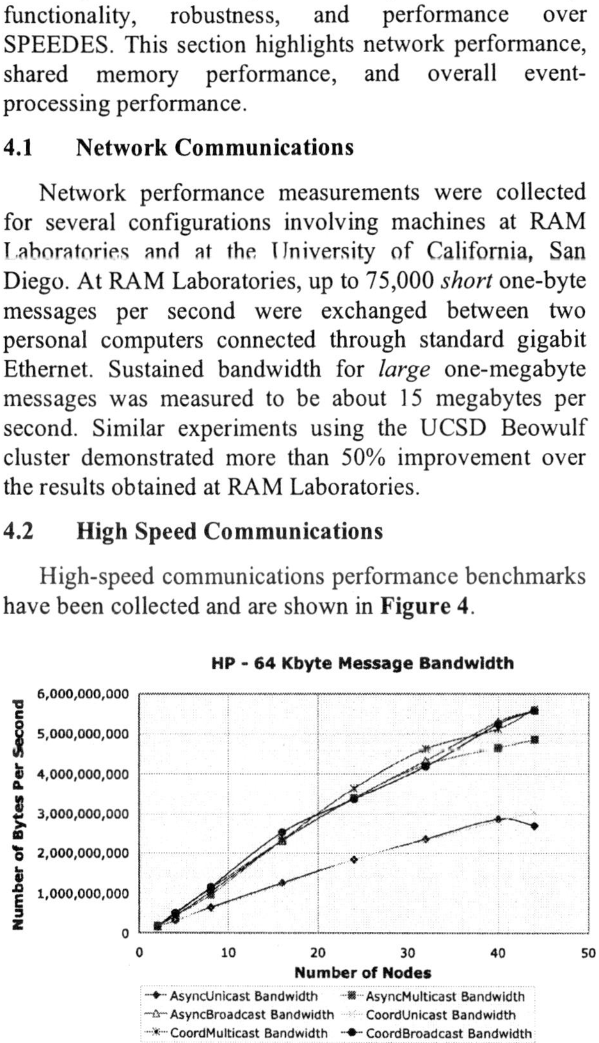

Figure 4: Message bandwidth performance.

These measurements were obtained on a legacy 48-processor HP Superdome at the SPAWAR Systems Center in San Diego. All of the shared memory benchmarks to date show nearly perfect scalability as a function of the number of nodes. This level of scalable performance is impossible to achieve on networked systems (e.g., Ethernet) using standard Internet protocols. Furthermore, all messages are transported reliably though shared memory, which is critical for high-performance parallel applications executing in logical time

4.3 Parallel Event Processing

A simple benchmark was constructed to demonstrate parallel event processing performance. **Figure 5** demonstrates performance for 1,000 simulation objects with 10 events per object executing on an HP Superdome computer with up to 44 processors. Each event randomly generated a new event with a random future time for another simulation object as it was processed. Even with low event granularities, the test application was able to achieve a significant level of parallelism.

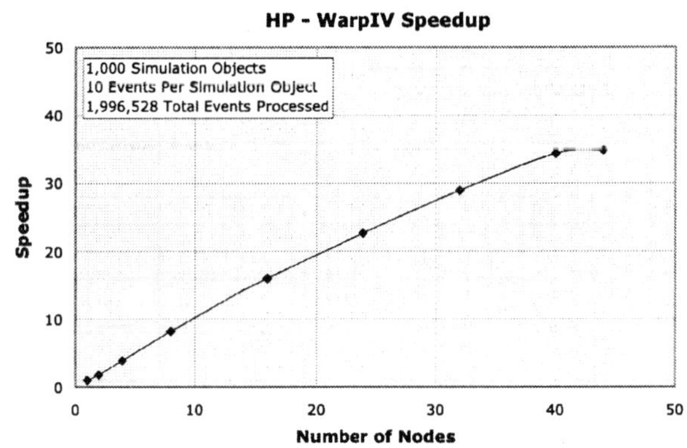

Figure 5: WarpIV parallel event-processing performance.

While it would be interesting to study the performance of other WarpIV services (e.g., rollback overheads, event management, time management flow control techniques, container classes, persistence, GVT updates, Data Distribution Management, HPC-RTI, and HLA Interoperability), this paper focuses on presenting the core performance drivers such as communications and overall performance of a simple test model. Future work will report on the performance of other WarpIV services.

5 Summary and Conclusions

This paper provided a high-level overview of the WarpIV Simulation Kernel. WarpIV was designed to provide next-generation capabilities based on 15 years of lessons learned using the SPEEDES framework. Through its backward compatibility layer, WarpIV supports SPEEDES-based applications while providing new capabilities for future programs.

RAM Laboratories will open the source code for WarpIV in the near future, with the goal of forming a basis for the Standard Simulation Architecture. This will help grow a larger user-base and research community. One of the benefits of this will be to help jump-start research and development programs.

6 References

1. Jefferson David, 1985. "Virtual Time." ACM Transactions on Programming Languages and Systems, Vol. 7, No. 3, pages 404-425.
2. Wieland Fred et al. 1989. "The Performance of a Distributed Combat Simulation With the Time Warp Operating System." *Concurrency: Practice and Experience*. Vol. 1, No. 1, Pages 35-50.
3. Steinman Jeff, 1991. "SPEEDES: Synchronous Parallel Environment for Emulation and Discrete Event Simulation." In proceedings of *Advances in Parallel and Distributed Simulation*. Pages 95-103.
4. Steinman Jeff, 1992. "SPEEDES: A Multiple-Synchronization Environment for Parallel Discrete-Event Simulation." International Journal in Computer Simulation. Vol. 2, Pages 251-286.
5. Steinman Jeff, 1994. "Discrete-Event Simulation and the Event Horizon." In proceedings of the *1994 Parallel And Distributed Simulation Conference*. Pages 39-49.
6. Steinman Jeff, 1993. "Breathing Time Warp." In proceedings of the *7th Workshop on Parallel and Distributed Simulation (PADS93)*. Vol. 23, No. 1, Pages 109-118.
7. Steinman Jeff, 1993. "Incremental State Saving in SPEEDES Using C++." In proceedings of the *1993 Winter Simulation Conference*. Pages 687-696
8. Steinman Jeff, 1996, "Scalable Synchronization of Distributed Military Simulations." In proceedings of the *1996 Object Oriented Simulation Conference*. Pages 247-252.
9. Steinman Jeff and Wieland Fred, 1994. "Parallel Proximity Detection and the Distribution List Algorithm." In proceedings of the *1994 Parallel And Distributed Simulation Conference*. Pages 3-11.
10. Steinman Jeff, 1996. "Discrete-Event Simulation and the Event Horizon Part 2: Event List Management." In proceedings of the *1996 Parallel And Distributed Simulation Conference*. Pages 170-178.
11. Steinman Jeff, 1991. "Interactive SPEEDES." In proceedings of the *24th Annual Simulation Symposium*. Pages 149-158.
12. Van Iwaarden Ron, Steinman Jeff, Blank Gary, 1999. "A Combined Shared memory – TCP/IP Implementation of the SPEEDES Communications Library", In proceedings of the *1999 Fall Simulation Interoperability Workshop*, Paper 99F-SIW-095.
13. Steinman Jeff, Nicol David, Wilson Linda, and Lee Craig, 1995. "Global Virtual Time and Distributed Synchronization." In proceedings of the *1995 Parallel And Distributed Simulation Conference*. Pages 139-148.
14. "SPEEDES User's Guide." April 20, 2003, No S024, Rev. 4, Metron Inc.
15. Steinman Jeff, 1998. "Time Managed Object Proxies in SPEEDES." In the proceedings of the *Object-Oriented Simulation Conference* (OOS'98), pages 59-65.
16. Steinman Jeff, Tran Tuan, Burckhardt Jacob, Brutocao Jim, 1999. "Logically Correct Data Distribution Management in SPEEDES", In proceedings of the *1999 Fall Simulation Interoperability Workshop*, Paper 99F-SIW-067.
17. Joint Simulation System (JSIMS) System Subsystem Design Document.
18. Kuhl Frederick, Weatherly Richard, and Dahmann Judith, 2000. "Creating Computer Simulation Systems, An Introduction to the High Level Architecture." Prentice Hall PTR, Upper Saddle River, NJ 07458.
19. Joint Simulation System (JSIMS) Common Component Simulation Engine (CCSE) Software Design Document (SDD).
20. Joint Simulation System (JSIMS) Common Component Simulation Engine (CCSE) Software User Manual (SUM).
21. Bailey Chris, McGraw Robert, Steinman Jeff, and Wong Jennifer, 2001. "SPEEDES: A Brief Overview" In proceedings of *SPIE, Enabling Technologies for Simulation Science V*, Pages 190-201.
22. Clark Joe, Capella Sebastian, Bailey Chris, Steinman Jeff and Peterson Larry, 2002. "The Development of an HLA Compliant High Performance Computing Run-time Infrastructure" In proceedings of the *2002 Spring Simulation Interoperability Workshop, Paper 02S-SIW-016*.
23. Steinman Jeff and Hardy Doug, 2004. "Evolution of the Standard Simulation Architecture." In proceedings of the Command and Control Research Technology Symposium, paper 067.
24. "Mersenne Twister: A 623-Dimensionally Equidistributed Uniform Pseudo-Random Number Generator". ACM Transactions on Modeling and Computer Simulation, vol. 8, no. 1, 1998, pp. 3-30.
25. Lammers Craig, Mayo Kristy, Steinman Jeff, 2004. "The SPEEDES CASS Motion Library." In proceedings of the 2004 International Symposium on Collaborative Technologies and Systems, vol. 36, no. 1, pages 277-283.
26. Steinman Jeff 2003, "Statistical Algebra Package - Programming Guide: Version 1.0." Copyright © 2003, RAM Laboratories, Inc. 10525 Vista Sorrento Parkway, Suite 220, San Diego, CA 92121.
27. Lammers Craig, Steinman Jeff, 2004, "JSIMS CCSE Performance Analysis." In proceedings of the Fall 2004 Simulation Interoperability Workshop, paper 04F-SIW-34.
28. Steinman Jeff, 2004, "Hierarchical Grids Design Document." RAM Laboratories, Inc.
29. Steinman Jeff, 2004, "High Speed Communications Design Document." RAM Laboratories, Inc.
30. Steinman Jeff 2003, "High Speed Communications Package - Programming Guide: Version 1.2." Copyright © 2003, RAM Laboratories, Inc. 10525 Vista Sorrento Parkway, Suite 220, San Diego, CA 92121.
31. Henning Michi, and Vinoski Steve, 1999, "Advanced CORBA Programming with C++." Addison-Wesley Professional Computing Series.
32. Tuecke S., et. al., 2003. "Open Grid Services Infrastructure, Version 1.0." June 27, 2003.
33. Steinman Jeff, 2003. "The SPEEDES Persistence Framework and the Standard Simulation Architecture." In proceedings of the Parallel and Distributed Simulation (PADS03) conference.
34. Plauger P.J., Stepanov Alexander, Lee Meng, Musser David, 2001. "The C++ Standard Template Library." Prentice Hall PTR, Prentice-Hall Inc., Upper Saddle River, NJ 07458.
35. Chandy, K., and Misra, J., 1979. "Distributed Simulation: A Case Study in Design and Verification of Distributed Programs." IEEE Transactions on Software Engineering. Vol. SE-5, No. 5, pages 440–452.
36. Fujimoto Richard, 2000. "Parallel and Distributed Simulation Systems." John Wiley & Sons, Inc., 605 Third Avenue, New York, NY 10158-0012.
37. Steinman Jeff, 2004. "The Distributed Simulation Management Services Layer in SPEEDES." In proceedings of the Spring 2004 Simulation Interoperability Workshop, paper 04S-SIW-98.
38. U.S. Department of Defense, "High Level Architecture Interface Specification, Version 1.3"
39. Steinman Jeff, 2005, "WarpIV Kernel: Real Time HPC-RTI Prototype." In proceedings of the Spring Simulation Interoperability Workshop, 05S-SIW-071.
40. Wilson Linda and Nicol David, 1995. "Automated Load Balancing in SPEEDES." In proceedings of the *1995 Winter Simulation Conference*, Pages 590-596.

Transparent State Management for Optimistic Synchronization in the High Level Architecture

Andrea Santoro and Francesco Quaglia
Dipartimento di Informatica e Sistemistica
Università di Roma "La Sapienza"
via Salaria 113, 00198 Roma, Italy

Abstract

In this paper we present the design and implementation of a software architecture, namely MAgic State Manager (MASM), to be employed within a Run-Time Infrastructure (RTI) in support of HLA federations. MASM allows performing checkpointing/recovery of the state of a federate in a way completely transparent to the federate itself, thus providing the possibility of demanding to the RTI any task related to state management in optimistic synchronization. Differently from existing proposals, through our approach the federate programmer is neither required to supply modules for state management within the federate code, nor to explicitly interface the federate code with existing, third party checkpointing/recovery libraries. Hence, the federate programmer is completely relieved from the burden of facing state management issues. Some experimental results demonstrating minimal run-time overhead introduced by MASM are also reported for two case studies, namely an interconnection network simulation and a personal communication system simulation.

1 Introduction

The High Level Architecture (HLA) is a standard for the integration of autonomous simulators into a single, distributed simulation system [13]. The autonomous simulators are usually known as *federates*, while the resulting distributed simulation system is known as *federation*. Each federate interacts with the rest of the federation employing a middleware called Run-Time Infrastructure (RTI), which provides a general set of services [14].

A key service of RTI is the Time Management, which is required to synchronize the federates. Although Time Management offers an interface to accommodate both conservative and optimistic synchronization, most work in the HLA context is oriented towards conservative simulation. A reason is that, according to the HLA specification, the RTI interface does not offer to the federate any access to functionalities to log and/or recover its state. Hence, optimistic synchronization requires checkpointing and state recovery mechanisms built in the federate code.

Recent works attempted to tackle issues related to optimistic synchronization in HLA federations via the introduction of so called rollback managers (or controllers) [28, 30]. The objective is to move the handling of most part of rollback procedures (e.g. the retraction, or cancellation, of events) to the middleware in support of the federation. However, these solutions still make use of *GetState* and *SetState* callbacks to the federate code in order to let the federate collect a snapshot of its state and pass it to the middleware or reload its state to a value passed by the middleware via the callback. In other words, the federate software is still required to implement modules for handling state related actions in support of optimistic synchronization. Moreover, such callbacks are not prescribed by HLA standards.

In this work we propose a software architecture to be embedded within the RTI, which allows supporting checkpointing and recovery actions of the state of the federate without the need for having modules for state management within the federate software. Additionally, activation of checkpointing and recovery actions is done in a way completely transparent to the federate. Specifically, such an activation does not pass through any explicit interfacing between the federate and RTI, thus not even requiring the federate to offer state management callbacks to RTI. The interface of RTI is therefore maintained compliant to the HLA standard.

As we shall detailedly describe, the software architecture, which we refer to as MAgic State Manager (MASM), has been developed for LINUX systems and is composed of a set of user level and kernel level modules. These modules allow:

(i) Identification of the portion of the memory image of the federate (i.e. the federate state) at any time, within the memory image of the whole application, namely federate plus RTI.

(ii) Checkpointing/recovery of the portion of the memory

1087-4097/05 $20.00 © 2005 IEEE

image related to the federate at a given simulation time.

Actually, the capabilities of MASM rely on low level management of the application address space, which allows MASM to treat the federate state independently of the semantic of the specific simulation model. Additionally, low level management of the page table within the operating system, also performed by MASM, allows supporting checkpointing of the federate state efficiently by performing snapshots based on the incremental copy of the modified (dirty) pages only.

As hinted above, the target of MASM is to allow the implementation of optimistic synchronization without the need for having state management modules within the federate code. Therefore, the objective is to achieve transparency for state management at the level of the federate programmer. A direct consequence is that MASM can be used for designing an RTI capable to support optimistic synchronization even in case of federates only interfacing to the conservative portion of Time Management services (like typically occurs for most COTS simulation packages, whether they be based on parallel or sequential simulation approaches). This could be achieved by having the RTI deliver unsafe events to the federate, even if the federate is originally designed for conservative synchronization (or simple sequential execution). In case of timestamp order violations, rollback actions can be executed by the RTI code transparently to the federate through checkpointing and recovery functionalities offered by MASM and, for instance, the rollback controller approach previously discussed for handling retractions. This approach would allow simplification of simulation software production since federate programmers could rely on timestamp ordered delivery of events independently of the fact that applications will be federated according to the optimistic synchronization scheme.

In other words, beyond transparency, our proposal is in the direction of enlarging the spectrum of possibilities for synchronization within HLA federations independently of the specific nature (conservative or optimistic) of the involved federates. This has the strong advantage of allowing to cope with performance problems related to (i) poor or zero lookahead within the specific federation and (ii) large costs for the preventive computation of event safety in case the simulation system is hosted by an infrastructure with, e.g., non-minimal delivery delay among the different instances of the RTI.

The remainder of this paper is structured as follows. In Section 2 we describe MASM, including implementation details. In Section 3 we discuss relations between MASM and prior works. An experimental evaluation of the proposed architecture is presented in Section 4.

2 MAgic State Manager (MASM)

In this section we present the architecture of MASM. At first we provide a high level description of the main approaches used by MASM to support checkpointing and recovery of the state of a federate. Then we enter details of the implementation for LINUX systems.

2.1 Main Approaches for Checkpointing and State Recovery

In typical implementations (see, e.g., [12]), both the federate and the RTI are parts of a same process within the operating system. However, as we shall discuss later while presenting implementation details, exploiting appropriate techniques (such as assembler and linker options) and ad-hoc management of dynamic memory allocation within RTI, it is possible to identify all the virtual memory regions reserved for either RTI data or federate data. We refer to those regions as **MD** (Middleware Data) and **FD** (Federate Data). Furthermore, those regions can be obtained as aligned to the page within virtual addressing so that each virtual memory page either belongs to **MD** or to **FD**. The only exception is the application stack, since its pages might contain data related to both RTI and the federate due to the fact that RTI software can be activated by the federate via standard function calls and, similarly, software modules within the federate can be activated by RTI via callbacks.

By the previous arguments, we are able to identify the entries of the page table associated with virtual pages within each of the regions **MD** and **FD**. Hence, except for the stack that needs a special treatment we shall present later, the page table can be seen as logically divided into two different data sections referring to mapping of virtual to physical addresses for the two regions **MD** and **FD**. A schematization of this is shown in Figure 1. We note that MASM is designed to be used as a software component for RTI, hence in our schematization the **MD** region is also used to denote virtual memory areas accessed by MASM, e.g., for keeping the values of proper data structures it requires.

Based on this schematization, the MASM architecture allows copying the content of virtual memory pages belonging to **FD** within memory buffers belonging to **MD**, i.e. memory buffers managed by MASM (hence by RTI), to perform checkpointing. At the same time, MASM allows restoring the content of virtual memory pages belonging to **FD** by reloading data previously saved into memory buffers belonging to **MD**.

We have designed MASM in order to let it deal with checkpointing of the federate state efficiently for what concerns both CPU time and memory usage. Specifically, on the top of the LINUX virtual memory system, we have developed software modules allowing MASM to take a complete snapshot of the federate state, i.e. of the content of **FD**, by copying only those virtual pages that have been modified since the last snapshot.

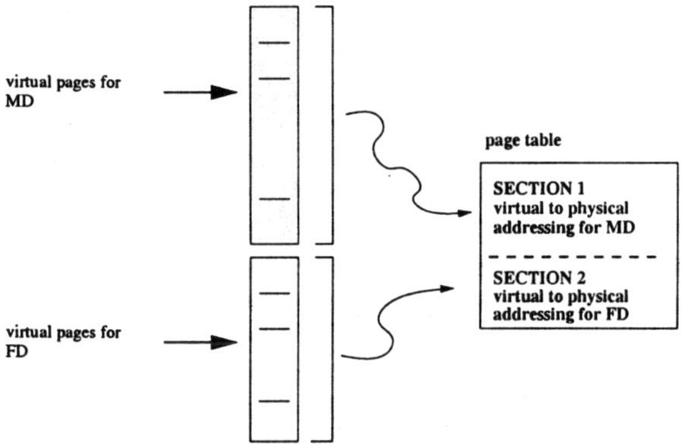

Figure 1. Virtual Memory Addressing and Page Table Sections.

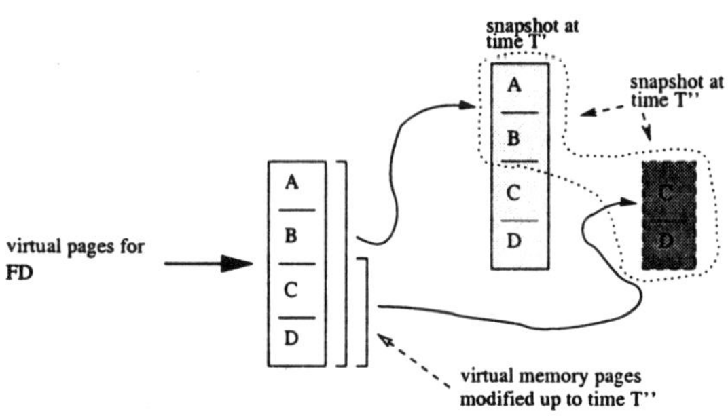

Figure 2. Snapshots of the Federate State at Simulation Time T' and T''.

This is achieved by exploiting standard protection mechanisms within the LINUX virtual memory system together with the previously hinted logical partitioning of the page table into separate sections for **MD** and **FD**. Specifically, we have embedded within MASM software modules that allow marking as write-protected into the page table all the virtual memory pages belonging to **FD**. Also, we have augmented the standard page fault handler for LINUX with the capability to detect a page fault occurring due to MASM memory protection on any page within **FD**. Hence, we are able to identify all those virtual memory pages within **FD** that have been updated (one or more times) since the last mark operation. This allows the identification of all the federate data that have been modified due to the execution of one or more simulation events since the last mark operation. Copying those modified pages within MASM buffers allows taking a checkpoint of the whole federate state by only copying the incrementally modified virtual memory pages within **FD**. This is shown in Figure 2, where the grey pages denote the initial snapshot of the content of **FD** at simulation time T' and the dark grey pages denote a copy of those virtual pages within **FD** that have been modified due to event executions up to time T''. As shown by the dotted line, the union of the dark grey pages C and D, plus the additional grey pages A and B within the snapshot at time T' constitutes the snapshot of the federate state at simulation time T''. Hence, in case of future rollback occurrence, we can reload the federate snapshot at either T' or T'' depending on the simulation time for the causality violation. An important observation we would like to bring to the reader's attention is that, even though the snapshot of the federate state is built incrementally, we do not need to backward apply all the incremental logs to perform state recovery. We simply need to identify for each virtual page to be recovered within **FD** the corresponding page to reload from the log. As we shall show, this can be performed by adequately designing data structures allowing, for each logged virtual page, the identification of the virtual memory interval for which its content is valid. As an example, the logged grey page A is valid (i.e. can be reloaded into the corresponding page within **FD** upon state recovery) in case of rollback to either time T' or T'', hence it is valid within such a whole interval of simulation time. Instead, the logged dark grey page C cannot be reloaded in case of rollback to time less than T'', hence exhibiting a different interval of validity within simulation time.

2.2 Stack Management

In the previous section we have outlined the basic mechanism used to cope with checkpointing and recovery of the memory image of the federate for what concerns all the federate data that are outside the application stack. This section is instead just devoted to the stack management, and to techniques we have adopted to support checkpointing and recovery of this region of the address space of the application.

In an HLA federation the execution always starts within federate software, and RTI software is activated on demand through calls to proper services provided by RTI. As a consequence, the application stack is always organized in a way that the initial portion contains data (including flow control information) related to the state of the federate. Also, in the case of a federate that needs synchronization supports, like, e.g., a time-constrained federate in the HLA terminology, RTI provides grants to the federate in order to let its simulation clock advance. As a consequence, each time we enter RTI software, we know that the initial stack portion related to the federate represents part of the federate snapshot at a given simulation time. An example is shown in Figure 3, where we have three different configurations for the stack at different simulation times T, T' and T''.

By the previous consideration, the same basic scheme used for the **FD** portion of the address space, which has been described in Section 2.1, can be adopted to support checkpointing of the stack portion related to the federate. Specifically, once RTI has control, we can perform the in-

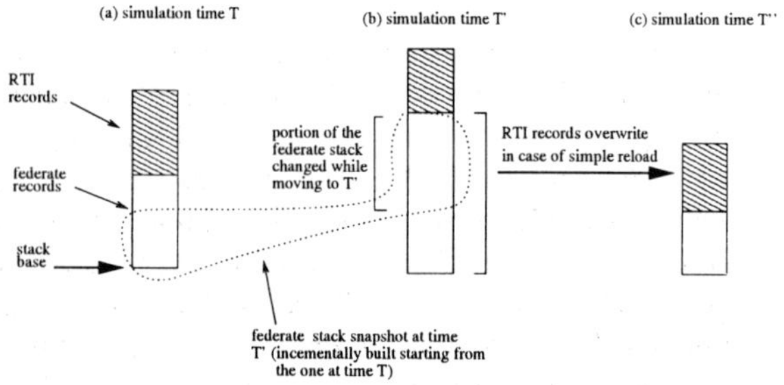

Figure 3. Application Stack at Simulation Time T, T' and T''.

cremental copy of modified virtual pages belonging to the federate stack portion into proper buffers maintained by MASM. This is shown in Figure 3.b where the snapshot of the stack portion related to the federate at time T' can be built incrementally by combining part of the snapshot at time T, and the portion of the stack that has been modified while the federate simulation clock has moved from T to T'.

However, the problem with the application stack is state recovery for the federate since the stack portion related to the federate might have different sizes at different simulation times. As a consequence, simple reload of virtual memory pages related to the federate stack content at an earlier simulation time might compromise the correct execution flow within RTI software. This problem can be more clearly explained through the following example, still referring to Figure 3. Consider the case of federate having simulation clock T'', and suppose RTI has now control, hence the application stack contains at least one record for RTI data. This case corresponds to Figure 3.c. Also, suppose RTI decides that we need to perform rollback of the federate state at simulation time T'. If we perform state recovery by simply copying back the stack snapshot for the federate taken at simulation time T', then we incur the problem of overwriting RTI data within the application stack itself. This is just because the size of the stack referring to the federate at time T' is larger than the one at current simulation time T''.

To address this problem we have decided to design MASM in order to support a switch of the stack when we enter within RTI software. As we shall detailedly describe later, this solution is based on the preventive allocation of a virtual memory region to be used as the stack when entering RTI, and on the use of a proper assembly layer allowing the manipulation of stack pointer registers. With this solution we can avoid overwriting RTI records within the stack even in case the federate portion of the stack is recovered to a larger stack size compared to the current one.

As a final observation, similarly to the case of **FD** described in the previous section, the use of an adequate data structure within MASM, which we shall illustrate in the sequel, allows performing recovery of the federate stack without the need for backward applying all the incremental logs of virtual memory pages. Specifically, the data structure permits, for each logged virtual page belonging to the federate stack, the identification of the virtual memory interval for which its content is valid.

2.3 Implementation Details

In this section we present details related to the implementation of MASM. Actually the implementation has been developed on top of LINUX kernel 2.6.6 with machine dependent portions of the software developed for IA-32 compliant hardware. We recall however that machine dependent modules, required for the manipulation of the page table and CPU registers, represent a minimal portion of the whole MASM architecture. Hence MASM might be adapted to different hardware systems with minimal programming effort. Anyway we are currently investigating on the possibility to increase the level of portability by avoiding machine dependent modules and kernel patches at the expense of limited additional overhead. Also, the implementation is tailored to classical mono-thread and asynchronous multithread RTI process models, supported by many commercial and non-commercial implementations (e.g., [8, 12, 29]) ([1]).

We proceed in this section by first describing solutions dealing with the separation of **FD** and **MD** into two different sections within the page table. Then we provide details related to the stack management. Finally, we overview modules for the management of the page table (including those modules augmenting the LINUX page fault handler) and then provide a description of the main data structures used to maintain logs of virtual memory pages for the federate.

2.3.1 Separation and Identification of FD and MD

MASM must be aware of which virtual addressing memory ranges are part of **FD**. Also, the **FD** region must not share virtual pages with **MD**. To achieve this, our solution relies on:

- The observation that **FD** can simply be viewed as "all the allocated virtual memory not belonging to **MD**". Hence knowing the start and the end points of **MD** automatically allows the determination of the **FD** region.

[1] To our knowledge there is a single RTI commercial implementation employing a pure multi-thread process model [18] according to which the RTI performs callbacks to the federate code while the federate concurrently proceeds with computation in a separate thread. The current implementation of MASM cannot cope with this type of process model since it assumes the federate does not touch its state while checkpointing is in progress, i.e. it assumes that the log of the federate data is taken as an atomic action. We plan to cope with this type of process model in future implementations.

```
#define PAGE_SIZE 4096

.data
.align PAGE_SIZE
.global __data_RTI_start
__data_RTI_start:

.bss
.align PAGE_SIZE
.global __bss_RTI_start
__bss_RTI_start:
```

Figure 4. The START Module to Mark data and BSS Portions for RTI.

- The use of proper techniques to force adequate collocation of **MD**, i.e. page aligned, within virtual addressing.

We base our solution on the so called *incremental linking*. This linking technique allows the building of a single relocatable object starting from all the RTI object files (including MASM files), with the advantage that each of its sections (text, data and BSS) is collocated within a contiguous virtual addressing range. In other words, with incremental linking, we are able to ensure that **MD** is composed of a few virtual memory blocks instead of being non-deterministically scattered throughout the whole virtual addressing range for the application.

To make MASM aware of start and end addresses for those virtual memory blocks and to ensure that those blocks are aligned to the virtual page, we have exploited again incremental linking plus two simple assembler modules we have developed. Specifically, a START module, is used to mark the start of the data and BSS sections. An END module is used to mark the end of those sections. To perform the mark operation, each of the two modules contains a symbol for the data section and a symbol for the BSS section. This is shown in Figure 4 for what concerns the START module, where the symbols `__data_RTI_start` and `__bss_RTI_start` are used. The modules also contain alignment assembler directives, so that the start and end points of **MD**, identified by the corresponding symbols, are aligned to the page.

Incremental linking with START and END modules linked at the head and at the tail, respectively, allows us to collocate those symbols at the head and the tail of their related sections within virtual addressing. Thus MASM does only need to reference those symbols to identify virtual addressing ranges destined for data maintained by RTI, namely those forming the **MD** region. Also, it knows that those regions are automatically aligned to the virtual page.

Now, to determine the virtual page ranges forming the **FD** region, we only need to consider the whole virtual addressing for the application and exclude the regions associated with the previous symbols. This is achieved in our implementation by considering that the whole virtual addressing for the application can be completely identified since the linker automatically inserts symbols to mark the start and end of each section in the memory address space of the executable file (e.g. the `__end` symbol for the end of the whole virtual addressing area).

Actually, the solution proposed above is used by MASM to identify and keep track of the static (i.e. compile-time defined) portion of **FD**. However it is common for applications to dynamically allocate memory, e.g. through the `malloc` library. This is accomplished by extending the area destined to the heap by using the proper system call, i.e. `brk()` on LINUX, and organizing this additional memory space by maintaining a directory of free and allocated memory segments. MASM is confronted with the following two different issues concerning dynamic memory allocation.

The first issue is that, during its computation, the federate might decide to extend the heap area. However, a state recovery might need to recover a snapshot of **FD** whose heap area had a limit different from the current one. We have addressed this problem by considering the value of the heap area limit as part of a snapshot of the federate at a given simulation time. Upon state recovery, we set the limit back to the value it had at the time the snapshot was taken. `sbrk()` and `brk()` were used by MASM to read the limit and set it back (if necessary) ([2]).

The second issue is connected to the fact that both the federate and RTI might require dynamic memory allocation, but the data maintained by the `malloc` library must only be located within **FD** to allow correct state recovery for the federate (i.e. to allow correct undo of dynamic memory allocation performed by the federate). This also means that the RTI cannot use directly the `malloc` services, since any memory allocation by the RTI might be reverted in case of a state recovery for the federate. To allow the RTI to still use dynamic memory, any call to the `malloc` library from the RTI object file is intercepted at linking time and redirected towards a memory allocator internal to MASM. Actually, the memory allocator we currently provide within MASM has a simple implementation, possibly subject to future improvements, based on static memory reserved by MASM at compile time and managed according to the first fit policy for what concerns "free holes" of virtual memory to be assigned to RTI.

It is important to note that the previous issues related to the `malloc` library can be framed by the more general problem related to the handling of third party libraries employed by both the federate and RTI. If we collocate data managed by those libraries within **FD**, then it means those

[2]Critical situations in which the `malloc` library might use the `mmap()` system call to reserve additional memory outside the heap when `brk()` fails have not yet been addressed.

data belong to the recoverable portion of the application. This, however, does not mean we can really recover any action performed by a call to a function within the library since it might have an interaction with the operating system whose actions cannot be assumed to be recoverable. Considering for example the `stdio` library, state recovery on data managed by this library does not mean we are able to recover an I/O operation on the terminal (this is the well known problem of the output commit in rollback recovery [9]). With respect to this point, except for the `malloc` library, we suggest to the RTI developer who decides to use MASM to link all the libraries having an interaction with the operating system to the RTI portion of the code through the incremental technique described above. This allows imposing that data maintained by those libraries are not recoverable.

As a final observation, the approach we have taken of allowing recovery of a third party library by collocating its data within **FD** has straightforward application in case of static linking of libraries. Otherwise, modification of the loader of dynamic libraries is required to properly place data related to a dynamic library within **FD**.

2.3.2 Implementation of Stack Switch

As already pointed out in Section 2.2, the stack cannot be recovered by simply reloading its logged virtual memory pages at a given simulation time. This is because the size of the stack portion to be recovered cannot be assumed to be the same size of the stack portion being replaced, which might cause overwriting of RTI records currently within the stack itself when RTI has control and attempts to perform a state recovery for the federate. As also pointed out, to solve such a problem, anytime we enter an RTI function that can ultimately yield to a checkpoint (or, equivalently, a rollback) we perform a stack switch, moving the RTI stack portion in a different memory area, statically allocated by MASM. Note that, once the stack switch is performed, we can proceed deeper into nested calls within RTI without the need for switching again.

Our implementation of stack switch relies on a proper option in the linker (e.g. the `--wrap` option if the linker is `ld`) which allows the redirection of the RTI function (or functions) into proper wrappers we have developed, which are available within MASM. Actually, we need a different wrapper for each RTI function whose activation needs stack switch. This is because the wrapper itself needs to keep the name of such RTI function, which is defined at compile time (anyway we only need the function prototype to generate the wrapper). We are currently investigating on the possibility to support wrapping of multiple RTI functions with a single parameterized wrapper.

Each wrapper performs the following steps:

1. It saves the stack and frame pointers of the current stack, i.e. the federate stack, into proper locations, namely `federate_stack_pointer` and `federate_base_pointer` managed by MASM. This is achieved through assembly instructions nested within the wrapper. The same occurs for general purpose registers.

2. It copies into the new stack region a small portion at the top of the original stack, containing the parameters passed by the federate to the currently invoked RTI function, and the local variables. Actually, to ensure that parameters are really passed through the stack we can use the `regparm(0)` compiler directive (we note this is actually the default choice for standard `gcc` compilers).

3. It performs the real stack switch operation by loading adequate values onto the stack and frame pointers within the architecture. This is also achieved through assembly instructions nested within the wrapper.

4. It invokes the RTI function originally invoked by the federate through a `call` instruction. The same parameters originally specified by the federate are passed to the function, since they have already been copied (see Point 2) into the new stack area.

5. It puts the original stack back in place together with general purpose registers (as though nothing happened) when the invoked RTI function returns.

Every time a checkpoint of the federate takes place, MASM takes as part of the checkpoint also the stack and frame pointers, and the general purpose registers, saved in Step 1. When a recovery takes place, the stack and frame pointers are copied back in place, together with the virtual memory pages to be recovered within the federate stack. Therefore when the RTI releases control after a recovery, the federate will resume with the same stack content and the same stack/frame pointers it had before the checkpoint.

2.3.3 Tracking Modified Pages

The checkpointing operation itself is directly demanded to the application level of MASM. However, to perform the checkpoint by incrementally logging only the modified pages of the federate portion of the application as depicted in Section 2.1, MASM relies on the following kernel level mechanism.

MASM maintains in its memory space a bitmap representing the mapping of all user-memory pages of the application. This bitmap is initialized to zero and its address is notified to the kernel by a system call `notify_bitmap(void *addr)` we have added to the kernel API. We have also developed an additional system call, namely `mark()`, which allows MASM to mark all the entries in the page table corresponding to pages of **FD** and of the federate stack as write-protected. Actually, to keep the kernel modifications to a minimum, we do not mean for these pages to be Copy-on-Write (CoW) pages, thus we need a mechanism to distinguish them from simple CoW pages. In the IA-32 architecture (as in other architectures) we have unused bits inside the page table entries, which are available for kernel designers. We have reserved one of these bits to distinguish between a real CoW and MASM write protection ([3]). When the federate attempts to write in one of its write-protected pages, it will generate a page fault. Thus, the page fault handler will be run, and by checking both the write-protection, and the bit reserved for MASM within the page table, it will be able to decide whether the fault is a real CoW, or a MASM related fault. In the latter case it will run the MASM fault handler which performs the following two steps:

1. Sets to one the bit corresponding to the faulting page into the bitmap.
2. Sets the page as unprotected, so that no other fault will occur on that page until a subsequent mark operation is executed.

At this point the program resumes as if nothing happened, except that when a federate page is write accessed at least once after a mark operation, the corresponding bit in the bitmap is set to one. By checking the bitmap, MASM detects which pages changed since the last checkpoint and saves only those modified pages so to support checkpointing incrementally. After taking a checkpoint, the bitmap is reset, and a new mark operation is executed so to allow the MASM fault handler to be able to notify future changes of the federate state occurring after the current checkpoint operation.

2.3.4 Data Structures Keeping Track of Checkpoints

As pointed out, MASM performs checkpointing of the whole federate state by incrementally logging only the modified pages. However, upon state recovery, we need to identify all the logged pages that need to be reloaded to reconstruct the federate state at a given simulation time. As hinted in Section 2.1, this is achieved by associating with each logged copy of the x-th page within virtual addressing a simulation time interval for its validity. Specifically,

[3]For generality, we note that in architectures that do not reserve bits for designer usage, one could simply allocate another bitmap into the kernel telling, for each page, whether the protection is used by MASM or by the kernel.

```
struct log_entry{
    double start_time;
    double end_time;
    void * page_address;
    struct log_entry * next;
    struct log_entry * prev;
}
```

Figure 5. Data Structure for the Double Linked List of Logged Versions of each Virtual Page.

MASM maintains for each federate page within virtual addressing a double linked list of entries structured as in Figure 5, where the fields `start_time` and `end_time` identify the simulation time interval for the logged page validity, and the `page_address` field points to the logged page (recall this page is maintained within MASM managed buffers). When we need to perform state recovery at simulation time T, MASM scans the list associated with any page to be recovered and determines the logged version of the page that is valid at time T. Such a page is copied back into its original virtual addressing location (recall this location is uniquely identified by the index of the page we are recovering). Actually, to determine which pages need to be recovered MASM exploits both (i) the logged value of the stack pointer valid at time T, which determines how many pages need to be recovered starting from the stack base, and also (ii) the logged value of the limit of the **FD** area at time T (see the discussion on dynamic memory allocation and virtual addressing boundaries in Section 2.3.1), which determines how many pages need to be recovered for data/BSS and heap portions related to the federate. Those logged values are also maintained by MASM through adequate lists.

3 Related Work

Apart from the already discussed results on the rollback controller approach (i.e. [28, 30]) recently proposed just in the context of HLA, our work is also related to a number of other results in the field of checkpointing in the context of both traditional Parallel Discrete Event Simulation (PDES) and fault tolerance. However, it exhibits significant differences from any of those results as we shall discuss below.

For PDES systems, several checkpointing solutions have been introduced which are based on logging the whole state of a simulation object (at each event execution or after an interval of executed events) [10, 21, 22, 23, 24], or on incremental logging of changes of state variables occurring at each event execution [3, 25, 27, 31], or on a mix of the two approaches [11, 26]. All these solutions require anyway the application programmer (i) to supply the necessary code to collect snapshots of the objects state, or (ii) to employ calls to functions within the API of proper checkpointing libraries, or (iii) to explicitly declare which portions of the address space need to be considered part of the state. In all cases, transparency is not supplied since the programmer must necessarily be faced with issues related to the state snapshot collection. Also, explicit declaration of which portions of the address space need to be part of a snapshot makes some of these solutions unfeasible in case of dynamic memory allocation for the object state. Our solution tackles previous issues by supporting checkpointing without the need for specific log/recovery modules within the application code, or for explicit interfacing with checkpointing libraries, and by allowing checkpoints of an object state even in case it is scattered on dynamically allocated memory chunks. Differently from those approaches, our solution is therefore well suited for usage within a middleware component, e.g. RTI, that aims at managing simulation object states with generic structure in a way completely transparent to the application level programmers.

Another approach to support optimistic synchronization in PDES is the so called reverse computation [6], where state recovery is achieved by performing the inverse of the operations that were performed during forward event computation. However, with this solution, the application programmer is required to provide both the reversible and the reversing code, which again limits transparency compared to our approach. With respect to the latter assertion, even in the case of employment of compiler supports for the automatic production of the reversing code as suggested in [6], the level of transparency achievable is still bound by the one related to classical checkpointing techniques for PDES. This is just because reverse computation still requires to checkpoint the portions of the object state that are modified through non-reversible operations (e.g. plain assignments).

In the context of fault tolerance, several solutions have been proposed to support checkpointing of a process state by exploiting memory protection and operating system facilities to detect dirty pages and incrementally log them [16, 19, 20]. However, differently from our approach, those solutions cannot be employed in the context of a single process logically partitioned into a recoverable portion (i.e. the federate in the HLA context) and a portion that is not subject to rollback operations (i.e. the RTI). The novelty of our proposal resides therefore in the ability to manage separate data/BSS/stack areas for the two different portions, and to recover one of these portions selectively whenever required. Also, although some of those solutions might exhibit higher portability, e.g. by exploiting UNIX standard system calls for protecting memory and detecting write access at the application level through UNIX signals, our approach is expected to provide higher performance effectiveness by executing low level operations related to the ad-hoc memory management scheme directly within the kernel.

4 Evaluation

We base the evaluation of MASM on the observation that this software architecture has not been designed to improve performance compared to optimized checkpointing/recovery mechanisms built in the federate code, or available to the federate programmer through proper libraries. Instead, its target is transparency, which would even allow optimistic synchronization in case of federates equipped with no state management module and interfacing with no state management library. Recall this is the case of both federates programmed to be employed with conservative synchronization and federates resulting from adaptation of sequential (legacy) simulation software (i.e. federates designed with the assumption of delivery of safe events only by the RTI). In this context, advantages from MASM should be assessed when considering that it can avoid the computation of event safety in case of HLA federations including those types of federates. With respect to the latter point, we note that, as also recently discussed in [17], computation of event safety (i.e. of the so called LBTS for a federate) is a distributed reduction to be performed by the RTI, whose latency depends on the timely participation of all other processes in the system and on the timely delivery of messages. Both these dependencies make such a computation a performance dominating factor, especially in the case of federations with poor lookahead and/or deployed on an infrastructure where the speed of different processes can diverge while performing the reduction, and/or there are periods during which the latency of message delivery can get unexpectedly long. For those situations, optimistic synchronization might offer better performance if we are able to provide an underlying checkpointing mechanism with limited overhead. For these considerations, we concentrate in this section on evaluating the checkpointing overhead imposed by MASM. Anyway, this evaluation can also provide indications on the relation between the efficiency of MASM and that of any optimized checkpointing mechanism built in the federate code. Specifically, if the overhead by MASM is limited, then the system performance should not be significantly different by the one achievable with the optimized built-in approach.

We have not yet integrated MASM with an existing RTI (this is actually the objective of future work), therefore the checkpoint overhead evaluation has been carried out by using a stub-RTI simulating the presence of HLA middleware. The stub-RTI simply collects *Time Advance Request* (TAR) invocations by the application level code and delivers TAG callbacks granting an advance at simulation time equal to the one requested by the application via TAR. Once the stub-RTI has taken control through TAR, it can activate MASM checkpointing routines before passing control back to the federate.

We have used two different case studies for what concerns the application level code (i.e. the federate code). In the first one, the application level code simulates an interconnection network with packets transmitted according to wormhole switching and deadlock-free Planar Adaptive Routing (PAR) [7]. In the second case study, the application level code simulates a personal communication system with fixed base stations offering communication services to mobile devices and performing power regulation based on the Signal-to-Interference Ratio (SIR) evaluated considering cross channel interference within a same cell [15].

Both simulators have been integrated with the stub-RTI with few modifications. Specifically, a TAR call to the stub-RTI has been inserted before the execution of any new event. The argument for this call is the next event time in the local event queue of the federate. The next event is then executed after the receipt of the TAG callback originated by the stub-RTI. In other words, anytime the federate wants to advance its simulation time to the timestamp of the next event in its local queue, the stub-RTI takes control so that a checkpoint of the federate state can be taken ([4]).

In our experiments we have decided to let the stub-RTI perform checkpointing of the federate state upon each TAR request, which, according to our software organization, means at each event execution. This choice allows a worst case analysis for the checkpointing overhead, which is significant for the following two main reasons: (i) It is representative of situations guaranteeing the minimal state recovery latency (hence exclusion of the recovery latency by the experimental study does not limit the generality of the observations we can draw on the overhead) and (ii) It is representative of the overhead we need to pay in case of non-determinism of the application level software (where log of the state taken on a sparse basis is unfeasible due to non-reproducibility of state values in a coasting forward).

For what concerns the wormhole switching simulation model, the network has a mesh topology with wrap-around connections, and PAR is supported through two virtual channels for each routing direction. Transmitted packets have an average size of 10 data flits (each of size 1 byte), plus head and tail flits. The inter-arrival time of packets to be transmitted follows an exponential distribution with mean value of 500 units per node while the flit transmission delay has been set to 1 unit. Also, packets are equally likely destined to whichever node in the network. Finally, we have varied the size of the simulation model from 10×10 to 100×100 interconnected nodes. For what concerns the personal communication system simulation model, we have used hexagonal cells, each with 100 channels, and have set the threshold SIR to be achieved by power regulation at about 10 DB, similarly to what happens in standard GSM transmission. The movement of mobile devices follows a classical random walk model [1] with cell switch time exponentially distributed with mean 10 minutes. The average call holding time has been set to 2 minutes and the inter-arrival time of calls per each cell follows an exponential distribution [2, 4, 5] with mean value 2 seconds (this yields to channel utilization factor of about 50% for this specific configuration). Also, we have varied the size of the simulation model from 100 to 10000 cells within the coverage area.

We have measured both the average execution cost of the events (evaluated by considering all the execution time spent within the application level code) and the average execution cost of any checkpointing related action performed by MASM. The latter cost includes the time for incrementally logging dirty pages, the time to manage data structures maintained by MASM and also the time for the page fault caused by the MASM protection mechanism described in Section 2.3.3. These costs have been measured for a Pentium 2.8GHz CPU (512KB cache - 1GB RAM) running LINUX (kernel version 2.6.6) and are reported in Figure 6. Each value, expressed in microseconds, is the average over a number of samples ensuring confidence interval of 10% around the mean at the 95% confidence level. By the obtained results, we get that, for the personal communication system simulation application, the checkpointing overhead per event is low or negligible independently of the simulation model size. On the other hand, it is kept low also for the case of the finer grain wormhole switching simulation application, except for the case of reduced network size. We note however that the relative overhead by MASM would be even lower in case it were evaluated with a real RTI implementation providing supports for a (complete) set of HLA services (instead of a stub-RTI with negligible run-time cost), which additionally contributes to the performance effectiveness of our proposal.

[4] Actually, taking a checkpoint within RTI upon the issue of a TAR request might be a way to allow the RTI to deliver TSO (timestamp ordered) messages to the application even if those messages are still unsafe. Then, in case the RTI discovers a timestamp order violation, the application level can be rolled back at the point of the TAR request, and the TSO messages, including those originating the violation, can be delivered again as though nothing happened as a result of the original TAR request. This is one possible way to support optimistic synchronization in case of federates originally designed for the conservative approach.

References

[1] I. F. Akyildiz, Y. B. Lin, W. R. Lai, and R. J. Chen. A new random walk model for PCS networks. *IEEE Journal on Selected Areas in Communications*, 18(7):1254–1260, 2000.

[2] A. Boukerche, S. K. Das, A. Fabbri, and O. Yildz. Exploiting model independence for parallel PCS network simulation. In *Proceedings of the 13th Workshop on Parallel and Distributed Simulation*, pages 166–173. IEEE Computer Society, May 1999.

[3] D. Bruce. The treatment of state in optimistic systems. In *Proceedings of the 9th Workshop on Parallel and Distributed Simulation*, pages 40–49. IEEE Computer Society, June 1995.

[4] C. D. Carothers, R. M. Fujimoto, P. England, and Y. B. Lin. Distributed simulation of large-scale PCS networks. In *Proceedings of the 2nd IEEE*

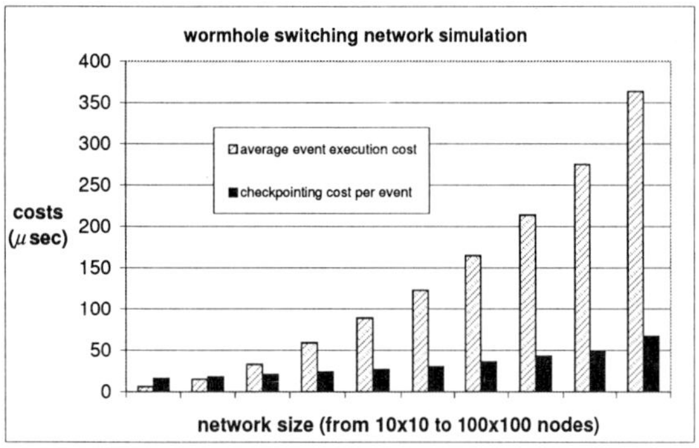

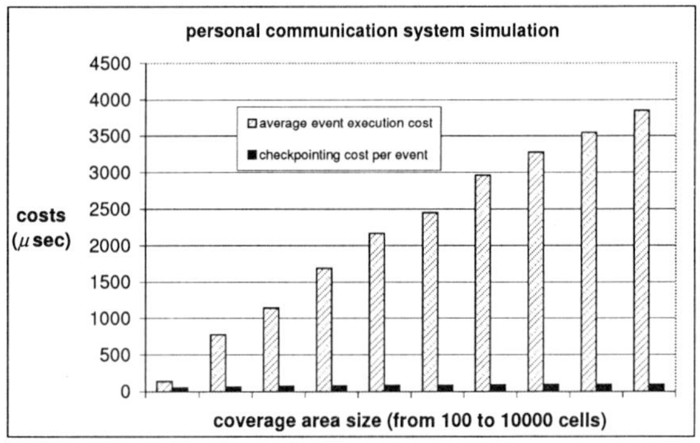

Figure 6. Event and Checkpointing Costs for the Two Case Studies.

International Workshop on Modeling, Analysis, and Simulation of Computer and Telecommunication Systems, pages 2–6. IEEE Computer Society, 1994.

[5] C. D. Carothers, R. M. Fujimoto, and Y. B. Lin. A case study in simulating PCS networks using Time Warp. In *Proceedings of the 9th Workshop on Parallel and Distributed Simulation*, pages 87–94. IEEE Computer Society, June 1995.

[6] C. D. Carothers, K. S. Perumalla, and R. Fujimoto. Efficient optimistic parallel simulations using reverse computation. *ACM Transactions on Modeling and Computer Simulation*, 9(3):224–253, 1999.

[7] A. A. Chien and J. H. Kim. Planar-adaptive routing: Low-cost adaptive networks for multiprocessors. *Journal of the ACM,*, 42(1):91–123, 1995.

[8] DMSO. Runtime Infrastructure (RTI). *https://www.dmso.mil/public/transition/hla/rti*, 2004.

[9] E. N. Elnozahy, L. Alvisi, Y.-M. Wang, and D. B. Johnson. A survey of rollback-recovery protocols in message-passing systems. *ACM Computing Surveys*, 34(3):375–408, 2002.

[10] J. Fleischmann and P. Wilsey. Comparative analysis of periodic state saving techniques in Time Warp simulators. In *Proceedings of the 9th Workshop on Parallel and Distributed Simulation*, pages 50–58. IEEE Computer Society, June 1995.

[11] S. Franks, F. Gomes, B. Unger, and J. Cleary;. State saving for interactive optimistic simulation. In *Proceedings of the 11th Workshop on Parallel and Distributed Simulation*, pages 72–79. IEEE Computer Society, June 1997.

[12] Georgia Tech Research Corporation. FDK - Federated Simulations Development Kit. *http://www.cc.gatech.edu/computing/pads/fdk/*, 2003.

[13] IEEE Std 1516-2000 (2000). IEEE Standard for Modeling and Simulation (M&S) High Level Architecture (HLA) – Framework and Rules. New York, NY, Institute of Electrical and Electronics Engineers, Inc.

[14] IEEE Std 1516.1-2000 (2000). IEEE Standard for Modeling and Simulation (M&S) High Level Architecture (HLA) – Federate Interface (FI) Specification. New York, NY, Institute of Electrical and Electronics Engineers, Inc.

[15] S. Kandukuri and S. Boyd. Optimal power control in interference-limited fading wireless channels with outage-probability specifications. *IEEE Transactions on Wireless Communications*, 1(1):46–55, 2002.

[16] K. Li, J. Naughton, and J. Plank. Low latency concurrent checkpointing for parallel programs. *IEEE Transactions on Parallel and Distributed Systems*, 5(8):474–479, 1994.

[17] T. McLean and R. M. Fujimoto. Predictable time management for real-time distributed simulation. In *Proceedings of the 17th Workshop on Parallel and Distributed Simulation*, pages 89–96. IEEE Computer Society, 2003.

[18] PITCH. pRTI 1516^{TM}. *http://www.pitch.se/prti1516/default.asp*, 2004.

[19] J. Plank, M. Beck, and G. Kingsley. Libckpt: Transparent checkpointing under UNIX. In *Proceedings of USENIX Winter Technical Conference*, pages 213–223. USENIX Association, 1995.

[20] J. Plank, J. Xu, and R. H. Netzer. Compressed differences: an algorithm for fast incremental checkpointing. *Tech. Rep. CS-95-302, University of Tennessee at Knoxville*, 1995.

[21] B. R. Preiss, W. M. Loucks, and D. MacIntyre. Effects of the checkpoint interval on time and space in Time Warp. *ACM Transactions on Modeling and Computer Simulation*, 4(3):223–253, July 1994.

[22] F. Quaglia. A cost model for selecting checkpoint positions in Time Warp parallel simulation. *IEEE Transactions on Parallel and Distributed Systems*, 12(4):346–362, Feb. 2001.

[23] F. Quaglia and A. Santoro. Non-blocking checkpointing for optimistic parallel simulation: Description and an implementation. *IEEE Transactions on Parallel and Distributed Systems*, 14(6):593–610, 2003.

[24] R. Ronngren and R. Ayani. Adaptive checkpointing in Time Warp. In *Proc. of the 8th Workshop on Parallel and Distributed Simulation*, pages 110–117. Society for Computer Simulation, July 1994.

[25] R. Ronngren, M. Liljenstam, R. Ayani, and J. Montagnat. Transparent incremental state saving in Time Warp parallel discrete event simulation. In *Proceedings of the 10th Workshop on Parallel and Distributed Simulation*, pages 70–77. IEEE Computer Society, May 1996.

[26] H. Soliman and A. Elmaghraby. An analytical model for hybrid checkpointing in Time Warp distributed simulation. *IEEE Transactions on Parallel and Distributed Systems*, 9(10):947–951, 1998.

[27] J. Steinman. Incremental state saving in SPEEDES using C plus plus. In *Proceedings of the Winter Simulation Conference*, pages 687–696. Society for Computer Simulation, 1993.

[28] F. Vardanega and C. Maziero. A generic rollback manager for optimistic HLA simulations. In *Proceedings of the 4th Workshop on Distributed Simulation and Real-Time Applications*, pages 79–85. IEEE Computer Society, 2000.

[29] Virtual Technology Corporation. RTI NG Pro^{TM} version 2.0.2. *http://www.virtc.com/Products/prdFulltext.jsp?ID=1z_RTI*, 2004.

[30] X. Wang, S. J. Turner, Y.-H. Low, and B. P. Gan. Optimistic synchronization in HLA based distributed simulation. In *Proceedings of the 18th Workshop on Parallel and Distributed Simulation*, pages 123–130. IEEE Computer Society, May 2004.

[31] D. West and K. Panesar. Automatic incremental state saving. In *Proceedings of the 10th Workshop on Parallel and Distributed Simulation*, pages 78–85. IEEE Computer Society, May 1996.

XTW, a parallel and distributed logic simulator

Qing XU
School of Computer Science
McGill University
Montreal, Quebec H3A 2A7
Email: qxu2@cs.mcgill.ca

Carl Tropper
School of Computer Science
McGill University
Montreal, Quebec H3A 2A7
Email: carl@cs.mcgill.ca

Abstract— **In this paper, a new event scheduling mechanism XEQ and a new rollback procedure rb-messages are proposed for use in optimistic logic simulation. We incorporate both of these techniques in a simulator XTW. XTW groups LPs into clusters, and makes use of a multi-level queue,XEQ, to schedule events in the cluster. XEQ has an O(1) event scheduling time complexity. Our new rollback mechanism replaces the use of anti-messages by an rb-message, and eliminates the need for an output queue at each LP. Experimental comparisons to Time Warp reveal a superior performance on the part of XTW, while experimental results over large circuits (5-million-gate to 25-million-gate) shows XTW scales well with both the size of circuits and the number of processors.**

1 Introduction

In the competitive arena of VLSI design, the size of circuits has increased as Moore's law predicted -the transistor density on integrated circuits doubles every couple of years. One result of this is the steadily increasing computational requirements for circuit simulation and verification. Parallel and distributed simulation has the potential to provide a solution to this problem.

The fundamental problem in distributed simulation is one of synchronizing the processes involved in the simulation. The two major approaches to synchronization are referred to as conservative and optimistic. We focus upon the optimistic algorithms in this paper, of which Time Warp [1] is the most visible. In Time Warp (TW) causality errors are corrected by rolling back the state of the simulation to a previous correct state and eliminating erroneously sent messages and their effects by the sending of anti-messages.

Logic and behavioral simulation is a low granularity and tightly coupled computational task which poses a significant challenge to the development of a distributed simulator. Clustered Time Warp (CTW) [2], [3] was developed with these problems in mind. As the name implies, in CTW LPs (representing gates) are gathered into clusters. Several techniques were developed for use to obtain checkpoints and to roll back the LPs in a cluster. The algorithms described in this paper are intended for use with clusters of gates and are an outgrowth of CTW.

A number of other efforts have been directed at logic simulation including [4] which employs optimistic algorithms and [5], which employs conservative algorithms. [5] contains a good survey of work before 1995.

In this paper, a new optimistic synchronization mechanism, XTW, is proposed to improve the performance of Time Warp. XTW was inspired by several characteristics of discrete event logic simulation. XTW consists of a new event scheduling algorithm, *XEQ*, and a new rollback mechanism, *rb-message*. XEQ has an O(1) cost bounded on the number of simulated entities (not on the number of events). *Rb-message* not only reduces the computing cost of annihilating previously sent messages, but also dramatically reduces the memory cost by eliminating the output queue in each LP.

The remaining sections of the paper are organized as follows. Section2 describes the motivation for XTW. Section 3 contains a detailed description of XEQ and rb-messages along with an analysis of their complexity. Section 4 contains our experimental work, in which XTW is compared to CTW as well as to a sequential version of XTW. The concluding section of the paper follows.

2 Motivation for XTW

Discrete event simulations of circuits, whether at the logic, behavioral or register-transfer level, share certain characteristics, among which are:

1) Events generated by an LP are produced in chronological order(See figure 1).
2) An LP receives events from another LP in chronological order(See figure 1).
3) In a parallel discrete event simulation which uses a communication facility guaranteeing FIFO order, the messages(events) from a specific LP(source) arrive at the destination LP in chronological order.
4) LPs are *sparsely connected.*
5) The LP topology is static during the simulation.

Observations 1, 2 and 3 show that events are naturally sorted with "zero-cost" when they are generated and propagated. These observations are the keys to our approach and inspire us to create a new event scheduling algorithm, XEQ, which utilizes these "zero-cost" sorted events. We make use of XEQ to create the *rb-message* mechanism in order to reduce the rollback cost in TW. Observations 4 and 5 make it feasible to implement XEQ and rb-message in large circuit simulations.

2.1 Utilizing "zero-cost" sorted events

In this section, we will explore how to utilize "zero-cost" sorted events in discrete event circuit simulation. [6] has

1087-4097/05 $20.00 © 2005 IEEE

a good analysis on the same phenomena and proposed an *append-queues* input queue sturcture.

First, we examine a simple situation– a parallel discrete event circuit logic simulation which has two components residing on two simulation nodes. One component is an event-generator and resides on Node1, while another component is a NOT gate residing on Node2. Each component is modeled as an LP and communicates with each other via FIFO order communication facility.(See figure 1). In figure 1, we can see

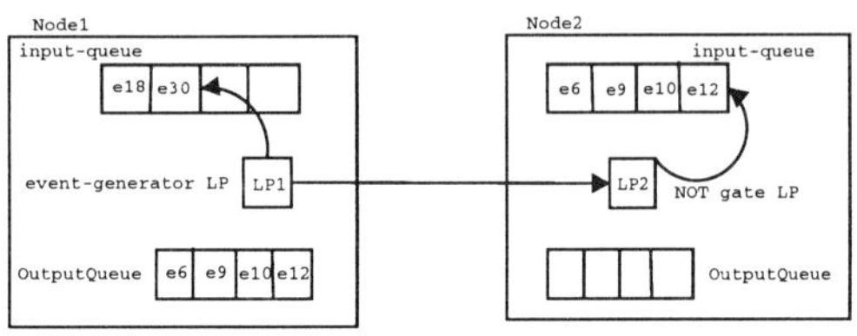

Fig. 1. a single LP, single InCh model in PDES

that the event scheduling cost at Node1 is O(1), consisting of the cost to append the generated events into the input queue and to de-queue the head event from input-queue. At Node2, the event scheduling cost is also O(1), consisting of the cost to append the events coming from Node1 to the input-queue and to de-queue the head event from the input-queue. In this example, observations 1, 2 and 3 are made use of to give an O(1) cost event scheduling algorithm.

When there are a large number of LPs residing in one node and multiple input sources at one LP, the situation is totally different. Events generated by different LPs and coming from different sources have to compete with other to be inserted into the input-queue.(see figure 2) The naturally occurring "zero-cost" sorted events are lost by this competition. In TW, an LP can be rolled back and generate out of order events, further complicating matters. In the next section we describe a data structure, XEQ, which makes it is possible to preserve the "zero-cost" sorted events and has an O(1) event-scheduling cost. A new rollback mechanism, rb-message, is proposed to make it possible to utilize "zero-cost" events to reduce the rollback overhead. We call the Time-Warp simulation system which implements XEQ and rb-messages XTW.

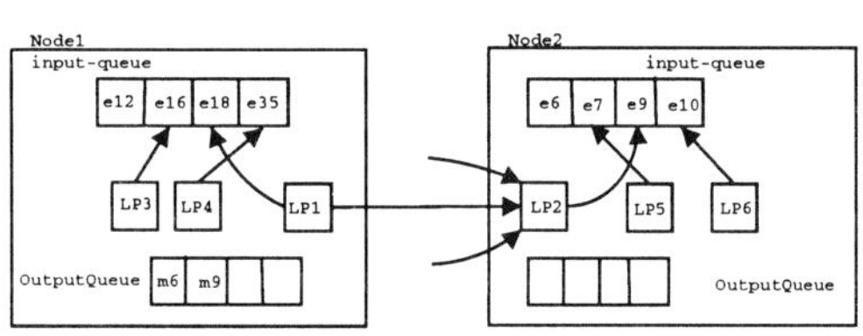

Fig. 2. a multiple LPs, multiple InChs model in PDES

3 XTW

XTW makes use of clusters of LPs. The clusters are intended to represent the grouping of gates according to the functional units to which they belong. Each cluster has a multi-level event queue, *XEQ*, associated with it whose purpose is event scheduling. A cluster level event queue (*CLEQ*) is part of XEQ and stores events which are sent to other clusters. XTW is an outgrowth of CTW [2]. Three techniques for checkpointing and rolling back in CTW are described in [2], each occupying a different point in a memory vs. execution time trade-off. XTW makes use of one of these techniques, *local rollback,local checkpoint*. Local checkpoint means that an LP saves its state only if it receives a message from an LP in another cluster. Local rollback refers to each LP rolling back individually, as opposed to requiring all of the LPs in a cluster to roll back (one of the techniques in CTW).

This section contains a detailed description of XEQ and the rb-message mechanism, along with an analysis of their complexity. We organize the section as follows. Section 3.1 introduces the *Input-Channel* structure. Section 3.2 presents the structure of *XEQ*. Section 3.4 presents the XTW event scheduling mechanism and its cost analysis. Section 3.5 presents the *rb-messages* mechanism.

3.1 Input-Channel

In XTW, a new structure,the *input-channel*(InCh) is added to LPs. Each InCh models an unique input of a circuit component and is subject to *Rule 1* as follows:

Rule 1: Each InCh can only have one unique incoming source.

Figure 3 shows how the *Input-Channel* models the connection edge of gates. In figure 3, G1 has two inputs from G2 and G3. G2 has one input. G3 has one input from itself and another from others. Each input is modeled as an InCh.

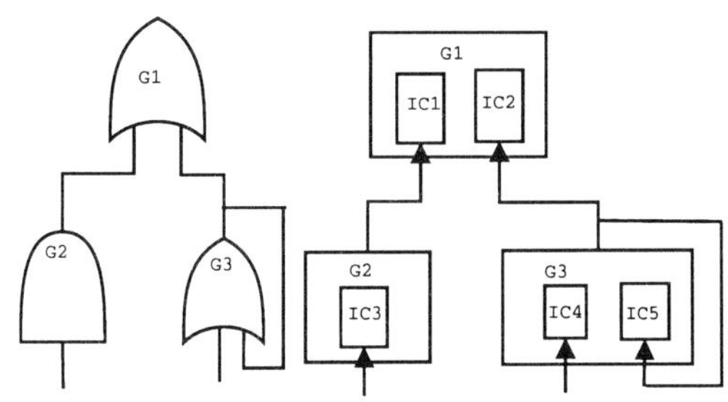

Fig. 3. Input Channel Model

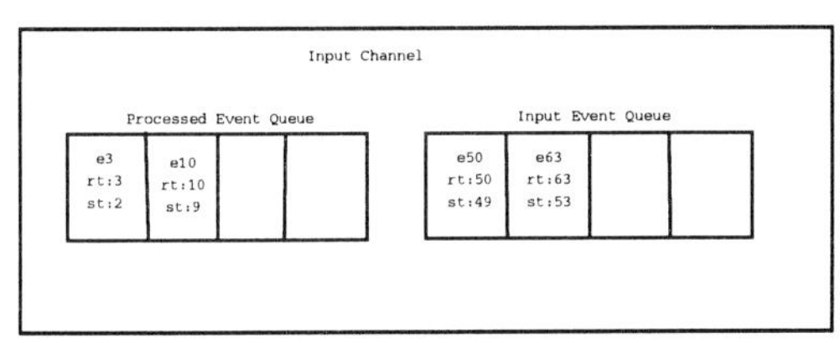

Fig. 4. The Structure of Input Channel

Figure 4 shows the structure of InCh. Each InCh contains one input event queue(ICEQ) and one processed event queue(ICPQ). Newly arrived events are put in the ICEQ. After an event is processed, it is put in the ICPQ. Each event has two timestamps: a)receive-time stamp is the time stamp indicating when the event occurs(conventional definition of time stamp) b)the send-time stamp is the Local Virtual Time(LVT) of the

LP when it scheduled E . LVT is equal to the receive-time of the latest processed event.

As a result of observations 1, 2, and 3 (the *FIFO communication assumption*) and *Rule 1*, all of the events must arrive at each ICEQ in chronological order and be naturally sorted in the ICEQs(see Figure 4).

3.2 The Structure of XEQ

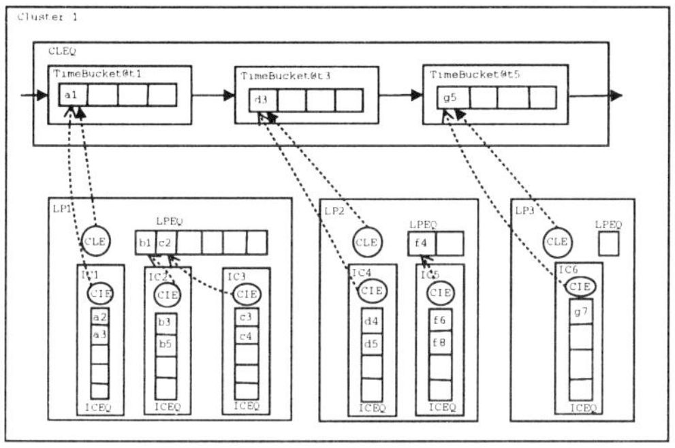

Fig. 5. The Structure of XEQ

Figure 5 shows the structure of XEQ. In XEQ, there are event queues at the Input-Channel level, the LP level and the Cluster level.

- At the *Input-Channel* level, the event queue is called the *ICEQ* and is implemented as a list of events sorted in increasing timestamp order.
- At the LP level, the event queue is called the *LPEQ* and is implemented as a list of events sorted in increasing timestamp order.
- At the cluster level, the event queue is called the *CLEQ* and is implemented as a list of *time-buckets* sorted in increasing timestamp order. A *time-bucket* is a list of events which have the same time-stamp.

In addition, the following two event pointers are added respectively for each *Input-Channel* and each LP.

- CIE: At each *Input-Channel*, a CIE(current-IC-event) pointer points to the event which is de-queued from its ICEQ and is currently stored in the LPEQ or the CLEQ. This pointer is used to remove the (pointed-to) event from the LPEQ or the CLEQ in the event of rollback.
- CLE: At each LP, a CLE(current-LP-event) pointer points to the event which is de-queued from its LPEQ and is currently stored in the CLEQ. This pointer is used to move the (pointed-to) event from the CLEQ back to LPEQ in the event of a rollback at the LP.

3.2.1 Rules for XEQ: The following rules are enforced in XEQ:

- *Rule 2: An InCh can submit only one event to its hosting LP's LPEQ if and only if the ICEQ is not empty. This event has the lowest time-stamp in the ICEQ and is called the* current IC event. *Its pointer value is assigned to CIE.*
- *Rule 3: An LP can submit only one event to its hosting cluster's CLEQ if and only if the LPEQ is not empty. This event has the lowest time-stamp in the LPEQ, It is called the* current LP event *and its pointer value is assigned to CLE.*

3.3 Event Node Structure, Space Cost of XEQ

Figure 6 shows the structure of an event node and how an event node moves around among the different levels of the event queue.

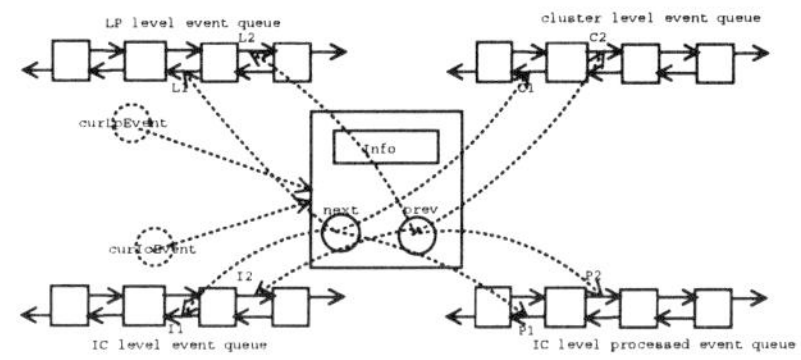

Fig. 6. an event node structure and its movement

Moving an event node from one event queue to another event queue is accomplished by changing the values of the next and the prev pointer of the event node. No copying is necessary and as a consequence, extra memory is not required at each of the event queues. An example is depicted in figure 6. When e1 is moved from the ICEQ to the LPEQ, the only operation necessary is changing the next and prev pointer of e1 from I1,I2 to L1, L2. Similarly, moving e1 to the CLEQ or ICPQ just involves changing the next and prev pointer value to C1, C2 or P1, P2.

XEQ can be viewed as a Time Warp *input queue* broken into small pieces. The total space cost of XEQ is approximately the same as that of the Time Warp *input queue* structure.

3.4 XTW O(1) Event Scheduling Mechanism

XEQ is used to implement a smallest timestamp first event scheduling mechanism within clusters which has an O(1) time complexity.

An event is scheduled and processed in XTW via the following steps:

1) After an event is generated, it is propagated to its destination InCh and is appended into the respective ICEQ.
2) According to *Rule 2*, if the ICEQ is not empty, it will submit the smallest receive-time event to its LPEQ. Since the ICEQ is naturally sorted, the smallest timestamp event is just the head event of ICEQ. Thus, we can simply de-queue the head event at a cost of 1.
3) The event from the ICEQ is inserted into the LPEQ. The cost of finding the correct position into which to insert the event is N_e. N_e is the number of events stored in LPEQ. Based on *Rule 2*, in the worst case, the maximum value of N_e is C_{ic}, where C_{ic} is the number of InChs at an LP.
4) According to *Rule 3*, if the LPEQ is not empty, it will submit the head event to its CLEQ. The cost of finding the correct position in the CLEQ is N_{tb}, where N_{tb} is the number of time-buckets in the CLEQ. Based on *Rule 3*, in the worst case, the maximum value of N_{tb} is C_{lp}, where C_{lp} is the constant number of LPs in a cluster.

Putting the above observations together, the cost of scheduling an event in XTW, SC, is:

$$SC = 1 + N_e + N_{tb} \quad (1)$$

In the worst case the cost of scheduling an event is :

$$SC = 1 + C_{ic} + C_{lp} \quad (2)$$

Since both C_{ic} and C_{lp} are constant, the complexity of scheduling an event is O(1). In reality, C_{ic} is far less than C_{lp} in most discrete event circuit models and making use of an O(lgN) data structure in the CLEQ, results in an event scheduling cost of $O(\log C_{lp})$.

Comparing XEQ other event-list data structures we first note that their time complexity is bounded by the number of events in the queue. Standard event list structures and their time complexities include the calendar queue O(1), the splay-tree($O(\log n)$), the red-black tree($O(\log n)$), the skip-list($O(\log n)$) and the heap($O(\log n)$)r. XEQ has more stable performance because it is bounded by the number of LPs, which is static during the simulation. It is not sensitive to the distribution of events as is the calendar queue. Moreover, XEQ can be used in both parallel and sequential discrete event circuit simulation and is easily implemented.

3.5 Rollback with Rb-messages

3.5.1 Motivation for the Rb-messages *Mechanism:* We begin with the 2-LP example shown in figure 1. This time, we assume that a rollback occurs in LP1- event e8 is generated after e12 in LP1 and is sent to LP2. In Time-Warp, anti-messages for e9, e10 and e12 will be sent out one by one to annihilate the events in LP2. However, in this example, LP2, upon the arrival of e8 can annihilate e9, e10 and e12 without the necessity of anti-messages. Consequently, the output-queue can be eliminated from each LP, since no anti-messages are required to annihilate the previous sent messages.

The advantage of above scenario is obvious – we can not only can reduce rollback overhead by eliminating anti-messages, but can also save memory by not saving any output-events. We extend the simple 2-LP scenario to the general case via the use of *rb-messages*, described in the following section.

3.5.2 The Rb-messages *Mechanism :* In XTW, each event has two timestamps: a)receive-time stamp is the time stamp indicating when the event occurs(conventional definition of time stamp) b)the send-time stamp is the Local Virtual Time(LVT) of the LP when it scheduled E. All events in ICEQs and ICPQs are maintained in receive-time chronological order. According to Observations 1, 2 and 3, all events are also in the send-time chronological order. The event which has the smallest receive-time in an event-queue is called as the head event. The event which has the largest receive-time in an event-queue is called as the tail event. We do not distinguish between "messages" and "events" in the rest of the paper.

In Time-Warp, an event causing rollback is called a *straggler.* After receiving a straggler, an LP must be rolled back to a previous time point. We call the time point that the LP is rolled back to as the *rollback-time* and call the first event submitted by an LP after rolling back as a *rollback event.* In XTW the following "Propagation Rule" is enforced in addition to the normal propagation rule:

- *Rule 4: If a rollback event is processed, the output events must be propagated.*

The output-events, which are generated by the *rollback event* and forced to propagate, are mainly used to propagate the rollback and thus called as *rb-messages* in this paper.

In the following, we describe how the *rb-messages* mechanism works in the XTW rollback procedure:

When a new event, E_{new}, arrives at an LP, it is checked if its receive-time is smaller than LVT. If the receive-time of E_{new} is larger than or equal to LVT, it is a normal event and will be scheduled in the way described in section 3.4. If the receive-time of E_{new} is smaller than LVT, it is a straggler(e.g. E6 at LP1 in fig 8). Then, the LP which receives the straggler is rolled back as follows:

1) Step 1: The *rollback-time* is set equal to the receive time of E_{new}.
2) Step 2: The *current LP event* which is pointed by CLE is moved from CLEQ to the LPEQ.
3) Step 3: The *current InCh events* pointed by respective CIEs are moved from LPEQ to the head of respective ICEQs.
4) Step 4: Every *Input-Channel* is rolled back. There are two cases to be considered:
   a) Case 1: The *Input-Channel* is the one which receives the straggler. This *Input-Channel* erases all events in its ICEQ if any, and all ICPQ events which have receive-time larger than the *rollback-time*.
   b) Case 2: The *Input-Channel* is not the one receiving the straggler. This *Input-Channel* is rolled back by moving all ICPQ events which have receive-time larger than the *rollback-time* from ICPQ to ICEQ.
5) Step 5: The LP restores the states to the first state that has time-stamp smaller than or equal to the *rollback-time*.
6) Step 6: E_{new} is en-queued at the head of its arriving ICEQ.
7) Step 7: Every *input-channel* submits one event to LPEQ if its ICEQ is not empty. LP submits one event to CLEQ. This event is the *rollback-event*.
8) Step 8: After the *rollback-event* is processed, according to *Rule 4*, the output events(rb-messages) must be propagate to subordinate LPs. There are five cases to consider when an LP receives a rb-message. Fig 7 states all five cases. Fig 8 depicts concrete examples of these five cases.
   In fig 8, LP3 has two *input-channels*, InCh1 receives events from LP1, InCh2 receives events from LP2. We assume LP1 has two different service-time, 1 and 10. So if LP1 processes an event at LVT 6 using service time 1, the output event will be E7 with receive-time at 7(rt:7) and send-time at 6(st:6); if LP1 processes an

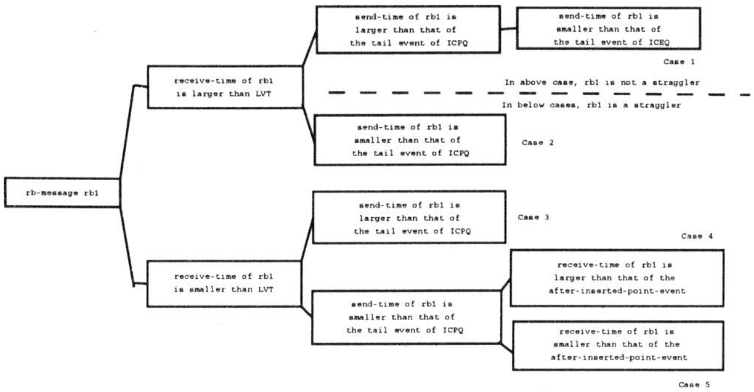

Fig. 7. five rb-message arriving cases

event at LVT 6 using service time 10, the output event will be E16 with receiver-time at 16(rt:16) and send-time at 6(st:6).

Each of five cases is handled respectively as follows:

a) Case 1: In this case, the rb-message is not a straggler. The *input-channel* which receives the rb-message erases all events which have send-time larger than that of the rb-message from its ICEQ. In fig 8, rb23 is in this case. Rb23 is propagated from LP1 to LP3 after the *rollback event* e23 is processed with service time 1 in LP1.

b) Case 2: In this case, the rb-message is a straggler. The send time of the rb-message is used to find the *cut-point* in ICPQ, such that all events with send-time larger than the send-time of the rb-message is after the *cut-point*. The LP sets the *rollback-time* equal to the receive-time of the first event after the *cut-point*. Then the LP recusively applies the rollback procedure following Step2-Step8 as described above.
In fig 8, rb16 is in this case. Rb16 is propagated from LP1 to LP3 after the *rollback event* e6 is processed with service time 10 in LP1. Using the send-time of Rb16, st:6, the *cut-point* is found before E10 in ICPQ. The LP3 *rollback-time* is then set to the receive-time of E10 at 10. Fig 9 shows the LP3 after rolled back by rb16.

c) Case 3: In this case, the rb-message is a straggler. The LP sets the *rollback-time* equal to the receive-time of the rb-message. Then the LP recusively applies the rollback procedure following Step2-Step8 as described above.
In fig 8, rb11 is in this case. Rb11 is propagated from LP1 to LP3 after the *rollback event* e10 is processed with service time 1 in LP1. In this case, the LP3 *rollback-time* is set to 11 after receiving rb11.

d) Case 4: In this case, the rb-message is a straggler. The send time of the rb-message is used to find the *cut-point* in ICPQ. The LP sets the *rollback-time* equal to the receive-time of the first event

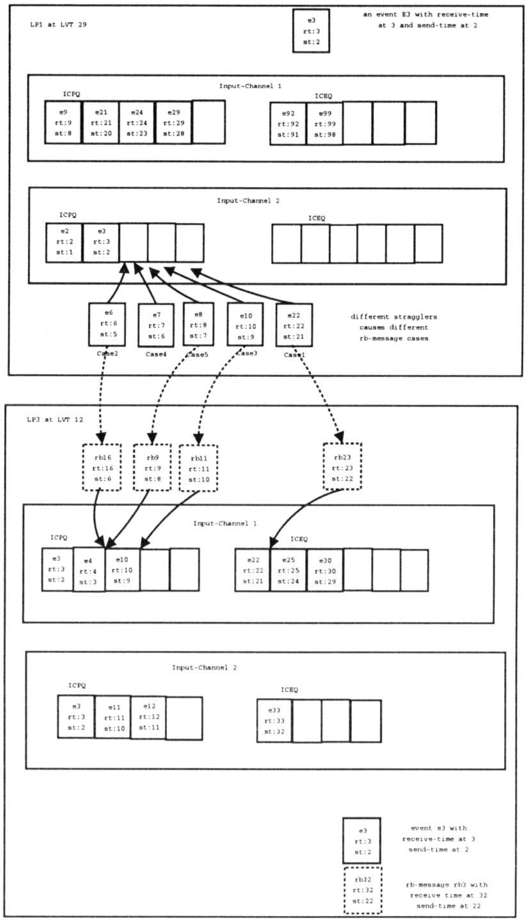

Fig. 8. concrete examples of five rb-message arriving cases

after the *cut-point*. Then the LP recusively applies the rollback procedure following Step2-Step8 as described above.
In fig 8, we assume following activities happened: 1) E33 in LP3 has been processed and LP3 is at LVT 33. 2) The *rollback-event* e7 is processed in LP1 with service time 10, and a rb-message, rb17, is generated with receive-time at 17 and send-time at 7. 3) rb17 is propagated to LP3.
When rb17 arrives at InCh1 of LP3, its receive-time(rt:17) is smaller than the LVT(33). Rb17 is a straggler. Using the send-time of rb17, st:7, the *cut-point* is found before E10 which has the send-time at 9. Since the receive-time of rb17(rt:17) is larger than that of E10(rt:10), LP3 sets the *rollback-time* to the receive-time of E10, at 10.

e) Case 5: In this case, the rb-message is a straggler. The LP sets the *rollback-time* equal to the receive-time of the rb-message. Then the LP recusively applies the rollback procedure following Step2-Step8 as described above.
In fig 8, rb9 is in this case. Rb9 is propagated from LP1 to LP3 after the *rollback event* e8 is processed with service time 1 in LP1. In this case, the LP3

rollback-time is set to 9 after receiving rb9.

Recursively applying the above "roll back, send rb-messages" procedure will eventually erase all incorrect computations resulting from the original incorrect message send.

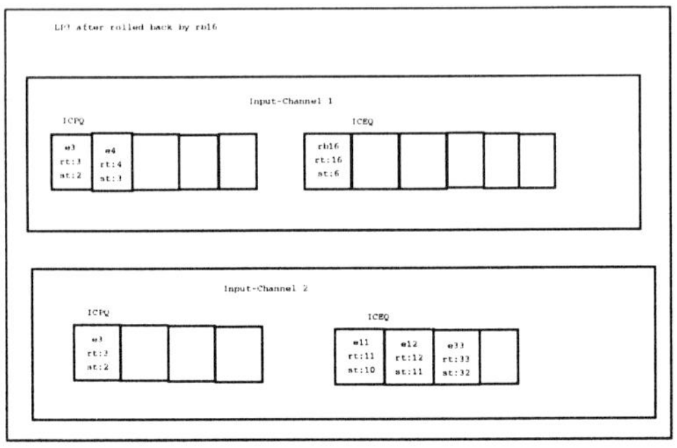

Fig. 9. *rb-messages*, an LP receives a straggler rb-message

3.5.3 Eliminating the Output Queue *and the* anti-messages*:* From the above description, we can see that the *anti-messages* mechanism is eliminated in XTW, and therefore the *output queue*, which is used to store all of the anti-messages, can be obviated in XTW as well. Since an anti-message is saved for every output event, considerable time and space are expected to be saved with the elimination of the *output queue*. This is one of the fundamental virtues of the *rb-messages* mechanism.

4 Experimental Evaluation of XTW

In this section, two sets of experiments are presented. In subsection 4.1, a set of experiments is described which compares CTW and XTW, while in subsection 4.2, a set of experiments examines the scalability of XTW.

All of the results reported in this paper are the average values of 10-100 runs. XTW employs MPI as the software communication platform, thereby guaranteeing a FIFO order of message communication.

4.1 XTW vs. Time Warp(CTW)

In this subsection, we present results comparing the performance of XTW and CTW [2] [3]. We compare XTW to CTW because CTW is oriented towards logic simulation, and exhibits a superior performance to Time Warp [2] in this domain.

The XTW-CTW experiments were conducted on a Myrinet network of seven personal computers. Each computer is equipped with dual Pentium III 450 processors and 256 Megabytes of internal memory.

In our experiments, the *local roll back, local checkpoint* mechanism is made use of in CTW. Local checkpoint means that an LP saves its state only if it receives a message from an LP in another cluster. Local rollback refers to each LP rolling back individually, i.e. the same technique used in Time Warp.

We conducted experiments on various benchmark circuits. The results show that CTW has the best performance on the circuit s90k – a combination circuit which consists of ISCAS89 benchmark circuits s38584 and s38417, and has around 90,000 gates. In the following, we present the XTW-CTW comparisons making use of s90k.

The following metrics are used for the performance comparison:

- *Simulation Time*: *Simulation Time* is defined as the elapsed real time for the simulation.
- *Speedup*: *Speedup* is defined as the ratio of the simulation time of a simulator using one processor to the simulation time of the same simulator using more than one processor.
- *Throughput*: *Throughput* is defined as the number of processed events per second.
- *Goodput*: *Goodput* is defined as the number of committed processed events per second.
- *Committed Rate*: *Committed Rate* is defined as the ratio of the *Goodput* and the *Throughput*.

Both CTW and XTW use the same partitioning algorithm. The time to perform the partitioning is not included in the simulation time.

Since CTW crashes when more than 3 processors are used in a simulation, all of the CTW results are presented with up to 3 processors.

4.1.1 Simulation Time: Figure 10 shows *the simulation time vs. the number of processors*. The results demonstrate that XTW outperforms CTW in all parallel simulations with any number of processors.

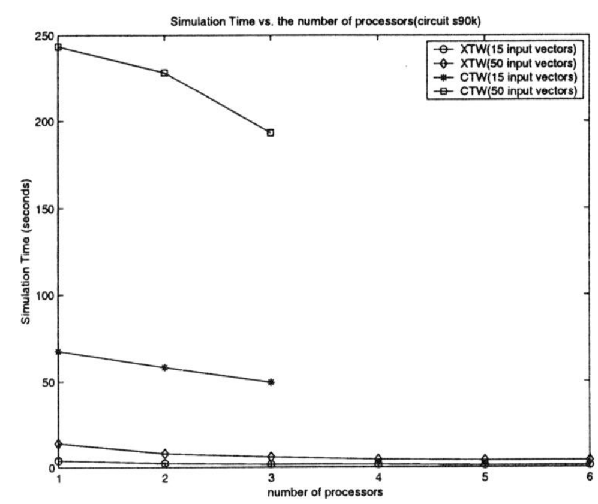

Fig. 10. simulation time vs. number of processors

4.1.2 Goodput and Committed Rate: Figure 11 depicts the good-put vs. the number of processors. Figure 12 shows the committed rate vs. the number of processors. Figure 11 shows that XTW has an almost linear increase in the good-put, while CTW has a relatively flat one. Figure 12 reveals the reason behind this phenomenon- XTW has a higher committed event rate than CTW. Moreover, XTW has an almost flat reduction in committed event rate when more processors are used, while CTW has a relatively steep reduction in its committed event rate. *These results indicate that XTW has a more efficient rollback mechanism.*

4.1.3 Speedup: Figure 13 shows *speedup vs. the number of processors*. It should be noted that the larger the throughput of a simulator, the harder it is to obtain a good speedup.

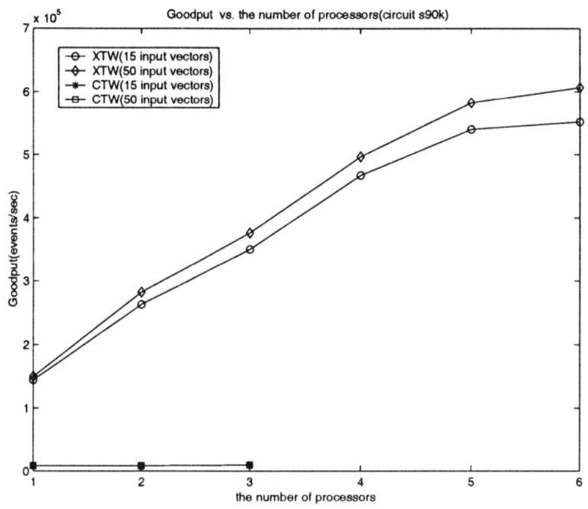

Fig. 11. goodput vs. the number of processors

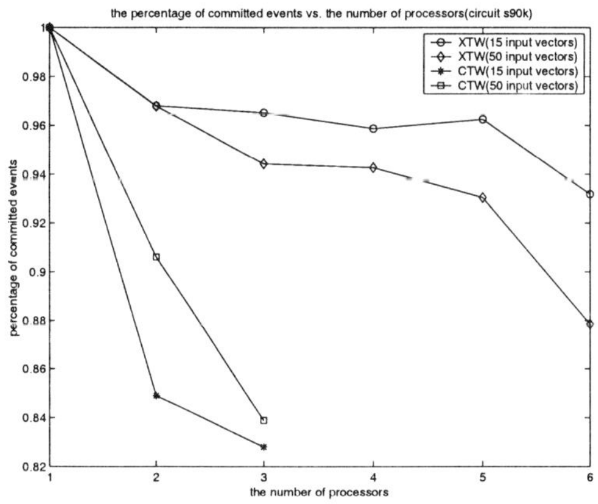

Fig. 12. committed events rate vs. the number of processors

Although XTW has a much larger goodput than CTW, the results indicate that XTW still has a bigger speedup than CTW in all the cases. Moreover, XTW has an almost linear increase in speedup while CTW has a relatively flat one. This clearly demonstrates that XTW has a smaller overhead than CTW.

4.2 XTW Scalability Experiments

In this section we explore the scalability of XTW with respect to the size of the circuit and the number of processors. Three circuits(5-million-gate, 10-million-gate and 25-million-gate) are simulated on CLUMEQ [7], a Beowulf cluster with 128 Appro 1100i 1U nodes connected by a Myrinet. Each CLUMEQ node has dual Athlon 1900+ processors and 3G memory. Because CLUMEQ is a shared platform, the number of compute nodes which we used was limited to 40.

4.3 A Hierarchical Synthetic Benchmark Circuit Generation

There is an absence of large benchmark circuits described as gate-level netlists in the public domain. Consequently, we developed a hierarchical mechanism to generate the synthetic circuits which we used in the experiments described in this section.

The benchmark circuits were generated as follows:

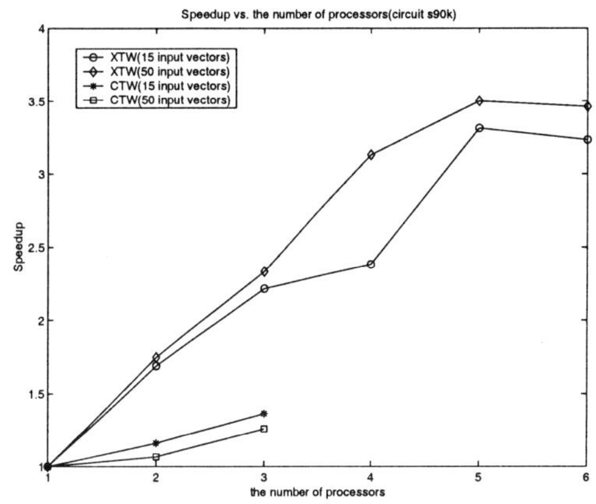

Fig. 13. speedup vs. the number of processors

1) A modular-level netlist, consisting of real world circuits (which can be described in Verilog or VHDL) is created. This modular-level netlist is used to describe the connections among modules of the benchmark circuit.
2) Each node(module) of the modular-level netlist is instantiated into a gate-level netlist.

By making use of this hierarchical approach, we can generate a synthetic benchmark circuit of any size.

4.4 A modular-level partition algorithm

The design of a large circuit follows a "divide and conquer" approach, in which the design is broken into a collection of individual modules and in which the interfaces between individual modules are clearly defined. As a consequence of this approach, most communication occurs within (as opposed to between) the modules.

Based upon this observation, we made use of a straightforward DFS-modular partitioning algorithm in our experiments- the algorithm partitions the modules of the circuit design. One shortcoming of this approach is that it can result in an unbalanced partition, i.e. different numbers of gates can be assigned to different computers.

Table I shows the simulation time of three circuits simulated over 8 to 40 CLUMEQ nodes. The simulations of 25-million-gate over 12 and 8 nodes did not complete because of swapping. From the data in Table I, we see a consistent trend of a decrease in simulation time as the number of processors increases.

Figure 14 shows the speedup vs. the number of processors. In Figure 14, we see that XTW scales almost linearly with the number of processors and scales well with the size of the circuits.

5 Conclusion

In this paper, two new mechanisms for improving the efficiency of distributed logic simulation were introduced. The first, *XEQ* is a a multi-level input queue, which lies behind an $O(1)$ event scheduling algorithm. The second, *rb-messages*, reduces the rollback costs. It also reduces the cost of saving events by eliminating the output queue at each LP. Both of

number of nodes	5-Million-gate	10-Million-gate	25-Million-gate
40	48.04	107.50	495.97
36	51.92	117.67	606.30
32	58.98	142.46	756.52
28	64.62	161.24	832.09
24	78.12	207.76	1058.69
20	106.36	261.49	1264.55
16	134.98	422.07	2187.50
12	200.59	1120.54	N/A
8	403.00	1324.84	N/A

TABLE I

SIMULATION TIME(SECONDS) VS. PROCESSOR NODES

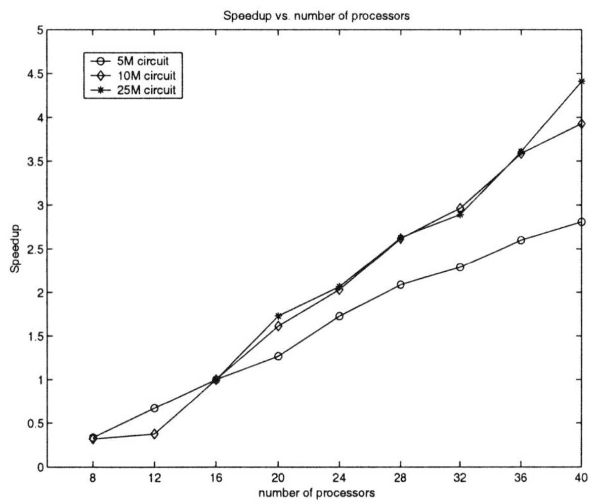

Fig. 14. Speedup vs. the number of processors

these mechanisms presume the use of clusters of LPs. These mechanisms were combined with a version of Clustered Time Warp to produce a simulation framework which we call *XTW*.

The cost of these algorithms were analyzed in theory. Comparisons to CTW revealed that XTW has a far superior performance. Experimental comparisons to a sequential version of XTW suggested that it is scalable, while experiments with large, synthetic circuits further support this claim.

It is certainly desirable to make use of XTW on large, real circuits and to modify it for use in behavioral and mixed behavioral/logic simulations. In addition, the development of efficient partitioning and/or load balancing algorithms is vital for the further development of XTW. We hope to continue our work in these directions.

REFERENCES

[1] D. Jefferson, "Virtual time," *Programming Languages and Systems*, 1985.

[2] H. Avril and C.Tropper, "On rolling back and checkpointing in time warp," *IEEE Trans. on Par. and Distr. Systems, vol.12, no.11, Nov.2001, pp. 1105-1122*, 2001.

[3] H.Avril and C.Tropper, "Scalable clustered time warp and logic simulation," *VLSI Design, Special Issue on Current Advances in Logic Simulation, Gordon-Breach, vol.19, no.3, lpp.291-313*, 1999.

[4] D.Martin and et al, "Analysis and simulation of mixed technology vlsi systems," *JPDC, Slpecial Issue Parallel and Distributed Discrete Event Simulation, pp. 468-493*, 2002.

[5] M. J. R.Chamberlain, "Parallel logic simulation of vlsi systems," *ACM Computing Surveys, vol.26, no.3, Sept. 1994, pp. 255-295*, 1994.

[6] J.Dahl, M. Chetlur, and P. Wilsey, "Event list management in distributed simulation," in *European Parallel Computing Conference*, 2001.

[7] www.clumeq.mcgill.ca, "Clumeq infrastructure," 2003.

(MMSM) Analysis of Worms

A Preliminary Simulation of the Effect of Scanning Worm Activity on Multicast

Ihab Hamadeh, Jason Hart, George Kesidis
Department of Computer Science and Engineering
Department of Electrical Engineering
Pennsylvania State University
University Park, PA
hamadeh@cse.psu.edu, jth214@psu.edu,
kesidis@engr.psu.edu

Venkat Pothamsetty
Critical Infrastructure Assurance Group
Cisco Systems
Austin, TX
vpothams@cisco.com

Abstract

Previous scanning worms have been significant sources of network congestion and have had catastrophic effects on switches, routers and end-systems. In this paper, we focus on the simulation of the secondary resource-exhaustion effects that scanning worms cause on network protocols operating in Internet routers. Specifically, we describe a preliminary simulation study on the effect of the spread of the Ramen and SQL Slammer/Sapphire worms on the multicast infrastructure.

1. Introduction

The Internet has recently experienced several serious outbreaks of scanning worms. Scanning worms are those that exploit a software vulnerability to gain access/control of an end system. Unlike e-mail worms, scanning worms require no human intervention to propagate. An infected end-system scans (dispatches suitably crafted packets often to randomly chosen IPv4 addresses of) potential victim end-systems. If the scanned end-system is susceptible to the exploit, it is subsequently infected and begins scanning (spreading the worm) in turn. Some scanning worms (e.g., Witty [17]) were more malicious than others in the sense that they harmed the end-systems they infected. Others were relatively benign to their hosts (e.g., SQL Slammer/Sapphire [16]). Several, including Slammer and Witty, propagated so rapidly that all potential susceptibles were infected before (human initiated) responses could be mounted.

Most existing worm research has focused on finding ways to mitigate the spread of a worm. Several worm detection and containment solutions have been proposed [25, 22, 19, 27, 3, 4]. However, scanning worms have had significant secondary (indirect) effects on some enterprise networks and on the Internet core. For instance, Code Red II indirectly caused serious ARP storms resulting in high router CPU utilization and memory allocation failure [20] that lead, in turn, to the meltdown of many access routers. The SQL Slammer/Sapphire worm, using a single UDP packet to both scan and infect, propagated very rapidly and was consequently able to saturate various links on the Internet. The link congestion caused router adjacencies to be lost resulting in BGP route withdrawals which propagated across the Internet.

In this paper, we are interested in the effect of worms on multicast. The SQL Slammer/Sapphire worm and the Ramen worm [15] generated large volumes of scans destined to multicast addresses creating a storm of Source Active (SA) messages that propagated across Multicast Source Discovery Protocol (MSDP) enabled networks. The SA messages filled up the memory of some routers and dramatically increased their CPU utilization causing resource exhaustion. The Abelene Internet2 community (consisting of 220 university, corporate, and affiliate member institutions in the United States) along with the largest research and education backbone in Europe have already deployed and are utilizing multicast. Increasing numbers of ISPs have begun implementing a multicast infrastructure. In the near future, the Internet may provide full multicast connectivity among any end systems.

The security vulnerabilities of multicast protocols have not been fully explored. Some research has concentrated on source authentication and group management [9, 18, 10, 24, 26]. Rajvaidya et al. [14] explored and proposed detection and deflection mechanisms to miti-

1087-4097/05 $20.00 © 2005 IEEE

gate the effect of multicast Denial-of-Service (DoS) attack including that indirectly caused by worms. In this paper, we describe a preliminary simulation study that recreates the resource exhaustion effect of worms on a router memory. Our ultimate goal is to create a realistic simulation platform to evaluate and tune techniques to mitigate the effects of scanning worms on network protocols.

This paper is organized as follows. In section 2, we review some of the multicast protocols and describe the operation of today's multicast infrastructure. The effect of scanning worms on multicast is explained in section 3. Our preliminary simulation study is covered in section 4 followed by a concluding section on future work.

2. Multicast Protocols

Multicast protocols are either intra-domain or inter-domain. Intra-domain multicast protocols manage the multicast network within a domain while inter-domain multicast protocols insure that domains are interconnected and that multicast sources in one domain are reachable to receivers in other domains.

2.1. Intra-domain Multicast Protocols

There are two categories of intra-domain multicast forwarding protocols: Dense Mode (DM) and Sparse Mode (SM).

DM protocols assume that a large number of receivers exist within a network domain. These protocols flood the links with multicast data until downstream routers send Prune messages to upstream routers to stop the data flow. This mechanism is mostly known as flood and prune. Distance Vector Multicast Routing Protocol (DVMRP) [23], Multicast Open Shortest Path First (MOSPF) [11], and Protocol Independent Multicast - Dense Mode (PIM-DM) [1] are examples of DM protocols. DVMRP was the first-generation multicast routing protocol to be widely accepted. It is a distance vector protocol that allows multicast traffic to be forwarded within Routing Information Protocol (RIP) unicast network. DVMRP's hop count limitations and its periodic updates make it unsuitable for today's largescale internetworks. Nowadays, DVMRP is implemented in some routers only for backward compatibility with existing DVMRP enabled infrastructure [6]. MOSPF is another DM protocol similar to DVMRP but requires an OSPF unicast protocol to operate. Another DM protocol, PIM-DM, has also many similarities with DVMRP and MOSPF. But, unlike DVMRP and MOSPF which require specific routing protocol to make forwarding decision, PIM-DM is protocol independent (i.e., it can use the route's unicast routing tables populated by any routing protocol such as IGRP, EIGRP, RIP, and OSPF).

SM protocols, on the contrary, do not flood the network with multicast data. Multicast packets are sent when explicitly requested by downstream routers. An SM-capable network requires the existence of a central router, called a Rendezvous Point (RP), that receives registration requests from receivers interested in certain multicast groups. Protocol Independent Multicast - Sparse Mode (PIM-SM) is an example of an SM protocol. PIM-SM tries to constrain the multicast data distribution only to interested receivers. It is protocol independent and can use either the router's unicast routing tables or separate routing tables dedicated to multicast.

In general, SM protocols are becoming the preferred multicast protocols even in networks dense with receivers [13].

2.2. Inter-domain Multicast Protocols

Multicast Source Discovery Protocol (MSDP) is the current solution for inter-domain multicast routing. It was developed to interconnect multiple PIM-SM domains in order to allow domains to learn about other domains' multicast sources. As soon as a multicast source appears in a domain, the MSDP-speaking router within the same domain, which is also an RP of that domain, advertises the existence of a new source by sending a Source Active (SA) message to its RP peers in other domains. After receiving the SA messages, the RP peers check if any recipient members within their domains are interested in the new multicast source.

2.3. Operation of Today's IP Multicast Infrastructure

The current IP multicast infrastructure in the Internet is mainly based on four protocols:

- the Internet Group Management Protocol (IGMP) [5] to allow multicast receivers to request group join and leave operations,
- the PIM-SM protocol to manage the distribution of multicast data between sources and receivers,
- MSDP to advertise the multicast source information to neighboring domains, and
- the Multiprotocol Border Gateway Protocol (MBGP) [2] for IP multicast to enable multicast routing policy throughout the Internet and to connect multicast topologies within and between BGP autonomous systems.

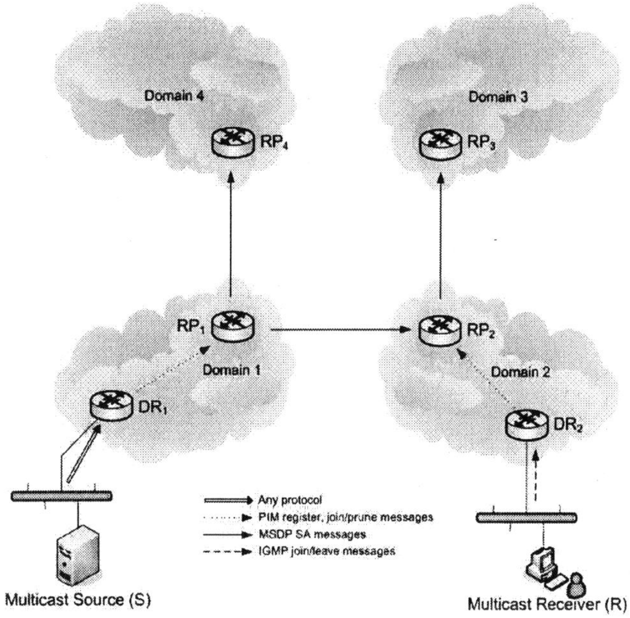

Figure 1. Multicast Infrastructure.

Figure 1 illustrates a simplified scenario of how today's multicast infrastucture operates.

When a multicast source S sends its first packet to a multicast group G, the Designated Router (DR_1), which is the first hop router, recognizes that a new multicast source has just joined in. Consequently, DR_1 creates a register message according to the PIM-SM protocol, encapsulates the packet sent by the source S into that message and then unicasts the message to the domain's Rendezvous Point RP_1. RP_1 caches the new source address and group address (S,G) and starts a data-timeout timer (default is 210 seconds [7]). The data-timeout represents the time after which the (S,G) state for a silent source will be deleted. RP_1 also creates a connection oriented session with its adjacent MSDP peers (RP_2 and RP_4) and advertises (S,G,RP) by sending SA messages as per the MSDP protocol. When the MSDP peer RP_2 receives the SA message, it checks if there exist any receivers in its domain which are interested in the multicast group G. Regardless, RP_2 will cache (S,G), (the SA cache timeout should not be less 90 seconds [8]) and forwards the unmodified SA message to RP_3.

Now, if a multicast receiver R is interested in any multicast group G, it conveys its membership information using IGMP to its DR_2 which, in its turn, creates a (*,G) PIM Join message and forwards it to RP_2. If group G is in the cache of RP_2, RP_2 sends the necessary information back to enable receiver R to connect to source S.

It is important to note that, in addition to the initial SA message, RP_1 periodically advertises (every 60 seconds [8]) the portion of its (S,G) cache which contains the active sources within its own domain.

3. Vulnerability of Multicast Infrastructure to Worms

The ability to become a multicast source requires no membership, no extra software or protocols. Unlike receivers which require the use of IGMP to announce their interest in joining a multicast group, a multicast source may start transmitting any data with a class D destination address whenever it needs to. This open permission to become a source on a multicast-capable network was unintentionally exploited by worms, namely SQL Slammer/Sapphire and Ramen, which crafted a percentage of packets with multicast destination IP address. These packets were believed to be multicast sources and resulted in having DRs, with attached infected machines, flood their RPs with PIM register messages. Consequently, RPs started advertising an SA message for each register message, flooding the multicast infrastructure with unnecessary data (Figure 2). In addition to that, each RP needs to maintain a list of its active sources in its cache and to advertise them periodically prolonging the residence of bogus (S,G,RP) entries in memory of its MSDP peers. Under normal conditions, the number of unique SA announcements seen is on the order of

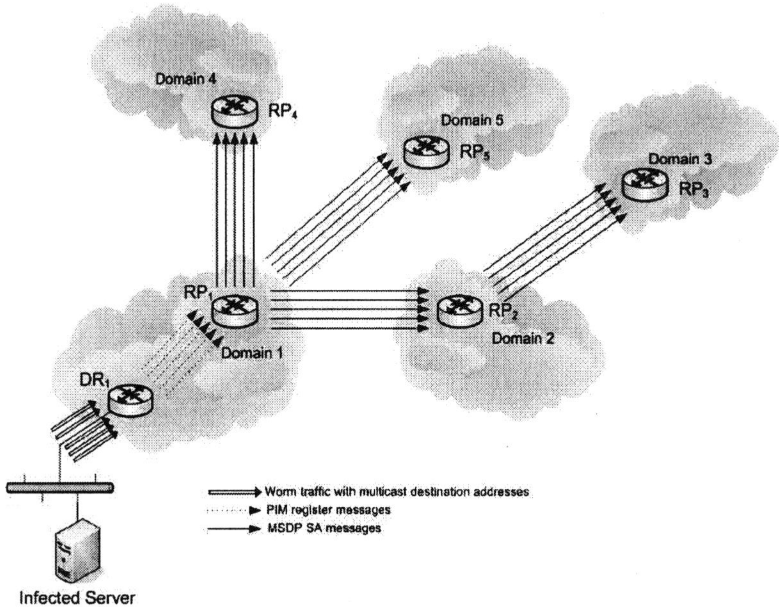

Figure 2. Multicast flooding due to worm scanning activity.

a few thousand. During the spread of a worm, the number of unique SA announcements could dramatically increase the state information to be cached in RPs which not only caches the (S,G) state of their own sources but also the (S,G,RP) state sent by other RPs.

Today's high-speed routers are composed of a data plane used for queuing/scheduling, classifying and forwarding datagrams at line-speed and a control plane for routing and signaling (e.g., managing routing tables and executing routing protocol). Traffic that engages the control plane is not usually time critical and requires limited CPU and memory resources. In the case of multicast, both SA message and PIM register messages require the intervention of the control plane to lookup (S,G,RP) states in its cache, creating/updating states, crafting multicast control and signalling messages. During the spread of worm, the excessive amount of PIM register messages and SA messages from other peers could overwhelm the control plane, causing memory depletion and high CPU utilization. Both memory exhaustion and CPU utilization could inhibit the processing of critical routing protocols causing the router to lose connectivity and even its maintenance sessions to hang. For example, during the SQL Slammer outbreak, Indiana University's Juniper M20 router failed, and lost connectivity between the university and the commodity Internet, including a connection to the Abilene (Internet2) network and the university's DDoS monitoring systems [21]. The router failed because it was not able to withstand the ingress of multicast state from the Abilene network and experienced hung maintenance sessions and multiple memory faults.

4. Simulation Setup and Results

Currently, we are developing simulations of a router's multicast state cache memory subjected to scanning worm traffic. Figure 3 shows the router of interest (RP_2). It is important to note that an RP with a worm infection in its domain would suffer less than its peer RP to which it will send SA messages. For illustration, given the default timers introduced in Section 2.3, an RP with a worm infection in its domain caches (S,G) states for 210 seconds, while its peers (to which it sends correspondent SA messages) will cache the (S,G,RP) states for an amount of time ranging from 240 to 300 seconds (because of the 90 seconds timeout for (S,G,RP) states advertised through SA messages). Therefore, we are interested in the multicast states created by SA messages arriving from other RPs which have infections within their own domains. Moreover, we assumed that in each domain there exists a single infection (i.e., a single RP with a single infection transmitting SA messages to its peers). We simulated the effect of 1, 5, and 10 infected domains (each domain has a single RP and a single worm infection) on an RP of an uninfected domain including all the necessary timers described in section

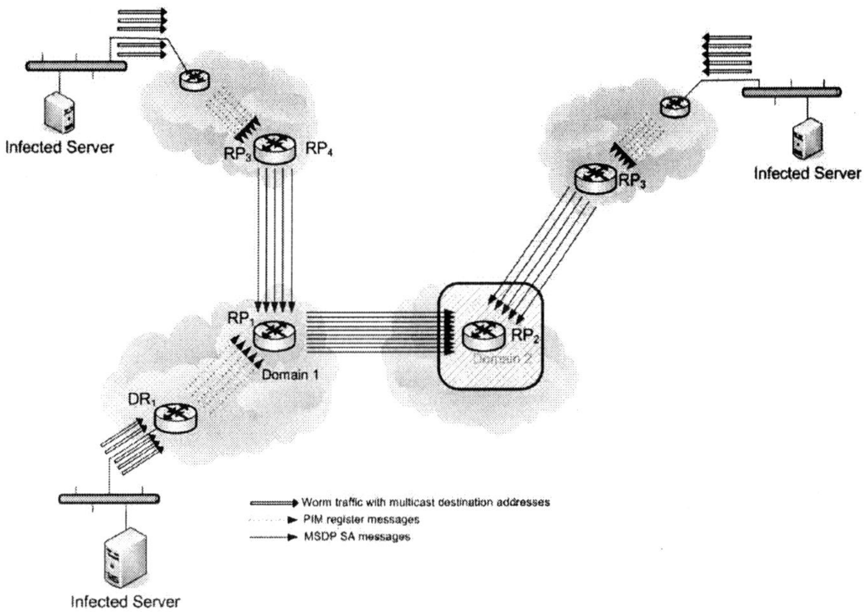

Figure 3. The effect of worm scanning activity on a single Rendezvous Point RP_2.

2.3. For this purpose, we wrote a time-driven C simulator and noted the growth of the (S,G,RP) entries inside the cach of the uninfected domain's RP. Because the purpose of the simulation is to depict how (S,G,RP) entries may increase while a worm is propagating, we assume the memory of a router to be infinite to study the backlog created by worm activity without considering dropped entries due to buffer overflow.

We studied the effect of three types of worms on multicast:

- ***The Ramen worm*** generated destination IP addresses between 13.0.0.0 and 242.255.255.255. It selected the value of the first two bytes randomly and thereafter linearly scanned the /16 subnet. As a TCP worm, Ramen spread relatively slowly. It completely scanned a /16 subnet in about 20 to 25 minutes, i.e., approximately 50 scans per second.
- ***The SQL Slammer/Sapphire worm*** generated destination IP addresses randomly. Because Slammer used a single UDP packet to scan and infect and because its victims tended to have high-bandwidth uplinks (being servers), its spread was very rapid. An infected machine on a 10Mbps network could generate about 2900 scans per second (averagely 170 multicast scans per second).
- ***The Ramen-Slammer hybrid worm*** is our hypothetical hybrid that incorporates the fast scanning rate of Slammer and the linear scanning strategy of Ramen. The first two bytes of a generated destination IP address are randomly chosen. After generating the first two bytes, the worm will scan the /16 subnet.

Since the control plane of a router processes packets slower than the data plane, it is important to note that the fidelity of the simulation study depends on the processing time of the PIM register message and the propagation and transmission times of the corresponding SA message. For the results of our simulation to be somewhat realistic, the delay between two consecutive SA messages should be at most 20ms in the case of Ramen, 6ms in the case of SQL Slammer, and 0.35ms for the Ramen-Slammer hybrid worm. Figures 4, 5 and 6 illustrate the number of (S,G,RP) entries cached in an RP router assuming an infinite memory size. Obviously, the behavior of each worm and the number of infected interconnected domains dictate how an RP router cache is being populated. The Ramen worm was a slow worm. A single domain with one instance of that worm would cause an RP of a neighboring domain to cache around 14000 entries. The dark area where the number of entries seem to be constant is actually an oscillation caused as some entries were deleted (because of entry time out) while others were added. As the number of infected domains increased, the number of (S,G,RP) entries did not grow proportionally. This result was expected as the Ramen worm has a slow scan rate and a /16 linear scanning strategy which lowers the chance of having two or more

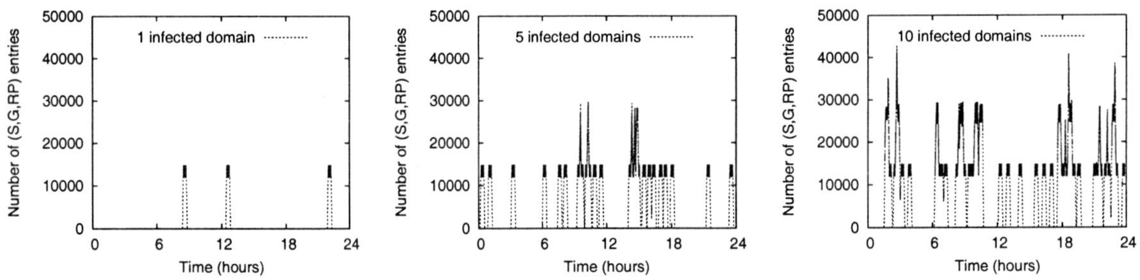

Figure 4. Ramen Worm.

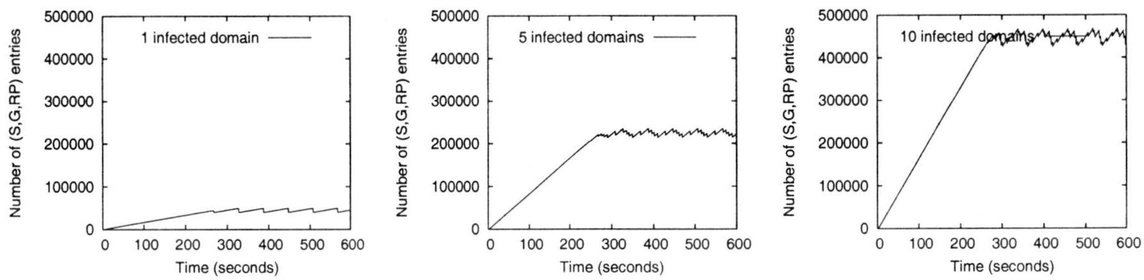

Figure 5. Slammer Worm.

infected domains scanning the multicast addresses at the same time. Unlike the SQL Slammer/Sapphire worm which congested many stub links and crashed many switches and routers, the Ramen worm was stealthy (because of its scan rate and the scarcity of vulnerable machines in the Internet) and thus infected machines remained up and running for days and caused few spikes in in memory consumption of RP routers. This is why we simulated the Ramen worm over a 24-hour period.

On the other hand, the SQL Slammer simulation was conducted over a period of 10 minutes. The SQL Slammer worm was able to infect around 75000 vulnerable machines within 10 minutes. The effect of SQL Slammer on RP router memory consumption is shown in Figure 5. A single infected domain could create around 45000 new entries in the neighboring peer RPs. Unlike the Ramen worm, the number of entries of the SQL Slammer worm was proportional to the number of infected domains (note that as mentioned before, we assume a single infection in each domain). Moreover, a few minutes after outbreak, the number of entries remained approximately constant with a clear upper and lower bound.

We also simulated the hypothetical hybrid worm that combined the scanning rate of the SQL Slammer worm (i.e. 2900 scans/s) and the /16 linear scanning rate of Ramen. A single instance of this worm could cause over 100,000 (S,G,RP) entries to be created in a peer RP. Note, however, that the maximum number of (S,G,RP) entries a worm could cause depends greatly on the amount of time an RP router needs to process a PIM register message and to send the corresponding SA message to its peer. The slower the RP processing time is, the better it is for its RP peers under such circumstances. Also the data timeout timers need to be small. Some vendors use over 600 seconds instead of 210 seconds as recommended by the RFCs and that could cause bogus multicast entries due to worm spread to remain in memory much longer and speed up the problem of memory exhaustion.

5. Discussion Future Work

In summary, we described a preliminary simulation of the secondary effects of the spread of scanning worms on the multicast infrastructure of the Internet. In the future, we will expand our simulation to encompass more routers. Also, we will model how different protocols compete and consume routers resources (memory, CPU cycles, transmission bandwidth) and simulate a router subjected to scanning worm traffic and back-

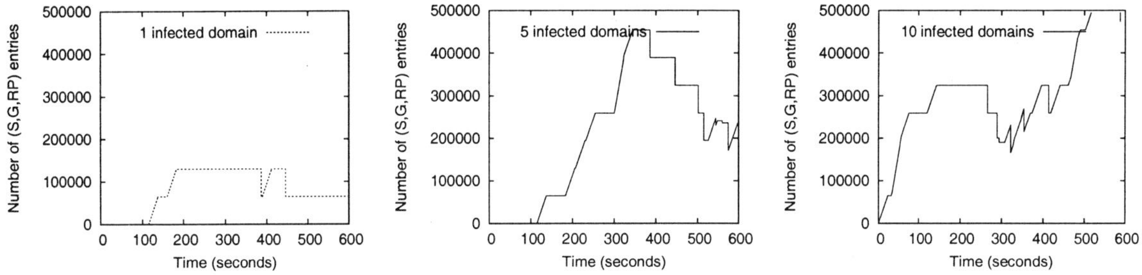

Figure 6. Ramen-Slammer hybrid Worm.

ground (nominal) traffic. Our ultimate goal is to test and fine-tune defense strategies some of which have already been incorporated in routers such as PIM register messages and rate-limiting of SA messages. An ideal defense strategy would, however, aim to stop worm attacks at their sources. In multicast, any source can send multicast traffic to as many multicast groups as it wants without authorization. Unlike multicast receivers that require join message for each multicast group, a multicast source does not need to send any message to the DR to become the source of that group. One defense strategy would have DRs set a limit on the number of multicast groups per attached source (there are many ways to implement this idea and a simulation study could help evaluate and compare the approaches). However, this protection could be evaded by a single-packet UDP worm spoofing its source IP address. Another solution would be to build a new protocol or expand IGMP to include authorization/signalling for sources that wish to send multicast packets. In the long-term, these approaches may be deployed and, as a result, RPs will not be subjected to potentially malicious multicast traffic and push the problem of the multicast infrastructure denial-of-service to the network edge (i.e., to the DRs).

A new multicast routing protocol called Protocol Independent Multicast source specific mode (PIM-SSM) [12], that is robust in the presence of scanning worm activity, has been introduced. PIM-SSM is intended to support the mostly available one-to-many audio and video broadcast applications (e.g., TV and radio broadcast). PIM-SSM takes advantage of the PIM-SM features while requiring no RPs at all and thus no MSDP protocol (i.e., no SA messages flooding the network). PIM-SSM is to be initially available on multicast addresses 232.0.0.0/8. Because of its simplicity and usefulness, it might replace today's multicast infrastructure by supporting many-to-many group communication by using relay nodes.

References

[1] A. Adams, J. Nicholas, and W. Siadak. Protocol independent multicast-dense mode (PIM-DM): Protocol specification (revised). *RFC 3973*, January 2005.

[2] T. Bates, Y. Rekhter, R. Chandra, and D. Katz. Multiprotocol extensions for BGP-4. *RFC 2858*, June 2000.

[3] V. Berk, G. Bakos, and R. Morris. Designing a framework for active worm detection on global networks. In *Proceedings of the IEEE International Workshop of Information Assurance*, March 2003.

[4] V. Berk, R. S. Gray, and G. Bakos. Using sensor networks and data fusion for early detection of active worms. In *Proceedings of the SPIE Aerosense Conference*, April 2003.

[5] B. Cain, S. Deering, I. Kouvelas, B. Fenner, and A. Thyagarajan. Internet group management protocol, version 3. *RFC 3376*, October 2002.

[6] M. Crane and D. E. Knuth. *Cisco CID Exam Certification Guide*, chapter 5. Cisco Press, 2001.

[7] D. Estrin, D. Farinacci, A. Helmy, D. Thaler, S. Deering, M. Handley, V. Jacobson, C. Liu, P. Sharma, and L. Wei. Protocol independent multicast-sparse mode (pim-sm): Protocol specification. *RFC 2362*, June 1998.

[8] B. Fenner and D. Meyer. Multicast source discovery protocol (msdp). *RFC 3618*, October 2003.

[9] H. Harney and C. Muckenhirn. Group key management protocol (GKMP) architecture. *RFC 2094*, July 1997.

[10] S. Mitra. Iolus: A framework for scalable secure multicasting. In *ACM SIGCOMM '97*, September 1997.

[11] J. Moy. MOSPF: Analysis and experience. *RFC 1585*, March 1994.

[12] Juniper Networks. Pim-ssm. http://www.juniper.net/techpubs/software/junos/junos60/swconfig60-multicast/html/pim-intro7.html.

[13] D. Price and S. Spence. IP multicast on JANET. http://www.ja.net/documents/tg-IPMulticast.pdf.

[14] P. Rajvaidya, K. Ramachandran, and K. Almeroth. Managing and securing the global multicast infrastructure. *Journal of Network and Systems Management*, September 2004.

[15] Symantec Security Response. Linux.ramen.worm. http://securityresponse.symantec.com/ avcenter/venc/data/linux.ramen.worm.html, January 2001.

[16] Symantec Security Response. W32.sqlexp.worm. http://securityresponse.symantec.com/ avcenter/venc/data/w32.sqlexp.worm.html, January 2003.

[17] Symantec Security Response. W32.witty.worm. http://securityresponse.symantec.com/ avcenter/venc/data/w32.witty.worm.html, March 2004.

[18] A. T. Sherman and D. A. McGrew. Key establishment in large dynamic groups using one-way function trees. *IEEE Transactions on Software Engineering*, 29(5), 2003.

[19] S. Staniford. Containment of scanning worms in enterprise networks. 2004.

[20] Cisco Systems. Dealing with mallocfail and high CPU utilization resulting from the code red worm. http://www.cisco.com/warp/public/63/ ts_codred_worm.shtml, October 2001.

[21] G. Travis, E. Balas, D. Ripley, and S. Wallace. Analysis of the SQL slammer worm and its effects on indiana university and related institutions. http://www.anml.iu.edu/downloads/ SLAMMER.pdf, March 2004.

[22] J. Twycross and M. M. Williamson. Implementing and testing a virus throttle. In *Proceedings of the 12th USENIX Security Symposium*, August 2003.

[23] D. Waitzman, C. Partridge, and S. Deering. Distance vector multicast routing protocol. *RFC 1075*, November 1988.

[24] D. Wallner, E. Harder, and R. Agee. Key management for multicast: Issues and architectures. *RFC 2627*, June 1999.

[25] M. M. Williamson. Throttling viruses: Restricting propagation to defeat mobile malicious code. In *Proceedings of the 18th Annual Computer Security Applications Conference*, December 2002.

[26] C. K. Wong, M. Gouda, and S. S. Lam. Secure group communications using key graphs. *IEEE/ACM Transactions on Networking*, 8(1), 2000.

[27] Wormscout. http://www.forescout.com/wormscout.html.

Routing Worm: A Fast, Selective Attack Worm based on IP Address Information

Cliff C. Zou[†], Don Towsley[‡], Weibo Gong[†], Songlin Cai[†]
[†]Department of Electrical & Computer Engineering
[‡]Department of Computer Science
University of Massachusetts, Amherst MA 01003
{czou,gong,scai}@ecs.umass.edu, towsley@cs.umass.edu

Abstract

Most well-known worms, such as Code Red, Slammer, Blaster, and Sasser, infected vulnerable computers by scanning the entire IPv4 address space. In this paper, we present an advanced worm called "routing worm", which implements two advanced attacking techniques. First, a routing worm uses BGP routing tables to only scan the Internet routable address space, which allows it propagate three times faster than a traditional worm. Second, and more importantly, the geographic information of BGP routing prefixes enables a routing worm to conduct pinpoint "selective attacks" by imposing heavy damage to vulnerable computers in a specific country, company, Internet Service Provider, or Autonomous System, without collateral damage done to others.

Because of the inherent publicity of BGP routing tables, attackers can easily deploy routing worms, which distinguishes the routing worm from other "worst-case" worms. Compared to a traditional worm, a routing worm could possibly cause more severe congestion to the Internet backbone since all scans sent out by a routing worm are Internet routable (and can only be dropped at the destinations). In addition, it is harder to quickly detect a routing-worm infected computer since we cannot distinguish illegal scans from regular connections without waiting for traffic responses. In order to defend against routing worms and all scanning worms, an effective way is to upgrade the current Internet from IPv4 to IPv6, although such an upgrade will require a tremendous effort and is still a controversial issue.

1. Introduction

Computer worms are malicious programs that self-propagate across a network exploiting security or policy flaws in widely-used services [26]. Most previously wide-spreading worms, such as Code Red, Slammer, Blaster, and Sasser [7], are scanning worms that find and infect vulnerable machines by probing IP addresses in the entire IPv4 Internet address space. How fast a worm can propagate is determined by many factors. Among them, three major factors could be improved by attackers:

(1). The number of initially infected hosts;
(2). A worm's scan rate η, defined as the number of scans an infected computer sends out per unit time;
(3). A worm's hitting probability p, defined as the probability that a worm's scan hits any computer that is either vulnerable or already infected.

"Hit-list worm" presented by [23] exploits the first factor above to improve a worm's propagation speed by containing a large number of IP addresses of vulnerable hosts in the worm code. The second factor, worm scan rate, is determined by the efficiency of a worm's code and also the network bandwidth. If attackers want to improve a worm's propagation speed, another effort is to increase the worm's hitting probability p, i.e., to waste fewer scans on obviously empty IP space.

In order to defend against Internet worm attacks, we need to anticipate and study how attackers will improve their attacking techniques. In this paper, we present an advanced scanning worm called "routing worm", which increases its propagation speed by removing many empty IP addresses from its scanning space based on information of BGP *routable* addresses. We define two types of routing worms — one based on "/8" prefix (x.0.0.0/8) address allocation, another based on BGP routing prefixes. We call them "/8 routing worm" and "BGP routing worm", respectively. Without missing any potential target in the Internet, a /8 routing worm and a BGP routing worm can reduce their scanning space to 45.3% and 28.6% of the entire IPv4 address space, respectively. In this way, attackers can increase

1087-4097/05 $20.00 © 2005 IEEE

the spreading speed of their worms by a factor of two to more than three without adding much complexity to the worm codes.

The IP address information of BGP routing prefixes provides geographic information about which IP addresses belong to which country, company, Internet Service Provider (ISP), or Autonomous System (AS). With such information, attackers could deploy a routing worm to selectively impose heavy damage to compromised hosts if they belong to a specific entity (country, company, ISP, or AS) and leave the compromised hosts belonging to others intact. Such a "selective attack" property makes a routing worm tremendous dangerous considering the potential attacks initiated by terrorists, revengers, or business rivals.

Because of the inherent publicity of BGP routing tables, attackers can easily deploy a routing worm without much extra effort — this distinguishes the routing worm from other theoretical "worst-case" worms. In addition, compared to a traditional worm that scans the entire IPv4 space, a routing worm could possibly cause more congestion trouble to the Internet backbone, and also makes it harder to quickly detect infected computers. We will explain these challenges in detail later in this paper.

To defend against the threat of routing worms and all scanning worms, we show that upgrading the current IPv4 Internet to IPv6 is an effective way, although such an upgrade will require a tremendous effort and is still a controversial issue.

The rest of this paper is organized as follows. Section 2 surveys related work. In Section 3, we discuss how routing worms can use various types of IPv4 address information to improve their spreading speed. In Section 4, we point out that attackers can use routing worms to conduct selective attack based on geographic information of IP addresses or BGP prefixes. Then in Section 5, we point out two additional challenges brought up by routing worms. In Section 6, we present modeling and analysis of routing worms based on uniform-scan worm model [31]. Then we propose to upgrade IPv4 to IPv6 to defend against scanning worms in Section 7. In the end, Section 8 concludes this paper.

2. Related work

At the same time when we proposed the "routing worm" in this paper, Wu *et al.* [28] independently presented a "routable scan" strategy that is similar to the reducing scanning space idea of the routing worm. However, the routing worm presented in this paper is not only a simple "routable scan" worm, but also a worm that could be used by attackers to conduct selective attack to a specific country or company (ISP, AS, etc), which is more dangerous and important to attackers than simply improving a worm's propagation speed. Staniford *et al.* [23] presented several possible fast spreading worms such as "Warhol" worm and "hit-list" worm right after the 2001 Code Red incident. [23][30][29][8][22][18][14] provided the major research work on how to model and analyze a worm's propagation under various situations.

Many people have studied how to derive the geographic information of ASes, ISPs, IP addresses, or domain names from public available information. The Skitter project provides detailed information of the AS number, name, longitude and latitude for every AS in the Internet [6]. In [5], CAIDA provides the mapping between AS number and the country it belongs to. Furthermore, there are location mapping commercial services, such as EdgeScape from Akamai [9] and the free IP-to-location service from Geobytes [17].

The Route Views project [20] and the Routing Information Service from RIPE NCC [19] provide detailed BGP routing information of the Internet. In 1997, Braun [3] first used BGP routing tables to determine the fraction of IP space that has been allocated. CAIDA also studied this issue in 1998 [4].

Some people have proposed upgrading IPv4 to IPv6 as a defense against scanning worms [25][24][29], but have not explained this issue in detail. Thus most people have not paid attention to the inherent capability of IPv6 in preventing attacks from scanning worms.

3. Routing Worm: A Fast Spreading Worm

The central idea of the spreading speed improvement of a routing worm is to make the worm's target-finding more efficient without ignoring any potential vulnerable computer in the Internet.

3.1. BGP routing worm

One simple way to reduce the scanning space is to use the information provided by Border Gateway Protocol (BGP) routing tables. Both the Route Views project [20] and RIPE NCC [19] provide complete snapshots of BGP routing tables several times per day. BGP routing tables contain all Internet routable IP addresses. A "*BGP routing worm*" is an advanced worm that contains BGP routing prefix information to only scans BGP routable IP addresses. In this way, the worm effectively reduces its scanning space without missing any target.

A BGP routing *prefix* is a chunk of IP addresses that have the same n most-significant bits in their addresses where n is called *prefix length* for this prefix. Because of multihoming, many prefixes in a BGP routing table overlap with each other — one prefix of shorter length contains all of the IP addresses in another prefix of longer length. To determine the percentage of IPv4 space that is BGP routable, we download BGP routing tables from Route Views [20], extract routing prefixes, and remove all overlapping prefixes that are contained by others. We illustrate in Fig. 1 how the utilization of IP space has evolved in the six-year period from 1997 to 2003.

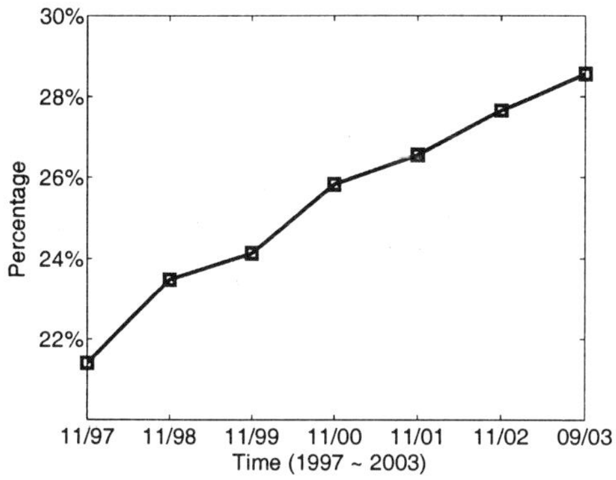

Figure 1. Percentage of BGP routable address space over the entire IPv4 space from 1997 to 2003 (data from Route Views project [20])

Although the number of computers connected to the Internet has increased greatly from 1997 to 2003, due to the usage of Classless Inter-Domain Routing (CIDR), Network Address Translation (NAT), and Dynamic Host Configuration Protocol (DHCP), the allocated routable IP space has not increased much. Fig. 1 shows that about 28.6% of IPv4 addresses are BGP routable on Sept. 2003. By including the information of BGP routing prefixes, a BGP routing worm can reduce its scanning space by 71.4% without ignoring any potential vulnerable computer.

3.2. /8 routing worm

BGP routing tables in September 2003 contain more than 140,000 prefixes. After removing overlapping prefixes, a BGP routing worm still needs to include about 62,000 prefixes. To avoid adding a big payload to a routing worm, attackers could possibly use IPv4 "/8" address allocation information instead of BGP routing prefixes.

The Internet Assigned Numbers Authority (IANA) provides public information about how "/8" prefix (x.0.0.0/8) of IPv4 has been assigned [12]. Each "/8" prefix contains 2^{24} IP addresses and there are 256 (2^8) "/8" prefixes in IPv4. By combining the IANA "/8" allocations with the information of BGP routing prefixes (BGP data from September 22, 2003), we find that 116 "/8" prefixes contain all BGP routable IP addresses. In other words, from an attacker's point of view, a worm does not need to waste its scans on IP addresses belonging to the other 140 "/8" prefixes.

A *"/8 routing worm"* is defined as an advanced worm that only scans those "/8" prefixes that contain BGP routable addresses. According to the BGP data from September 2003, a /8 routing worm only needs to scan 45.3% of IPv4 space by adding a small 116-byte prefix payload.

In fact, Code Red II [1] has already used part of IANA address allocations to reduce its scanning space: if an IP address generated by a Code Red II worm belongs to 127.0.0.0/8 (loopback addresses) or 224.0.0.0/4 (16 "/8" multicast addresses [12]), then the worm skips that address and generates a new address to scan. In this way, Code Red II scans 93.4% of the entire IPv4 space (239 out of 256 "/8" address space).

3.3. Routing worm based on prefix aggregation

A BGP routing worm scans a potentially smaller space than a /8 routing worm, but its routing prefix payload is much larger. In order to have a good trade-off between the size of the scanning IP space and the payload requirement for a routing worm, attackers could aggregate BGP routing prefixes. Here "aggregation" means that many BGP prefixes can be combined into one that has a shorter prefix length by adding the empty IP space between those original ones. In this way, the newly generated prefix covers all the IP space in those original prefixes. Through aggregation, a routing worm would need to scan a larger IP space but store fewer prefixes in its payload.

One simple aggregation method is to aggregate all prefixes that have prefix lengths longer than n to be "$/n$" prefixes ($8 \leq n \leq 32$), which can be called "$/n$ aggregation". If $n = 32$, no prefixes need to be aggregated and a BGP routing worm is derived; if $n = 8$, a /8 routing worm is derived.

Fig. 2 shows the aggregation impact on a routing worm's scanning space and prefix payload. For clarity, we only show the aggregation results from "/16" aggregation to "/8" aggregation in this figure. It shows that, as a routing worm aggregates more BGP prefixes together, it increases its scanning space while reducing the size of its payload. For example, if a routing worm uses "/16" aggregation, the worm increases the scanning space from the original 28.6% of a BGP routing worm to 30.9% of the IPv4 space, while reducing the prefix payload dramatically from the original 175KB to 24KB.

By using prefix aggregation, attackers have the freedom to choose a suitable "$/n$" aggregation according to their needs, or to the desired spreading properties of their routing worms.

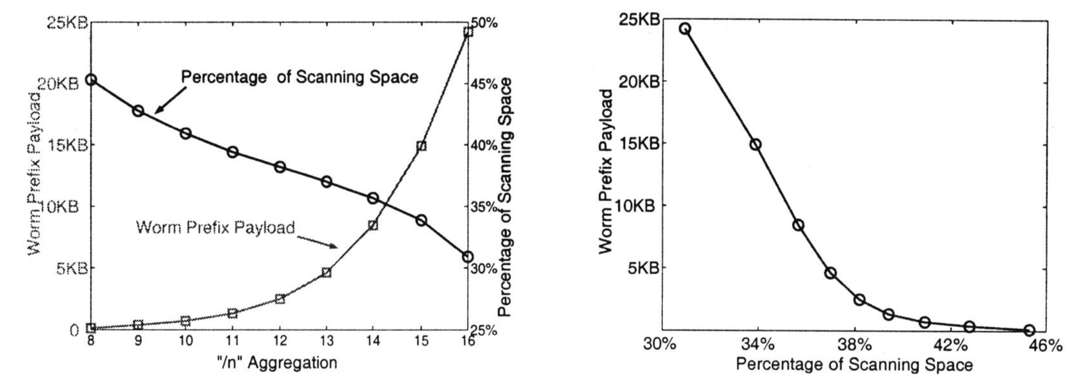

(a). "/n" aggregation ($n = 8 \sim 16$)

(b). Payload and scanning space trade-off

Figure 2. Prefix aggregation impact on a routing worm's scanning space and prefix payload (In the left-hand figure, the left Y-axis represents a routing worm's prefix payload; the right Y-axis represents the percentage of scanning space over the entire IPv4 address space. In the right-hand figure, each point from left to right represents "$/n$" aggregation where $n = 16, 15, \cdots, 8$, respectively.)

4. Routing Worm: A Selective Attack Worm

By considering IP address information, a routing worm not only increases its propagation speed, but also can use such information to conduct selective attacks, which is a more important property to attackers. "Selective attack" means that hackers or terrorists can selectively impose heavy damage to vulnerable computers in a specific country, company, ISP, or AS with little collateral damage done to others.

4.1. Selective attack based on IP geographic information

IANA provides limited information about who owns a "/8" network [12]. For example, 214.0.0.0/8 and 215.0.0.0/8 are allocated to the US Department of Defense; 56.0.0.0/8 is allocated to "US Postal Service"; 43.0.0.0/8 is allocated to "Japan Inet", etc [12]. Such information can be possibly used by attackers in their /8 routing worms.

Meanwhile, BGP routing tables provide detailed information about what Autonomous System (AS) owns a specific network prefix. Since many people have studied how to derive geographic information from BGP routing prefixes [6][5], hackers, revengers, or terrorists can use routing worms to conduct pinpoint heavy attacks to vulnerable computers in a specific country, company, ISP, or AS with little collateral damage to others.

Attackers can program a routing worm to exhibit different behaviors based on the location of the compromised computers. For example, if a compromised computer belongs to a specific country or company, the routing worm can impose heavy damage to this computer; otherwise, the compromised computer will be simply used as a stepping stone to scan and infect other vulnerable computers without being destroyed. For another example, attackers can program a routing worm to have a higher scanning preference for IP prefixes belonging to a specific target — this "target preference" scanning method is an extension of the "local preference" used by Code Red II [7].

4.2. Selective attack: a simple but general attacking idea

In fact, "selective attack" is a simple but very general attacking idea for any large-scale spreading virus or worm. Viruses or worms can use any information they can get from compromised computers to conduct selective attacks. Such information of a compromised computer includes the computer's IP address, time zones, Operating System, installed software, CPU, memory, network connection type and speed, etc. For example, a worm can selectively impose heavy damage on compromised computers if they have installed illegal Windows Operating Systems, or a specific peer-to-peer file sharing program, or video cards from a specific manufacturer.

Besides inflicting damage, attackers can also use the "selective attack" idea to improve a worm's spreading speed. For example, on any compromised computer, Code Red always generates 100 threads to scan and infect others simultaneously [16]. However, some compromised computers that have a small-size memory or a slow network connection cannot support those 100 threads without crash; on the other hand, many compromised computers that have powerful CPU, large memory, and high connection speed may be able to support thousands of threads generated by the worm. Therefore, attackers can program a worm to generate different number of scanning threads based on computer resources to speed up the worm's overall spreading speed.

In fact, a primitive selective attack has already been implemented by Code Red II — the worm generates 300 threads if a compromised computer runs non-Chinese Windows and 600 threads if the computer runs Chinese Windows [1].

5. Other Challenges from a Routing Worm

Besides its fast spreading speed and selective attack properties as explained in the above two sections, a routing worm imposes two additional challenges to the Internet and our defense systems. In this section, we discuss these two challenges in detail.

First, when an ordinary scanning worm is transformed into a routing worm, it may cause more severe congestion to the backbone of the Internet. Since about 70% of IPv4 space is not BGP routable, around 70% of scan packets sent out by an ordinary worm, which target IP space that is not Internet routable, will be quickly dropped at "default-free" routers[1] before entering the backbone links of the Internet. Thus a major part of worm scan traffic will not appear on the Internet backbone. On the other hand, all scans sent by a routing worm are BGP routable, and hence, will travel across the Internet backbone and reach the routers of the destination ASes or local networks. Therefore, a routing worm, especially a bandwidth-limited routing worm, will cause more severe congestion trouble to the Internet backbone than current scanning worms that scan the entire IPv4 space. For example, Slammer worm has caused severe congestion in many parts of the Internet [15]. If this worm writer had changed the worm code to be a routing worm, it would possibly have caused severe congestion to the entire Internet instead of just congestion in some local area networks.

Second, a routing worm makes it harder to quickly detect and then quarantine internal infected computers in an enterprise network. As explained in [22], in order to defend an enterprise network against a fast worm attack, the defense system of the enterprise network must be able to identify and then quarantine an internal infected computer as quickly as possible. One general detection method is to detect the abnormal level of illegal traffic sent out by an infected computer due to the random scans generated by a scanning worm [13][22][27]. For an ordinary worm that scans the entire IPv4 space, because a large percentage of the worm's random scans target non-routable address space, we can quickly detect an internal infected computer based on its outgoing connection destinations without waiting for the traffic response. On the other hand, for a routing worm infected computer, we have to wait a while for its traffic response (such as TCP timeout or ICMP error messages from routers) in order to detect its illegal traffic. For the defense of a fast spreading worm such as the Slammer worm, such a detection time difference might be critical for shutting down the worm infection process before it is too late.

1 A default-free router is a router that "actively decides where to send packets with a destination outside the AS to which the router belongs, and not forward it, by default, to another router" [2].

6. Routing Worm Propagation Modeling and Analysis

In our previous paper [31], we have presented a uniform-scan worm model that is described by worm propagation parameters:

$$\frac{dI_t}{dt} = \frac{\eta}{\Omega} I_t(N - I_t) \quad (1)$$

where I_t is the number of infected hosts at time t; N is the total number of vulnerable hosts in the system before the worm spreads out. At $t = 0$, I_0 hosts are infected and the remaining $N - I_0$ hosts are vulnerable. η is the worm's average scan rate and Ω is the size of the worm's scanning space.

If a routing worm uniformly scans its scanning space and has the same average scan rate as a traditional uniform-scan worm, then according to (1), a routing worm will propagate faster due to its smaller scanning space Ω. To show how much faster a routing worm can propagate, we use Code Red as the example of a traditional worm, which has a scan rate $\eta = 358$ per minute and a vulnerable population $N = 360,000$ [29]. We assume that there are $I_0 = 10$ initially infected hosts. Fig. 3(a) shows the numbers of infected hosts I_t of the Code Red worm, a /8 routing worm, and a BGP routing worm as functions of time t, respectively. It shows that by using IP routing information, routing worms clearly increase their spreading speed.

Staniford *et al.* [23] introduce a "hit-list" worm that has an address list of a large number of vulnerable hosts in the Internet. Since a hit-list worm can infect all vulnerable hosts in its hit-list within a few seconds [23], we ignore this hit-list infection time and assume that a hit-list worm begins to propagate with a large number of initially infected hosts where I_0 equals to the size of the hit-list. When a hit-list worm uniformly scans the Internet after its hit-list scanning phase, its propagation can be modelled by (1) with $\Omega = 2^{32}$.

To study the propagation differences between a hit-list worm and routing worms, Fig. 3(b) compares a BGP routing worm, a /8 routing worm, with a hit-list worm that has a hit-list of $10,000$ vulnerable hosts and the same scan rate $\eta = 358$/min as Code Red. This figure shows that the hit-

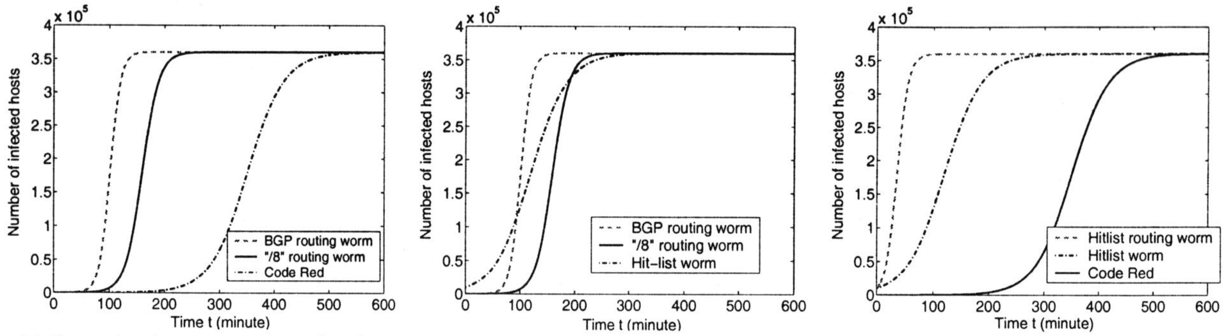

(a). Comparison between two types of routing worms and Code Red

(b). Comparison between two types of routing worms and a hit-list worm

(c). Comparison between a hit-list routing worm, a hit-list worm, and Code Red

Figure 3. Worm propagation comparisons

list worm can infect a larger number of hosts in a short time, but its infection growth rate is smaller than routing worms.

A hit-list worm and a routing worm try to improve their spreading speed through two different approaches. These two approaches do not conflict with each other and can be easily combined together to generate a new worm, called a "hit-list routing" worm, that has both a large number of initially infected hosts and a fast propagation speed. Fig. 3(c) shows the propagation of a hit-list routing worm, which has a 10,000 hit-list and the BGP routing prefixes. Compared with a traditional worm and an ordinary hit-list worm, the hit-list routing worm spreads out much faster.

The famous *Warhol* worm presented in [23] is a hit-list worm that uses "permutation scan" instead of uniform scan. Permutation scan provides a form of coordination among infected hosts to avoid multiple scanning on the same IP addresses [23], which cannot be modeled by the uniform-scan worm model (1). Due to the coordination mechanism, Warhol worm propagates faster than a uniform-scan hit-list worm after most vulnerable hosts have been infected (as shown in Figure 3 in [25]). However, a routing worm and the original Code Red can also deploy the same permutation scan instead of uniform scan without any problem. If a routing worm and Code Red implement the same permutation scan as a Warhol worm, these three worms will have the similar propagation relationship as what shown in Fig. 3 (although the pattern of propagation curves will change slightly as shown in Figure 3 in [25]).

Authors in [23] also present a *flash* worm that contains IP addresses of all vulnerable hosts in the worm's hit list, which can infect all vulnerable computers in the Internet within tens of seconds [23]. However, it is very hard or impossible to collect up-to-date IP addresses of all vulnerable hosts in the global Internet, especially for the vulnerabilities of computers that do not advertise their addresses (such as SQL database servers attacked by Slammer, or the ISS security products attacked by Witty worm [21]). Therefore, flash worms exist in theory, not likely to be generated by attackers in an Internet scale attack (although it is possible for attackers to use a flash worm to attack a local area network).

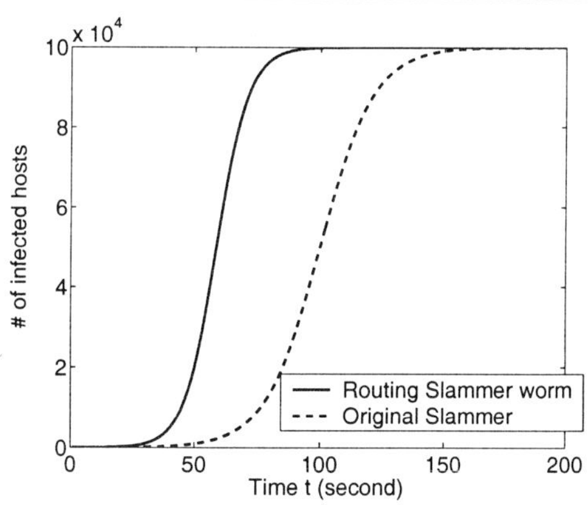

Figure 4. Worm propagation comparison of the original Slammer with the /8 routing worm transformed from Slammer

Due to its tiny payload requirement, a "/8 routing worm" might be used by attackers in their future bandwidth-limited worms. A "bandwidth-limited worm" is a worm that fully uses the link bandwidth of an infected host to send out infection traffic. For example, SQL Slammer is a bandwidth-limited worm with an average scan rate $\eta = 4000$ scans/second [15]. Because Slammer is a UDP-based worm that puts the complete worm code into one single UDP packet, the BGP routing worm idea is not realistic for this worm. Each UDP infection packet sent out by Slammer is 404 bytes [15]. if the worm author transformed Slammer into a /8 routing worm, which is called a "routing Slammer worm", the

UDP infection packet would be 520 bytes (by adding a 116-byte prefix payload). After transforming into a /8 routing worm, the routing Slammer worm would have an average scan rate $\eta = 4000 \times 404/520 = 3108$ scans/second. Fig. 4 shows the worm propagation of the original Slammer and the new routing Slammer worm as functions of time (the other parameters are $N = 100,000$, $I(0) = 10$, the same as what used in [29]).

7. Defense Against Routing Worms: Upgrading IPv4 to IPv6

It is very hard to prevent attackers from generating a routing worm due to the following two reasons: (1) both IANA "/8" allocations and BGP routing tables are public available information that are difficult or impossible to hide from attackers; and (2) a routing worm is very easy for attackers to implement, much easier than the hit-list worm presented in [23]. Once attackers obtain BGP routing prefixes, they can use the same BGP data for all scanning worms to attack various vulnerabilities. On the other hand, to program a hit-list worm, attackers need to put effort to collect a hit-list of vulnerable computers and have to repeat such work for different vulnerabilities. Such a hit-list is especially hard to collect for vulnerable hosts that do not advertise their addresses (e.g., Windows SQL servers attacked by Slammer). Because of the real threat coming from routing worms, we must find a way to prevent a routing worm from quickly spreading out.

A routing worm increases its propagation speed by reducing its scanning space. Fig. 3 shows how much faster a routing worm can propagate when the worm reduces its scanning space by only half to two thirds. Therefore, if we use the same principle to dramatically increase a worm's scanning space, we can significantly slow its propagation speed. For this reason, we believe that an effective defense against routing worms and all scanning worms is to upgrade the current IPv4 Internet to IPv6 — the vast address space of IPv6 (its BGP table does not reveal address information of networks with less than 2^{64} IP addresses) can prevent a worm from spreading through scanning.

IPv6 has dramatically increased IP space from 32-bit addresses to 128-bit addresses. Because of this huge IP address space, IPv6 implements a hierarchical addressing theme where the smallest network has 2^{64} IP addresses (with prefix /64) [10][11]. In other words, the smallest network in IPv6 BGP routing tables contains the number of IP addresses equal to that of *4 billion* IPv4 Internet.

Some people might think that allocating such a big address space for a smallest network wastes too much IP resource. Actually, it does not. Suppose there are *1000 billion* people on earth, then on average each person can own 2.3 million the smallest networks (/64) mentioned above for unicast usage.

Attackers can still use BGP routing tables to program a routing worm. However, they cannot know address allocation information inside any /64 network from BGP routing tables since the longest prefix in BGP routing table is /64. A local network might uses smaller address space for address allocation internally, but such local address allocation information will not show up in BGP routing table. Such local address allocation is confidential to the local network administrators that attackers cannot know without port-scanning beforehand.

Even one single /64 network in IPv6 will have sufficient IP space to defeat scanning worms. Suppose there are $N = 1,000,000$ vulnerable hosts in one single /64 network and a worm has a scan rate $\eta = 100,000$/second with $I_0 = 1000$ initially infected hosts. If the worm only scans and infects hosts in this /64 network, then $\Omega = 2^{64}$. Based on (1), the worm will need to spend *40 years* to infect half of the vulnerable hosts in this single /64 network.

Of course, upgrading IPv4 to IPv6 is not the omnipotent solution for defending all kinds of worm attacks. It is only useful for defending worms that find victims by random scanning, such as Code Red, Slammer, Blaster, Sasser and Witty worm. In addition, IPv6 is still a controversial issue and there are many important economic and technical details to be solved before we can upgrade the current IPv4 to IPv6.

8. Conclusions

In this paper, we present a new advanced scanning worm called "*routing worm*". Based on BGP routing prefix information, a routing worm not only propagates faster, but also is able to conduct pinpoint selective attacks to specific country, company, ISP or AS. Because of the inherent publicity of BGP routing tables, attackers can easily deploy routing worms in the future. Compared to a traditional worm, a routing worm could possibly cause more severe congestion trouble to the Internet backbone, and makes it harder to quickly detect infected computers. An effective way to defend against routing worms and all scanning worms is to upgrade the current IPv4 to IPv6, although such an upgrade will require a tremendous effort and is still argued by many people.

Acknowledgements

This work was supported in part by ARO contract DAAD19-01-1-0610, NSF Grant EEC-0313747, EIA-0080119, ANI-0085848 and CNS-0325868.

References

[1] eEye digital security: CodeRedII worm analysis. http://www.eeye.com/html/Research/Advisories/AL20010804.html, 2001.

[2] A. Antony and H. Uijterwaal. Routing information service R.I.S. design note. http://www.ripe.net/projects/ris/Notes/ripe-200/, 1999.

[3] H. Braun. BGP-system usage of 32 bit Internet address space. http://moat.nlanr.net/IPaddrocc, November 1997.

[4] CAIDA. IPv4 address space utilization. http://www.caida.org/outreach/resources/learn/ipv4space, 1998.

[5] CAIDA. IPv4 BGP geopolitical analysis. http://www.caida.org/analysis/geopolitical/bgp2country, 2003.

[6] CAIDA. Visualizing Internet topology at a macroscopic scale. http://www.caida.org/analysis/topology/as_core_network, 2003.

[7] CERT. CERT/CC advisories. http://www.cert.org/advisories/.

[8] Z. Chen, L. Gao, and K. Kwiat. Modeling the spread of active worms. In *Proceedings of the IEEE INFOCOM*, March 2003.

[9] Akamai service: EdgeScape. http://www.akamai.com/en/html/services/edgescape.html.

[10] R. Hinden and S. Deering. RFC-3513: Internet protocol version 6 (IPv6) addressing architecture. April 2003.

[11] R. Hinden, S. Deering, and E. Nordmark. RFC-3587: IPv6 global unicast address format. August 2003.

[12] IANA. Reserved IPv4 addresses. http://www.cidr-report.org/v6/reserved-ipv4.html, January 2004.

[13] J. Jung, S. E. Schechter, and A. W. Berger. Fast detection of scanning worm infections. In *Proceedings of the 7th International Symposium on Recent Advances in Intrusion Detection (RAID)*, September 2004.

[14] G. Kesidis, I. Hamadeh, and S. Jiwasurat. Coupled kermack-mckendrick models for randomly scanning and bandwidth-saturating internet worms. In *Proceedings of 3rd International Workshop on QoS in Multiservice IP Networks (QoS-IP*, Feburary 2005.

[15] D. Moore, V. Paxson, S. Savage, C. Shannon, S. Staniford, and N. Weaver. Inside the Slammer worm. *IEEE Magazine on Security and Privacy*, 1(4), July 2003.

[16] D. Moore, C. Shannon, and J. Brown. Code-Red: a case study on the spread and victims of an Internet worm. In *Proceedings of the second ACM SIGCOMM Workshop on Internet Measurement*, November 2002.

[17] Net world map project: IP address locator tool. http://www.geobytes.com/IpLocator.htm?GetLocation.

[18] D. Nicol and M. Liljenstam. Models of Internet worm defense. IMA Workshop 4: Measurement, Modeling and Analysis of the Internet. http://www.ima.umn.edu/talks/workshops/1-12-16.2004/nicol/talk.pdf, January 2004.

[19] RIPE NCC routing information service. http://www.ripe.net/ris.

[20] University of Oregon route views project. http://www.routeviews.org.

[21] C. Shannon and D. Moore. The spread of the Witty worm. http://www.caida.org/analysis/security/witty/, March 2004.

[22] S. Staniford. Containment of scanning worms in enterprise networks. *Journal of Computer Security*, 2003.

[23] S. Staniford, V. Paxson, and N.Weaver. How to own the Internet in your spare time. In *Proceedings of USENIX Security Symposium*, August 2002.

[24] M. H. Warfield. Security implications of IPv6. Internet Security Systems, Inc. White Paper, 2003.

[25] N. Weaver. Warhol worms: The potential for very fast Internet plagues. http://www.cs.berkeley.edu/~nweaver/warhol.html, 2001.

[26] N. Weaver, V. Paxson, S. Staniford, and R. Cunningham. A taxonomy of computer worms. In *Proceedings of ACM CCS Workshop on Rapid Malcode (WORM'03)*, October 2003.

[27] N. Weaver, S. Staniford, and V. Paxson. Very fast containment of scanning worms. In *Proceedings of 13th USENIX Security Symposium*, August 2004.

[28] J. Wu, S. Vangala, L. Gao, and K. Kwiat. An efficient architecture and algorithm for detecting worms with various scan techniques. In *Proceedings of the 11th Annual Network and Distributed System Security Symposium (NDSS'04)*, February 2004.

[29] C. C. Zou, L. Gao, W. Gong, and D. Towsley. Monitoring and early warning for Internet worms. In *Proceedings of 10th ACM Conference on Computer and Communications Security (CCS'03)*, October 2003.

[30] C. C. Zou, W. Gong, and D. Towsley. Code Red worm propagation modeling and analysis. In *Proceedings of 9th ACM Conference on Computer and Communications Security (CCS'02)*, October 2002.

[31] C. C. Zou, D. Towsley, and W. Gong. On the performance of Internet worm scanning strategies. Technical Report TR-03-CSE-07, Umass ECE Dept., November 2003.

REQUIREMENTS ON WORM MITIGATION TECHNOLOGIES IN MANETS

Robert G. Cole and Nam Phamdo*
JHU Applied Physics Laboratory
{robert.cole,nam.phamdo}@jhuapl.edu

Moheeb A. Rajab and Andreas Terzis†
Johns Hopkins University
{moheeb,terzis}@cs.jhu.edu

Abstract

This study presents an analysis of the impact of mitigation on computer worm propagation in Mobile Ad-hoc Networks (MANETS). According to the recent DARPA BAA - Defense Against Cyber Attacks on MANETS *[4], "One of the most severe cyber threats is expected to be worms with arbitrary payload that can infect and saturate MANET-based networks on the order of seconds". Critical to the design of effective worm counter measures in MANET environments is an understanding of the propagation mechanisms and the performance of the mitigation technologies. This work aims to advance the security of these critical systems through increased knowledge of propagation mechanisms, performance and the effect of mitigation technologies. We present both analytic and simulation analysis of mitigation effectiveness. The ultimate goal of these studies is to develop an accurate set of performance requirements on mitigation techniques to minimize worm propagation in tactical, battlefield MANETS.*

1. Introduction

The Defense Advanced Research Program Agency (DARPA) believes that computer worms present a severe security threat against tactical, battlefield Mobile Ad Hoc Networks (MANETS). There is much emphasis within the recently released DARPA Broad Agency Announcement on Digital Cyber-Attacks in MANETS [4] on computer worm propagation, mitigation and isolation. For this reason we have initiated a program to study computer worm propagation and mitigation in tactical, battlefield MANETS. In this paper, we extend previous work [3] by investigating the effectiveness of mitigation technologies in military MANETs. The primary goal of this research effort is the generation of a set of performance requirements on mitigation technologies in order to ensure their success in tactical, battlefield MANETS. This objective drives some of the modeling parameters we choose to investigate in this study. We present both analytic and computer simulation studies of mitigation effectiveness in minimizing the spread of the computer worm under a variety of conditions. We study the effects of mitigation response time, nodal mobility and channel congestion on the final state of the worm propagation.

Our initial studies in [3] investigated the impact of communications and mobility effects on worm propagation mechanisms in MANETS. There we found that network delays and channel congestions had a large impact on the worm propagation effects. We also found that a set of relatively simple analytic models reproduced these communications effects quite well. In this paper, we extend our previous work by focusing on the impact of mitigation on worm propagation in MANETS under various network conditions. We also present a simple analytic model of mitigation, discuss its predictions and compare these to simulation results. Our main results in this paper are:

- There are network conditions, i.e., channel congestion, under which mitigation technologies can actually promote the spread of infection by reducing competition between probes on common communications channels.
- Our simple analytic model of mitigation does a reasonable job of estimating the steady state infection probability when compared to our simulation results and may eventually be useful in developing engineering tools for the design of mitigation techniques.
- The analytic model of mitigation has some rather interesting properties: a) it has multiple stationary state solutions, one $c(\infty) = 1$ and $c(\infty) < 1$ where $c(t)$ is the probability of infection by time t, b) a critical $c(0)$ exists, $c_c(0)$, for which $c(0) < c_c(0)$ implies that $c(\infty) = c_c(\infty) < 1$ independent of $c(0)$, while $c(0) > c_c(0)$ implies that $c(\infty) > c_c(\infty) < 1$ which monotonically increases as $c(0)$ increases.

* Power Projection Systems Department, 11000 Johns Hopkins Road., Laurel, Maryland 20723.
† Computer Science Department, 3400 N. Charles Street, Baltimore, Maryland 21218.

1087-4097/05 $20.00 © 2005 IEEE

The rest of this paper is organized as follows. Section 2 provides a brief overview of previous work related to our studies within this paper. Section 3 provides an analysis of the Standard Epidemic Model, discusses its assumptions and relationship to worm propagation in communications networks. This section also analyzes our simple analytic model of mitigation. Simulation studies are then presented in Section 4, followed by a brief discussion on mitigation in Section 5. We end the paper with conclusions.

2. Previous Studies

Previous studies have analyzed and modeled the propagation of computer worms in digital communications networks. [13] provides an extensive investigation into the mechanisms of worm propagation and their performance, addressing specifically the Code Red I and II worms as well as the Nimda worm. They also provide an interesting discussion on potential strategies to build better worms and efforts necessary to mitigate worm propagation throughout the Internet. [6] and [7] provide an investigation of the Code Red worms propagating through the Internet. Relevant to our work, they provide an interesting discussion and analysis of performance requirements on several mitigation technologies through simulation studies of Internet-like networks.

[16] provides an excellent analysis of mathematical models of worm propagation through the Internet. Notably, they discuss the Kermack-Mckendrick model for the removal of infected nodes from the system. They also propose a heuristic expression for inter-worm competition for Internet bandwidth and develop a "Two Factor Worm Model" for their studies.

[14] addresses the issues of finite propagation times and infected node removal (or death) on propagation rates. They provide both analytic models and simulation results of these effects for Internet-like environments. [12] provides a thorough literature review of worm propagation models and studies. Interestingly, they also review various models of mitigation techniques of computer worm propagation.

[10] presents an analysis and simulation study of the performance of a novel, distributed mitigation technology referred to as *Network Telescopes*. This study demonstrates the value of this distributed and collaborative technique for rapid identification of worm infection and its role in mitigation. [11] investigates, through analysis and simulation, the impact of the non-uniform distribution of nodes within the Internet.

3. Analytic Models

In this section we discuss a relatively simple analytical model of worm propagation and mitigation in computer networks. We draw upon previous models, but derive simplified forms while maintaining their critical aspects. Our hope being to encourage the development of explicit solutions useful to engineers in future studies.

The standard analytic model used in the literature to analyze worm propagation in computer networks is the Standard Epidemic Model, see, e.g., [1]),

$$\frac{dI(t)}{dt} = \beta I(t)[N - I(t)]/N \tag{1}$$

where N is the total size of the susceptible population, $I(t)$ is the number of infected nodes at time t, and β is the rate at which a given infected node probes the total, susceptible population of nodes.

Key assumptions in the derivation of the Standard Epidemic Model applied to worm propagation in computer networks are:

- *Uniform Medium* - all nodes, their nature and distribution, are assumed equivalent. In the MANET environments we focus on here, this is true. However, details of the nodal distribution and non-uniformity can have a large impact on the nature of the worm propagation and counter measures to prevent its spread, see, e.g., [11].
- *Action at a Distance* - as soon as an infected probe is queued for transmission to another host, it is immediately received by that host. This implies that all hosts always have routes established to all other hosts and hence there exists no time required for the route discovery process. It also implies that there exists no queuing, transmission or propagation delays within typical, bandwidth constrained, tactical, battlefield MANETS. This effect can be significant in MANETS.
- *Independent Infection Agents* - there exists no interaction between the infection probes propagating through the infection media, i.e., the communication network. In networks, and prominently in MANETS, this ignores two effects, a) sharing access to a common radio channel and b) probe losses due to overloading the limited bandwidth and finite sized communication buffers. These effects can be quite large in MANETS.
- *Zero Death Rate* - once a node is infected it never dies or gets cured. Instead, it is forever infected and generating infection probe packets. This assumption is related to the modeling of mitigation mechanisms within the MANETS and to the determination of their effectiveness in protecting the network nodes.
- *No Incubation Period* - as soon as the infection probe packet reaches the susceptible computer hosts, it can immediately begin transmitting infection probes to the

other hosts. This may be significant in modeling stealth worms.

The Standard Epidemic Model is derived from the following difference equation,

$$I(t+\Delta t) \approx I(t) + \beta I(t)\Delta t[N - I(t)]/N + O((\Delta t)^2) \quad (2)$$

where $O((\Delta t)^2)$ represents terms of order $(\Delta t)^2$. Here, $\beta I(t)\Delta t$ is the effective number of probes which are sent into the target network and $[N - I(t)]/N$ represents the probability that a probe encounters a susceptible, non-infected node. In the limit that $\Delta t \to 0$, dividing through by Δt, we get

$$\frac{dI(t)}{dt} = \beta I(t)[N - I(t)]/N \quad (3)$$

Defining the probability of infection as $i(t) = I(t)/N$, we rewrite the equation as

$$\frac{di(t)}{dt} = \beta i(t)[1 - i(t)] \quad (4)$$

An explicit solution to the Epidemic Model, obtained by factoring and integration, is given by

$$i(t) = \frac{e^{\beta(t-T)}}{1 + e^{\beta(t-T)}} \quad (5)$$

where T is determined by the initial condition $i(t = 0)$.

Typically, β is written as

$$\beta = \beta_0(\frac{N}{2^{32}}) \quad (6)$$

where β_0 represents the rate at which an individual, infected node probes for other nodes and $N/2^{32}$ represents the likelihood that a randomly chosen 32-bit IPv4 address is a susceptible node. Other strategies are employed and modeled accordingly through appropriate definitions of β. In order to concentrate on those aspects unique to MANET networks, we assume that the infected worms only generate probes to nodes within the MANET. In this case, β will be set to the rate at which an individual infected node generates and transmits probes. This represents a worse case strategy from the perspective of generating performance requirements on mitigation techniques and assumes that the worms will have access to a table of nodes comprising the MANET. However, it is somewhat artificial in the sense that the infected nodes choose from the table of nodes randomly. Clearly, additional node selection strategies should be the subject of future investigations.

The Kermack-Mckendrick model [5] addresses the issue of the removal process of infected nodes. In the context of computer worm propagation, [16] applied the Kermack-Mckendrick model in their study of the Code Red worm. This extension to the Standard Epidemic Model addresses

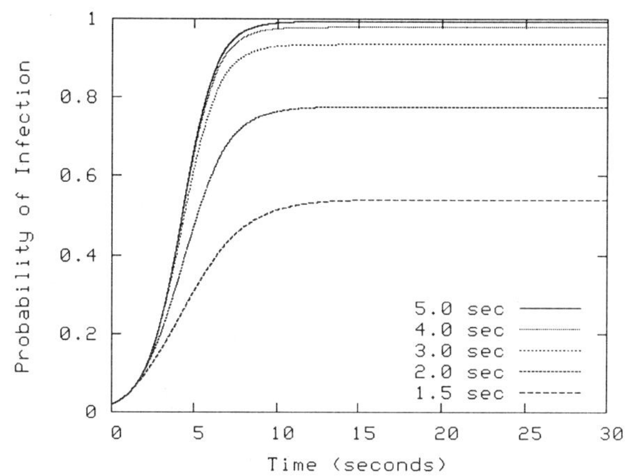

Figure 1. The baseline MANET worm propagation results in the presence of a mitigation technology.

the *Infinite Lifetime* assumption discussed above and is important in the context of our mitigation technology discussion below. We can derive a relatively simple analytic model of the performance of mitigation technologies as follows. Let $c(t)$ be the probability that a host has been infected by the worm by time t. This represents both the probability of hosts currently infected, $i(t)$, and the probability of hosts either quarantined or rehabilitated (and no longer susceptible to further infection), $r(t)$. Let us assume a simple model of the mitigation technology, i.e., that it takes a fixed amount of time, δ, for the mitigation response to act on the infected hosts. Then, following the same argument to derive the Standard Epidemic model above, we get

$$(t < \delta) \quad \frac{dc(t)}{dt} = \beta c(t)[1 - c(t)] \quad (7)$$

$$(t > \delta) \quad \frac{dc(t)}{dt} = \beta(c(t) - c(t-\delta))[1 - c(t)] \quad (8)$$

Note, this equation can also be derived from the more complex "Two Factor Worm Model" found in [16], by substituting $c(t) = i(t) + r(t)$. Further, given that infected nodes older than δ seconds are rehabilitated, then $r(t) = c(t - \delta)$. Finally, we implicitly assume that $c(0)$ consists of newly infected nodes, i.e., $c(0) = i(0)$. The expression in Eq.(8) modifies the Standard Epidemic model above by arguing that the total probe rate within the network is modified by the removal of the nodes which had been infected prior to $t - \delta$ seconds ago.

This equation is written for two separate time regimes due to the discontinuity in the slope of $c(t)$ at $t = \delta$,

$$\lim_{\varepsilon \to 0} \frac{dc(\delta+\varepsilon)}{dt} - \frac{dc(\delta-\varepsilon)}{dt} = -\beta c(0)[1 - c(\delta)] \quad (9)$$

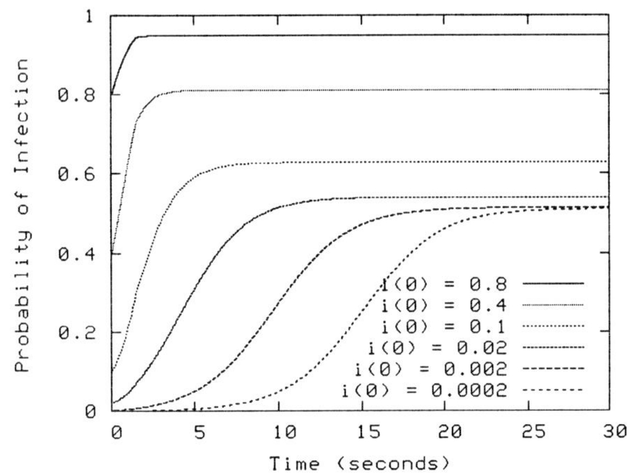

Figure 2. The effects of initial conditions on the final system state - 1.5 second mitigation response time.

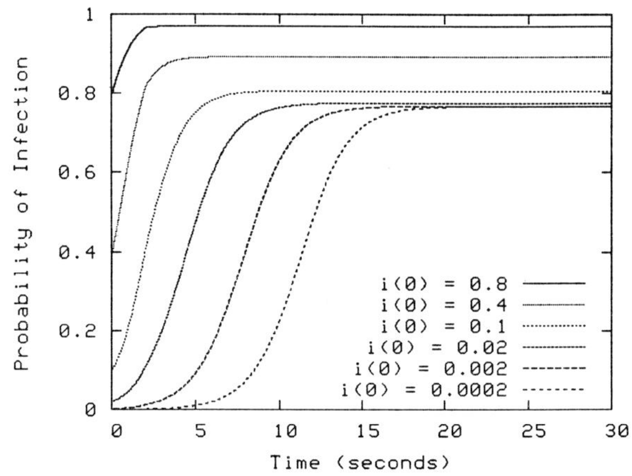

Figure 3. The effects of initial conditions on the final system state - 2.0 second mitigation response time.

The value of analytic models of relative simplicity is the explanation of the system dynamics which they afford. The steady state ($t \longrightarrow \infty$) solution to the Standard Epidemic Model is $i(\infty) = 1$, which is apparent from Eq.(1) by setting the RHS of the equation to 0 yielding $1 - i(\infty) = 0$. The mitigation equation above affords the same solution for $c(\infty)$. The interesting question is whether the mitigation equation affords other steady state solutions as well. If we perform a Taylor Series expansion of $c(t - \delta)$ in Eq.(7) in terms of $c(t)$, we get

$$\frac{dc(t)}{dt} = \beta(\delta \frac{dc(t)}{dt})[1 - c(t)] \tag{10}$$

Canceling the derivatives on both side of this expression yields

$$c(\infty) = 1 - (\beta\delta)^{-1} \tag{11}$$

Therefore, we suspect that there exist steady state solutions to Eq.(7) where $c(\infty)$ is less than unity, implying that the mitigation technology was effective in stopping the spread of the infection before the entire population was affected. Further, the faster the mitigation technology in detecting a infected node, the more effective the technology in limiting the final infection probability.

In Figure 3 we show the results of a numerical integration of Eq.(7). Here, we set $c(0) = 0.01$ and use 10,000 integration points over the range of the plot. We see that indeed there are steady state solutions where $c(\infty) < 1$ and that the final value of $c(\infty)$ decreases as the value of δ decreases.

In Figures 2 and 3 we show the results of varying the initial conditions on the final steady state solution. These plots exhibit some interesting behavior. For small values of $c(0)$, i.e., $c(0) < c_c(0)$, the steady state solution is independent of the initial condition. However, for larger initial conditions, i.e., $c(0) > c_c(0)$, the steady state solution uniformly increases with larger initial conditions until finally the steady state solution of $c(\infty) = 1$ is approached. Based upon this behavior, we know that our simple expression in Eq.(11) is wrong, as it is independent upon initial conditions. We know this not to be the case from these figures. Further, if we try to interpret Eq.(11) as $c_c(\infty)$, we see from Table 1, that it does not well represent this value either. In Table 2, we investigate the impact of integration step sizes in determining $c_c(\infty)$. From these results, we are confident that the numerical integration results are correct. It remains an open area of investigation as to why the Taylor Series expansion of $c(t)$ fails to find the correct steady state.

Table 1. Numerical tests for $c_c(\infty)$.

δ	No. Int. Pts.	$c(0)$	$c_c(\infty)$
1.5	$2x10^5$	$2x10^{-12}$	0.51
2.0	$2x10^5$	$2x10^{-12}$	0.77
3.0	$2x10^5$	$2x10^{-12}$	0.93
4.0	$2x10^5$	$2x10^{-12}$	0.98
5.0	$2x10^5$	$2x10^{-12}$	0.99

Table 2. Numerical tests in search of $c_c(\infty)$.

δ	No. Int. Pts.	$c(0)$	$c_c(\infty)$
1.5	$2x10^5$	0.04	0.57
1.5	$2x10^5$	0.02	0.54
1.5	$2x10^5$	0.002	0.51
1.5	$2x10^5$	$2x10^{-4}$	0.51
1.5	$2x10^5$	$2x10^{-8}$	0.51
1.5	$2x10^5$	$2x10^{-12}$	0.51
1.5	$2x10^7$	$2x10^{-12}$	0.51

4. Simulation Studies

We present a comparison of the above model to a set of mitigation simulation studies. The NS2 simulation tool [8] was used to simulate the spread of the worm infection throughout a MANET. The version 2.27 of NS2 already contained an application which simulated the spread of a computer worm. We modified the NS2 application in order to a) simulate an isolated MANET, b) allow us to plant the initial infection seed at random in the MANET at time zero and c) allow us to define a fixed, finite lifetime to an infected node (which dies at a lifetime of δ).

Because the dynamics specific to a MANET are of interest, we simplified the simulation and analysis in the following ways:

- Simple Worm Model - we assume the worm propagates through the transmission of a single UDP packet of size P. We simulate the effects of bandwidth competition by varying the channel bandwidth while holding the size of the infection data constant.
- MANET Aware Model - the worm chooses nodes at random to infect, but only targets nodes within the MANET. We wanted to focus this study on MANET specific issues, without the added complexity of modeling and simulating on-MANET versus off-MANET probe traffic.
- Modified Random WayPoint Mobility Model - we assume that the nodes move independent of one another according to the Random WayPoint model, modified in order to address the concerns raised in [15]. Other, more realistic, mobility models will be studied in the future, see, e.g. [2].
- AODV Routing Protocol - the NS2 simulation tool supports a number of MANET routing protocols. For our initial studies we choose the AODV routing protocol [9]. Future studies will include other routing protocols.

Table 3. Baseline case parameter definitions.

Parameter Description	Range	Base Case
Number of Hosts	50	50
Address Block Search	50	50
Transmission Rate (Mbps)	0.1 - 2.0	2.0
Transmission Range (m)	250	250
Topographic Range (m^2)	1000^2	1000^2
Nodal Mobility (mps)	1 - 10	1
Routing Protocol	AODV	AODV
Probe Size (bytes)	400	400
Probe Rate (probes/sec)	1	1

- 802.11 MAC and Physical Layer - The NS2 simulation tool provides models of the 802.11 MAC and Physical layer protocols. Further, we utilized the NS2 Two Ray radio propagation model with an effective transmission range of 250 meters.

The parameters in Table 3 define our Baseline MANET simulation model.

Several simulations of the Baseline Case were conducted for δ values of 1.5, 2.0, 3.0, 4.0 and 5.0 seconds. For each set of conditions, we ran thirty independent simulation runs and averaged their results. These averaged results are presented in Figure 4. These simulation results show the same qualitative behavior as shown in the numerical results of Figure 3. We see that the impact of a mitigation technology applied to this environment is negligible for response times, i.e., δ's, larger than 3 seconds. Remember that we have assumed a focused search strategy for our infection agents and that the probe rate per infected node, i.e., β, is unity. In Figure 5 we overlay the model predictions from Figure 3 onto the simulation results from Figure 4. The model seems to do a reasonable job in predicting the steady state value for the infection probability for values of δ equal to 2 seconds and higher. However, for the case of $\delta = 1.5$ seconds, the model over estimates the steady state value of the infection probability.

We know from our discussion of the Standard Epidemic Model in the Section 3, that Eq.(7) is an extremely simplified model within the context of its application to MANET environments. In [3] we explicitly discussed the impact of the various assumptions inherent to the Standard Epidemic Model and analyzed the effectiveness on enhanced models incorporating the effects of network delays and bandwidth competition on worm propagation. As an example, in Figure 6 we modeled the impact finite network delays using Eq.(6) from [3]. Here we set $\delta = 2$ seconds and varied the network delays, ranging from 0 seconds (implicitly assumed previously in this paper) to 0.5 seconds. We see that

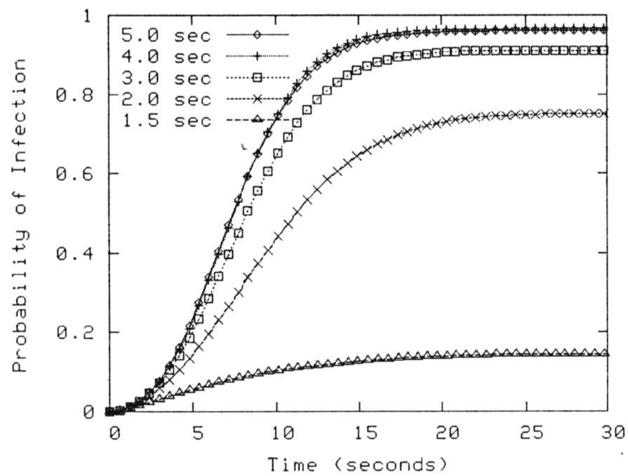

Figure 4. The results from the simulation studies of the MANET.

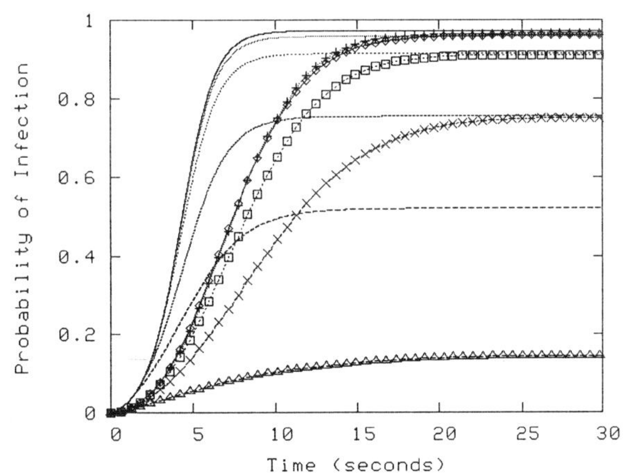

Figure 5. Overlay of the analytic model results on the simulation results.

the finite network delay slows the initial spread of the worm due to the finite delays in time between an infected node sending out an infection probe and an infected node receiving the probe. This propagation delay reduces the resultant overall infection probability. Other effects impact the longer term behavior of the worm propagation, e.g., mobility and bandwidth competition.

In Figure 7 we investigate the impact of nodal mobility. Our baseline case set the nodal mobility to 1.0 meters per second (mps). The mobility model used is the Random Way Point model modified according to the discussion found in

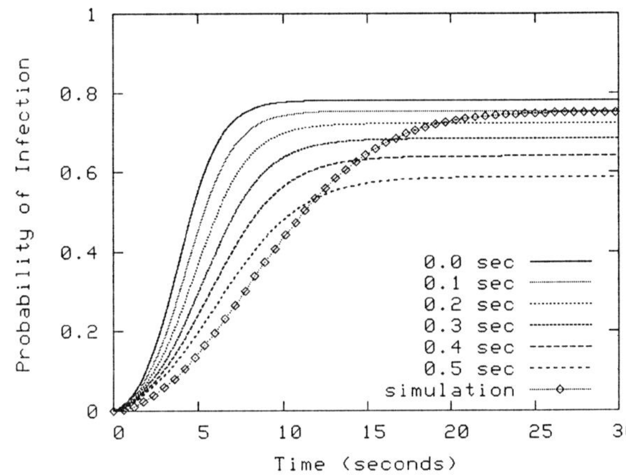

Figure 6. Effects of network delay on worm infection results.

[15]. We present simulation results for mobilities ranging from a low of 1.0 mps to a high of 10.0 mps. Here we set the mitigation response time to 2.0 seconds, which seems to be within the range of interesting effects for the baseline parameter set. The impact of mobility within the range investigated, seems to have little impact of the nature of the worm propagation. For low probabilities of infection, the curves are essentially indistinguishable. At high probabilities of infection, there may be some slight differences in $c(\infty)$ between the various mobilities, but not enough to see any clear relationship.

In Figure 8 we present results for channel bandwidth of 200 Kbps. We discussed the effects of competition between worm probes under conditions of limited bandwidth in the MANET in [3]. In this study, we choose to reduce the channel bandwidth 10 fold, from our baseline of 2.0 Mbps down to 200 Kbps. Our previous investigations showed this bandwidth to result in severe channel congestion due to the relatively high number of infection probes being injected into the network as the probability of infection grows. All other parameters are set to their baseline parameter set values. In this figure we vary the mitigation response time from a high of $\delta = 20$ seconds to a low of $\delta = 1.5$ seconds. From above, we expect that a mitigation response time greater than 5.0 seconds will have little impact on the final infection probability. From the figure we see little difference between the $\delta = 20.0$ and the $\delta = 5.0$ seconds behavior; perhaps the $\delta = 5.0$ seconds showing a slightly higher final infection probability as compared to the $\delta = 20.0$ seconds results. This trend continues as we reduce the mitigation response time down to a $\delta = 2.0$ seconds. Finally, when $\delta = 1.5$ seconds, the final probability of infection drops way down as

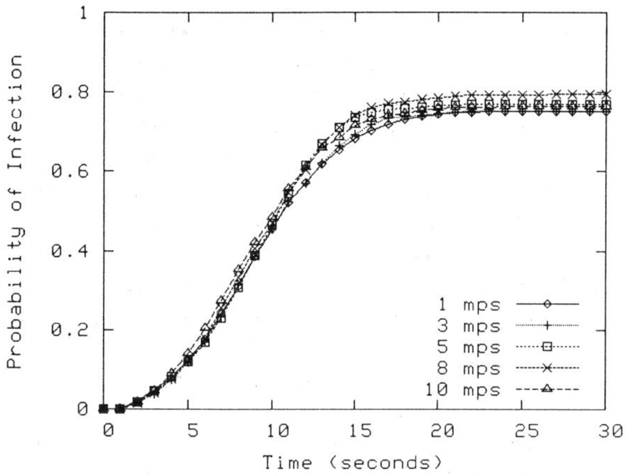

Figure 7. Effects of mobility on the performance of the mitigation technology.

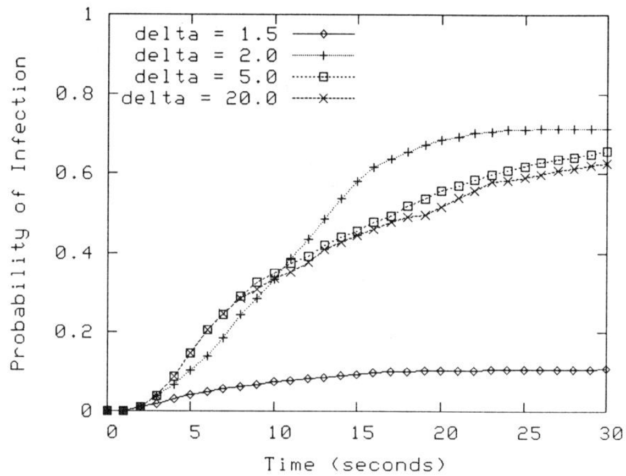

Figure 8. Effects of congestion on the performance of the mitigation technology.

we initially would expect. Therefore it seems that there is a range of δ's for which a mitigation technology may actually increase the performance of the worm propagation under conditions of channel congestion. This effect is similar to the situation in population dynamics where the presence of predation actual improves the health of the population. In our study, the predation is the mitigation technology and the population is the infected nodes. Future studies are necessary to a) better analyze the conditions under which this behavior occurs and b) develop analytic models for the prediction of this behavior.

5. Discussion of Mitigation Technologies in MANETS

Modeling investigations presented thus far have focused on greedy worm propagation mechanisms whereby the worms propagate at a high rate, eventually stressing the underlying communication infrastructure. In these situations, it is reasonable to expect that intrusion detection monitoring systems would detect the worm propagation traffic patterns and could be used to initiate some form of response, e.g., nodal quarantines, nodal patches, etc. However, as our discussion of impact of congestion on worm propagation rates above suggests, there may be conditions where the presence of a mitigation technology actually encourages the propagation of the worms by reducing channel congestion. More work is necessary to better understand this effect.

The above numerical model addresses only the mean behavior of the propagation. In order to derive meaningful requirements for mitigation technologies, we need to investigate the effectiveness of the mitigation technologies in keeping the worm infection probability below some value, say, 95 percent of the time. [7] studied this question in the context of the larger, wired Internet. They examined, through simulation of several potential mitigation technologies such as *Address Blacklisting* and *Content Filtering*, the spread of a computer virus through a large scale network. The focus of [7] was on the effectiveness of these mitigation technologies in reducing the worm infection versus the probing rate of the worm. They evaluated the effectiveness of these technologies in terms of various confidence levels.

Clearly this is the direction we need to take our studies in order to generate performance requirements on potential mitigation technologies. Figure 9 gives us an idea of the variability in the worm propagation in our baseline MANET by plotting out the individual histories from a set of 30 simulation runs. The parameters used for this set of runs were the *Baseline Case* with the $\delta = 4$ seconds. The mean value numerical models may not satisfy our needs to generate useful requirements on mitigation technologies. Our future investigations will require further simulation studies and perhaps the development of meaningful stochastic differential equations for worm propagation in computer networks.

6. Conclusions

We have presented a brief study of mitigation of computer worm propagation in MANETS. We investigate the validity of a simple mitigation model through simulation studies. Our simple model, however, is shown to have rather interesting behavior. We suspect that models of this type will be useful in developing engineering rules for design

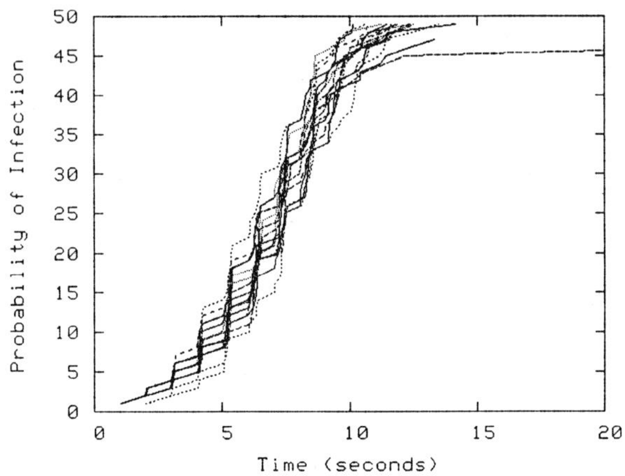

Figure 9. The individual state traces from the simulation study of the MANET with a mitigation response of 4 seconds.

and deployment of mitigation technologies. We discussed efforts to extract steady state solutions from this model. Clearly further work in this area is warranted. We compared the model predictions with simulations of an idealized mitigation technology in a MANET environment. The simplified analytical model of these environments predicted reasonably well the long term effectiveness of the mitigation technologies. Or simulation studies showed conditions under which the presence of mitigation actually aided the overall spread of the worm.

Our ultimate goal is to generate performance requirements on potential mitigation technologies in these MANET environments. We concluded this report with a brief discussion of the effectiveness of mitigation technologies and future investigations. Clearly, there is a subtle interplay between the worm agent, the mitigation technology and the communications infrastructure. More work is necessary to better understand these subtleties.

Acknowledgements

We would like to acknowledge Sue Lee of JHU/APL for suggesting this investigation and for her initial encouragement, beneficial discussions and a host of references on the topic. We also wish to acknowledge the support and encouragement of Don Duncan at JHU/APL.

References

[1] Bailey, N.T., *The Mathematical Theory of Infectious Diseases and it's Applications*, Hafner Press, New York, 1975.

[2] Camp, T., Boleng, J. and V. Davies, "A Survey of Mobility Models for Ad Hoc Network Research", *Wireless Communication and Mobile Computing (WCMC)*, vol. 2, no. 5, 2002.

[3] Cole, R.G., "Initial Studies of Worm Propagation in MANETs for Future Combat Systems", *The Army Science Conference 2004 (ASC2004), Orlando, FL, November 2004.*

[4] Ghosh, A.K., Technical POC, *Defense against Cyber Attacks on Mobile, Ad Hoc Network Systems (MANETS)*, BAA04-18 Proposer Information Pamphlet (PIP), Defense Advanced Research Projects Agency (DARPA) Advanced Technology Office (ATO), 16 April 2004.

[5] Frauenthal, J.C., *Mathematical Modeling in Epidemiology*, Springer-Verlag, New York, 1980.

[6] Moore, D. and C. Shannon, "Code-Red: a Case Study on the Spread and Victims of an Internet Worm", in *Proceedings of the 2002 SIGCOMM Internet Measurement Workshop*, Marseille, France, pp. 273-284, November 2003.

[7] Moore, D., et al., "Internet Quarantine: Requirements for Containing Self-Propagating Code", in *Proceedings of the 2003 SIGCOMM Internet Measurement Workshop*, Marseille, France, pp. 273-284, November 2003.

[8] The Network Simulator - 2, *http://www.isi.edu/nsnam/ns/*, 2004.

[9] Perkins, C.E. and E.M. Royer, "The Ad Hoc On-Demand Distance-Vector Protocol", in *Ad Hoc Networking*, C.E. Perkins (ed.), Addison-Wesley, 2001.

[10] Rajab, M.A., Monrose, F. and A. Terzis, "An Evaluation of Collaborative Monitoring for Worm Defense", *HiNRG Technical Report 2004-03*, 2004.

[11] Rajab, M.A., Monrose, F. and A. Terzis, "On the Effectiveness of Distributed Worm Monitoring", *HiNRG Technical Report 2005-01*, 2005.

[12] Serazzi, G. and S. Zanero, "Computer Virus Propagation Models", *preprint*, 2001.

[13] Staniford, S., Paxson, V. and N. Weaver, "How to Own the Internet in Your Spare Time", in *Proceedings of the 11th USENIX Security Symposium*, 2002.

[14] Wang, Y. and C. Wang, "Modeling the Effects of Timing Parameters on Virus Propagation", in *WORM'03*, Washington D.C., October 2003.

[15] Yoon, J., Liu, M. and B.D. Noble, "Random Way Point Considered Harmful", in *INFOCOM '03*, San Francisco, April 2003.

[16] Zou, C.C., Gong, W. and D. Towsley, "Code Red Worm Propagation Modeling and Analysis", in *CCS'02*, Washington, D.C., November 2002.

Advanced Simulation Techniques

Sequential Performance of Asynchronous Conservative PDES Algorithms

Roger Curry, Cameron Kiddle, Rob Simmonds and Brian Unger
{curry,kiddlec,simmonds,unger}@cpsc.ucalgary.ca
Department of Computer Science
University of Calgary
Calgary, Alberta, Canada

Abstract

The widespread use of sequential simulation in large scale parameter studies means that large cost savings can be made by improving the performance of these simulators. Sequential discrete event simulation systems usually employ a central event list to manage future events. This is a priority queue ordered by event timestamps. Many different priority queue algorithms have been developed with the aim of improving simulator performance.

Researchers developing asynchronous conservative parallel discrete event simulations have reported exceptional performance for their systems running sequentially in certain cases. This paper compares the performance of simulations using a selection of high performance central event list implementations to that achieved using techniques borrowed from the parallel simulation community. Theoretical and empirical analysis of the algorithms is presented demonstrating the range of performance that can be achieved, and the benefits of employing parallel simulation techniques in a sequential execution environment.

Keywords: *Sequential Discrete Event Simulation, Parallel Discrete Event Simulation, Conservative Synchronization*

1 Introduction

Discrete event simulation (DES) is used to test and analyze the behavior of many systems. Events are used to model changes in the system that occur at discrete points in time. Each event has a timestamp to indicate the time that the state change should occur.

Most sequential DES systems employ a single *central event list* (CEL) to manage future events. The CEL is implemented as a priority queue ordered by event timestamps. In many cases the simulator performance depends on on the efficiency of insert and remove operations on the CEL. Many different priority queue algorithms and implementation techniques have been explored in the literature.

Parallel discrete event simulation (PDES) systems have been developed that can decrease the run length of individual simulation runs. However, they do this at the expense of extra complexity and decreased efficiency. It is often the case that many thousands of individual simulation runs are required to complete a study. In this case the efficiency of use of the available resources has a far greater impact on the time taken to complete the study than the speed of any individual run.

Some publications have reported performance advantages using PDES systems over CEL based systems when running sequentially. For the *ATM Traffic and Network Simulator* (ATM-TN) performance improvement of three times was achieved using a PDES system over using a splay tree CEL based system [16]. For the *IP Traffic and Network Simulator* (IP-TN), a performance improvement of up to four times that of a heap CEL based system was reported [8]. In each case the PDES system employed the *Critical Channel Traversing* (CCT) algorithm [17]. CCT is an asynchronous conservative PDES algorithm based on the *Chandy-Misra-Bryant* (CMB) algorithm [3, 5].

This paper examines the conditions under which CMB based systems can exhibit improved sequential performance over CEL based systems. A synthetic workload model is used to facilitate the comparison of the CMB and CEL based algorithms. The effect of manipulating model parameters is analyzed theoretically and empirical performance results are presented that confirm the theoretical analysis.

The rest of the paper is organized as follows. Section 2 provides an overview of several CEL algorithms and Section 3 provides an overview of CMB based algorithms. The complexity of CMB based algorithms in a sequential environment is analyzed in Section 4. The experimental methodology used to compare the sequential performance of CEL and CMB based algorithms is presented in Section 5, with the experimental results given in Section 6. Conclusions and future work are presented in Section 7.

1087-4097/05 $20.00 © 2005 IEEE

2 CEL Algorithms

Most sequential discrete event simulation systems use a single central event list (CEL) to manage all future events. Events are removed from the CEL and executed in nondecreasing timestamp order. During the execution of an event, new events could be created that are inserted into the CEL. Many studies have been performed that compare the costs associated with inserting and removing events from the CEL by using different priority queue algorithms [7, 10, 15]. Several of these algorithms are described in this section.

The most basic priority queue implementation is a sorted linked list. This is rarely used in modern DES systems since scaling with respect to the size of the queue is poor. The cost of removing an event is $O(1)$, but the cost of inserting an event is $O(P)$, where P is the number of events in the queue. For very small queue sizes, a linked list can perform well in comparison to more sophisticated priority queue implementations.

A heap is a type of balanced binary tree. The cost of inserting or removing an event is $O(\log P)$. Empirical results suggest that heaps are relatively insensitive to different distributions [7], which provides good motivation for their use in general purpose sequential simulation systems.

The splay tree priority queue [13] is a self-adjusting binary search tree. A single operation can cost $O(P)$ in the worst case, but amortized over a sequence of operations the behavior is $O(\log P)$. With each operation the structure of a splay tree is modified to improve the access time for future operations. Splay trees have been shown to achieve very good performance in comparison to many other CEL algorithms [7].

Calendar queues [2] are based on the concept of a desk calendar. In practice, the cost of inserting and removing an event is $O(1)$ on average. A calendar queue consists of an array of sorted linked lists, with one sorted linked list for each *day* of the *year*. Performance is ideal when the number of events is equal to the number of days in the year and events are uniformly distributed across the days in the year. The number of days in a year and the length of each day are automatically adjusted as the queue size grows and shrinks. The calendar queue may perform sub-optimally when the distribution of event timestamps changes while the queue size remains fixed.

Table 1 provides a summary of the per event costs of the CEL algorithms discussed in this section. The per event cost is the cost of inserting and removing the event from the priority queue.

Table 1. Per event cost of CEL algorithms.

linked list	heap	splay tree	calendar
$O(P)$	$O(\log P)$	$O(\log P)$	$O(1)$

3 CMB Based Algorithms

Most asynchronous conservative PDES systems employ algorithms derived from the Chandy-Misra-Bryant (CMB) [3, 5] algorithm. In conservative PDES algorithms, causality errors where events that affect the same state item are executed out of order are strictly avoided. This is in contrast to optimistic PDES algorithms that can execute related events out of order, but employ mechanisms to recover when this situation is detected [6].

These simulators use the logical process modelling methodology [5] to describe the system being modelled. With this, the system is viewed as a set of physical processes that only interact by exchanging messages. Each physical process is mapped to a *logical process* (LP) in the simulation system and messages are mapped to events. CMB based simulators use a channel based view of messaging. Unidirectional channels are set up between any pair of LPs that could communicate with each other. Events are inserted in nondecreasing timestamp order on each channel and are removed by the destination LP in FIFO order. This guarantees that the timestamp of the last event received from the channel is a lower bound on the timestamp of any future events that will be received. As long as an LP has an event on each input channel, it is safe to execute the event with the smallest timestamp. However, if an input channel is empty, the LP must wait as the timestamp of the next event to arrive on the channel is unknown.

Associated with each channel is a clock that represents the lower bound on the timestamp of future events to be received on the channel. Each event has a *lifetime* represented by the difference between the timestamp of the event whose execution caused this event to be generated, and the timestamp given to the event. A minimum lookahead value is also associated with each channel representing the minimum lifetime of any event that could be sent on the channel.

To avoid deadlock in the absence of events, LPs send *NULL messages* on output channels to update channel clocks to a new lower bound on the timestamp of any future event that will be sent. The value of the timestamp given to a NULL message is calculated using the LP's clock. An LP's clock is the minimum of the timestamp of any future event it currently has waiting to be processed and the clocks of all its input channels. The timestamp of the NULL message is set to the value of the current LP clock plus the minimum lookahead value for the channel it will be inserted into. Note that in sequential and shared memory parallel computers it is not necessary to explicitly send NULL messages. The channel clock variable can simply be updated by the sender LP.

4 Sequential Cost Analysis of CMB

This section examines the per event cost for sequential execution of CMB based algorithms that use the following approach. Each LP has its own priority queue that holds events it has generated for itself and at most one event from each of its input channels. The remaining events are kept on channels until needed to keep queue size to a minimum. LPs are scheduled in a priority queue and are executed in order of LP clock values. An LP execution session involves scanning input channels to determine the time up to which it is safe to execute, executing the events up to this time and updating output channel clocks. Terms used for the cost analysis are defined in Table 2.

Table 2. Definitions used in CMB cost analysis.

Term	Definition
P	event population (total # events)
N	# LPs
D	event density = P/N (avg # events at each LP)
C	avg # channels per LP
L	minimum lookahead of all channels
E	avg # events per LP execution
μ	avg lifetime of event

The simulation overhead per event for CEL algorithms is the cost to insert and remove the event from the central event list. Determining the per event cost of CMB based algorithms is more complicated. For simplicity, the following assumptions are made:

1. Events are uniformly distributed among LPs.
2. The event population P and number of LPs N are constant. This implies that when an event is executed exactly one new event is generated. This also implies that the event density D is constant.
3. Channels are statically allocated at the beginning of the simulation with no channels deleted and no new channels created. (i.e., C is constant)

For CMB based algorithms the sequential simulation overhead cost per event can be divided up into three parts as follows:

1. **Channel Scanning Cost** $O(\frac{C}{E})$: This is the cost of scanning channels each LP execution session to determine the time up to which it is safe to execute events and to update channel clocks. This is proportional to the number of channels C. The per event cost depends on the number of events E executed each LP execution session.
2. **LP Scheduling Queue Cost** $O(\frac{\log N}{E})$: Assuming that a heap is used as the priority queue, this is the cost to insert and remove an LP from the LP scheduling queue which is done once per LP execution session. The per event cost depends on the number of events E executed each LP execution session.
3. **Local Event Priority Queue Cost** $O(\log D)$: Assuming that a heap is used as the priority queue, this is the cost to insert and remove an event from an LP's local priority queue. If all events that are generated are sent on channels (i.e., no local events) then this reduces to $O(\log C)$ if $C <= D$, as at most one event from each channel is kept in the local priority queue. In a system where events are not uniformly distributed among LPs then the worst case scenario is actually $O(\log P)$ as it could be possible that all events are located on the same LP. Sorting of the event queue alone would cost the same as for the CEL approach in this case and thus a CMB based algorithm would not be suitable. For experiments in this paper a linked list is used as the event priority queue so the cost is $O(D)$. If D is very large then another priority queue implementation would be more appropriate.

It should be noted that there is also a cost to insert and remove an event from a channel. This cost is ignored however as it is constant due to the FIFO behavior of channels. Combining all three costs together gives:

$$\text{Per Event Cost} = O\left(\frac{C + \log N}{E} + \log D\right)$$

Ignoring the channel scanning costs gives $O(\frac{\log N}{E} + \log D) = O(\log(N^{\frac{1}{E}} D))$ for the per event cost of a CMB based algorithm. This assumes that heaps are used for the priority queues. A CEL algorithm using a heap priority queue has a per event cost of $O(\log P) = O(\log(ND))$. This indicates that the number of events per LP execution E must be greater than 1 for a CMB based algorithm to exhibit better asymptotic behavior. Note that this is a necessary condition but might not be sufficient as channel scanning costs must still be taken into account.

When $E > 1$ the LP scheduling queue is accessed less frequently, reducing sorting costs in comparison to the CEL algorithms. Also, better cache behavior is expected as the LP state remains in cache for the execution of E events. When $E < 1$ the LP scheduling queue is accessed more than once per event on average, giving rise to greater sorting costs in comparison to CEL algorithms.

If μ is the average lifetime of an event, then the rate of events being generated at each LP, with respect to simulation time, is D/μ. For a sequential simulation using a priority queue to sort LPs, LPs will be executed in LP clock order. When an LP executes, the clocks of all LPs will be greater than or equal to the clock of the current LP. The minimum amount of simulation time that the LP will be able to advance will be the minimum lookahead L in the model. Therefore the expected minimum time advance per LP execution session will be L on average. This gives the expected minimum value of $E_{min} = \frac{LD}{\mu}$ events per LP execution.

The per event cost of a CMB based algorithm can now be expressed as follows:

$$\text{Per Event Cost} = O\left(\frac{\mu(C + \log N)}{LD} + \log D\right)$$

The above cost expression is influenced by the number of LPs, the event density, the connectivity, the minimum lookahead and the average lifetime of an event. Table 3 summarizes the expected behavior when modifying a given parameter and keeping the other parameters constant.

Table 3. Expected behavior when modifying model parameters.

N	D	C	L	μ
$O(\log N)$	$O(\frac{1}{D} + \log D)$	$O(C)$	$O(\frac{1}{L})$	$O(\mu)$

5 Experimental Methodology

This section describes the experimental methodology used to evaluate the sequential performance of CMB based algorithms with respect to CEL algorithms. Included are descriptions of the experimental environment, simulation model, experimental design and performance metrics.

5.1 Experimental Environment

The CEL and CMB based algorithms that are examined in experiments are implemented as part of the same simulation kernel and make use of the same model code. The CMB based implementation uses a heap for the LP scheduling queue and a linked list for the local event queue at each LP.

Experiments were run on a Dell desktop computer with an 866 MHz Pentium III processor and 128 MB of RAM. This has a 16KB, 4-way associative first level (L1) instruction cache with a 32 byte line size, a 16KB, 4-way associative first level (L1) data cache with a 32 byte line size, and a 256KB, 8-way associative second level (L2) cache with a 32 byte line size. It was running Red Hat Linux 7.3 with the v2.4.18 kernel. The GNU g++ V2.96 compiler was used with the "-O2" optimization flag.

The *Cachegrind* tool (part of the *Valgrind 2.0.0* [14] suite) was used to determine instruction counts and analyze cache behavior. Cachegrind was configured to simulate a cache with the same specifications as the computer that the experiments were run on, as described above.

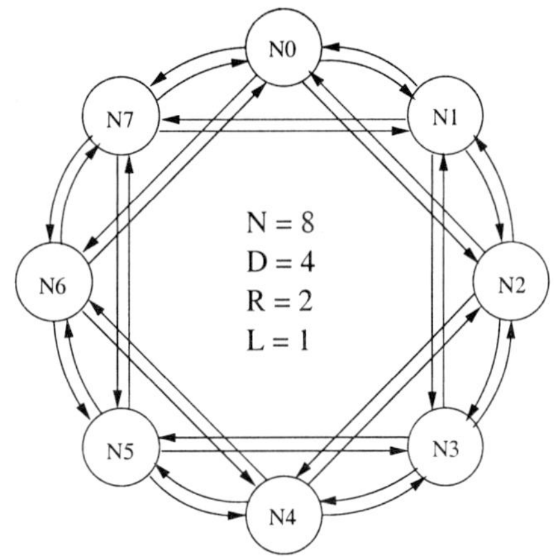

Figure 1. Example ring model.

5.2 Simulation Model

A ring model, similar to models described in [9, 12] was used for the experiments. The ring model does not implement any real system, but it allows the effects of model size, event density per LP, connectivity and lookahead to be examined. An example ring model can be seen in Figure 1. The model is parameterized with $N = 8$ LPs, an average event density of $D = 4$ events per LP, a connection radius $R = 2$, and a minimum channel lookahead $L = 1$ simulation time unit. Each LP is connected to R LPs ahead in the ring and R LPs behind in the ring with channel lookahead L.

Before the simulation is started, the system is populated with $N \times D$ events with timestamps selected independently from an exponential distribution with a mean of 1 simulation time unit. The events are uniformly distributed among LPs such that on average, each LP is populated with D events. The initial events are considered to be local events.

Upon processing a local event, an output channel is selected randomly with uniform probability. A new external event is generated with a timestamp equal to the timestamp of the current event plus the minimum lookahead L assigned to the selected output channel. Upon receiving an event from a neighbouring LP a local event is generated with a timestamp equal to the timestamp of the current event plus an increment drawn from an exponential distribution with a mean of 1 simulation time unit. The total event population P in the system remains constant at $P = N \times D$ throughout the simulation.

5.3 Performance Metrics

Four metrics are used to analyze the performance of the algorithms, namely the *instructions per event, L2 cache miss rate, events per LP execution* and *event rate*. The first three metrics are obtained while running the simulator with

Cachegrind, whereas the event rate metric is obtained while running the simulator without Cachegrind.

Instructions per event is the total number of instructions divided by the total number of events executed. Only instructions after initialization are taken into account.

The *L2 cache miss rate* is the percentage of data references missed by the L2 data cache. Only misses after initialization of the simulation are taken into account. L1 cache misses are not examined as the cost of an L2 cache miss is much larger.

Events per LP execution is the total number of events divided by the total number of LP execution sessions. This is easily calculated for the CMB based algorithm. For the CEL algorithms this is taken to be the average number of events executed consecutively at the same LP.

Event rate is the total number of events processed divided by the wallclock time (i.e., execution time) taken to run the simulation. Only wallclock time after initialization is taken into account. This metric is taken from runs where the simulator is run without Cachegrind so that the performance overhead of Cachegrind does not affect the results.

5.4 Experimental Design

Table 4 summarizes the experimental parameters and levels used in the experiments. Only one parameter is varied at a time for a given set of experiments with the others having fixed values marked by an asterisk in the table. Each experiment is run for three central event list algorithms, heap, splay tree and calendar queue, and also for the CMB based algorithm.

Table 4. Experimental parameters and levels.

Parameter	Levels
N	16, 128, 1024, 8192*, 65536
D	0.25, 0.5, 1, 2, 4*, 8, 16, 32, 64
R	1*, 2, 4, 8, 16, 32
L	0.015625, 0.0625, 0.25, 1*, 4

Each test was run twice with Cachegrind and once without it. One of the Cachegrind runs used a simulation end time of 100 simulation units and the other Cachegrind run was terminated after initialization so that the effects of initialization could be eliminated from the results. The run without Cachegrind was executed for 60 seconds of wallclock time, excluding initialization. The three runs were repeated 5 times using different random number seeds. The metrics were averaged over the 5 runs and corresponding 95% confidence intervals calculated. The half-width of the confidence interval was less than 5% of the sample mean for all metrics in all cases.

6 Experimental Results

This section compares the performance of a simulation system using three different CEL implementations and the same simulation system using a CMB based approach. In each of the four experiments a single model parameter was varied while holding all others constant. The four experiments vary the number of LPs, the event density, the connectivity, and the lookahead.

6.1 Number of LP Results

The first set of experiments examine the effects of varying the number of LPs on the CEL and CMB based algorithms with event density $D = 4$, connection radius $R = 1$ and minimum channel lookahead $L = 1$. Figure 2(a) shows a plot of the instructions per event versus the number of LPs. Expected behavior of the heap and splay tree algorithms is $O(\log P) = O(\log(ND))$. For the calendar queue algorithm $O(1)$ behavior is expected. For the CMB based algorithm the expected behavior as given in Table 3 is $O(\log N)$ since a heap is used for the LP scheduling queue. In all these cases the expected behavior was observed.

If a different priority queue implementation was used for the LP scheduling in the CMB implementation, a different behavior would result. The CMB based algorithm exhibits the lowest instructions per event initially but does start to surpass the instructions per event for the calendar queue for larger numbers of LPs.

Figure 2(b) shows a plot of the L2 cache miss rate versus the number of LPs. The model fits into the cache for 16 and 128 LPs. After this point the cache miss rate increases as the number of LPs increases for the CEL algorithms. The cache miss rate of the CMB based algorithm remains constant at just above 1% and is up to 4 times lower than the cache miss rate for the calendar queue algorithm and up to 6 times lower than for the splay tree algorithm.

The cache behavior of the algorithms is explained by the plot of events per LP execution versus the number of LPs shown in Figure 2(c). A single line is plotted for all of the CEL algorithms as the events per LP execution values are the same for all of these algorithms. The number of events executed consecutively at the same LP is one on average. This means that the next event in the central event list most often occurs at a different LP. The LP might not be in the cache so the cache miss rate increases. The CMB algorithm achieves nearly 8 events per LP execution, improving the cache locality.

Due to the nature of the ring model, the CEL algorithms achieve one event per LP execution on average for all of the test sets in this paper. It should be noted that there are cases where CEL based algorithms can achieve greater than one event per LP execution which are not captured by this model.

The expected minimum number of events per LP execu-

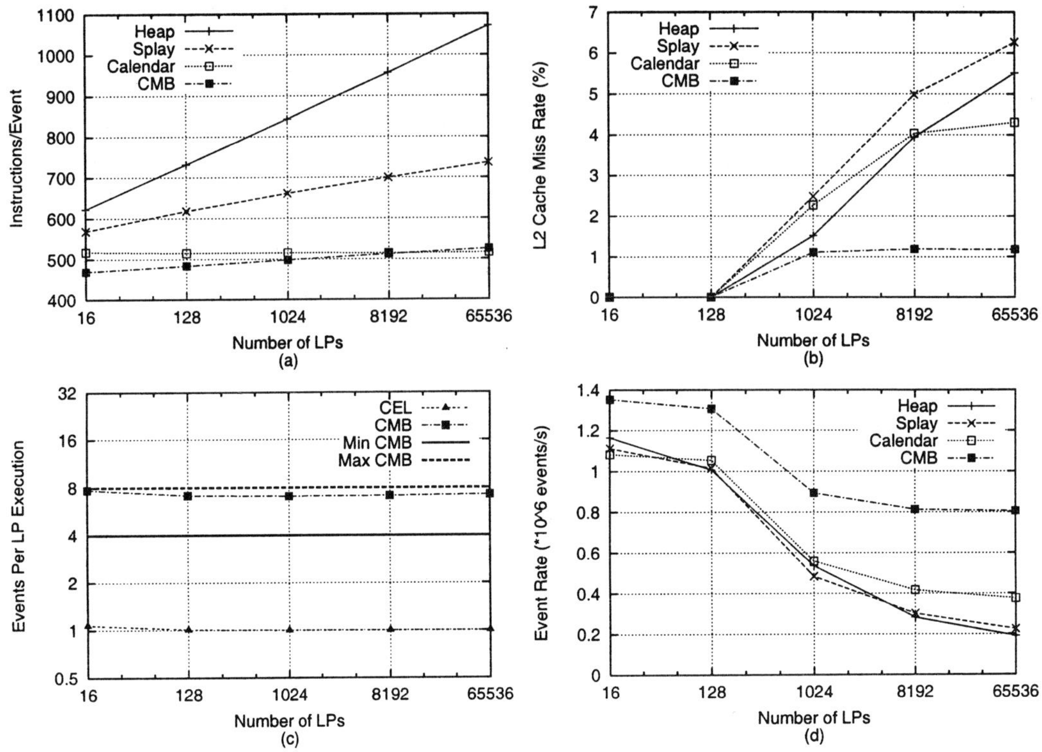

Figure 2. Plots of (a) instructions per event, (b) L2 cache miss rate, (c) events per LP execution and (d) event rate vs the number of LPs for D=4, R=1 and L=1.

tion is also plotted for the CMB algorithm. This is based on the derivation of $E_{min} = \frac{LD}{\mu}$ in Section 3. For the ring model, half of the events are generated locally with a timestamp increment based an exponential distribution with mean 1, and half are sent on channels with a timestamp increment of L. This gives $\mu = \frac{1+L}{2}$ and $E_{min} = \frac{2LD}{1+L}$. For this set of tests $L = 1$ and $D = 4$ so $E_{min} = 4$.

Since all events sent on channels have timestamps of at most the current LP clock plus L, when an LP starts an execution session neighbouring LPs can be at most L simulation time units ahead. Therefore, the maximum amount of time that an LP can advance in an execution session for the ring model is $2L$. This gives an expected maximum number of events per LP execution of $E_{max} = \frac{4LD}{1+L} = 2E_{min}$. For these tests this works out to $E_{max} = 8$. This is also plotted in Figure 2(c). The E_{min} and E_{max} curves are also plotted on the events per LP execution graphs for the remaining test sets in this paper.

Figure 2(d) shows a plot of the event rate versus the number of LPs. The plot clearly shows the effect of cache behavior on the performance. The highest event rates for all algorithms are observed when the model fits in the cache. The event rates drop significantly at 1024 LPs, as the model no longer fits in the cache. The CMB based algorithm exhibits the best performance, having an event rate up to twice that of the calendar queue algorithm and four times that of the heap and splay tree algorithms. The performance improvement of the CMB based algorithm over the calendar queue algorithm occurs even though the number of instructions per event are close. This is due to the much lower cache miss rate of the CMB based algorithm. The number of instructions per event still plays an important role. The heap exhibits more instructions per event than the splay tree, but the splay tree has a higher cache miss rate than the heap. The result is a similar event rate for the two algorithms.

6.2 Event Density Results

The second set of experiments examine the effects of varying the event density with number of LPs $N = 8192$, connection radius $R = 1$ and minimum channel lookahead $L = 1$. Figure 3(a) shows a plot of the instructions per event versus the event density. The expected behavior of the heap and splay tree algorithms is $O(\log P) = O(\log(ND))$ and is observed in the plot. The expected behavior of the calendar queue algorithm is $O(1)$ and this is also observed. The expected behavior of the CMB based algorithm as given in

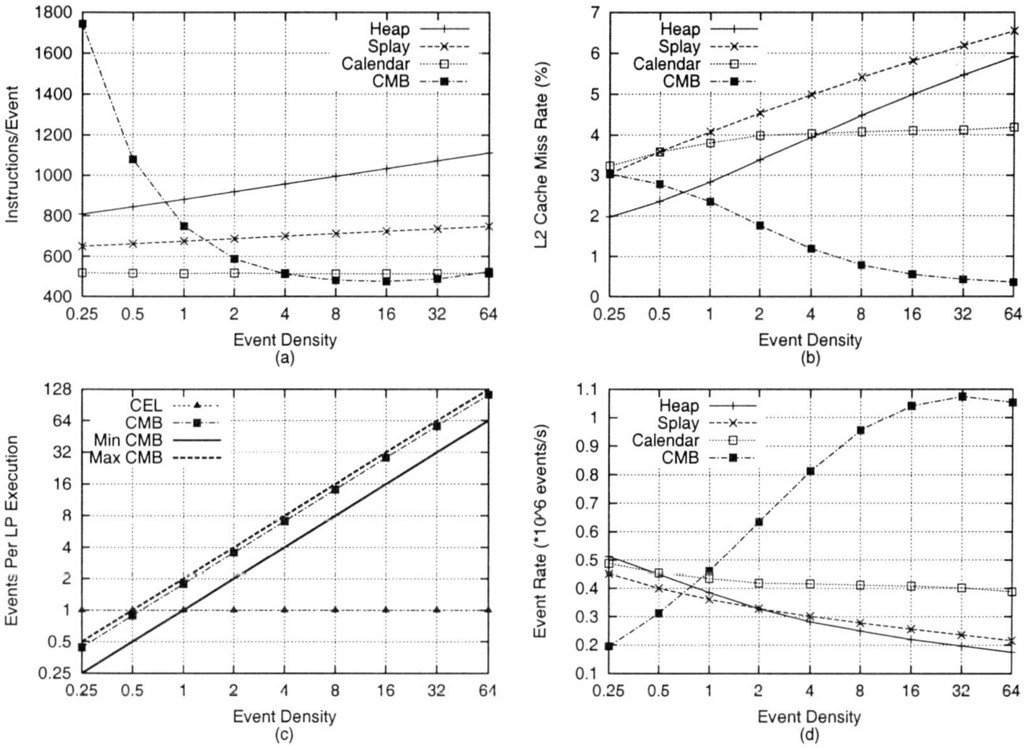

Figure 3. Plots of (a) instructions per event, (b) L2 cache miss rate, (c) events per LP execution and (d) event rate vs the event density for N=8192, R=1 and L=1.

Table 3 is $O(\frac{1}{D} + \log D)$. It is actually $O(\frac{1}{D} + D)$ since a linked list is used for an LP's local event priority queue. The $O(1/D)$ behavior dominates initially with the $O(D)$ behavior appearing after an event density $D = 16$. As was the case for the LP scheduling queue, a different priority queue implementation could be used for an LP's local priority queue to get different behavior. When event density is low the instructions per event becomes quite high for the CMB based algorithm. Many LPs are void of events when they are scheduled for execution resulting in additional scheduling overhead.

Figure 3(b) shows a plot of the L2 cache miss rate versus the event density. At low event density the CEL and CMB based algorithms have similar cache miss rates. With increasing event density the cache miss rate generally increases for the CEL algorithms, although more slowly for the calendar queue algorithm. The cache miss rate decreases as event density increases for the CMB based algorithm. This behavior is due to the improved cache locality obtained when a larger number of events are executed per LP execution session, as shown in Figure 3(c). The cache miss rate of the CMB based algorithm is up to 18 times less than that of the splay tree algorithm and up to 12 times less than that of the calendar queue algorithm.

A plot of the events per LP execution versus the event density is shown in Figure 3(c). The events per LP execution increases with event density for the CMB based algorithm and stays quite close to the expected maximum value. When the event density is quite low the number of events per LP execution drops below one indicating that there were many LP execution sessions in which no events were executed. This resulted in the state of more LPs being accessed increasing the cache miss rate.

Figure 3(d) shows a plot of the event rate versus the event density. The event rates for the heap and splay tree algorithms decrease as the event density increases, due to the greater cost of maintaining the priority queue and the larger number of cache misses. Even though the instructions per event remains constant, the event rate for the calendar queue algorithm decreases as result of the increasing cache miss rate. The event rate for the CMB based algorithm increases as event density increases, smoothing off and then decreasing as the $O(D)$ cost behavior begins to dominate. At high event density the CMB based algorithm has an event rate of about 3 times that of the calendar queue algorithm and about 5.5 times that of the heap algorithm. However, at low event density the event rate of the CMB based algorithm is about

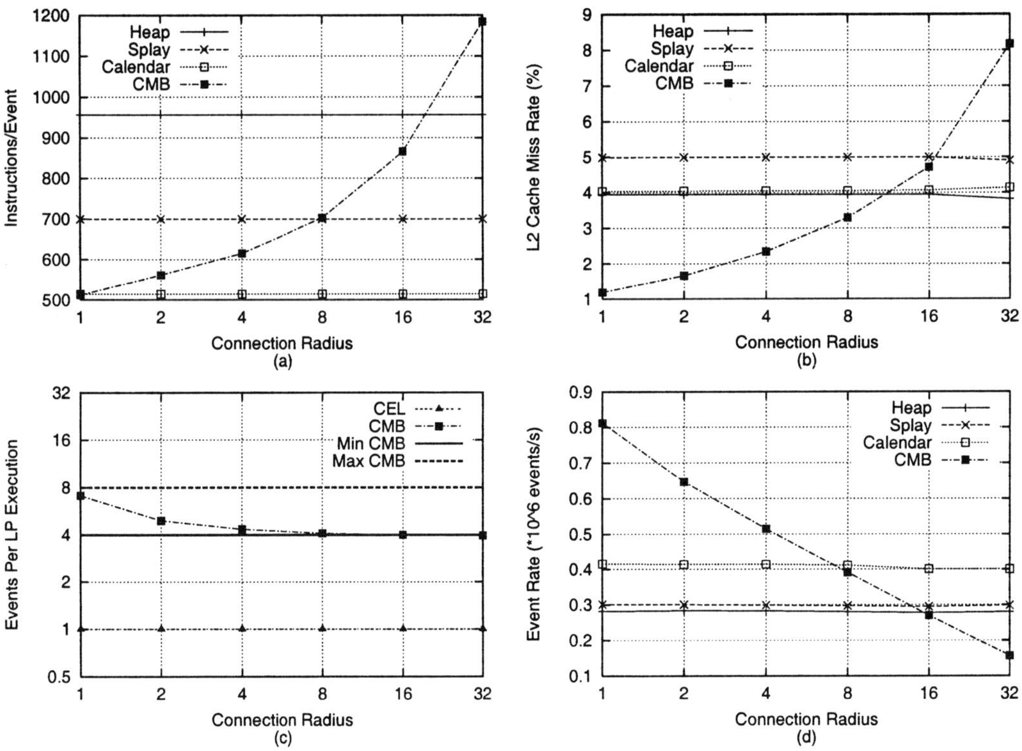

Figure 4. Plots of (a) instructions per event, (b) L2 cache miss rate, (c) events per LP execution and (d) event rate vs the connection radius for N=8192, D=4 and L=1.

2 times lower than that of the CEL algorithms. The CMB based algorithm does not perform better than any of the CEL algorithms until the number of events per LP execution is greater than one as was predicted in Section 3. This illustrates the importance of having greater than one event per LP execution to obtain good performance from CMB based algorithms.

6.3 Connectivity Results

The third set of experiments examines the effects of varying connectivity on the CEL and CMB based algorithms with number of LPs $N = 8192$, event density $D = 4$ and minimum channel lookahead $L = 1$. Figure 4(a) shows a plot of the instructions per event versus the connection radius. All three CEL algorithms exhibit constant behavior since they do not scan channels. Expected behavior of the CMB based algorithm as given in Table 3 is $O(C)$ which equals $O(R)$ for the ring model. The linear behavior of the CMB algorithm indicates how the cost of channel scanning becomes significant as connectivity increases. The CMB based algorithm starts off with the same number of instructions per event as the calendar queue algorithm but eventually surpasses the instructions per event of all CEL algorithms.

Figure 4(b) shows a plot of the L2 cache miss rate versus the connection radius. The CEL algorithms do not need to access additional state as connectivity increases and therefore the cache miss rate remains constant. The CMB based algorithm must access additional channel state as connectivity increases resulting in a greater cache miss rate.

A plot of the events per LP execution versus the connection radius is shown in Figure 4(c). The events per LP execution for the CMB based algorithm starts out near the expected maximum value but approaches the expected minimum value as the connection radius increases. As the connection radius increases, an LP has more neighbours so it is unlikely that all neighbours are L simulation time units ahead. It is more likely that there will be one or more neighbours that are close in time allowing the LP to advance only L simulation time units instead of $2L$ simulation time units.

Figure 4(d) shows a plot of the event rate versus the connection radius. The event rate is unaffected by the connection radius for the CEL algorithms as expected. The event rate for the CMB based algorithm decreases as the connection radius increases, eventually becoming worse than that of the CEL algorithms. Even though the instructions per event is greater for the CMB based algorithm than for the calendar queue al-

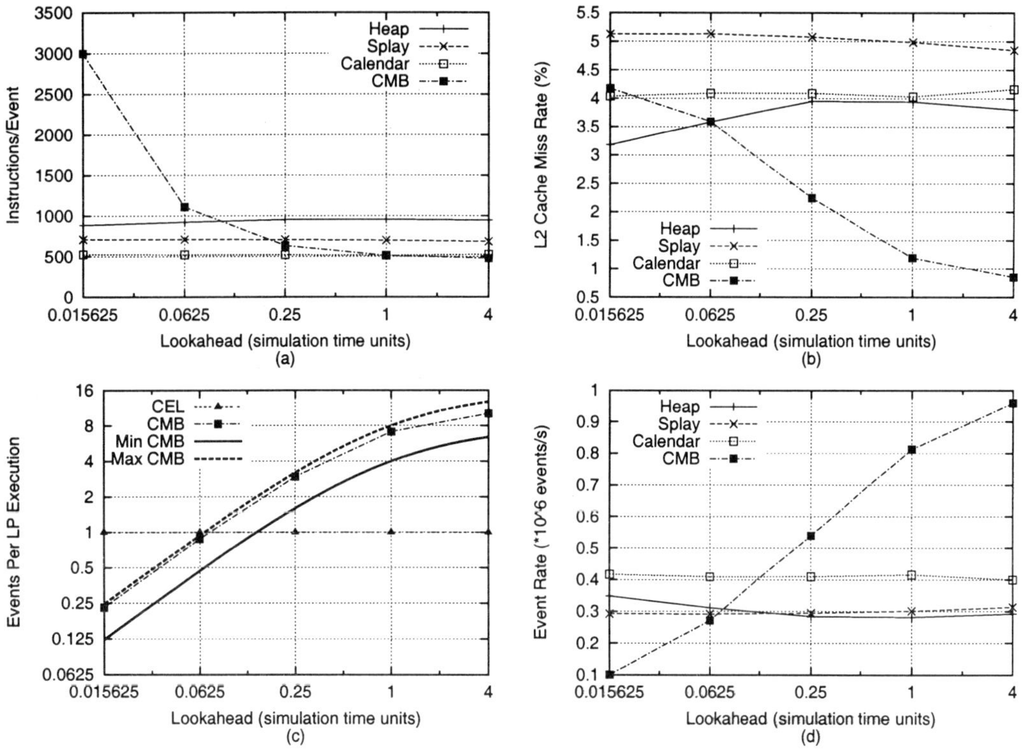

Figure 5. Plots of (a) instructions per event, (b) L2 cache miss rate, (c) events per LP execution and (d) event rate vs the lookahead for N=8192, D=4 and R=1.

gorithm for a connection radius less than 8, the CMB based algorithm still outperforms the calendar queue algorithm in terms of event rate. This is due to the lower cache miss rates of the CMB based algorithm at these points, further illustrating how cache behavior can have a significant impact on performance.

6.4 Lookahead Results

The fourth set of experiments examines the effects of varying the minimum channel lookahead on the CEL and CMB based algorithms with number of LPs $N = 8192$, event density $D = 4$ and connection radius $R = 1$. Figure 5(a) shows a plot of the instructions per event versus the minimum channel lookahead. Nearly constant behavior is observed for the CEL algorithms. The expected behavior of the CMB based algorithm as given in Table 3 is $O(\frac{1}{L})$ is also observed. As the lookahead decreases, instructions per event for the CMB algorithm becomes very high, up to six times that of the calendar queue algorithm. This is due to the temporal separation of events being much greater than the minimum lookahead resulting in low lookahead cycles. In this situation LPs execute many times to advance simulation time to the timestamp of the next event.

Figure 5(b) shows a plot of the L2 cache miss rate versus the minimum channel lookahead. Overall, the cache miss rate for the CEL algorithms is close to constant. The observed variation could be due to the distribution of event timestamps being dependent on the lookahead since half of the events are generated with a lifetime equal to the lookahead. The cache miss rate for the CMB based algorithm decreases as lookahead increases. At low lookahead, many LPs must be executed to advance simulation time to the timestamp of the next event, resulting in more model state being accessed. As the lookahead is increased this becomes less of a problem, requiring less model state to be accessed and improving cache behavior.

A plot of the events per LP execution versus the minimum channel lookahead is shown in Figure 5(c). The events per LP execution for the CMB based algorithm increases as the lookahead is increased but to a bound. The maximum events per LP execution session is approaching 16 and the minimum events per LP execution is approaching 8. Events per LP execution for the CMB based algorithm stays close to the expected maximum value. At low lookahead the number of events per LP execution session can drop below one for the CMB based algorithm.

Figure 5(d) shows a plot of the event rate versus the minimum channel lookahead. Event rates for the CEL algorithms are approximately constant. The event rate for the CMB based algorithm increases with increasing lookahead. Once again, it does not perform better than any of the CEL algorithms until the number of events per LP execution is greater than 1. The plot indicates how low lookahead can result in poor performance of the CMB based algorithm with the calendar queue algorithm achieving up to 4 times the event rate when L=0.015625.

7 Conclusions and Future Work

This paper explored the range of performance that can be achieved sequentially by Chandy-Misra-Bryant (CMB) based systems, originally developed for parallel simulation. The performance of a CMB based system was compared with three central event list (CEL) implementations namely the heap, splay tree, and calendar queue. Both the number of instructions executed and the cache behavior were found to have a significant impact on performance. In some situations, superior cache performance was able to make up for a larger number of instructions executed. Experimental results confirmed predictions of the asymptotic behavior derived from a theoretical analysis of CMB based algorithms. In particular, such algorithms are shown to excel in cases of high event density, high lookahead and low connectivity.

One condition that is necessary, but not sufficient, for improved sequential performance of CMB based algorithms over CEL based algorithms is having greater than one event per LP execution on average. When this condition holds, cache locality improves as the same LP state is accessed repeatedly, reducing the cache miss rate. Also, sorting costs are reduced as the LPs are inserted and removed from the LP scheduling queue less often. When this condition does not hold, multiple LP execution sessions are required to execute a single event. This negatively impacts cache behavior and increases the frequency of both channel scanning and sorting of the LP scheduling queue.

This paper has examined the performance of CEL and CMB based algorithms for a particular workload model. Studies using different models, parameters and event distributions would be useful. Many techniques have been developed to improve performance of CMB based algorithms in a parallel environment. These include techniques that address the low lookahead cycle problem such as *Carrier NULL Messages* [4] and *Cooperative Acceleration* [1] and techniques that address channel scanning costs such as *composite synchronization* [11] and *Receive Side CCT* [12]. Optimization of these techniques for a sequential environment could be explored.

Acknowledgments

Financial support for this research was provided by ASRA (Alberta Science and Research Authority) and NSERC (Natural Sciences and Engineering Research Council of Canada).

References

[1] T. D. Blanchard, T. W. Lake, and S. J. Turner. Cooperative acceleration: Robust conservative distributed discrete event simulation. In *Proceedings of the 8th Workshop on Parallel and Distributed Simulation*, pages 58–64, 1994.

[2] R. Brown. Calendar queues: A fast $O(1)$ priority queue implementation for the simulation event set problem. *Communications of the ACM*, 31(10):1220–1227, 1988.

[3] R. E. Bryant. Simulation of packet communication architecture computer systems. Technical Report TR-188, MIT Labratory for Computer Science, 1977.

[4] W. Cai and S. J. Turner. An algorithm for distributed discrete-event simulation – the "carrier null message" approach. In *Proceedings of the SCS Multiconference on Distributed Simulation*, volume 22 of *SCS Simulation Series*, pages 3–8, 1990.

[5] K. M. Chandy and J. Misra. Distributed simulation: A case study in design and verification of distributed programs. *IEEE Transactions on Software Engineering*, SE-5(5):440–452, 1979.

[6] D. R. Jefferson. Virtual time. *ACM Transactions on Programming Languages and Systems*, 7(3):404–425, 1985.

[7] D. W. Jones. An empirical comparison of priority-queue and event-set implementations. *Communications of the ACM*, 29(4):300–311, 1986.

[8] C. Kiddle. *Scalable Network Emulation.* PhD thesis, Computer Science Department, University of Calgary, 2004.

[9] J. Liu, D. M. Nicol, and K. Tan. Lock-free scheduling of logical processes in parallel simulation. In *Proceedings of the 15th Workshop on Parallel and Distributed Simulation*, pages 22–31, 2001.

[10] W. M. McCormack and R. G. Sargent. Analysis of future event set algorithms for discrete event simulation. *Communications of the ACM*, 24(12):801–812, 1981.

[11] D. Nicol and J. Liu. Composite synchronization in parallel discrete-event simulation. *IEEE Transactions on Parallel and Distributed Systems*, 13(5):443–446, 2002.

[12] R. Simmonds, C. Kiddle, and B. Unger. Addressing blocking and scalability in critical channel traversing. In *Proceedings of the 16th Workshop on Parallel and Distributed Simulation*, pages 17–24, 2002.

[13] D. D. Sleator and R. E. Tarjan. Self-adjusting binary search trees. *Journal of the ACM*, 32(3):652–686, 1985.

[14] Valgrind. Available from http://valgrind.kde.org/.

[15] J. G. Vaucher and P. Duval. A comparison of simulation event list algorithms. *Communications of the ACM*, 18(4):223–230, 1975.

[16] Z. Xiao, R. Simmonds, B. Unger, and J. Cleary. Fast cell level ATM network simulation. In *Proceedings of the 2002 Winter Simulation Conference*, pages 712–719, 2002.

[17] Z. Xiao, B. Unger, R. Simmonds, and J. Cleary. Scheduling critical channels in conservative parallel discrete event simulation. In *Proceedings of the 13th Workshop on Parallel and Distributed Simulation*, pages 20–28, 1999.

Merging Parallel Simulation Programs

Abhishek Agarwal and Maria Hybinette

Computer Science Department
University of Georgia
Athens, GA 30602-7404, USA

maria@cs.uga.edu

Abstract

In earlier work cloning is proposed as a means for efficiently splitting a running simulation midway through its execution into multiple parallel simulations. In simulation cloning, clones usually are able to share computations that occur early in the simulation, but as their states diverge individual LPs are replicated as necessary so that their computations proceed independently. However, if, over time the state of the clones (or their constituent LPs) converges there is, as of yet, no means for recombining them. In this case some efficiency is lost because they will execute identical events. This idea is the reverse of cloning, as we merge logical processes that have been previously cloned and we show that this can further increase efficiency because the new uncloned LPs will complete computations that would otherwise be duplicated. We discuss our implementation of merging, and illustrate its effectiveness in several example simulation scenarios.

1. Introduction

In this work we introduce simulation merging as the converse of cloning and we show that for efficient parallel simulations merging is as important cloning. To put merging in context, we must first briefly review simulation cloning.

In earlier work we introduced simulation cloning as a means of gaining efficiency in the execution of parallel simulations. Simulations are cloned at decision points. As simulation time progresses, the decision points are analogous to forks in the time-line where the state of the executing simulations begins to diverge. Cloning is efficient because all simulations after a fork benefit from shared computations made before the fork. In fact, because our cloning scheme is incremental, clones continue to benefit from shared computations after a decision point, depending on how quickly the change in state propagates among the constituent LPs.

We refer to a simulation clone as fully diverged when all of its LPs have been cloned. Even though computations were saved before diverging, after diverging the continuing simulation is as expensive as a separate stand-alone simulation. However, as simulations continue to run, it is possible, perhaps likely, that the state of separate clones that were once distinct may converge. This is possible, for instance, in simulations of stable systems that tend to converge to an equilibrium, or of cyclic systems that "reset" each day (e.g. the air traffic network).

It is natural to wonder, if once clones have converged to similar states, might they be recombined or merged? In other words, can forked time lines be recombined? In this way a simulation could benefit again from shared computations in the same way that it did before the fork.

Consider that a single simulation clone may comprise hundreds or thousands of LPs distributed over dozens of processors. At first it would seem that merging simulations is a bit like putting the proverbial genie back in the bottle. How could we efficiently evaluate the state of such a vast process, then compress it back together with its sibling? In fact, the answer is simple, flexible and dynamic. Our approach is to recombine simulations gradually, in the same way that they are cloned in the first place: one LP at a time.

Specifically, LPs occasionally compare their state with the state of their peers. If the states are identical (or "close enough") the LPs recombine. This enables a clone to be fully diverged or fully re-converged with another, or anywhere between these two extremes.

2. Problem statement

In order to provide context for the problem, we must first review our approach to simulation cloning in more details. After that, we describe the need for and challenge of simulation merging.

For cloning and merging we assume that simulations consist of multiple *logical processes* (LPs) that communi-

1087-4097/05 $20.00 © 2005 IEEE

cate exclusively by time stamped messages. Conceptually, one may consider that the simulation is composed of virtual logical processes, physical logical processes, and messages. The relationship between physical and virtual LPs is similar to that between physical and logical (virtual) address space in modern virtual memory systems. The cloning software maps the simulation programmer's virtual logical processes and messages to their corresponding "real" physical logical processes and messages. We introduced this approach in [12]. Virtual LPs and messages do not have a physical realization. Instead, each virtual LP maps to one *physical* LP that has a physical realization in the parallel simulation system. Similarly, each virtual message maps to a single physical message.

Computations common between two or more clones are completed by a physical LP and shared by the virtual LPs in the clones that are mapped to the physical LP. Similarly, virtual messages among different clones are mapped to a single physical message to avoid duplication. Sharing of common computations may proceed until the state of one of the virtual LPs diverges from the others. At this point the LP must be replicated and it becomes a physical LP.

If replication is "one way" only, all cloned simulations will eventually end up in a fully replicated state. Once in this state, efficiency from shared computations is no longer feasible. However, it may be the case that cloned simulations converge back to similar or identical states. It may be possible to reclaim efficiency by merging (invert cloning) simulations back together.

Our problem is twofold:

1. How can we identify clones that may be merged safely? and
2. How can we accomplish the merging?

Our approach is to consider merging at the LP level – in much the same way that cloning is accomplished at the LP level. Accordingly a clone, composed of many LPs, is merged with another one LP at a time.

As an example, consider an air traffic simulation. Suppose that cloning was being used to evaluate whether to restrict traffic at the Sacramento airport (which is represented as an LP in our simulation). Later, the restriction is lifted. After the restriction is lifted, flights may gradually return to a normal pattern, and be similar to the original simulation without a restriction. In this case, during the period of the restriction, the states of simulated airports (LPs) near the Sacramento airport may diverge. However, after the restriction is lifted they may gradually converge to the state of a simulation without a restriction.

A number of sub-problems arise as we consider how merging should be implemented. For example, there are situations in which unexpected thrashing may occur. Suppose we have fully replicated the air traffic simulation and the cloned simulations are now beginning to converge. Specifically, suppose that the Sacramento airport can now be merged and the merge is performed. After the merge, the Sacramento airport can accept arrivals of aircraft from airports that are still diverged, which would lead to an immediate re-cloning of the LP. However if that aircraft arrival did not cause the airport to diverge, or differ, it becomes an immediate candidate for merging again. We can quickly wind up in a merge/clone cycle wasting enormous amounts of CPU effort.

Another consideration is when or how frequently we should check for re-convergence. One solution is to consider merging a cloned logical process at any time that it receives a message, this has the benefit that after a merge, LPs will avoid being cloned again as in our previous example. However, this may result in too much overhead. A more practical approach is to check en masse at specific check point times. The frequency of checks could be specified by the simulation application designer.

To reduce the cost of full LP state comparisons we envision the merging system to use heuristics or statistical methods that gauge the most likely elements to be different, and to compare those elements first. In our initial implementation however we assume that LPs have a limited amount of state to compare. This is a reasonable assumption for optimistic simulations; otherwise system memory would be quickly exhausted by the simulation's state saving features.

The several problems we must address then, are:

- How and when can we detect that logical processes reconvergence?
- How can we avoid merge clone thrashing?
- How frequently should we test for merging?
- How can we implement merging so that the resulting simulation outcome is correct?

We address these questions in the sections that follow. Our earlier work showed that cloning can provide a significant application performance advantage for a wide class of simulation executions. In this work our initial results indicate that clone merging can similarly provide improved performance.

3. Implementation

Merging is implemented together with cloning in a layered fashion with the operating system at the bottom, the simulation executive in the middle, and the simulation application at the top. The code that implements merging and cloning is layered between the simulation application and the simulation executive. This approach allows cloning and merging to run on top of various underlying simulation executives. From the point of view of the executive cloning and merging software is simply part of the simulation application. Cloning is independent of the synchronization mechanism (optimistic or conservative), however our implementation is using an optimistic simulation kernel.

An efficient implementation of merging requires us to pay careful attention to two issues: comparisons and thrashing. Merging of course, requires state comparisons, but state comparison is expensive, so our implementation must consider how to minimize them. Additionally, we must avoid merge/clone thrashing cycles, where an LP is merged and then immediately re-cloned due to receiving a message from an LP that has not yet been merged. We address these issues at the application level and within the cloning/merging library.

We observe that it is difficult to estimate how long it might take for cloned LPs to converge without knowledge of the application. Accordingly, in order to reduce the number of comparisons, we rely on the application programmer to provide a recommendation for how frequently LPs should be checked to see if they have converged. This information is provided by the application programmer using an API given later in this section.

Thrashing occurs when a cloned LP is merged then quickly re-cloned. This happens when the cloned LP receives a message from another LP that is still cloned, even though the sender's LP state may not have diverged from it's corresponding cloned physical logical process. Thrashing may be further aggravated when merging runs on an optimistic simulation engine. Our solution to the first part of the problem is to delay replication (cloning) until it can be determined that the sender's virtual logical processes are indeed diverged. Observe that identical sender virtual logical processes send identical messages. Thus one can rely on message checking to detect situations where replication is necessary. We addressed this issue in previous work in which we introduced just-in-time cloning. Just-in-time cloning delays replication of cloned logical processes until it is absolutely necessary, thus avoiding unnecessary replication. Merging uses Just-in-time cloning to avoid unnecessary re-cloning.

When merging is implemented on an optimistic executive we may find situations where LPs are merged, but then the merging event is rolled back. Clearly, this behavior could contribute to merge/clone/merge thrashing. We address the problem by scheduling merging events conservatively at physical logical processes at global virtual time.

Now we introduce the API for merging that is provided to the simulation application programmer. The API also includes calls to support cloning which are described in CITATION. There are three merging functions available. We list the function names below, then describe them in detail later. The functions are prefixed with the letters CM to indicate that they are functions from the clone merge library:

```
CM_Enable( check-frequency );
CM_Disable();
CM_RegisterFunction( mergefunc );
```

`CM_Enable()` and `CM_Disable` enable and disable merging. `CloneMerge_Enable()` turns on a timer (in simulated time) in the simulation executive, and each time the timer expires, a clone merge check performed. When the simulation is completely merged `CloneMerge_Disable` is called automatically. The `check-frequency` parameter defines how regularly the merging library checks for merging after the simulation is cloned.

`CM_RegisterFunction( mergefunc )` registers a user defined function defined by its parameter. This function is provided by the application programmer to compare two LPs so that it can be determined if they are ready for merging. `mergefunc` returns either `True` or `False` depending on whether the LPs should be merged or not. We require this function from the user because it is possible that the state of two LPs may be bit-wise different, but still equivalent. The kernel cannot resolve these ambiguities without help from the application level. Also note that since the user defines the function that determines the *similarity* between the states, this function may also relax the constraint on "equivalence", which consequently can increase the efficiency of merging.

The merging library uses the `merge_time[LP][clone]` data structure to store the time to make a comparison to test for merging for each physical logical process. The matrix is indexed by logical process and clone and set by the merge library. It is initialized by the time given by the parameter check-frequency in `CM_Enable( check-frequency )` and is reset every time the timer expires. In general the comparison time of clones of a particular logical process should be set to the same time in order to synchronize the merging event. Observe that different logical process may schedule merging asynchronously, especially if they do not communicate without any impact on performance.

The merging library also uses two functions internally (transparent to the simulation application):

```
CM_ScheduleMergeEvent();
CM Merge( parent_lp, child_lp );
```

`CM_ScheduleMergeEvent() )` is scheduled by a logical process on itself by the merging library when the timer for state checking expires. This is done by sending a blocking message to itself. In general, parent and descendant virtual logical processes should schedule comparisons simultaneously to that their states are synchronized. In order to prevent indefinite blocking, priority is given to the parent process.

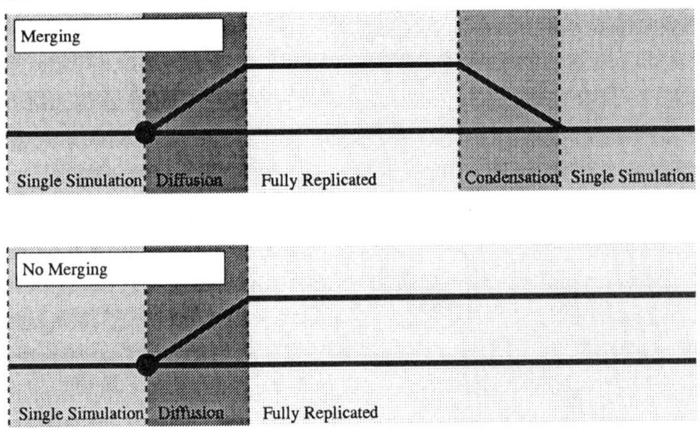

Figure 1. Sequence of Events in Simulation Cloning and Simulation Cloning with Merging: *Top:* A simulation that can be merged benefits from sharing computations after the simulation converges and merges into one single simulation. The LPs are incrementally merged. *Bottom*: A simulation that can be merged but that remains cloned cannot benefit from shared computations.

If two LPs are equivalent they are merged by `CM_Merge( parent_lp, child_lp )`, This function changes the mapping of the virtual logical processes so that their corresponding physical logical process are now equivalent. The child's old physical logical process is set to inactive and returned to the pool of physical logical processes.

4. Performance

In this section we experimentally evaluate the performance of merging simulations. We observed in earlier experiments with cloning that the performance depends significantly on when in simulated time a simulation is cloned (or in this, case merged). Performance is maximized when cloning occurs late in a simulation because all computations up to that point can be shared. Conversely, we expect that merging will have the best impact on performance when merging occurs early in the simulation.

A cloned simulation passes through three distinct phases: (1) before cloning (2) diffusion (before the simulation is fully replicated) and (3) fully replicated. When merging is enabled, the simulation transitions back from fully replicated to partly replicated and finally, fully re-converged. Merging most likely most beneficial the earlier the merging point.

The performance of merging was evaluated using the benchmark application P-Hold. P-Hold provides synthetic workloads using a fixed message population [7]. Each LP is instantiated by an event. Upon instantiation, the LP schedules a new event with a specified time-stamp increment and destination LP. In all our experiments P-Hold is configured with 512 logical processes and a message population of 4, 096. The sender is configured to chose a recipient LPs from a uniform distribution. We conducted the experiments on an SGI Origin 2000 with 24 X 300 MHz MIPS R12000 processors with 4MB cache memory and 8 GB of system main memory. All experiments used two processors.

Performance improvement due to merging over pure cloning can be measured in terms of the progress of virtual time as a function of real time, i.e. the independent variable for this experiment is execution time and the metric is simulation progress (virtual time). Larger values indicate better performance. For this experiment the simulation is run for a total of 2, 000 simulated seconds. The simulation is cloned when approximately 25% of the simulated time is complete (i.e. at simulation time 500). We manipulated the simulation application so that LPs could merge at a specific point in simulated time. We ran three experiments, with three different merging times. Performance in these simulations is illustrated in Figure 2.

The plot in Figure 2 shows three curves: the left-most

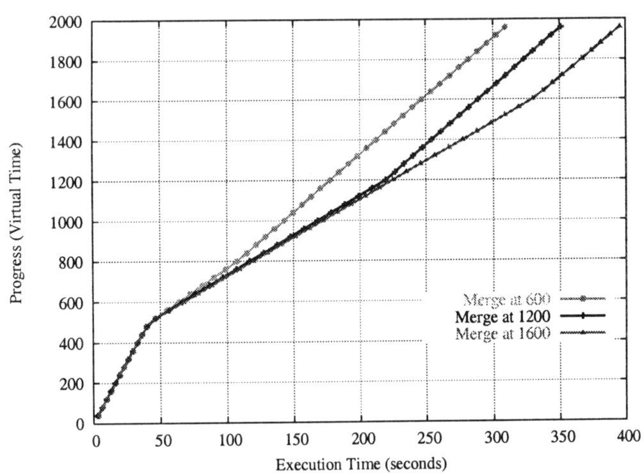

Figure 2. Performance of P-Hold. Larger numbers indicate better performance.

curve shows a run where merging occurs at simulated time 600, the middle curve shows a run where merging occurs at simulated time 1, 200 and the right-most curve merging occurs at simulated time 1, 600.

We observe that performance degrades upon instantiation of new clones. This is evident by a more shallow slope of the curves at the cloning time. The simulations then continue with linear progress after simulated time 500. All three curves show similar performance until simulated time 600, when the left-most curve accelerates. This is a result of merging starting at time 600 and completing at time 800. The acceleration of simulated time for the middle curve is noticeable at simulated time 1, 200 and the right most curve at simulated time 1, 600.

In these experiments, in the best case, merging improves performance by about 24% over a non-merged simulation (which ran for 418 seconds, but is not shown in the plot).

In a second experiment, we investigate the impact of merging on speedup in the performance on P-Hold. For comparison, a pure cloning scheme (i.e. no merging), is compared against merging. Performance is evaluated as speedup of the run time of merging versus pure cloning. Speedup is the total running time of pure cloning divided by the running time of merging.

The independent variable in this experiment is the merging point. The plot of this experiment is shown in Figure 3. The results indicate that merging outperforms pure cloning

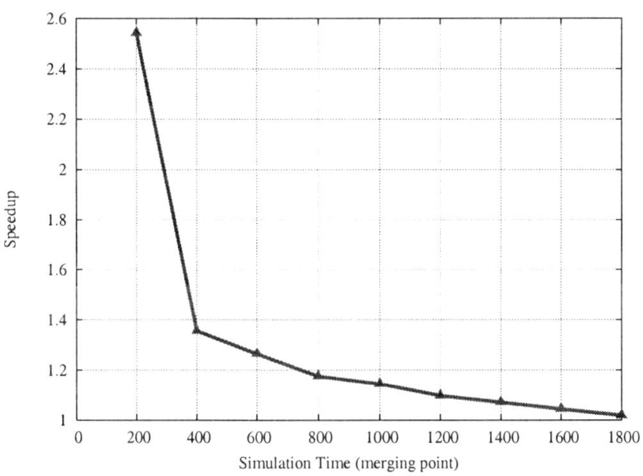

Figure 3. Speedup of cloning with merging over pure cloning with P-Hold. Larger numbers indicate better performance.

for all merging points. As expected, merging is more beneficial the earlier the merging point. The results show that merging can achieve up to 2.5 speedup (when the merging point is instantiated at the time of cloning). However, we would expect speedup in this case to be capped at 2.0 because the comparison between two clones that run to completion and two clones that merge, then run as one. We believe that the speedup exceeds 2.0 due to additional overhead incurred by cloned simulations.

The benefit of merging depends on the frequency of state comparisons and the size of the state. It should be noted that in our initial implementation there is an overhead associated with merging that we measured in the worst case. Merging overhead averages 9.4% of the application run time. The worst case occurs when the application test for merging fails frequently because the state is still diverged.

5. Related work

Simulation cloning has been shown to improve performance of interactive applications such as simulations of the ground transportation [15, 16] and air-traffic control [12]. Cloning and extensions of cloning has been implemented both in conservative [1, 15, 16] and optimistic [12] simulation executives.

With respect to cloning in general, related work in interactive parallel simulation include [6] and [5]. The approach of [6] allows for the testing of what-if scenarios provided they are interjected before a deadline. Alternatives are examined sequentially using a rollback mechanism to erase exploration of one path in order to begin exploration of another. [5] create a new simulation from a previous base-line simulation by executing forward. They can determine if a computation can be reused by using a predicate function that is tested on the baseline simulation, however as in [6] only the testing of one alternative at a time is allowed. A drawback of this latter approach is that one must manage the entire state-space of the baseline simulation.

Cloning has been used to improve accuracy of simulation results, i.e., to run multiple independent replications then average their results at the end of the runs. For example, in [9] research focuses on how to achieve statistical efficiency of replications spread on different machines. In [17] replications are synchronized via a shared clock. In this way the same event occurs at the same time at all replicas.

Cloning is also used in sequential simulations to propagate faults in digital circuits [13], modeling of flexible manufacturing systems [3] or to fork transactions in simulation languages [10]. Sequential simulation languages typically clone dummies ("shadows") to do time-based waiting [14].

Our approach that avoids redundant computations is similar to approaches (but in the reverse) that reduce the cost of rollbacks: Lazy cancellation [8], Lazy re-evaluation [18] the aggressive no-risk (ANR) [4] protocol or exploiting "lookback" [2] for example. Lazy cancellation uses message comparisons and consequently delays sending anti-messages until the event that originally scheduled them is guaranteed not to be re-generated. Lazy re-evaluation is a technique that avoids state recomputation when process state is un-altered after a rollback. ANR delays delivering messages until the event that created them is guaranteed not to be rolled back (the sender event), this technique avoids cascading rollbacks. Lookback is a techniques that identifies situations where one can avoid rollback.

Our approach is applicable both to optimistic and conservative protocols. It uses state and message comparison as in the lazy cancellation and revaluation protocols. However, the number of state comparisons is minimal and only occurs infrequently. After merging, it uses just-in-time cloning [11], which uses message comparisons, that was proposed earlier, to avoid cloning immediately after an LP is merged, but it only compares messages if the LP is again subject to replication.

6. Conclusion

Merging parallel simulations enables cloned simulations to recapture computational time wasted by unnecessary clones in a cloned or replicated simulation. The efficiency of cloning is provided by shared computations before the LPs are replicated. Merging enables simulations to recapture the efficiency of shared computations after LPs merge.

We demonstrated the potential benefit of merging using the parallel simulation benchmark, P-Hold. The impact of merging on performance depends on when in the simulation merging occurs. Results indicate that merging can improve the performance of simulation cloning by a factor of 2.5 when merging occurs at an advantageous time. At best, when a clone is immediately followed by a merge operation the overhead is insignificant. Over all run time is virtually the same as that for a *a single simulation* run. These initial performance results indicate that merging may significantly reduce the time required to compute multiple simulations.

At present we have only evaluated the approach in a synthetic application. In future work we will investigate performance in more typical simulation tasks, such as ground and air transportation (e.g. D-PAT [19]). Additionally, we assume that the cost of state comparison is low. This may be reasonable since we only need to to compare state at irregular, user defined intervals. In future work we will examine the impact of varying the state size and also also explore heuristic methods, such as hierarchical comparison of data specified by the simulation application designer. The idea is that the designer could define an ordered comparison of the LP state data in order to make the comparison run very efficiently (by efficiently, we mean able to come to a negative decision quickly, since this will be presumed to be the most common case). One adaptive approach we are considering is to record the locations within the LP state which caused the most recent failures, and to check those locations first.

A final point of interest for future work concerns the issue of how similar simulations must be in order for them to be considered "equivalent" and thus eligible for merging. It may be that relaxing the requirement that LP state must be identical will provide even more speedup. It may be that portions of the state have significant tolerance for variation that will have no significant impact on the simulation outcome. If so, a designer could specify such tolerances through an API.

References

[1] D. Chen, S. J. Turner, B. P. Gan, W. Cai, J. Wei, and N. Julka. Alternative solutions for distributed simulation cloning. *Simulation: Transactions of The Society for Modeling and Simulation International*, 79:299–315, 2003.

[2] G. Chen and B. K. Szymanski. Four types of lookback. In *Proceedings of the seventeenth workshop on Parallel and distributed simulation*, page 3. IEEE Computer Society, 2003.

[3] W. J. Davis. On-line simulation: Need and evolving research requirements. In J. Banks, editor, *Handbook of simulation: Principles, methodology, advances, applications, and practice*. John Wiley & Sons, August 1998. Co-published by Engineering and Management Press.

[4] P. Dickens and P. Reynolds. SRADS with Local Rollback. In *Proceedings of the SCS Multiconference on Distributed Simulation*, pages 161–164, 1990.

[5] S. L. Ferenci, R. M. Fujimoto, M. H. Ammar, and K. Perumalla. Updateable simulation of communication networks. In *Proceedings of the* 16th *Workshop on Parallel and Distributed Simulation (PADS-2002)*, pages 107–114, May 2002.

[6] S. Franks, F. Gomes, B. Unger, and J. Cleary. State saving for interactive optimistic simulation. In *Proceedings of the* 11th *Workshop on Parallel and Distributed Simulation (PADS-97)*, pages 72–79, 1997.

[7] R. M. Fujimoto. Performance of Time Warp under synthetic workloads. In *Proceedings of the SCS Multiconference on Distributed Simulation*, volume 22, pages 23–28. SCS Simulation Series, January 1990.

[8] A. Gafni. Rollback mechanisms for optimistic distributed simulation systems. In *SCS Multiconference on Distributed Simulation*, volume 19, pages 61–67, February 1988.

[9] P. W. Glynn and P. Heidelberger. Analysis of parallel replicated simulations under a completion time constraint. *ACM Transactions on Modeling and Computer Simulation (TOMACS)*, 1(1):3–23, 1991.

[10] J. O. Henriksen. An introduction to SLX. In *Proceedings of the 1997 Winter Simulation Conference*, pages 559–566, December 1997.

[11] M. Hybinette. Just-in-time cloning. In *Proceedings of the* 18th *Workshop on Parallel and Distributed Simulation (PADS-2004)*, pages 45–51. ACM Press, 2004.

[12] M. Hybinette and R. M. Fujimoto. Cloning parallel simulations. *ACM Transactions on Modeling and Computer Simulation (TOMACS)*, 11(4):378–407, 2001.

[13] K. P. Lentz, E. S. Manolakos, E. Czeck, and J. Heller. Multiple experiment environments for testing. *Journal of Electronic Testing: Theory and Applications*, 11(3):247–262, December 1999.

[14] T. J. Schriber and D. T. Brunner. Inside discrete-event simulation software: How it works and why it matters. In *Proceedings of the 1997 Winter Simulation Conference*, pages 14–22, December 1997.

[15] T. Schulze, S. Strassburger, and U. Klein. On-line data processing in simulation models: New approaches and possibilities through hla. In *Proceedings of the 1999 Winter Simulation Conference*, pages 1602–1609, December 1999.

[16] T. Schulze, S. Strassburger, and U. Klein. Hla-federate reproduction procedures in public transportation federations. In *Proceedings of the 2000 Summer Computer Simulation Conference*, July 2000.

[17] P. Vakili. Massively parallel and distributed simulation of a class of discrete event systems: a different perspective. *ACM Transactions on Modeling and Computer Simulation (TOMACS)*, 2(3):214–238, 1992.

[18] D. West. Optimizing Time Warp: Lazy rollback and lazy re-evaluation. M.S. Thesis, University of Calgary, January 1988.

[19] F. Wieland. Parallel simulation for aviation applications. In *Proceedings of the IEEE Winter Simulation Conference*, pages 1191–1198, December 1998.

Concurrent Replication of Parallel and Distributed Simulations

Luciano Bononi, Michele Bracuto, Gabriele D'Angelo, Lorenzo Donatiello
Dipartimento di Scienze dell'Informazione, Università degli Studi di Bologna,
Mura Anteo Zamboni 7, 40126, Bologna, Italy
{bononi, bracuto, gdangelo, donat}@cs.unibo.it

Abstract

Parallel and distributed simulations enable the analysis of complex systems by concurrently exploiting the aggregate computation power and memory of clusters of execution units. In this paper we investigate a new direction for increasing both the speedup of a simulation process and the utilization of computation and communication resources. Many simulation-based investigations require to collect independent observations for a correct and significant statistical analysis of results. The execution of many independent parallel or distributed simulation runs may suffer the speedup reduction due to rollbacks under the optimistic approach, and due to idle CPU times originated by synchronization and communication bottlenecks under the conservative approach. We present a parallel and distributed simulation framework supporting Concurrent Replication of Parallel and Distributed Simulations (CR-PADS), as an alternative to the execution of a linear sequence of multiple parallel or distributed simulation runs. Results obtained from tests executed under variable scenarios show that speedup and resource utilization gains could be obtained by adopting the proposed replication approach in addition to the pure parallel and distributed simulation.

1. Introduction

Many fields of research currently adopt simulation-based techniques for the analysis, in order to obtain deep insight of new systems' design, tuning and optimization. Many systems of interest for the analysis may be characterized by complex model definition and dynamic interactions among a possibly huge set of model components. The accuracy of simulation results requires a detailed definition and simulation of every single model component of the whole complex system model. To overcome the computation and memory bottlenecks of mono-processor architectures [22, 23], many practical experiences have demonstrated that a solution for the simulation of such systems is achievable by using parallel and distributed models and architectures, i.e. a Parallel or Distributed Discrete Event Simulation (PDES) approach [14, 16]. The IEEE 1516 Standard for Modeling and Simulation High Level Architecture (HLA) is a recently approved standard dealing with component-oriented distributed simulation [7, 12]. It defines rules and interfaces allowing for heterogeneous model components' interoperability in distributed simulation.

In presence of a complex dynamic system, the implementation of a parallel or distributed simulation would lead to synchronization and communication overheads [3, 4]. The research on the optimization and overheads reduction in parallel and distributed simulations has gained a great interest, leading to the design and implementation of parallel and distributed models and simulation frameworks [3, 10, 17, 22, 24]. In general, an inverse tradeoff exists that determines a mutual worsening in the speedup: i) by reducing the degree of parallelism in the computation or, conversely, ii) by the communication bottlenecks and blocking synchronization primitives among many heterogeneous simulation components. Many research activities dealt with dynamic balancing of logical processes' executions (both cpu-loads and virtual time-advancing speeds) by trading-off communication, synchronization and speedup, both in optimistic and conservative approaches [8, 10, 17]. Adaptive behavior in the management of the model at runtime, to control the overheads due to the model dynamics, have been considered in [3]. A perfect load balancing over the execution units is difficult to obtain, due to the model dynamics and the asymmetry of the physical execution units. For these reasons, a majority of rapidly executed components (Logical Processes, LPs) may be idle waiting the synchronization of at least one single late component. This means that the execution of a majority of execution units is often blocked (by wasting local CPU time), and the whole simulation process proceeds with the speed of the slowest components. The frequent synchronizations are usually implemented as message passing primitives, and may be heavily affected by the overheads for communication management and communication bottlenecks.

In this paper we investigate a new direction for trying to maximize the speedup of the simulation processes and the

This work is supported by MIUR FIRB funds, under the project: "Performance Evaluation of Complex Systems: Techniques, Methodologies and Tools" utilization of computation and communication resources in the system architecture supporting the parallel or distributed simulation. Our assumption, based on a common analysis rule, is that a simulation-based analysis requires many independent parallel or distributed simulation runs, to collect many independent set of observations for a correct and significant statistical analysis of results. Our proposal is to realize a parallel and distributed simulation framework which is able to implement Concurrent Replications of Parallel and Distributed Simulations (CR-PADS), rather than executing a sequence of multiple parallel or distributed simulation runs. The replication concept [11, 13, 15, 20, 21, 22, 24] is intended here as a mechanism that duplicates the logical processes (LPs) of parallel and distributed simulation runs starting from the initialization phase of every single run. Every replica is based on the common model definition, and realizes an independent execution (i.e. replicas do not require mutual synchronization) based on local initial parameters, variable factors for the analysis, and different random number generation seeds. The CR-PADS is intended as a way to maximize the speedup and utilization of system resources when implementing a set of parallel and distributed simulations of complex dynamic system models. This approach is substantially different from the simulation Cloning concept [6, 18]. Simulation cloning has been demonstrated as a good technique for supporting "faster than real time" simulation [18] and "what if" analysis [6] being based on the active cloning of multiple instances of the initial simulation process at "decision points" that may be met during the simulation. The CR-PADS approach is not intended as a way to investigate all the possible evolutions from a "decision point", like in the Cloning approach. The CR-PADS replication approach is also different from the Multiple Replications in Parallel (MRIP) approach adopted for the concurrent execution of independent sequential simulation runs, like in the Akaroa2 framework [1, 2, 11, 13, 15, 22]. The aim of MRIP in Akaroa2 is basically to give a simple way to the modeller for initiating multiple independent runs of sequential simulators over different processors. To the best of our knowledge, Akaroa2 offers a controlled environment for launching multiple independent sequential simulations, each one executed over a single CPU, without managing the concept of parallel and distributed simulation. With respect to CR-PADS approach, Akaroa2 and the MRIP approach may have limitations in exploiting the aggregate resources of a cluster of execution units, and the adoption of distributed models, which are some of the motivations in favour of the parallel and distributed simulation.

The implementation of the CR-PADS mechanism has been defined and tested over the Advanced RTI System (ARTÌS) framework [5]. The ARTÌS framework is a middleware currently under implementation, whose design is inspired to the High Level Architecture (HLA) design and IEEE 1516 Standard. Results obtained for the simulation of a complex dynamic system model (i.e. a wireless ad hoc network model) demonstrate that a speedup gain can be obtained by adopting the proposed replication approach as an alternative to a sequence of standalone parallel and distributed simulations. The speedup is obtained up to a given amount of replicas and has evidenced a dependence on the model characteristics. Basically, trashing effects are introduced when the saturation of the computation power of all the CPUs has been achieved. An excessive number of replicas would result in additional trashing effects under the management viewpoint. Given the light and efficient implementation of CR-PADS the number of replicas causing trashing is in a range that exceeds the typical amount of runs required to achieve a good statistical relevance, i.e. thin confidence intervals, from the collected observations.

The paper structure is the following: in section 2 we outline some concepts about the parallel and distributed simulation cloning and replication; in Section 3 the key issues for the replication mechanism implementation and the ARTÌS middleware are defined; in section 4 a prototype wireless system's model and a set of simulation results are presented to evaluate the concurrent replication approach; in section 5 we summarize our conclusions and future work.

2. Cloning and Replication of Parallel and Distributed Simulations

The Multiple Replications in Parallel (MRIP) is a technique that we cite here as a reference for our work [1, 2, 11, 13, 15, 20, 21]. This technique consists in launching multiple runs of independent sequential simulations in parallel over a set of concurrent CPUs. Every simulation run is executed from the beginning up to the end on the same CPU, under the control of a single scheduler (i.e. a monolithic sequential simulation). Some frameworks like Akaroa2 provide support for the MRIP when launching simulations based on common sequential simulation tools like PTolemy, NS2, OMNET++ [13, 22]. To the best of our knowledge, the MRIP approach for parallel and distributed simulations is still to be investigated.

2.1. Parallel and Distributed Simulation

The architecture of the physical execution units (PEUs) can be organized in different ways: from a parallel multi-processor architecture with shared memory up to a distributed cluster of PCs interconnected by LANs or even by the Internet. The research community called a parallel simulation the concurrent execution of a single simulation run over a tightly coupled multi-processor architecture, and a distributed simulation the concurrent execution of a single simulation run over a loosely coupled set of execution units, each one running on a possibly different HW architecture and separate local memory. In the optimistic approaches for implementing parallel and distributed simulations, several simulation components may bet on forecasting and computing one out of the possible evolutions, in order to obtain a maximum exploitation of the parallel execution. In solutions like the Time Warp [19], many model components advance their evolution without worrying about causality maintenance at least until a violation of causality is revealed: in such case a costly process called rollback is executed to restore the processes states to a global safe-state. Such optimistic implementations were thought as a way to maximize the utilization of expensive computation architectures. The efficiency of optimistic implementations would depend heavily on the evolutionary characteristics of the models: highly independent, predictable or self-correlated models would behave better than unpredictable ones, since independent sub-models may have few common "decision points" affecting each others' evolution, and the choices made at "decision points" could be performed on the basis of more effective "oracles" that could reduce the need for frequent rollbacks. Needless to say, rollbacks can reduce the efficiency of the simulation process in significant way. In the conservative approach, each "time advance" in the model evolution is made under the conservative assumption that all previous events have been processed in correct timestamp order, by all the parallel and distributed model components. Frequent synchronizations (i.e. blocking and unblocking event executions) of all the model components are performed for ensuring a conservative implementation of the causal order of events.

2.2. IPC Communication for Parallel and Distributed Simulation

The communication among LPs in a parallel simulation is usually efficient and reliable because it can be supported by the classical mechanisms for local inter-process communication (IPC) like pipes, FIFO channels and Shared Memory. Possible advantages given by local IPC communication mechanisms are: reliable communications, ordering maintenance of messages, and efficiency, intended as high bitrate and low latency channels among LPs. The shared memory solution requires a control of the concurrent accesses to mutual exclusive areas: the efficient implementation of control primitives by the operating system is a necessary condition for the efficiency of the communication.

The distributed simulation approach is based on the implementation of concurrent LPs executed over distributed physical execution units (PEUs). The advantages of distributed simulation architectures can be summarized as: i) theoretical scalability, given by the arbitrary extension of the PEU architecture, ii) the possible geographical distribution of PEUs, which could be exploited to deal with management and reliability issues, and iii) the fault tolerance based on the possible substitution of unreliable or disconnected PEUs. The communication among LPs can be supported typically by external inter-process communication mechanisms, i.e. message passing based on packet-based communication over heterogeneous interconnection networks. External IPC solutions are usually less reliable and efficient than local IPC. The assumptions about the network infrastructures to be adopted ranges from efficient LANs up to unreliable and high-latency Internet-based communication. In some scenarios, both parallel and distributed PEUs can be used to execute simulations. Given the low performance and reliability of network based communication, it is clear that local IPC is preferable (if available) to be exploited over parallel architectures.

2.3. Parallel and Distributed Simulation Cloning

The simulation cloning technology was introduced as a concurrent evaluation mechanism, in the context of parallel simulation [18]. Simulation cloning allows the creation of copies of a simulation process (clones) at "decision points", which are evaluated at runtime, but need to be defined preliminary in the model design phase. When a set of clones is created, each clone would execute a different possible evolution of the current scenario, each one related to any choice made at the decision point. The main flow of events of a simulation may be recursively split in separate flows characterizing a different evolution of clones, starting from the decision points. The advantage of simulation cloning is basically obtained by the concurrent investigation of alternative choices, by exploiting the concurrent computation of parallel and distributed architectures. Clones' evolutions originated by bad choices can be killed at runtime to reduce the overheads.

The cloning approach includes the management of different time axes in parallel, in order to support a runtime forecasting functionality [24]. In [6] the aim to support users willing to run existing complex simulation models, gave to reusability and transparency issues a top role while enabling simulation cloning. This is the reason for cloning design on HLA-compliant distributed simulations, which led to the introduction of the concept of virtual federates [6, 18]. A preliminary discussion of the design and implementation challenges and solutions, like virtual logical processes (VLPs) and virtual messages (VMs), can be found in [6, 18]. The design and implementation of runtime support for cloning of HLA-based parallel and distributed simulations is quite complex and challenging effort. This is even more critical under HLA-based and Data Distribution Management (DDM) based implementations.

2.4. The Concurrent Replication of Parallel and Distributed Simulations

The replication concept is intended here as a mechanism that duplicates the logical processes (LPs) of parallel and distributed simulation runs starting from the initialization phase of every single run. Each replica is based on a common model definition, and realizes an independent run execution based on local initial parameters, variable factors for the analysis, and different random number generation seeds. In other words, many independent simulation runs are executed concurrently by replicating them (just as clones) only at the beginning of the simulation process.

2.4.1. Motivations for the Concurrent Replication. In the following we are going to explain the motivations for our proposal of a Concurrent Replication mechanism for Parallel and Distributed Simulation (CR-PADS) by sketching the differences among the MRIP, the PDES and the CR-PADS approaches, under the computation and communication viewpoints.

In figure 1, by assuming that a set of N CPUs are made available for computation (no matter if they belong to parallel or distributed architectures) we want a set of many independent runs to be executed (only two in the figure for clarity). Obviously, the aim is to have the completion of the overall simulation process in the lowest time and with the maximum utilization of computation and communication resources. By focusing on the MRIP approach (figure 1a), the independent runs can be executed by launching in parallel the sequential simulations over the available CPUs. It results that the possible concurrency of the model execution cannot be exploited to obtain simulation speedup, because every computation is linearly executed as a sequence of tasks. In this scenario, the model data structures and computation must fit on the CPU system and may suffer memory and computation limitations. Moreover, as the figure 1a illustrates, if the available resources are more than the number of runs required, the potential associated to some resources may remain unexploited.

The parallel (or distributed) discrete event simulation (PDES) approach (see figure 1b) may introduce advantages, because every independent run could exploit the whole computation architecture, by mapping and exploiting the degree of parallelism inherent to the model over the concurrent CPUs. This implies that a single run may complete in less time than a sequential run. On the other hand, the linear execution of two (or many) runs in the scenario of figure 1b may result in a speedup depending on the number of resources and the number of runs required under MRIP and PDES, respectively. It is worth noting that the advantages of the aggregate memory architecture may assist the model data structures management, and that the whole set of computation resources (CPUs) can be exploited in parallel.

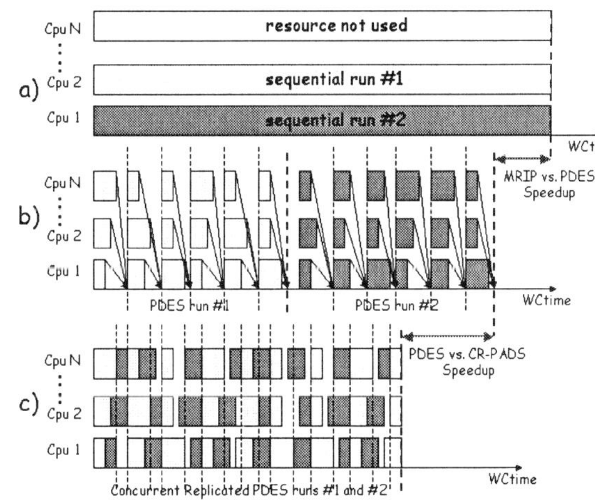

Figure 1. Comparing MRIP vs. PADS vs. CR-PADS

The problem arising under the PDES scenario is represented in the figure 1b, where frequent synchronizations are required among the model components (by assuming a conservative event-based or time-stepped implementation). Every synchronization barrier initially unblocks the concurrent computation of CPUs. As soon as the computation phase is terminated, every process starts a message passing phase to synchronize again its execution with other processes. This implies that i) the whole set of processes advance with the speed of the slowest (or more computation intensive) one, and ii) the final phase before the synchronization barrier is communication-intensive and may suffer additional delays due to the congestion and delays of the inter-process communication infrastructure. The communication delay may result in a high percentage of the whole synchronization delay, under loosely coupled distributed architectures (e.g. over CPUs interconnected by LAN or Internet technology). In other words, as shown in figure 1b, every simulation process may result in a sequence of mixed and interleaving bottleneck phases originated i) by the CPU computation and ii) by synchronization and communications, respectively.

In this work we investigate how to obtain a more fluent computation and communication by merging the execution tasks of more than one parallel or distributed simulation replica over the computation and communication architecture. By launching multiple, independent and concurrent parallel or distributed simulation runs, idle CPU time could be avoided by switching to the execution of computation requests by the other replicas which already completed their synchronization phase. The same principle could be exploited under the communication system viewpoint, because the message passing from all the replicas may increase the uniform utilization of the communication system. As a result, idle CPU phases, and idle or congested communication phases, could be smoothed over time. This may result in additional speedup with respect to the time required for completing the whole set of simulation runs. The risk in this approach is to spend too much time in switching processes' executions, and in the creation of communication bottlenecks and livelocks, resulting in trashing effects. Our design is based on a set of guidelines that we followed in order to obtain the maximum advantage from the replication mechanism, by opportunely managing the processes executions and communications, and by keeping under control the overheads introduced.

2.4.2. Advantages of the Replication approach. Among the advantages of a concurrent replication approach for parallel and distributed simulations, at the top layer we identify the possible speedup obtainable when executing a set of many independent runs, or the possible concurrent analysis of different scenarios (defined at the beginning of the run). Specific implementation guidelines could lead to additional advantages. As an example, we defined the structure of the ARTÌS framework such that a separation of the simulation and replication management is specifically devoted to a clean design and to the exploitation of management techniques that reduce the communication overheads.

Replicas are created by replicating virtual LPs that realize a simulation run. A set of replicas of virtual LPs is managed as a single LP by the runtime management. This simplifies the management under the ARTÌS viewpoint and allows an optimization and balancing of the utilization of communication resources, based on queue management, priority and fairness protocols. The management of Random Numbers Generators (RNGs) is simpler than in the cloning approach, because seeds can be chosen at the beginning of the runs, without originating correlated sequences whose effect could bias the analysis of results at the end of a set of simulation runs.

3. The CR-PADS Implementation

Recently proposed and implemented middleware solutions based on the IEEE 1516 Standard have shown that the parallel and distributed simulation of massive and complex systems can result in relevant overheads [3, 4]. Overheads are due to the complex and full management of a wide set of runtime services and to the latency due to distributed communication bottlenecks. Specifically, the implementation of the interprocess communication services has been implemented in sub-optimal way, without considering the heterogeneity of the simulation execution platforms [3, 4].

The HLA implementation criticisms [3, 4, 7, 9] and the lack of efficient Open Source runtimes are the main motivations behind the design and implementation of a new parallel and distributed simulation middleware named Advanced RTI System (ARTÌS) [5]. The aim of the ARTÌS middleware is to support parallel and distributed simulations of complex systems, based on a minimal set of efficiency-oriented middleware services. The ARTÌS design is oriented to support the model components' heterogeneity, distribution and reuse, and to increase the simulation performances, scalability and speedup, in parallel and distributed simulation scenarios. Another design issue of the ARTÌS framework is the dynamic adaptation of the interprocess communication layer to the heterogeneous communication support offered by possibly different simulation-execution units. Specifically, the ARTÌS design is based on the adaptive evaluation of the communication bottlenecks and support for multiple communication infrastructures and services, from shared memory to Internet-based communication.

The ARTÌS implementation follows a component-based design, that results in easily extendable middleware (see figure 2a). The solutions proposed for time management and synchronization in distributed simulations have been widely analyzed and discussed in the design phase. Currently, ARTÌS supports the conservative time management based on both the time-stepped approach, and the Chandy-Misra-Bryant (CMB) algorithm. The extension of ARTÌS to support optimistic time management algorithms (Time Warp) is ongoing work.

3.1. Implementation of Replication in ARTÌS

Given the top level structure of ARTÌS shown in figure 2a, ARTÌS supports the execution of LPs over the RTI kernel. The RTI kernel implements time management policies, object ownership and declaration management, data distribution management, federation management and other functions. At the bottom layer of the RTI, the Runtime Communication layer (RTIComm) manages the communication based on the underlying communication system that connects the PEUs' architecture. Specifically, communication is implemented over shared memory for parallel processors, over Reliable-UDP for LANs and TCP/IP for Internet-based communication.

In ARTÌS, many design optimizations have been applied to obtain adequate protocols for synchronization and communication over Local Area Networks (LAN) or Shared Memory (SHM) multiprocessor architectures. In our vision the communication and synchronization middleware should be adaptive and user-transparent about all the optimizations required to improve performances. The current scheme adopts an incremental straightforward policy: given a set of LPs on the same physical host, such processes always communicate and synchronize via read and write operations, performed within the address space of LPs, in the shared memory (see PEU X on figure 3). To implement these services we have designed, implemented and tested many different solutions, based on inter-process communication (IPC) semaphores and locks, busy-waiting, and "wait on signals" with a limited set of temporized spin-locks. The latter solution has demonstrated very low latency and limited CPU overhead, good performances obtained in multi-CPU systems, good scalability, and no need to reconfigure the operating system kernel level.

Two or more LPs located on different hosts (i.e. no shared memory available), on the same local area network segment, communicate by using a light Reliable-UDP (R-UDP) transport protocol over the IP protocol. Two or more LPs located on Internet hosts rely on standard TCP/IP connections (see PEUs X and Y in figure 3).

Given the ARTÌS design, the abstractions of LPs, messages, channels and simulation-runs appear as objects implemented over the RTI kernel. In order to manage efficiently the management of messages among LPs, an active thread is waiting for messages on each channel, and demultiplexes messages to the above layers by adopting an efficient callback mechanism. The time management layer also adopts callback techniques to avoid polling techniques over the RTIComm layer, that may reduce performances.

The Replication mechanism has been inserted in ARTÌS directly over the RTIComm layer. This facilitates the need to maintain transparency to the LPs, and light implementation of the replication mechanism. The choice to realize replication at the above layers would have given benefits under the optimization viewpoint, at the additional expenses of ad hoc re-implementation of the replication services for each time management policy.

The Replication management layer is the funnel for replicas over the RTIComm layer (see figure 2b). The Replication layer generates the replicas of each LP, and manages messages from/to LPs of each replica. The set of processes and threads of each simulation replica has been designed as a tree-like structure, whose inter-process communication is based on highly efficient UNIX pipes. UNIX pipes have been preferred to shared data structures, because messages have limited size and the consistency management of shared data structures would introduce latency and additional overheads.

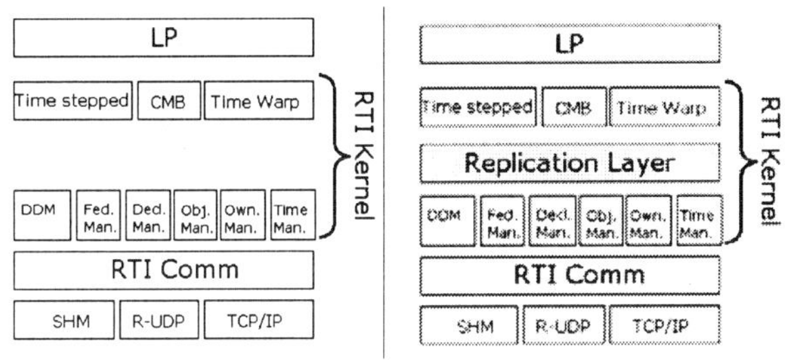

a b

Figure 2. The ARTÌS and Replication architecture

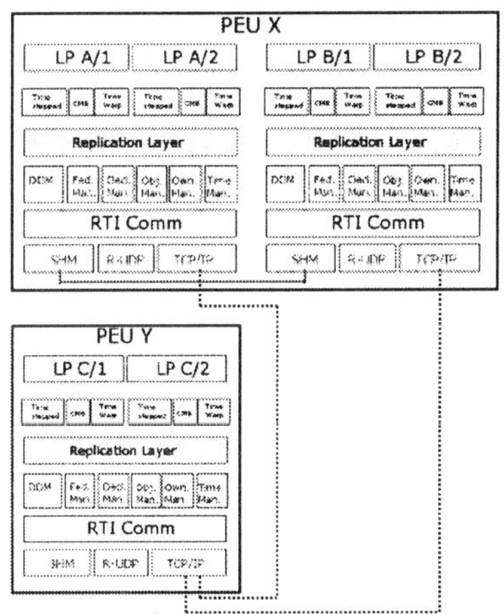

Figure 3. Parallel and distributed CR-PADS structure

The proposed implementation architecture allows optimization of the communication management locally to the LPs. Alternative architectures aiming to reduce the communication bottleneck are currently under evaluation. In the following, we sketch the dynamic behavior of the Replication management layer when replicating a LP in a parallel or distributed simulation run.

1) *the user's simulator code is compiled with ARTÌS*
2) *the simulation run is started*
   a) *execute initialization*
   b) *call ARTIS_init() API who creates LP_father*
3) *ARTIS_init() calls Replication_init()*
4) *LP_father calls RTI_kernel_init()*
   a) *RTI_kernel_init() creates threads for communication and initialization of LP replicas that will be created by the LP_forker thread*
   b) *each LP replica create a new pipe_listener thread to receive messages from the LP_father*
5) *the LP_father creates the LP_forker process*
   a) *LP_forker process generates new replicas (upon request from the user)*
6) *LP_father waits on its own communication pipes*
7) *Simulation run starts*

a) once LP replicas send messages, the Replication layer sends the message to the LP_father pipe

b) once the LP_father receives messages, it adds headers for multiplexing and manage the message by adopting the standard RTI kernel functions to send the message to the receiver LP.

c) once a message is received by the thread of the receiver LP, the receiver LP demultiplexes the message to the pipes of the LP replicas, where the message is handled

The set of operations 7.a.b.c is executed until the LP process terminates, and all its resources are freed.

4. Performance Evaluation

To test our framework we implemented a time-stepped, conservative, parallel and distributed discrete-event simulation of a mobile wireless system.

4.1. Simulation system and simulation model

Our simulation testbed consists of two different environments: i) parallel and ii) distributed discrete-event simulation of model components. In the parallel environment for simulation the model components are executed as logical processes over a dual processor physical execution unit (PEU). Specifically, the PEU is an Intel Dual Xeon Pentium IV 2800 Mhz, with 3 GB RAM, Debian GNU/Linux OS with kernel version 2.6.

In the distributed environment the logical processes are mapped over a set of physical execution units (PEUs), connected by a physical LAN network. Specifically, the execution architecture is composed by three homogeneous units defined like the aforementioned PEU.

As a testbed for our replication framework, we realized a conservative, time-stepped simulation of a complex and dynamic model. The simulation model we considered for the simulations is a wireless mobile ad hoc network model. The mobile ad hoc network is realized by Simulated Mobile Hosts (SMHs), each one characterized by random mobility and CBR traffic (that is, ping messages sent to all the neighbor SMHs in their reception area). The number of simulated SMHs has the effect of controlling the average SMH density in the system. The SMH mobility causes changes in the network topology and the SMH dynamics. Since the model design is out of scope in this paper, we simply characterize the model execution by noting that: i) the computation required for each SMHs per timestep is in the order of O(#SMH^2) and, ii) the communication and synchronization required among SMHs is in the order of O(K*#SMHs) per timestep. All the model choices have been defined in order to realize a stressing test for our simulation framework.

4.2. Performance results

In this section we present the results of some testbed simulation experiments executed to analyze the performance of the proposed CR-PADS approach in presence of parallel and distributed environments.

We performed multiple runs of each experiment, and the confidence intervals obtained with a 95% confidence level are lower than 5% the average value of the performance indices shown.

In the following we define M as the number of physical execution units (PEUs) supporting the simulation execution, and N as the total number of logical processes (LPs) implemented for each simulation run. As mentioned above, each PEU is composed by a dual processor machine. With the "CR-PADS OFF" label we identify a legacy parallel and distributed simulation approach: that is, simulation runs are executed in sequential order, by activating N LPs at a time. With "CR-PADS ON" we identify a parallel or distributed simulation executed under the effect of the CR-PADS replication approach described in previous sections. The "number of replications" is intended as the number of independent simulation runs executed (both sequentially when CR-PADS is OFF, and in concurrent way when CR-PADS is ON).

In figures 4, 5 and 6 we report results for the parallel simulation environment (M=1, N=2). Each figure shows the Wall Clock Time (WCT) required for completing the x simulation processes. Figure 4 shows the effect of 500 SMHs involved in the simulation (250 SMHs over the N=2 LPs executed over the M=1 dual processor PEU). Figure 5 and 6 show the same index with 1000 and 2000 SMHs, respectively. Results confirm that the CR-PADS approach outperforms the sequential approach by considering the WCT required to complete a whole set of simulation runs. Each run is defined with fixed size of 300 timesteps. In figure 4, by increasing the number of concurrent replications (up to 20), the CR-PADS results are better than the traditional parallel simulation approach. By increasing the number of SMHs up to 1000 (fig. 5) and 2000 (fig. 6) we are increasing the percentage weight of local computation, with respect to the percentage weight of communication, in the sequence of synchronization steps, for each SMH during the simulation runs. This means that we are pushing the computation to saturate all the CPUs computation power. When the computation load for LPs asymptotically saturates the CPU computation power, the CR-PADS approach becomes less efficient than the legacy PADS approach, because it does not longer exploit any idle CPU time in order to execute more concurrent replicas.

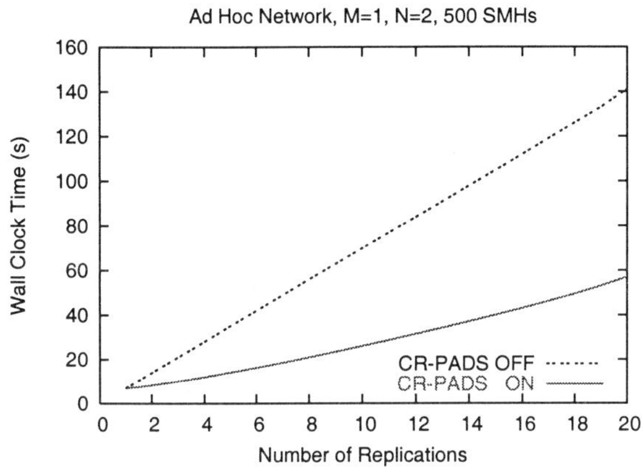

Figure 4. Total WCT vs. Number of runs (replications) Parallel simulation scenario: M=1, N=2, 500 SMHs

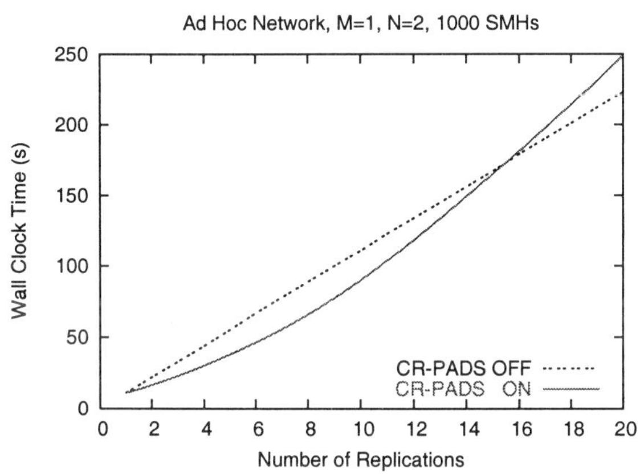

Figure 5. Total WCT vs. Number of runs (replications) Parallel simulation scenario: M=1, N=2, 1000 SMHs

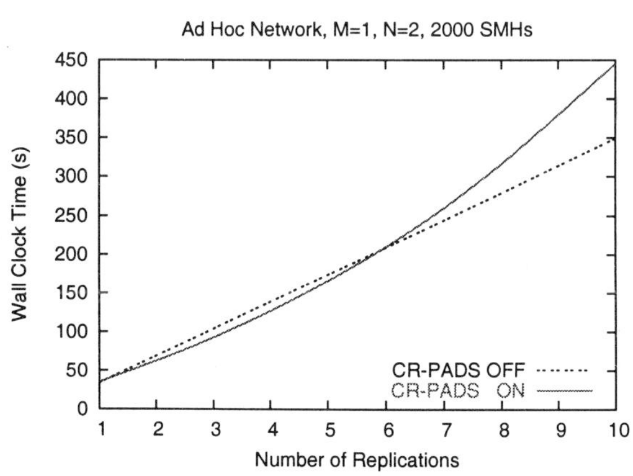

Figure 6. Total WCT vs. Number of runs (replications) Parallel simulation scenario: M=1, N=2, 2000 SMHs

It is worth noting that the break-even in the number of replicas is around 15 in figure 5 and around 6 concurrent replicas in figure 6. As it was expected, the CR-PADS approach introduces overheads when the number of replicas is high and the computation of few replicas saturates the computation power of all PEUs. It is worth noting that in all the proposed scenarios, the CR-PADS approach can give a speedup effect, at least limited to the initial subrange in the number of concurrent replicas. By focusing our attention to the distributed environment (with M=3 and N=6), in figures 7, 8 and 9 we illustrate the same results shown for the parallel simulation scenario.

It is worth noting that the average communication latency of distributed environments is at least one order of magnitude bigger than the average latency experienced in the parallel architecture.

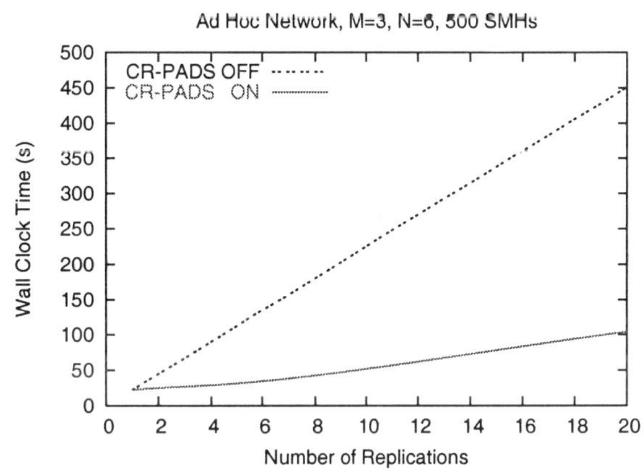

Figure 7. Total WCT vs. Number of runs (replications) Distributed simulation scenario: M=3, N=6, 500 SMHs

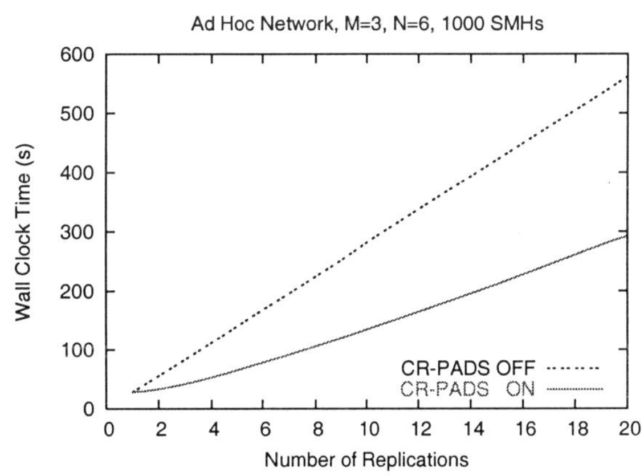

Figure 8. Total WCT vs. Number of runs (replications) Distributed simulation scenario: M=3, N=6, 1000 SMHs

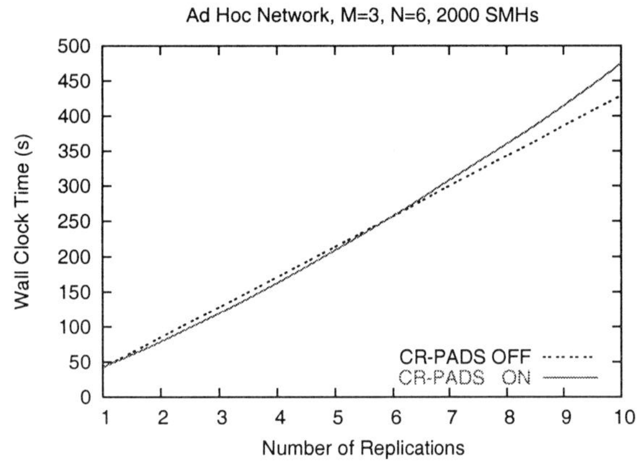

Figure 9. Total WCT vs. Number of runs (replications) Distributed simulation scenario: M=3, N=6, 2000 SMHs

A significant latency implies long time required to achieve synchronization at every timestep. This would translate in better opportunities for CR-PADS to optimize the concurrent execution of many runs, by exploiting a better utilization of the PEU computation power, and by reducing the global WCT required for completing the simulations. The results confirm the expectations: for a number of concurrent runs ranging from 1 up to 20, the CR-PADS mechanism is able to give significant speedup both in the 500 and 1000 SMHs scenarios (figures 7 and 8). When the scenario becomes computation-intensive (2000 SMHs in figure 9) the CR-PADS approximates the same results than the legacy PADS approach, and does not introduce significant overheads in the range of 1 up to 10 concurrent replications.

Figure 10 illustrates the rate of event processing under both parallel and distributed scenarios obtained for 10 simulation runs executed with and without the CR-PADS framework in background. By looking at the figure 10, CR-PADS allows a high event computation density when the computation load in each timestep does not saturate the available CPUs (that is, when SMH=500..1000). When the computation load increases (SMH=2000) the trashing effect of CR-PADS appears, basically because there is not space for additional concurrency in the computation. In the distributed scenario, the high latency of communication reduces the computation concurrency in legacy distributed simulations. As expected, the CR-PADS mechanism is able to maintain a high computation concurrency.

Figure 11 shows the effect of the communication layer during the execution of distributed simulations. It is clear how the CR-PADS mechanism is able to increase the throughput of communication channels even when the computation load is low. Conversely, when CR-PADS is off, the communication channels are under-utilized. When the computation load asymptotically saturates the available CPUs, both the CR-PADS On and CR-PADS Off implementations converge to the same network utilization. This is due because the network communication is generated as a function of the events processed (that is the computation performed, which is the system bottleneck in the current scenario).

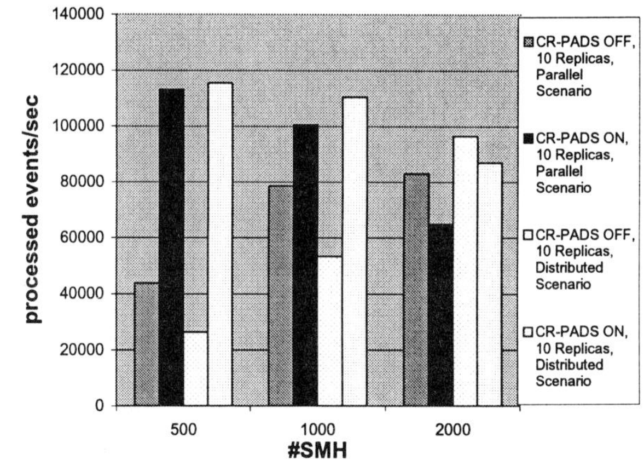

Figure 10. Analysis of event processing rate

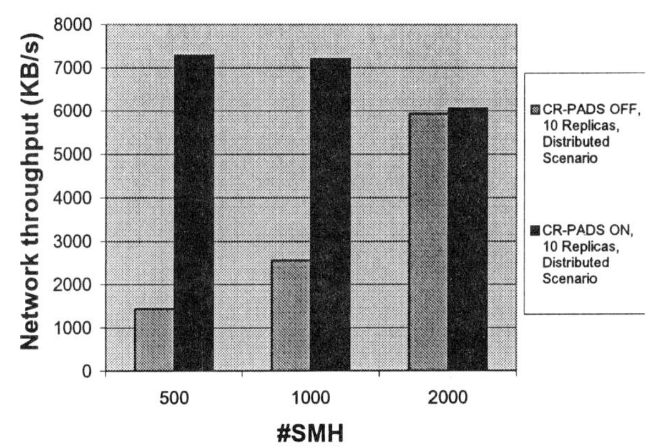

Figure 11. Analysis of communication throughput

5. Conclusions and future work

In this paper we propose and investigate a new direction for increasing both the speedup of a parallel or distributed simulation process and the utilization of computation and communication resources. A typical implementation of a simulation-based investigation requires to collect many independent observations for a correct and significant statistical analysis of results. On the other hand, the execution of many independent parallel or distributed simulations may suffer the speedup reduction due to rollbacks under the optimistic approach, and due to idle CPU times originated by synchronization and communication bottlenecks under the conservative approach. We present a parallel and distributed simulation framework supporting Concurrent Replication of Parallel and Distributed Simulations (CR-PADS), as an alternative to the execution of a linear sequence of multiple parallel or distributed simulation runs. The implementation of the CR-PADS mechanism has been defined and tested over the Advanced RTI System (ARTÌS) framework, which is inspired to the HLA architecture. Results obtained from tests executed under variable scenarios show that speedup gains could be obtained by adopting the proposed replication approach in addition to the pure parallel and distributed simulation. Our future work will include the optimization of the proposed framework, and the investigation of adaptive automation of concurrent replication. We plan to investigate the adoption of CR-PADS under other conservative and optimistic approaches for parallel and distributed simulation, and under massive parallel computation architectures. We also plan to integrate CR-PADS with a framework for adaptive load balancing and migration of simulated entities, and with the components for runtime transient and steady-state analysis of data, confidence interval estimation, and run termination management.

6. References

[1] D. Anagnostopoulos and M. Nikolaidou, "Executing a Minimum Number of Replications to Support the Reliability of FRTS Predictions", proc. 7-th IEEE DS-RT 2003, Delft, The Netherlands, Oct. 2003

[2] W. Biles and J.P.C. Kleijnen, "Statistical Methodology for WEB-Based Simulation", proc. 7-th IEEE DS-RT 2003, Delft, The Netherlands, Oct. 2003

[3] L. Bononi, G. D'Angelo and L. Donatiello, "HLA-Based Adaptive Distributed Simulation of Wireless Mobile Systems", in Proceedings of IEEE/ACM Int'l Workshop on Parallel and Distributed Simulation (PADS'03), San Diego, CA, 06/2003

[4] L. Bononi, M. Bracuto, G. D'Angelo and L. Donatiello, "A New Adaptive Middleware for Parallel and Distributed Simulation of Dynamically Interacting Systems", proc. 8-th IEEE Int'l Symposium on Distributed Simulation and Real Time Applications (DS-RT 2004), Budapest, Hungary, Oct. 2004

[5] L. Bononi, M. Bracuto, G. D'Angelo and L. Donatiello, "ARTIS: a Parallel and Distributed Simulation Middleware for Performance Evaluation", in LNCS 3280 - 2004 Proc. of the 19-th International Symposium on Computer and Information Sciences (ISCIS 2004), Antalya, Turkey, Oct. 2004, 627-637

[6] D. Chen, S.J. Turner, B.P. Gan, W.T. Cai, J. Wei and N. Julka "Alternative Solutions for Distributed Simulation Cloning", Simulation, Vol. 79, No. 5-6, 299-315 (2003)

[7] J. Dahmann, R.M. Fujimoto, and R.M. Weatherly, "High Level Architecture for Simulation: an update", Winter Simulation Conference, December 1998

[8] S.R. Das, "Adaptive protocols for Parallel Discrete Event Simulation", Proc. of Winter Simulation Conference, 1996

[9] W.J. Davis and G.L. Moeller, "The High Level Architecture: is there a better way?", proc. Winter Simulation Conf., 1999

[10] E. Deelman and B.K. Szymanski, "Dynamic load balancing in parallel discrete event simulation for spatially explicit problems", Proc. of the 12-th workshop on Parallel and distributed simulation PADS'98, July 1998

[11] E. de Souza Mota, K. Pawlikowski and A. Wolisz. "A Perspective of Batching Methods in Simulation Environment of Multiple Replications in Parallel", Proc. Winter Simulation Conf. 2000, Orlando, Florida, USA, Dec. 2000, pp. 761-766

[12] DMSO: Defence Modeling and Simulation Office (1998), High Level Architecture RTI Interface Specification, Ver. 1.3

[13] G. Ewing, K. Pawlikowski and D. McNickle. "Akaroa2: Exploiting Network Computing by Distributing Stochastic Simulation", Proc. European Simulation Multiconference ESM'99, Warsaw, ISCS, June 1999, pp. 175-181

[14] A. Ferscha, "Parallel and Distributed Simulation of Discrete Event Systems", In Handbook of Parallel and Distributed Computing, McGraw-Hill, 1995

[15] F.Fitzek, E. Mota, E. Ewers, A. Wolisz, and K. Pawlikowski, "An Efficient Approach For Speeding Up Simulation Of Wireless Networks", In Proc. of WMC 2000, San Diego, California, USA, January 2000.

[16] R.M. Fujimoto, "Parallel and Distributed Simulation Systems", John Wiley & Sons, 2000

[17] B.P. Gan, Y.H. Low, S. Jain, S.J. Turner, W. Cai, W.J. Hsu and S.Y. Huang, "Load balancing for conservative simulation on shared memory multiprocessor systems", Proc. of the 14-th workshop on Parallel and distributed simulation (PADS'00), May 28-31, 2000, Bologna, Italy, p.139-146

[18] M. Hybinette and R.M. Fujimoto. "Cloning parallel simulations". ACM Trans. Model. Comput. Simul., 11(4), 2001.

[19] D.R. Jefferson, "Virtual Time", ACM Trans. on Prog. Languages and Systems, Vol.7 No.3, pp. 404-425, 1985

[20] K.G. Jones and S.R. Das, "Parallel Execution of a sequential network simulator", Proc. of the 2000 Winter Simulation Conference, 2000

[21] Y.B. Lin, "Parallel independent replicated simulation on a network of workstations", In proc. of the 8-th workshop on Parallel and distributed simulation, pp. 73--80, 1994.

[22] G.F. Riley, R.M. Fujimoto and M.H. Ammar, "A generic framework for parallelization of network simulations", Proc. of MASCOTS'99, College Park, MD, October 1999

[23] G.F. Riley and M.H. Ammar, "Simulating Large Networks How Big is Big Enough?", Proc. of First Intern.l Conference on Grand Challenges for Modeling and Simulation, Jan. 2002

[24] T. Schulze, S. Straßburger, and U. Klein, "HLA- federate reproduction procedures in public transportation federations" proceedings of the 2000 Summer Computer Simulation Conference, July, Vancouver, Canada

(MMSM) Malware Defense

Software Diversity as a Defense Against Viral Propagation: Models and Simulations

Adam J. O'Donnell*, Harish Sethu
ECE Department
Drexel University
3141 Chestnut St.
Philadelphia, PA, USA

E-mail: {adam, sethu}@ece.drexel.edu

Abstract

The use of software diversity has often been discussed in the research literature as an effective means to break up the software monoculture present on the Internet and to thus prevent malcode propagation. However, there have been no quantitative studies that examine the effectiveness of software diversity on viral propagation. In this paper, we study both real (an IPv6 BGP topology) and synthetically generated (an Erdös-Rényi random graph) network topologies and employ a popular metric called the epidemic threshold to measure resistance to viral propagation in the presence of software diversity. We show that one can increase the epidemic threshold of a network even with a naïve, random distribution of diverse software on the nodes of a network. We also show that an algorithm-driven diversity assignment further increases the epidemic threshold. These results confirm the value of strategic topology-sensitive assignment of diversity to improving the tolerance of a network to malcode propagation.

1. Introduction

The field of viral propagation modeling has garnered a great deal of attention in recent years as computer security researchers attempt to find ways of mitigating rapid malcode propagation. A variety of techniques have been suggested which can delay the spread of a worm, including rate-limiting network cards [23], targeted immunization of highly connected nodes [17], and a combination of address blacklisting and content filtering [14]. In complementary work, researchers have been focusing on the software monoculture on the Internet and its relationship to viral epidemics. The value of software diversity to computer security comes from the fact that an attack written for one piece of software rarely works for a different but functionally equivalent software package. By increasing the number of diverse software packages present on the network, the research argues, the chances that an attack will be effective against a randomly selected node will decrease.

The research literature in software diversity suggests that the introduction of different software packages is an effective method of disrupting the activities of an attacker or a worm, particularly one which repeatedly utilizes a pre-written and unchanging attack to compromise machines. However, there have been no quantitative evaluations of the impact of software diversity on malcode propagation in real network topologies. In this paper, we use a popular metric called the *epidemic threshold* [22] to measure a network's resiliency against malcode propagation and study the steady state prevalence of computer viruses in the presence of software diversity. We show, through both modeling and simulation, that even a simple randomized distribution of diverse software packages can increase the epidemic threshold of both real and synthetically generated computer networks. This paper also shows that an algorithm-driven distribution of diverse software packages [15] can further increase the epidemic threshold and serve as an effective method for preventing worm epidemics.

2. Problem Statement

In previous work [15], we showed that the location of diverse software packages on a network is as critical to effectively diversifying a network as the creation of diverse software packages. A visual example of this is provided in Figure 1, where the introduction of an alternative software package is able to minimize the number

* The author's work was supported by the NSF Graduate Research Fellowship and the Koerner Family Fellowship.

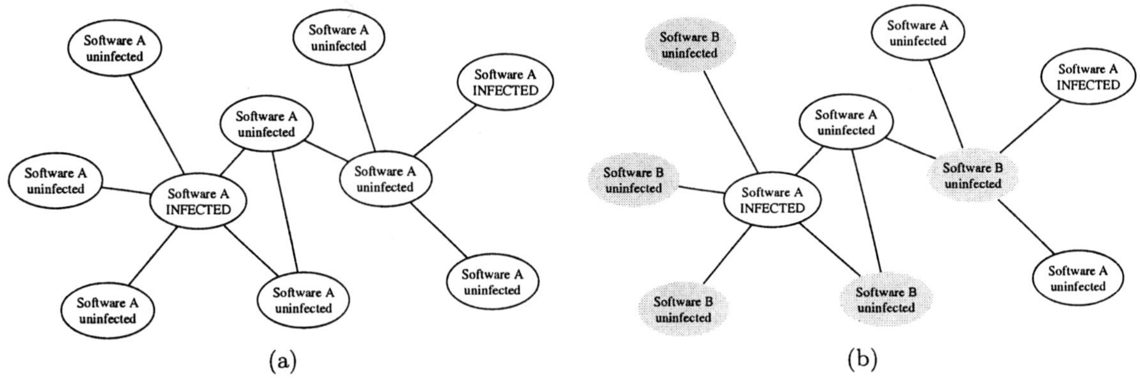

Figure 1. The networks presented above are both infected with a computer virus. The network shown in (a) consists of nodes running the same software package. The nodes in the network shown in (b) are allowed to run two different operating systems. While topologically equivalent, the network shown in (b) provides only a single link for an infectious agent to traverse by reducing the number of vulnerable nodes by half.

of edges across which a virus can traverse. Assuming that different software packages are represented by different colors, this problem translates to that of the distributed coloring of a graph while minimizing the number of monochromatic edges, i.e., the number of homogeneous pairs of neighbors.

While the number of monochromatic edges is an effective metric as an optimization goal, it does not directly express the ability of the diversity assignment algorithm to limit the virulence of a worm. This paper, on the other hand, quantifies the quality of a software diversity assignment by focusing on the effect that network assignments of diverse software has upon the propagation of worms. Given a worm whose rate of propagation from an infected node to each of its vulnerable neighbors is β and the rate at which infected nodes are disinfected is δ, we study the *epidemic threshold*, or the ratio of β/δ below which an infectious agent will burn itself out (i.e., the ratio below which there will be no infected nodes in the network at steady state).

One of the goals of any virus mitigation technique should be to increase the epidemic threshold of the network. In this paper, our goal is to study:

1. The epidemic threshold with a randomized distribution of diverse software packages to nodes in a real network (an IPv6 BGP topology) as well as a synthetically generated (an Erdös-Rényi random graph) network topology.
2. The relationship of the above results to the number of different software packages available to distribute among the nodes.
3. The epidemic threshold on the same networks with a topology-sensitive algorithm-driven distribution of diverse software packages.

Consider a network of computers represented by graph G, a set of diverse software packages C which can be assigned to nodes on the network, and a contagion which can infect only a single software package in C. Assume that the number of software packages available in C is greater than or equal to the chromatic number of the graph $\chi(G)$. If the software packages are randomly distributed to the network, then a portion but not all of the nodes will be rendered immune to the infection. However, if a graph coloring algorithm is used to assign the software in C to the nodes in G, then no edges will be left to spread the infection, and the infection is guaranteed to die out.

This paper is organized as follows. Section 3 describes related work in the fields of software diversity and viral propagation modeling. A generalized analysis of the viral propagation models and the impact of diversity upon them is presented in Section 4. In Sections 4.1 and 4.2, we extend both the statistically derived and graph theoretic viral propagation models to incorporate the impact of random as well as algorithm-driven diversity assignments. We validate these models using simulations of virus propagation on both synthetic and *real* network topologies in Sections 4.1.1 and 4.2.1. The simulations show that the improvement in the epidemic threshold experienced under an algorithm-driven diversity assignment algorithm is significantly higher than that predicted by the bounds generated by our models for real-world graphs. Finally, we present our concluding comments in Section 5.

3. Related Work

The research discussed in this paper is based upon work from two independent but related fields, *software diversity* and *viral propagation modeling*. Software diversity research focuses on the creation and distribution diverse software packages to limit the exploitability of a security vulnerability by a worm, known as the *wormability* of a vulnerability [18]. While software diversity focuses on the interaction between a worm and a system at the moment of infection, the field of viral propagation research focuses on the modeling of large scale behavior of worms once they are established in the network.

3.1. Software Diversity

Position papers that assess the inherent value of a heterogeneous population of software packages have been published in both peer-reviewed conferences [24] and in more public forums [7–9, 19]. Literature on the topic contains numerous methods for artificially introducing diversity to software, including the use of source code modification [3, 6, 20], virtual hardware modification [1, 11], and compile time randomization techniques [2, 4, 6]. Just and Cornwell [10] provided a survey of these techniques, and characterized them as a method of breaking the "virtual specification" for attack used by attackers to write worms and viruses. A further classification of diversity techniques is provided by Keromytis and Prevelakis in [13].

In many practical situations, the number of diverse software packages may be insufficient to guarantee that every node is different from every other node on the network. Our previous work [15] showed that careful assignment of a limited set of diverse software packages reduces, and in some cases prevents, an attacker's ability to leverage a single vulnerable system in order to attack additional systems running the same software. In the paper, we equate different software packages to colors on a graph, and then propose a series of distributed graph coloring algorithms for the assignment of diverse software packages, each of which can be used in conjunction with one another to reduce the impact on the algorithm of disinformation from malicious nodes.

3.2. Viral Propagation Modeling

All of the models discussed below are based upon the SIS, or Susceptible-Infected-Susceptible paradigm, where the individual vertices on a graph are either in one of two states: *susceptible* to infection or *infected*. A node moves from the susceptible state to the infected state when an infected neighbor, with the probability β, passes on its contagion. A node moves from the infected state to the susceptible state, independent of its number of neighbors, with the disinfection probability δ. As discussed before, if the ratio β/δ is below the epidemic threshold, the infection will eventually die out.

Kephart and White [12] considered viral propagation on a Erdös-Rényi random graph in an early contribution to the study of computer virus epidemiology. Their assumptions regarding the homogeneity of the nodes in the communication network allowed the authors to model the behavior of an infectious agent using a first order differential equation. A steady state solution for the differential equation is found which provides a bound on the epidemic threshold as a function of the average degree in the graph. They show that the ratio of the infection rate to the disinfection rate must be less than the inverse of the average node degree, $\langle k \rangle$, in order to prevent an epidemic:

$$\frac{\beta}{\delta} < \frac{1}{\langle k \rangle}$$

Pastor-Satorras and Vespignani produced a model which provides insights into the propagation of viruses on graphs with arbitrary degree distributions [16]. Their analysis provides a bound on the epidemic threshold in terms of the node degree's first and second order statistics:

$$\frac{\beta}{\delta} < \frac{\langle k \rangle}{\langle k^2 \rangle}$$

The authors leveraged statistical mechanics to determine closed-form expressions of the second-order statistics of degree distributions for specific classes of graphs. When applied to synthetic graphs which are statistically similar to real world networks, the model predicts that every infection will become an epidemic as the number of nodes tends to infinity. On graphs sampled from real-world data, the number of nodes is finite, and while small, the epidemic threshold is non-zero and can be evaluated numerically.

Y. Wang and others [21] created a discrete time model which is then converted to vector-space notation, which encapsulates the infection state of each node on the network. Using algebraic manipulation, they isolate a system matrix which determines the current infection state based upon the previous system state using a method similar to solving discrete time Markov chains. Spectral decomposition bounds the epidemic threshold of a virus propagating on the network to the inverse of the largest eigenvalue of the graph's adjacency matrix $\mathbf{A}$:

$$\frac{\beta}{\delta} < \frac{1}{\max\limits_{\forall i}\{\mu_i(\mathbf{A})\}}$$

Each of the different models examined here have seemingly different methods to determine the upper bound on the epidemic threshold. For the Kephart and White model, the epidemic threshold can be maximized by minimizing the average number of adjacent systems which are vulnerable to a worm. The epidemic threshold will be increased in the Pastor-Satorras and Vespignani model by minimizing the second order statistic while maximizing the first order statistic. The Wang model's epidemic threshold can be maximized by minimizing the largest eigenvalue of the diversified network's adjacency matrix. We show, however, through modeling and simulation, that all of these goals can be met by reducing the number of edges across which a virus can traverse in a diversified network.

4. Viral Propagation and Software Diversity

It is possible to show that, regardless of the underlying viral propagation model, an assignment of software packages to a graph such that the assignment forms a perfect graph coloring will force the epidemic threshold to infinity. Consider a perfect coloring, where there are no edges across which a virus can propagate. The only infected hosts that exist are those which are initially infected by a virus. Because this set cannot increase, the disinfection rate of systems will continually decrease the number of infected systems until all systems are uninfected.

As pointed out in [15], it may not be possible to guarantee that a sufficient number of software systems will be available to perfectly color the network. It would then be more appropriate to assign the limited amount of diversity so as to limit the number of monochromatic edges and thus increase the epidemic threshold. To achieve this goal, we use the COLOR FLIPPING algorithm described in [15]. The distributed algorithm has each node choose an initial software package, or color, and, at random intervals, communicate with their immediate neighborhood of nodes to discover their current color. The node initiating the communication will then switch to the neighborhood's minority software package if it finds a majority of its neighbors are running the same software package.

The introduction of a graph coloring algorithm removes some of the assumptions of randomness that underpin the statistical models discussed, which results in loose bounds on the epidemic threshold on networks colored using the COLOR FLIPPING algorithm. Rather than providing only loose bounds, we examine the effect of algorithm-driven color assignments on the epidemic threshold primarily through the use of simulation.

4.1. Statistical Models

We can consider nodes which run software packages which are different from their neighbor to be relatively immune to attack from their neighbor. Assuming a randomized distribution of diverse software packages, if there are c software packages available for n nodes, it is expected that $n - n/c$ nodes will be relatively immune to the n/c vulnerable nodes.

The effective infection rate, or the rate any given infected node can infect a neighboring homogeneous node, becomes:

$$\beta' = \beta \frac{1}{c}$$

with an epidemic threshold given by:

$$\frac{\beta}{\delta} < \frac{c}{\langle k \rangle}$$

For a given β and δ, the critical number of software packages needed to ensure that a worm infection does not become an epidemic is:

$$c_{crit} = \left\lceil \frac{\beta}{\delta} \langle k \rangle \right\rceil$$

A similar analysis can be done for the Pastor-Satorras and Vespignani model, which shows an increase in the epidemic threshold by a similar factor.

4.1.1. Simulation In order to test the utility of diversity assignments for increasing the epidemic threshold, it is necessary to either generate or measure a network topology for simulation study. Our first network was generated by collecting a list of the BGP peers present in the IPv6 network by accessing the routing table from IPv6 capable Looking Glass routers. A second network was created using an Erdös-Rényi random graph generator. Both graphs contain 266 nodes and approximately 7500 edges. The distribution of the individual node degrees is shown on a log-log scale in Figure 2. While both graphs have similar average degree, the degree distribution for both graphs is dramatically different. The distribution plot of the synthetic graph, shown in Figure 2(a) corresponds to a standard random graph, while the distribution of the sampled graph's topology, shown in Figure 2(b), shows the same self-similar characteristics that have been observed in previous literature [5].

The rest of the simulation studies presented in the paper follow a standard methodology; a single color is tagged as being vulnerable to infection, and the graph is assigned an initial coloring. A high percentage of the nodes assigned the vulnerable color are randomly chosen to be the nodes which initially contain the infection. We experimentally determine the epidemic threshold by progressively changing β relative to a fixed δ until a persistent infection is not seen over numerous simulation runs with both the same initial infection set and with alternate initial infection sets.

The simulation exercises shown in Figures 3(a) and (b) examine the effect that the number of colors has upon theoretically derived and experimentally-

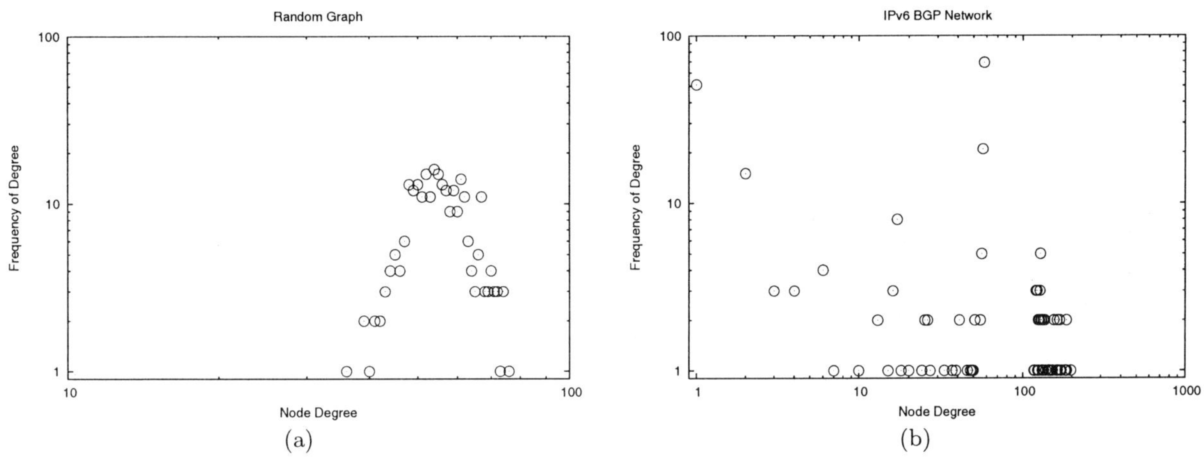

Figure 2. Plot of the degrees of nodes found in the examined networks versus the frequency of the occurrence of the degree. The graph examined in (a) was constructed from a standard random graph model, and contains 266 nodes and 7448 edges. The graph examined in (b) was sampled from the IPv6 BGP topology, and contains a similar number of nodes and edges.

evaluated epidemic thresholds. For each color, we compute the diversity-aware variants of the Kephart and White (KW) model and the Pastor-Satorras and Vespignani (PV) model presented in Section 4.1 for the random graph and the IPv6 graph, respectively. Additionally, both randomized and algorithm-driven color assignments, based upon the COLOR FLIPPING algorithm presented in [15], are performed on the graph for each color count examined.

The data shows that the bound on the epidemic threshold of a randomized coloring provided by the statistical models is below the experimentally determined epidemic threshold. The result allows us to conclude that the epidemic threshold of a diversified network will be higher than the epidemic threshold of a homogeneous network even if diversity is assigned randomly. It is noteworthy that the epidemic threshold is significantly increased by allowing an algorithm to assign diverse software packages to nodes on the network; this leads us to conclude that a planned diversity assignment is a worthwhile undertaking in order to maximize the epidemic threshold of a network.

4.2. Graph Theory Derived Models

In a fashion consistent with Wang's model, we are able to restate the goal of the software assignment in terms of graph partitions and the subsequent eigenvalues of the subgraphs. We denote our software assignment as $f : V(G) \mapsto C, C = \{1, 2, ..., c\}$, where C is the set of available software packages. Let $G_i := G[f^{-1}(i)] : i \in C$, where G_i are the subgraphs induced by color i. Define $\mu_{max}(G_i)$ as the maximum eigenvalue of subgraph G_i's adjacency matrix. Therefore, we wish to find a software assignment f_{opt} where:

$$f_{opt} = \arg\min_{\forall f} \left\{ \max_{i \in C} \{\mu_{max}(G_i)\} \right\}$$

which minimizes the maximum eigenvalue across all subgraphs induced by each color.

Loose bounds for general graphs and hard bounds on regular graphs can be determined for the largest eigenvalue of the adjacency matrix of a diversified network. Rather than relying upon the loose bounds, we directly measure the eigenvalue of a network which is actively undergoing diversification to predict the epidemic threshold.

4.2.1. Simulation To examine the impact the number of monochromatic edges has upon the epidemic threshold, we simulate a homogeneous network of systems, then allow each system to minimize its number of monochromatic neighbors by executing the COLOR FLIPPING algorithm presented in [15]. At each timestep, we compute the epidemic threshold predicted by the Pastor-Satorras and Vespignani model and Wang's eigenvalue model. The Kephart and White model is inappropriate for use with networks using an algorithm-driven diversity assignment as the application of the algorithm to the network removes the homogeneous degree distribution on the network.

Figures 4(a) and (b) show the impact that decreasing the number of monochromatic edges has upon the statistical, eigenvalue-derived, and experimentally

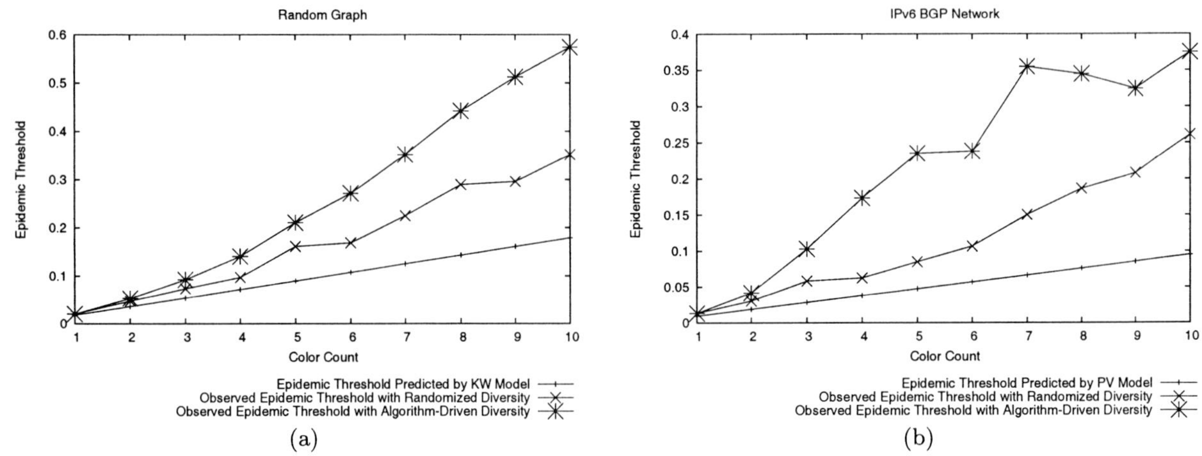

Figure 3. Comparison of the effect of the number of colors on the experimentally determined epidemic threshold. In both (a) and (b), a graph is assigned either one color for every node, multiple colors via a randomized algorithm, or multiple colors via the described COLOR FLIPPING algorithm. It can be seen in both graphs that the epidemic threshold increases as the diversity-assignment algorithms become progressively more sophisticated.

found epidemic thresholds. It is clear from the simulation studies that reducing the number of monochromatic edges in the network is an extremely effective method of increasing the epidemic threshold. The simulation studies confirm the utility of recomputing the eigenvalue-derived epidemic threshold with each step of the graph coloring operation is an effective method of approximating the epidemic threshold. Furthermore, the experiment shows that decreases in the number of defective edges go hand in hand with increases in the epidemic threshold.

5. Concluding Remarks

While a wide variety of techniques for mitigating rapid malware propagation have been analyzed and simulated using standard virus modeling techniques, the contributions of the software diversity community have not yet been fit into this framework. In this paper, we make the first contributions toward analyzing viral propagation modeling in the presence of software diversity. We use both models and simulations to show that on both simulated and real networks of systems, a naïve, randomized software diversity assignment is able to increase the epidemic threshold. Simulations also show that an algorithm-driven diversity assignment is able to further increase the epidemic threshold beyond that seen with a randomized assignment. These results provide quantitative insight into the impact of software diversity on the tolerance of a network to viral attack.

Acknowledgments: Finally, we would like to thank Dave Richardson of Drexel's CS Department for his comments on the early drafts of the paper, and Madhusudan Hosaagrahana of Drexel's ECE Department for alerting us to this conference.

References

[1] E. G. Barrantes, D. H. Ackley, T. S. Palmer, D. Stefanović, and D. D. Zovi. Randomized instruction set emulation to disrupt binary code injection attacks. In *Proc. of the 10th ACM Conference on Computer and Communication Security*, pages 281–289. ACM Press, 2003.

[2] S. Bhatkar, D. C. DuVarney, and R. Sekar. Address obfuscation: An efficient approach to combat a broad range of memory error exploits. In *Proc. of the 12th USENIX Security Symposium*, pages 105–120, Washington D.C., USA, August 2003.

[3] C. Collberg, C. Thomborson, and D. Low. Breaking abstractions and unstructuring data structures. In *Proc. of the IEEE International Conference on Computer Languages*, pages 28–38, Chicago, IL, May 1998.

[4] H. Etoh. GCC extension for protecting applications from stack-smashing attacks, 2004. http://www.trl.ibm.com/projects/security/ssp/.

[5] Michalis Faloutsos, Petros Faloutsos, and Christos Faloutsos. On power-law relationships of the internet topology. In *Proc. of the Conference on Applications, Technologies, Architectures, and Protocols for Computer Communication*, pages 251–262. ACM Press, 1999.

[6] S. Forrest, A. Somayaji, and D. Ackley. Building diverse computer systems. In *Proc. of the 6th Workshop on Hot*

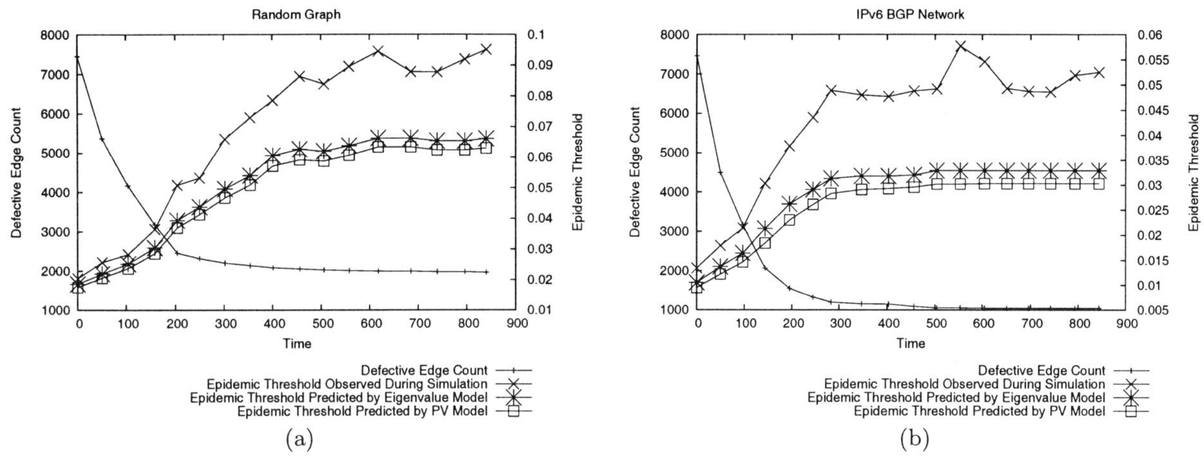

Figure 4. Comparison of the effect of the number of defective edges on the epidemic threshold. In both (a) and (b), the nodes of the graphs all begin at the same color, and the COLOR FLIPPING algorithm from [15] is executed to find a 3-color assignment which reduces the number of monochromatic edges. As the number of monochromatic edges decreases, the experimentally determined epidemic threshold increases beyond what is predicted by statistical models and by the eigenvalue model.

Topics in Operating Systems (HotOS-VI), pages 67–72. IEEE Computer Society, 1997.

[7] D. Geer. Monopoly considered harmful. *IEEE Security & Privacy Magazine*, 1(6):14–16, December 2003.

[8] D. Geer, R. Bace, P. Gutmann, P. Metzger, C. P. Pfleeger, J. S. Quarterman, and B. Schneier. Cyberinsecurity: The cost of monopoly. Tech report, CCIA, 2003. http://www.ccianet.org/papers/cyberinsecurity.pdf.

[9] G. Goth. Addressing the monoculture. *IEEE Security & Privacy Magazine*, 1(6):8–10, December 2003.

[10] J. E. Just and M. Cornwell. Review and analysis of synthetic diversity for breaking monocultures. In *Proc. of the 2nd Workshop on Rapid Malcode*, Washington, D.C., October 2004.

[11] G. S. Kc, A. D. Keromytis, and V. Prevelakis. Countering code-injection attacks with instruction-set randomization. In *Proc. of the 10th ACM Conference on Computer and Communication Security*, pages 272–280. ACM Press, 2003.

[12] J. O. Kephart and S. R. White. Directed-graph epidemiological models of computer viruses. In *Proc. of the IEEE Symposium on Security and Privacy*, Oakland, CA, May 1991.

[13] A. D. Keromytis and V. Prevelakis. Dealing with system monocultures. In *Proc. of the NATO IST Panel Symposium on Adaptive Defense in Unclassified Networks*, Toulouse, France, April 2004.

[14] D. Moore, C. Shannon, G.M. Voelker, and S. Savage. Internet quarantine: Requirements for containing self-propagating code. In *IEEE INFOCOM*, pages 1901–1910, March – April 2003.

[15] A. J. O'Donnell and H. Sethu. On achieving software diversity for improved network security using distributed coloring algorithms. In *Proc. of the 11th ACM Conference on Computer and Communications Security*, pages 121–131, Washington, D.C., October 2004.

[16] R. Pastor-Satorras and A. Vespignani. Epidemic dynamics and endemic states in complex networks. *Phys. Rev. E*, 63(066117), 2001.

[17] R. Pastor-Satorras and A. Vespignani. Immunization of complex networks. *Phys. Rev. E*, 65(036104), 2002.

[18] A. Powell. Internet worms. Tech Report 00727, NISSC, 2003. http://www.niscc.gov.uk/niscc/docs/re-20030805-00727.pdf.

[19] M. Stamp. Risks of monoculture. *Commun. ACM*, 47(3):120, 2004.

[20] C. Wang, J. Davidson, J. Hill, and J. Knight. Protection of software-based survivability mechanisms. In *Proc. of the International Conferece on Dependable Systems and Networks*, pages 193–202, July 2001.

[21] Y. Wang, D. Chakrabarti, C. Wang, and C. Faloutsos. Epidemic spreading in real networks: An eigenvalue viewpoint. In *22nd Symposium on Reliable Distributed Systems*. IEEE Computer Society, October 2003.

[22] Y. Wang and C. Wang. Modeling the effects of timing parameters on virus propagation. In *Proc. of the 2003 ACM Workshop on Rapid Malcode*, pages 61–66. ACM Press, 2003.

[23] M. M. Williamson. Throttling viruses: Restricting propagation to defeat malicious mobile code. In *Proc. of the 18th Annual Computer Security Applications Conference*, page 61. IEEE Computer Society, 2002.

[24] Y. Zhang, H. Vin, L. Alvisi, W. Lee, and S. K. Dao. Heterogeneous networking: a new survivability paradigm. In *Proc. of the 2001 Workshop on New Security Paradigms*, pages 33–39. ACM Press, 2001.

Microscopic Simulation of a Group Defense Strategy

Linda Briesemeister and Phillip Porras *
SRI International, 333 Ravenswood Ave., Menlo Park, CA 94025
first.lastname@sri.com

Abstract

We introduce a novel worm containment strategy that integrates two complementary worm quarantine techniques. The two techniques are linked, with one strategy employing the other as an indicator of worm infection. A group defense mechanism shares such indicators among neighboring networks, and when enough corroboration occurs, the network engages in traffic filtering to halt infection attempts.

We present an SSFnet-based microscopic simulation of the containment strategy against random scan worms, and explore various performance characteristics of the group defense mechanism. The simulation results help to characterize the conditions and degree to which the integrated quarantine strategy can both slow worm propagation and prevent the worm from reaching its full saturation potential.

1. Introduction

The increasing speed and sophistication of Internet worms has offered strong motivation toward the development of automated worm defense strategies. Some strategies seek to delay worm propagation by restricting the consumption of resources that a worm utilizes as it attempts to propagate [20, 16, 21]. Some strategies attempt to disrupt or thwart the ability of the worm to discover new susceptible hosts within its search space [13, 18, 5]. Other defenses propose to block worm propagation through cooperative information sharing that allows defensive filtering to leap ahead of the worm as it propagates across the network seeking new victims [1, 11].

In [12] we examined the potential synergies that exist between two competing worm defense strategies by overlaying them within an enterprise network simulation. We observed how the independent overlay of a resource-limiting strategy with a cooperative leap-ahead (LA) defense provides a synergistic effect that reduces worm infection growth rates significantly more than either approach could independently achieve. We presented an analytical argument to explain the basis of this synergy.

In this study, we examine an integrated worm defense strategy, where connection rate limiting (RL) serves as the input source to an LA approach. Here, the RL algorithm is used to identify local worm infections and slow their propagation attempts to remote addresses. Each threshold violation is monitored and shared by the local network using an LA protocol. Each local network attempts to corroborate the occurrences of reported RL threshold violations across the greater network. The repeated experiences of RL threshold violations among peer network domains may cause a local network to enter a defensive posture, such as enabling a filter to suppress incoming infection attempts. We describe how dynamic filters could be derived through the examination of RL-suppressed packets, and suggest how this approach provides substantial worm growth suppression in the presence of random scanning worms at different speeds. For some classes of worms, this solution offers a signature-free approach to both slow the infection growth rate and prevent the worm from reaching its full saturation potential within a group of peer networks.

We examine the effectiveness of this integrated and interdependent worm defense strategy through microscopic network simulations of various random scan worms using the Scalable Simulation Framework (SSF) [15]. We call this approach a microscopic worm simulation not because of the size of the network, but rather that we do not aim to abstract the whole Internet or even an autonomous system (AS) backbone. While we admittedly employ a simplified and abstract network topology, we examine other subtleties of the integrated combination strategy by incorporating into our simulation common network protocols, greater implementation detail of the worm and our algorithms, and modeling of finer network traffic and link characteristics.

* This material is based upon work supported by the National Science Foundation under Grant No. ANI-0335299, through a subcontract with the University of California at Davis, Contract No. 01RA0052.

1087-4097/05 $20.00 © 2005 IEEE

2. Related Work

Worm containment research to combat the growing threat of large-scale malware epidemics is an active field of study. By *worm containment* we refer to methods that attempt to isolate infected computing assets from the uninfected segments of a network. Detection may be one step in the containment process, followed by techniques such as traffic filtering or address blacklisting, which could be directed at either inbound or outbound communications.

Resource limitation strategies have been proposed to suppress the speed at which worms propagate by throttling the resources that they are known to consume as they seek out new infection targets. In particular, the monitoring and prevention of outbound network connections has been widely studied as an effective strategy to suppress the infection growth rate of worms. Connection rate limiting at the end host [20], the network gateway [16], and within backbone routers [21] has been proposed. Rate limiting through process-based monitoring of outbound connection rates across the total population of processes or from a preselected group of known benevolent processes has also been proposed [6]. Ganger et al. [3], and more recently [19], suggest that limiting the number of network connections not facilitated through DNS lookups provides an effective defense for certain classes of worms. The simulation presented here implements outbound connection rate limiting at the egress of each local network.

Several cooperative sharing algorithms have been proposed to allow networks to recognize the emergence of propagating attacks. These algorithms can employ a hierarchical coordination center to model threats that span multiple networks. GrIDS [17] is an early example of a hierarchical detection scheme to identify coordinated worm activity and coordinated floods or sweeps. More recently, peer-sharing schemes have been described to allow individuals to independently corroborate the emergence of worm activity and take defensive actions before the worm can compromise their networks. We refer to these as *leap-ahead (LA)* defenses, in that networks have the potential to activate a defensive posture before the worm reaches them, and thus can slow or prevent the worm from reaching its full saturation potential.

COVERAGE [1] is an example peer-sharing scheme, in which each participating network randomly polls a set of remote hosts for reports of worm activity at periodic intervals. Friends [11] is a peer-sharing scheme similar to COVERAGE. However, under the Friends protocol the peer groups are pre-selected, and alerts are pushed to friends asynchronously rather than pulled at periodic intervals. The LA strategy incorporated into our integrated strategy operates in a way similar to Friends, but with several key differentiators. We prevent our sharing protocol from allowing a single detector from inducing filter modes across a group of peer networks, we do not allow a domain to enter defensive mode based solely on local alerts, and we integrate RL thresholds violation monitoring as the worm detection mechanism.

Many worm defense studies evaluate their proposed solutions by analyzing traffic traces or omit more details about the simulation framework they used. Riley et al. [14] employ the Georgia Tech Network Simulator (GTNetS) to simulate worm infection on the scale of the Internet. The paper reports on the detailed implementation of TCP and UDP worms and on the enhancements of the simulator to achieve the desired scale. In contrast to our paper, the authors do not study worm mitigation strategies and in turn, we focus less on the scale of the simulated network.

Liljenstam and Nicol [9] tackle the challenge of worm simulation on the scale of the Internet. The authors use a mixed abstraction-level technique that uses epidemic models to abstract from the details of the worm behavior. In subsequent papers [7, 8] the simulation framework is used to compare so-called active (such as counterworms) with passive (such as patching) worm defense strategies.

3. Group Defense Strategy

The integrated group defense strategy employs an outbound connection rate limiting algorithm at the egress router of each local network. An LA algorithm shares control of the egress router with a rate limiter, and uses RL threshold violations to identify potential worm infections among the local end hosts. The LA protocol broadcasts alerts about RL threshold violations to its peers. The corroboration of RL threshold violations from multiple group members may cause an LA process to enable inbound traffic filters, which may be derived through an examination of the suppressed packets (see Subsection 3.2). Once in the defensive posture, the LA process continues to maintain filtering while peer networks contribute RL threshold violations, and transitions out from this posture if no alerts are raised over time.

Figure 1 depicts our algorithm in more detail. First, two counters, a (alert level) and c (hold-off), are initialized to zero. In every time step, both counters are decremented but never fall below zero (the right logic branch). It is through this temporal decay of a that the LA process transitions from the defensive posture back to the normal state when it fails to receive continued alerts of worm activity.

When a local RL threshold violation occurs, the local LA process sends an alert to its selected peers weighted by a

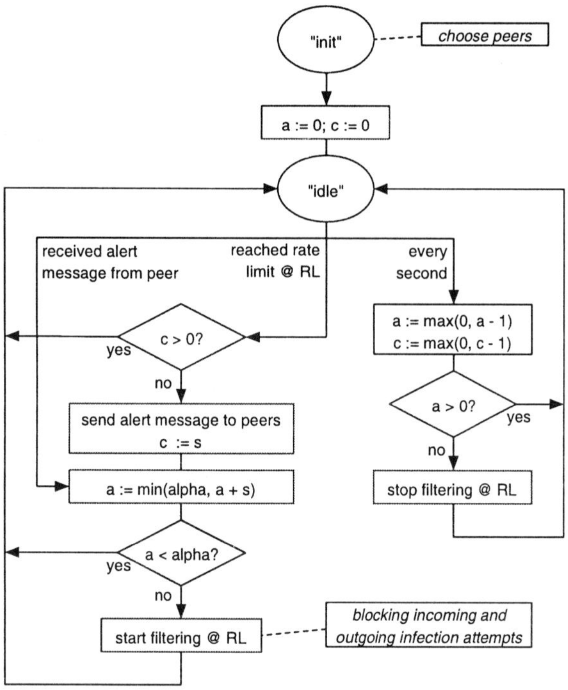

Figure 1. LA flow diagram

parameter s (severity). A hold-off counter c is employed by the LA process to suppress repeated RL threshold warnings for a period of s seconds. This mechanism prevents a single end host that generates a stream of RL threshold violations over multiple seconds from causing the entire group to enter the defensive posture. Rather, the algorithm requires corroboration from multiple peer contributors before any network may enter the defensive posture.

When receiving alerts or when the RL threshold is violated outside of the hold-off period ($c = 0$), the alert level a increases by s, but never above the alert threshold $\alpha = r \cdot s$. When the alert level reaches α, we say that the host is in defensive posture, which may include the enabling of a filter that selectively blocks traffic matching the characteristics of the packets that are suppressed by the rate limiter (see Subsection 3.2). With respect to the simulations performed in this study, we assume that the filtering mechanism will completely block subsequent worm traffic, which in practice may not be achievable without the use of broad traffic filters and may itself be subject to worm countermeasures. Once the alert level decays to zero, the defensive posture is abandoned. For our simulation, this means that we drop our guards and let traffic flow freely within the limits of the RL component.

The alert threshold α defines the corroboration required to

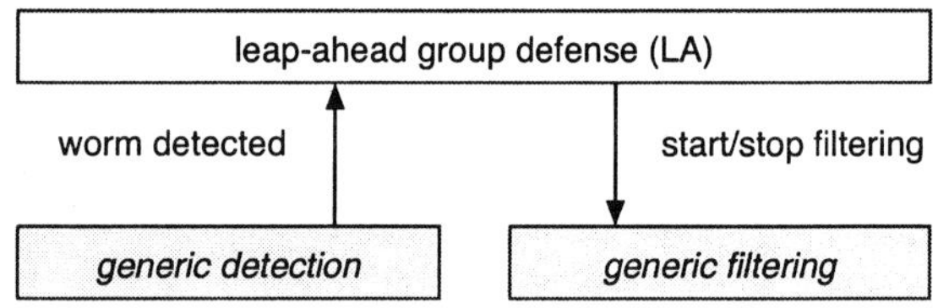

Figure 2. LA interaction with generic modules

enter defensive posture. This may prove more effective in preventing false positives from impacting the defense strategy. On the other hand, a smaller α permits defenders to react much more quickly to arising alerts and gives the defense a better chance of leaping ahead of the spreading worm.

Another parameter of LA is the size of the group of peers that exchange alert messages. Each LA selects $F = G - 1$ peers at the beginning of operation. To reach optimal coverage over the population of LA hosts, we employ the following scheme to ensure that each LA host becomes a peer of the same number of other LA hosts. We arrange the IP addresses of all known LA hosts in a ring of ascending order and then select the next $G - 1$ addresses from a given LA's address to be the peers to which this LA sends messages. In this study, we deploy the RL/LA functionality at routers that serve as a gateway for a group of end hosts.

3.1. Generic Worm Detection and Filtering

In principle, our group defense strategy works with any kind of worm detection and filtering mechanism. One could replace the RL portion in our algorithm—which currently implements both, detection and filtering—simply by altering the notification "reached rate limit @ RL" in the flow diagram of Figure 1 to suit another worm detection. In the same manner, the filtering component that implements defensive posture, can be exchanged for example, with an implementation of the scheme described in detail in Subsection 3.2. The specification of the LA algorithm then directs the notifications "start filtering @ RL" and "stop filtering @ RL" to the appropriate module. Figure 2 shows how our LA algorithm can interact with generic worm detection and filtering components.

3.2. Dynamic Filter Generation

The basis for connection rate limiting algorithms is the observation that a surge in end host transmissions to unique remote addresses offers a reasonable heuristic to diagnose a potential infection of certain classes of worms. While refinements of this approach have been suggested, which include considerations such as DNS assistance [3, 19], the approach is by no means free of false positives. In practice, non-worm-related threshold violations may produce delays in end host operations that should not cause permanent harm.

We leverage the RL threshold violation as one potential data point for worm activity, where it is the corroboration of multiple RL threshold violations from across the peer group that provides the leap-ahead algorithm with an opportunity to potentially formulate and insert an inbound connection filter.

For connection filtering to be applicable, the LA component must observe some degree of correlation among the packets of the end hosts that trigger the RL violations. For example, consider the Slammer worm, which employs a buffer overflow packet on UDP port 1434 and a random scan propagation strategy. Each locally infected end host will cross the RL threshold as its instantiation of Slammer attempts to propagate. For worms that similarly produce a strongly correlated infection packet, a dynamic filtering strategy for assisting the LA component could be implemented as follows.

When end host E triggers RL threshold at time t:

- Select port/protocol pair (A/B) as the dominant target port/protocol used by E's outbound packets during t
- Select datagram size S as the average datagram and D as the standard deviation of datagrams sent by E during t
- Report an RL threshold violation to LA with E, A/B, S, D

When the LA process at Router N observes $a \geq \alpha$:

- Construct filter F such that F denies incoming A/B packets
- When $D < \epsilon$, augment F to filter packets of size $S \pm \epsilon$

Regardless of whether inbound worm filtering is formulated through automated or manual processes, the selectiveness of the filters will greatly depend on the degree to which the worm produces a common traffic pattern. However, selective filter generation may be substantially more difficult when worm infections manifest greater packet diversity.

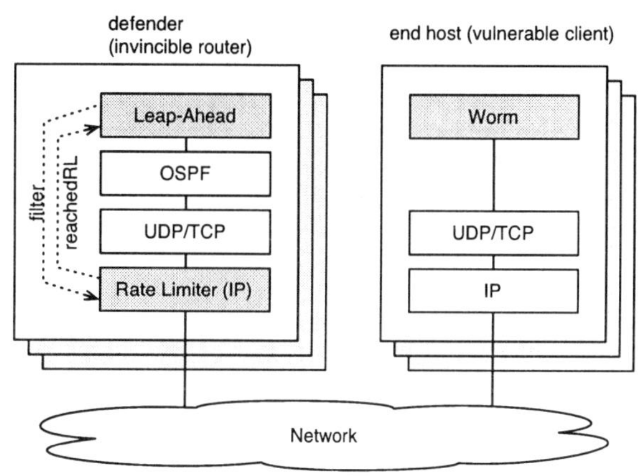

Figure 3. Protocol stacks implemented in SSFNet

4. Simulation and Results

We study our group worm defense using a simulator written in Java implementing the SSFNet [15]. In contrast to many worm simulations, we focus on the worm behavior at a microscopic level. Our motivation here is to study the behavior of the worm defense at the edge of the network rather than the propagation of the worm in the context of the broader Internet.

Figure 3 shows how we implemented—gray colored boxes denote our additions to SSFNet—the proposed algorithms RL and LA on a defender host. Both protocols communicate with each other in the following situations. First, the rate limiter notifies LA when the rate limit has been reached. Second, the leap-ahead algorithm instructs RL when to start filtering packets in defensive posture. We also implemented an application-layer random-scanning UDP worm that runs on vulnerable hosts.

The network topology consists of $M = 100$ LANs, each containing one egress router acting as the defender of this LAN and $k = 10$ vulnerable end hosts. These 100 LANs are connected through a small backbone network of 24 routers. The backbone network is organized into two tiers with 20 routers in an outer ring each connecting to five LANs and four routers in an inner ring each connecting to four routers of the outer ring.

The worm implementation uses only one UDP packet to infect other hosts. It scans the address space between 0 and $2^{16} - 1$ randomly with three different rates: 10 (low speed), 100 (medium speed), and 1000 (high speed) scans per second.

The RL component running at the IP layer of the egress router allows each end host of the connected LAN to communicate with at most 10 different remote IP addresses per second. Packets to other remote IP addresses get dropped after this limit has been reached during one time step. The RL protocol also implements inbound and outbound filtering of worm messages on behalf of the LA component when the router activates defensive posture. This filtering occurs independently of the rate limiting.

The LA algorithm chooses nine peers ($G = 10$) to which to send alerts. It employs a severity of $s = 3$ to alerts and incidents, and varies $r = 2, 3, 4, 5$, which results in values for $\alpha = 6, 9, 12, 15$, respectively.

Each simulation run starts with one end host being initially infected and runs for 200 simulated seconds or until all vulnerable end hosts are infected. We compare simulation runs without any defense (baseline), with a rate-limiting defense only, and with the combined RL/LA approach. We carry out 100 runs per parameter set.

For each run, we collect the following metrics over time. First, we measure the percentage of vulnerable end hosts currently infected, ρ. Second, we record the number of defenders whose rate limit was reached (at one or more end hosts) during the past second. Our metric R then denotes the percentage of defenders who reached the rate limit. Third, we count the number of defenders who are filtering at each second. For filtering and not filtering defenders, we also count the number of defenders having none and at least one infected end host in their LANs. The metric L captures the percentage of defenders who are in filtering mode at the end of each time step.

Figure 4 shows the simulation results of ρ for a high-speed and medium-speed worm. We compare our approach to simulations without any defense and to simulations employing rate limiting only. The rate limiting slows the spreading of the worm, but eventually the whole population becomes infected. For different values of α our approach successfully curbs the spreading of the worm. As expected, a small value of α leads to slower infection spread than a large value of α because a low alert threshold permits defenders to switch into defensive posture (filtering) much more quickly. However, with a high value of α we achieve greater corroboration and thus believe the strategy to be more resilient to false positives.

Given the results in Figure 4 for high-speed and medium-speed worms, the results of ρ for the low-speed worm (Figure 5, top) seem surprising at first. Why does our approach not leap ahead of a slow worm even better than a fast worm? The answer lies in the underlying rate-limiting component that works at the scanning rate of the simulated worm. However, comparing RL alone to a defenseless network, the rate

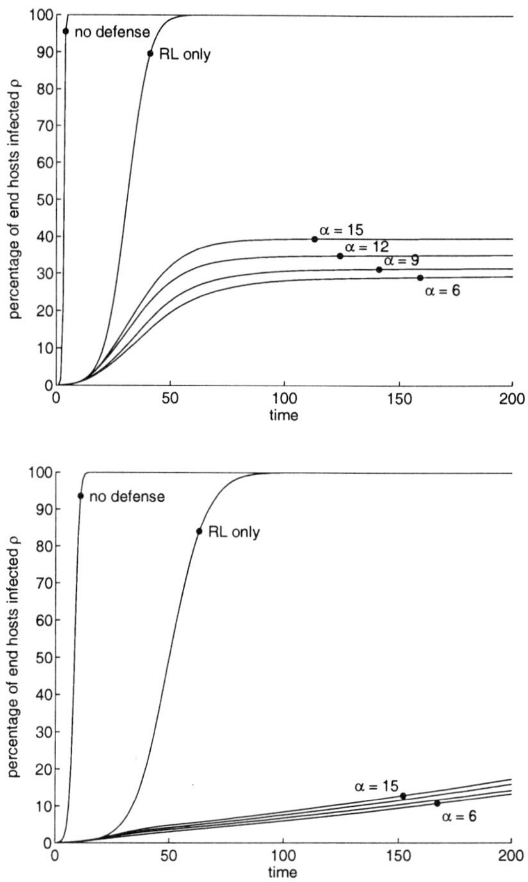

Figure 4. Results for ρ under high-speed (top) and medium-speed worm (bottom) for $\alpha = 6, 9, 12, 5$ compared with defenseless network and rate limiting only

limiting does not seem to have much of an impact. Hence, it seems unusual that the combined approach curbs worm spreading at all. The simulation traces show us that even though the worm sends only 10 packets per second, these packets get scheduled and delayed in the network and may turn up later at the defending router and then potentially trigger the rate limit. Figure 5, bottom, depicts the percentage of defenders who have at least one associated end host exceeding the rate limit threshold. As more and more end hosts become infected the rate limit metric R grows, meaning that more defenders become aware of it and eventually activate filtering to curb the spread of the infection.

Taking a closer look at the behavior of the defenders, we plot the percentage of defenders in filtering mode L as a thick line in Figure 6. The top graph of Figure 6 shows L

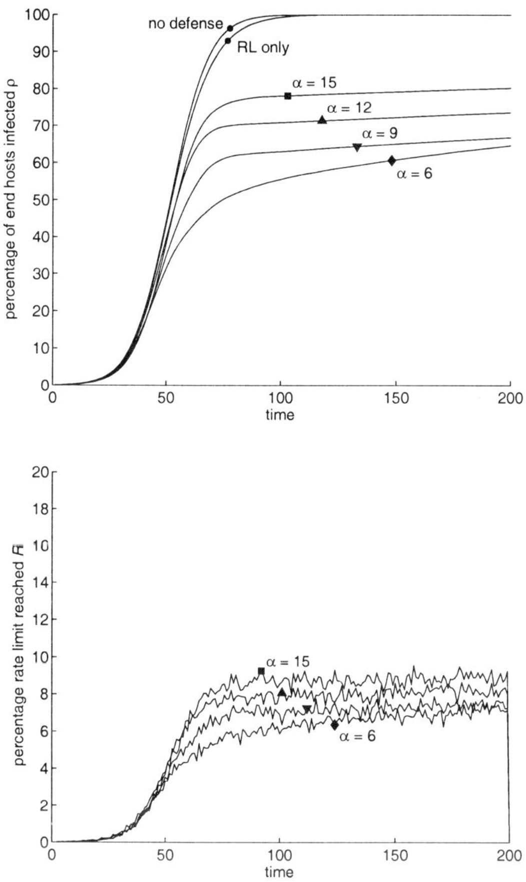

Figure 5. Results for ρ (top) and R (bottom) under low-speed worm for $\alpha = 6, 9, 12, 5$; ρ compared with defenseless network and rate limiting only

for the case of a slow worm and $\alpha = 6$, which corresponds to the situation in Figure 5. Indeed, as the percentage of defenders whose rate limit has been reached increases, more and more defenders switch into active filtering of inbound and outbound worm traffic.

In Figure 6, we also distinguish, within each group of filtering and not-filtering defenders, between those guarding a network without any infection (lighter gray) and a network with at least one end host infected (darker gray). The area above the thick line corresponds to defenders not filtering, whereas the area below denotes filtering defenders. With this distinction, we conclude the following. Many defenders reach their defensive posture after about 80 seconds but with just occasional triggers from a slow worm operating at the detection level. However, the defensive posture

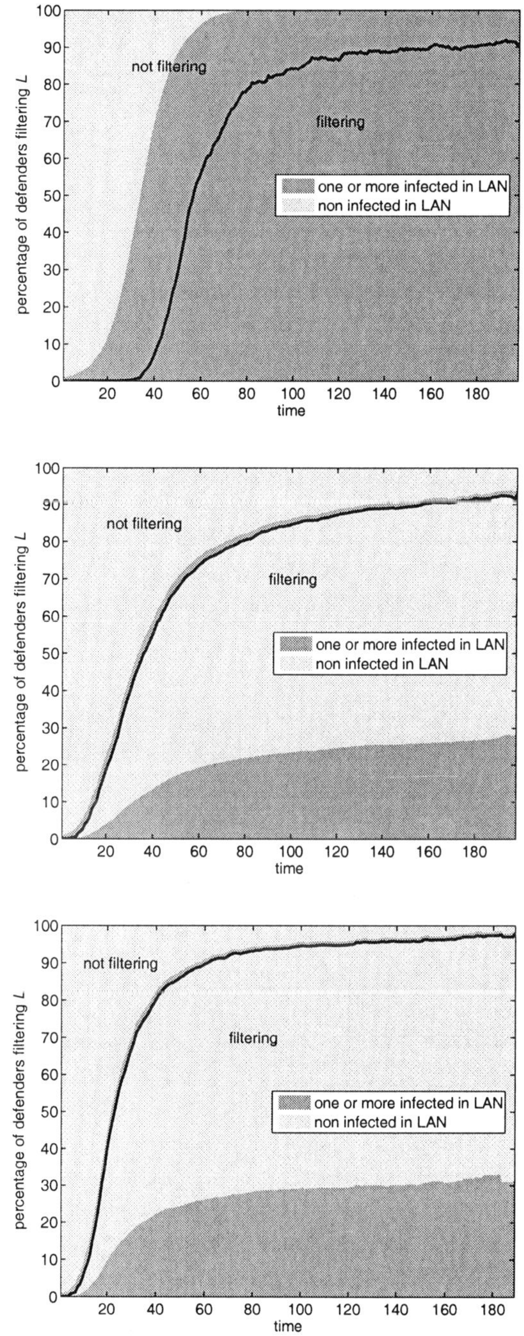

Figure 6. Results for L (thick line) under a low-speed (top) and medium-speed (middle) and high-speed (bottom) worm for $\alpha = 6$

comes too late, as each filtering defender has at least one infection in its own network. These infections continue to spread locally even while defenders are filtering outgoing traffic. Therefore, the leveled curves of ρ in Figure 5 are deceiving in that the worm will reach saturation eventually, albeit much more slowly. Note that even when the combination of both dark areas add up to 100%, which means that all defenders have infected hosts in their networks, the metric ρ does not have to reach 100% at the same time as some of the end hosts in an "infected" LAN may still not be infected.

In Figure 6, the middle and bottom graphs show L and how the defenders' states are locally infected or not for the medium-speed and high-speed worm, respectively. Again, we display the results for $\alpha = 6$. In contrast to the graph at the top, the majority of filtering defenders do not have an infected end host in their networks. This metric demonstrates that our RL/LA approach indeed leaps ahead of the worm and causes defenders to move into defensive posture *before* their networks become affected. The results for other values of α are similar and are omitted here.

4.1. Confidence Intervals

We determine the quality of the simulation output by using independent replications analysis [4, 2]. We stopped every simulation run when a certain criterion was met. Thus, these runs fall into the category of terminating simulations. For each run, the pseudo random number generator (Mersenne Twister [10]) starts with a new initial seed and hence produces a replication independent from other runs. If the number of independent replications is large enough, a central limit theorem allows us to assume that the replicate outputs are approximately i.i.d. (independent, identically distributed) normal. We then compute the half-width of the $100(1-\alpha)\%$ confidence interval as stated in (1) where $t(d,p)$ represents the p quantile of Student's t distribution with d degrees of freedom. We set the confidence level to 95% corresponding to $\alpha = 0.05$.

$$M_p \pm t(n-1, 1-\frac{\alpha}{2}) \cdot \sqrt{\frac{V_p}{n}} \quad (1)$$

where M_p : mean of data with parameter p
V_p : standard deviation of data with parameter p
n : number of independent replications

It is beyond the scope of this paper to report on all confidence intervals obtained through our simulation. As an example, we list in Table 1 the confidence intervals for metric ρ at the end of the simulation runs. These confidence intervals are roughly maintained over the course of a simulation run. For 100 independent runs that we carried out for each parameter set, the margin of error of ρ varies between 2.8 and 4.1 around the mean values determined for ρ.

5. Conclusion

We examine an integrated worm defense strategy, where connection rate limiting (RL) serves as the input source to a leap-ahead (LA) approach. We present the algorithms in detail and discuss some possible extensions such as constructing dynamic filters.

We carry out microscopic simulations of our defense strategy against random scanning worms of various speed. A combination of metrics shows that the defense leaps ahead of medium-speed and high-speed worms and effectively curbs the spread of infection. For a slow worm scanning at the connection rate limit, the threshold is violated less often. Still, the defense can achieve corroboration, shifting the defenders across the network into defensive posture. However, a closer look at a combination of simulation metrics reveals that in the case of a slow worm, all local networks in defensive posture contain at least one infected host, which will eventually lead to full saturation of the network. We conclude that in this case the defense is not able to leap ahead of the worm for the lack of infection indicators.

References

[1] K. G. Anagnostakis, M. B. Greenwald, S. Ioannidis, A. D. Keromytis, and D. Li. A cooperative immunization system for an untrusting internet. In *Proceedings of the 11th IEEE International Conference on Networks (ICON'03)*, October 2003.

[2] J. M. Charnes. Statistical analysis of output processes. In *Proceedings of the 25th Winter Simulation Conference*, pages 41–49. ACM Press, December 1993.

[3] G. R. Ganger, G. Economou, and S. M. Bielski. Self-securing network interfaces: What, why and how. Technical report, Computer Science Department, Carnegie Mellon University, 2002.

[4] D. Goldsman. Simulation output analysis. In *Proceedings of the 24th Winter Simulation Conference*, pages 97–103. ACM Press, December 1992.

[5] S. P. Gorman, R. G. Kulkarni, L. A. Schintler, and R. R. Stough. Least effort strategies for cybersecurity. Technical report, George Mason University, 2003.

[6] M. Gualtieri and D. Mossé. Limiting worms via QoS degradation. Technical report, Computer Science Department, University of Pittsburgh, 2003.

[7] M. Liljenstam and D. M. Nicol. Comparing passive and active worm defenses. In *Proceedings of the First International Conference on the Quantitative Evaluation of Systems (QEST)*, pages 18–27, September 2004.

α	slow-speed worm $\rho(t = 200)$ [%]	medium-speed worm $\rho(t = 200)$ [%]	high-speed worm $\rho(t = 200)$ [%]
6	64.6 ± 3.1	13.2 ± 2.9	29.3 ± 3.9
9	66.8 ± 4.1	14.2 ± 2.8	31.5 ± 3.8
12	73.5 ± 4.0	15.9 ± 3.1	35.1 ± 3.6
15	80.2 ± 4.0	17.2 ± 3.2	39.6 ± 3.7

Table 1. Example of confidence intervals for ρ

[8] M. Liljenstam and D. M. Nicol. Comparing passive and active worm defenses. In *Proceedings of the 1st International Conference on Quantitative Evaluation of Systems (QEST)*, pages 18–27, 2004.

[9] M. Liljenstam, Y. Yuan, B. J. Premore, and D. M. Nicol. A mixed abstraction level simulation model of large-scale Internet worm infestations. In *10th International Workshop on Modeling, Analysis, and Simulation of Computer and Telecommunication Systems (MASCOTS)*, pages 109–116. IEEE Computer Society, 2002.

[10] M. Matsumoto and T. Nishimura. Mersenne Twister: A 623-dimensionally equidistributed uniform pseudo-random number generator. *ACM Trans. Model. Comput. Simul.*, 8(1):3–30, 1998.

[11] D. Nojiri, J. Rowe, and K. Levitt. Cooperative response strategies for large scale attack mitigation. In *DARPA Information Survivability Conference and Exposition*, pages 293–302, 2003.

[12] P. Porras, L. Briesemeister, K. Skinner, K. Levitt, J. Rowe, and Y.-C. A. Ting. A hybrid quarantine defense. In *Proceedings of the 2004 ACM workshop on Rapid malcode (WORM)*, pages 73–82. ACM Press, 2004.

[13] N. Provos. A virtual honeypot framework. In *Proceedings of the 12th USENIX Security Symposium*, pages 1–14, August 2004.

[14] G. F. Riley, M. I. Sharif, and W. Lee. Simulating internet worms. In *Proceedings of the 12th International Workshop on Modeling, Analysis, and Simulation of Computer and Telecommunication Systems (MASCOTS)*, pages 268–274, 2004.

[15] Scalable Simulation Framework. http://www.ssfnet.org/.

[16] S. Staniford. Containment of scanning worms in enterprise networks. *Journal of Computer Security*, 2004.

[17] S. Staniford-Chen et al. GrIDS—A graph based intrusion detection system for large networks. In *Proceedings of the 19th National Information Systems Security Conference*, volume 1, pages 361–370, October 1996.

[18] H. Wang, C. Guo, D. Simon, and A. Zugenmaier. Shield: Vulnerability-driven network filters for preventing known vulnerability exploits. Technical report, Microsoft Research, Technical Report MSR-TR-2003-81, 2004.

[19] D. Whyte, E. Kranakis, and P. van Oorschot. DNS-based detection of scanning worms in an enterprise network. In *Proceedings of the 12th Network and Distributed System Security Symposium (NDSS)*, pages 181–195, February 2005.

[20] M. M. Williamson. Throttling viruses: Restricting propagation to defeat malicious mobile code. In *Proceedings of the 18th Annual Computer Security Applications Conference*, page 61. IEEE Computer Society, 2002.

[21] C. Wong, C. Wang, D. Song, S. Bielski, and G. R. Ganger. Dynamic quarantine of Internet worms. In *Proceedings of the International Conference on Dependable Systems and Networks DSN-2004*, June 2004.

Simulation and Analysis on the Resiliency and Efficiency of Malnets

Jun Li
University of Oregon
lijun@cs.uoregon.edu

Toby Ehrenkranz
University of Oregon
tehrenkr@cs.uoregon.edu

Geoff Kuenning
Harvey Mudd College
geoff@cs.hmc.edu

Peter Reiher
University of California, Los Angeles
reiher@cs.ucla.edu

Abstract

Future network intruders will probably use an organized army of malicious nodes (here called "malnodes", or collectively a "malnet") to deliver many different attacks, rather than recruiting a disorganized set of compromised nodes per attack. However, partly due to the lack of understanding of the resiliency and efficiency a malnet can have, countering malnets has been ineffective.

This paper begins to address this deficiency. Through calculation and simulation for three representative malnets—random, small-world, and Gnutella-like—we show that extremely resilient malnets can be formed to deliver attack code quickly. In particular, we show that disconnecting malnets is possible, but extremely naive approaches such as randomly disinfecting malnodes will not suffice, and effective defenses must either happen very quickly during a second-wave attack, or take effect prior to it.

1. Introduction

An increasingly important problem in network security is the emergence of large numbers of networks of malicious nodes (here called "malnodes", or collectively a "malnet"). A single malnet can be used repeatedly for various nefarious purposes, such as launching DDoS (distributed denial-of-service) attacks, sending spam, or simply stealing computing cycles. Although such networks are not new, recent malnets have increased in number and sophistication.

For example, trinoo, a distributed denial-of-service attack tool, builds a simple three-layer *trinoo network* [1] in which the attacker controls one or more "master" servers, each master controls many "daemons," and the daemons are all instructed to coordinate an attack against one or more victim systems (Figure 1(a)).

Botnets and their variants [2] can also be harmful. For example, a botnet can use IRC channels to connect a collection of IRC bots, where each bot is executable (malicious) code on an IRC client [3]. The study in [4] reported two main types of IRC botnet structures: the *Hub-Leaf* structure in which all bots connect through a hub, resulting in a star architecture (Figure 1(b)), and the *Channel* structure in which a bot needs to join an IRC channel to listen to commands issued by the controller (Figure 1(c)). According to [2], security experts identify botnets with 10 to 100 compromised hosts several times a day, and botnets with 10,000 or more hosts weekly. Botnets with 100,000 computers have also been found.

It is also known that malnodes of a worm can form a *worm network* through which an attacker can issue commands and perform remote control [6]. In this worm network, every malnode keeps a list of other worm malnodes, and can create encrypted communication channels with them; therefore, the command from the attacker can be injected into any malnode and then propagated further toward all remaining malnodes. Furthermore, redundancy can be used to keep the worm network connected even if some malnodes are disinfected and thus removed from the network.

In this paper, we generalize all of these networks as "malnets", which are overlay networks of malnodes. A malnet can be built by malicious code (such as a worm or a Trojan horse) during its infection phase. Further overlay construction can continue even if that malicious code stops propagating.

These malnets can be very sophisticated. Once an intruder has recruited and organized its malnode army, the overlay network it has built can serve as a superhighway for code propagation, including the distribution of upgraded versions for maintaining the malnet it-

1087-4097/05 $20.00 © 2005 IEEE

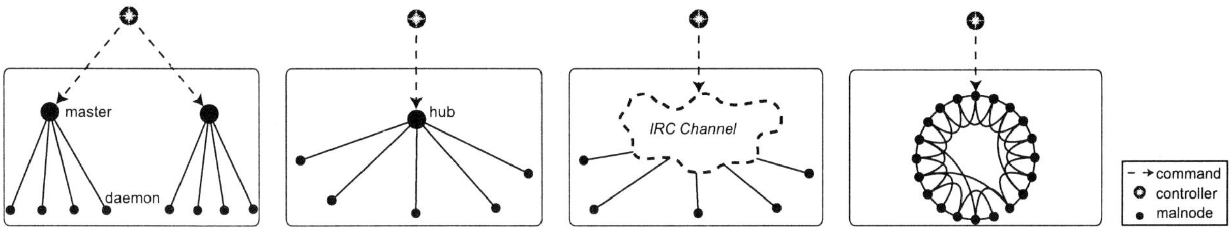

(a) trinoo network

(b) IRC botnet with a Hub-Leaf structure

(c) IRC botnet with a Channel structure

(d) WS model [5] small-world network

Figure 1. Example malnets.

self. In addition to the first wave of attack in which vulnerable nodes are converted to malnodes and recruited into the malnet, second-wave attacks can be launched. The new danger of such a malnet is that it offers the attacker a surreptitious "anytime, anywhere, any flavor" capability: attacks can be launched at a moment's notice, injected at any point in the overlay, and can be crafted to any purpose. Attackers could create a network of compromised machines that would allow them to perform arbitrary, "useful" activities. In addition to sending spam and launching DDOS attacks, for instance, malnets could be used to break cryptographic keys by brute force, store and distribute stolen software or data for fun and profit, or allow malicious "customers" to rent the malnet to perform any desired activity that requires a large number of nodes.

Furthermore, malnets not only can perform dangerous operations, but can also employ mechanisms to manage their own network structures. For example, a malnet might constitute itself as a small-world network (see Figure 1(d)). Recently, malnets have also been found [7] that utilize WASTE [8], an open source P2P communication framework that allows anonymous, secure, and encrypted communication. Malnets can maintain themselves so that they can easily incorporate newly recruited malnodes or forget old departed ones. Moreover, even if they are large networks of many malnodes, malnets can have small diameters so that disseminating commands or new exploits is fast. They can also be made resilient so that disinfecting a subset of malnodes might not disconnect the whole malnet. As a result, those malnets could become hard to defeat.

In this paper, we first justify why it is important to understand the efficiency and resiliency of malnets, and then use calculation and simulation to study the efficiency and resiliency characteristics of three types of malnets. The implications of the simulation results will also be discussed. We will also present some related work and then conclude the paper.

2. The Importance of Understanding the Efficiency and Resiliency of Malnets

In order to defend against malnets, effective solutions must be designed. Note that the focus of this paper is not to discuss approaches to the difficult problem of defense. Instead, we touch upon defense here only to justify our study of two important properties of malnets: *efficiency* and *resiliency.*

The life cycle of a malnet has many interesting phases, each of which offers defensive opportunities. We can attempt to limit the growth of malnets; we can find and disinfect the malnodes; or we can insulate uninfected machines from the damage that existing malnodes try to inflict.

Limiting the growth of malnets and insulating the uninfected from infection are similar to combating the spread of worms or other malware. These approaches are currently of limited efficacy, and are not expected to be completely effective any time in the near future. At best, these mechanisms will cut down on the size of malnets, but will not eliminate them.

Thus, since malnets can be formed even in the face of defensive measures, it is critical to be able to locate and disinfect malnodes. Malnet-specific approaches such as the following offer the hope of at least some success, either individually or in combination:

- Searching for malnet command listeners (since malnodes need to listen to malnet commands)
- Searching for heartbeats (since neighboring malnodes in sophisticated malnets will probably periodically ensure the liveness of their neighbors)

- Traffic analysis (since malnodes will come alive in second-wave attacks and will exchange data with their neighbors)
- Tracing malnets (since each malnode must maintain certain information about other malnodes)
- Having users inspect their computers and look for malnets

Many defensive approaches will have to rely on the detection of malnodes in the middle of second-wave attacks. Examples include searching for malnet command listeners, traffic analysis, and tracing. As a second-wave attack propagates, the sooner defenders can detect the propagation, the sooner they can search as many listeners as possible, conduct thorough traffic analysis, and trace malnets to find more malnodes. Clearly, understanding the efficiency of malnets is essential when considering the defensive reaction-time requirement. If the spread of malnet commands is sufficiently slow, early detection could act as a warning allowing defenders to effectively preempt the attack. If the spread is very fast, there may not be enough time for a warning to be of much use.

Furthermore, assuming certain malnodes can be found, they should then be cleaned. Unfortunately, past experience suggests that while many owners of infected machines are eager to disinfect them as soon as the problem is discovered or reported to them, a significant number of them are either unaware of the problem, unable to perform disinfection, or unconcerned by the infection. For instance, there are still large numbers of machines infected with CodeRed years after its introduction to the Internet [9, 10]. Therefore, if malnets will be formed anyway (although perhaps to a lesser degree), we probably will not be able to clean all the malnodes on a malnet, so it will be important to know how many malnodes must be disinfected to achieve a certain level of disconnection or partitioning. This naturally leads to studying the resiliency of malnets, which is the focus of the present paper.

In Sections 3 and 4, we try to understand the efficiency and resiliency of malnets by simulating three different types of malnets:

- *Random malnet* where every malnode randomly adds r (a constant) malnodes on average to its neighborhood.
- *Small-world malnet* where a malnet is actually a small-world graph.
- *Gnutella-like malnet* where malnodes are connected through a Gnutella-like peer-to-peer network.

These three malnets actually map to three possible paradigms for forming malnets by attackers. Small-world malnets have strong local clustering characteristics, corresponding to the locality feature when a malnet grows. This is particularly true when the infecting code first explores vulnerabilities in the same subnet or administrative domain before attempting to propagate to other places.

In contrast, random malnets do not rely on local knowledge; instead, every malnode infects a certain number of victims throughout the entire Internet. As an example construction paradigm for random malnets, every vulnerable node might choose 1–5 other nodes throughout the network with the same vulnerability (here, the amount of probing needed to discover these nodes is irrelevant to our analysis).

Gnutella-like malnets have a more stringent formation requirement: a two-level hierarchy will be formed, where "ultrapeer" nodes have a relatively high connectivity to each other, and every leaf node connects to a small number (say 3) of ultrapeers.

3. Efficiency Analysis of Malnets

When the controller of a malnet wishes to launch a second-wave attack, how long does it take for the attack code or command to reach all the malnodes through the malnet? We answer this question by studying random malnets, small-world malnets, and Gnutella-like malnets in the following. As the dissemination speed is directly related to the distance between two malnodes, our study will focus on the diameter of a given malnet.

3.1. Random malnet

Through simulation, we estimated how long it would take for exploit code or a command from an attacker to reach all the nodes on a malnet. Figure 2(a) shows the average and maximum diameter of random malnets in which every malnode has an average of four neighbors, i.e. $r = 4$. (4 is a typical number; for example, [6] reports the average node degree to be 4–5.5 in a 1-million-node worm network formed through permutation scanning.) We have found that the maximum and average hop count between any two malnodes closely follow a logarithmic trend with respect to the number of malnodes. Assuming the trend is sustained when a malnet has 1 million nodes, at most 17 hops are needed between any two nodes. Plugging in the average latency between two nodes on the Internet and considering factors such as congestion, our study shows that starting from any member node, the mas-

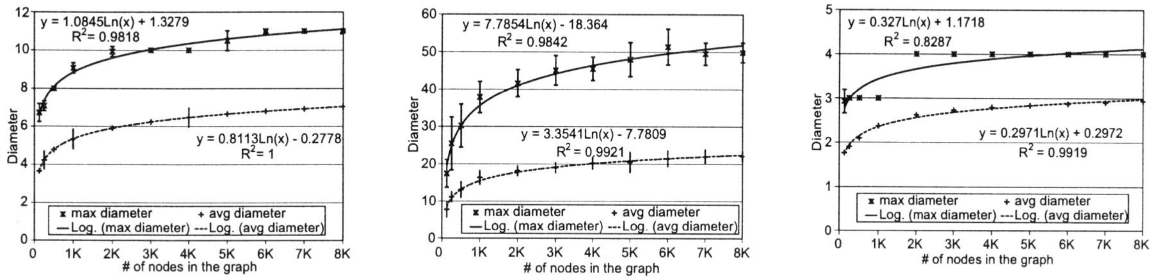

(a) random malnet (average node degree 4)

(b) small-world malnet (average node degree 4)

(c) Gnutella-like malnet (only ultrapeer level presented, average node degree 30 for ultrapeers)

Figure 2. Malnet diameter evaluations.

ter of a malnode army could disseminate a 1-megabyte exploit to 1 million malnodes in less than six minutes [11].

3.2. Small-world malnet

Using methods and formulas from Comellas et al. [12], we have calculated the diameters of some *deterministic* small-world-based malnets. These deterministic small-world graphs are created by starting with a "circulant" graph where nodes are arranged in a ring topology with edges to the closest r neighbors, half in the clockwise direction and half in the counter-clockwise direction. For a network of 8,192 nodes arranged in a circulant graph where every node has degree 6, the diameter is 1,366. A hub graph can then be overlaid on top of the circulant graph to create shortcuts between distant clusters of nodes. If we overlay a complete hub graph with 265 nodes (3.2% of the total) on top of the above circulant graph, the diameter is reduced to 11. Since it is not reasonable to have each hub node connect to every other hub node, we recalculated the diameter when a double loop graph is used as the hub graph. This results in a larger diameter of 21 when applied to the above circulant graph, but only increases the degree of hub nodes by 4 as opposed to 264 (265 − 1) when using a complete graph.

We also introduced random factors in our simulation to study the diameters of small-world malnets. We followed the methods described by Watts and Strogatz [5] in forming small-world graphs in the simulation. First, a circulant graph is created with each node connected to its r closest neighbors, the same as above. Then a node is chosen, and the edge that connects to its nearest clockwise neighbor is considered. This edge has probability p of being reconnected to any random node in the ring, as long as the new connection would not be a duplicate. This process continues on for the rest of the nodes in a clockwise manner, then repeats for the second closest neighbor, and so forth. This process is done until each edge has been considered once. For our small-world simulations we set $p = 0.03$.

Figure 2(b) shows the average and maximum diameter of small-world malnets from the simulation. Here, if the trend reported in the figure continues, when there are 1 million malnodes and every node has four neighbors on average, the maximal distance between any two nodes would be 90, while the average maximal distance from one node to another would be 39.

3.3. Gnutella-like malnet

A malnet could be built using Gnutella-like peer-to-peer techniques. To analyze the diameter of such a malnet, we studied the measurement results of the real Gnutella. As reported in [13], which contains the most recent Gnutella measurements, Gnutella has grown to have around 800,000 peers with a network diameter of 11. However, the vast majority of peers are reachable within 6 hops or less. Such short paths stem from the use of the two-level hierarchy. In current implementations of Gnutella, every ultrapeer tends to have around 30 ultrapeer neighbors, and every leaf node connects to a small number of ultrapeers (around 3).

Figure 2(c) shows the average and maximum diameters of the ultrapeer level of Gnutella-like malnets, where we evaluated random graphs as the ultrapeer-level connection graphs and each ultrapeer had an average of 30 neighbors. Note that the distance between two leaf nodes is the distance between their ultrapeer nodes, plus two. If the trend is taken out to 1 million nodes with $\frac{1}{14}$ being ultrapeers, and if every leaf has one ultrapeer, the total number of links will be approximately the same as that in a 1-million-node random malnet where the average node degree is 4. The maximum diameter will be 4.8 between ultrapeers or 6.8 between leaf nodes. This is consistent with the results reported by previous researchers: in [13], 99.5% of the ultrapeer nodes were within 5 hops of each other.

4. Resiliency Analysis of Malnets

Do we really have to monitor malnets closely to learn their structures and properties in order to effectively disrupt them? While it is clear that any achievable degree of disinfection should reduce the damage a malnet can do, can we just *randomly* disinfect malnodes or convert some of them into firewalls or filters to effectively disrupt the malnet, at least with a high probability? For example, the trinoo network, often used for DDoS attacks, does not offer much resiliency. With two masters and five daemons, for instance, randomly dropping two nodes has a 52.4% probability of dropping a master node.

We have designed a simulation to study the resiliency of random malnets, small-world malnets and Gnutella-like malnets, aiming to answer two questions: (1) For a given malnet, if x nodes are randomly disinfected, what percentage of remaining nodes will remain connected? (2) What is the impact of a malnet's size on its resiliency?

Here, we assume that a malnet does not attempt to reconnect any nodes after the disinfection. Also, since disinfection is often about cleaning up malnodes, not links between malnodes, our resiliency study will focus on dropping nodes, not links, from a malnet.

We first define a resiliency metric, the *maximal reachability* of a graph, which is the percentage of nodes that belong to the largest partition of the graph. It indicates the percentage of malnodes that are reachable by the attacker if the exploit injection point is from the largest partition.

4.1. Random malnet

Despite the lack of directed organization, a random malnet can have good connectivity. For different values of node degree r, we tested twenty 10,000-node malnets; for each network, we tested different values of x; and ten different random cuts were measured for each value of x. Figure 3(a) shows the maximum reachabilities for those 10,000-node graphs with x nodes cut. For example, when 1,024 nodes are randomly cut and $r = 2$, the maximum reachability will decrease from 100% to roughly 43.30%; but if $r = 4$, the maximum reachability will only drop from 100% to 99.80%. Furthermore, while a higher value of r clearly leads to a higher maximum reachability, Figure 3 shows that a small value of r can already lead to high reachability, and thus high resiliency. With $r = 10$, even if 80% of the malnodes were disinfected, 70% of the remainder would remain connected and ready to receive new exploits.

4.2. Small-world malnet

As in Section 3.2, we first conduct a deterministic analysis of small-world malnets to calculate the number of nodes that must be removed to disconnect small-world graphs. Recall that in small-world graphs as considered by Comellas et. al [14], when a node has r neighbors there will be $\frac{r}{2}$ in either direction around the circulant graph, and a hub graph is overlaid on top of the circulant graph. Assuming that nodes have degree r, it is easy to see that if $\frac{r}{2}$ nodes on both sides of a given node v are removed then v will become disconnected. If v is part of the hub graph, another r_h nodes must be removed (r_h is the degree of nodes in the hub graph). So to disconnect a single node, either r or $r+r_h$ nodes must be removed. As an upper bound, suppose we want to ensure there are no connected components larger than the distance between nodes which make up the hub graph. We can simply take out blocks of $\frac{r}{2}$ nodes, with each block centered around a hub. Taking our example from Section 3.2 with 8,192 nodes of degree 6 and a hub graph consisting of 265 nodes, we should remove $3 \times 265 = 795$ nodes to create disconnected networks of size $\lceil \frac{8192-795}{265} \rceil = 28$. It is important to remember that we are assuming the removal of nodes is focused, rather than being random.

To compare this analysis with our statistics on random malnets, we also ran simulations. We again adopted the Watts and Strogatz model for the simulation, as in Section 3.2. Figure 3(b) shows the small-world malnet reachability results, where each malnet has 10k nodes but r varies. Note that for the small-world malnet we cannot consider graphs with $r = 2$, since otherwise there could be no clustering while maintaining connectivity. A graph must have a high level of clustering to be considered small-world, so our simulations start with $r = 4$ as a minimum. The figure shows that in general, the maximal reachability begins to decrease when 1,000 nodes, or 10% of the total nodes in a malnet, are dropped. Dropping around 7,000-8,000 nodes will almost completely partition the malnet, in

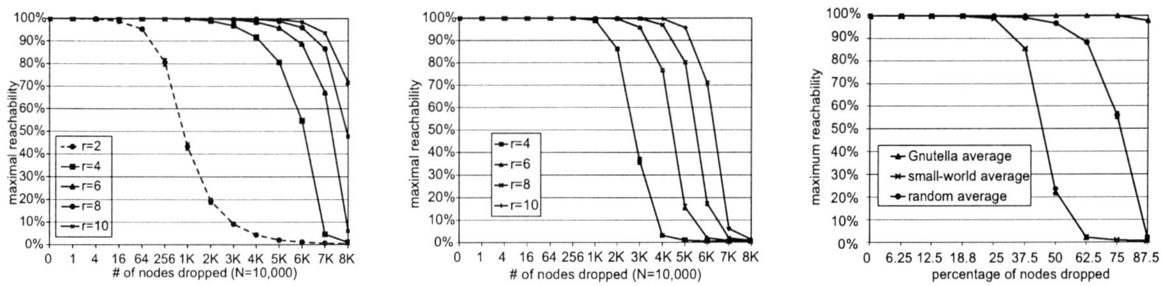

(a) Reachability after disinfection of a random malnet (10,000-node graphs with varying node degree)

(b) Reachability after disinfection of a small-world malnet (10,000-node graphs with varying node degree)

(c) Average reachability for random malnets, small-world malnets, and Gnutella-like malnets, with varying N

Figure 3. Malnet resiliency evaluations.

contrast to only needing to drop 795 carefully selected nodes from the 8,192-node deterministic small-world malnet.

4.3. Gnutella-like malnet

A previous study [15] found the Gnutella overlay to be very robust, requiring an estimated 60% of the overlay's nodes to be randomly dropped before the network fragments. More interestingly, the study also found that the Gnutella network fragments rapidly when the highest-degree nodes were removed (as opposed to random node failures). This can be attributed to earlier observations that the degree of Gnutella nodes exhibits a power-law distribution. However, more recent studies of modern Gnutella do not show a power-law distribution [13], suggesting that the current overlay has a higher resiliency.

Our simulation also shows that Gnutella-like malnets stay very well connected even after a high percentage of nodes is randomly dropped. For example, Figure 3(c) shows that even dropping 75% of the nodes will still leave the remainder unpartitioned, and dropping 87.5% will leave about 97% still connected.

4.4. Malnet size impact on resiliency

We also studied the impact of the size of a malnet on its resiliency and found that it is minimal. Figure 3(c) shows the results for malnets with a constant value of r ($r = 6$ for small-world and random networks and $r = 30$ for Gnutella-like malnets) but different sizes of N, where $N = 1,024$ to $16,384$ in powers of two. Clearly, with the same percentage of nodes cut, the maximal reachability will be approximately the same for malnets of different sizes. This implies that even malnets with a relatively modest number of nodes, say 1,000, can still be very well connected.

5. Discussion

We have presented results for three different types of malnets. Section 3 shows that for the same number of malnodes and the same average node degree, small-world malnets have larger diameters than those of random malnets, whereas small-world malnets tend to be easier to form. This is largely due to the clustering feature of small-world graphs. The diameter and amount of clustering present in a small-world graph varies with the probability p that an edge will be reconnected to a random node. When $p = 0$ there is no reconnection and the graph remains a regular circulant graph with a high amount of clustering and large diameter. As p increases, the clustering and diameter decrease; when $p = 1$, the graph becomes a random graph.

As N increases, Gnutella-like malnets achieve even smaller diameters than random malnets by exploring more sophisticated formation procedures, even when the same number of links is used. By having a more densely connected core, malnodes can in general get even closer to one another.

The resiliency evaluation in Section 4 further shows that randomly dropping nodes will typically not be able to effectively partition a malnet. Selective dropping, on the other hand, can be much more effective, as shown in Sections 4.2 and 4.3.

Moreover, even though small-world malnets are less resilient and efficient compared to the other two types of malnets, note that they are already fast in that the master of a malnode army could still disseminate a 1-megabyte exploit or upgrade to a million malnodes, starting from any member node, in less than 30 minutes. They are also resilient in that randomly disinfecting malnodes cannot effectively disconnect the remaining nodes in a small-world malnet.

Although it is true that Gnutella-like malnets may be hard for attackers to code, the chance of such malnets happening is non-trivial. In addition, malnodes could use the existing Gnutella network for covert communications, rather than creating their own Gnutella-like overlay. In the latter case the malnet overlay would be composed of mostly neutral nodes, which means that instead of "dropping" malicious nodes, we would have to filter or block them at the neutral points, which must be able to handle both the second-wave attack traffic and the legitimate Gnutella traffic.

Superficially, some of the results presented so far would seem to suggest that disconnecting a malnet is a hopeless task. However, we must emphasize that these results address the question of *random* malnode disinfections. Rather than proving the task impossible, our results indicate that disconnection may be possible, but that extremely naive approaches will not suffice. Meanwhile, as discussed in Section 3, there is a very real and serious threat from malnets because of the speed with which new attacks can be disseminated. Thus, it is critical that we find ways to combat these networks.

6. Related Work

Studies focusing on malicious networks have been rare. In terms of distributing information to a large number of recipients, malnets share some features with legitimate distribution mechanisms, such as broadcasting, multicasting, content-delivery networks, etc. Malnets are especially similar to legitimate delivery services based on overlay networks. There are tree-structured overlays for delivery service that are often regarded as application-level multicast [16, 17, 18, 19, 20, 21]. There are also non-tree-structured overlays; for example, Bullet [22] provides high-bandwidth data dissemination through an overlay mesh, and Revere [23] supports large-scale security update delivery through resilient self-organized overlay networks. A malnet can in principle have the same form as any of above. The essential difference is that a malnet program often tries to infect unprotected and uninfected machines to form or expand its network, without any prior agreement. This difference makes it possible to design solutions such as honeypots that can lure malnet programs and even join malnets to disrupt their operations, or at least gather information on them [7].

There has also been significantly related research on graph-theoretical models. One is the rich area of the structure of interconnection networks, including those evolving in a fairly random manner [24, 25, 26, 5], and those exhibiting controlled growth patterns [12]. Some researchers have also conducted studies on the resiliency of small world networks, but these are not directly applicable to our research. For example, research in [27] created networks of degree 20 and compared the resiliency of small-world networks to that of random networks; but in investigating disconnection, they considered the removal of graph edges, whereas we remove nodes.

7. Conclusions

Our paper addresses a major problem in the modern Internet: the threat of malicious "armies" of co-opted computers being used for illegal or even warlike activities. Many different types of malnets have appeared, and more sophisticated ones can be expected in the future. In fact, some highly sophisticated malnets are already feasible today and could be designed by an attacker of no more than moderate sophistication. Most component parts of such malnets have already been observed in released worms or other malicious code. The remaining parts resemble other popular and well-known programs (such as peer-to-peer file-sharing networks) and are not tremendously challenging to implement.

Prior work in the area has not developed effective methods for disabling these armies, partly due to the lack of understanding of the resiliency and efficiency features a malnet can have, and partly due to the lack of proper countermeasures to deal with these features. As an important step in addressing this deficiency, we have combined theoretical analysis and simulation to characterize the resiliency and speed of three representative types of malnets, corresponding to different paradigms of forming malnets. We have shown that it is not feasible to counteract such malnets by simply randomly dropping nodes, even if a large percentage of malnodes is dropped from the network, *i.e.*, disinfected or even converted to a firewall or filter node. Instead, the malnodes to be dropped need to be selected in a sophisticated way. Moreover, since second-wave attacks of malnets can be launched quickly, an effective defense must either happen very quickly during a second-wave attack, or take effect prior to the attack.

Future work on malnets must combine both theory and practice to address the problem at the source. A radically new approach must be designed to defend against malicious network intruders so that they can be shut down in an effective and efficient manner. To use a military analogy, rather than building tall walls around our city and trying to withstand a long siege, we need to locate the enemy commander and cut the lines of communication between him and his troops.

8. Acknowledgments

We thank Xun Kang for his early work on helping simulate random malnets.

References

[1] Computer Emergency Response Team, "Distributed denial of service tools," http://www.cert.org/incident_notes/IN-99-07.html, 1999, cERT IN-1999-07.

[2] D. Geer, "Malicious bots threaten network security," *IEEE Computer*, vol. 38, no. 1, pp. 18–20, January 2005.

[3] C. Kalt, "RFC 2810: Internet Relay Chat: Architecture," RFC 2810, IETF, April 2000.

[4] J. Jones, "BotNets: Detection and mitigation," Federal Computer Incident Response Center, Tech. Rep. FCIRC, February 2003.

[5] D. J. Watts and S. H. Strogatz, "Collective dynamics of 'small-world' networks," *Nature*, vol. 393, pp. 440–442, 1998.

[6] S. Staniford, V. Paxson, and N. Weaver, "How to 0wn the Internet in your spare time," in *Proceedings of the 11th USENIX Security Symposium (Security '02)*, 2002. [Online]. Available: citeseer.nj.nec.com/staniford02how.html

[7] Honeynet Project, "Know your enemy: Tracking botnets," http://www.honeynet.org/papers/bots, March 2005.

[8] WASTE Development Team, "WASTE: Anonymous, secure, encrypted sharing," http://waste.sourceforge.net.

[9] B. N. Chun, J. Lee, and H. Weatherspoon, "Netbait: A distributed worm detection service," Intel Research Berkeley, Tech. Rep. IRB-TR-03-033, September 2003, http://netbait.planet-lab.org/.

[10] S. Costello, "Nimda, Code Red still crawling, threatening the Net," http://www.nwfusion.com/news/2002/0506code.html, May 2002.

[11] P. Reiher, J. Li, and G. Kuenning, "Midgard worms: Sudden nasty surprises from a large resilient zombie army," UCLA Computer Science Department, Tech. Rep. UCLA-CSD-040019, April 2004.

[12] F. Comellas, J. Ozón, and J. G. Peters, "Deterministic small-world communication networks," *Information Processing Letters*, vol. 76, no. 1-2, pp. 83–90, 2000.

[13] D. Stutzbach and R. Rejaie, "Characterizing today's Gnutella topology," http://www.cs.uoregon.edu/~reza/PUB/tr04-02.pdf, Department of Computer Science, University of Oregon, Tech. Rep. CIS-TR-04-02, December 2004.

[14] F. Comellas, M. Mitjana, and J. G. Peters, "Epidemics in small-world communication networks," http://citeseer.ist.psu.edu/623969.html, School of Computing Science, Simon Fraser University, Tech. Rep. SFU-CMPT-TR 2002-09, October 2002.

[15] S. Saroiu, K. P. Gummadi, and S. D. Gribble, "Measuring and analyzing the characteristics of Napster and Gnutella hosts," *Multimedia Syst.*, vol. 9, no. 2, pp. 170–184, 2003.

[16] Y. D. Chawathe, "Scattercast: An architecture for Internet broadcast distribution as an infrastructure service," Ph.D. dissertation, University of California, Berkeley, 2000, chair: Eric A. Brewer.

[17] Y. H. Chu, S. G. Rao, and H. Zhang, "A case for end system multicast," in *Measurement and Modeling of Computer Systems*, 2000, pp. 1–12.

[18] P. Francis, "YOID: Your own Internet distribution," http://www.icir.org/yoid/, April 2000.

[19] J. Jannotti, D. K. Gifford, K. L. Johnson, M. F. Kaashoek, and J. W. O'Toole, Jr., "Overcast: Reliable multicasting with an overlay network," in *Proceedings of the Fourth Symposium on Operating System Design and Implementation (OSDI)*, October 2000, pp. 197–212.

[20] D. Pendarakis, S. Shi, D. Verma, and M. Waldvogel, "ALMI: An application level multicast infrastructure," in *Proceedings of the 3rd USENIX Symposium on Internet Technologies and Systems (USITS '01)*, San Francisco, CA, USA, March 2001, pp. 49–60.

[21] S. Q. Zhuang, B. Y. Zhao, A. D. Joseph, R. H. Katz, and J. D. Kubiatowicz, "Bayeux: An architecture for scalable and fault-tolerant wide-area data dissemination," in *Proceedings of NOSSDAV*, June 2001.

[22] D. Kostić, A. Rodriguez, J. Albrecht, and A. Vahdat, "Bullet: High bandwidth data dissemination using an overlay mesh," in *SOSP '03: Proceedings of the nineteenth ACM symposium on Operating systems principles*. ACM Press, 2003, pp. 282–297.

[23] J. Li, P. Reiher, and G. Popek, "Resilient self-organizing overlay networks for security update delivery," *IEEE Journal on Selected Areas in Communications, special issue on Service Overlay Networks*, 2003.

[24] P. Erdős and A. Rényi, "On random graphs. I," *Publicationes Mathematicae Debrecen*, vol. 6, pp. 290–297, 1959.

[25] A.-L. Barabási and R. Albert, "Emergence of scaling in random networks," *Science*, vol. 286, pp. 509–512, 1999.

[26] B. M. Waxman, "Routing of multipoint connections," *IEEE Journal on Selected Areas in Communication*, vol. 6, no. 9, pp. 1617–1622, December 1988.

[27] K. Sun and Q. Ouyang, "Distance distribution and reliability of small-world networks," *Chinese Physics Letter*, vol. 18, pp. 452–454, Mar. 2001.

HLA and Virtual Environments

An Adaptive Interest Management Scheme for Distributed Virtual Environments

Rob Minson and Georgios Theodoropoulos
School of Computer Science,
University of Birmingham, UK
E-Mail: {rzm|gkt}@cs.bham.ac.uk

Abstract

Traditionally Interest Management (IM) in distributed environments has been performed through a 'top-down' expression of interest patterns in the model. For many models the interest patterns are complicated or highly dynamic and are not suitable for expression in this way. Top-down expression also forces the model to contain data about the network communication which should strictly be encapsulated by the infrastructure. We propose a system, based on a Distributed Shared Variable abstraction, capable of automatically deriving interest expressions at the infrastructure level in a 'bottom-up' manner. We demonstrate through a simulated testbed that for certain access patterns this dramatically improves the precision of the IM system without sacrificing transparency from a modeller perspective.

1 Introduction

A Distributed Virtual Environment (DVE) can be characterised as a system of simulation nodes such that each node in the system is responsible for the modelling of a subset of a shared environment. An update occuring at a given node is therefore likely to have immediate significance for only a subset of the other nodes in the system. Interest Management (IM) is the process by which one exploits this *interest* of each node to minimise the number of update messages that must be propagated.

IM systems are found in all forms of distributed virtual environment including large-scale distributed simulations [11, 8]; virtual reality systems [13, 10, 2]; and multiplayer networked games [15, 5]. All such systems currently adopt an approach in which nodes can express interest in ('subscribe to') some subset of the model, all updates pertaining to this subset are forwarded to the node. The task of formulating these expressions is left to the model and hence we can term this class of IM system *top-down* .

In many situations top-down IM schemes actually provide inefficient solutions to the problem of bandwidth reduction whilst introducing development overhead by making these low-level issues of network communication part of the model specification. We propose a bottom-up framework that uses infrastructure-level observation of the access patterns of the model to automatically and continuously derive and maintain a node's data subscriptions.

The remainder of this paper is organised as follows. Section 2 gives a brief survey of the current state of the art in top-down IM schemes. Section 3 gives a more formal expression of the problem of interest management. Sections 4 and 5 outline our proposed use of a Distributed Shared Variables abstraction to address this problem through pattern prediction. In sections 6 and 7 we describe the design and testing of a simplistic example of such a pattern prediction algorithm and section 8 describes experimental results for a these tests. Finally sections 9 and 10 discusses related research in this area and the probable direction of this research in the immediate future.

2 Top-Down IM Schemes

The following general IM schemes all provide some mechanism by which the model expresses interest patterns for each node. The precise details of these mechanisms effect the precision, transparency and flexibility of the scheme in general.

2.1 Grid-Based Schemes

These schemes divide the universe of data in a model into an n-dimensional grid of interest cells, requiring individual nodes to subscribe to some set of cells. Updates are sent only between nodes who share some subset of cell subscriptions. The most historically influential grid-based scheme was NPSNET [8], implemented for the Distributed Interactive Simulation protocol (DIS) [6].

The advantages of a grid-based IM scheme are relatively clear. The world is decomposed into fairly intuitive interest landscape where the semantic of an area of interest at model level (i.e. a physical area of space) is easily mapped on to the interest expression that the executive requires. Also, because the decomposition of the world is static, a very close mapping on to multicast groups can be statically defined, creating a highly optimised network layer.

Cell-granularity is the primary issue for grid-based schemes. Too large a cell size creates imprecise interest expressions while too small a size means that fast moving entities provoke thrashing in the network layer by constantly changing their multicast group memberships. These disadvantages of static, grid-based schemes have been explored by the NPSNET group in [1].

2.2 Class-Based Schemes

The DIS protocol itself [6] performs data exchange between nodes through the propagation of Protocol Data Units (PDUs). These PDUs are split in to classes depending on the information to which they pertain. Nodes in such a scheme may express their interest through subscription to some set of classes.

This approach is potentially extremely flexible but requires a large amount of machinery at the model level for taking advantage of certain interest patterns. The work of Sorroche and Szulinski [14] demonstrates the complexity involved in enabling large DIS models to take advantage of limited spatial interest regions for bandwidth reduction. This work demonstrates that a purely class-based IM scheme cannot easily express interest in a discrete area of continuous space.

2.3 Region-Based Schemes

Region-based schemes, such as HLA's Data Distribution Management (DDM) [16], are similar to grid-based schemes in that they require nodes to explicitly subscribe to notional areas of the data-space. Region schemes are more general however, in the sense that they do not assume a static decomposition of the data space but instead allow the nodes themselves to define arbitrary regions of data in which they are interested.

Because both update and subscription regions can be created and modified arbitrarily at runtime and because of the arbitrary dimensionality of regions, DDM is very expressive in comparison to both grid- and class-based schemes. This expressivity does come with a significant overhead, however. Because update-regions may not map directly to subscription-regions, and because of the arbitrary dimensionality of these regions, algorithms for calculating update-groups in region-based IM are costly. Research by Morse on minimising these recalculations [12] and on finding optimal multicast mappings [11] clarifies the problems and offers solutions. However, such solutions generally trade flexibility and transparency for performance.

2.4 Bespoke Schemes

Outside of the distributed simulation domain most distributed environments use bespoke IM systems tightly coupled to the specific modelling task.

Virtual Reality research has explored very intricate algorithms for visibility based IM [2, 10]. Architectures have also been proposed in [13] and [3] to combine these algorithms with graceful degradation of fidelity in the event of network overload. Such sophisticated techniques generally rely on a large number of model-specific heuristics.

This is also the case with network game engines such as Unreal [15] which relies on an intimate knowledge of the behaviour of entities in the virtual environment for its calculation of a client's 'relevance set'.

In general these 'hard-tuned' systems are clearly inappropriate for flexible distributed simulation platforms where a-priori knowledge of interest patterns is unavailable. More significantly, because these systems rely on these static definitions they are unable to adapt to situations in which heuristics prove inaccurate.

3 Levels of Precision

The problem of interest expressions in general is to find some way of expressing a set of data items which will be used (read) by the modelling process at a node within some time interval. We can define the *precise* sphere of interest $SOI(n, [T])$ to be the set of variables that are accessed (read) by the node n during the notional time interval $[T]$[1].

In the schemes reviewed in section 2 the definition of an interest expression in these terms is in fact a two-stage process. First the model expresses some range of *values* to the IM infrastructure (e.g. a set of object classes, or a range of integer values in a coordinate space). At runtime the infrastructure then evaluates each update message in the rest of the system against this expression and transmits only the matching ones. We can define $u(ie, [T])$ for a given interest expression ie as the set of variables for which at least one update is returned by this procedure over the time interval $[T]$.

If we represent a theoretical interest expression that will evaluate to $true$ for *any* update as ∞ then a given interest expression ie in any of the schemes described above is *valid* for a given node n iff

$$u(ie, [T]) \supseteq (u(\infty, [T]) \cap SOI(n, [T]))$$

In other words the expression is valid only if it generates a set of variables which contains all the variables which experienced updates *and* were read by n.

[1] At this abstract level, whether our time system is virtual or real is immaterial.

The process of formulating an interest expression is in fact the process of conservatively predicting the size of this intersection. The overlap:

$$u(ie, [T]) - (u(\infty, [T]) \cap SOI(n, [T]))$$

for any such valid expression is the set of variables whose updates have been sent erroneously as a result of too conservative an estimation of the size of the intersection. In the schemes discussed in section 2, the size of this set is generally relative to the dynamism of the model and expressivity of the IM scheme.

An immediate solution to eliminate this overlap is to switch from *push*-processing, where updates to a variable at the owner node are immediately sent to other nodes, to *pull*-processing [4], where accesses to variable values cause a request-reply exchange between the 'remote' node and the 'owner' node, while updates at the owner node simply modify the local copy.

The problem with pull-processing is that it trades one overlap for another. A pull performed on some variable v at time t_r is only necessary if a write on v has occurred since the previous read. The overlap in pull-processing is not between one set of variables and another, but between the set of necessary pulls and the set of actual pulls.

An optimal interest management scheme is one which can ensure an empty overlap between the necessary messages and the actual messages. In the case of push-processing this implies that over any time interval:

$$u(ie, [T]) \equiv SOI(n, [T])$$

In the case of pull-processing it implies some scheme whereby queries are only sent if the owner's value has changed since the last read. Both of these optimal schemes are precluded due to the properties of uncertainty in distributed systems. The remainder of this paper therefore discusses a bottom-up framework capable of automatically deriving a sub-optimal approximation of these schemes.

4 A problem statement based on DSVs

Our framework is based on a runtime analysis of read and write patterns. In order to gain access to these data we make use of Distributed Shared Variables (DSVs) to represent the shared state in a distributed environment. The DSV abstraction is used largely as means of providing the infrastructure with the access information it requires from the model. Note at this point that the framework itself is reliant on no particular distributed consistency model such as those discussed by Mehl and Hammes [9]. The possibilities of extending the scheme for different consistency models are discussed in section 10. For the sake of simplicity in this discussion our model is based on the central server approach, where one node in the system is the *owner* of the variable and holds the *master* copy, all other nodes are *replicators* of the variable and hold *proxies*.

We start from the position that both push-processing and pull-processing alone will produce large amounts of redundant messages. For a given model, one algorithm may give less redundancy than another, but even during a single run this balance will change over time, this general pattern scales down to the level of a single DSV during a discrete time interval.

This general idea is illustrated in fig. 1. This figure shows a single master/proxy pair, in the first case the communication is managed by push-processing, in the second by pull-processing. An example sequence of operations at each variable is also presented[2].

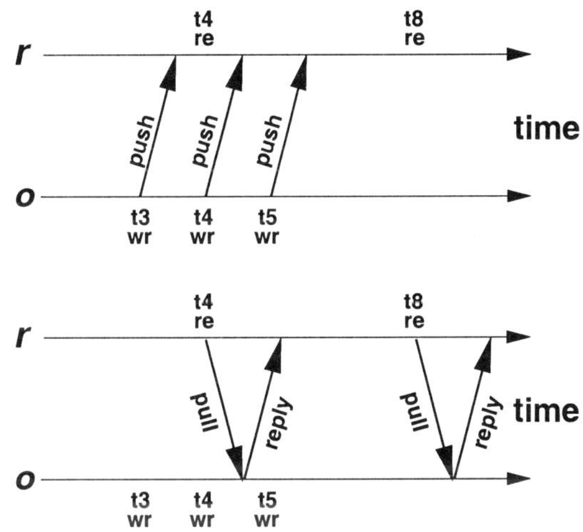

Figure 1. Messages exchanged between a replicator r and an owner o given a sequence of reads (re) and writes (wr) for both push-processing (above) and pull-processing (below)

By counting the number messages each processing scheme produces for a given sequence of operations we can determine which would be preferable for the time interval enclosing these operations. From table 1 it is clear that push processing is preferable over the entire interval $[t_0, t_8]$, but the opposite is true over the interval $[t_0, t_7]$.

This problem of segmenting known sequences to minimise messages is in itself a non-trivial problem as the search space of possible segmentations increases polynomially with the size of the sequence. The problem we face however, is to do so *on the fly* by predicting the evolution of

[2]Note that in the central server approach, writes to proxies must *always* be communicated to the owner, while reads on masters are *never* communicated to the replicators. Because of this imperative these operations are a static cost and hence are unimportant for our analysis.

Scheme	t_1	t_2	t_3	t_4	t_5	t_6	t_7	t_8	Total
Push	0	0	1	1	1	0	0	0	3
Pull	0	0	0	2	0	0	0	2	4

Table 1. Push vs. Pull performance for a given operation sequence

the sequence.

It is at this level that we propose to perform our analysis and it is by modulating a single DSV between push- and pull-processing based on pattern prediction that we propose to automatically effect interest management.

5 The Push-Pull Framework

Initially we define the basic machinery of the infrastructure:

- The system consists of a set of *nodes*, all viewing a common set of variables in the form of DSVs. For each DSV, one node is the *owner* and all others are *replicators*.
- A DSV is a single *master* variable at the owner and n *proxies*, one at each replicator.
- Each <master, proxy> pair represents an update *edge*, this being an abstraction of some virtual channel in a communication system
- At any point in real time an edge is in one of two *update states*, *push* or *pull*.
- The update state is implemented by boolean flags at the master and proxy forming this edge, describing whether writes at the master should be pushed and whether reads at the proxy should be pulled. The update state can be *flipped* from one state to another by a message-based handshake operation.

The task is to define some mechanism for managing the update states to minimise the number of messages. In considering algorithms for this management, understanding the memory access model used by the application is vital. We consider here two of the most common models.

5.1 Support for a Reference-Space Memory Access Model

A reference-space access model is one in which data items are accessed by specifying some unique identifier for that item, such as the name of a variable. There are a number of different levels at which support can be provided for managing update state given such an access model.

At the level of a *single edge* the task is to define a prediction model for a single operation sequence such as the one given in section 4, and apply update state flips based on this model, taking into account the cost of the handshake messages. The *demand-push* algorithm outlined in section 6 is a simplistic example of such a prediction model.

Moving one level up through the machinery, we can perform a prediction analysis based on correlative behaviour between *groups of edges*. Whilst correlation analyses are relatively expensive, identifying sets of edges whose operation patterns are related may make further prediction cheaper and more meaningful with regard to certain models.

Beyond the level of groups of edges, the prediction of patterns of behaviour begins to rely on some higher-level understanding of the model itself. A prediction model may be constructed at this level, but it is likely that it would have some kind of heuristic component.

This framework in general does have the possible disadvantage of high memory demands. Let v be the number of master variables, and N be the number of nodes in the system, then each node will have to record $v(N-1)$ update-states (one for each proxy). Depending on the prediction model, prediction data may also have to be recorded in similar quantities. It is clear from this that in very large networks with a large number of local variables at each node, available memory may become a factor.

In such cases it may be necessary to investigate clustering nodes together in push-pull groups, which would decrease the number of update-states for local variables to $(n/s)+s-2$ for an n node network with a cluster-size of s. However, it is probable that this would incur a cost of increased network messages as the accuracy of the node-to-node interest approximation is worsened. Note that this scheme is comparable to the hierarchical routing structures for shared-state data proposed in [7].

5.2 Support for an Associative Memory Access Model

If one considers the realities of modelling it is unlikely that data-gathering will take place solely on the basis of individual read operations. Just as important a facility for a model, is the ability to determine the identities of variables whose value matches some predicate (e.g. *the position of all people within* 5 *yards of point* (x,y)).

This abstract memory access model is the *associative* model and it is present in the push-pull framework in the form of the *range query* operation, it can be expressed more formally by:

$$rq(c, ?id, V \mid or \mid [x,y])$$

Where c is a given variable class, V is a non-empty set

of values or predicates and $[x, y]$ is a value interval in the domain c such that $x \leq y$. The $?id$ symbol denotes that these commands will return a set of *id* values of variables whose value is equal to the given value.

Upon receiving a range query invocation we can simply perform a read of each variable of class c, comparing the returned value to the predicate and returning the satisfying set. This algorithm - the serial-read algorithm - sends a number of messages equal to twice the number of proxies of class c whose update state is currently set to *pull*.

The operation can be optimised by defining an extra virtual edge between each node which we term the *bulk-read* edge. This edge is specifically for performing range-queries. When a range query is executed by the model, the following algorithm is executed by the infrastructure:

1. The querying node r passes the rq parameters down the bulk-read edges to all other nodes O such that there exists an edge (o_i, r) with a variable-class of c, and an update-state of *pull*.
2. Upon receiving the query o_i checks each variable of class c whose update-edge to r is set to *pull*, for equality with the query-predicate and returns the satisfying set S of $<var\_id, value>$ tuples.
3. Meanwhile r performs the same operation locally, by evaluating a satisfying set from its own master variables of class c *and* from all proxy variables of class c where the update state is set to $push$.
4. Once all satisfying sets have been received from O at r they are combined and returned as the result of the query.

Using the bulk-read algorithm one reduces the number of messages for each range query in comparison to the serial-read algorithm. A range query at node n_i will send one message for each node n_j (where $j \neq i$) such that there exists a proxy at n_i with an update state of *pull* and a class of c. Because a serial-read would send a message for each of these proxies anyway, the worst performance of the bulk-read algorithm is exactly equal to the serial-read algorithm. Bulk-reads also have a scaling property since the evaluation of predicate equality is evenly distributed across all nodes and executed in parallel.

The bulk-read algorithm provides reasonable performance support for associative memory access. As is identified in section 10, using infrastructure level pattern prediction to optimise associative memory access is an important but very complex area of future work.

6 The Demand-Push Algorithm

This section presents a basic algorithm of the type proposed in section 5. We assume a reference-space memory access model only, so range queries can never be issued by the model. The algorithm works by managing the update-state of a single edge over time.

The demand-push algorithm works in a similar way to demand-paging in virtual memory systems. When a read is performed upon a proxy, a timer T is set running on the proxy, taking a period of length k to reach 0. While $T > 0$ the proxy's edge is left in push mode, when T reaches 0 the replicator node sends a message flipping the edge back to pull-mode. If a read occurs on a proxy in push-mode this is not communicated to the owner, T is simply reset to k.

The demand-push algorithm is likened to a demand-paging algorithm in the sense that remote reads are taken to be analogous to page-faults in a paged-memory system. In both cases the caching of recently accessed localities is an attempt to minimise the number of future faults.

In both cases caching also incurs a cost, in the case of demand-paging the cache is of a limited size, so for every page cached another must be selected for removal. With demand-push the cost is rather that for every proxy 'cached' $k(w/s)$ push messages will be sent along the edge where w/s is the number of writes per second (assuming k is expressed in seconds).

7 The Simulated Testbed

We have produced a simulated testbed for examining properties of the push-pull framework in general and of given algorithms specifically. This testbed is a virtual-time based simulation of the framework which presents an interface (based on DSVs) to a virtual-time based model (the 'input model'). The general system is described pictorially in fig. 2. The input model defines the set of simulation nodes, the set of variables and the ownership of variables by nodes. The framework simulation models the communication that takes place between nodes given a) a set of read/write operations from the model and b) a particular algorithm for managing update state of the edges.

In our case the input model was a set of traces collected over 1000 virtual time 'ticks' of a simplistic stochastic multi-agent model. This model is a grid environment where each grid cell has a variable integer 'value' which changes periodically through time. Simple agents move around the grid sensing the values of the cells according to that agent's visual range. The model uses the DSV interface provided by the push-pull infrastructure, hence grid cells change their values using an explicit *write* operation and agents read the value of a cell using an explicit *read* operation.

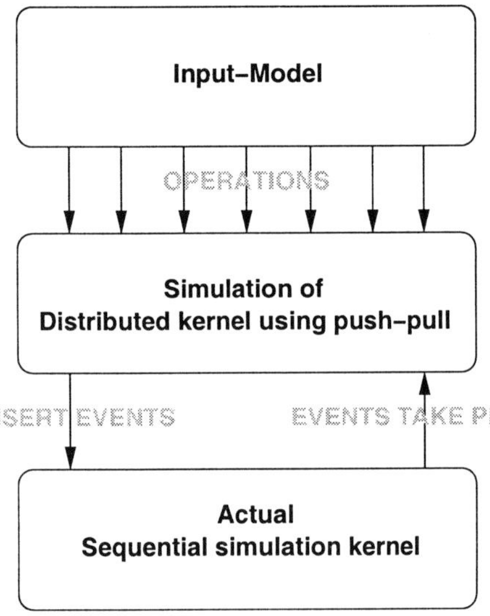

Figure 2. Architecture of the Testbed

8 Results

The traces generated by the process described in section 7 produce a single read-write sequence for each edge. To test each algorithm the same sets of traces were input to the testbed a number of times, each time a different algorithm was used to manage the update-state of the edges.

Figures 4-7 compare the performance of the three different algorithms; push-processing; pull-processing; and demand-push with various values of k. The performance is represented in these graphs as samples of the number of messages sent along all edges during consecutive 50-tick periods.

In order to evaluate the performance of the demand-push algorithm some understanding of its probable behaviour is necessary. Messages are generated on an edge under demand-pushing in 4 situations:

1. When a read occurs on a proxy and $T = 0$.

2. When a write occurs on a master and $T > 0$.

3. When a master receives a pull request (at the start of the period k) and replies with the current value and a confirmation of the flip to push.

4. When T times out and the edge is flipped back to pull mode by the replicator node sending a notification to the owner node.

Given these properties, the performance in terms of total aggregate network activity of the demand-push algorithm is not simply dependant on the ratio of reads to writes, though this is clearly a factor.

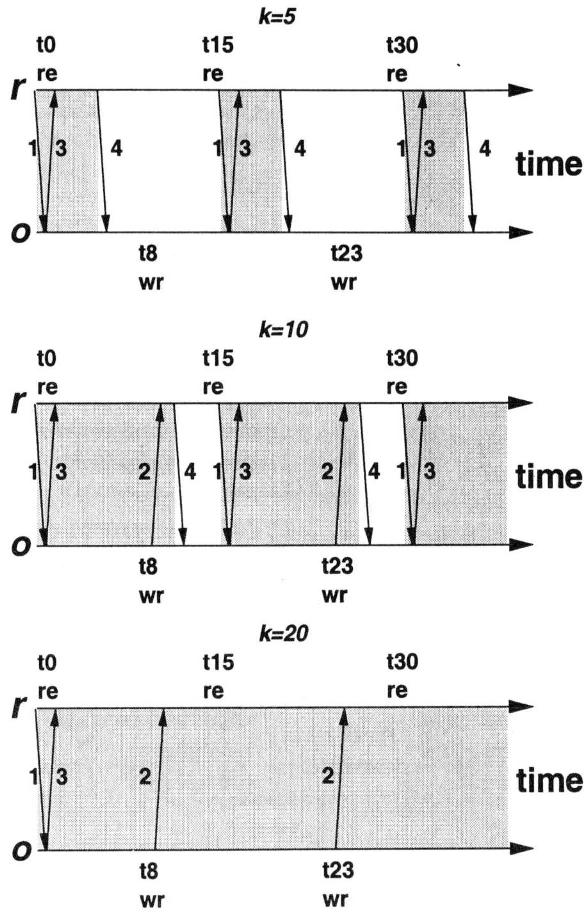

Figure 3. The behaviour of the demand-push algorithm for a single operation sequence with various values of k. Shaded areas of each graph denote periods of push-processing. The numerical annotations on each message denote the cause of the message, as given in the enumeration above.

In fig. 3 three different values of k are shown for the same input sequence. In both cases where $k \leq 10$, the edge is reset to pull mode before the next read can reset T to k. In effect the algorithm is thrashing because more messages are being used for the management of update-state than for the communication of modelling information. However, increasing k is not necessarily the best solution to this problem. This is demonstrated by the increase in messages where $k = 10$ in comparison to where $k = 5$. The thrashing issue is still present, but unused push messages are now increasing the total communication.

Because the cost of thrashing is a coefficient of the read-frequency r/s of a given sequence, its significance will reduce in proportion to the write frequency of the same sequence. For example, were there to be a write every 2 ticks in the above figures, $k = 5$ would out perform the other two values, despite thrashing. Likewise an increase in the read-frequency will increase significance of thrashing up to a point at which $r/s = k$ when it will disappear.

To relate these observations to the results, we used the two variables of aggregate read frequency and aggregate write frequency, producing four permutations.

In general the worst performer is one of the two pure push- or pull-processing algorithms, for high read frequencies pull-processing produces the most messages, for high write frequencies, push-processing. Also in general, for higher values of k, demand-push out performs both pure-processing forms. Although there is little difference between them, $k = 25$ generally performs better for higher ratios of reads/writes while the opposite is true for $k = 100$. This fits with the analysis as $k = 100$ is more likely to leave a scarcely-read variable in push mode, causing more wasted messages in a high write-frequency model.

The effects of thrashing are abundantly clear for $k = 10$ where the read frequency is low. In fig. 6, all other algorithms result in almost no messages, demonstrating how few data are actually being exchanged from a modelling perspective. Conversely, and as speculated above, where the read frequency is high this thrashing component is not present, and $k = 10$ has a very similar profile to larger values of k. In fact it can be seen to out-perform both the other values at many points in fig. 7, where the write frequency is also high.

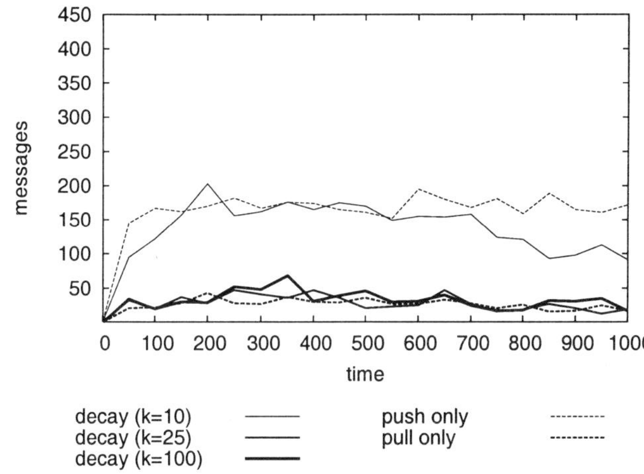

Figure 4. Low read frequency/High write frequency

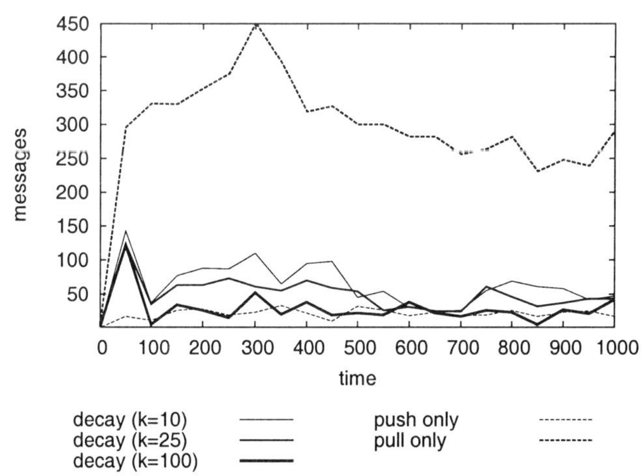

Figure 5. High read frequency/Low write frequency

9 Related Work

As mentioned in section 5, the push-pull framework in general is inspired by the PDES-MAS (Parallel and Discrete Simulation of Multi-Agent Systems) framework described by Logan and Theodoropoulos in [7]. This system also aims to achieve optimisation through bottom-up analysis of access patterns. The framework in this case is a graph of owner nodes, each responsible for some set of shared-

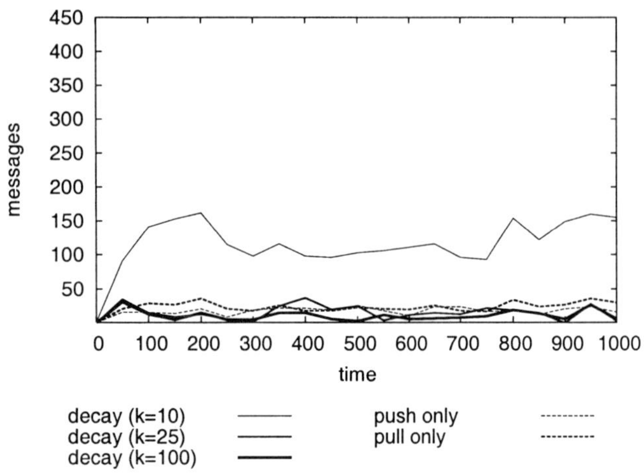

Figure 6. Low read frequency/Low write frequency

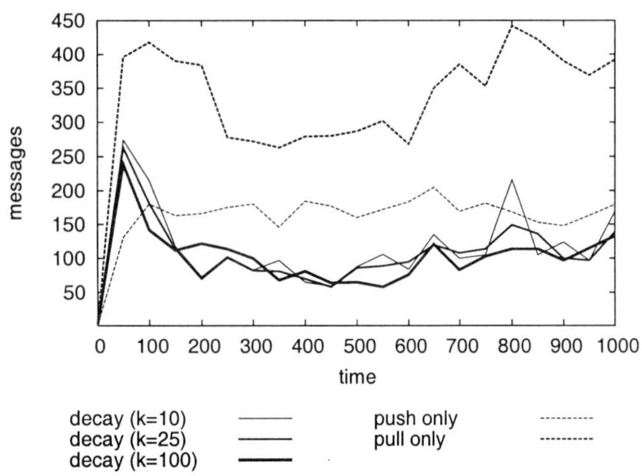

Figure 7. High read frequency/High write frequency

state variables. The primary aims are balancing of the computational load between these nodes, rather than minimisation of communication costs.

Work done by Yellin at IBM [18] presents a competitive algorithm for solving the problem of selecting a policy (in the form a component) for serving an application request based on previous performance profiles. This 'delta' algorithm is applied to the push-pull problem - termed the 'pub/sub' (publication/subscription) problem in Yellin's work - and identified as optimal within the limit. However, Yellin's approach does not explore the use of prediction models and we expect to find algorithms inspired by this area which outperform delta for a number of sequence types.

Vitter and Krishnan by comparison have done extensive work in the use of discrete sequence prediction models for improving prefetching strategies in virtual memory systems [17]. The modelling itself is directly applicable to the push-pull problem whilst its use to generate prefectching strategies is less so, due to the differences between push-pull and traditional caching mentioned in section 6.

10 Summary and Future Work

This paper has proposed a bottom-up approach to Interest Management in DVEs. Our work is currently in a continuing experimental stage with the essential machinery defined and proof-of-concept simulations completed.

Of most immediate interest is improving on the performance of the demand-push algorithm given in section 6. This algorithm is inelegant from the perspective of pattern-prediction and is susceptible to non-linear behaviour as shown in section 8, making it a poor choice for robust systems. Mature research exists in the area of discrete sequence prediction and we propose to use this research in the development of more elegant, robust algorithms.

Implementing range queries to support an associative memory access model is another priority. A general technique for this support is given in section 5.2. Expanding on this support to include prediction of associative access sequences is a much more demanding challenge than that for reference-space access sequences.

Currently this work deals purely with real time applications. Future work will extend this to enable the framework to perform IM in as part of a larger virtual-time simulation framework. Mehl and Hammes work into implementing DSVs for virtual-time simulation systems [9] is a very useful starting point for this considerable task, particularly as it speculates on performance profiles for each architecture given properties of the model.

References

[1] Howard Abrams, Kent Watson, and Michael Zyda. Three-tiered interest management for large-scale virtual environments. In *Proceedings of the ACM Symposium on Virtual Reality Software and Technology*, pages 125–129, 1998.

[2] John Barrus, Richard Waters, and David Anderson. Locales: Supporting large multiuser virtual environments. *IEEE Computer Graphics and Applications*, 16(6):50–57, November 1996.

[3] Chris Faisstnauer, Dieter Schmalstieg, and Werner Purgathofer. Scheduling for very large virtual environments and networked games using visibility and priorities. In *Fourth IEEE International Workshop on Distributed Simulation and Real-Time Applications (DS-RT'00)*. IEEE, 2000.

[4] Richard M. Fujimoto. *Parallel and Distributed Simulation Systems*. Wiley Interscience, 2000.

[5] GarageGames.inc. openTNL - torque network library. World Wide Web, `http://www.opentnl.org`, 2004.

[6] IEEE. 1278: Standard for distributed interactive simulation, 1995.

[7] Brian Logan and Georgios Theodoropoulos. The Distributed Simulation of Multi-Agent Systems. In *Proceedings of the IEEE - Special Issue on Agent-Oriented Software Approaches in Distributed Modelling and Simulation*, 2000.

[8] Michael Macedonia, Michael Zyda, David Pratt, Donald Brutzmann, and Paul Barham. Exploiting reality with multicast groups: A network architecture for large-scale virtual environments. *IEEE Computer Graphics and Applications*, 15(3):38–45, 1995.

[9] Hosrt Mehl and Stefan Hammes. Shared variables in distributed simulation. In *Proceedings of the 7th Workshop on Parallel and Distributed Simulation*, pages 68–75, 1993.

[10] Graham Morgan and Fengyun Lu. Predictive interest management: An approach to managing message dissemination for distributed virtual environments. In *Proceedings of the First International Workshop on Interactive Rich Media Content Production:Architectures, Technologies, Applications, Tools (Richmedia2003)*, 2003.

[11] Katherine Morse. *An Adaptive, Distributed Algorithm for Interest Management*. PhD thesis, University of California, Irvine, 2000.

[12] Katherine Morse and Jeffrey Steinman. Data distribution management in the HLA: Multidimensional regions and physically correct filtering. In *Proceedings of the 1997 Spring Simulation Interoperability Workshop*, 1997.

[13] Dieter Schmalstieg and Michael Gervautz. Demand-driven geometry transmission for distributed virtual environments. In *Proceedings of EUROGRAPHICS 1996*, volume 15, pages 421–433, 1996.

[14] Joe Sorroche and Jerry Szulinski. Bandwidth reduction techniques used in DIS exercises. In *Proceedings of the 2004 European Simulation Interoperability Workshop*, 2004.

[15] Tim Sweeney. The Unreal networking architecture. World Wide Web, `http://unreal.epicgames.com/Network.htm`, 1999.

[16] US Defence Modelling and Simulation Office. HLA Interface Specification, version 1.3, 1998.

[17] Jeffrey Scott Vitter and P. Krishnan. Optimal prefetching via data compression. *Journal of the ACM*, 43(5):771–793, September 1996.

[18] Daniel M. Yellin. Competitive algorithms for the dynamic selection of component implementations. *IBM Systems Journal*, 42(1):85–97, 2003.

Service Provisioning for HLA-based Distributed Simulation on the Grid

Yong Xie[1], Yong Meng Teo[1,2], Wentong Cai[3], Stephen John Turner[3]
[1]Singapore-Massachusetts Institute of Technology Alliance
[2]Department of Computer Science, National University of Singapore, Singapore 117543
[3]School of Computer Engineering, Nanyang Technological University, Singapore 639798
smaxy@nus.edu.sg, teoym@comp.nus.edu.sg, {aswtcai, assjturner}@ntu.edu.sg

Abstract

Modeling and simulation permeate all areas of business, science and engineering. With the increase in the scale and complexity of simulations, large amounts of computational resources are required, and provisioning of the services is becoming increasingly difficult. The Grid provides a platform for coordinated resource sharing and application development and execution. In this paper, we focus on extending the High Level Architecture (HLA) to the Grid. More specifically, we propose a distributed simulation framework, called HLAGrid. The framework uses a Federate-Proxy-RTI architecture, which allows resources on the Grid to be utilized on demand by using Grid services. The architecture also supports federation discovery, security of the simulator logic, and flexible federation construction, such as hierarchical federations. The architecture hides the heterogeneity of the simulators, simulators' execution platforms, and how the simulators communicate with the RTI. All interfaces used in the framework comply with the standard HLA interface specification, which provides reusability to simulators. A prototype of the framework is implemented using DMSO's RTI 1.3NG version 6 and the Grid system runs the Globus Toolkit.

1. Introduction

Modeling and simulation provide a low cost and safe alternative to real-world training, experiments, analysis of natural phenomena, etc. The High Level Architecture (HLA), approved by US Department of Defense (DoD) in 1995, provides an architecture for interoperability and reuse in distributed simulation [5], and it was adopted as an open standard through the IEEE Standard 1516 in September 2000.

A simulation, or a *federation* in HLA's terminology, consists of a set of logically related simulators, called *federates*. Federates communicate with each other through the *Run-Time Infrastructure* (RTI). HLA defines the rules and specifications to support reusability and interoperability amongst the simulation federates. The RTI software supports and synchronizes the interactions amongst different federates that conform to the standard HLA specification [5].

In order to run a distributed simulation over the Wide-Area-Network (WAN) using the IEEE HLA/RTI directly, special arrangements have to be made beforehand to ensure the availabilities of the required hardware and software. Such arrangements are typically made with a centralized control or simply within an organization, because inter-organizational sharing of resources involves issues such as security. With the increase in the scale and complexity of simulations, large amounts of resources are required, and provisioning of services becomes more and more difficult. In the case of HLA-based distributed simulation, the resources of RTI, the simulation model, and/or the underlying infrastructure may not be available when they are needed.

The concept of "Grid" computing was proposed by Ian Foster as secure and coordinated resource sharing and problem solving in dynamic, multi-institutional virtual organizations [9]. Much effort has been made in the area of Grid computing since 2001. Many systems and middleware for Grid computing have been proposed in the past few years, and Globus [10] is becoming the de facto standard middleware for Grid computing. The third version of the Globus Toolkit [12] is based on the concept of *Grid Services*, which is defined by the Open Grid Services Architecture (OGSA) [11], and is specified by the Open Grid Services Infrastructure (OGSI) [21]. The Grid Services architecture enables resources to be dynamically discovered and shared on demand, thus supports the provisioning of services for large-scale Grid applications, such as HLA-based distributed simulation.

In this paper, we aim to extend the IEEE HLA to the Grid, and more specifically we focus on the provisioning of services to support HLA-based distributed simulation on the Grid. We present a distributed simulation framework

1087-4097/05 $20.00 © 2005 IEEE

to address several important issues, such as HLA/RTI service provisioning, heterogeneity, federation discovery, federation construction, and security. The framework supports the provisioning of the RTI service by using a Federate-Proxy-RTI architecture, in which a remote proxy acts on behalf of the federate in interacting with the RTI. It hides the heterogeneity of the simulators, simulators' execution platforms, and how the simulators communicate with the RTI. Moreover, RTI services are exposed as Grid services, and the communications are through Grid service invocation, which provides more secure, scalable and coordinated management. The architecture also supports dynamic discovery of the federation, and hierarchical federations. All interfaces used in the framework comply with the standard HLA interface specification, which provides reusability to simulators. A prototype of the framework is implemented using DMSO's RTI 1.3NG version 6 and the Globus Toolkit Version 3. The DMSO HLA's benchmark programs have been converted from C++ to Java, and are used in the testing of the prototype.

The rest of the paper is organized as follows: Section 2 presents the literature review on related work. Section 3 discusses the design of the Federate-Proxy-RTI architecture and our prototype implementation. In Section 4, we describe the experimental results. Section 5 presents further discussion on the merits of our proposed architecture. Our concluding remarks and plan for future work are in Section 6.

2. Literature Review

In the literature on improving the HLA, some researchers [13, 22] focus on building tools to ease the process of modeling and simulation using HLA, and some [24] focus on adding auxiliary systems to make HLA more useful in a wide-area-network (WAN), while others [7, 8, 19, 20] have a more ambitious objective to reinvent HLA to be model-driven and composable, or replace HLA with a new framework.

Some researchers focus on the extension of HLA's interoperability. For example, in [19, 20], Tolk, et al. propose a framework to integrate HLA into the Model-Driven Architecture (MDA) [18] defined by the Object Management Group (OMG) to improve interoperability.

Wytzisk, et al. [22] propose a solution that brings HLA and the Open GIS Consortium (OGC) [15] standard together. It provides external initialization of federations, controlled start up and termination of federates, interactions with running federates, and access of simulation results by external processes. Zajac, et al. [24] propose a system to enable HLA-based simulations on the Grid, but they focus on migrating federates. The system also includes discovery, and information indexing services. However, the communication between RTI and federates is based on the original HLA communication, which requires predefined ports to be open. Fitzgibbons, et al. [8] present a distributed simulation framework, called IDSim, based upon OGSI [21]. It makes use of Globus's Grid service data elements as simulation states to allow both pull and push modes of access. It also aims to ease the integration and deployment of tasks through inheritance.

The distributed simulation communities initiated a plan, called the Extensible Modeling and Simulation Framework (XMSF) [7], which defines a set of Web-based technologies, applied within an extensible framework, that enables a new generation of modeling and simulation applications to emerge, develop and interoperate. Morse, et al. [14] propose an architecture using Web Services for web based federates communicating with the RTI. Their approach is based on formatting the RTI calls via Simple Object Access Protocol (SOAP) [17] and employing the Blocks Extensible Exchange Protocol (BEEP) [2] communication layer to enable bi-directional calls and callbacks via web services.

Compared with all the previous work, we have different focuses, which are the provisioning of services and flexible construction of federations. We believe these are the characteristics that will differentiate a Grid-enabled HLA-based distributed simulation from the traditional IEEE HLA/RTI based distributed simulation.

3. Design and Implementation

3.1. Overview

To provide services to support HLA-based distributed simulation on the Grid, we leverage on the existing Grid infrastructure, and the layered framework is shown in Figure 1. The ideal framework for distributed simulation over the Grid should sit on top of our HLAGrid and various other Grid projects, such as Access Grid [1], Semantic Grid [16], and Data Grid [6]. Our specific goals include:

- to support RTI service to be used on demand
- to support dynamic discovery of federations
- to provide a standard HLA API, for reasons of interoperability and reusability.
- to overcome the limitation of firewalls in traditional HLA/RTI implementations.
- to support hierarchical federations

The HLAGrid framework includes a Federate-Proxy-RTI architecture, in which different participants (clients) in the same simulation run their federate codes at their local sites, and the RtiExec and FedExec are executed on the remote resource. A new entity, *proxy*, is introduced to act on behalf of the clients' federate code to communicate with

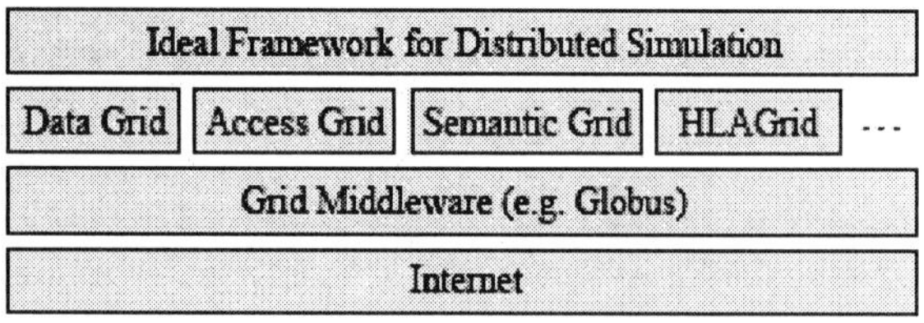

Figure 1. A layered framework for distributed simulation on the Grid.

proxies of other clients through the RTI. Proxies are executed at remote grid resources. Federate codes and their respective proxies communicate with each other through Grid services, and a Grid-enabled HLA API, which provides the standard HLA API to the federate codes, is implemented to translate the communications into Grid services invocations. Our framework also includes additional Grid services to support the creation of the RTI and discovery of federations. As a result, the RTI resource can be created, discovered, and used on demand. Moreover, hierarchical federations can be constructed by using the proxy in a way similar to the mechanisms used in [3, 4]. Users have the flexibility to join the federation locally, remotely (using the Federate-Proxy-RTI architecture), or hierarchically.

In this framework, clients can run their simulator anywhere on any type of machine architecture. This framework hides the communication over the Grid network, and provides user transparency and simulator reusability. It also facilitates migration of federates without affecting other parts of the simulation, and the Proxy-RTI backbone can also be migrated, as it does not involve any simulation logic. Different RTI services can be exposed as separate Grid services, which provide standard state management schemes that are required for Grid service composition. This framework incurs additional communication cost and overhead in embedding HLA communication into Grid service invocations, which will be quantified in the experiments of our implementation.

3.2. Detailed Design

The framework consists of two major components: client and resource (proxy-RTI backbone) together with supporting Grid services, which are interconnected through the Grid network, as shown in Figure 2.

3.2.1. Client Side The client side provides the standard HLA API to the federate code, while allowing communication through the Grid. We make use of the Globus Grid middleware as the lower level communication channel, and provide a Grid-enabled API to translate federate-RTI communication into Grid service invocations, as illustrated in Figure 2.

To translate federate-RTI communication, all the method calls in the *RTIambassador* class and the callback functions provided in the *FederateAmbassador* need to be exposed to Globus. The *RTIambassador* method calls across the Grid are achieved using remote Grid service invocations by embedding the parameters inside invocations. When there is a *FederateAmbassador* callback from the RTI, the proxy will deliver the callback through Grid service invocation to the client. Figure 3 provides the conceptual view of the interactions between the client side and the proxy.

Note that, the proxy decouples the client and the RTI, and the simulation logic is maintained securely at the client side. The Proxy-RTI only provides mechanisms for simulation management, such as federation management and time management. This architecture facilitates migration of the federate without affecting other parts of the simulation, because during the migration of the federate, the proxy could still respond to the RTI. There is no need for other federates to suspend their executions, which is required in [24]. Moreover, the proposed framework also supports migration of the Proxy-RTI backbone, because in the proposed framework, the Proxy-RTI backbone does not involve any simulation logic.

3.2.2. Resource Side At the resource side, the *proxy* acts on behalf of the client and communicates with the RTI through the Local Area Network (LAN), as shown in Figure 4. The proxy is responsible for translating *RTIambassador* Grid service invocations into normal federate initiated RTI services, as well as embedding *FederateAmbassador* callbacks into Grid service invocations to the client's *FebAmb* Grid service.

3.2.3. Other Grid Services Besides the Grid services to enable the communication between the client's federate code and the remote RTI, other Grid services are required for creating the RTI and discovering the federation.

- RTI services: persistent RTI service factories are needed to create instances of RTI services.
- Indexing service: a persistent indexing service is needed for maintaining the mapping between federations and handles of corresponding RTI services instances.

For how these services are created, managed and coordinated to provide various services for distributed simulation on the Grid, please refer to [25] for more details.

3.3. HLA Simulation on the Grid Walk-through

We describe the detailed steps involved in a HLA simulation on the Grid.

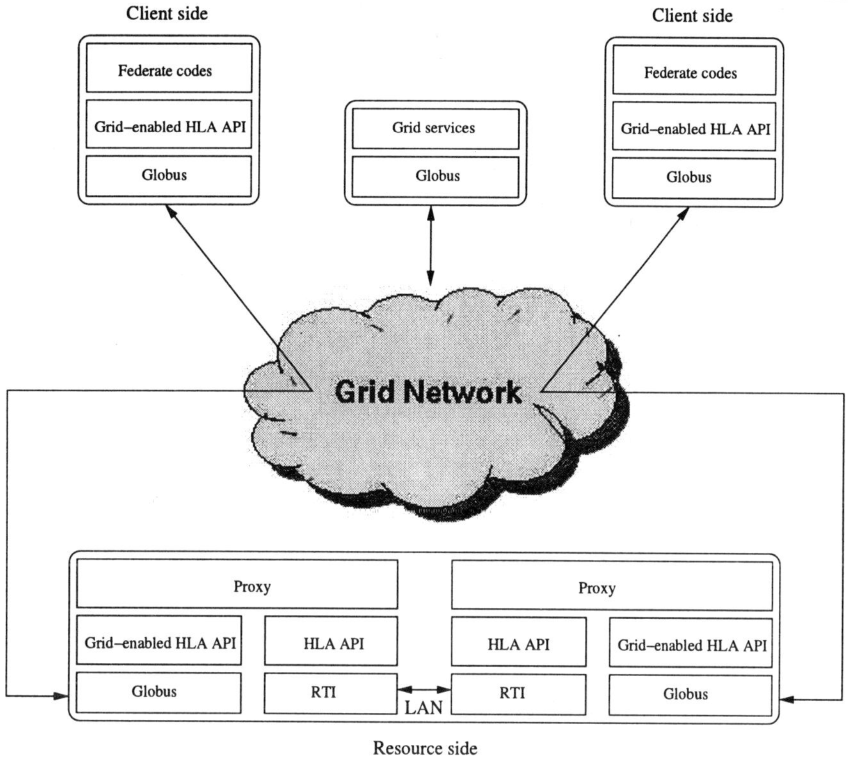

Figure 2. Architecture of Proxy-based HLA simulation on the Grid.

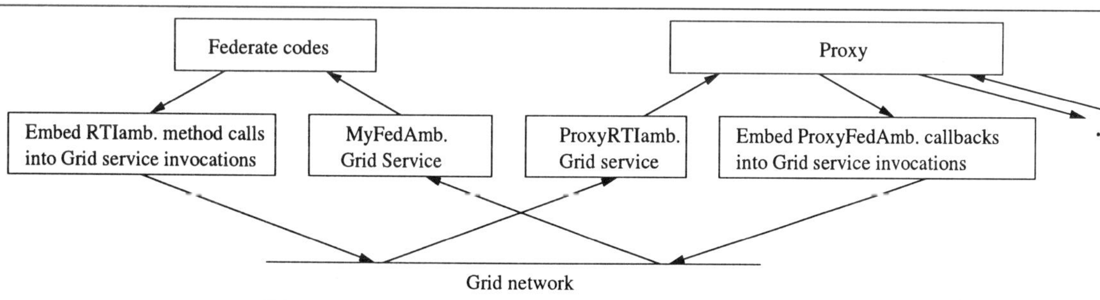

Figure 3. Interaction between client side and the proxy in the framework.

- Startup stage: steps 1 to 5

  1. Create RTI: the federate code will invoke the persistent RTI service factory to create a RTI service instance, and use the instance to run *rtiexec* at the resource side. The newly created RTI instance and the federation name need to be registered with the index service, so that other federates in the same federation will be able to look up the correct RTI instance. Note that, there is a concurrency issue involved in creating the RTI and registering the RTI with the index service. It can be resolved using a reservation table and a reference table, and the details are in [25].

  2. Create federate ambassador and RTI ambassador: the *Proxy* is created, and its associated *RTIambassador* and *FederateAmbassador* will be created at the resource side, so that they will communicate with the RTI locally.

  3. Create and join federation execution: two *RTI-ambassador* method calls will be made at the client side and translated into Grid service invo-

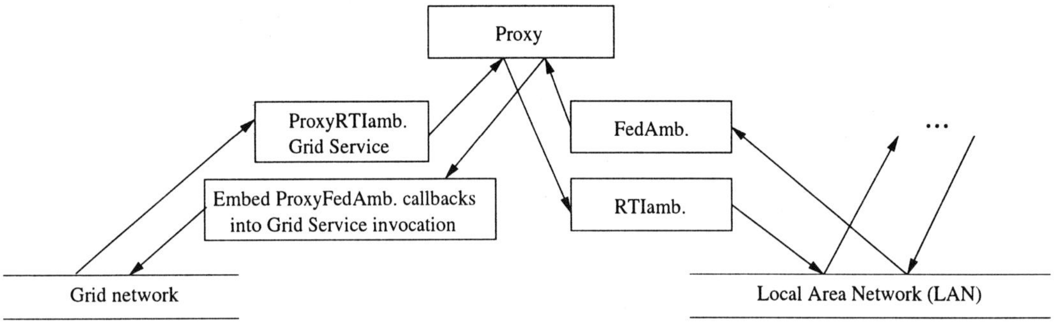

Figure 4. Interaction between the proxy and the RTI at the resource side.

cations to the resource side.

4. Initialize, publish and subscribe: all simulation settings will be initialized by invoking the *RTI-ambassador* at the resource side.
5. Enable time constrained and time regulating if required as in step 4.

- Main loop: step 6

6. This is the main body of the federate code, which includes *RTIambassador* method calls and *FederateAmbassador* callbacks, as shown in Figure 5 and Figure 6.

- Shutdown: steps 7 to 9

7. Resign from federation: this involves a method call to the remote *RTIambassador*.
8. Destroy federation execution: besides the Grid service invocation to destroy the federation, the federation should be deregistered in the index service.
9. Destroy RTI: this will be done according to the administrative rules at the resource side.

3.4. Implementation

A prototype of our proposed framework is implemented in Java, and the Grid system runs the Globus Toolkit version 3.

At the client side, three main classes are implemented, as shown in Figure 7:

- *HLAGridNullFedAmb* class extends the default *NullFederateAmbassador* class provided in the DMSO's HLA implementation, and all the interfaces remain the same.
- *ClientProvider* class is a Grid service. An instance of the *ClientProvider* class will be able to receive Grid service invocation from the Proxy and translate them into callbacks of *MyFedAmb*.

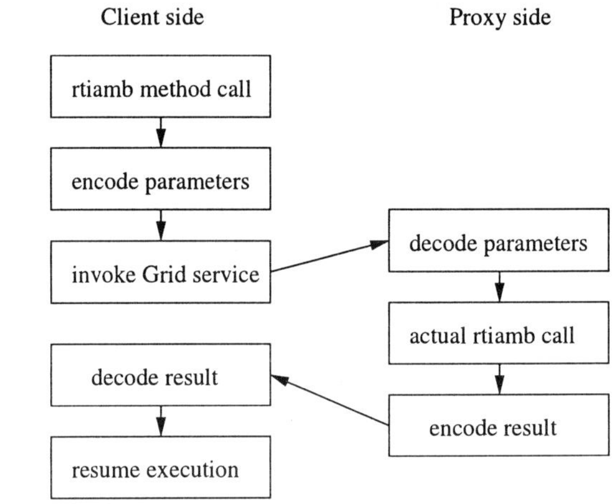

Figure 5. Executing a *RTIambassador* method call through Grid service invocation.

- *HLAGridRTIAmb* embeds all the *RTIambassador* calls into a Grid Service invocation.

The client's own code should contain an instance of *HLAGridRTIAmb* and an instance of the client-defined *MyFedAmb* which extends the *HLAGridNullFedAmb* class.

At the resource side, five main classes are used:

- *ProxyServiceProvider* class implements the Grid service class *OperationProvider*. It accepts remote invocations of *RTIambassador* method calls, and delivers *FederateAmbassador* callbacks to the client by invoking the Client's Grid service.
- *ProxyNullFedAmbassador* extends the default *NullFedAmbassador* in the DMSO's HLA implementation.
- *ProxyRTIComponent* contains a *RTIambassador* to communicate with the RTI.

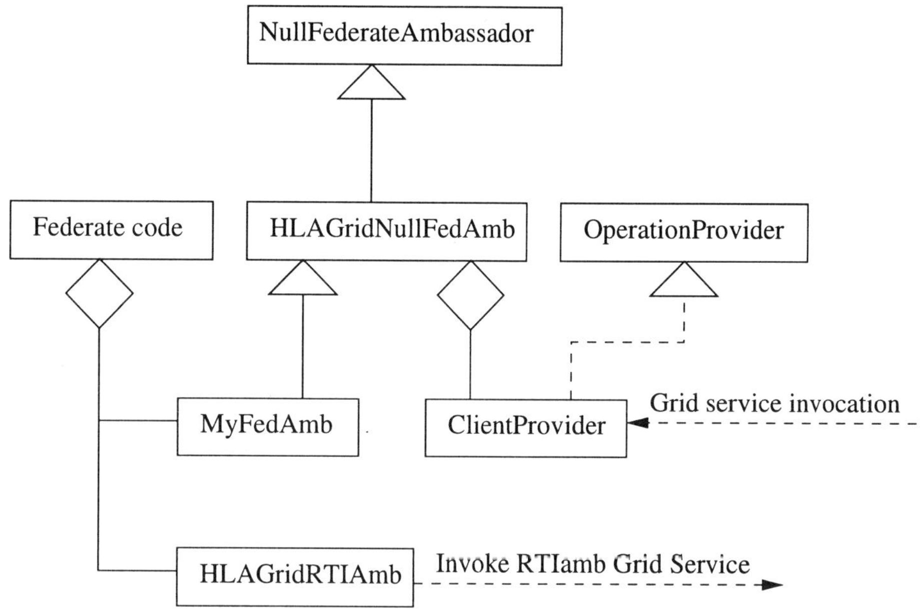

Figure 7. The class diagram of the client side.

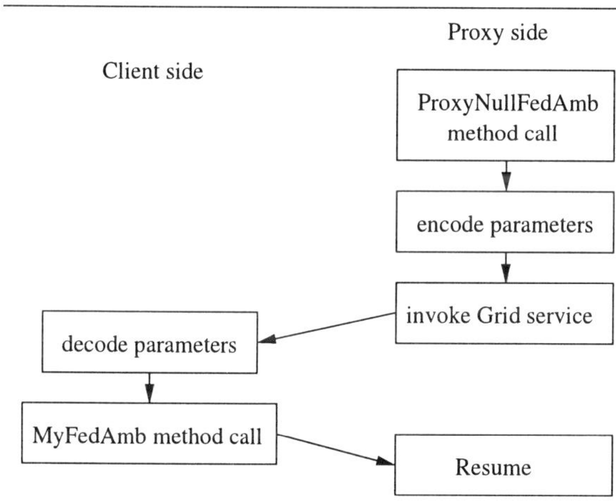

Figure 6. Executing a *FederateAmbassador* callback through Grid service invocation.

- *ProxyFedComponent* also contains a *ProxyNullFedAmbassador*, which embeds callbacks into Grid Service invocations.

We have implemented the *RTIambassador* services' API for Federation Management, Time Management, Object Management, Declaration Management, and Ownership Management. As mentioned in [14], to implement the Data Distribution Management (DDM), we need to keep the state and context for each region and its dimension handles. We plan to implement the DDM in future. A detailed description of the implementation can be found in [23].

4. Experiments and Results

In order to investigate the overhead incurred in the proposed framework, we converted the benchmark programs from DMSO's HLA package into Java programs, and tested them under different network configurations. We focused on two main benchmarks, i.e. Latency and Time Advancement.

The latency benchmark program measures RTI performance in terms of the latency of federate communications. More specifically, the benchmark program measures the elapsed time it takes for federates to send and receive an attribute update. The benchmark uses two federates, and it works as follows: one federate sends an attribute update, and upon receiving this update, the other federate sends it back to the sending federate. The elapsed time of this communication is calculated by using the real time taken at the sending and reflecting federates. All parameters used are the default values given in the DMSO package. There is no queuing of messages involved, and the communication payload is assumed to be negligible. The communication protocol used is reliable.

The time advancement benchmark program measures RTI performance in terms of the rate at which time advance requests are processed. The benchmark uses two federates with timestep cycle of 10, all other parameters are the default values from the DMSO package.

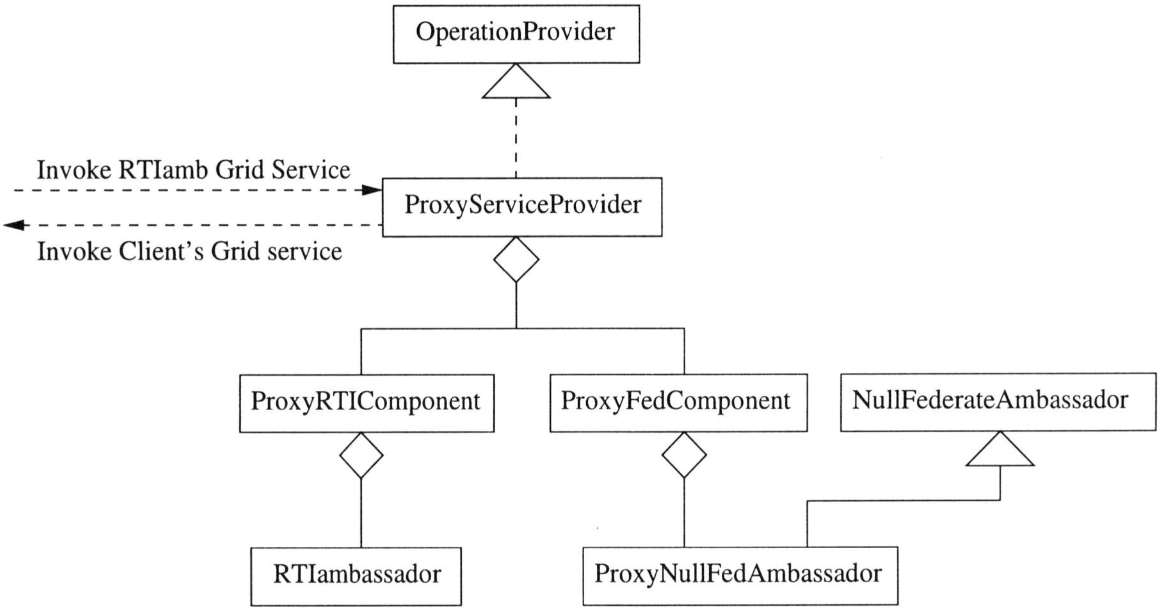

Figure 8. The class diagram of the resource side.

The testing is done using the Linux cluster in the Parallel and Distributed Computing Centre at the School of Computer Engineering of Nanyang Technological University in Singapore and a Linux workstation in the School of Computer Science at Birmingham University in the United Kingdom.

There are five components in the experiment: RTI, two federates $Federate1$ and $Federate2$, two more corresponding proxies $Proxy1$ and $Proxy2$ required by the HLAGrid software. The processes $RtiExec$ and $FedExec$ are executed in Singapore on machines M_{rti}. The processes $Federate1$, $Proxy1$, and $Proxy2$ are executed in Singapore on machines M_{fed1}, M_{proxy1}, and M_{proxy2} respectively. The process $Federate2$ is executed on M_{fed2}-SG in NTU, and on M_{fed2}-UK in Birmingham as a comparison. All machines in NTU are inter-connected using ethernet. There is a connection between machine M_{proxy2} in NTU to machine M_{fed2}-UK in Birmingham through the Grid network. The experiment hardware configuration is shown in Figure 9. Individual machines' specifications are shown in Table 1. Figure 10 shows the configuration of the latency benchmark and the major communication involved. As a comparison study, the same benchmark programs are executed in the cluster and Wide-Area-Network (WAN) using both the DMSO HLA's implementation and our HLAGrid prototype. Besides the configuration shown in Table 1 for benchmark experiments, we have also demonstrated our HLAGrid on more heterogenous platforms between Singapore and UK Midland e-Science center at Birmingham University. For example, in the e-Science cluster at Birmingham University, each node has 2 GBytes of memory and 2 Intel Xeon 3GHz processors, with Red Hat Enterprise Linux (RHEL) system version AS 3 as the operating system.

The experimental results are shown in Table 2. The cluster version of the latency benchmark shows that our prototype incurs about 40 millisecond of overhead in a cluster, and this is mainly due to the use of Globus, the encoding/decoding of parameters/result, and the communication cost. The overhead of Globus and the encoding/decoding of parameters/result are relatively fixed. But the communication cost varies significantly between the WAN version and the cluster version. From the comparison between HLA's cluster and WAN version, we can calculate the difference in communication cost is roughly 300 millisecond. Also, we can observe that in the HLAGrid's cluster and WAN latency benchmark comparison, the difference in communication cost is around 1150 milliseconds, which is about 3-4 times that of the HLA case. To understand this, we use the Unix command TCPDUMP to monitor the traffic (SOAP messages) involved in Grid service requests/responses. We observe that the size of the SOAP message is around 1-2 KByte per Grid service request/response, which is much larger than the attribute size used in the benchmark (128 byte), and the overheads involved are the namespace information and XML tags. The increase of the number of packets for the communication through Grid service invocation as compared to the pure socket connection in the existing HLA significantly affects the communication efficiency. The time-advancement benchmark also shows similar results.

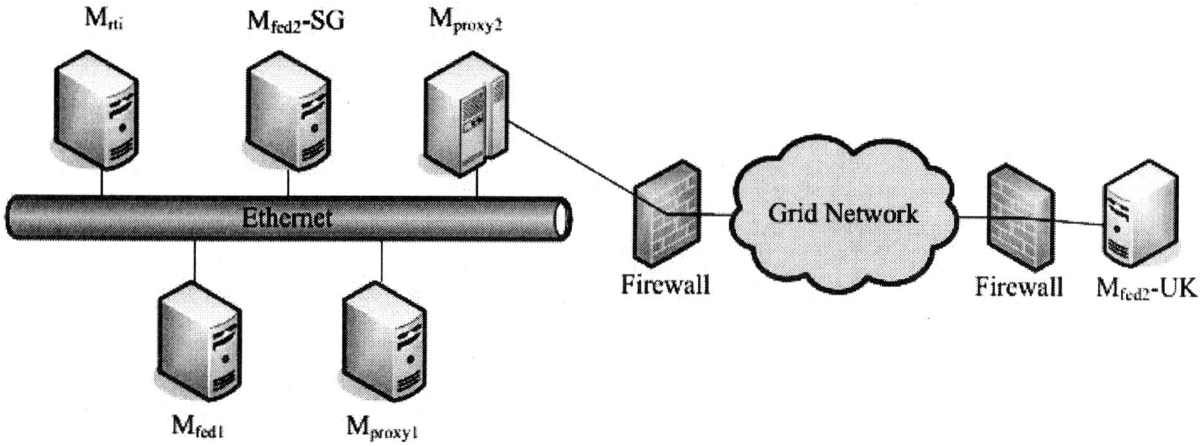

Figure 9. Experiment hardware configuration.

	M_{proxy2}	M_{rti}, M_{fed1}, M_{fed2}-SG	M_{proxy1}	M_{fed2}-UK
CPU	4xPentiumIII 500MHz	PentiumIII 733MHz	2xPentiumIII 733MHz	AMD Athlon 1.5GHz
Memory	1 Gbyte	1 Gbyte	1 Gbyte	2 Gbyte
OS	Redhat Linux 7.0	Redhat Linux 7.0	Redhat Linux 7.0	Redhat Linux 7.3
gcc	3.0.2	3.0.2	3.0.2	3.0.2
HLA	DMSO NG 1.3 V6	DMSO NG 1.3 V6	DMSO NG 1.3 V6	DMSO NG 1.3 V6

Table 1. Specification of machines for experiments.

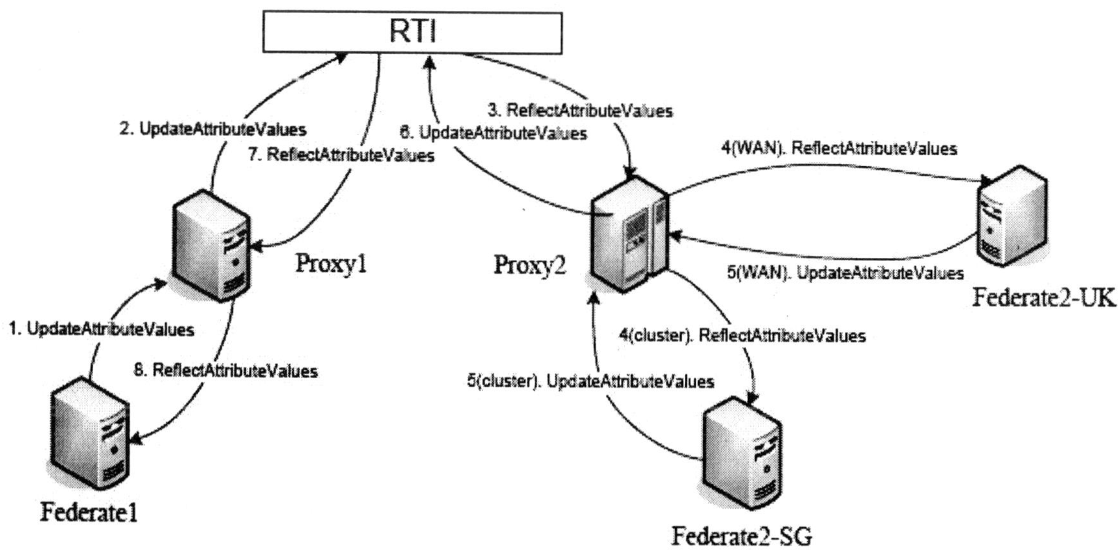

Figure 10. Benchmark configuration.

		HLA	HLAGrid
Latency	Cluster	10 millisecond	50 millisecond
	WAN	305 millisecond	1200 millisecond
Time Advancement	Cluster	680 grants/second	150 grants/second
	WAN	2 grants/second	0.41 grants/second

Table 2. Experiment results

5. Benefits of the Architecture

Despite the rather lackluster performance results, the proposed architecture supports service provisioning for HLA-based distributed simulation on the Grid in several aspects.

Firstly, clients only need the Grid-enabled HLA library for the federates to collaborate with other ones. This library differs from the HLA/RTI JavaBinding, because it does not require the HLA/RTI runtime executable code, while the HLA/RTI JavaBinding executes such code via Java Native Interface (JNI). Thus, the Grid-enabled HLA Library does not rely on any HLA/RTI implementation, providing more flexibility to the users. Moreover, the Grid-enabled HLA library is implemented using Java, and it hides the heterogeneity of the platforms (CPU, Operating System, etc) where federates can be executed.

Secondly, as one of the main features of the proposed framework, the actual HLA/RTI services are provided over the Grid, rather than provisioned by the clients who need to run the federates. From the architecture's point of view, this feature allows users to run simulations without having to manage the RTI service. Also, the entire simulation can be provided as a service, so that other clients can discover and use this service via the Grid-enabled HLA library. For example, if there exists a HLA-based supply chain management simulation available on the Grid, a wafer fab federate can make use of the proposed framework to get involved in the simulation without the knowledge of the HLA/RTI version and the details of how the supply chain management simulation is constructed, or how other federates are implemented. The proposed framework provides transparency not only between federates and the RTI, but also between a federate and the rest of the federation because of the provisioning of services (both RTI service and the simulation as a service).

Besides, multiple copies of the HLA/RTI services can serve multiple federations. The HLA/RTI service could be provided by different parties on heterogenous platforms, and this increases the availability of the HLA/RTI services. Clients can choose which HLA/RTI service to use, which provides more flexibility to the users. Furthermore, with the availability of multiple HLA/RTI services, load balancing among the service providers is possible. Even if one HLA/RTI service fails due to reasons like a hardware crash, other services can still be used by clients, providing fault-tolerance to the system as a whole.

Furthermore, clients can discover services and join a federation dynamically. In the traditional HLA-based distributed simulation, special arrangement has to be made beforehand. But, with the proposed architecture, the HLA/RTI service is discovered dynamically, and federates can join into an existing federation without prior arrangement. This feature is especially suitable for interactive simulation such as war-game simulation, where federates (aircrafts, tanks, troops, etc) join and leave the federation dynamically.

Lastly, the proxy and the Grid-enabled HLA library in the proposed architecture provides transparent HLA/RTI method calls and callbacks through Grid service invocations, and can be used as gateway/bridge to support hierarchical federations by connecting multiple RTIs [3, 4].

6. Conclusion and Future Work

In this paper, we propose a framework to extend the HLA to support Grid-wide distributed simulation. More specifically, we focus on provisioning of resources through Grid services and flexible construction of hierarchical federations. The framework achieves interoperability between different simulators (federates) by using a Federate-Proxy-RTI architecture. This architecture allows federates with heterogenous platforms to dynamically discover the RTI service and join a federation on the Grid. Moreover, the RTI services are exposed as Grid services, which provides more secure, scalable and coordinated management. All interfaces used in the framework comply with the standard HLA interface specification, which provides reusability to simulators. A prototype of the framework is implemented using DMSO's RTI 1.3NG version 6 and the Grid system runs the Globus Toolkit Version 3 to achieve compatibility and interoperability. Experimental results show that the our prototype incurs more overhead than the DMSO HLA/RTI, and is suitable for coarse-grained applications. Much work remains to be done, such as federate migration, fault-tolerance, and integration with security.

References

[1] Access Grid Project. http://www.accessgrid.org/, 2004.

[2] BEEP. Blocks extensible exchange protocol, http://www.ietf.org/rfc/rfc3080.txt, 2003.

[3] W. Cai, G. Li, S. J. Turner, B.-S. Lee, and L. Liu. Automatic construction of hierarchical federations architecture. In *Proceedings of Seventh IEEE International Symposium on Distributed Simulation and Real Time Applications (DS-RT 2002)*, pages 50–58, 2002.

[4] W. Cai, S. J. Turner, and B.-P. Gan. Hierarchical federations: an architecture for information hiding. In *Proceedings of Fifteenth Workshop on Parallel and Distributed Simulation*, pages 67–74, 2001.

[5] J. S. Dahmann, F. Kuhl, and R. Weatherly. Standards for simulation: as simple as possible but not simpler-the high level architecture for simulation. *Simulation*, 71(6):378–387, June 1998.

[6] Data Grid Project. http://www.globus.org/datagrid/, 2004.

[7] Extensible Modeling and Simulation Framework (XMSF). http://www.movesinstitute.org/xmsf/xmsf.html, 2004.

[8] J. B. Fitzgibbons, R. Fujimoto, D. Fellig, D. Kleban, and A. J. Scholand. IDSim: An extensible framework for interoperable distributed simulation. In *Proceedings of the IEEE International Conference on Web Services (ICWS2004)*, pages 532–539, 2004.

[9] I. Foster. The anatomy of the Grid: Enabling scalable virtual organizations. *Lecture Notes in Computer Science*, 2150:1–12, 2001.

[10] I. Foster and C. Kesselman. Globus: A metacomputing infrastructure toolkit. *The International Journal of Supercomputer Applications and High Performance Computing*, 11(2):115–128, Summer 1997.

[11] I. Foster, C. Kesselman, J. Nick, and S. Tuecke. The physiology of the grid: An open grid services architecture for distributed systems integration, http://www.globus.org/research/papers/ogsa.pdf., 2002.

[12] Globus Toolkit version 3. http://www.globus.org/.

[13] L. Granowetter. RTI interoperability issues – API standards, wire standards, and RTI bridges. In *Proceedings of the 2003 European Simulation Interoperability Workshop*, number 03S-SIW-063, 2003.

[14] K. L. Morse, D. L. Drake, and R. P. Brunton. Web enabling an *RTI* - an *XMSF* profile. In *Proceedings of the IEEE 2003 European Simulation Interoperability Workshop*, number 03E-SIW-046, 2003.

[15] Open GIS Consortium (OGC). http://www.gis.com/software/ogc.html, 2004.

[16] Semantic Grid Project. http://www.semanticgrid.org/, 2004.

[17] SOAP. Simple Object Access Protocol, http://www.w3.org/tr/soap/, 2003.

[18] R. Soley and the OMG Staff Strategy Group. Model-driven architecture. Technical report, Object Management Group (OMG), November 2000.

[19] A. Tolk. Avoiding another green elephant - a proposal for the next generation HLA based on model driven architecture. In *Proceedings of the 2002 Fall Simulation Interoperability Workshop*, number 02F-SIW-004, 2002.

[20] A. Tolk and J. A. Muguira. The levels of conceptual interoperability model. In *Proceedings of the 2003 Fall Simulation Interoperability Workshop*, number 03F-SIW-007, 2003.

[21] S. Tuecke, K. Czajkowski, I. Foster, J. Rey, F. Steve, and G. Carl. Grid service specification, www.globus.org/research/papers/gsspec.pdf, 2002.

[22] A. Wytzisk, I. Simonis, and U. Raape. Integration of HLA simulation models into a standized web service world. In *Proceedings of the 2003 European Simulation Interoperability Workshop*, number 03E-SIW-019, 2003.

[23] Y. Xie, Y. M. Teo, W. Cai, and S. J. Turner. A distributed simulation backbone for executing HLA-based simulation over the internet. In *Workshop on Grid Computing & Applications, Proceedings of the 2nd International Conference on Scientific and Engineering Computation*, pages 96–103, June 2004.

[24] K. Zajac, M. Bubak, M. Malawski, and P. M. A. Sloot. Towards a grid management system for *HLA*-based interactive simulations. In *Proceedings of Seventh IEEE International Symposium on Distributed Simulation and Real Time Applications (DS-RT 2003)*, pages 4–11, Delft, The Netherlands, October 2003.

[25] W. Zong, Y. Wang, W. Cai, and S. J. Turner. Grid services and service discovery for HLA-based distributed simulation. In *Proceedings of the IEEE/ACM Distributed Simulation-Real Time Application Symposium*, pages 116–124, 2004.

Dynamically Adaptive Partition-based Data Distribution Management*

Bora İ. Kumova

İzmir Institute of Technology; Department of Computer Engineering; 35430 Turkey
borakumova@iyte.edu.tr; iyte.edu.tr /~borakumova

Abstract

Performance and scalability of distributed simulations depends primarily on the effectiveness of the employed data distribution management (DDM) algorithm, which aims at reducing the overall computational and messaging effort on the shared data to a necessary minimum. Existing DDM approaches, which are variations and combinations of two basic techniques, namely region-based and grid-based techniques, perform purely in the presence of load differences. We introduce the partition-based technique that allows for variable-size partitioning shared data. Based on this technique, a novel DDM algorithm is introduced that is dynamically adaptive to cluster formations in the shared data as well as in the physical location of the simulation objects. Since the re-distribution is sensitive to inter-relationships between shared data and simulation objects, a balanced constellation has the additional advantage to be of minimal messaging effort. Furthermore, dynamic system scalability is facilitated, as bottlenecks are avoided.

1 Introduction

Establishing and maintaining network connections for the purpose of satisfying the mutual information requirements of the participants of a distributed system is called data distribution management (DDM) [14]. Alternative denominations are relevance filtering [8], data subscription management, focus [1] data dissemination management [7] or interest management (IM) [16]. In this text we shall use these terms interchangeably. The principle goal of DDM is to deliver objects of a given distributed system the exact amount of data they are interested in, no more and no less.

The two basic filtering techniques, region-based and grid-based, have been discussed in the literature [10], [14], [2], combined with other techniques and refined extensively, in order to improve performance. In region-based filtering, simulation objects specify interest areas on the shared data, in form of update and subscription regions (*Figure 1*). Where intersecting regions represent potential communication between related objects. This technique is inherently parallelisable upon the shared data, if the data is represented as a homogeneous multi-dimensional hyperspace, like in High Level Architecture (HLA) DDM 1516 [17]. The upper bound time complexity is $O(n^2)$, for comparing in the worst case every subscription region with every update region, and $O(n \log n)$ in case of recursive interest matching algorithms [17]. In grid-based filtering, shared data is subdivided into equal-sized value ranges and interest matching is performed implicitly, when interest regions fall into the same grid. Parallelism is exploited here by performing independently within each grid.

Synchronous Parallel Environment for Emulation and Discrete Event Simulation (SPEEDES) operating system [19] and Synthetic Theater of War Europe (STOW-E) [9] were early implementations of the grid approach. Where the latter combined both techniques for filtering the data difference between an intersecting region and the grid region, which seeks reducing the network transmission of unnecessary data. Some HLA DDM implementations have also adopted this approach, like U.S. Defense Modeling and Simulation Office (DMSO) Runtime Infrastructure (RTI) [5] and Pitch RTI (pRTI) [18].

*This research was partially supported by Ege University, International Computer Institute.

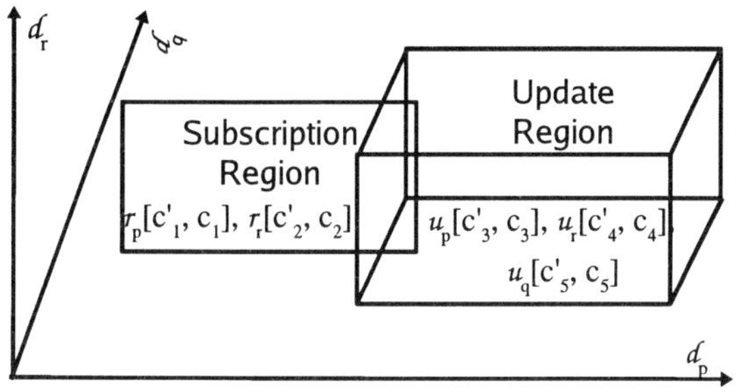

d_p: Data d Dimension p

r_p, $u_p[c'_1, c_1]$: Read r, Update u Interval c'_1 through c_1 on d_p

Figure 1. Sample Update/Subscription Regions in the Multi-dimensional Hyperspace as of HLA DDM 1516

While the above techniques aim at reducing the messaging load on the network, multicasting can reduce the computational load on a node, by delegating it to the related hardware unit of the network. Assigning each intersection region or grid a multicast group [15], [3] can reduce the computational load for replicating a data update propagation.

Sources for computational imbalances in distributed simulation are clusters of federates and/or clusters of data access regions. Where cluster formations are unpredictable, particularly in non-deterministic application domains. For instance, the load balancing approach proposed for HLA implementations in [4], interprets an overloaded node as a cluster of federates and resolves imbalances by migrating whole federates. Data access clusters are identified based on simulation objects' position and extents of interest on the shared data, such as focus [1], visibility [13], spheres of influence [12]. Connected intersections of such interest regions then imply data access clusters.

Dynamically adaptive partition-based DDM is a new approach for load balanced distributed simulation that assembles and extends the above ideas. This model is introduced here in the context of the distributed simulation platform Adaptive Parallel Discrete Event Simulator (APDES) [11] for non-deterministic applications. It possesses the following properties:

- Identifying multi-dimensional clusters within the multi-dimensional state variable (SV) space.
- Adapting the boundaries of a multi-dimensional SV partition to encapsulated clusters.
- Migrating a SV partition to an imbalanced neighbouring host and splitting/merging the partitions.
- Migrating an LP to its interest region with the highest access cost for this LP.

The principle structure of the model is introduced below. We shall use the following terms interchangeably, shared data, data dimension and state variable (SV) and refer to as d_i and the terms federate, logical process (LP) and simulation object, although sometimes an LP may represent several simulation objects.

2 Principle Structure of the Model

The principle idea of the new DDM model is to distribute the shared data of an application over a given set of hosts, by assigning each host one partition of each data dimension and by preserving adjacency information between partitions. Since one partition has at most two adjacent partitions, changing interest region boundaries need to be communicated to at most one host, as we assume continues value changes on SVs. Partition sizes are dynamically calculated based on emerging data clusters and distributed, depending on the contained regions' access costs.

2.1 State Variable Conceptualisation

SVs are normalised within the value range [0..1], as this facilitates homogeneous and variable-sized partitioning over dynamically varying numbers of hosts. Values of a SV are assumed to change continuously to the maximum extent of the local data partition size. An LP^e may declare at most one update region $u^e_i[c'_1, c_1]$ and at most one subscription region $r^e_i[c'_2, c_2]$ per SV d_i, where $c'_1 \le c_1$, $c'_2 \le c_2$ and $c'_1, c_1, c'_2, c_2 = [0..1]$.

2.2 Data Access Evaluation

Statistics over the access to SV regions provide qualitative information about regions and enable the DDM to dynamically adapt to the application behaviour, thus facilitating load balancing and scalability. Therefore every access region is attributed with following statistical values, which are additionally stored at the owning LP's site.

Region access frequency. In the course of a simulation the access frequency of SVs may change dynamically, depending on changing interests and interactions between LPs. The access frequency $\mathcal{F}(a_i[c'_1, c_1])$ of an update or subscription region $a_i[c'_1, c_1]$ of LP^e on SV i, gives information about how often it was accessed in the most resent time interval $[t', t_0]$, where $t' = t_0 - \Delta f$, t_0 is the last global state change and Δf the number of some most resent global state changes. Δf may be adapted to the overall region access frequency of a particular application. This information is used to optimise the distribution of the shared data and the LPs.

Region access latency. The average time to access a region is updated with every access to that region with

$$\mathcal{L}(a_i) = (\mathcal{L}'(a_i)\ \mathcal{F}(a_i) + |a_i|_{time}) \ / \ (\mathcal{F}(a_i) + 1)$$

a_i is an abbreviation for $a_i[c'_1, c_1]$, $\mathcal{L}'$ is the previous access frequency and $|a_i|_{time}$ the time required for the most resend access. The access latency of local regions is always set to zero. In case of remote regions, the time stamp of the incoming message is compared with local time.

2.3 Data Cluster Detection

A cluster C_i is identified as an ordering relation of access region boundaries on SV d_i:

$$C_i[c_{z'1}, c_{z1}] = \{(a_i[c_{z'2}, c_{z2}], b_i[c_{z'3}, c_{z3}]) \mid c_{z'1} \le c_{z'2} \wedge c_{z'2} \le c_{z2} \wedge c_{z'3} \le\le c_{z3} \wedge c_{z'3} \le c_{z2} \wedge c_{z3} \le c_{z1} \wedge c_{z'1}, c_{z1}, c_{z'2}, c_{z2}, c_{z'3}, c_{z3} = [0..1] \wedge i = [1..s]\}$$

For any access region a_i, b_i. Where two clusters $C_i[c_{z'1}, c_{z1}]$ and $C_i[c_{y'1}, c_{y1}]$ on the same SV d_i do not intersect, iff $c_{z1} < c_{y'1}$. The number of regions in a cluster $|C_i[c_{z'1}, c_{z1}]|_{size}$ is stored separately. The smallest possible cluster is a single region without intersections $|C_i[c_{z'1}, c_{z1}]|_{size} = 1$. Cluster detection is processed simultaneously with interest matching, as both share a similar algorithmic structure.

2.4 Interest Matching

Matching interest is calculated by intersecting two boundaries of two access regions $a_i[c'_1, c_1]$ and $b_i[c'_2, c_2]$ on SV d_i, such that

$$a_i[c'_1, c_1] \cap b_i[c'_2, c_2] \neq \emptyset \rightarrow c'_2 \le c_1$$

Only c_1 and c'_2 need to be compared for each region, as the boundary values c'_1, c_1, c'_2, c_2 are sorted. Additionally, the algorithm simultaneously calculates the clusters C_i. For this purpose, region boundaries on each SV are kept sorted in ascending order, which requires an additional computational effort. The time complexity for inserting one region into the sorted list of regions is O(log n).

2.5 Basic Data Partitioning Concepts

Data management starts initially with gridded partitioning the shared data in form of a table and continues with some primitive operations on the table.

Initial partition distribution. A data dimension d_i is sub-divided into s equal-sized partitions $d_{i,j}$ and each partition assigned to a different host h_j of the distributed system with n hosts (*Table 1*).

Table 1. Initial Assignment of Data Partitions to Hosts

$d_{i,j}$ at h_j	h_1	...	h_n
d_1	$d_{1,1}$	...	$d_{1,n}$
...	...	...	...
d_s	$d_{s,1}$	...	$d_{s,n}$

The table entry at $h(i, j)$ contains the actual network address of the hosts h_j with partition $d_{i,j}$. This schema allows to find the network location of a partition $d_{i,j}$ with a single direct access. Depending on the semantics of a data dimension and the location of LPs, adjacent partitions $d_{i,j}$ and $d_{i,j+1}$ may be stored at physically closer located hosts h_j and h_{j+1} in the network, as region boundaries of access regions can move only to adjacent partitions.

Note however that in the initial configuration, the partition index j in $d_{i,j}$ and the host index j in h_j are the same, hence $h_j = h(i, j)$. Below, an extension to this schema is introduced with variable-size partitioning and partition migration, where the equality $h_j = h(i, j)$ does not hold any more for any j.

Primitive partitioning operations. In the course of a simulation, a partition $d_{i,j}$ may be merged or split with adjacent partitions $d_{i,j-1}$ or $d_{i,j+1}$. This is exemplified below on a disengaging/engaging host, where a column j that consists of partition j on all SVs d_i with i = [0..s], is merged/split with adjacent partitions, respectively.

By default, each partition $d_{s,k}$ of a disengaging host h_k is joined with one of its adjacent partitions, either $d_{i,k-1}$ or $d_{i,k+1}$ (*Table 2*).

Table 2. Merging Data Partitions from a Disengaging Host with Neighbouring Partitions

O$d_{i,j}$ at h_j	...	h_{k-1}	h_k	h_{k+1}	...
d_1	...	$d_{1,k-1}$; $d_{1,k}$ ←	$d_{1,k}$	$d_{1,k+1}$	...
...	...	... ←	...	...	...
d_s	...	$d_{s,k-1}$; $d_{s,k}$ ←	$d_{s,k}$	$d_{s,k+1}$	...

By default, a partition d_i on host h_{k-1} is split into two, $d_{i,k-1}$ and $d_{i,k}$, and assigned to the new host h_k. (*Table 3*).

Table 3. Splitting Data Partitions and Re-assigning to a New Engaging Host

$d_{i,j}$ at h_j	...	h_{k-1}	h_k	h_{k+1}	...
d_1	...	$d_{1,k-1}$; $d_{1,k}$ →	$d_{1,k}$	$d_{1,k+1}$	...
...	...	.. →	...	...	...
d_s	...	$d_{s,k-1}$; $d_{s,k}$ →	$d_{s,k}$	$d_{s,k+1}$	...

Partition size. The size of data partitions are directly affected by the number of available hosts. Depending on the context of a SV d_i and performance considerations during a particular application, initially equal-sized partitions $d_{i,j}$ may become variable or zero-sized. Variable size partitioning allows adapting to clusters of intersecting access regions. However, a cluster that is split over more than one partition, can cause additional network messaging, as intersecting interests represent potential communication relationships. Zero partition size of $d_{i,j}$ indicates that host h_j does currently not maintain any value range of that SV, which may change during an application for load balancing purposes.

A performance issue is the ratio between partition length and access region length, respectively:

$$m_j = |d_i[c'_1, c_1]| \; / \; |d_{i,j}|$$

For $m \leq 1$ one message is required. For $1 < m$, m split regions of d_i need to be maintained at m hosts, which implies an additional network overhead of m -1 messages and an additional local overhead at m -1 hosts for pointing to the host with the owning LP^e of d_i. At the site of LP^e an additional local overhead of m-1 pointers to further m-1 hosts is required.

Access region replication. For the purpose of minimising messaging effort, for each subscribed remote SV region, a local copy is maintained. Where one DDM objective is to minimise the total number of replica within a simulation, as each replica requires one message for synchronising with each update on the original remote data.

2.6 Multi-dimensionality of State Variables and Data Clusters

By default all SVs are homogeneous and no semantics are defined between value ranges of a SV or between different SVs. However supporting such semantics helps identifying multi-dimensional data clusters in the context of user model semantics. Consider for instance the state variables d_p and d_r in (*Figure 2*). If they are evaluated independently, then following LP clusters would result: (LP^1, LP^4) and (LP^2, LP^3) on d_p and (LP^1, LP^2, LP^4) and (LP^3) on d_r. A somehow logically combined evaluation of d_p and d_r however, for instance as physical area, apparently results in different LP clusters (*Figure 2*). In this case, LP^2 does no more appear in the cluster with LP^1 and LP^4, as it is not intersecting with them on the physical area.

Declaring compound SVs. A group of SVs $d_1, .., d_q$, with $1 \leq q \leq s$, where s is the total number of SVs of

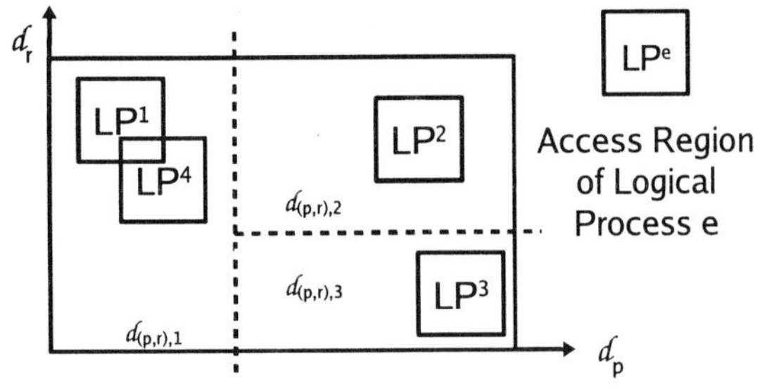

$d_{(p,r),(i,j)}$: Partition (i,j) of SV $d_{(p,r)}$

Figure 2. Sample Relationships Between Access Regions of Logical Processes in a Two-dimensional Data Space

the application can be introduced as one compound SV (d_1, .., d_q) by declaring

$$d_{(1,\ldots,q)} = \{(d_1, \ldots, d_q) \mid q \leq s\}$$

In general, the more SVs are bound to each other by grouping relationships, the smaller the probability for involving access regions incorrectly in multi-dimensional data clusters. Hence, the smaller the probability for LPs to depend on each other over shared data.

A particular SV d_k may be grouped multiple times. Resulting consistency relationships between groups however is in the responsibility of the user application. For instance whether updates on d_k over one group should have consistent interpretation in an other group that includes d_k as well.

Detecting multi-dimensional data clusters. A multi-dimensional data cluster $C_{(1,\ldots,q)}[c_{z'1}, c_{z1}, \ldots, c_{z'q}, c_{zq}]$ is detected in two steps: Firstly, the above described cluster detection algorithm is applied to all SVs, independently from whether a SV is bound or not. Secondly, for each compound SV $d_{(1,\ldots,q)}$, related access regions $d^e_{(1,\ldots,q)}$ and $d^f_{(1,\ldots,q)}$, of LP^e and LP^f respectively, are compared pairwise, if they intersect on at least one SV d_1, ..., d_q, such that

$$[c_{z'1}, c_{z1}] \cap [c_{y'1}, c_{y1}] \neq \emptyset \vee \ldots \vee [c_{z'q}, c_{zq}] \cap [c_{y'q}, c_{yq}] \neq \emptyset \rightarrow C^{e,f}_{(1,\ldots,q)}[c_{z'1}, c_{z1} \vee c_{y1}], \ldots, [c_{z'q}, c_{zq} \vee c_{yq}]$$

The time complexity for detecting q-dimensional clusters is $O(q * g) = O(n^2)$, for comparing in the worst case all g LPs' access regions on all q SVs. With a recursive algorithm, the complexity reduces to $O(n \log n)$.

Space complexity for variable-size and multi-dimensional partitions. On one hand, less dependent LPs require less messaging effort and can be re-located more independently. On the other hand, bound SVs increase the space requirement at each host. For instance, the number of adjacent multi-dimensional rectangular partitions increases exponentially with $s^3 * 2^s$ for increased number of s dimensions, which is a space complexity of $O(n^3 2^n)$. It enables however encapsulating an s-dimensional cluster within an s-dimensional SV partition. of variable edge size. For instance, for a 3-dimensional partition, the addresses of $3 * 2^3 - 3 = 21$ to 24 hosts need to be stored at each host, depending on the location of a partition at SV boundaries. The number increases with the number of adjacent partitions at each edge or surface.

2.7 Optimisation of Partition Distribution

Partition distribution over the hosts is dynamically optimised through variable-size partitioning, for adapting to cluster formations, and partition migration, for balancing the messaging load between hosts.

Variable-size partitioning. A single partition $d_{i,j}$ is split between two clusters $C_i[c_{z'1}, c_{z1}]$ and $C_i[c_{z'2}, c_{z2}]$ at $(c_{z1} + c_{z'2}) / 2$. A multi-dimensional partition $d_{(1,\ldots,q)}$ is split between two clusters $C_{(1,\ldots,q)}[c_{z'1}, c_{z1}, \ldots, c_{z'q}, c_{zq}]$ and $C_{(1,\ldots,q)}[c_{y'1}, c_{y1}, \ldots, c_{y'q}, c_{yq}]$ at each SV partition (1, ..,q), such that $(c_{z1} + c_{y'1}) / 2, \ldots, (c_{zq} + c_{y'q}) / 2$. Consequently, variable-size partitions may emerge in the course of a simulation (*Table 4*).

Table 4. Sample Variable-size Data Partitions

$d_{i,j}$ at $h(i,j)$	$h(i,j)$				
d_1	$d_{1,1}$ at h_1	$d_{1,2}$ at h_4	$d_{1,3}$ at h_3	$d_{1,4}$ at h_5	
d_2	$d_{1,1}$ at h_3	$d_{1,2}$ at h_2	$d_{1,3}$ at h_1	$d_{1,4}$ at h_4	$d_{1,5}$ at h_5
d_3	$d_{1,1}$ at h_2	$d_{1,2}$ at h_3	$d_{1,3}$ at h_5	$d_{1,4}$ at h_1	$d_{1,5}$ at h_4

Note again the two kinds of indexing a host with $\mathcal{h}_j$ for referring to all partitions on that host and with $\mathcal{h}(i,j)$ for referring to the same partition index j of all SVs i. Accordingly, index j of two partitions $d_{i1,j}$ and $d_{i2,j}$ may be equal for different SVs $i1 \neq i2$, but not necessarily located on the same host $\mathcal{h}(i1,j) \neq \mathcal{h}(i2,j)$.

Partition migration. Variable-size partitioning allows adapting to data clusters, but can cause growing clusters in several partitions $\mathcal{d}_{i,j}$ to concentrate on one host $\mathcal{h}(i,j)$, which in turn can lead to load imbalances. In order to balance the load in such a case, clusters on that host are migrated to hosts $\mathcal{h}(i,j-1)$ or $\mathcal{h}(i,j+1)$ and merged with their adjacent partitions $\mathcal{d}_{i,j-1}$ or $\mathcal{d}_{i,j+1}$, respectively.

Candidates for migration are chosen from the list of all clusters $\mathcal{C}[c_{z'1},c_{z1}]$ on host $\mathcal{h}_j$, which is sorted in descending order after cluster access cost $sort_{desc}(\mathcal{A}(\mathcal{C}[c_{z'1},c_{z1}]))$. Clusters with relative high access cost are those, whose owning LPs are located remote, thus migrating them will at least not increase the overall messaging effort of the application. Note that in this process a cluster is not distinguished from a single access region that has no intersections. The migration is continued for all clusters, until the accumulated cluster access costs of neighbouring hosts are equal, relative to their local load:

$$\Delta\mathcal{H}_{j-1} * \mathcal{H}_{j-1} = \Delta\mathcal{H}_j * \mathcal{H}_j = \Delta\mathcal{H}_{j+1} * \mathcal{H}_{j+1}$$

for hosts $\mathcal{h}_{j-1}$, $\mathcal{h}_j$ and $\mathcal{h}_{j+1}$, respectively. Where

$$\mathcal{H}_j = \Sigma^s{}_i\Sigma_z\mathcal{A}(\mathcal{C}_i[c_{z1}, c_{z2}])$$

Where z denotes the number of regions on SV $\mathcal{d}_i$. Partition migration is initiated for all hosts in every second phase of 2 * Δf state changes, alternating with the task for optimal placement of LPs. This schema balances the load in a simulated annealing fashion, where the grade of annealing is adapted over Δf for a given application. $\Delta\mathcal{H}_j$ is the load factor of host j and is re-calculated based on the local processor load.

Cluster splitting. In cases where the above equality for load balancing cannot be achieved on the overloaded host, the next cluster in the list that exceeds the equality is split, just like a partition is split. A split cluster is principally undesired, as it increases messaging effort, but is unavoidable, if balanced load is required. This capability enables the DDM to adapt to applications that may develop increasingly growing clusters or, in the worst case, even a single "all-one-cluster".

2.8 Optimal Placement of Logical Processes

For the purpose of balancing the process load between the hosts, each LP^e is placed on host k with the highest access cost $\mathcal{A}^e{}_k$ for LP^e:

$$\max_v(\Sigma^s{}_i(\mathcal{A}_k(r^e{}_{i,k}) + \mathcal{A}_k(u^e{}_{i,k}))\ \text{iff}\ r^e{}_{i,k} \cap u^f{}_{i,k} \neq \emptyset$$

Where $v \leq s$ is the total number of regions of LP^e, e, f = [1..g] and $e \neq f$, and $\mathcal{A}^e{}_k = \mathcal{F}^e{}_k * \mathcal{L}^e{}_k$ with $i \leq s$ of s SVs. A subscription region without any intersections with update regions is excluded from the calculation, as it has always zero access cost, wherever LP^e is located.

A sample distribution of access regions and LP placement for hypothetical access costs is sketched in (*Figure 3*). Note that, for instance subscription region $r^f{}_{s,1}$ was not included in the calculation for the placement of LP^f, as it does not intersect with any update region. Also, compound SV $\mathcal{d}_{(1,2,3)}$ is depicted as one-dimensional region, for simplicity, but is to be interpreted as cubical region.

2.9 Primitive Operations on Shared Data

LPs can access the shared data over three primitive operations: reading and updating a region and changing region boundaries. Each operation initiates a well defined sequence of messages for keeping the shared data globally consistent, by complying with the above sketched data distribution schema [11].

Message content. The network message sent for synchronising a remote SV is uniform. It contains the SV value and a local time stamp.

Reading subscribed data. When LP^e subscribes to a region $r^e{}_i[c'_1, c'_1]$ within partition $\mathcal{d}_{i,j}$ on host $\mathcal{h}(i, j)$, then the region is copied to the host where LP^e is located. Any following read operation from LP^e within $r^e{}_i[c'_1, c_1]$ is then performed locally. Thus two messages are required for each new subscription, if the partition is remote. Hence the messaging overhead $\mathcal{P}$ for reading subscribed data is $\mathcal{P}_r = 2$.

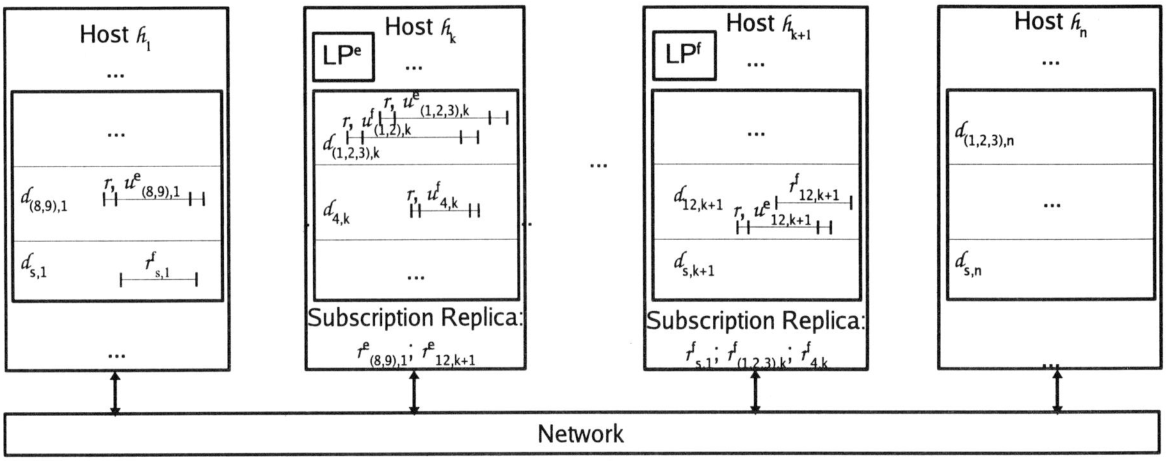

$d_{i,j}$: Partition j of State Variable i — $r, u^g_{i,j}$: Subscription/Update Regions r/u on $d_{i,j}$ of LP^g

$h(i, j)$: Network Address of Partition j of SV d_i on Host $h(i, j)$

$\max(A_1(r, u^e_{(8,9),1}), A_{k+1}(r, u^e_{12,k+1}), A_k(r, u^e_{(1,2,3),k})) = k$: Placing LP^e on Host $h((1,2,3), k) = h_k$

$\max(A_k(r, u^f_{(1,2,3),k}), A_k(r, u^f_{4,k}), A_{k+1}(r^f_{12,k+1})) = k+1$: Placing LP^f on Host $h(12, k+1) = h_{k+1}$

Figure 3. Sample Data Distribution and Optimised Placement of Two Logical Processes for Given Data Access Schema

Updating associated data. If an update within a region $u^e_i[c'_1, c_1]$ is remote, with respect to the associated LP^e, then one message is required. If the update region intersects with a total number of v remote subscription regions, then further v messages are required to propagate the update on the original data to v replica, where v = [0..n] and n is the total number of hosts. Thus at most v + 1 messages are required. The messaging overhead for updating associated data becomes than $P_u = v + 1$.

Updating region boundaries. Changing region boundaries, caused for instance by a moving simulation object, requires a new calculation of intersections with other regions. If the change on the boundary is within the boundaries of this partition, then no messages are required. Otherwise, one message is send to the host with the related adjacent partition. One further message is sent back to the region owner, if the new boundary has crossed an adjacent partition on an other host. Thus at most two messages are required for this operation, yielding a messaging overhead of $P_b = 2$.

2.10 Performance Evaluation

The overall performance of the DDM model in terms of messaging and time complexity for primitive operations on shared data is sketched in (*Table 5*) and compared with the region and grid-based algorithms for the following two cases:

- Evenly distributed interest: interest regions and the overall access cost of the LPs are evenly distributed over the hosts (peers).
- Single-clustered interest: interest regions and the overall access cost of the PLs are concentrated on one host (server).

Server. All techniques perform equal for the case that all s SVs are maintained at a server. For read operations, the worst case is assumed, where each read is preceded by an update on the original data and therefore requires a message for replication. Messaging complexity is only O(n), as in the worst case all n hosts may send a message to the server in one state change. Time complexity is O(n log n), since interest matching is performed only on the server. For instance, the region technique combined with the grid on a server has been proposed in [20].

Region; peer. If all SVs are fully replicated at all peers, peer-to-peek communication is required with the region technique. Interest has to be matched at all n hosts over all s SVs, no matter whether all interest regions are single-clustered or not.

Table 5. Messaging, Time and Space Complexity of Operations of DDM Techniques for Evenly Distributed and Single-clustered Interests

Technique	Distribution	Operation				Data Connectivity (Space)
		Read or Update (Messaging)		Move (Messaging/Time)		
		Evenly Distributed	Single Cluster Evenly	Distributed/Matching	Cluster/Matching	
All	Server	O(n)	O(n)	O(n)/O(n log n)	O(n)/O(n log n)	O(0)
Region	Peer	$O(n^2)$	$O(n^2)$	$O(n^2)$/O(n log n)	$O(n^2)$/O(n log n)	O(0)
Grid	Peer	$O(n^2)$	O(n)	$O(n^2+G)$/O(0)	O(n)/O(0)	$O(n\ 2^n)$
Partition	Peer	$O(n^2)$	$O(n^2)$	$O(n^2+P)$/O(0)	$O(n^2)$/O(0)	$O(n^3\ 2^n)$
Grid with Region	Peer	$O(n^2)$	O(n)	$O(n^2+G)$/O(log n)	O(n)/O(n log n)	$O(n\ 2^n)$
Partition with Region	Peer	$O(n^2)$	$O(n^2)$	$O(n^2+P)$/O(log n)	$O(n^2)$/O(log n)	$O(n^3\ 2^n)$

Grid or partition; peer; read or update. In case of gridded or partitioned distribution of the SVs, peer-to-peer communication complexity is equal for read/update operations. It reduces to O(n) for the single cluster located at a single peer in the grid, but remains equal, if the cluster is split over all peers within partitions.

Grid or partition; peer; move. In case of move operations, peer-to-peer communication complexity is principally equal with the grid and partition techniques, as the administrative messaging overheads $\mathcal{G}$ and $\mathcal{P}$ are principally equal. Interest matching reduces to O(log n) at each host. If an application develops a single cluster, then messaging reduces to O(n) in the grid, assuming that moving interest regions will remain within the cell on that peer. If the single cluster is split over all peers within partitions however messaging remains at $O(n^2+\mathcal{P})$. Interest matching increases to O(n log n) within the single grid cell and reduces to O(log n) within each peer's partition.

3 Conclusions

The introduced IM model inherits its adaptability from the dynamics of the data distribution schema, particularly the partition adaptation to data cluster formations and the optimal LP placement, by considering network latencies. Where LP clusters are recognised indirectly through the local processor load. The model benefits from the fact that no receiver-side filtering is required, as all LPs receive the exact amount of messages they require. The administrative overhead is restricted to a few network messages for maintaining partition adjacency information. These capabilities of the model facilitate further load balancing as well as scalability. The local overhead for interest matching and cluster detection is notable, but does not introduce more administration than the grid approach. The additional administration for adjacency maintenance does scale with increased partition granularity, but remains still minimal and therefore does not dramatically influence the scalability. In fact, the administrative overhead is expected to scale almost linear with increased number of peers.

Remarkable is the nearly constant performance of the partition technique that converges in all cases to the messaging complexity $O(n^2)$ and time complexity O(log n), which facilitates dynamic adaptability. Although the grid technique outperforms the partition technique in some cases, adaptability and dynamically scalability are the significant advantage over the grid technique. Achieving continuously balanced load throughout an application is the only way to guarantee real-time response at all times.

Our next goal is to examine the practical performance of the partition-based DDM technique for some representative deterministic and non-deterministic applications in critical constellations. The space complexity $O(n^3\ 2^n)$ of a partition, for pointing to variable-size adjacent partitions, might prove critical in practice, especially for the case where clusters are closely located, even for only s = 3 dimensions. The performance however is expected to improve in general for increased partition granularity.

4 References

[1] Benford, Steve; Fahlen, Lennart; 1993; "A Spatial Model of Interaction in Virtual Environments", *Proc. Third European Conference on Computer Supported Cooperative Work* (ECSCW'93)

[2] Boukerche, Azzedine; Roy, Amber; 2002; "In Search of Data Distribution Management in Large Scale Distributed Simulations"; *Summer Computer Simulation Conference*

[3] Boukerche, Azzedine; Amber, Roy; 2002; "Dynamic Grid-Based Approach to Data Distribution Management"; *Journal of Parallel and Distributed Computing* (JPDC); Elsevier

[4] Cai, W.; Turner, S. J.; Zhao, H.; 2002; "A Load Management System for Running HLA-Based Distributed Simulations over the Grid"; *Workshop on Distributed Simulation and Real-Time Applications* (DS-RT'02)

[5] HLA 1.3; U.S. DoD DMSO; 1996; "HLA Data Distribution Management Design Documentation Version 0.5, 1997"; http: // hla.dmso.mil

[6] Helfinstine, B.; Wilbert, D.; Torpey, M.; Civinskas, W.; 2001; "Experiences with Data Distribution Management in Large-Scale Federations"; *Winter Simulation Interoperability Workshop* (SIW), Orlando

[7] Horling, Bryan; Mailler, Roger; Lesser, Victor; 2004; "Farm: A Scalable Environment for Multi-Agent Development and Evaluation"; *Advances in Software Engineering for Multi-Agent Systems*; Springer

[8] van Hook, Daniel J.; Rak, Steven J.; Calvin, James O.; 1994; "Approaches to Relevance Filtering"; *Distributed Simulation* (DIS) Workshop

[9] van Hook, Daniel J.; Calvin, James O.; Newton, Michael K.; Fusco, David A.; 1994; "An Approach to DIS Scaleability"; 11th Workshop on Standards for the Interoperability of Distributed Simulations

[10] van Hook, Daniel J.; Calvin, James O.; Spring 1998; "Data Distribution Management in RTI 1.3"; *Simulation Interoperability Workshop* (SIW); IEEE

[11] Kumova, Bora İ.; 2005; "Scalable Interest Management in Distributed Simulation of Intelligent Systems"; *Symposium on Design, Analysis, and Simulation of Distributed Systems* (DASD'05); The Society for Modelling & Simulation International (SCS)

[12] Logan, B.; Theodoropoulos, G.; 2000; "Dynamic Interest Management in the Distributed Simulation of Agent-Based Systems"; Proceedings of 10th AI, Simulation and Planning Conference (RAE2001); Society for Computer Simulation International

[13] Merchant, F.; Bic, L. F.; Dillencourt, M. B.; 1998; "Load Balancing in Individual-Based Spatial Applications"; *Conference on Parallel Architectures and Compilation Techniques* (PACT'98)

[14] Morse, Katherine L.; Steinman, Jeffrey S.; 1997; "Data Distribution Management in the HLA Multidimensional Regions and Physically Correct Filtering"; *Summer Simulation Interoperability Workshop* (SIW); IEEE

[15] Morse, Katherine L.; Bic, Lubomir; Tsai, Kevin; 1999; "Multicast Group for Dynamic Data Distribution Management"; *Proc. Of the 31st Society for Computer Simulation Conference* (SCSC)

[16] Morse, Katherine L.; 2000; "An Adaptive Distributed Algorithm for Interest Management"; *PhD Thesis*; University of California, Irvine

[17] Petty, Mikel D.; 2001; "Comparing high level architecture data distribution management specifications 1.3 and 1516"; *Simulation Practice and Theory*; Elsevier

[18] pRTI; "Pitch RTI"; http:// www.pitch.se

[19] Steinman, Jeff S.; Wieland, Frederick; 1994; "Parallel Proximity Detection and the Distributed List Algorithm"; *Workshop on Parallel and Distributed Simulation* (PADS); New York IEEE

[20] Tan, Gary; Zhang, Yu Song; Ayani, Rassul; 2000; "A Hybrid Approach to Data Distribution Management"; *Workshop on Distributed Simulation and Real-Time Applications* (DS-RT); IEEE Computer Society

Author Index

PADS 2005

IEEE COMPUTER SOCIETY

IEEE

Press Operating Committee

Chair
Roger U. Fujii
Vice President
Northrop Grumman Mission Systems

Editor-in-Chief
Donald F. Shafer
Chief Technology Officer
Athens Group, Inc.

Board Members

Mark J. Christensen, *Independent Consultant*
Richard Thayer, *Professor Emeritus, California State University, Sacramento*
Ted Lewis, *Professor Computer Science, Naval Postgraduate School*
Linda Shafer, *Professor Emeritus, University of Texas at Austin*
James Conrad, *Associate Professor, UNC-Charlotte*
John Horch, *Independent Consultant*
Deborah Plummer, *Manager, Authored Books*
Thomas Baldwin, *Manager, Conference Publishing Services (CPS)*

IEEE Computer Society Executive Staff

David Hennage, *Executive Director*
Angela Burgess, *Publisher*

IEEE Computer Society Publications

The world-renowned IEEE Computer Society publishes, promotes, and distributes a wide variety of authoritative computer science and engineering texts. These books are available from most retail outlets. Visit the CS Store at *http://computer.org/cspress* for a list of products.

IEEE Computer Society *Conference Publishing Services* (CPS)

The IEEE Computer Society produces and actively promotes conference publications for more than 175 acclaimed international conferences each year in a variety of formats, including soft-cover books, hard-cover books, CD-ROMs, video, and on-line publications. For information about the IEEE Computer Society's *Conference Publishing Services* (CPS), please e-mail tbaldwin@computer.org or write to Proceedings, IEEE Computer Society, P.O. Box 3014, 10662 Los Vaqueros Circle, Los Alamitos, CA 90720-1314. Telephone +1-714-821-8380. Fax +1-714-761-1784. Additional information about the IEEE Computer Society's *Conference Publishing Services* (CPS) can be accessed from our web site at: *http://www.computer.org/proceedings/*.

IEEE Computer Society / Wiley Partnership

The IEEE Computer Society and Wiley partnership allows the CS Press authored book program to produce a number of exciting new titles in areas of computer science and engineering with a special focus on software engineering. IEEE Computer Society members continue to receive a 15% discount on these titles when purchased through Wiley or at: *http://wiley.com/ieeecs*. To submit questions about the program or send proposals, please e-mail dplummer@computer.org or write to Books, IEEE Computer Society, 10662 Los Vaqueros Circle, Los Alamitos, CA 90720-1314. Telephone +1-714-821-8380. Additional information regarding the Computer Society's authored book program can also be accessed from our web site at: *http://computer.org/cspress*.

Revised: 03 January 2005